PRACTICAL DATABASE MANAGEMENT

TONY FABBRI
University of Louisville

A. ROBERT SCHWAB, JR.
Provident Life Insurance

PWS-KENT PUBLISHING COMPANY

Boston

PWS-KENT
Publishing Company

20 Park Plaza
Boston, Massachusetts 02116

Sponsoring Editor: Jonathan Plant
Assistant Editor: Mary Thomas
Production Editors: Chris Crochetiere/Kirby Lozyniak
Manufacturing Coordinator: Lisa Flanagan
Production and Interior Design: Editorial Services of New England, Inc.
Cover Designer: Kirby Lozyniak
Typesetter: Grafacon, Inc.
Printer and Binder: Arcata Graphics/Halliday
Cover Printer: New England Book Components
Cover Image: Ellen Schuster. Courtesy of The Image Bank

PWS-KENT Publishing Company is a division of Wadsworth, Inc.

Library of Congress Cataloging-in-Publication Data

Fabbri, Tony.
    Practical database management / Tony Fabbri and A. Robert Schwab, Jr.
       p.   cm.
    Includes index.
    ISBN 0-534-92592-8
    1. Data base management. I. Schwab, A. Robert. II. Title.
QA76.9.D3F22 1992   91–39170
005.74—dc20   CIP

Printed in the United States of America
92 93 94 95 96—10 9 8 7 6 5 4 3 2 1

Contents

CHAPTER 13   SQL AND THE PROGRAMMER   372

CHAPTER 14   NETWORK DATABASES   408

Preface

Database textbooks come in many varieties and all of them contain an abundance of information. Many of the textbooks are designed strictly for the business student, while others are designed for the computer scientist. This text is designed for both the business student who wants practical usage of database concepts, and the computer science major who needs to become exposed to the business side of data processing. Throughout the text, we include state-of-the-art database concepts as they apply to the business environment. Database theory throughout the text includes practical applications of that theory as it applies to the business world.

We wrote the text keeping in mind that the student reader will someday be using this information in his or her job function. We try not to include theory that has no practical usage in the real world. Because none of us knows what the future will create, however, we must include concepts and principles that look to the future of databases. Most computer facilities provide services to the business aspect of the corporation. Therefore, the concepts and principles in this text work for both the business major and the computer science major. The business major needs exposure to database concepts if he or she is to survive in today's business world, and the computer science major needs exposure to the underlying principles and needs of the business community if he or she plans to effectively function in the corporate world.

It is our belief that relational databases will dominate the database environment for the next few decades. This does not mean we can abandon the other types of databases. Remember, in the commercial world things are done based on the bottom line. Even though relational databases are the current pet of the computer industry, most industrial data centers will convert to them slowly—ever so slowly. Because most computer shops have substantial dollar investments in network and hierarchical databases, they must approach relational databases as they would any other new concept or product. They will perform a feasibility study, an in-house test, and then slowly build a library of relational programs and systems while maintaining their existing investment in older database structures.

Apple Corporation introduced its first "home" computer in the late 1970s; but personal computers were not prevalent in the business world until the late 1980s. And even now, many PCs are not used to their full potential. This span of over a decade reflects the business world's caution toward new technology and its inability to absorb any new technology quickly. A similar scenario will occur for relational databases. In our treatment of database concepts, we must include topics dealing with all three types of database structures: relational, hierarchical, and network. Because we feel relational databases will be the logical choice of most computer shops, we slant this textbook toward the relational model and devote only a few chapters to the other two database models.

Because many students are computer neophytes, the first three chapters of the text provide an introduction to computers. These chapters introduce the concepts students will need for understanding the remaining chapters of the text. If the reader already knows an idea or principle we discuss, however, he or she can ignore that section of the text and proceed to the next topic. Likewise, if the reader already has an excellent background in the mainframe and microcomputer environment, he or she can skip the first three chapters. These chapters provide an overview of files, databases, the mainframe and micro environments, and data structures. Students with only an elementary knowledge of computers should read Chapters 1, 2, and 3 more thoroughly.

Databases can be resident on a mainframe, minicomputer, or a microcomputer or some combination of the three. Most business environments include one or more mainframes to handle the bulk of the company's data processing needs and a battery of PCs to handle other data processing demands of the organization. The text includes detailed treatment of databases as they appear in both the mainframe and PC environments. The vast majority of computer shops are IBM mainframe oriented and most business organizations have hundreds if not thousands of IBM PCs and their compatibles. Because most business majors and information science majors will be on an IBM mainframe and an IBM PC (or compatible) when they reach the business world, this text leans heavily to these two computer environments.

We chose to concentrate on IBM's version of SQL throughout the text's treatment of relational databases. We did this for two reasons. First, IBM's treatment of SQL is becoming a de facto standard for SQL. Second, IBM's consortium agreement with most colleges and universities permits all colleges with IBM minis and mainframes to get SQL/DS virtually free. Because SQL/DS runs on many of IBM's minis (e.g., the AS 400 and the 9370), many colleges and universities can have access to SQL/DS for the price of a minicomputer. Although this is not a small sum of money, it still is within the budgetary framework of most colleges and universities.

After each chapter we include questions for the student to answer. In addition, many chapters include one or more case studies for the student to work. These studies are directed toward the PC environment and the mainframe environment. The commercial world uses both these environments, so the student should be exposed to both environments in the classroom. Remember, some solutions to real problems might exist only in the vastness of the mainframe setting, while other solutions might be ideally suited to the PC world. Students, therefore, need the tools and knowledge of both cultures to effectively function in today's computerized business world.

In some parts of the text we include COBOL examples and record formats to illustrate a concept or to define a record. Appendix A gives a brief summary of file description formats using the COBOL language.

In addition to the case studies and the problem exercises, we have included several minilabs for the student to work. We feel it is important for the student to have hands-on experience and the minilabs will give them some practical experience using database concepts.

Tony Fabbri
A. Robert Schwab, Jr.

1 | Overview of Files and Databases

To understand database management, you must first develop a sense of the context in which databases are used. The purpose of these first three chapters is to present three components of that context. This chapter examines the similarities and differences between databases and traditional (nondatabase) files. Chapter 2 examines the machine environment by focusing on hardware and its operating system software, because their combination determines the way in which a database can be used. Chapter 3 examines the data structures and data access methods that are used by databases.

This chapter begins by examining traditional files, because they are the foundation of databases. We then examine the advantages and disadvantages of using databases instead of traditional files. We examine briefly the three major types of databases that have evolved for the storing of data.

TRADITIONAL FILES

In the typical business environment the computer provides a variety of reports to a company's management. A few of these include the following:

1. Reports on the financial status of the company
2. Reports on the company's customers, clients, and competitors
3. Reports on the operational status of the company and its employees
4. Reports providing documentation to various government regulators

In each of these cases the computer converts data into usable information by processing the data using a computer program. Data can be divided into several levels, called a **data storage hierarchy** (see illustration on page 2). The bit is the smallest and simplest entity in the hierarchy, and the database is the most complex. The discussion starts with the simplest entity—a bit.

Database
File
Record
Field
Character or byte
Bit

Bits and Bytes

A **bit,** or binary digit, is a single-digit number represented by either 0 or 1, and it is the smallest unit of storage in the computer. A **character,** or **byte,** is a combination of eight consecutive bits. A character represents one storage location in the computer where we can store either **alphabetic characters** (*A* through *Z,* and *a* through *z*), **numeric characters** (0 through 9), and **special characters** (+ , %, $, and so forth). An **alphanumeric character** is any alphabetic, numeric, or special character. Because the smallest bit configuration for a character is 0000 0000 and the largest bit configuration is 1111 1111, we can store any one of a possible 256 different symbols in one character or byte. (Note that binary numbers usually are written in groups of four: The binary number for 25 (decimal) is 11001; this figure is written as 0001 1001. This is done for purposes of readability, just as we typically separate decimal numbers into groups of three, separated by commas: for example, 195,674,890.)

We convert the 256 possible 8-bit codes into a character using either the Extended Binary Coded Decimal Interchange Code (EBCDIC) or American Standard Code for Information Interchange (ASCII) encoding standards (see Figure 1.1).

Typically, large IBM mainframes use the EBCDIC coding standard, and minicomputers and microcomputers use the ASCII coding standard. The bit configuration for the character A in EBCDIC (1100 0001) is different from the bit configuration for the A in ASCII (0100 0001). Consequently, when transferring data from one computer that uses ASCII to a computer that uses EBCDIC, (such as transferring data from a PC to a mainframe), you must "massage" the data before or after transferring it. This massaging of the data is done through a special program called a **utility program** (Figure 1.2). A utility program performs a special service or function that is needed by several applications. For example, it makes no difference whether you are transferring data for a billing system, a management report, or a budgeting system; you still must translate the data, and the same translation program can be used by each application. A special program or routine must transform each character stored in the ASCII coding system to a character in the EBCDIC coding system.

The capacity of primary and secondary memory in computer systems is measured in kilobytes (K), megabytes (M or meg), gigabytes (G or gig), or terabytes (T). A **kilobyte** is 1024 bytes or characters and a **megabyte** is 1024K, or 1,048,576 bytes or characters. On the other hand, a **gigabyte** is 1024M (about one billion) characters and a **terabyte** is 1024G (about one trillion). Hence, a 640K PC computer system with a 1.2-meg floppy disk drive and a 50-meg hard disk drive has 655,360 bytes of main memory, about 1,258,000 bytes available on a floppy diskette and about 50,000,000 bytes or locations available on the hard drive.

Parity Check Because machines have a tendency to break down and memory units can fail, many manufacturers include a parity check as part of the

Character	EBCDIC code Hex	Binary	ASCII code Hex	Binary	Character	EBCDIC code Hex	Binary	ASCII code Hex	Binary
A	C1	1100 0001	41	0100 0001	5	F5	1111 0101	35	0011 0100
B	C2	1100 0010	42	0100 0010	6	F6	1111 0110	36	0011 0110
C	C3	1100 0011	43	0100 0011	7	F7	1111 0111	37	0011 0111
D	C4	1100 0100	44	0100 0100	8	F8	1111 1000	38	0011 1000
E	C5	1100 0101	45	0100 0101	9	F9	1111 1001	39	0011 1101
F	C6	1100 0110	46	0100 0110	a	81	1000 0001	61	0110 0001
G	C7	1100 0111	47	0100 0111	b	82	1000 0010	62	0110 0010
H	C8	1100 1000	48	0100 1000	c	83	1000 0011	63	0110 0011
I	C9	1100 1001	49	0100 1001	d	84	1000 0100	64	0110 0100
J	D1	1101 0001	4A	0100 1010	e	85	1000 0101	65	0110 0101
K	D2	1101 0010	4B	0100 1011	f	86	1000 0110	66	0110 0110
L	D3	1101 0011	4C	0100 1100	g	87	1000 0111	67	0110 0111
M	D4	1101 0100	4D	0100 1101	h	88	1000 1000	68	0110 1000
N	D5	1101 0101	4E	0100 1110	i	89	1000 1001	69	0110 1001
O	D6	1101 0110	4F	0100 1111	j	91	1001 0001	6A	0110 1010
P	D7	1101 0111	50	0101 0000	k	92	1001 0010	6B	0110 1011
Q	D8	1101 1000	51	0101 0001	l	93	1001 0011	6C	0110 1100
R	D9	1101 1001	52	0101 0010	m	94	1001 0100	6D	0110 1101
S	E2	1110 0010	53	0101 0011	n	95	1001 0101	6E	0110 1110
T	E3	1110 0011	54	0101 0100	o	96	1001 0110	6F	0110 1111
U	E4	1110 0100	55	0101 0101	p	97	1001 0111	70	0111 0000
V	E5	1110 0101	56	0101 0110	q	98	1001 1000	71	0111 0001
W	E6	1110 0110	57	0101 0111	r	99	1001 1001	72	0111 0010
X	E7	1110 0111	58	0101 1000	s	A2	1010 0010	73	0111 0011
Y	E8	1110 1000	59	0101 1001	t	A3	1010 0011	74	0111 0100
Z	E9	1110 1001	5A	0101 1010	u	A4	1010 0100	75	0111 0101
0	F0	1111 0000	30	0011 0000	v	A5	1010 0101	76	0111 0110
1	F1	1111 0001	31	0011 0001	w	A6	1010 0110	77	0111 0111
2	F2	1111 0010	32	0011 0010	x	A7	1010 0111	78	0111 1000
3	F3	1111 0011	33	0011 0011	y	A8	1010 1000	79	0111 1001
4	F4	1111 0100	34	0011 0100	z	A9	1010 1001	7A	0111 1010

FIGURE 1.1 *The EBCDIC and ASCII encoding systems.*

FIGURE 1.2   *Using a utility program to convert EBCDIC data to ASCII and vice versa.*

hardware storage procedure. The manufacturer associates an extra bit with each byte to check for certain kinds of internal errors. This ninth bit is called a **parity bit** and is transparent to everyone except computer repair personnel.

The computer can be set to check for an **odd parity** or an **even parity** setting. If the computer is set for odd parity, then each character must be represented by an odd number of 1 bits. That is, if the eight-bit code for any character has an odd number of 1s in the byte, the parity bit will be set to 0 to maintain this odd number. However, if the eight-bit code for a character has an even number of 1s, the parity bit is set to a 1 to maintain an odd number of 1s in the byte. For example, the letter A has the eight-bit EBCDIC configuration 1100 0001; hence its parity bit is set to 0 (1100 0001 0). However, the letter C has the eight-bit configuration 1100 0011. Hence, its parity bit is set to 1 (1100 0011 1) which maintains an odd number of 1 bits in the byte.

When a memory units fails on minicomputers and mainframes the machine issues a parity-error warning at the operator's console. The operator can bypass the faulty unit and call the necessary repair personnel. However, on microcomputers, any parity error immediately terminates processing and the computer stops. In most cases, the owner of the microcomputer must have the machine repaired before any further processing can take place.

Words, Halfwords, Fullwords, Doublewords, Longwords, Quadwords Many computer systems use something in addition to a byte to store characters. On IBM machines, a grouping of two consecutive bytes is called a **halfword** and a grouping of two halfwords is called a **fullword** (or **word**). Hence, a halfword contains 16 bits, a fullword contains 4 bytes or 32 bits. A **doubleword** consists of 8 consecutive bytes, or a total of 64 bits. When these machines store, transfer, and compare data, they do these operations via bytes, fullwords, and doublewords. Remember, most mainframe machines are 64-bit machines and therefore store, transfer, and compare objects using doublewords (see Figure 1.3A).

Digital Equipment Corporation (DEC) machines are either 32-bit or 64-bit machines. On DEC machines, a grouping of 2 consecutive bytes is called a **word** (16 bits), a grouping of 4 bytes is a **longword** (32 bits), and a grouping of 8 bytes is a **quadword** (64 bits). These machines store, transfer, and compare data using halfwords (bytes), words, longwords, and quadwords (see Figure 1.3B).

Most PCs based on the 8086/8088 chip are 16-bit machines and consequently move, store, and compare items using 16 bits. Newer PCs based on the 80286, 80386, and 80486 chips can store, move, and compare items using

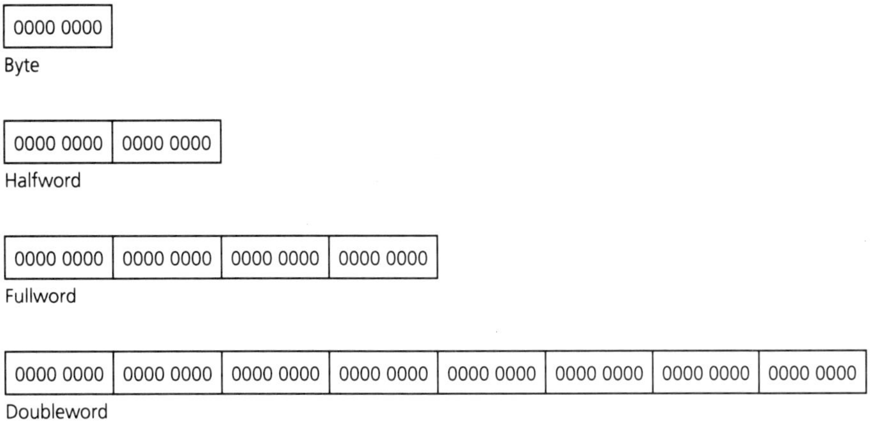

0000 0000

Byte

0000 0000	0000 0000

Halfword

0000 0000	0000 0000	0000 0000	0000 0000

Fullword

0000 0000	0000 0000	0000 0000	0000 0000	0000 0000	0000 0000	0000 0000	0000 0000

Doubleword

FIGURE 1.3A   *Byte, halfword, fullword, and doubleword.*

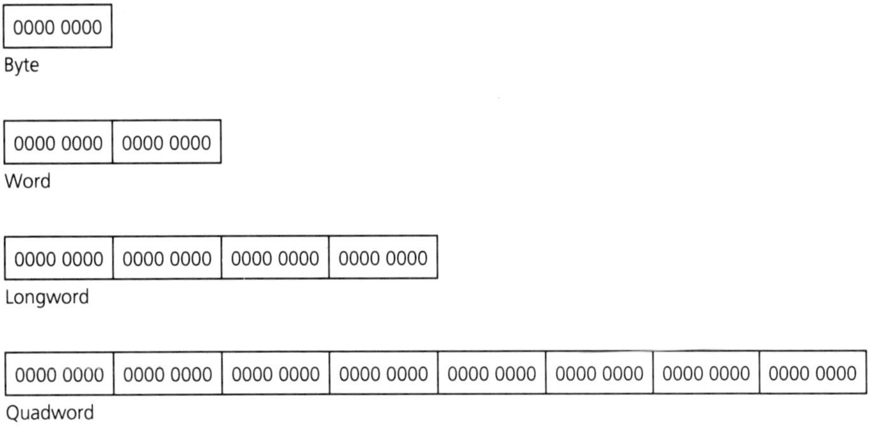

0000 0000

Byte

0000 0000	0000 0000

Word

0000 0000	0000 0000	0000 0000	0000 0000

Longword

0000 0000	0000 0000	0000 0000	0000 0000	0000 0000	0000 0000	0000 0000	0000 0000

Quadword

FIGURE 1.3B   *Byte, word, longword, quadword.*

16, 32, or 64 bits. Graciously, the manufacturers of these machines, in co-ordination with their writers of the operating system, have made the internal physical structure of the PC transparent to most users.

Fields, Records, and Files

A **field** is any collection of related characters. A person's name can be composed of a first-name field, a middle-initial field, and a last-name field. A field is the smallest unit of data storage that has meaning to the user. Fields can consist of only one character, for example, a field used to denote the sex of an employee might contain only F or M. Each of these fields can contain any alphanumeric character. Fields are defined to be alphabetic fields, numeric fields, and alphanumeric fields depending on the type of characters the field contains. A numeric field can contain a decimal point and sign. For some software products numeric fields might not allow the use of negative numbers and decimal points.

When you write a computer program, each field must be defined to the system. For example, in COBOL, you could define a person's name as

```
05 PERSON-NAME     PIC X(50).
```

However, describing a person's name in general terms does not permit you to use the first name or last name as a separate entity. To differentiate a person's first name from his or her last name, you might use the COBOL definition

```
05 PERSON-NAME.
    10 LAST-NAME        PIC X(29).
    10 FIRST-NAME       PIC X(20).
    10 MIDDLE-INITIAL   PIC X(01).
```

Here, you can extract the last name, for example, and use it in a sort routine or to find other data. Obviously, you could rearrange the field's structure by placing FIRST-NAME, MIDDLE-INITIAL, and LAST-NAME in first, second, and third positions, respectively. But how do you know in what order to place a person's name? In many cases you have a great deal of latitude on how you define the fields within a computer program. However, if your program is to merge with other programs on the system or if it calls an already existing field structure from some disk device, you might be required to define a field in a particular way so that it will be compatible with other data on the system.

A **record** is a collection of related fields. An employee's weekly employment record can contain, for example, fields concerning his or her name and address, hours worked, and deductions for union dues, credit union, and United Fund. Each field will be classified as to its type (alphabetic, alphanumeric, or numeric) and length (number of characters). A numeric field must not contain alphabetic data because the arithmetic unit in the computer cannot, for example, add 123 to 2R6. Such an attempt will generate an error message and the computer, in most cases, will terminate the processing of the program. This abnormal termination of processing is called an **abend,** or abnormal end.

Programs convert input data into the EBCDIC version of it before it is stored in a file. The program must also pack the numbers before they are sent to the arithmetic unit. Later, they must be edited for output before they can be redisplayed on a screen or sent to a printer. Editing routines during data entry must prohibit the inclusion of nonnumeric data in numeric fields. It requires a great deal of programming time and effort to write the necessary editing routines to validate the data (Figure 1.4). As far as the computer is concerned, the name George Was&*47$@# is a valid name. The error does not produce an abend and the machine will continue to process. Later, when

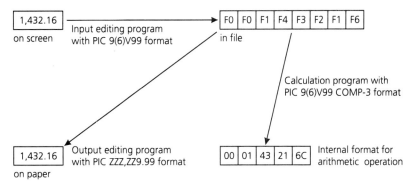

FIGURE 1.4   *Program editing of data.*

you check the fields for correctness, any incorrect data can be modified and reentered properly into the computer.

The computer must know the lengths of the various fields. An employee's employment record could contain the following fields, their type, and their lengths:

Field	Type	Length
Last name	alphanumeric	25
First name	alphanumeric	25
Middle initial	alphanumeric	1
Address	alphanumeric	20
City	alphanumeric	20
State	alphanumeric	2
ZIP (USA only)	alphanumeric	5
Date of birth	numeric	6
Date employed	numeric	6
Marital status	numeric	1
Number of dependents	numeric	2

The record for one employee has a length of 113 characters and is stored in a 113-byte contiguous area of memory (Figure 1.5).

A **file** is a collection of records where each record contains specific data and the data is related in some way. Typically, you create a file or modify an already existing file to hold the data so you can process it later into usable facts and figures. Files usually are stored on secondary memory storage devices, such as floppy disks, tapes, or hard drives. You access a file that resides on a secondary storage unit by reading one record from that file and then processing that record. If you want to read multiple records from the file, you must do the following:

1. Search the file for a particular record
2. Read the record
3. Process that record
4. Begin again at step 1 until you exhaust your quest for records

First record

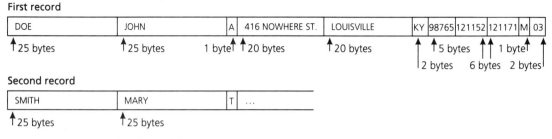

FIGURE 1.5   *Sample record in memory.*

DATABASES

A **database** is an integrated system of files designed primarily to minimize the repetition of data. The files of a database are part of an overall software package that creates, manages, and accesses the database files. Some of the major database software systems include IMS, IDMS/R, DB2, Oracle, Focus, Ingres, and dBASE III and IV.

Remember, the files in a database are different from standard files because database files are linked together logically via some database structure. However, a database is not just the arrangement of files in a particular order and the use of specialized software. Because a database is only a collection of data or facts, you must have a system to create and manage a database.

A Database Management System (DBMS) is a collection of software and other tools available from software or hardware vendors. A DBMS also might require the purchase of additional hardware and software, the design and implementation of standards and procedures, the implementation of security guidelines and standards for using the database, and the financial commitment to train and develop personnel to use it efficiently.

Fixed-length and Variable-length Records

So far, we have only illustrated records that are **fixed-length records,** which means each record contains the same number of bytes. For example, the employee record shown in Figure 1.5 is always 113 bytes long, regardless of which employee's record you access. Although fixed-length records are easy to understand (and program), they can be wasteful of storage space. In Figure 1.5, the employee record specifies 25 bytes for the last name; however, all employees will not have a 25-character last name. In fact, most employees will have a last name that is considerably less than 25 characters long. However, to be able to store data for those few who have 25-character last names, 25 bytes was allocated for all employee names. If, for example, the average length of a last name is only 12 bytes, you waste an average of 13 bytes of storage space for each record. These records would contain blanks or some other meaningless character, such as **low values** (the byte 0000 0000) or **high values** (the byte 1111 1111).

Although wasting 13 bytes per record might be acceptable if you are keeping data on a dozen employees, it can become a serious problem if you are keeping data on many thousands of employees. The main disadvantage of fixed-length records is that the maximum amount of space must be allocated for each record, regardless of whether a particular record needs that space.

Variable-length records make better use of storage space. Here, only the space actually required for each record is allocated. In addition, you must choose some method of indicating where the field ends and store that information as well. To process a record, first access the information regarding where each field ends, and then access each field within the record.

Let us look at how to store the variable-length field LAST-NAME. If the name is SMITH, store the length of the name (which is 5) and the name logically as follows:

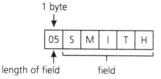

On IBM mainframes using the EBCDIC code, the field becomes

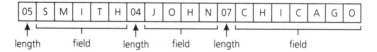

You can store multiple variable-length fields using the same concept. Store the three fields SMITH (LAST-NAME), JOHN (FIRST-NAME), and CHICAGO (CITY) logically as

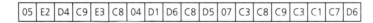

This translates into the internal representation of

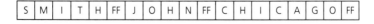

This technique has many drawbacks, however, including having to convert decimal lengths into hexadecimal lengths and vice versa. You can resolve this problem by placing some standard symbol (e.g., hexadecimal FF) after each field. The previous three fields would be stored logically as

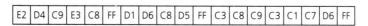

and physically as

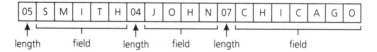

Note that, in this example, you have dealt with variable-length fields. You also can create variable-length records even when the fields are fixed-length fields. For example, assume that you are keeping data on employee payroll deductions. You might have in your record the following fields, their types, and their lengths:

Field	Type	Length
Retirement plan deduction	numeric	5
Life insurance deduction	numeric	5
Health insurance deduction	numeric	5
401K deduction	numeric	5
Parking fee deduction	numeric	5
United Fund deduction	numeric	5

Because not all the employees will have all the deductions, space is wasted by storing unused values in the fields—especially those fields with a zero deduction. Here, you would use the same strategy as above, but on a field level rather than on a character level. You only allocate space for those fields that represent actual deductions for an employee and indicate in the record which fields you have stored. (We will discuss specific methods of doing this in Chapter 3.)

There are advantages and disadvantages to using fixed-length and variable-length fields. Fixed-length fields are easier to understand and define in a program, but they waste space. Variable-length fields can save space, but require more computer resources to process. Here, extra program logic must execute for each record to determine where fields end or which fields are included. The type of record used depends on the application and the amount of computer resources available for that application.

FILE TYPES

There are eight major types of data files classified according to their use (Figure 1.6). These include the following:

- *Master files* contain current data of a permanent nature
- *Transaction files* contain data of a temporary nature, usually used to update master files
- *History files* contain historical data; they can represent an audit trail of activity that has transpired
- *Backup files* are identical copies of another file to ensure against mishap
- *Input files* are any files used for inputting of data
- *Output files* are any files used for outputting of data
- *Print files* are files specially formatted for printing
- *Sort files* are files having one or more records in sorted order

Figure 1.6 shows different file types. The master file has both a backup copy on tape cassette for immediate recovery due to damage and an archive

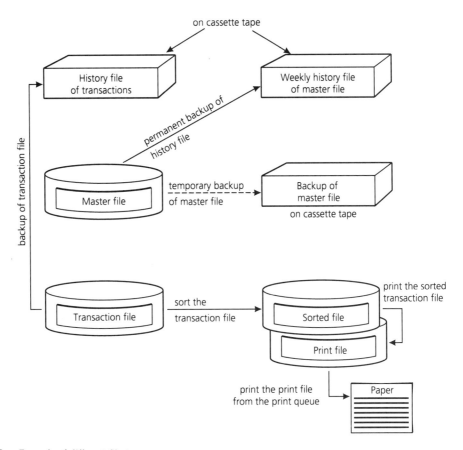

FIGURE 1.6 *Example of different file types.*

copy as a history file. The transaction file has an archive copy as a history file. The user sorts the transaction file and prints a report. The sort and print files are immediately deleted after the report prints. The transaction file is deleted after the successful updating of the master file. If the master file fails to update properly, then it is reinstated to its original state using its backup copy. The archive copy of the master is saved for audit trail purposes.

Master Files

A **master file** contains data of a permanent nature. The master file is updated on an ongoing basis because it contains vital data and that data must remain current. The number of master files on a corporate mainframe can be enormous because the company might have multiple master files for each activity it pursues. Table 1.1 contains a partial list of some of the common master files of a corporation.

TABLE 1.1   *Example of typical corporation's master files*

Customer information	Employee attendance	Building maintenance
Field office sales	Union	Fixed assets files
Internal auditing	OSHA	Inventory
Federal, state, local tax	Product evaluation	Supplies
Accounts receivable	Potential clients/customers	Government regulation
Cost/payback	Customer credit history	Expense analysis
Word processing	Payroll	Future needs analysis
Land acquisition/real estate	Insurance	Salespeople commission
Office building	Retired workers	Employee savings plan
Company equity	Customer payment	Employee benefits
Building and facilities	Accounting	Charitable contributions
Vendor suppliers	Company stockholders	Affirmative action
Office and equipment location	Budget	Market penetration
Utility management	Accounts payable	Previous clients/customers
Employee medical history	Marketing files	General ledger
Travel cost	Stocks and bonds	Credit union
Entertainment	Financial strategy/math models	Unemployment
Employee salary	Depreciation	Employee benefits
Salary review files	Mortgage	

Most companies have a large number of master files on the computer system. The list in Table 1.1 contains only a small portion of the actual files in existence within a large company. Most of the files listed in the table can be subdivided further into more master files. That is, the company's payroll file is not just one file, but several files. These files allow for hourly workers, salaried workers, salespeople who are paid commissions, consultants, and employees who are paid at different time cycles (weekly, biweekly, and monthly). In addition, there could be multiple variations of each of the files for each division or subsidiary within the parent company.

Transaction Files

Transaction files contain data of a temporary nature and are used to update master files. Transaction files contain nondynamic data. The data in transaction files need not immediately update the data in a master file. The actual merging of the transaction file with the master file could occur a fews hours to a few months after the transaction file's creation, depending on the nature of the data. After the updating of the master file by the transaction file, the transaction file is either destroyed or saved for a short period of time.

History Files

If you want to save the data used to update the master file, you can create a history file. A **history file** is a file created for the long-term storage of data and can represent an audit trail of all activities that have transpired. Suppose a credit card company wants to keep track of customers' payments on their accounts, how much they paid, and when they made the payment. After a clerk opens the envelope containing payment, he or she would enter the account number and payment into the system as part of a transaction file. At the end of the clerk's shift, an auditing program would merge this daily transaction file with the customer master file to update the master. This auditing program would retain a copy of the transaction file as a history file to resolve any possible problem at a later date. Many months later when a customer complains about a payment not being credited to his or her account, the history files are scanned to resolve any data-entry errors that might have occurred. History files can be retained for years because of various legal requirements.

Backup Files

A **backup file** is an identical copy of a file to ensure against loss of data because of lost or damaged files. The backup copy is used to recreate the original file if the original file is destroyed.

Most computer installations have a regular schedule for creating backup copies of important files. Most installations now use cassette tape for storing the backup files and these tapes are retained in a secure area. Remember, any serious damage to files caused by programming errors, fire or other natural disasters, or terrorist activities by strangers or dissatisfied employees can seriously hamper the company's ability to function. Hence, all major files must have backup copies to maintain an orderly business environment in case of mishap. Many companies have instituted a Disaster Recovery Plan to ensure the orderly salvaging of data files and continuing operation of the data center in case of a major disaster.

Input, Output, Print, and Sort Files

Files that are sent to the printer are called **print files.** The computer makes a copy of the file to be printed and formats it by placing headers, footers, dates, and page numbers in their proper places and aligning the margins. This copy is called a print file and contains all the information the printer needs to print it. The system's print queue places the print file in queue for printing. After it is printed, the print file is deleted from the print queue.

When a program creates a file to be used by another program, the created file is called an **output file.** When a program uses another file for the inputting of data, that file is called an **input file.** A **sort file** is any file having one or more records in some sorted order. You create sort files using systems software (a SORT utility), a COBOL sort program, or other software designed to sort data based on one or more fields within a file.

━━━━━━━━━━━   ## FILE ACCESSING METHODS

So far we have discussed the types of files available on computer systems. Now let us look at how to access these files. The operating system of most computers has a built-in file management system as part of the Data Manager. This system manages the files by doing the following:

- Storing files on the storage media
- Retrieving files when they are accessed
- Updating files when instructed
- Creating keys or indexes depending on the type of file
- Using keys and indexes depending on the type of file
- Preventing unauthorized access to the files
- Providing communication routines between the files and programs

In fact, the Data Manager is responsible for all activity on the Direct Access Storage Devices (DASD) or hard disks. You can license or purchase other file-accessing systems from third-party vendors. The most popular of these accessing methods is Virtual Storage Access Method (VSAM), a file manager from IBM.

Standard file processing has several disadvantages, including the following:

- The data can be duplicated in multiple files
- Programs can be dependent on the file format (the location of fields within the record)
- Files are not integrated
- Security is haphazard and inefficient
- Multiple file usage is difficult
- Files are independent
- The data is not readily accessible to users
- The data is dependent on prewritten programs

File Storage and Access

There are three major commonly used methods for storing and retrieving files on disks or DASD. These methods are:

- Sequential file organization where the file contains records in sequential order
- Direct file organization where the file contains records in random or nonsequential order, also called random access files
- Indexed file organization where the file contains a key field in each record so the record can be accessed either randomly or sequentially

You use one of these organizational structures to store and retrieve records in files. The system developers decide the method for storage based on the available resources, programming requirements, and the current and future needs of the application.

You use **sequential file** organization for files where you want to access all records in sequential order. These records appear in the file one after another in the order each was entered and stored on the system.

You use **direct access files,** or **random files,** where you want to access specific records in the file quickly. Direct or random access files have a key field, called a primary key, which lets the computer locate, retrieve, and update any record in the file based on some key value. The records in direct access files do not have to be read sequentially to access the desired record. Instead, the system uses the primary key to find the location of the record on DASD using a technique or algorithm designed by the vendor of the software.

To access random files, enter a value for the primary key field (e.g., part number). The computer determines if a record exists for that key value. If a record exists for that value, the system retrieves the record. If a record does not exist for that value, the system returns a message indicating the record does not exist. You have the option to create a new record by loading data for that record into the system or you can attempt to access another record using a different primary key value.

You might want to create a file that can be accessed either sequentially or directly. This is particularly true if you want a listing of all the records in a random access file. Surely, you would not want to enter the primary key values for each record to read the records. You would not want two separate files, a sequential file and a random file, for the same data. You need a file that sometimes acts like a sequential file and sometimes acts like a random file. These files are called **indexed sequential files.**

When you create an indexed sequential file, you also produce a second file called an index file. An **index file** contains the relative addresses of a master file's records on DASD along with the primary key value for that record. Whenever you attempt to access the record, the access method must first search the index file to locate the record's physical location on DASD (Figure 1.7). Once it finds the DASD address, the system can obtain the desired record. When using an indexed sequential file, you can access any record at random using a key value or you can access the entire file sequentially, either in ascending or descending order.

Hashing

Hashing is a technique computers use to calculate an address for storage of a record on DASD. The computer uses a mathematical formula or algorithm using the key field value to produce a unique logical address using a random number generator (Figure 1.8). If the value in the key field contains alphabetic or special characters, the computer uses its numeric equivalent as the initial value for the random number generator. The random number produced from

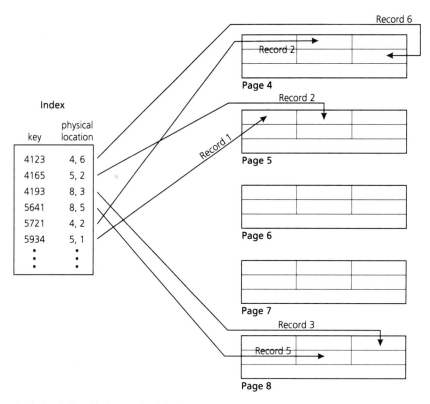

FIGURE 1.7   *An indexed file with its associated index.*

hashing is translated into a physical address on the DASD medium. Each time you attempt to access the record on DASD, the computer generates the same unique random number for that record's key value and gives the same unique DASD record location. Because you want one and only one record stored on disk for each key value in the file, the value in the key must be unique. Files created using this technique are referred to as hash files.

Hash files cause some problems. Because hashing randomly spreads the

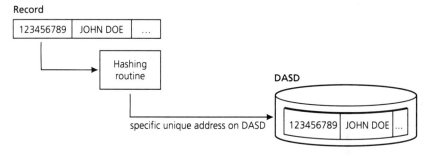

FIGURE 1.8   *Using hashing to place record on disk.*

records over some area of DASD, the sequential accessing of those records can prove to be difficult. This can be particularly annoying if you frequently need records in the file in either ascending or descending order. Because the records are randomly distributed over multiple regions of DASD, however, disk contention problems can be reduced or eliminated. Disk contention occurs when the system has a request to access or store more than one record on DASD at the exact same time. The read/write head of the disk drive can be in one location only at any one time. Hence, every record, except the one currently being accessed or stored, must wait in a queue until the device is ready to access or store the next record.

DATABASE CONCEPTS

To correct some of the problems with using classical file structures, many companies are utilizing database systems to save and store their vital data. Remember, a database is an integrated system of files specially designed to decrease the repetition of data. In addition, database files have an ordered structure that links the files together.

These integrated files are components in a complete system that includes software to manage the database records (that is, their deletion, creation, and modification). This system of software modules is a DBMS. Some of the more popular DBMS products include IMS, DB2, and IDMS/R (for the mainframe environment) and dBASE IV, Oracle, Focus, and Ingres (for the PC environment). These systems not only manage the database records but have built-in report generators allowing either the technical staff or the end user the opportunity to produce reports quickly and easily.

THE COMPLETE DATABASE ENVIRONMENT

Establishing a database environment requires more than just purchasing specialized software and creating database files. You must consider several other ingredients to guarantee a successful database environment. These ingredients include establishing the following:

- Procedures and standards for using the database
- Security criteria
- Training personnel
- Computer programs
- Measures to maintain error-free data

Procedures and Standards

You must develop procedures and standards for using the database. Most database systems are huge, both in the number of files within the database and in the number of people who can access its data. With the possibility of thousands of files within the database, you must initiate naming conventions and standards for the database file names to prevent mass confusion and their duplicity. In addition, you must establish procedures for backing up the data in the database files, identify who can access or modify the data in the files, and identify who can delete data in the files. Formal procedures for requesting accounts on the database might need management approval before they become established corporate policy.

Security Criteria

You must create security criteria for granting individuals the authorization to access the data in the database. All sensitive data that exist within the database must be safeguarded against unauthorized access. Corporate data about sales volume, pricing policies, and other sensitive data must be protected. Obviously, if sensitive medical information about an employee were made available to the general employee population because of a lack of security or carelessness on the part of the database designers, the company and the designers could find themselves in serious legal difficulty.

Training

Training must be provided for both the development staff and the end user on how to access and use the database. A database is a complex set of programs and files that requires training to use efficiently and effectively. The training of the existing programming staff on how to design, develop, and access the database files is crucial in the early stages of the implementation of the database. Later, after applications using the database become ready for the production mode, the end users will need training on how to access the data in the database and generate their own reports using the built-in report generators of the database.

Computer Programs

You might need to write new computer programs or convert current programs so they can access data in the database. Remember, once the database is functionally on line, the existing programs access classical files and must be rewritten so they will access the database files instead. In addition, you might need to convert the data in classical files to a database structure and load the data into multiple database files using utility programs.

Error-free Data

Measures and standards need to be established to keep the data in the database accurate and error free. One advantage of switching to a database environment is the ability of the end users to generate their own reports using the database software without programming staff intervention. Hence, if the end user departments can enter, modify, and delete data in the database, someone in the user departments must take the responsibility to ensure the data being modified is correct and accurate. You must make the end users responsible for errors in their own database files. Using databases can be a dynamic environmental change for the user departments who were dependent on the developers and programming staff for many years to provide them with accurate, error-free reports. This new responsibility, when thrust onto the user departments, can cause serious social and political repercussions within each of the user departments.

Remember, most user-department personnel might not be aware of backup files and how and when to create them. Most are inexperienced in the design of editing and error-trapping routines. Also, many database systems allow the end user freedom from developers or other members of the programming staff. Most database systems contain vehicles for end users to trash their own data, making it susceptible to damage or loss. Therefore, you must take certain measures and create certain standards to ensure the orderly creation, modification, and retention of database data.

ADVANTAGES OF DATABASES

Utilizing a database instead of classical files has many advantages. The advantages include the following:

- Reduced data redundancy
- Data integrity
- Data independence
- Data security
- Data consistency
- Easier use of data
- Less storage

Reduced Data Redundancy

Data redundancy is reduced by cross-referencing the data within the integrated database system. For example, an employee's name and address will appear only once in the database. In a classical file structure, each file is independent of any other file. Therefore, an employee's name and address could appear in multiple files depending on the need for that data. It is not uncommon to find an employee's name and address scattered among 10 to 20 files in a typical company's computer system (Figure 1.9). Any change in a name due to a marriage or divorce or a change in an employee's address would require modifying the data in these numerous files—and their backup copies. By utilizing classical files, there is no guarantee that all the backup and historical files reflect current modifications to their records. Remember, backup files

File 1

Tony Fabbri	Chicago	IL
Sue Smith	Peoria	IL
Don Jones	Lakeport	KY
•		
•		
•		

File 2

Tony Fabbri	Chicago	IL
Don Jones	Lakeport	KY
Mary Driver	Dunlap	CA
•		
•		
•		

FIGURE 1.9 *Data redundancy. Multiple files contain the same data. The Employee History File (File 1) contains data also found in the Employee Medical History File (File 2).*

should be current and some history files also should contain current data. Obviously, if the company's "history file of customer orders" does not contain the customer's new corporate name or new shipping location, great confusion could arise when that history file is later accessed.

Because a particular piece of data appears only once in the database, however, the reduction in the duplication of the data will decrease the amount of disks and tapes needed to retain the data. The database design eliminates duplicate data and reduces the time it takes to perform backups or recovery of the system. Yet, redundancy elimination can impose other costs. For example, if someone in the personnel department wants to query a database about the address of an employee's manager, the computer would have to access the Employee record (to find the employee's department), the Department record (to find the manager), and then the Employee record for the manager. These additional accesses translate into additional processing time and hardware utilization and increased cost.

Data Integrity

Because data appears only once in the database, you can be certain that changes to the data will be reflected in all future use of that data. For example, you need to change the address of an employee in only one location in the database and that change will appear in all future use of the data.

Data Independence

The structure of the database requires that data be independent of other data in the database and the software used to access the database. If you modify or delete data in the database, other data in the database should not be adversely affected. For example, deleting an employee from the database who resigns should not affect other data in the database. When deleting the employee from the database file of current employees, you should not lose information about year-to-date salary paid or federal tax payments withheld. Likewise, data about that employee's office, telephone number, desk, chairs, and so on should not be affected.

Because the database files have a predefined structure, programs written in different languages can access the same database file without difficulty. Remember, if you create a classical file using COBOL, the structure of the file on DASD might be different than if you created a similar file using FORTRAN. Here, the data is dependent on the software that creates it. By using a database, you eliminate the dependency between software and data. Because the program accesses the data through the database software, records are stored and accessed independently of the programming language that accesses the database records.

Data Security

A database system can have additional security measures as part of the database software product. Most database systems maintain their own independent security environment. When database data is centrally located, security is easier to regulate and control. In classical file usage, maintaining security is difficult because security measures are based on the ability of someone to access a particular file. If redundant data is spread over multiple files on multiple disk packs, then to have access to all occurrences of a field, you might need access to all the files. This might not be desirable. For example, why should a data-entry clerk taking orders over a phone have access to another individual's medical history files simply to make an address change? Remember, security in classical file structures is based on the file, not the fields in the file. Once you can access the file, you have the capability of accessing all fields within that file.

Typically, the database software system contains its own accessing procedure. Before someone can use the database software, he or she must have a special account on that database system. After he or she has general access to the database system, the database administrator gives that person a certain view of the database. The database user can access certain screens within the database software, use certain commands within the database (to read, update, create, and/or delete data) and access certain files, records, and fields within the database. Here, a database administrator is an individual or group of individuals whose primary responsibility is the management of the database.

Security is further enhanced in the database environment with the expanded use of audit trails. In classical file structures, the programming staff typically has to write software code to provide a trace of who accesses the system and what changes were made to the files. Most mainframe database packages automatically provide a complete audit trail of all activity against the database.

Data Consistency

Data consistency is maintained in a database environment. The name and size of data is consistent for all applications. For example, the size of FIRST-

NAME field is the same for all applications using the database. If the FIRST-NAME field was created as a 20-character field, the database will always access it as a 20-character field. In classical files, one programmer can assign a FIRST-NAME field in his or her file a length of 20 characters, while another programmer creating a different file can dictate the FIRST-NAME field to be 25 characters (Figure 1.10). Figure 1.10 shows that programs not containing a PIC X(20) clauses for FIRST-NAME cannot access the data in File 1 and similarly, programs not containing a PIC X(25) clause for FIRST-NAME cannot access the data in File 2. When each file and programmer works independently, there is no vehicle for uniformity among the programming staff. Even data dictionaries, which we will discuss later, do not fully remedy this problem. Files created 20 years ago can still contain inconsistent sizes for the same type fields.

In classical files, naming conventions are not generally uniform. For example, the COBOL name for an employee's first name could include EMPL-FIRSTNAME, E-FIRSTNAME, EMPLOYEE-F-NAME, EMPLOYEE-FIRST-NAME, EFN, FNAME, or E-F-N, to name just a few. However, in a database environment, when a name is first assigned to a field, that particular name endures for the life of the structure.

Easier Use of Data

Data is easier to use in the database environment. Most relational databases contain a user-friendly query language as part of the database software package. In these types of databases, with a little training, users can easily make queries on the data without programming staff intervention. Because the database user has a view of selected fields and files within the database, the

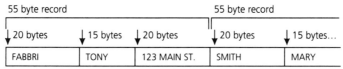

Physical layout of File 1 with records containing LAST-NAME, FIRST-NAME, and STREET as PIC X(20), PIC X(15), and PIC X(20), respectively

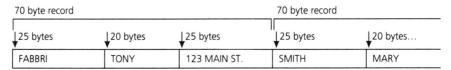

Physical layout of File 2 with record containing LAST-NAME, FIRST-NAME, and STREET as PIC X(25), PIC X(20), and PIC X(25), respectively

FIGURE 1.10   *Data consistency. The same fields stored by different programs where each program created a different length field for the same data.*

user has more power and versatility than under classical file structures. Now the user does not have to ask "permission" via a formal request to the programming staff to access the data and manipulate his or her own reports. Of course, this ease of use will inherently cause problems because errors have a tendency to magnify and grow with use by inexperienced personnel. Only after the end user becomes an experienced user of the database system will the true clout of his or her database usage unfold.

The programmer's use of the data by coding applications also is enhanced. Most database systems provide for access via a **database language** that is interfaced with program code in some other language, for example, COBOL, FORTRAN, or PL/I. These database languages are easier to use than traditional programming languages because much of the file processing is done behind the scenes by the database software; the programmer does not have to program these functions himself or herself. Such functions include opening and closing each file, creating a logical record from several physical files, and so forth.

Both programmers and end users find data access simpler with a database due to isolation from physical changes to the database. Typically, any user of a database, including programmers, "sees" the database through a **view,** which is a logical record created by the database administrator or the programming staff. For example, an employee database might include data about salary and medical claims on group insurance. End users and programmers working with and creating salary administration applications would work through a view containing only the salary data (Figure 1.11).

When you use a view of the file, changes are easier to implement. Suppose you want to change the way the medical claim data is stored in Figure 1.11. You can add a field for income tax withholding on disability payments because of changes in tax laws. In a traditional file, you would have to change all of the programs that access the main file because you changed the structure of the file. However, when you use a view in a database, only those programs that use the view containing the change would have to be modified. All other programs would remain the same.

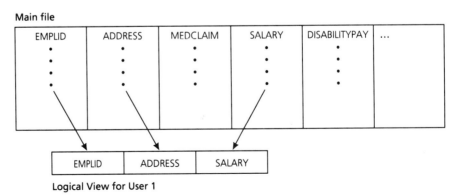

Main file

| EMPLID | ADDRESS | MEDCLAIM | SALARY | DISABILITYPAY | ... |

Logical View for User 1

| EMPLID | ADDRESS | SALARY |

FIGURE 1.11   *Using a view.*

Less Storage

Obviously, if you eliminate data redundancy, the data consumes less storage space. Instead of someone's name residing in 20 to 25 files, the name only resides in one file. However, as end users begin to appreciate the ease and versatility of databases, they begin to use them more frequently. Hence, productivity increases and storage space decreases as a result of the improved utilization. Of course, this is exactly what you want. Remember, the purpose of computer systems is to increase productivity and accomplish more business with the same employee resources. You might need to swap disk space for user productivity, which is an excellent trade off.

DISADVANTAGES OF DATABASES

There are several disadvantages of using databases due to their:

- Complexity
- Expense
- Vulnerability
- Size
- Training cost
- Compatibility
- Locking in of technology
- Lack of lower-level control

Complexity

Databases and their associated DBMS are extremely complex. They require special skills to implement and use. On large systems the selection and training of one or more database administrators is not a trivial expense. The developers and programming staff personnel will need special training on the design, use, and implementation of a particular DBMS. The End User Support Center must design classes or courses for the user departments so they can understand how to access the database using the DBMS built-in report generator.

Expense

The installation of the DBMS and its databases onto the current system requires careful planning because of the possibility of the need for additional hardware. The interfacing of the database software with the existing operating system might require additional systems programming by the systems support team. Because database systems consume massive amounts of storage both in primary and secondary memory, most companies must upgrade their hardware by purchasing additional DASD units, more memory, and in many cases, a bigger and faster CPU unit requiring millions of dollars in capital outlay. In fact, management's approval to purchase a particular DBMS might require an entirely different computer configuration in both the hardware required and operating system mandated by the database software package.

Database software is not cheap. Even a DBMS for personal computers would cost from five hundred to several thousand dollars depending on the database. In addition to the one-time purchase price, which in reality is a one-time lease price, a company might be required to pay an additional service fee costing thousands of dollars per month. These database software maintenance contracts require the company to pay a fixed percentage per year for software maintenance. This yearly percentage is usually 10% of the current purchase or lease price for the product. A database product that sold for $125,000 several years ago might be now selling for $350,000. In this example, the differential increases the company's expenditure for maintenance by $22,500 per year. However, typical maintenance contracts authorize the company to receive free upgrades and corrections to the database software as they appear on the market.

For PC-based products, the story is similar. As new and more advanced releases appear on the market for a particular PC-based DBMS, the purchaser of the outdated software will have to spend additional money to upgrade his or her current copy of the database system to the new version. For many DBMS owners, this is not a trivial sum of money.

Remember, if productivity of employees increases by 1% per person in a 500 man/woman computer shop because of the use of a database, that 1% easily translates into 5 additional workers with no increase in personnel. The savings in salary and fringe benefits for not having to hire five more people can offset any cost attributed to the database. If productivity increases by 10% to 30%, the cost of the database seems small when compared to the cost of hiring new employees over many years.

Vulnerability

Because data in databases is in a central location, it is vulnerable to partial or complete destruction when a breakdown of hardware components occurs—in particular DASD or in a software mistake. Obviously, an unauthorized invasion of the database by a person determined to disrupt the normal processing cycle will cause havoc to the database and its files. For such a person to permanently destroy the database, however, he or she will need to bypass the normal logon process to the main operating system, the accessing process to the database account, the built-in security device created by a view, the logging of all activity on the database by the automatic audit trail feature of the database software, and the normal backing up of database files by the operations team.

On PC-based systems, the database resides on hard disk. The PC user should take adequate precautions to ensure the safety of the database files. This includes making backup copies of the data on a timely basis and keeping them in a secure place. It does no good to backup the database and leave the backup copy near the PC computer system. A fire will surely damage both the hardware unit and the nearby floppy disk containing the backups.

Any theft of the hardware also could include theft of any software in the vicinity of the machine. A common procedure is to make two backup copies and place one close to the machine in case of accidental destruction of database files. The other copy can be kept at an off-site location to guard against the most serious of disasters. Although creating a backup can be time consuming, it is far better to have a backup than to lose everything to an accident, theft, carelessness, or neglect.

In mainframe environments, the operations staff creates backup copies of the database daily. Some mainframe databases even make continuous backups by making a copy of the database and creating log files of all activity on the database. When a disaster occurs, the automatic backup process recreates the database using the last backup copy of the database and then accesses all log files since that backup to replicate the database. Of course, such activity has an associated cost in both personnel and hardware. However, most companies must preserve crucial files to remain in business.

Size

The typical mainframe database is very large. Many database applications in a corporate environment require hundreds of interlinked database files, each containing thousands of records. Large insurance companies handling group insurance claims can have their group-claims database spanning 20 to 30 DASD devices each containing multigigabytes of memory. Obviously, large databases have special problems associated with their massive size. Backing up these large databases can require additional equipment and procedures. Recovery from a disaster can be very time consuming and difficult. If a company is processing one or two million transactions a day on one database, the audit trail log files quickly become huge. These files might need to be backed up to tape or cassette on a continuous basis, requiring additional hardware, tape librarians, computer operators, and storage facilities.

Part of the planning for the purchase of the database includes the study of the capacity of the existing system, a process called **capacity planning.** This study indicates that the database software and the projected use of the database might warrant the purchase of an additional CPU unit and additional DASD devices. This study is crucial because the database software can consume enormous amounts of both primary and secondary memory. Placing the database on the existing computer system can have an adverse effect on the response time, and thereby, the users of the system. It is the capacity planner's job to predict the projected response time for the applications on the system. He or she might find that the projected database configuration on the current system will degrade the performance of that system. Hence, the decision to purchase a database software product also might include the decision to purchase an additional mainframe computer system.

For PC-based databases, the prospective purchaser must determine if his or her existing computer system has the necessary minimum configuration for a particular database software product. Many PC-based databases require one to two megabytes of primary memory and at least five megabytes of available hard disk space. PC owners should be mindful that this minimum configuration is just that—a minimum configuration for the software. If the PC user intends to create multiple large databases, he or she should allow for the storage of the projected database files and their associated indexes on the hard disk. This requires the PC owner to forecast his or her possible utilization of the database. This analysis might result in the PC owner abandoning the purchase of the database because it will not fit properly on his or her system or it might involve additional expense of upgrading the owner's current system. However, there are numerous PC-based DBMS products on the market that do not require massive amounts of memory and disk storage. For small applications, these products are versatile and perform adequately.

PC owners also should be conscious of the speed of the DBMS he or she plans to purchase. A PC-based DBMS on an older PC (for example, Intel's 8086-based machine) might execute significantly slower than the same software on a more modern PC, such as Intel's 80386. Response time on the newer machines can be subsecond, while the response time on the older version of the PC can be multisecond or multiminute. It is always wise to question known users of the database system to get an indication of the benefits and pitfalls associated with the database software product.

Training Costs

When a company purchases a database, it must first train one or more individuals to be the database administrator for that database product. This training usually occurs off site at the database vendor's training location and requires several weeks of training. Next, the systems analysts need training on how to design and use the database structure associated with that particular database. The programming staff then needs training on how to program efficiently and effectively using the database's programming language. The training time for analysts and programmers usually is two to three weeks. In many cases this training involves out-of-town travel for weeks at a time. The expenses associated with travel, lodging, food, and the training fees can be costly both in dollars and loss of productivity of the developer during the training period.

For companies with large programming staffs, the company might need to hire a Director of Education to implement an orderly and complete database training program in house. This will involve creating classrooms and training materials, along with training the Director in the database software product.

When the developers are ready to place database applications in an on-line production mode, the end-user departments might need training on how to use the built-in report generators associated with the database system. This can involve creating an End User Support Center to handle training the nontechnical staff. Of course, these added expenses are associated with the initial purchase of the database software product and should be included in the budget for the purchase of the database system.

Compatibility

One of the pitfalls of most database systems is their incompatibility with other database systems. Files created in one database product are not easily transferred to another database product. This is particularly true of DB2 and IDMS/R, two popular databases for mainframes. Database files created using IDMS/R are not easily transported to DB2 database files, and vice versa. This problem results from trying to integrate files created by database products from two different vendors of software. In this case, IBM markets DB2 and Computer Associates markets IDMS/R.

This problem usually does not exist when you try to integrate files from different database products from the same software vendor. For example, database files from IMS are easily converted to DB2 database tables. Here, IBM is the vendor supplier of both the IMS and the DB2 database product.

The same problem exists in the PC environment. Many PC-based databases are not compatible with other PC-based databases. In addition, PC databases might not be transported readily to mainframe databases and vice versa. Although many PC-based database systems provide utility programs to massage the files to make them transportable, there is no assurance that this process will result in an acceptable migration to another database system. Many database software products are available that include a PC version and a mainframe version, which guarantees successful integration of the database files.

Locking In of Technology

One serious objection to databases is the locking in of technology. If, for example, a company invests millions of dollars in the design and development of a database using one vendor's product, that company has made a huge financial commitment to that database product. If the vendor supplying the database product falls on hard times, abandons the software market, or expresses a desire to abandon the support of that database product, the company might find itself facing serious financial losses. The entire company's computer operation is dedicated to a now possibly antiquated database system, and the cost of migration to another system might be prohibitive.

Also, if you purchase a database product and realize later that the database will not perform as had been expected, you have little recourse other than to accept the loss. This loss can involve large financial write-offs for the cost of the software, training cost, and salaries of personnel associated with the database product.

The true expense of a database is not in the purchase of the database software or the hardware to run it. The true expense is in the development cost, where the company pays salaries to highly trained computer professionals to design and develop programs using the database software. A company's database system can include thousands of worker years in salary payouts, all dedicated to one vendor's database product.

The databases on the market today probably will not be the databases on the market 10 or 15 years from now. As new technology develops both in hardware and software, newer, faster, and easier-to-use systems will appear on the market. Remember, there is no ultimate database technology that will be the best forever. Hence, the systems you purchase today have a finite life and their cost of implementation is a depreciating item.

Lack of Lower-level Control

With a system based on traditional files, the programmer has considerable control over the way the data is physically stored. Such control can include choice of which DASD volume to store the data on, whether to access the files via the system catalog, and whether and how to block the records so that several records are accessed with each physical read operation. Such lower-level control allows the programmer to fine-tune the systems using the data for optimal use of the computer. With a database, the programmer typically does not have such control. Fine tuning is accomplished either by the database software itself (for example, IBM's DB2 software "decides" whether to use any indexes to the data) or by the database administrator or operating system programmers. Centralizing such control can result in "bottlenecks" that cause necessary fine tuning not to be done in a timely manner.

PROGRAMMER AND PROGRAMMING CONSIDERATIONS

The developers of software must be properly trained to use the database. The programming logic to perform database reads, changes, deletes, and inserts must be understood by the programming staff. In some cases, the database product is in actuality a systems development tool in addition to being a database generator. This is true for Computer Associates' IDMS/R product. Here, the developers must learn an entirely new procedure for systems generation. The writing of a database's accessing commands is only one part of the procedure. This learning process is very time consuming and costly because of the technical staff's loss of productivity during the learning mode.

Even in the PC environment, the database user must learn the rituals and language of the database product. It is not uncommon for a PC database user to spend hundreds of hours learning to use a PC database and master its idiosyncrasies. Although PC-based databases are handy and useful, the PC user might have to rely on the development staff to design the database efficiently. Very few nontechnical users have the expertise and logic training to design efficient database systems. The typical PC database owner's initial concern is to master the commands of the product in a few short weeks. Remember, experienced systems analysts spend one or more weeks at a database vendor's training site to master the design features of a database. Therefore, it is not prudent to expect the typical nontechnical user to master database design in a few hours or days.

DATABASE STRUCTURES

Entity Relationships

Before we begin our discussion on the three database structures, we must first investigate the relationship between data, called an entity-to-entity relationship. In classical files we often create a primary key for a record. This primary key accesses one record if it is a unique key or multiple records if it is a nonunique key.

If each key has a unique record associated with it and if each record has a unique primary key value, the relationship is said to be a **one-to-one relationship** (1–1). The relationship between a social security number and the person assigned it is a one-to-one relationship (Figure 1.12). Each person has one and only one social security number and each number has one and only one person assigned to it. When you access a record using the social security field as a primary key, you know you will access the same person's data each and every time.

However, if a primary key value has multiple records associated with it, the relationship is said to be a **one-to-many relationship** (1–N) (Figure 1.13). Obviously, if you choose LASTNAME as a primary key in an employee file, you must create it as a nonunique key to allow for the storage of multiple records of persons with the same last name (for example, multiple Smiths). Here, you have a one-to-many relationship between the name field and multiple records in storage. Each LASTNAME field has multiple records associated with it, but each record has one and only one key value—SMITH.

If the relationship is nonunique for both the key and the record, it is said to be a **many-to-many relationship** (N–N). Here, each key has multiple records and each record has multiple key values associated with it. The relationship

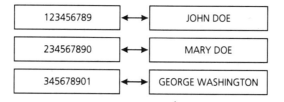

FIGURE 1.12 *Example of a one-to-one relationship.*

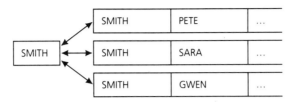

FIGURE 1.13   *Example of a one-to-many relationship.*

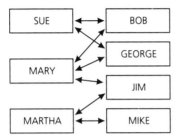

FIGURE 1.14   *Example of a many-to-many relationship.*

between teenage boys and teenage girls is a classic example of a many-to-many relationship. Each teenage boy has multiple girlfriends and each teenage girl has multiple boyfriends (Figure 1.14).

STRUCTURES TO EXPRESS ENTITY RELATIONSHIPS

There are three primary types of database structures:

- Hierarchical
- Network
- Relational

Hierarchical databases typically are found only in a mainframe environment, while network and relational databases are found in both mainframe and PC environments.

Hierarchical Databases

The data in a hierarchical database can be either a one-to-one relationship or a one-to-many relationship. Here, instead of grouping data into records and files, we group data into segments resembling a tree structure (Figure 1.15). This database has four segments, each with a specific field description defined much like a record. Each segment contains one or more fields and there can be multiple occurrences of each segment. In Figure 1.15, there are four segment

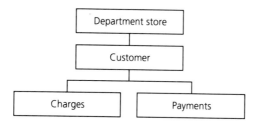

FIGURE 1.15   *Example of hierarchical segments.*

```
01   DEPARTMENT–STORE–BRANCH–SEGMENT.
     05 BRANCH–NAME                      PIC  X(20).
     05 BRANCH–MANAGER–LASTNAME          PIC  X(20).
     05 BRANCH–MANAGER–FIRSTNAME         PIC  X(20).
     05 BRANCH–STREET–LOCATION           PIC  X(20).
     05 BRANCH–CITY–LOCATION             PIC  X(25).
     05 BRANCH–STATE–LOCATION            PIC  X(2).
     05 BRANCH–ZIP–LOCATION              PIC  X(5).
     05 BRANCH–PHONE–NUMBER              PIC  X(10).


01   CUSTOMER–SEGMENT.
     05 CUSTOMER–SOC–SEC–NUMB            PIC  X(09).
     05 CUSTOMER–LASTNAME                PIC  X(20).
     05 CUSTOMER–FIRSTNAME               PIC  X(20).
     05 CUSTOMER–STREET–ADDRESS          PIC  X(20).
     05 CUSTOMER–CITY                    PIC  X(25).
     05 CUSTOMER–STATE                   PIC  X(02).
     05 CUSTOMER–ZIP                     PIC  X(05).
     05 CUSTOMER–PHONE                   PIC  X(10).
     05 DATE–OF–FIRST–ACTIVITY           PIC  9(6).
     05 STATUS–CODE                      PIC  X.
     05 CUSTOMER–CREDIT–CARD–NUMB        PIC  X(08).
     05 CUSTOMER–HIGH–BALANCE            PIC  9(9)V99.


01   CHARGES–SEGMENT.
     05 CUSTOMER–SOC–SEC–NUMB            PIC  X(09).
     05 CUSTOMER–CHARGES–TYPE            PIC  X(10).
     05 CUSTOMER–CHARGES–AMOUNT          PIC  9(9)V99
     05 CUSTOMER–CHARGES–ITEM–CODE       PIC  X(07).
     05 SALES–CLERK–NUMB                 PIC  X(09).


01   PAYMENTS–SEGMENT.
     05 CUSTOMER–SOC–SEC–NUMBER          PIC  X(09).
     05 CUSTOMER–CREDIT–CARD–NUMB        PIC  X(08).
     05 CUSTOMER–CREDIT–TYPE             PIC  X(10).
     05 CUSTOMER–PAYMENT                 PIC  9(9)V99.
     05 DATE–PAID                        PIC  9(6).
     05 FINANCE–CHARGE–PAID              PIC  9(8)V99.
```

FIGURE 1.16   *Field description for department store segments.*

types: department store, customer, charges, and payments. Each segment has a description of the fields within the segment (Figure 1.16).

Each segment in the database can have multiple occurrences to represent, for example, the following:

- The number of different branches for the department store
- The number of different customers at each branch
- The number of different charge accounts for each customer
- The number of payments for each customer

See Figure 1.17. As in a record, each segment contains one or more fields. In addition, as in a record, we insert, delete, and modify the data within each segment.

The segment at the top of the hierarchy is called the **root segment.** Department store is the root segment in Figure 1.18. The remaining segments in the tree are called **dependent segments.** Each dependent segment is the **parent** of the segment(s) immediately under it or a **child** of the segment immediately above it. In Figure 1.18, DEPARTMENT STORE is the parent of CUSTOMER and CUSTOMER is the parent of both children CHARGES and PAYMENTS. CHARGES and PAYMENTS are siblings. Multiple occurrences of DEPARTMENT STORE, CUSTOMERS, CHARGES, and PAYMENTS are twins, respectively. Parent segments have children segments: CUSTOMER is the child of DEPARTMENT STORE and CHARGES and PAYMENTS are children of CUSTOMER.

Remember, each parent in the database has one or more children and each child has one and only one parent. If a parent has more than one child, then those children are called **siblings.** Remember, hierarchical databases contain either one-to-one or one-to-many relationships between data. Hence, a parent with one child represents a one-to-one relationship, while a parent with siblings represents a one-to-many relationship. In hierarchical database

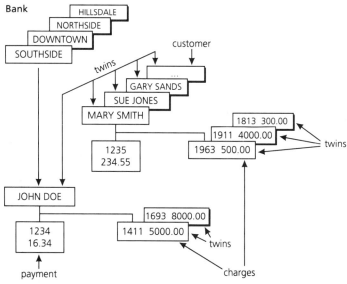

FIGURE 1.17   *Multiple occurrences of segments. Each bank branch has multiple customers and each customer has payments and charges.*

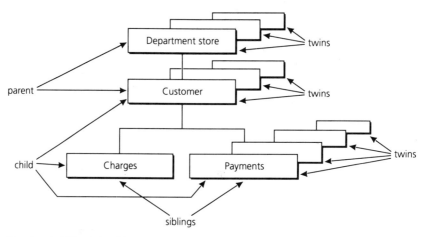

FIGURE 1.18   *Parent and child relationships.*

structures, we do not have a many-to-many relationship between the data. That is, children do not have multiple parents. Obviously the root segment (the one at the top of the structure) is never a child and the bottom-most segment in the hierarchy is never a parent.

If there are multiple occurrences of a segment in a parent or child, those occurrences are called **twins.** In our department store example, multiple charges for a customer (i.e., John Doe) are twins. Similarly, the many customers of the department store's branch location Southside are twins.

You access the segments in the database in a certain path or order, called the **access path.** Because each child is dependent on its parent, we must access the corresponding parent segment before we access any children. In particular, we must first access the root segment and then access each parent-child segment in the sequence in which they appear in the hierarchy. We can never access a child without first accessing the parent above it and we must access all parent-child segments from the root segment to the desired segment.

Network Databases

Network databases contain many-to-many relationships. A many-to-many relationship exists when the relationship between data requires that each parent accesses one or more children records and a child record accesses multiple parent records. In Figure 1.19 hospitals have multiple physicians and patients. Physicians have access to multiple hospitals and treat multiple patients. A patient can have multiple physicians. Each network record contains fields similar to hierarchical segments. In network systems, we refer to the parent records as **owners** and the child records as **members.** The owner records contain keys or pointers to each of their member records. Typically, you first access an owner record and then access each of its member records (Figure 1.20). This can require accessing numerous records requiring multiple disk

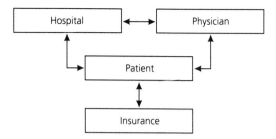

FIGURE 1.19 *Network structure using a many-to-many relationship.*

I/Os and considerable computer time. This becomes particularly cumbersome if a particular owner-record contains thousands or tens of thousands of member records.

In network databases you can establish keys or indexes on the member records and access them using the key or index. These additional steps can involve additional programming steps and procedures. Typically, network databases are difficult to construct because of the many-to-many relationships

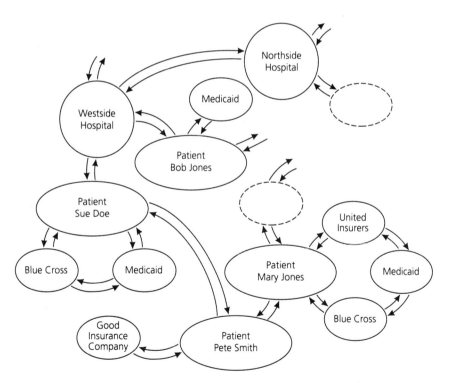

FIGURE 1.20 *Accessing strategies in owner-member relationships. We access the hospital record to extract data about a particular patient or group of patients. We then access a particular patient to extract data about his or her insurance coverage.*

between the owner records and their member records. Network databases require skilled systems analysts to define and construct the records and their relationships.

Relational Databases

One of the main pitfalls of hierarchical and network databases is the inability of end users to create, construct, and change the records within the database. In addition, because both types of database require a skilled programming staff to write programs accessing the respective database, end users are completely dependent on the development staff for systems modification and report generation. This is particularly true of the hierarchical database IMS where all queries must appear in programs written by skilled programmers. Also, many network databases (such as IDMS/R) have no useful end user query facility or the facility they provide has limited functionality.

What end users need is an easy-to-use system where they can create and modify records within the database and generate the reports they need and generate the reports when needed—independent of the software development staff. Relational databases solve some of these problems.

Data in relational databases is stored in tables (files) containing rows (records) and columns (fields). We use the concept of rows and columns because end users are familiar with them in the reports they encounter. Figure 1.21 is an example of two tables: one an EMPLOYEE table and the other a DEPARTMENT table. The EMPLOYEE table contains the columns EMPLOYEEID, LASTNAME, FIRSTNAME, ADDRESS, CITY, STATE, SEX, and DEPTNUMB. Each row in the table represents an employee enrolled in the company. The DEPARTMENT table contains the columns DEPTNUMB, NAME, MANAGERID, and ASSISTNT-

EMPLOYEE

EMPLOYEE ID	LAST NAME	FIRST NAME	ADDRESS	CITY	STATE	SEX	DEPT NUMB
123456789	DOE	JOHN	123 E. 3RD	CHICAGO	IL	M	ACCT
234567890	SMITH	MARY	34 N. HOLLY	DENVER	CO	F	ACCT
324566776	GROVER	SUE	56 W. 5TH	DENVER	CO	F	MARK
432143211	SMITH	ANDY	34 N. HOLLY	DENVER	CO	M	PERS
432234432	MARKUM	MIKE	194 W. 43RD	CHICAGO	IL	M	PERS

DEPARTMENT

DEPT NUMB	NAME	MANAGER ID	ASSISTNT MANAGER ID
ACCT	Accounting	123456789	346565432
MARK	Marketing	902902902	898989898
PERS	Personnel	432143211	453453453
AUDT	Auditing	848484848	122221122
TRNG	Training	980980980	878767777

FIGURE 1.21   *Data in relational tables.*

MANAGERID. Each row in the DEPARTMENT table represents a different department in the company. Each table uses codes to cross-reference data in one table with data in another table. Here, the DEPTNUMB of the EMPLOYEE table and the DEPTNUMB of the DEPARTMENT table are codes referencing the department names.

We create tables and columns using Data Definition Language (DDL) and access the data in the tables using Data Manipulation Language (DML). Because end users can learn these languages in a relatively short period of time, they have the capability of creating and modifying the structure of a database and extract data from it. Hence, the end user has the power to work independently of the programming staff.

SUMMARY

A character or byte is composed of eight consecutive bits. Multiple characters are grouped together to form a field. Because characters can be either numeric, alphabetic, or alphanumeric, the fields containing them also can be numeric, alphabetic, or alphanumeric. When the data in the field is to be used in some arithmetic operation, the field containing that data must be defined as a numeric field. Generally, all other nonnumeric fields are defined as alphanumeric fields.

A grouping of related fields composes a record. Multiple records grouped together form a file. In the mainframe environment, files also are referred to as data sets. These data sets reside on Direct Access Storage Devices (DASD) and are used by programs to produce usable information. Files on microcomputers reside on floppy disks or hard disks.

Records can be of fixed length or of variable length depending on the application. Fixed-length records are easier to use and program, but consume valuable disk space. Variable-length records, on the other hand, consume less disk space but are harder to program.

Master files contain data of a permanent nature, and transaction files are temporary. When master files or transaction files are archived, the archival copy is called a history file. These history files are kept by the installation for long periods of time and represent the history of the company's business activity.

In addition to making archival copies of the more important files, all installations also make backup copies of the files on the system. These backup files are only temporary copies. If the original file is damaged or destroyed, the backup copy can be used to recreate the original file. In large mainframe installations, the operations staff has elaborate procedures to ensure the creation of the backup of all files that are on the system. Typically, these procedures include a Disaster Recovery Plan in case a major accident occurs to on-line electronic data. On PCs, the backing up of important files is left to each individual user of the PC. Hence, to ensure that valuable company data will not be lost, many companies dictate security procedures and standards for using software on PCs.

Databases are specially designed integrated systems of files. These files are created and managed by a software package called a Database Management System (DBMS). Companies and individuals can purchase or lease a DBMS software product for their computer systems. PC versions of DBMS typically cost less than $1,000 and require a hard disk on the owner's PC. Mainframe DBMS software packages are leased from database vendors and are more complex than the PC version. Because companies will be investing significant sums of money into creating and maintaining a database and, because multiple individuals will be accessing and using the database, many companies develop an entire corporate environment based on the DBMS. This involves the following:

- Establishing standards and procedures for accessing data through the DBMS
- Training the technical staff on how to program using the DBMS product
- Training the nontechnical staff on how to query the database
- Creating security rules and procedures for the data in the database
- Writing new or modifying existing programs to access the database
- Establishing measures to maintain error-free data

Databases are classified as to the relationship between the data, called an entity-to-entity relationship. There are three types of entity-to-entity relationships: one-to-one (1–1), one-to-many (1–N), and many-to-many (N–N). Hierarchical, network, and relational databases use both the 1–1 and 1–N relationships, and network and relational databases also use the N–N relationship. However, system developers can design hierarchical databases so that they can indirectly use N–N relationships.

Hierarchical databases contain segments that are similar to records. The top-most segment in the hierarchy is called a root segment and the remaining segments are called dependent segments. Each dependent segment is a parent of the segments under it (each called a child). Hence, parents have zero or more children and the children, in turn, can be parents of other segments. If there are multiple occurrences of segments in a parent or child, those occurrences are called twins. Segments are accessed using a certain path called the access path. In network databases the parent records are called owners and the child records are called members. In relational databases files are called tables. These tables contain columns (fields) and rows (records).

Hierarchical and network databases have been available since the early 1970s and represent older software technology. The two most popular mainframe databases for that era are IMS (hierarchical) and IDMS/R (network). Both require large programming staffs and end users must rely on the programming staff to produce even the simplest of reports. Relational databases have been available since the early 1980s and give the end user more independence because the users can create their own reports without technical staff intervention. The most popular relational databases use Structured Query Language or SQL, with DB2 and SQL/DS being the most popular mainframe relational DBMS; and dBASE III, dBASE IV, and Oracle being the most popular PC-based DBMS.

Although relational databases are easier to use and provide features popular with end users, most installations must continue to support their older DBMS systems because of the large dollar investment they have in them.

QUESTIONS

1. What is the difference between a file, field, record, and character?
2. What is the difference between a bit and a byte?
3. How is the number 345 stored?
4. What is the difference between a backup file and a history file?
5. What is the main difference between the EBCDIC and the ASCII coding system? Why are there two different systems instead of one unified system?
6. What is the difference between a sequential file, a direct file, and an indexed sequential file?
7. What is meant by hashing? Why do we not create all files as hash files?
8. How do we determine which fields to use for the primary key in indexed files?
9. Why do we create a history file?
10. How do you create a backup copy of a file stored on a PC? On a mainframe?
11. Explain the steps in recovering from a destroyed master file.
12. What are some reasons for a transaction file failing to update a master file?
13. A large corporation is considering the takeover of another corporation. What data processing considerations must the larger corporation include in determining the cost of such a takeover?
14. XYZ Corporation intends to purchase a database system. What training needs will they have?
15. List the costs of acquiring a database system.
16. What are the three kinds of relationships that can exist between data?
17. Which database structures allow us to directly express many-to-many relationships?
18. There are four methods of storing organized data on a computer: relational databases, traditional files, network databases, and hierarchical databases. In what order do you think these methods were historically developed? Why?
19. What are the differences between parents, children, owners, and members?
20. Compare the accessing strategies for each type of database.

CASE STUDY

The HEAR-IT-NOW record shop, located in a small Louisville shopping center sells audio tapes, records, and compact discs. The current owner wants to upgrade his business and plans to install a computer system to keep track of the store's invoices, inventory, and sales. In addition, the owner wants the computer to provide timely reports on the business activity of the store. The current owner plans to use the store's invoicing forms to capture the data for the computer files. An example of a typical invoice follows.

				UNIT	SUGGESTED	
TITLE	ARTIST	TYPE	QUANTITY	PRICE	RETAIL	TOTAL
I'm Coming Home	Rockers	CAS	4	3.50	6.99	14.00
No You're Not	Rollers	CD	9	9.00	13.99	81.00
Be Mine	Country	CD	10	8.50	12.99	85.00
Get Lost	Westerns	REC	5	5.00	7.00	25.00

Buy It Now Suppliers, Inc.   June 3, 1991
1234 Happy Lane
Paris, Indiana

Amount Owed   205.00

Please remit within 30 days.

One of the files on the new computer system will be an invoice file of all records, compact discs, and tapes received. The owner will enter the data from the invoice into the computer each time the store receives a shipment from a supplier. At the end of each month, the owner wants the computer to do the following:

1. Print a report of all monies owed suppliers and issue those suppliers a check
2. List all items the store purchases for that month by type and by artist
3. List all the titles that are purchased each month, sorted by title and type

Questions

1. What type of file will we create?
2. What fields must the invoice file contain to satisfy the needs of the owner?
3. How many characters will each field contain? Each record contain?
4. Which fields will be the primary keys? Will any contain unique keys?

2 *Hardware and Operating System Considerations*

This chapter continues to examine how and when databases are used. The chapter will focus on the hardware and operating system environment for using databases. These factors determine what can and cannot be done by database software, so understanding them is essential to understanding database management. We will focus on both the mainframe and microcomputer environments, noting the differences and similarities between them.

THE MAINFRAME ENVIRONMENT

Operating Systems and Software Components

An **operating system** is a collection of programs and data files that is specifically created to utilize, manage, and optimize computer resources. These programs operate on a particular computer system and are unique to that system. The typical mainframe operating system contains both Control Programs and Processing Programs (Figure 2.1). Control Programs include Task Management, Job Management, and Data Management programs. Processing Programs include the various language translators on the system (e.g., COBOL, FORTRAN); the service programs (e.g., TSO, linkage editor); and user programs (e.g., Accounts Receivable, Payroll). All Processing Programs work under the supervision of Control Programs.

Overview of Task, Job, and Data Management

Task Management programs are those core-resident programs that supervise the operating system. These programs supervise the scheduling of all system activities and monitor their execution. In addition, they allocate and manage main memory and monitor and control all system interrupts. In essence, they are the traffic cops for the system. The collection of Task Management routines is called the Supervisor for the system.

    Job Management programs monitor and interpret all input commands,

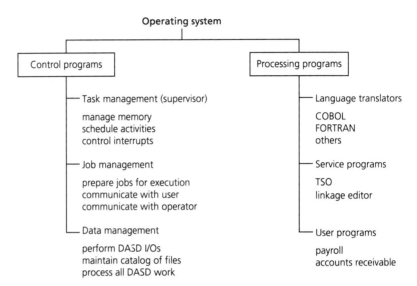

FIGURE 2.1   *Control and processing programs and their functions.*

prepare various jobs for execution, and obtain the needed resources for a job. All communication with the computer operator is controlled by Job Management software. The programs also provide the communication between the users and the operating system by interfacing the user's job with the Supervisor.

Data Management programs provide the communication routines between the system and external storage. They assign space on DASD, maintain the catalog of files for each DASD unit, and process all input and output to files resident on DASD units. Furthermore, Data Management programs initialize all work to be done on secondary storage devices, control the work's termination, and handle all their errors and interrupts.

Layers of Software

The typical operating system can be viewed as having a series of **software layers.** The hardware is controlled by a first layer of software, called the operating system. Normally this operating system is leased on a continuous basis from the manufacturer of the hardware system. Operating systems have such names as MVS/XA, MVS/ESA, VMS, VM, and DOS. Next, the system has a layer of specialized programs for application development. These include the various DBMS and other control programs that can be utilized to create application software. Programs in this layer are leased from various software vendors and include such products as DB2, IDMS/R, CICS, IMS, and TELON. The final layer of software on the system contains application software written for specific end-user problems. This layer includes payroll programs, accounts receivable programs, math simulations and models, and other data processing programs.

Multiprogramming

Prior to 1972, mainframe operators had to insert a stack of cards into a card reader, press some buttons on the console, and wait as the computer processed one job at a time. These were terminal-less days in the computer world. Operators could load only one job onto the system at any one time. After the one job terminated, the next job was loaded onto the system and was executed. The primitive operating system of those computers contained only the modules and routines needed to run the hardware. They had a small **throughput** because only one job was in the system and only one job could execute until completion. The throughput of a computer system is the amount of work it finishes over a certain period of time.

Modern operating systems are far more complex. The main job of a modern operating system is not to just run the hardware and communicate with a single user. Instead, it also must increase throughput by managing multiple users on the system and lowering the user's response time so the users can efficiently process jobs. The operating system must efficiently handle multiple jobs simultaneously, and effectively allocate systems resources to multiple users so that each user believes he or she is the only person on the system. These multiprogramming operating systems must contain elaborate management routines to supervise all resources on the system. They also prevent user contention for the same resource and eliminate deadlocks within the system. A deadlock occurs when two users or jobs need the same two resources (for example, a printer, DASD, or a terminal) and one job has one resource allocated to it and the other job has the other resource allocated to it; both jobs are deadlocked because each has something the other needs.

In a multiprogramming environment, each user's job gains control of the CPU unit via some scheduling algorithm built into the Supervisor. Once a user's job gains access to the CPU, it continues to execute until the program comes to a natural wait, such as during an Input/Output (I/O) to DASD or until the job exceeds the time allocated to it. Each job on the system is given a finite amount of CPU time. If this allocated time is exceeded, the system automatically terminates the job. The exact time restraint is designated by the installation's director of operations and guarantees equal CPU access to all users of the system.

Modern operating systems increase the throughput by decreasing the time the CPU is idle. When the CPU is not processing work, the operating system's scheduler gives the CPU some work to perform. This is accomplished through a priority system devised by the manufacturer of the operating system. Every job on the system is given a certain priority. Jobs with the highest priority are executed ahead of jobs with lower priority. Typically, the highest priority jobs are the various routines for the spooler of I/O devices. In this case, they demand CPU attention over all the other jobs on the system to maximize I/O throughput. A spooler is a software module that temporarily loads input or output to DASD because of some other busy device. The input or output then is reloaded as the other device becomes available.

The second highest job priority in the system is the software module controlling the operator's console. This gives the operator the power to interrupt and control activity on the system. Some operating systems even have a hierarchy of priority codes established for each user. For example, on a college or university's computer system, students could be given the lowest priority, and faculty and researchers could be given a higher priority. Jobs submitted by a higher priority user would access the CPU and its on-line input and output devices ahead of lower priority users. Here, each user has a preassigned priority code and would have certain rights and privileges based on that code. Typically, users are assigned a priority code from 0 (lowest) to 15 (highest). Operating system's modules have priority codes ranging from 16 to 31.

Data Sets, Partitioned Data Sets, and Libraries

A **data set** is any file on the system. You create a data set using either JCL, ISPF, or some other software tool. The mainframe hardware includes large DASD disk drives that can hold thousands of data sets. You need a technique to group the data sets into libraries; each library will contain a certain kind of data set. A library is called a **partitioned data set** (PDS) and contains one or more data sets and a directory of any and all the data sets within it (Figures 2.2A and 2.2B). You can store all your COBOL programs in one PDS and all your text files in another PDS.

Systems Software

Following is a brief discussion of some terms discussed in the Advanced Topic on pages 46–47.

TSO and ISPF/PDF Time Sharing Option (TSO) is a set of routines used to access the computer system. A valuable user interface that runs under TSO

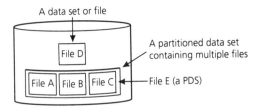

FIGURE 2.2A   *A logical view of data sets, libraries, and PDSs. File D is a data set residing on DASD. Files A, B, and C are data sets residing in library E, which is a partitioned data set.*

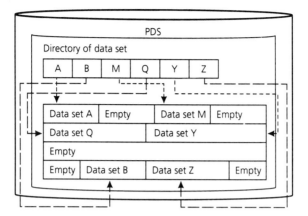

FIGURE 2.2B *Physical structure of a PDS. Addresses of the data sets (or members) within a PDS are stored in the PDS's directory. The PDS serves the same function as a directory for a building that indicates the location of all the tenants within the building.*

is Interactive System Productivity Facility/Program Development Facility (ISPF/PDF). ISPF/PDF includes a primary menu and numerous submenus that allow the user to perform the following:

- Allocate both data sets and partitioned data sets
- Delete an entire partitioned data set or any of its members
- Print the entire partitioned data set or any of its members
- Browse a data set
- Copy or move data sets
- Display catalog information
- Create or modify a data set using the system's editor
- Execute certain system utilities
- Perform a foreground or background compile
- Access DB2
- Access in-house routines
- Access other vendor software installed on the system
- Access a system tutorial

In essence, ISPF under TSO is the main vehicle most people utilize to access software and data on IBM mainframes. Because most company system software teams can customize the menus available in ISPF, both the technical staff and the user department personnel use this handy facility.

JES2 and JES3 JES2 and JES3 are two job schedulers in MVS. Because these systems are incompatible with each other, a company would use either JES2 or JES3. For simplicity, we will discuss JES in general because both are very similar. Programmers submit jobs to the system through JES. The programmer uses JCL to indicate to the system the activity he or she wants the system to perform (Figure 2.3). A job reader in JES places the submitted job in a job

The most popular operating system on IBM mainframes is Multiple Virtual Storage/Extended Architecture (MVS/XA), though the most recently developed is (MVS/ESA) Multiple Virtual Storage/Enterprise Systems Architecture. The MVS operating system contains three major facilities:

- Virtual Storage Management Facilities
- Program Development Facilities
- User Facilities

The Virtual Storage Management Facilities include page management, storage management, multiprogramming, multitasking, and JOB, TASK, and DATA Managers.

The Program Development Facilities include the various high-level languages available (e.g., COBOL, FORTRAN, or PL/I), the compilers for these languages, the linkage editors for these languages, libraries, and access methods for the data sets.

The User Facilities include the systems utilities and procedures, Job Control Language (JCL), a Time Sharing Option (TSO), a user interactive facility (ISPF, CMS), a job entry subsystem (JES2 or JES3), and various database systems (IMS, CICS, and DB2).

Smaller IBM mainframes can use DOS operating systems. DOS consists of the following:

- Control Programs
- Service Programs
- Language Translators

Control Programs manage main storage, jobs, and I/O. Service Programs include library management programs, as well as some utilities. Language Translators include compilers for languages such as COBOL.

An interesting IBM operating system is Virtual Machine (VM). VM is not so much an operating system as a control program that manages devices and other operating systems. VM can be used to partition one physical machine into several virtual machines. (A virtual machine is an environment that looks like a real machine, that is, a physical piece of hardware with its own operating system, to programmers and users, though it is actually a creation of software.) In such a configuration, one VM could run under one operating system, such as DOS, and another could run under a different operating system, such as MVS.

VM is composed of the Control Program, the Conversational Monitor System (CMS), the Remote Spooling Communications Subsystem, the Interactive Problem Control System, and the CMS Batch Facility. The Control Program is the interface between the real machine and one or more virtual machines. CMS is the equivalent of the Program Development Facilities of MVS. The Remote Spooling Communications Subsystem is used for managing files. The Interactive Problem Control System is a collection of monitoring and debugging tools. The CMS Batch Facility allows users to submit batch jobs for noninteractive processing.

---

queue. A job scheduler selects a job from the job queue for processing. An internal reader reads each JCL statement and executes it. When all JCL statements are read, the system terminates the job and accesses the job queue, looking for the next job (Figure 2.4).

For example, in Figure 2.4, the job reader places the JCL commands for job 23 into the job queue. The job scheduler reads a job from the job queue. The internal reader translates each JCL statement for that job and processes the commands. When all the statements for that job have been processed or if the job abends, the internal reader transfers control back to the job scheduler. (Recall, an abend is an abnormal end or an abnormal termination of a program or routine.)

A job scheduler must provide the necessary communications between the user and the system. In particular, it must perform three major functions or duties. First, it must read jobs and store them on DASD in a queue. Second, it must select jobs for execution and allocate the necessary memory and I/O devices before it executes. Third, it must load a program into memory, execute it, and write the output to DASD or spool the output for future processing.

When you submit a job for later processing, JES will schedule the job and execute it based on several factors. JES is working in the background performing the necessary functions for each submitted job that is to be executed by the system. For JES to work properly, it needs at least two pieces of information to schedule a job: a job class (A, B, C, D, H, L, T) and a job priority (0 through 15). Some typical job classes of JES3 are given in Figure 2.5. Each class is defined with a particular priority. The codes for job priority tell the system the order in which jobs are to process with the higher priority jobs processing first from the job queue. Job classes and their associated priorities are typically defined and maintained by the operating systems programming area.

```
//DPRSGENR   JOB   (1,DS,BW40RS),SCHWAB,CLASS=B,NOTIFY=$DPRS,
//                 MSGCLASS=3
//GENR0101 EXEC    PGM=IEBGENER
//SYSIN      DD    DUMMY,DCB=BLKSIZE=80
//SYSPRINT   DD    SYSOUT=*
//SYSUDUMP   DD    SYSOUT=*
//SYSUT1     DD    DSN=DP.INPUT.DATASET,DISP=SHR
//SYSUT2     DD    DSN=DP.OUTPUT.DATASET,
//                 DISP=(NEW,CATLG,DELETE),UNIT=3380,
//                 VOL=SER=EU8001,SPACE=(TRK,(1,1),RLSE)
```

FIGURE 2.3   *Sample JCL instructions. JCL statements include a JOB, EXEC, and one or more DD statements.*

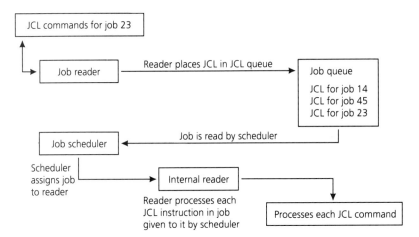

FIGURE 2.4   *Processing JCL commands.*

Data Storage on Mainframes

Real or Central Storage IBM mainframes have the architecture shown in Figure 2.6. Multiple CPU units access central storage via system controllers. These system controllers can access DASD and other I/O devices through a channel subsystem. A **channel** is a microprocessor that handles all I/O activity for the CPUs. It accesses its own programs, called **channel programs,** which run simultaneously and independently of the CPU units. This allows the operating system to send a request for I/O to a channel and allow the channel program to perform the I/O at the proper time; the operating system does not have to supervise the actual I/O performed by the device (Figure 2.7).

The steps for using a channel program are:

1. The CPU requests an I/O from the channel subsystem.
2. The channel, working independently from the CPU, accesses a channel program resident in central memory or on DASD and stores it in a channel buffer.
3. The channel executes the channel program that will perform the CPU's requested I/O.

A	Execute the job within the next 15 minutes
B	Execute the job within the next 30 minutes
C	Execute the job within the next 60 minutes
D	Execute the job overnight
H	Hold the job
L	Execute the job within the next 15 minutes, restrict job step times to 1 minute each
T	Job requires magnetic tape processing

FIGURE 2.5   *Sample job classes for JES.*

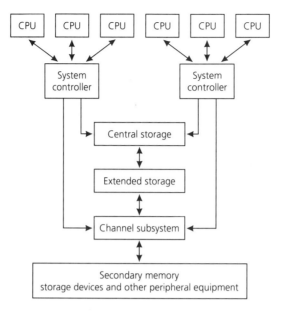

FIGURE 2.6 *Typical multiple-CPU IBM mainframe system. Six CPUs (or engines) can access central storage and the channel subsystem via various system's controllers. Central storage (or main memory) can access extended storage when needed. The channel subsystem accesses the DASD devices and other peripheral equipment.*

The main memory area or central storage area contains three sections (Figure 2.8). The first section is the **systems area** and contains the nucleus. The nucleus contains those operating system programs that are most frequently used and must be core-resident at all times. The Supervisor resides in this area. The second section is the **common area** and contains the various system queues, frequently used control programs, and a common service area.

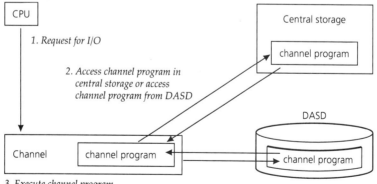

FIGURE 2.7 *Using a channel program.*

Systems area contains nucleus and supervisor	Extended systems area
Common area contains systems queues and selected control programs	Extended common area
Private area contains the user region and a systems region for users	Extended private area

FIGURE 2.8   *The three areas of central storage and their extensions.*

The third section is the **private area** and contains a user region and a system region. Typically, these three areas occupy a total of 16 megabytes of memory.

If modules or programs require additional space in central storage, the system creates an extended area for each of the three sections requiring additional memory space. These three areas are called the **extended systems area** (containing an extended nucleus), the **extended common area,** and the **extended private area,** respectively. All user regions are created by the system because they are needed either in the private area or the extended private area. The combined allocation of the original sections and their respective extensions consume a total of 2 gigabytes of central memory. This represents memory addressing using a 31-bit field.

When the mainframe is first powered on, the hardware performs an **initial program load** (IPL). During the IPL, the system creates the three sections of memory and initializes the Supervisor. After the system is IPLed, you can access the routines on the system using a variety of software. If for some reason the nucleus of the Supervisor is damaged or destroyed, the computer operator might have to re-IPL the system, a process requiring from 10 to 20 minutes to perform.

When you log onto the system or submit a batch job, you are given a fixed block of memory in which to operate, known as an **address space** (Figure 2.9). This block of memory usually is from 2K to 64K in size. The memory area assigned contains a protection key so other users cannot access this same area of memory. These protection keys prevent other users from both storing and reading data in your block of memory. You can read and write only to the areas assigned to you by the system.

Extended Memory

Paging You cannot execute a program unless it resides in central storage. Obviously, if a computer program contains, for example, 10,000 lines of code, the system does not place the entire code in memory all at once. In a virtual

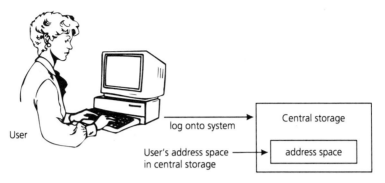

FIGURE 2.9   *Creating an address space.*

operating system environment, the system divides virtual storage into blocks of 4K of memory, called **pages.** The system only works with one page at a time, continually accessing one page after another as it executes instructions or accesses data (Figure 2.10). Pages are transferred between central storage and DASD storage. The 4K section of memory in central storage is called a **page frame** and the 4K section of memory on DASD is called a **page slot.** A page fault occurs when a program requires additional virtual storage for another page. The system locates the page on DASD containing the required data and transfers it to central storage (Figure 2.11). Thus, on a virtual storage system, real storage might be limited to 2 gigabytes, but the programmer or user can treat all virtual storage as if it were real storage; the operating system pages data from virtual storage into and out of real storage as needed.

It is possible for the system to steal a page. Say, for example, the system depletes all available central storage and needs an additional page to continue an already-started process. It will steal a page from some other application. The system writes some other page to auxiliary memory and overwrites the

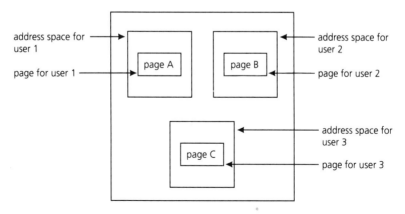

FIGURE 2.10   *Three pages of three different users in central storage. These pages are called page frames.*

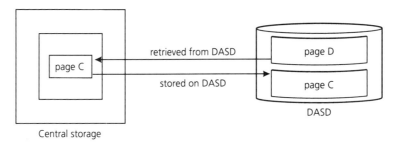

FIGURE 2.11   *Transferring pages between central memory and DASD. The page on DASD is called a page slot. Page C is stored on DASD and page D is retrieved and placed in the same memory location of central storage previously occupied by page C.*

stolen area with the desired page data. Unfortunately, page stealing is both time consuming and hardware consuming.

In older systems, page stealing required the system to write the stolen page to a DASD area before it rewrote over the stolen area. The system was slow because it had to do several things. It had to perform a disk I/O to write the stolen page to DASD, and another disk I/O to recall the stolen page from auxiliary memory. With the introduction of extended memory, the system rewrites the stolen page to extended memory (Figure 2.12). Once extended memory is filled, the system writes the stolen page to DASD. Then the system can use that region of extended memory for some other stolen page as it is needed.

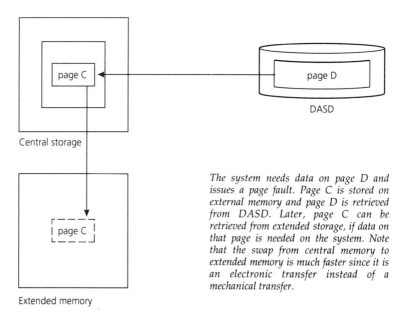

The system needs data on page D and issues a page fault. Page C is stored on external memory and page D is retrieved from DASD. Later, page C can be retrieved from extended storage, if data on that page is needed on the system. Note that the swap from central memory to extended memory is much faster since it is an electronic transfer instead of a mechanical transfer.

FIGURE 2.12   *Using extended memory for a page fault.*

However, if extended memory is sufficiently large, the system might not have destroyed the page in extended memory. A page steal in central storage might force the system to write the page to extended memory. If the extended memory area containing the page has not been overwritten by another job, the system can transfer the page from extended memory directly to central storage. The system only performs a disk I/O when it needs a page that has been previously overwritten.

Therefore, before the system recalls a page from DASD, it first checks extended memory for that page. If it finds the page unchanged, the system loads the unchanged page from extended memory and places it in central storage, saving a disk I/O (and time). Extended memory on large systems can contain terabytes of high-speed memory, providing for a very fast recall of stolen pages or the total elimination of page stealing.

Swapping. Sometimes the CPU is in a wait state because of a job's input or output operation. The job responsible for the wait will be swapped to disk so other jobs can use the CPU. When swapping occurs, all pages for that job are rewritten to extended memory or auxiliary memory (Figure 2.13). When the swapped job is reactivated by the scheduler, all of its pages are reloaded to central storage. At this point the processing of the job continues, beginning with the last instruction causing the swap. When the system swaps a job, the job no longer is resident in central storage and therefore is unavailable for processing.

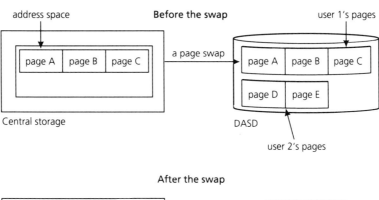

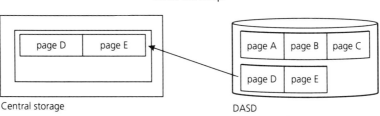

FIGURE 2.13   *One user's program swapped to DASD so that another user's program can execute. The CPU copies the contents of one user's address space to DASD and reloads another user's address space to central storage for execution.*

Virtual memory. When a programmer writes a program, compiles, and links it, the system creates a load module. This load module contains all the instructions the system needs to execute the code, along with the addresses of the memory locations where the code and data will reside. However, the load module contains only relative addresses of memory locations, not the actual addresses of central storage. The computer uses virtual addresses because it does not know where in central storage the code will reside until that code is actually loaded and placed in memory.

Remember, a mainframe is managing resources and is continually moving user areas and programs around in the system to maximize throughput within it. For example, one second your user area might be at address 123,456 and in another second it might be at address 1,234,567. Also, the system is continually swapping programs and data between the DASD units, extended memory, and central memory. So do not restrict the operating system to a certain memory location because that memory location already might be assigned to another user for some period of time.

To resolve addresses, the system uses an Address Resolution Table. Each load module contains the machine language version of your translated code. The first machine language instruction usually begins at relative address 0. When the system fetches the program for execution, it accesses the Address

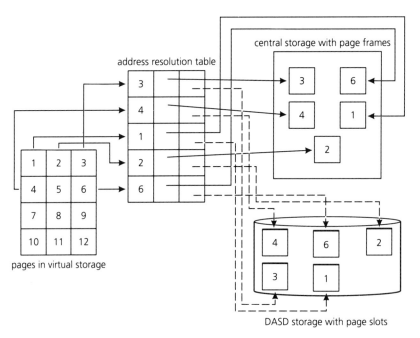

FIGURE 2.14 *Virtual storage address resolution. Pages in central storage are loaded to DASD using an address resolution table.*

Resolution Table to find where in memory to place the load module. Then it computes the actual memory locations of each instruction in the load module as it places the load module in central storage (Figure 2.14).

External Storage

Disk storage. A DASD contains a disk drive to read and write data on a disk pack or volume. A disk pack is an array of metal platters that hold a magnetic field. Modern DASD volumes are permanently sealed inside the drive and cannot be removed, although some of the older units still in use have mountable volumes. The DASD units are linked together to form a string of DASDs—usually a maximum of 10 DASD volumes per string. A DASD string controller accesses the DASD volumes on the string and communicates with the CPU through a high-speed selector channel (Figure 2.15). A group of up to 10 DASD units (called a string) are attached to a main controller (called a string controller) for that group. Each DASD unit has a DASD controller and a disk pack called a volume. Each string controller connects to the channel subsystem. The channel subsystem is connected to both central storage and extended storage and accesses them independently of the CPU units. When

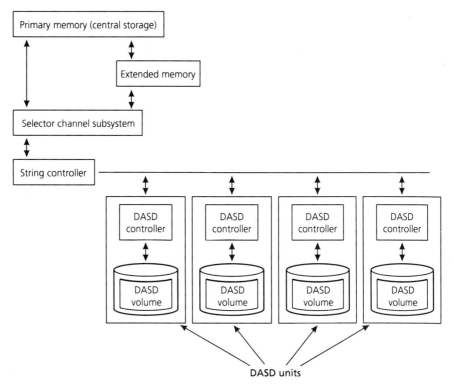

FIGURE 2.15   *DASD units, DASD string, DASD controller, and selector channel.*

each disk pack is first installed, it must be formatted. During this formatting process, the operator assigns it a logical name that becomes that pack's volume name. All future references to that volume will be via the volume name. This name is stored in the pack's VTOC at storage track 0, read/write head 0.

DASD and its associated string controller is expensive (Table 2.1). In fact, the philosophy of the majority of routines and algorithms in the operating system is to conserve disk space and keep the number of disk I/Os to a minimum to maximize utilization and decrease wear and tear of the disk packs.

Most DASD units have multiple platters, each with its own read/write head capable of reading both sides of the platter. Each platter is logically divided into concentric circles called a track. Each track is numbered sequentially beginning with the number 0 at the innermost track. Each track holds the same amount of data even though the outermost tracks are physically longer than the innermost tracks. A DASD unit with 10 platters, therefore, has 18 read/write heads located above and below each platter's surface. There is no read/write head at the topmost and bottommost sides of the platter's stack. When the read/write head positions itself over a track, the combined 18 tracks under the 18 heads is called a **cylinder** (Figure 2.16).

Tape storage. A tape drive reads and writes data to magnetic tape or cassette. The cassette tape is similar to the tape used by most video cassette recorders (VCRs). The cassette drive stores data in bits per inch (bpi), called its density. A cassette tape with a density of 20,000 bpi, for example, can store 20,000 bits in every inch of tape. The amount of data one cassette can store depends on its length. The longer the tape, the more data it can store.

We store a file's records on tape. Because the computer uses buffers for I/O transfers, we normally group records together into larger units called blocks (Figure 2.17). If a file is blocked, the system reads the entire block into a buffer area at one time, increasing the amount of data electronically available to the system. For the unblocked data, a single record is read and loaded into a buffer for later processing. In this case, the system will have to perform five separate reads to load five records into memory. However, for blocked data, the system performs a single read and loads all five records into memory for later processing. A buffer is memory the system reserves for a specific

TABLE 2.1   *Sample cost of DASD and tape units as of 1990*

Item	Initial Cost	Monthly Fee
IBM 3380-AK4 DASD	$134,000	$231
IBM 3380-BK4 DASD	$110,250	$169
IBM 3990 DASD CONTROLLER	$210,000	$800
IBM 3480 TAPE UNIT	$167,000	$1084
IBM 3480 CONTROL UNIT	$ 59,770	$435

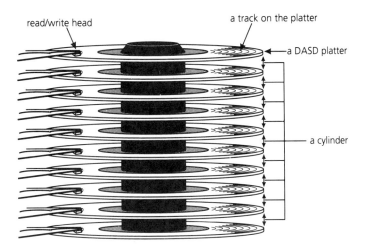

FIGURE 2.16 *Ten platters of a disk pack.*

function. In this case, the system can have a 64K buffer it uses for I/O transfers. When the system reads a record from some external storage device, it loads it first into a high-speed buffer area before it transfers it to central storage. Because the CPU is a continuously active device, our job that requested the I/O might have been swapped from central storage while the channel performed the I/O operation. Now the CPU is performing another user's job while it was waiting for the system to perform our auxiliary memory access. Once the system reswaps our job back into central storage, the data from the buffer is moved to central storage for processing.

We use blocking to load large segments of data from auxiliary storage

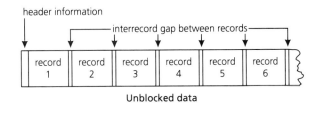

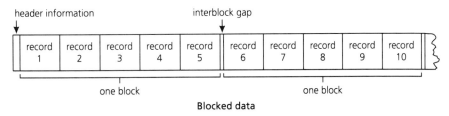

FIGURE 2.17 *Using blocking to increase throughput.*

```
FD     RECORD–IN
       LABEL RECORDS ARE STANDARD
       BLOCK CONTAINS 10 RECORDS
       RECORD CONTAINS 432 CHARACTERS
       DATA RECORD IS SALES–RECORD–IN.
```

FIGURE 2.18   *File definition clause indicating blocking factor.*

into a buffer area. Obviously, the amount of data we can read in one block is restricted by the size of the buffer area that will eventually hold the block. Figure 2.18 illustrates a part of a COBOL program that tells the system how many blocks to read and write into a buffer area at any one time. Each record contains 432 characters and the system will read 10 such records into an I/O buffer at one time.

Between each block on tape is a gap where no data is stored. When we group records together using blocking, the gap appears between the blocks instead of between the records and is called an **interblock gap** (IBG). See Figure 2.17.

One of the main pitfalls in using tape for data storage is that the records on tape must be processed sequentially. The tape must be mounted, requiring operator intervention. Most modern data processing centers use tape only for making backup copies and other archival purposes.

DASD and VTOC. Data management programs control DASD storage. These programs allocate space on DASD and store the data on one or more tracks on one or more platters. Each DASD volume contains a Volume Table Of Contents (VTOC). The VTOC contains information about the VTOC itself, information about each data set on the volume, and information about all the empty tracks available for storage. When the system needs to access a data set on a volume, it first accesses the VTOC and extracts information about that data set. The Data Manager makes sure that the user who is attempting to access the data set has the authorization to do so. It also checks the data set information to see if some other user is currently accessing the data set. The Data Manager prohibits concurrent updating of a data set, but in some cases it will permit concurrent reading of a data set.

Allocating data sets. To access a data set on DASD, the system needs the data set name, the identity of the device type (for example, IBM 3380, IBM 3350), and the volume name. The volume name is a logical name assigned to the volume when it is first initialized (such as, EU9001, RTT400, etc.). The first users of the volume can choose the name. In some cases, the operations team follows the company's policy for assigning a logical name to the volume.

Before the system can store data in the data set, the data set must be allocated by the system. You can allocate a data set using JCL, or you can use an option in the ISPF menu. After you allocate the data set, you can access it and store data in it. There are two types of data sets. Permanent data sets exist before and after a job and always must be given a name by the user. Temporary data sets are those data sets that a job creates, uses, and deletes before the job terminates. Temporary data sets usually are given a name that is generated by the system.

When you allocate a data set, you can specify on which volume you want the data set to reside. Some departments might have a departmental DASD volume and require all departmental personnel to save their data on that volume. If you simply want to store data somewhere on the system, you can make a nonspecific request for a volume and MVS will select the volume for you. If you request a volume name that is not currently on the system, MVS will send a message to the operator to mount the requested volume.

Deallocating a data set. When you deallocate a data set, the system removes the data set's name from the VTOC. It then updates the VTOC by listing the location of the data set in the VTOC's list of empty tracks available for storage. When you deallocate a data set, you do not erase it. The tracks containing the data set are simply released to the system for future use by any user. Remember, any sensitive information in the data set is still on the platter and can be accessed by another user (Figure 2.19). In fact, there are utility programs that permit experienced users to access the deallocated data set. Erase sensitive data using a systems utility program before you de-allocate it.

Cataloged data sets. You can catalog a data set if it needs to be used by several people. Cataloging a data set places the name of the data set and information about where it is located into a master index on the system. Once the data set is cataloged, you can reference it by name only and omit its volume name and device type identifiers. The company can have certain restrictions on who can catalog data sets and the names you assign them.

Disk caching. Each DASD unit has its own disk controller that is attached

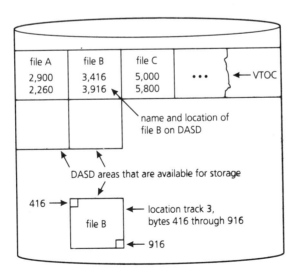

FIGURE 2.19 *Deallocating a data set.*

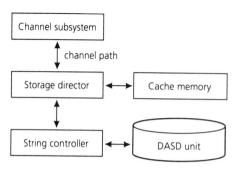

FIGURE 2.20   *Example of cache memory for DASD.*

to a DASD string controller. This string controller manages a string of DASD units. The string controller has a Storage Director containing information about all the DASD on the string. This Storage Director is attached to the channel (Figure 2.20). Disk caching keeps track of which records were accessed and their frequency of accesses. The more frequently accessed records are stored in cache memory, which serves as a buffer between DASD and the channels. When you request the system to access a record, the first thing it does is check cache memory for a copy of the record. If the record has not been modified or changed, the copy of the record in cache memory is used, thereby saving a disk I/O. However, if the record in cache memory has been modified or changed, then the system reads the record from disk. Keep in mind, each disk I/O requires movement of the disk read/write head to the proper location on the disk platter and this consumes time and resources.

Virtual Lookaside Facility. Virtual Lookaside Facility (VLF) is a recent IBM product that allows you to define certain data or programs to be cached automatically. This is particularly useful for programs that are frequently used, because it reduces the need to continually load the program from disk. In this case, the program will be loaded from disk only the first time it is used; thereafter, it will be kept in real storage. VLF also allows you to specify a threshold number of I/Os for data or programs; when that number has been exceeded, the data or program will be cached automatically.

Data spaces and hiperspace. Every job or user logon running under MVS has its own region of virtual storage called an **address space.** Usually, both a program's executing machine code and its internal data reside in its address space. Under MVS/ESA, IBM's latest mainframe operating system, a program can access data that resides in a **data space** outside of that program's address space. **Hiperspace** (high performance space) is a data space that can be made to act like DASD, though it can be accessed at a much higher I/O rate than normal DASD. The difference between data spaces and disk caching is that disk caching is managed by the operating system and is transparent to programs (including database managers); data spaces and hiperspace operate under program control.

Batch and On-Line Processing

Before 1972 all work on mainframes was accomplished in the batch mode. This is what happened: Programmers would write code and submit it to a computer operator. The code was keypunched onto data cards either by the programmer or by a keypunch operator. A computer operator would place the cards containing the program in the card reader, which was the main input device for the mainframe. The CPU executed one job at a time in what is now called a batch processing mode. Batch processing is the collection of data over time into files that are later processed as a group.

In 1972, IBM introduced its multiprocessing/multiprogramming mainframe, and called it the IBM 370. Not only did this mainframe have batch capability, but it also had an operating system that permitted real-time or on-line processing. Consequently, users and programmers could enter data into the system and command the CPU to execute their job immediately and concurrently with other jobs on the system. With on-line processing, users interact with the computer in a written conversational mode and the computer responds to the users' instructions instantaneously. In fact, most companies require their computer systems to have a one-second or sub-second computer response time for most of the users' computer transactions.

However, not all the work you do on a computer system requires immediate action by the CPU. So, for certain jobs, you can let the system execute the job at the computer's convenience as long as the job finishes in some predefined time frame.

Batch Processing The main function of the computer's scheduler of jobs is to ensure that the CPU is fully utilized. As soon as the CPU completes one job, the scheduler allocates another job. At most computer installations, the CPU is utilized only 60% to 80% of the time. As a result, a lot of time is wasted while the CPU is sitting idle waiting for work to perform. It would make sense if the CPU could be executing batch jobs during this idle time.

Batch initiator. You place job codes in your JCL JOB statement to indicate when you want your particular job to execute. Figure 2.21 lists the job classes available on most systems. You place one of these codes in the JOB card using the CLASS= option. The JOB statement

```
//DPRSGENR    JOB   (1,DS,BW40RS),SCHWAB,CLASS=B,NOTIFY=$DPRS,
//               MSGCLASS=3
```

indicates that you want the job to execute within the next 30 minutes (i.e., CLASS=B).

The mainframe contains a software module called a batch initiator, which schedules and controls batch jobs. Each day a computer operator activates one or more batch initiators and assigns it a series of job classes to execute. One batch initiator can be assigned the job classes of A, C, and T and a second one assigned the job classes A, B, and L (Figure 2.22). The system

A	Execute the job within the next 15 minutes
B	Execute the job within the next 30 minutes
C	Execute the job within the next 60 minutes
D	Execute the job overnight
H	Hold the job
L	Execute the job within the next 15 minutes, restrict job step times to 1 minute each
T	Job requires magnetic tape processing

FIGURE 2.21   *Job classes for execution of a batch job. These codes are used in the CLASS = n option of the JCL's JOB statement. Another application of these codes is demonstrated in Figure 2.5.*

can execute two batch jobs simultaneously, one from each batch initiator. In this example, jobs with job class A can be executed by either of the two initiators. If you submit a job containing a job class that has not been activated or is not currently in a batch initiator, that batch job can never execute. Only those batch jobs selected by a batch initiator can be scheduled for execution by the CPU. And each batch initiator starts jobs having only a certain job class.

Keep in mind, when you submit batch jobs to the system, the JCL statements contain the job class and priority code for that job. The job is placed in a queue for later handling by a batch initiator. The computer operator starts one or more batch initiators and tells the system which job classes are to execute in each of the batch initiators. The system's scheduler assigns the CPU one or more batch jobs for execution whenever the CPU is not busy. Make sure you always assign a priority code because jobs are picked according to the priority code.

When the on-line response time on the system starts to degrade, the computer operator can stop one or more batch initiators in hope of improving response time. In most installations, the production environment usually takes precedence over program development or reports generation. The production environment in this case refers to most on-line processing of the company's business.

One of the main benefits of batch processing is cost. During a company's normal business day the system is working at its peak load. The system is handling the maximum number of users and all of them are competing for system resources. Consequently, the cost per transaction generally is the highest for jobs on line during this peak load period. The cost per transaction can be reduced if the job executes either in the batch mode or at a nonpeak usage time.

In the business world, departments must work within a defined budget. The computer system is one entry in the department's budget. Most companies have a charge-back procedure for each user of the computer system. The department is charged automatically for using mainframe resources on a pro-rated basis. The charge-back cost includes a charge for using central storage and DASD space, and the CPU time. In addition, the charge-back fee includes a charge based on the time of day the transaction occurred.

batch initiator 1

batch initiator 2

FIGURE 2.22
Job classes in multiple batch initiators.

On-Line Processing On-line processing, also known as teleprocessing or On-Line Transaction Processing (OLTP), is interactive processing. Although batch processing is designed for programs that can run independently, on-line processing is used to create a dialog between the computer and the end user.

Let's look at how a master file might be updated in batch.

1. An input file (called a transaction file) would have to exist and would consist of data to be used to update the master file. Each record in the input file could be used to update a corresponding record in the master file. The input file must be sorted to the same order as the master file.

2. If a record is found in the input file with data that does not satisfy the program's edit routines, that record would not be used. Instead, the data would be output to an error report. The user would then have to correct the data, create a new input file with corrected data, and rerun the batch job.

3. This process might take place over several days, because most companies run production batch jobs at night, after normal working hours. The user would not produce an updated master file for perhaps many days.

On the other hand, a master file via an on-line system is updated in a different way. In an on-line system the following takes place:

1. The end user would input data into a terminal, one transaction (i.e., a record) at a time.
2. Editing of data would occur at that time. If any record contained invalid data, the user would receive an error message at the terminal and would have a chance to correct the data immediately.
3. The master file then would be updated.

The main advantage of on-line processing is currency of data. That is, programs can correct errors at the time that they are made and update files as soon as correct data is entered.

Major On-Line Systems

Some of the major on-line systems used on large mainframes are Information Management System (IMS), CICS, and TSO.

IMS IMS has two components:

1. A hierarchical database manager that uses a database language known as Data Language/I (DL/I)
2. A data communications manager

The database manager will be discussed in later chapters. This chapter is primarily concerned with the data communications manager.

Unlike TSO, which acquires an address space for each user who is logged on, IMS's data communications manager runs in several address spaces that are shared among users. Multiple copies of IMS can be started by the operator, each copy with its own set of address spaces. Typically, a company runs at least two copies of IMS—production IMS and test IMS. Production IMS is used for the company's transaction processing against "real" databases; test IMS usually contains smaller versions of those databases used for testing by programmers developing new applications.

It is also possible to run a copy of IMS that does not use DL/I; IBM's relational database, DB2, can be used instead. Also, the DL/I database manager can be run under the CICS communications manager. CICS is discussed more fully shortly.

Types of IMS programs. Some of the address spaces (Figure 2.23) used by IMS include those used to run the following:

> *Message Processing Program* (MPP). Also known as a data communication (DC) program, an MPP is an on-line program that runs under the control of IMS's data communications manager. The data communications manager handles requests for transactions from terminals, I/O to the terminals, and database I/O.
>
> *Batch Message Processing* (BMP) program. A BMP program is a batch job that runs under the control of IMS.
>
> *Control region.* The control region functions like a mini-operating system with regard to other address spaces, swapping programs in and out at certain times.

BMP programs are batch programs, although they run under control of IMS. As such, they can access three kinds of data:

- IMS databases
- Other, nondatabase files, such as sequential files and partitioned data sets
- The IMS message queue

IMS MPPs can write data into either IMS databases or a sequential message queue; BMP programs then can access either of these as well as nondatabase files. Thus, BMPs can serve as a bridge between IMS systems and other systems by "exporting" information in the form of sequential files from one to the other.

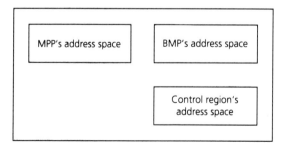

FIGURE 2.23   *IMS's three address spaces.*

BMP programs can read or update nondatabase files. They can also read or update IMS databases, but they can only read the message queue. The message queue is temporary storage; if IMS were to abend, or if the system were to require an IPL, data on the message queue would be lost. Data written out to a database would remain.

IMS uses the control region to swap programs in and out of memory. For example, when an MPP is waiting for terminal input from the user, IMS will swap it out to DASD or extended memory, place information about the MPP on a queue, and swap in another MPP. When the second MPP is waiting for terminal input, IMS will look at the queue and find another MPP (which is no longer waiting on terminal input) to swap in. Programs waiting on database I/O are not swapped out; IMS allows the control region to remain inactive until the database I/O is complete. BMP programs also are never swapped out, because they are noninteractive and thus never wait for terminal I/O.

DL/I. In addition to MPPs and BMP programs, there is one other kind of IMS program, the DL/I batch program. A DL/I batch program is similar to a BMP program, but it does not run under the control of IMS; it simply uses IMS DL/I services. This means a DL/I batch program can read or update IMS databases (under a certain condition) and read or update nondatabase files, but it cannot read the message queue. The condition that allows a DL/I batch program to access a database is that the operator issue a database release (DBR) command to IMS, which in effect removes the database from the control of IMS. After the DL/I batch job has run, the operator can restart the database, which again allows IMS to control it.

CICS Customer Information Control System (CICS) runs in a single address space and all users share the address space. Multiple copies of CICS can run; typically, there is a production copy and a test copy. The software in the CICS address space performs several functions: system services interface with the operating system, load application programs to run under CICS, and pass control to other parts of the address space as needed. Terminal control handles I/O between CICS and teleprocessing terminals. File control handles database I/O.

CICS can use VSAM files for its database, or can use IMS's DL/I as a database manager.

TSO Earlier in this chapter we briefly discussed TSO and ISPF, two tools available to us on IBM mainframes. TSO is a time sharing facility that permits multiple users to access the computer system at the same time. You use ISPF to create programs, edit files, and perform certain work on the computer. Under MVS, the system creates multiple background and foreground regions (i.e., address spaces) for running batch jobs and time-sharing jobs, respectively. Each of these regions is given slices of memory and each is granted a certain amount of CPU time. When the region's CPU accessing time has expired, the system swaps the jobs in that region to DASD or extended memory and loads another set of jobs into the region. This process continues until all jobs are processed. This process of time-sharing gives TSO its name: time sharing option. Each TSO job is given its own address space.

ISPF has two components:

- Program development facility (ISPF/PDF)
- Dialog management services (ISPF/DMS)

ISPF/PDF primarily is a programmer's tool. It can be used to edit or browse datasets; create, copy, or print datasets; compile and test program source code; submit batch jobs; and access DB2.

ISPF/DMS is the on-line system that was used by IBM to create ISPF/PDF. It allows programmers to create end-user systems that allow users to enter, browse, and edit data and that can process the data in various ways.

THE MICROCOMPUTER ENVIRONMENT

Hardware

In 1981, IBM introduced its first personal computer called the IBM PC. By 1984, the IBM PC had become the industry standard for personal computers. Since that time, numerous other microcomputer manufacturers have introduced their version of the IBM PC. These versions, if they are 100% compatible, are called PC clones or IBM PC compatibles. The PC itself consists of four distinctive parts.

1. *The computer's central processing unit (CPU).* It is based on either the Intel Corporation's 8086, 8088, 80286, 80386, or 80486 microprocessor.

2. *Primary memory or main memory.* Primary memory is electronic memory and is temporary. You lose anything that you store in primary memory whenever you turn off the machine or have a power interruption. The amount of primary memory in the computer is represented in groups of 64K. 1K is equal to 1024 characters or bytes. This memory is called Random Access Memory (RAM).

3. *Auxiliary memory.* This memory is usually magnetic and therefore represents a more permanent type of memory. When you turn off the computer's power, you do not lose whatever is stored on the magnetic media. Auxiliary memory is sometimes referred to as secondary memory or secondary storage. You perform work in primary or main memory and save it on some secondary storage media using a secondary storage device. These devices can be either a floppy disk drive for floppy disks or diskettes or a hard disk drive for metal disks. Tape backup units are also used occasionally.

4. *Connections to other devices, called interfaces.* Interfaces are other control boards installed on the system so the computer can perform other functions and activities. They typically include a parallel board, a serial board, a graphics board, a keyboard interface, and a terminal or monitor board. You connect your printer to the parallel port so you can get a paper copy of your work, called a hardcopy. You can connect either a mouse or a modem to the serial port. A mouse is a small rectangular device that moves a pointer on the screen. Some software packages require the installation of a mouse before that software can perform properly. A modem is a device that connects the computer to the telephone system for teleprocessing. You connect your monochrome computer screen to the monitor board and your keyboard to the keyboard interface. Obviously, you can purchase additional interfaces or controllers to perform numerous other functions or activities.

CPU, Main Memory, and the Motherboard The computer's motherboard is a large green board containing electronic circuits and is attached to the inside bottom of the computer's cabinet. It houses the Central Processing Unit (CPU), main memory, the bus, interface ports, and other circuitry to run the computer (Figure 2.24). Normally the motherboard contains multiple ports, called expansion slots, in case you need additional boards, called expansion boards. Certain expansion boards are standard equipment in some computer systems. Most expansion boards can be purchased separately from a variety of vendors and dealers. Typically, each board has an interface that sticks out of the back of the computer. You attach your printer, modem, mouse, and so on to these interfaces via cables. The bus connects all the expansion slots and primary memory to the CPU.

The CPU controls all the work in the computer because it contains electronic circuitry to process instructions and data. The CPU is a single silicon chip on the motherboard. A clock on the motherboard regulates the number of electronic pulses that occur per second within the computer. The speed of

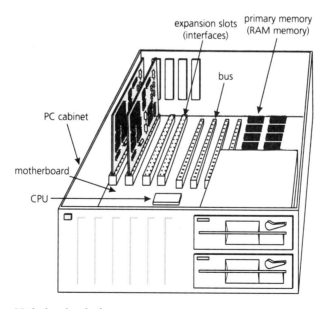

FIGURE 2.24 *Motherboard and other computer parts.*

the CPU is regulated by this clock—the faster the clock, the faster the CPU executes the instructions. The speed of the computer's clock is measured in megahertz (MHz). Other things being equal, an 8-MHz clock forces the CPU to process twice as many instructions per second as a 4-MHz clock. Of course, this faster CPU still would have to wait on slower devices such as disk drives, screens, and keyboards.

Monochrome and Color Screens Many computer systems use a monochrome screen because they are inexpensive. Monochrome screens can produce only a single color on a black or green screen. The most popular combinations are white on a black screen, green on a black screen, or amber on a black screen. These screens display characters in a 25-row by 80-column grid. They connect either to a built-in socket on the motherboard or to a female interface on the parallel expansion board. Monochrome screens can display only characters from the computer's predefined character set. In addition, each of the 2000 slots (25×80) on the screen can contain only one character from this predefined character set.

Color screens are more expensive than monochrome screens. Not only do they cost more but they also must be connected to a graphics expansion board costing hundreds of dollars. With a graphics expansion board on the system, you can generate color displays and produce geometric figures (pie charts, bar diagrams, circles, straight lines, and so on). Our color screen attaches to the female interface on the graphics expansion board that we must install in one of the expansion slots on the motherboard. We need a color screen to produce black and white geometric figures. Here, we are not restricted to a 25 by 80 grid but can generate characters and figures anywhere on the screen.

There are several different types of color screens including the following:

- Color Graphics Adaptor (CGA)
- Enhanced Graphics Adaptor (EGA)
- Video Gate Array (VGA)

The main difference among these three types, in practical terms, is the **resolution** of the monitor. Each character on the screen is composed of several lighted dots arranged in a particular pattern, which forms the character. (See Figure 2.25). These dots are technically known as **picture elements,** but are usually called **pixels** or **pels.** VGA monitors have more pels on each line of the screen than EGA monitors, which have more than CGA monitors. As a result, VGA monitors use more (and therefore smaller) pels to create letters, which causes the letters to be clearer and more sharply defined.

The PC The original version of the IBM PC in 1981 contained 16K of primary memory and had one single-sided floppy disk drive. Within a few months, IBM began selling its systems with double-sided disk drives. A double-sided disk drive has two read/write heads in the drive—one on the top and one

```
    #
   # # #
 # #   # #
 # #   # #
 # # # # #
 # #   # #
 # #   # #
```

FIGURE 2.25

The letter "A" composed of pels. Each pound sign ("#") represents a pel.

on the bottom. These drives are able to store twice as much as the original single-headed drives.

This version of the PC used Intel's 8088 microprocessor, which can address 16 bits at a time. The bus is a set of wires and circuits on the motherboard that connects the CPU to the other devices on the system. Because IBM only included an 8-bit bus in the 8086/8088 version of its PC, that PC is only a pseudo-16-bit machine.

The PC/XT In 1983 IBM changed some of the motherboard's circuitry and added a hard disk to its PC and called it an IBM/XT. These hard drives are nonremovable and can store millions of characters of data. The most popular XTs contain 10- and 20-megabyte hard disks. The XT still uses Intel's 8088 CPU and can access only the first 640K of primary memory.

The PC/AT In 1984 IBM introduced the PC/AT, which uses Intel's 80286 CPU unit. With the PC/AT came software that can access memory past the 640K limitations of the 8086/8088 CPU systems; typical PC/AT systems have 1MB to 2MB of memory. A 1MB system has 1024K of primary memory.

The PS/2 In 1987 IBM introduced the PS/2 series of computers. Some of the models (model 50 and 60) use the 80286 CPU, while the upper end of the series (model 80) uses the 80386 CPU. These upper-end models will also allow the 80386 to be replaced with the latest Intel CPU, the 80486.

Operating Systems

DOS Operating System As we discussed in Chapter 1, an operating system is a collection of programs specifically written for a computer system to manipulate and utilize the various hardware components on the system. When the IBM staff introduced their PC in 1981, they needed an operating system for it. Rather than spend precious time and resources to write one themselves, they obtained nonexclusive rights to Microsoft's MS-DOS operating system for 16-bit microprocessors. IBM renamed it the PC-DOS operating system. PC-DOS and MS-DOS are essentially the same operating system for 8086-based machines. The first version of DOS was named DOS 1.0 and cost $45 in addition to the cost of the hardware. As the hardware changes over time, the operating system also has to change so it can utilize the new features of the hardware. Table 2.2 lists the different versions of DOS and what precipitated the need for the change.

OS/2 Operating System The OS/2 operating system is designed to replace DOS as the standard operating system on the 80286 and 80386 CPU-based machines. Computer systems using OS/2 must have a hard disk and at least 2MB of primary memory. OS/2 can access up to 16MB of primary memory.

Most DOS applications will run under OS/2. However, because OS/2 re-

TABLE 2.2   *Various DOS operating systems*

Version of DOS	Year Introduced	Change Precipitating Need for New Version
DOS 1.0	1981	The introduction of the IBM PC.
DOS 1.1	1982	Change from single-sided floppies to double-sided floppies. Also, corrected certain errors in version 1.0.
DOS 2.0	1983	The addition of hard disks and the introduction of the PC/XT.
DOS 2.1	1984	The introduction of the IBM PCjr.
DOS 3.0	1984	The introduction of the IBM PC/AT, an 80286-based machine. Also, the introduction of high-density floppies with 1.2M capacity.
DOS 3.1	1985	Added support for local area networks.
DOS 3.2	1986	The introduction of the IBM PC Convertible. Also, the introduction of 3-1/2 inch floppies with 720K capacity.
DOS 3.3	1987	The introduction of the IBM PS/2 and 3-1/2 inch floppies with 1.4M capacity.
DOS 4.0	1988	The introduction of the DOS shell and support for hard disks having more than 32M capacity.

stricts all DOS applications to 512K rather than 640K as in standard DOS systems, some incompatibility can occur. In addition, if you must have both DOS and OS/2 on the system, you might have to reconfigure the machine because the system will boot OS/2 from the hard drive first. The reconfiguration will allow you to boot either DOS or OS/2 from the hard disk.

OS/2 also can run different applications at the same time, a process called **multitasking.** In addition, OS/2 can run multiple threads of the same application. A thread is a sequence of instructions or a series of code the computer executes. OS/2 can run a single application program with multiple users accessing the one application simultaneously. In this case, OS/2 accesses different lines of the same code for each of the users of that code. This in effect lets OS/2 perform networking, where one user on a server is protected from the other users on that server.

The ability of OS/2 to efficiently use the CPU in the creation of multiple tasks propels OS/2 from the microcomputer environment to a minicomputer environment. Instead of one user on the system performing one task, you can have multiple users on the system performing multiple tasks. OS/2 can process jobs in both the background mode and foreground mode. If you have a time-consuming job running on the system, you can let OS/2 continue to execute that job while you switch to a new process and begin a new job. The time-consuming job is running in background as you simultaneously process a new job in foreground.

Another feature of OS/2 is its ability to execute structured query language (SQL) commands and service these commands against a minidatabase built into OS/2.

Local Area Networks

Local area networks, or LANs, are microcomputers that are connected so they can share data. Each LAN consists of one or more file servers and one or more workstations. A file server is a PC, usually a 80286 or 80386 machine, which has one or more hard disks. Workstations are PCs that are connected to the file server by cables. When a user on a workstation needs to access data from the file server, the network software makes it appear to the user (and his or her software) that the data is actually on the workstation. In this way, it is possible for several users on different workstations to access one database.

The file server can be what is known as a **dedicated file server,** that is, it is not used as a workstation, or it can be a **nondedicated file server,** that is, it is also used as a workstation.

There are trade-offs involved in the decision to have a dedicated or nondedicated file server. A nondedicated file server might make it unnecessary to purchase one workstation. A nondedicated file server will reduce the data access speed for the entire network (because the machine has to do two tasks at once), which might unfavorably impact the productivity of all users of the LAN.

Most LAN software contains data security features, so the LAN administrator can limit access to certain files on the LAN to only those users who have authority to use them. The simplest security mechanisms involve a password for each sensitive file—only those users who know the password can access those files. More sophisticated schemes allow users to be defined as members of groups and files to be defined as available to certain groups but not to others (Figure 2.26). This method has two advantages over the password method. It makes security administration easier, because if a person transfers from one group to another, the LAN administrator only has to redefine the user's membership, as opposed to changing passwords for all files that person had access to. It also enhances security itself; if a group has several members, the password method requires that they all know the pass-

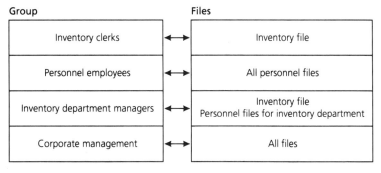

Group		Files
Inventory clerks	↔	Inventory file
Personnel employees	↔	All personnel files
Inventory department managers	↔	Inventory file Personnel files for inventory department
Corporate management	↔	All files

FIGURE 2.26 *A typical set of security groups for a LAN. Members of a given group can access the files defined for that group.*

words to the files they need to access. This increases the likelihood that someone will inadvertently disclose the password.

Real Storage on Microcomputers

RAM and ROM The main memory of the computer system is called Random Access Memory (RAM) because you can access any byte of memory and alter or change its contents. The operating system of the PC, PC/XT, and PC/AT can access a maximum of 640K of RAM. Some software products require you to access RAM memory beyond this 640K limitation. These packages either extend memory or expand memory using algorithms and techniques to accomplish the feat. However, these packages can be used only in isolated cases and for specific vendor software products.

Main memory is electronic memory and is temporary. Remember, RAM memory is like a fancy electric toaster in your kitchen. Once you cut the power to it, it loses its charge and cannot perform its duties.

Certain instructions and commands must be available to the system in a manner that is independent of the operating system. That is, the computer must know how to write the letter A or B on paper or display it on the screen. In addition, these instructions must remain as an integral part of the system whether or not the system has an electric current. You need memory locations that are permanent and cannot be changed by the user of the machine. This type of memory is called **read only memory** (ROM). ROM is scattered throughout the machine and handles such functions as providing graphics algorithms, calculating mathematical functions (such as computing square roots), and establishing the various fonts for the characters in its character set. These ROM chips are installed by the manufacturer of the computer system and give each machine a uniqueness by having some feature that might not be available on other machines.

PROM, EPROM, and EEPROM Suppose a computer manufacturer wants to introduce a new feature into its computer systems for competitive purposes. This new feature would need to be programmed into the ROM chips within the newly designed computer system. Because the instructions are permanently burned into a ROM chip, the old ROM chips in the manufacturer's inventory could not be used for this newly designed system. Instead of initially purchasing ROM chips, the manufacturer could have initially purchased **programmable read only memory** (PROM) chips instead. PROM is a version of ROM, but each chip can be individually programmed. The manufacturer can purchase PROM chips, store them in inventory, and program them as they are needed. However, once the PROM chip is programmed, its contents cannot be changed. The computer manufacturer has usable inventory and can introduce new systems as market conditions warrant, regardless of inventory cost-lost considerations.

If there is any error in the programs or instructions stored within a ROM or PROM chip, it cannot be corrected. If the manufacturer found a glitch or error in the ROM or PROM chip, it would have to unsolder the chip from the motherboard (or other control board) and solder the new chip back into its place. This process would involve recalling all computer systems it sold to make this costly and time-consuming correction. To prevent this problem, the computer manufacturer could use **erasable programmable read only memory** (EPROM) in its machines. The ROM memory can be erased or changed, but only with a special device or procedure—changes can be made without having to unsolder the chips. Typically this memory is ultraviolet light erasable and electrically programmable. Each chip contains a small window so it can be erased by an ultraviolet source and an interface so it can be electrically programmed.

Electrically erasable and programmable read only memory (EEPROM) is similar to EPROM except it can be both programmed and erased electrically. A utility program changes the contents of EEPROM chips. The utility program can be used by the computer manufacturer, the user, or any other third party. Many current computer systems have EEPROM memory to hold data on the type of hardware installed on that user's system. When you purchase additional hardware for your computer system, you run a special utility program. This program updates the EEPROM chips with data identifying the current computer system's hardware configuration. EEPROM is faster than EPROM, but both are slower than ROM.

Buffer Areas Most computer systems have a variety of different types of memory. In addition to having RAM, ROM, PROM, EPROM, and/or EEPROM, most systems have buffer storage or memory. The keyboard on most microcomputer systems, for example, uses a 15-character buffer area located in RAM memory. When you type characters on the keyboard, the characters first enter the buffer area and are then used by the system for processing in a first-in-first-out (FIFO) process. If the system is performing a disk read, you can still type up to 15 characters or commands into the keyboard. Once this buffer is filled, any continuing use of the keyboard results in the system broadcasting an audible sound, usually a small beep.

Many printers have a 1K to 64K buffer area installed within the printer. When you send a document to the printer for printing, that document is first stored in the printer's buffer area. When the size of the document is equal to or smaller than the buffer, the printer sends a "finished printing" command back to the computer system even though it has not finished printing. This frees the computer system's bus and allows it to continue processing other functions. The printer prints the document contained in its buffer area while you continue to use the computer system for other activities. If for some reason the printer loses power or encounters some other problem, you might have to reactivate the printing routine to rectify the problem. You have in effect produced a multitasking environment where two jobs are running at the exact same time.

External Storage on Microcomputers

Floppy Diskettes A floppy disk or diskette is a small flexible plastic disk coated with iron oxide. You store data on a disk. The original diskettes in the 1970s were single sided and stored data only on one side. They were 5-1/4 inches in diameter and could store about 180K characters. The first IBM PCs under DOS 1.0 used these single-sided diskettes for storaging data. When the reliability of the double-sided diskettes improved, most computer manufacturers switched from the single-sided to the double-sided diskettes. These were known as double-sided/double-density (DS/DD) floppies. DOS 1.0 and 1.1 formatted these diskettes into 40 tracks and 8 sectors per track for a total of 320 segments. Each sector could store 512 bytes of data. Because the diskette had two sides (side 0 and side 1), the diskette had a maximum capacity of 320K characters. All subsequent versions of DOS format the diskette into 9 sectors and 40 tracks for a total of 360 segments and have a capacity of 360K.

With the introduction of the PC/AT and PS/2, different formatting techniques became available. The PC/AT comes with an optional high-density floppy drive that requires a high-density floppy diskette. DOS formats these diskettes into 80 tracks with 15 sectors per track, giving a capacity of 1.2M of storage. Although these high-density drives can read standard DS/DD diskettes, they cannot reliably write to them in certain cases: A DS/DD diskette that is written to by a high-density floppy drive always can be read with a high-density drive, but cannot be read by about 15% of the DS/DD drives in existence.

You can format DS/DD diskettes on the high-density drive using the FORMAT A:/4 option. However, because the read/write head of the high-density drives is smaller than the DS/DD disk heads, the data you store on these diskettes is not dependable. That means sometimes you can access the data and sometimes you cannot. To ensure the integrity of the data on DS/DD diskettes, always place a write-protect tab over the cut-out slot on the DS/DD diskette whenever you place them in a high-density drive. This guarantees that the high-density drive will not write onto the DS/DD diskette and therefore prevents accidental trashing of the diskette.

Microfloppies or Microdiskettes The IBM PS/2 comes with another type of diskette—a 3-1/2-inch microdiskette or microfloppy. Unlike the 5-1/4-inch diskette which is wrapped in a flexible soft plastic wrapper, the 3-1/2 inch microdiskette is encased in hard plastic. This case contains a metal tab protecting the read/write surface of the floppy enclosed within it. Its hard shell makes it less susceptible to damage and destruction.

The DS/DD microdiskettes are formatted into 80 tracks giving you about 720K of memory. These microdiskettes also have a high-density version containing 1.44M of memory. Most potential purchasers of computer systems are facing a serious quandary: "Which of the many diskettes do I put on my system?" Although one purpose of the diskette is to provide a vehicle for backing up the hard drive, the main purpose of it is to provide a vehicle for transporting data and programs from one system to another system. The variety and incompatibility of the many types of diskettes on the market make the easy transportation of data and programs difficult.

There are several things to consider when you install a diskette drive on your computer system. Obviously, you want upward compatibility. That means the work you already have done on an older hardware system must be able to be transferred to a newer hardware system. In addition, the computer you purchase must be compatible with those of your colleagues and other business associates. If you have customers, clients, or a sales force using PCs, your system must be able to communicate with these other users. In a business with multiple computer systems and multiple generations of DOS and hardware, you might be forced to purchase multiple diskette drives for your system to maintain your compatibility with them.

The purchase of multiple diskette drives can involve the purchase of multiple disk controllers. Most disk controllers have the capability of handling two diskette drives. The addition of a third floppy disk drive requires the purchase of another disk controller. This cost is not a trivial amount to most users of computer systems.

Hard Disks A hard disk is a nonremovable small metal disk coated with iron oxide on which data is stored. The first authorized hard disk on IBM PCs appeared on the PC/XTs. The hard disk usually is housed in a vacuum encasement and demands its own separate controller board. The board fits into one of the expansion slots on the motherboard and the drive is attached to the main cabinet. The face of the hard drive extends out of the front of the computer cabinet and generally contains a small light to indicate when the drive's disk head is accessing the disk platter. Unlike floppy drives that make contact with the floppy disk's surface, the hard drive's read/write head never makes contact with the disk's metal surface, but floats on a cushion of air a fraction of an inch above it.

The most popular hard drives are the 20MB and 30MB systems. These systems require the use of directories and subdirectories to keep the massive amounts of data in some coherent order. You must use a special formatting procedure to format the hard drive. By common convention, the hard drive is drive C, with floppy drives allocated as drive A or drive B. When you boot a hard drive system, the operating system usually boots off the hard drive.

Because the hard drive revolves at a high rate of speed and the drive is balanced to prevent the head from touching the surface, most early computer systems with hard disk drives were never moved from their original setup location. Computer systems with floppy disks could be moved easily, but systems with hard drives should remain stationary at all times. Also, computers with hard drives should never be moved or jarred while the system is running. Virtually all hard drive systems on the market today can "park" the read/write head in a special location where no data will be stored. This is done so the machine can be moved.

Crashes There are several types of crashes we need to discuss at this time. A system crash occurs when the copy of the operating system in primary memory is damaged or destroyed. When this happens, reboot the system. When you reboot the system, you will lose all work that was not saved. A disk crash occurs when the copy of the operating system in secondary storage is damaged or destroyed. You use a backup copy of DOS to create a new copy of DOS. The contents of primary memory might or might not be destroyed by a disk crash. A head crash occurs when the read/write head of a hard disk makes contact with the disk's metal platter. The read/write head could be damaged or the metal platter could be permanently scratched. In either case, you have physical damage to the drive. Not only will you lose the data on the hard disk, you also will lose the hard disk itself and will have to purchase a new one.

Therefore, on hard disk systems, you should practice good data processing techniques. This includes performing a backup of the data on the hard drive on a timely basis. Remember the statement, "What would I do if my hard drive was destroyed in the next two seconds?" Remember, you can replace the hard drive in a matter of hours (assuming you have the money) but it might take weeks or months to recapture the data or recreate it as it appeared on the hard disk before the crash. The backup of a 20MB hard drive system takes about 45 minutes and requires about 10 to 15 high-density floppies to hold the backup data.

Tape Backup Systems Tape backup systems provide quicker, easier, and more efficient backup abilities. A tape backup system is a tape drive that uses cartridge tape to backup the hard drive. Tape backup is quicker than diskette backup, because the actual writing to the backup media does not have to be interrupted frequently to exchange a blank diskette for a full one. It is easier because you do not have to be present to continually swap diskettes. It is more efficient for the same reason: Because you do not have to be present, the backup can be started just before lunch or just before quitting time. This can be particularly important if the hard disk resides on a file server for a LAN; while backups are in progress, none of the LAN users have access to the files on the file server. Because of these productivity considerations a tape backup system can pay for itself in a short period of time.

Improving Performance: Virtual Storage, Caching, and RAM Disks Vendors have marketed products that give microcomputers many of the features of mainframes in regard to memory management. Virtual storage allows you to execute programs that might otherwise be too large to fit in RAM; caching and RAM disks can improve the speed of data I/O.

Virtual storage programs and caching programs are resident programs; RAM disks are device drivers. We will deal with resident programs and device drivers more fully later in this chapter; for now, you only need to know that these types of program execute in such a fashion as to, in effect, become part of the operating system.

With special software, a PC can implement virtual memory much like a mainframe. This can be important when you are executing a program that needs more memory for its data than is available on the system. An example is a word processing program that is designed to load an entire document into RAM. (This might be done for the sake of speed while manipulating the file; don't forget that RAM access is much faster than any kind of disk access.) If you are working on an extremely large document, even 640K might not be enough RAM to hold the document and the program. In this situation, a virtual memory program could swap portions of the document to disk while causing the word processing program to "think" it is really in RAM. Generally, virtual memory programs perform this swapping to hard disks, but some are capable of swapping to floppies as well.

Disk caching programs also work very much like a mainframe. When a portion of a disk is read into RAM, it is saved, or cached, until the next disk read request is received from a program. At this time, the caching software intercepts the read request and searches the cache in RAM; if the data is found there, it is returned to the program that requested the disk read as if it had been retrieved from disk. Again, this method of disk access relies on the fact that RAM access is much faster than disk access.

RAM disks work much like hiperspace on a mainframe. (Remember that hiperspace is a data space in main memory that can be made to act as disk space.) RAM disks are areas of RAM that act as another drive. Again, RAM disks take advantage of the fact that RAM access is faster than disk access. One difference between RAM disks and hiperspace is that, on a mainframe, hiperspace works under program control; on a microcompu.er, a RAM disk is transparent to an application program (a word processor, a database, etc.).

Program Processing on Microcomputers

On-Line Processing The large majority of microcomputer programs are on line, that is, they are interactive with the user. From the programmer's standpoint, there is a fundamental difference between on-line programs on microcomputers and on mainframes: A microcomputer gives the programmer considerably more control than a mainframe does. On a mainframe, terminal I/O usually is under the control of a communications manager, such as those of IMS or CICS. When a programmer wishes to display a screen on a terminal from his program, he or she must program a request to the communications manager and then turn control over to it. When the user has typed in the necessary data on the screen, he or she presses the "enter" key, "send" key, or some other key to tell the communications manager that he or she is finished entering data. Control then returns to the program to process the data.

On a PC, the programmer always has control over the terminal. To display a screen, he or she programs write commands to the terminal until the screen is formatted the way he or she wants it. These write commands are executed instantly, as each is encountered in the program. The programmer then programs a loop to look for and capture keystrokes by the user; the program then can either process each keystroke as it is entered or save the keystrokes for processing as a group.

These differences in programming capability can easily result in differences that are visible to the user, if programs are written to take advantage of the higher level of control. For example, a program that processes each keystroke as it is entered can trap errors as they occur and give the user a message while he or she is typing; on a mainframe, it is usually necessary to wait until the user has finished entering data for the entire screen to do this. Also, menus can make use of "hot keys." On a mainframe, the user must type the key corresponding to the menu selection desired and then press one other key, such as, "enter" or "send"; on a microcomputer, the user may only have to press the selection key to have the program immediately execute the desired selection.

Batch Processing From the user's standpoint, batch processing is done much the same way on microcomputers as on mainframes. In either case, a series of different tasks are executed, one after the other, in a batch. Some differences between batch processing on microcomputers and on mainframes are the way data files are specified and the amount of interaction with the user that is allowed. These differences are shown in Figure 2.27.

Figure 2.27 shows two jobs for backing up two disk units (C and D) to tape by using a program called TAPEBACK. The first job is designed to run on a mainframe and consists of MVS JCL (Job Control Language); the second consists of DOS batch commands.

The JCL statements each begin with two slashes ("//"). The first statement is a JOB statement, which identifies the job to the operating system and provides certain accounting information. An EXEC statement identifies the program to be run; note that we have two such statements, because we are running the program twice, once for each disk. Each EXEC statement is followed by one or more Data Definition (DD) statements, which specify the data sets that will be used by the program.

In the microcomputer batch job, we begin with a pair of ECHO statements to display messages to the user. This is followed by a command to execute a program called GETANS. GETANS is not a program supplied by DOS; in our example, the programmer would have had to code it. It would be designed to accept a keystroke from the user and return a code to indicate which key was pressed. In this example, a code of one is returned if the user pressed n; this return code can be detected by the DOS IF ERRORLEVEL command, which, in this case, causes control to be passed to the part of the job labeled :ABORT. Otherwise, the batch job executes TAPEBACK twice (once for each disk), prints some messages, and ends.

The way data files are specified differs between the two examples: In the

```
//DPTAPEBK   JOB    (1,DS,BW70RS),SCHWAB,CLASS=F
//STEP1      EXEC   PGM=TAPEBACK
//DISKFILS   DD     UNIT=DISK,VOL=SER=C
//TAPEFILS   DD     UNIT=TAPE,VOL=SER=MYTAPE,LABEL=1
//STEP2      EXEC   PGM=TAPEBACK
//DISKFILS   DD     UNIT=DISK,VOL=SER=D
//TAPESFILS  DD     UNIT=TAPE,VOL=SER=MYTAPE,LABEL=2
```

A. *A Mainframe's JCL Job*

```
ECHO TAPE BACKUP BEGINNING
ECHO TYPE "N" TO ABORT OR ANYTHING ELSE TO CONTINUE
GETANS
IF ERRORLEVEL 1 GOTO ABORT
TAPEBACK C: 1
TAPEBACK D: 2
GOTO GOODEND
:ABORT
ECHO TAPE BACKUP ABORTED.
GOTO EXIT
:GOODEND
ECHO TAPE BACKUP COMPLETED.
:EXIT
ECHO END OF BACKUP PROCEDURE.
```

B. *A Microcomputer's Job File*

FIGURE 2.27 *Examples of a tape backup job on a mainframe and on a microcomputer. Data sets are specified in different ways; the microcomputer job is also more interactive.*

mainframe job, TAPEBACK must be coded in such a way as to use a pair of labels on the DD statements (known as DDNAMES), DISKFILS and TAPEFILS; the JCL will specify the actual disks and tapes to be used, and the operating system will make the data available to the program. In the microcomputer job, however, TAPEBACK must be able to accept the disk specifications as input parameters, which are coded after the name of the program when it is invoked. TAPEBACK must then request DOS to make the data available.

The microcomputer batch job can be much more interactive than the mainframe batch job. Here, you can display messages to the user and get information back from him or her.

Resident Programs and Device Drivers A third set of programs that can be executed on microcomputers consists of memory-resident programs and device drivers. These programs are designed to work "behind the scenes," in such a way as to be transparent to application programs. Various memory-management programs that have been discussed are resident programs or device drivers. Various "pop-up" programs, such as Borland International's SideKick, also are resident programs. These programs are designed to be used in conjunction with other application programs, such as word processors or databases. When the user presses a certain combination of keys, for example, both shift keys at once, the resident program "pops up" on the screen, on top of the application program. Typically, resident programs provide such tools as notepads, calendars, or calculators that can be used in conjunction with the application program. Resident programs are also known as Terminate and Stay Resident (TSR) programs.

Resident programs make use of the fact that there are two ways that a microcomputer program can end: One way is to call the DOS TERMINATE function; this causes DOS to regain control and free the RAM that was occupied by the program, thus making it available for other programs. The other way is to call the DOS KEEP function; this causes DOS to regain control, but it does not free the program's RAM. Resident programs use the second method of ending.

There is one thing a resident program must do, however, before it ends. The 8086 family of processors (which includes the 80286, 80386, and 80486) are what are known as interrupt-driven processors. Approximately 18 times per second, the CPU interrupts what it is doing at the time (e.g., executing an application program), saves some data about what it was doing, and then performs other functions. These other functions include checking for keyboard input, updating the screen display, and updating the microcomputer's internal clock. To perform these functions, the CPU checks a list of interrupt vectors. An **interrupt vector** is simply the address in RAM of the code that the CPU must execute to service the interrupt. The CPU goes down this list and executes the code at each address pointed to by the list. An interesting feature of the list of interrupt vectors is that it resides in ROM but is copied to RAM when the microcomputer is powered on; it is the RAM version that the CPU uses. Because the list is in modifiable memory, the resident program can substitute its own address for one of the interrupt vectors and then end. Then, whenever the CPU services that interrupt, it will automatically execute the resident program that then can check for certain key combinations (for example, both shift keys) or certain aspects of the current system environment (such as an outstanding disk read request) and take appropriate action.

A class of programs that is similar to resident programs is device drivers. Although resident programs operate by, in effect, "fooling" DOS into thinking that they are part of a normal interrupt routine, device drivers operate more in conjunction with DOS. (Of course, DOS is quite willing to be fooled in this fashion; this is one of the purposes of the KEEP function.) When the microcomputer is first powered up, DOS looks in a special file (CONFIG.SYS), which is modifiable by the programmer or user, for a list of device drivers to load into RAM. When DOS gets a request for I/O to a device, DOS looks for the appropriate device driver in memory and executes it. As the name implies, device drivers are used to provide support for various devices, such as printers, disk drives, or monitors. DOS was not designed to be able to directly operate all I/O devices; instead, DOS was designed to be able to transfer control to device drivers. This allows new devices, which were not in existence when DOS was developed, to be added to the microcomputer. A typical example would be a RAM disk.

ADVANTAGES AND DISADVANTAGES OF MAINFRAMES AND MICROCOMPUTERS

It is nearly impossible to create a hard-and-fast list of advantages and disadvantages of mainframes and microcomputers, for two reasons. First, with the advent of faster CPUs, greater RAM addressability, bigger hard disks, LANs, multitasking, and so on, the differences between mainframes and microcomputers are becoming smaller and smaller. Second, whether a particular system is relatively more or less useful depends in large part on the applications to run on the system; what is a disadvantage for one application might not be a disadvantage for another. For these reasons, it is more useful to develop a set of considerations that should be taken into account when determining whether to implement a given system on a mainframe or on a microcomputer.

One obvious consideration is what is known as **connectivity.** Connectivity is simply the ability to share data among several users. Connectivity is easier to implement on mainframes, because most mainframe communications software (such as that found in IMS or CICS) is designed for multiple users. Microcomputers achieve connectivity through LANs, which typically do not have all of the functionality of mainframe communications managers. For a small number of users, however, they can be much cheaper.

Don't overlook the importance of **speed.** The speed of a mainframe's CPU is measured in millions of instructions per second (MIPS). The clock speed of a microcomputer's CPU is measured in hertz, an engineering term that means cycles per second; a 12-MHz CPU performs 12 million cycles per second. An instruction averages 13 cycles. This gives a microcomputer CPU a speed of .92 MIPS; this can be compared with a typical mainframe's speed of 50, 70, or even more than 90 MIPS. This would seem to suggest that, if execution speed of a system is important, the mainframe is the obvious choice. However, the situation is rarely so simple. Recall that mainframes almost always have multiple users and that they operate by time sharing, that is, each user's application executes for a certain period of time and is then swapped out while other users get a turn. Given this, the number of users on a mainframe system has a noticeable effect on response time for an application. In some cases, a microcomputer, which is typically dedicated to one user and one application at a time, can sometimes be faster than a mainframe.

Another consideration is **disk size.** Here, the situation tends to be clear cut. IBM PS/2s might have as many as four 130M hard drives, for a total of 520M while a single 3380 disk on a mainframe would have 630M—and mainframes have numerous disk drives. If truly massive amounts of data need to be stored at one time, a mainframe is the better choice.

You need to consider **address space size.** This is not a clear-cut issue. Extremely large programs might need a lot of RAM on a microcomputer. An IBM PS/2 might be expanded to 12M; a mainframe might have 64M of main storage (which could be expanded to, say, 256M). However, again, the number of users is a consideration; a mainframe with a large number of TSO users, for example, might be able to maintain acceptable response time only if the maximum TSO address space size were limited to, say, 2 to 4 meg. Again, the microcomputer might be a better choice in certain situations.

Don't forget to consider **cost,** and, again, the issue is not clear cut. A mainframe will have costs that a PC will not, such as large floor space requirements, large power requirements, high software costs, and large programmer/support staff costs. Again, however, the number of users is a factor: If a large number of users needs to be able to perform a large number of different tasks, economies of scale can make a mainframe cheaper, on a per-user basis, than a large number of microcomputers.

HYBRID SYSTEMS

So far, we have assumed that the choices are either mainframe or microcomputer; however, more and more companies are creating hybrid systems that make use of the advantages of both choices. Typically, such a system stores data on a mainframe and performs on-line processing on a microcomputer and batch processing (where a lot of power is required to sift through large amounts of data) on a mainframe. In this section, we will examine some of the aspects of sharing data between microcomputers and mainframes.

In Chapter 1, we dealt with the differences in data formats between ASCII and EBCDIC. Microcomputers almost always use ASCII; mainframes usually use EBCDIC. Therefore, some sort of data translation is needed if data is to be shared between the two systems. Although there are utilities that will translate from one format to the other, not all characters are translatable. ASCII can contain some characters that do not have a corresponding character in EBCDIC, and vice versa. Fortunately, there are few such characters and, in many cases, they are unimportant.

Internal representations of numeric data also can be different. ASCII and EBCDIC are used to store numeric data in what is known as display format; this format is designed to make the data easier to display on a terminal or print on a printer. There are other methods of storing numeric data that are designed to make calculations easier. For example, most mainframes make use of what is known as packed data; packed data "packs" two digits into each byte except for the last one, which contains one digit and a code for the sign of the number. Figure 2.28 shows the hexadecimal representation of the number 1467 in display and packed formats. Display format is used primarily for displaying the number on the terminal or the printer; packed format is used primarily for calculations. (Note that, in this case, the final F of the number in packed format represents a positive number.)

Microcomputers, however, typically use a different format for internally representing numbers for calculation purposes. In this case, the number 1467

Display format (EBCDIC)   Packed format

| F1 | F4 | F6 | F7 | | 01 | 46 | 7F |

FIGURE 2.28   *The number 1467 in display and packed formats.*

Display format (ASCII)   Internal format

| 31 | 34 | 36 | 37 | | 05 | BB |

FIGURE 2.29   *The number 1467 in display and internal formats on a microcomputer. Compare with Figure 2.28.*

probably would be stored as a binary number. Figure 2.29 shows a typical microcomputer representation of the number 1467 in display and internal formats.

A translation utility would have to be able to recognize different data formats on the machine it was copying from. This alone would be difficult: How would a utility be able to distinguish the number 14 in display format (31/34) from the number 12,596 in internal format (31/34)? A more difficult problem would be to determine the proper data format for the machine the utility is copying to. For example, suppose the utility detects the internally formatted number 05/BB on a PC; we have said that this usually is formatted as 01/46/7F on a mainframe. Indeed, this usually is the case, but not always; in some situations, the mainframe will format the data in the same manner as the PC, as in 05/BB.

One way of solving this problem is to impose the restriction that only display data can be transferred from one system to the other. This usually requires that the data be massaged in such a way as to translate from internal format to display format before inputting it to the ASCII/EBCDIC translation utility.

Once these problems have been surpassed, you then must face the question of how to actually transfer the data. The most common method involves **terminal emulation.** With the proper hardware and software, it is possible to use a microcomputer in place of a mainframe terminal; the hardware and software accepts signals from the mainframe that are intended for a mainframe terminal and uses them to display data on a microcomputer monitor. Input from the user is translated into the same signals that a mainframe terminal would send to the mainframe, and then those signals are sent to the mainframe. In effect, the hardware and software on the microcomputer make it "look" like a mainframe terminal to the mainframe. IBM and several other vendors market such emulators.

This feature allows you to transfer data to and from the mainframe. Transferring data to the mainframe is known as **uploading** the data. To do this the microcomputer sends signals to the mainframe which cause it to display a screen under some communications and data manager which requests data. The user might or might not see this screen; instead, the data is entered into the screen by the microcomputer, and signals are sent to the mainframe to cause it to process the data as if the user had entered the data. The reverse process, transferring data from the mainframe to the microcomputer, is known as **downloading** the data. To download data, the microcomputer sends signals to the mainframe that cause it to display data. Again, this data is never seen by the user; instead, the microcomputer reads it from the screen and writes it out to a file.

Our discussion of hybrid systems would not be complete without mentioning systems application architecture (SAA). SAA is not a method of transferring data, but is a standard and a statement of direction from IBM. SAA consists, primarily, of a set of guidelines for how end-user applications can be developed. SAA is designed to meet two goals. The first involves what is known as the common user access (CUA). CUA is based on the concept that all applications should "look and feel" the same to the user. That means screens should be formatted in the same fashion and the same keys should perform the same functions. For example, if a certain key is used to indicate that the user wants to add a record in one application, the same key should be used for that function in other applications; similarly, if the field where the record's key is to be inputted is at the top of the screen in one application, it should be at the top of the screen in other applications. The result is that users of one application will find it easier to learn the other applications.

The second goal of SAA is what is known as common programming interface (CPI). CPI is designed to make the machine that will execute the program transparent to the programmer. In other words, the programmer should be able to develop an application without knowing (or caring) whether it will be executed on a PC or a mainframe. It also should make no difference to the programmer whether the program will execute on a PC but store data on a mainframe, or execute on a mainframe but store data on a PC.

Currently, SAA is in its infancy; there are well-developed standards, which, if they are followed by the programmer, should allow the goals noted above to be met. Also, IBM has begun to market products that will conform to SAA. However, virtually all authorities in the field agree that all of this is simply a beginning; much more needs to be done in terms of definition and development. What is more important is that SAA is a statement of direction: IBM has promised to continuè to develop products that will make the goals of SAA a reality. As such, SAA is one of the most ambitious and far-reaching events in the computer field today.

SUMMARY

An operating system is a collection of programs and data files that manages the computer. Mainframe computers operate in a multiuser environment and have multiprogramming and multiprocessing capabilities. Most PCs operate in a single-user environment and normally execute one job at a time.

The most common mainframe operating systems are MVS/XA and MVS/ESA, which have three main sections: Virtual Storage Management Facilities (VSMF), Program Development Facilities (PDF), and user facilities.

VSMF's main function is to manage all the internal activity of the computer. PDF includes all the languages and routines to link programs written in some high-level language to the system. User facilities include all the routines and modules that allow someone to communicate with the computer, to schedule activity on the system, and to manage the database systems.

One way to access a mainframe is through TSO's ISPF. This facility is menu driven and is the principal vehicle many programmers use to access an IBM mainframe. Under TSO, a programmer uses job control language (JCL) to indicate the activity he or she wants the system to perform. The user then submits the JCL using either the job scheduler JES2 or JES3. The instructions in JCL include a JOB, EXEC, and DD statements. The JOB statement identifies the name of the job to be performed and contains the accounting information about the submitter of the job. The EXEC statement indicates the name of a program or procedure (called a PROC) that will be accessed. The DD statement identifies the data sets that will be accessed and includes codes and parameters concerning the status of those data sets.

The typical mainframe includes multiple CPUs connected to central storage and a battery of channels. A channel is a microprocessor that is designed to handle all input and output activity of the system. The CPU sends to a channel an instruction concerning some I/O operation. The channel then fetches a channel program from the operating system so it can accomplish the desired task. The channels run simultaneously and independently of the CPU.

In a virtual storage environment, the system divides central storage into 4K blocks of memory, called a page. When the system needs additional memory to hold additional pages, a page fault occurs. When this occurs, the system steals a slice of memory from some other job by swapping the other job to DASD or extended memory.

Each DASD unit has a device controller that is connected to a string controller. Typically, a string controller can have a maximum of ten DASD units attached to it. The string controller in turn is connected to a channel device. The channel device contains multiple channels, each capable of controlling an I/O request from the CPU. Each DASD unit contains a series of platters on which data is stored magnetically by modules found in the data manager section of the operating system. The system stores data on DASD either as a data set or as a member of some library. DASD libraries are called partitioned data sets (PDSs).

When the operations team members prepare a new DASD unit for use, they initialize it. During initialization, the system creates a virtual table of contents (VTOC) on the unit. The VTOC contains a unique logical name for the unit and the names and locations of all the data sets stored on the volume. Whenever the system needs to access a data set, it must first access the VTOC to extract needed parameters concerning the data set's location and its structure. The VTOC is updated whenever a data set is added to or deleted from the volume.

PCs contain a CPU, a bus, primary memory, and secondary memory devices. The speed of a computer system is based on the type of CPU that is installed in the PC. A bus is a set of wires that connects the CPU to the other devices on the system. The CPU uses the bus to send signals to these devices.

The first IBM PCs used Intel's 8088 CPU unit. Later models of PCs contained advanced versions of the original 8088. These include the 80286, 80386, and the 80486 processors. Earlier PCs relied on floppy disks for the permanent storage of data and could access up to 640K of primary memory. All of these early PCs contained at least one 5-1/4 inch floppy drive capable of holding about 360K of data on a diskette. Today's PC contains multiple megabytes of primary memory, a 20M or 30M hard drive, and one or more floppy drives.

The most common operating system for PCs is MS-DOS. A more powerful and sophisticated operating system is OS/2. It gives the PC additional functionality including multitasking and the ability to execute SQL statements. Multitasking is the ability of the computer to run different applications at the same time.

When multiple PCs are connected together using specialized hardware and software, the resultant system forms a LAN. One of the PCs on the LAN is given the responsibility of controlling and managing the entire network. This PC is called a file server and the others are called workstations.

The main memory of a computer is called RAM and is memory users can use and change. Memory that is read by the system and never changed is called ROM. Similar to ROM is PROM, EPROM, and EEPROM.

QUESTIONS

1. What determines the type of operating system that an installation installs on its mainframe?
2. What is the difference between a data set and a PDS? Between a PDS and a library? Between a library and a volume?
3. What is the difference between TSO and ISPF?
4. What is a batch initiator? Why do we have a batch initiator on the system?
5. What is meant by the term virtual storage?
6. How does cache memory improve the performance of the computer system?
7. What is the difference between swapping and paging?
8. What is a page fault?
9. What is the difference between the Job Manager and the Task Manager?
10. What is a page? How do mainframes use pages in manipulating data?
11. Discuss in detail how the system uses pages to access data.
12. Describe how the system uses the VTOC.
13. What type of jobs would you run in batch? What type of jobs would you run in an on-line environment?
14. What are some differences between the PC/XT and the PC/AT?
15. If computer speed was not an issue, why would you buy a PS/2?
16. Could you run programs stored on a DOS 3.0 formatted diskette on a system booted with DOS 2.0? Why or why not?
17. Would DOS 3.0 boot a PS/2? Why or why not?
18. What is the difference between PROM, EPROM, and EEPROM chips?
19. What are some of the advantages of using a hard disk rather than a floppy disk?

20. A user purchased a PC system having two hard disk drives and no floppy drives. What are some of the problems he or she might encounter? Why would this user create this configuration?
21. What are some of the advantages of DOS over OS/2? Of OS/2 over DOS?
22. If EEPROM is so great, why doesn't every computer system use it?
23. What are some of the facts you must consider in making a decision to purchase a PC?
24. Briefly describe the difference between a disk crash, a head crash, and a systems crash.

3

Data Structures and Access Methods

To complete our initial examination of databases, we will look at data structures and the various methods of accessing data. Both of these concepts are the building blocks of databases. Remember, no matter how complicated the database software is, or how many functions it provides, the computer system still must store and access the data within the database. We will see in later chapters, when focusing on specific database types, how these data structures and access methods are used.

PHYSICAL DATA STRUCTURES

Data Types

Data is any information that you can store and use in a computer system. There are several types of data including the following:

- *Integer data*—data containing only an integer (i.e., from the list 0, 1, −1, 2, −2, 3, −3, etc.)
- *Real data*—data containing only a real number (i.e., from the list 0.1, 1.789, −8.93, etc.)
- *Alphabetic data*—data containing only alphabetic characters
- *Alphanumeric data*—data containing alphanumeric characters

We use the notation INTEGER to identify integer data; CHAR to identify alphanumeric data having a fixed length; VARCHAR to identify alphanumeric data having a variable length; and FLOAT (for "floating point") to represent numeric data containing real numbers.

Storage of Data

Data that has an expressed value is said to be a constant. Examples are pi, the number of days in a week, or a flat tax rate. Conversely, data that does not have an expressed value is said to be a variable. Examples are the number of dependents an employee has (which varies from employee to employee), the number of working days in a month (which varies from month to month), or an income tax rate (which varies according to income). The computer stores numeric data in the following ways:

- Binary form
- Coded form (EBCDIC, ASCII)
- Some machine-specific internal format

The number 123, for example, can be stored as any of the following:

- The 8-bit binary field 0111 and 1011
- The 3-byte EBCDIC field F1 F2 F3
- The 2-byte packed field 12 3F

In these examples, we have been dealing with logical representations of data. However, recall that all data is physically stored by computers in binary format (base 2). That means the data is a series of electromagnetic charges that represent a string of ones and zeros. However, people frequently translate the binary representation into its hexadecimal (base 16) equivalent. Hexadecimal numbers are numbers containing the digits 0 through 9 and letters from A through F, with A through F representing the decimal numbers 10 through 15.

Let's look at how we could store the number 123. Consider the EBCDIC representation of the number 123: physically, the number is stored in the computer as:

1111 0001 1111 0010 1111 0011

The hexadecimal representation of this binary representation is:

F1 F2 F3

The reason we use hexadecimal notation is that hexadecimal numbers are much more convenient to work with for any but the smallest numbers. The number 123 is not a very large number, but it is much easier to write, perform arithmetic with, and understand if it is used as a hexadecimal number rather than a binary number. In this text, we will use both binary and hexadecimal numbers interchangeably.

There are certain restrictions on the size of data that the computer can process in the various formats. Table 3.1 lists the largest unsigned integer

TABLE 3.1 *Binary values for a byte, half-word, and fullword*

Bit Size	Integer Equivalent
8	$2^8 - 1$ or 255
16	$2^{16} - 1$ or 65,535
32	$2^{32} - 1$ or 4,294,967,296

that a computer system can store in either an 8-bit, 16-bit, or 32-bit binary field. We will examine size restrictions on other formats later in this chapter.

Integer Data Storage on Microcomputers

Microcomputers usually store integer data in binary format, although they do it in a fashion that would seem unnatural to most of us. For example, the hexadecimal representation of the number 495 is 01 EF. However, a microcomputer would store this number as EF 01.

This is known as least significant byte/most significant byte (LSB/MSB) format or, sometimes, low byte/high byte format. The least significant byte is stored first. The reason for this has to do with the way the CPU works. The computer's CPU is designed to process only machine-language instructions. All the commands you give a computer are first translated into a machine-language instruction before the CPU performs its command. Some of these machine-language instructions are designed to operate on only one byte of data, while others operate on multiple bytes. Obviously, for the first class of instructions, the least significant byte is always dealt with first, because it is the only byte processed. It is simpler to design a CPU if we can assume that the least significant byte always comes first, even for those instructions that process more than one byte.

The size restriction for integer data on a microcomputer is the amount of data that will fit in two bytes (for example, FF FF, which is the number 65,535). This is the case with **unsigned integers.** These are integers whose

TABLE 3.2 *Examples of integers in decimal, two's complement, and physical storage format*

Decimal Format	Two's Complement Format	Physical Storage Format
1	00 01	01 00
−1	FF FF	FF FF
2	00 02	02 00
−2	FF FE	FE FF
3	00 03	03 00
−3	FF FD	FD FF
10	00 0A	0A 00
−10	FF F6	F6 FF
16	00 10	10 00
−16	FF F0	F0 FF
12345	30 39	39 30
−12345	CF C7	C7 CF
32767	7F FF	FF 7F
−32768	80 00	00 80

mathematical sign is always assumed to be positive. Signed integers are stored in binary format using the **two's complement form.** The main effect of the two's complement form is to cause all bits from the beginning of the field to the first significant digit of the field to be set to 1 if the field is negative; otherwise, the bits are 0. As a side effect, the significant digits also are changed, but this is not important to your understanding at this point. For now, you need only understand that if the most significant bit (the leftmost bit) is set to 1, then the CPU will uncomplement the integer and treat it as a negative value. Table 3.2 shows examples of some numbers in decimal format, two's complement format, and physical storage format. The most significant bit is always 0 for positive numbers and always 1 for negative numbers.

If the leftmost bit in an unsigned two-byte number is 1, the number must be at least as large as 2^{16}, or 32768. This number, and all higher numbers, will have this bit set to 1; all lower numbers will have this bit set to 0. Because numbers with the leftmost bit set to 1 are considered to be negative, the range of signed integers that we can express is -2^{16} through $2^{16} - 1$, or -32768 through 32767.

Packed and Unpacked Data Storage on Mainframes

Most data you enter into the computer system is in display format meaning it is unpacked. You enter a number into a system using some computer program and that program stores the number in its coded form (EBCDIC on IBM mainframes, ASCII on microcomputers and non-IBM mainframes) in a variable. Figure 3.1 illustrates how a mainframe stores numeric data in its unpacked and packed form. All data must be packed before you use it in an arithmetic operation on a mainframe. When you compile a program, the compiler places packing and unpacking instructions in the load module before and after each use of the numbers in an arithmetic operation.

When you load data to tape or disk, the data has been edited and converted to packed format. The unpacked data in Figure 3.1 requires five bytes of storage, while the packed data only requires three bytes of storage. Here, not only do you prepare the data for arithmetic operations when you pack it, you also save substantial memory space. Fortunately, the compilers and other software programs generate code that performs these packing operations for us. However, COBOL programmers must follow certain rules and include certain procedures in their code to guarantee that all data sent to the arithmetic unit is in packed format.

What about size restrictions for packed data? The largest integer value you can manipulate on a computer system using data in packed form is dependent on the way a particular computer system manipulates data. On IBM mainframes, the machine language instruction the CPU uses to add two numbers together is given by the six byte code:

FALM RAAA RBBB

unpacked form

packed form

FIGURE 3.1
The number 12345 in packed and unpacked form.

FA tells the CPU to add two numbers where the first number is at relative address RAAA, the second number is at relative address RBBB, and the lengths of these two numbers in hexadecimal is L and M, respectively. You add 1 to the two one-byte hexadecimal numbers L and M to get the length of each number. This translates to each number occupying from 1 to 16 bytes. In packed format, the largest 16-byte number would be in the format:

99 99 99 99 99 99 99 99 99 99 99 99 99 99 99 9F

which would be:

9,999,999,999,999,999,999,999,999,999

in decimal.

This, however, does not guarantee that all software products available on the mainframe will process this large a number.

Alphanumeric Data

To determine the size restrictions for alphanumeric data on IBM mainframes, you have to look at the machine language instruction set. Some machine instructions exist that use only a single byte to indicate the length of alphanumeric data. The largest hexadecimal number you can store in one byte is FF or 255. Because these instructions add one to the length of the field they operate on, you can potentially access a 256-byte field of alphanumeric data. In certain circumstances, however, the computer system limits you to a smaller size than this absolute maximum. In fact, most database packages limit you to a maximum of 254 bytes for your alphanumeric fields. In these packages, the first byte of a field is a null-field indicator (contains 00 if it is a null field and FF if it is not) and the second byte contains the field's length (00 to FD).

On an IBM microcomputer, one instruction to move alphanumeric data is a one-byte instruction: A5. This instruction uses registers to indicate the source and destination of the data to be moved. However, unlike the mainframe instruction that allows the programmer to specify the registers that address the data, the microcomputer instruction uses a set pair of registers. Also, unlike the mainframe instruction that allows the programmer to specify the length of the data to be moved (in a pair of registers), the microcomputer instruction is limited to a single maximum length.

The largest alphanumeric field that a microcomputer CPU can move at any one time is two bytes. Surely, this would severely limit the database capabilities of a microcomputer; after all, two-byte fields are not very useful. However, this is a restriction on the physical amount of data that the CPU can manipulate at one time. The restrictions on the logical amount of data that computer programs can manipulate are very different. Most microcomputer database programs allow you to manipulate considerably more than two bytes of data at a time. This is accomplished by the computer moving data repetitively, two bytes at a time, until it moves the entire field of data.

ADVANCED TOPIC
More on Alphanumeric Data

The machine language instruction the CPU uses to move a piece of data from one relative storage address to another is given by OERS. This is move character long (MVCL) in the IBM 370 assembler set. OE instructs the computer to move the data at the relative address contained in the register S to the relative address contained in the register R. Registers are special storage locations within the CPU—they are used for certain addressing and mathematical operations. Because they are within the CPU, they can be accessed more quickly than other forms of storage. In this example, registers R and S are used to address the storage locations containing the data; two other registers that are not explicitly coded are used to specify the lengths of the data to be moved. The next register after S (S+1) is used to specify the length of the data to be moved. The next register after R (R+1) is used to specify the length of the storage to receive the data. Registers are 32 bits in length. Therefore, the largest number that can be stored in a register is

FF FF FF FF   *or*   4,294,967,295.

However, this instruction uses the last three bytes, or 24 bits, of the registers R+1 and S+1 to specify the length of the data to be moved.

To the user, it appears that the computer moves the entire field at once, even though the CPU must execute the alphanumeric move instruction several times. We will explore this concept of logical data restrictions versus physical data restrictions further when we consider real data in the next section in this chapter.

In all of the previous cases, we had to look at how the CPU manipulates data. To do this, we had to look at the predefined machine-language instruction set for a particular CPU to get a clue on how data is used inside the machine. Remember, the parameters of that computer's machine-language instruction set restrict what action the software can perform and how the system, in general, manipulates data. The machine-language instruction set, called its assembler language instruction set, is created by the vendor who manufactures the CPU.

Real Data

Most computer manufacturers indicate in their machine's specification sheets the various restrictions on the data that machine can handle. These specifications usually indicate the maximum and minimum values for integer and real data. You have to use some common sense in reading these specifications. If a manufacturer indicates its machine can handle real numbers of the magnitude 10^{123}, this information has little meaning in the real world. Remember, the largest usable real number is the distance from one end of the universe

3.14
10.578
20000.01

FIGURE 3.2

A set of floating-point numbers. The decimal point is in a different position in each number.

```
      3.14
     10.578
+20000.01
 20013.728
```

FIGURE 3.3

Floating-point numbers with decimal points aligned. The same set as in Figure 3.2 but you must know the position of the decimal point to align.

Number	Decimal places
314	2
10578	3
2000001	2

FIGURE 3.4

Fixed-point format. The numbers above are the same floating-point numbers as in Figure 3.2. Here, the number of decimal places must be stored separately.

to the other end, which astrophysicists tell us is only 10^{81} mm. Remember also that physical limits and logical limits might be different. We will discuss physical methods of manipulating real data soon. At the beginning of this chapter, we introduced a term, FLOAT, which can be used to describe data that contains real numbers, and we noted that this term stands for **floating point.** This simply means that the decimal point can "float" from place to place between different numbers (Figure 3.2).

For the numbers in Figure 3.2, the decimal point is in a different place in each number. When you add such numbers manually, you align the decimal points as shown in Figure 3.3.

To align the decimal points, you have to know the position of the decimal point in each number. Of course, you know where the decimal point is, because you can see it. Obviously, on computer systems you must use other means to locate the decimal point. There are two methods of doing this, fixed-point format and floating-point format.

Fixed-point Format   **Fixed-point format** is based on the concept of multiplying each number by an appropriate power of 10 so that the decimal point is always in a fixed location.

In Figure 3.4 each number has the decimal point in a fixed location (to the right of the last significant digit). In this case you store the actual position of the decimal point separately from the number itself. Using this technique you can store both the number and the decimal places field in integer format. Also, using this format the maximum size of a number would be the same as in integer format.

To add the numbers in Figure 3.4 you must multiply each number by an appropriate power of ten to align the decimal points properly. Because two of the numbers have two decimal places (314 and 2000001) and one has three (10578), you must multiply the numbers with the smaller number of decimal places (those with two) by ten raised to the power of the difference between the smaller number of decimal places and the larger number of decimal places, that is, by $10^{(3-2)}$, or 10^1, or 10. Then add the numbers as integers. You store the number by storing it as an integer along with the largest number of decimal places of any of the numbers you added (here, three). See Figure 3.5.

The CPU does not automatically do any of this fixed-point arithmetic for you—the software has to do it. For this reason, there are different ways of handling fixed-point data. Figure 3.5 is mainly for illustration purposes. Because software controls the handling of fixed-point addition, microcomputer and mainframe implementations of fixed-point format could be the same. Both machines are capable of implementing it in the fashion noted above. Of course, microcomputer and mainframe implementations also might be different. By implementing a process in software modules rather than in hardware mechanics you gain considerable flexibility.

Floating-point Format   In contrast, **floating-point format** on mainframes usually is different from that on microcomputers because it is implemented by

```
      3140
     10578
  +20000010
   20013728
Decimal places: 3
```

FIGURE 3.5
An example of fixed-point addition. The numbers are multiplied by an appropriate power of ten to align the decimal points.

hardware on both types of machines. On mainframes, the CPU has instructions to manipulate floating-point data. On microcomputers, floating-point data is implemented by an optional microchip known as an 8087 math coprocessor. It is possible that 80286 machines will use the 80287 math coprocessor, instead. Even on microcomputers without an 8087, if floating-point numbers are implemented by software, the software tends to emulate the methods used by hardware.

Floating-point numbers are used in scientific, not business, applications because these numbers allow you to specify extremely large numbers with considerable precision. They allow you to have a large number of significant digits in your problem and answers. Although this might be necessary for measuring the universe, you rarely need these numbers in measuring business performance. Because fixed-point data is usually sufficient for business, we will not deal with floating-point numbers any further.

ARRAYS

When data is arranged into cells or groups it is called an **array** or **subscripted data** (Figure 3.6). Each cell in the array is an element of that array and you use an index to identify individual elements. In Figure 3.6 the ten cells are identified using the index numbers 1 through 10 to represent cell 1 through cell 10. In this example, an integer value is in each of the cells of the array. Cell(5) has value 20, and cell(10) has value 54. You assign values to each cell in the array using the = symbol. For Figure 3.6 you load each cell's value using the notation:

cell(1)	= 21	or	$cell_1$ = 21
cell(2)	= 23	or	$cell_2$ = 23
cell(3)	= 22	or	$cell_3$ = 22
cell(4)	= 43	or	$cell_4$ = 43
cell(5)	= 20	or	$cell_5$ = 20
cell(6)	= 56	or	$cell_6$ = 56
cell(7)	= 43	or	$cell_7$ = 43
cell(8)	= 05	or	$cell_8$ = 05
cell(9)	= 77	or	$cell_9$ = 77
cell(10)	= 54	or	$cell_{10}$ = 54

You can initialize the array to zero using the algorithm

```
FOR A = 1 TO 10
    CELL (A) = 0
NEXT A
```

Here you increment A from 1 to 10 to create the cell's indexing.

When you work with arrays or subscripted variables you assign a meaningful name to the cells (rather than just calling it CELL). The array's name

FIGURE 3.6 *A ten-cell array. An index is used to identify each cell of the array.*

can be any variable name valid in the computer language you use to create the array.

Obviously, you are not restricted to linear arrays (single-indexed arrays) like the ones in Figure 3.6. You can create multiple indexes for arrays depending on your need for developing the array. For example, suppose you want to create an array for the data in Table 3.3. If the data represents the daily profits for a small business, you can use the variable name PROFIT for the array and index it using two indexes: one for day (DAY) and one for week (WEEK). Table 3.4 illustrates this array's cell structure.

To initialize the array to zero, use this algorithm:

```
FOR WEEK = 1 TO 4
    FOR DAY = 1 TO 5
        PROFIT(DAY,WEEK) = 0
    NEXT DAY
NEXT WEEK
```

In this case when you use the algorithm, WEEK initially is set to 1 and the second loop:

```
FOR DAY = 1 TO 5
    PROFIT(DAY,1) = 0
NEXT DAY
```

increments the index DAY from 1 to 5.

You can assign other values to the array using techniques dependent on the computer language you are using. Figure 3.7 illustrates different techniques to load the values in Table 3.3 into the array structure in Table 3.4.

You are not restricted to one-dimensional or two-dimensional arrays when you store data. Suppose, for example, a chemical dye house with 23 dyeing machines works three shifts a day, seven days a week, for 52 weeks a year.

TABLE 3.3 *A two-dimensional array*

	Monday	Tuesday	Wednesday	Thursday	Friday
WEEK 1	123.00	345.00	340.00	214.00	982.00
WEEK 2	388.00	944.00	542.00	99.00	190.00
WEEK 3	444.00	565.00	767.00	400.00	300.00
WEEK 4	300.00	300.00	593.00	344.00	554.00

TABLE 3.4 *Array structure for two-dimensional array for daily profits from a small business*

	Monday	Tuesday	Wednesday	Thursday	Friday
WEEK 1	PROFIT(1,1)	PROFIT(2,1)	PROFIT(3,1)	PROFIT(4,1)	PROFIT(5,1)
WEEK 2	PROFIT(1,2)	PROFIT(2,2)	PROFIT(3,2)	PROFIT(4,2)	PROFIT(5,2)
WEEK 3	PROFIT(1,3)	PROFIT(2,3)	PROFIT(3,3)	PROFIT(4,3)	PROFIT(5,3)
WEEK 4	PROFIT(1,4)	PROFIT(2,4)	PROFIT(3,4)	PROFIT(4,4)	PROFIT(5,4)

In FORTRAN
```
REAL PROFIT(5,4)
DATA PROFIT/123.00, 345.00, 340.00, 214.00, 982.00,
            388.00, 944.00, 542.00, 99.00,  190.00,
            444.00, 565.00, 767.00, 400.00, 300.00,
            300.00, 300.00, 593.00, 344.00, 554.00/
```

In BASIC
```
100 DIM PROFIT(5,4)
110 FOR A = 1 TO 4
120   FOR B = 1 TO 5
130     READ PROFIT(A,B)
140   NEXT B
150 NEXT A
900 DATA   123.00, 345.00, 340.00, 214.00, 982.00
910 DATA   388.00, 944.00, 542.00,  99.00, 190.00
920 DATA   444.00, 565.00, 767.00, 400.00, 300.00
930 DATA   300.00, 300.00, 593.00, 344.00, 554.00
```

In COBOL
```
01  ARRAY-DATA.
    03 FILLER    PIC 9(3)V99   COMP-3   VALUE 123.00.
    03 FILLER    PIC 9(3)V99   COMP-3   VALUE 345.00.
    03 FILLER    PIC 9(3)V99   COMP-3   VALUE 340.00.
    03 FILLER    PIC 9(3)V99   COMP-3   VALUE 214.00.
    03 FILLER    PIC 9(3)V99   COMP-3   VALUE 982.00.
    03 FILLER    PIC 9(3)V99   COMP-3   VALUE 388.00.
    03 FILLER    PIC 9(3)V99   COMP-3   VALUE 944.00.
    03 FILLER    PIC 9(3)V99   COMP-3   VALUE 542.00.
    03 FILLER    PIC 9(3)V99   COMP-3   VALUE  99.00.
    03 FILLER    PIC 9(3)V99   COMP-3   VALUE 190.00.
    03 FILLER    PIC 9(3)V99   COMP-3   VALUE 444.00.
    03 FILLER    PIC 9(3)V99   COMP-3   VALUE 565.00.
    03 FILLER    PIC 9(3)V99   COMP-3   VALUE 767.00.
    03 FILLER    PIC 9(3)V99   COMP-3   VALUE 400.00.
    03 FILLER    PIC 9(3)V99   COMP-3   VALUE 300.00.
    03 FILLER    PIC 9(3)V99   COMP-3   VALUE 300.00.
    03 FILLER    PIC 9(3)V99   COMP-3   VALUE 300.00.
    03 FILLER    PIC 9(3)V99   COMP-3   VALUE 593.00.
    03 FILLER    PIC 9(3)V99   COMP-3   VALUE 344.00.
    03 FILLER    PIC 9(3)V99   COMP-3   VALUE 554.00.
01  FILLER REDEFINES ARRAY-DATA.
    03 FILLER OCCURS 4 TIMES.
        05 PROFIT OCCURS 5 TIMES
                 PIC 9(3)V99   COMP-3.
```

FIGURE 3.7 *Examples of initializing arrays in BASIC, FORTRAN, and COBOL.*

A 4-dimensional array could be used to represent the amount of material dyed in each machine on each shift throughout the year. Here, the dye house would use the array

STUFF(MACHINE,SHIFT,DAY,WEEK)

where the values for the indices are

MACHINE   index has range 1 to 23
SHIFT   index has range 1 to 3
DAY   index has range 1 to 7
WEEK   index has range 1 to 52

You are limited to the number of indexes you can use in any one array. Many computer software programs restrict the maximum number of indices in any one array to 7. Also, the size of the array has certain restrictions as to the number of cells it can contain. The chemical dye house's subscripted variable has a total of 25,116 (23 × 3 × 7 × 52) cells in the array. Because each cell occupies one or more memory locations in central storage, large arrays might exceed central storage's capacity to handle them.

FIXED-LENGTH AND VARIABLE-LENGTH RECORDS

Records are a heterogeneous mixture of different fields. The fields within a record could contain alphanumeric data, numeric data, and arrays. As far as the computer is concerned, the record is one contiguous stream of characters between two special control characters representing the beginning and the end of the record. It is up to the programmer or analyst to design and interpret the characters within a record.

Records can have a fixed length or a variable length. Fixed-length records have a predefined length for each field within them and a predefined number of fields in each record; the sum of these field lengths is the length of the record.

Variable-length Fields

When the fields within a record do not have a predefined length, the field is said to be a variable-length field, or a VARCHAR field. Let's look at how you could store a person's first name in memory. If the FIRSTNAME field has a fixed length of 20 characters, the name TONY could be stored in memory as

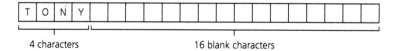

In this example, you are wasting 16 storage locations. At first this might not appear to be significant. However, if your file or database is to hold 10 million names, then you are in essence wasting 16 × 10,000,000 locations, or about 8% of a DASD volume.

An alternate way to store data in the FIRSTNAME field is to let FIRSTNAME be a variable size field. Many database software packages have a limit of 254 bytes for the size of your alphanumeric fields. Therefore, the first two characters of FIRSTNAME will be the null-indicator field and the length of the field, both in hexadecimal, respectively. The remaining characters in the field will contain the data. In VARCHAR fields all blanks to the right of the data will be deleted. To store TONY as a VARCHAR field, the name is loaded into the field as

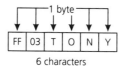

Keep in mind that the computer's hardware restricts you to storing a maximum of 256 alphanumeric characters in any one field. Therefore, because you will consume one character to identify a null field and one character to indicate the field's length, you must restrict the size of data you place in variable-length fields to 254 characters. The first character in any field will be hexadecimal 00 or FF to indicate nulls or not nulls. The second character in any field will be hexadecimal 00 to FD and indicates the field's length in hexadecimal (1 to 254 characters). Our program, therefore, might have to contain the following:

1. A routine to translate hexadecimal numbers into decimal numbers and vice versa
2. A routine to compute the length of the alphanumeric data that is to be stored in the field
3. A routine to compress the data by eliminating all blanks to the right of the right-most character in the field
4. A routine to extract the length of the field when you use the record containing the field
5. A routine to extract the data using its length
6. A routine to uncompress the data so it fits into other fields in the program

Fortunately, many software packages already contain the algorithms to handle variable-length fields. All you have to do is define the variable as VARCHAR and the system will handle its compression and decompression and store it efficiently on DASD.

```
FD   STUDENT–CLASS–FILE
     LABEL RECORDS ARE STANDARD.
     RECORD CONTAINS 34 TO 78 CHARACTERS.
01   STUDENT–RECORD.
     05  TYPE–OF–RECORD–1          PIC X.
          88 STUDENT               VALUE 'S'.
          88 CLASS                 VALUE 'C'.
     05  STUDENT–ID–NUMBER         PIC X(9).
     05  STUDENT–LASTNAME          PIC X(20).
     05  STUDENT–FIRSTNAME         PIC X(20).
     05  STUDENT–MI                PIC X.
     05  STUDENT–STREET            PIC X(20).
     05  STUDENT–STATE             PIC XX.
     05  STUDENT–ZIP               PIC X(5).


01   CLASS–RECORD.
     05  TYPE–OF–RECORD–2          PIC X.
     05  CLASS–ID                  PIC X(7).
     05  CLASS–GRADE               PIC X.
     05  CLASS–TEXT                PIC X(25).
```

FIGURE 3.8   *COBOL description of variable-size record.*

Variable-length Records

A variable-length record occurs when a file contains one or more records having a different length than other records in the same file. This generally occurs when you need to process two types of records in the same file. One type of record has the function of being a parent record and the other type record has the function of being the child record. Variable-length records are restricted to classical file structures and are independent of any database software technique.

```
FD   STUDENT–CLASS–FILE
     LABEL RECORDS ARE STANDARD.
     RECORD CONTAINS 79 TO 419 CHARACTERS.
01   STUDENT–RECORD.
     05  CLASS–VARIABLE–INDICATOR

                                   PIC S9(4)      COMP.
     05  STUDENT–DATA.
          10  STUDENT–ID–NUMBER    PIC X(9).
          10  STUDENT–LASTNAME     PIC X(20).
          10  STUDENT–FIRSTNAME    PIC X(20).
          10  STUDENT–MI           PIC X.
          10  STUDENT–STREET       PIC X(20).
          10  STUDENT–STATE        PIC XX.
          10  STUDENT–ZIP          PIC X(5).
     05  CLASS–DATA OCCURS  10
                    DEPENDING ON CLASS–VARIABLE–INDICATOR.
          10  TYPE–OF–RECORD–2     PIC X.
          10  CLASS–ID             PIC X(7).
          10  CLASS–GRADE          PIC X.
          10  CLASS–TEXT           PIC X(25).
```

FIGURE 3.9   *Another way of handling variable-size records.*

```
READ STUDENT–RECORD
    AT END ...
PERFORM PROCESS–STUDENT–DATA.
PERFORM PROCESS–CLASS–DATA
        CLASS–VARIABLE–INDICATOR TIMES.
```

FIGURE 3.10   *Processing a variable record. These statements process the record shown in Figure 3.9. You must loop in order to process the class data.*

Graciously, COBOL has a technique to handle variable-length records. Let's look at a common file found at most colleges and universities. Each student takes one or more classes each semester. The file, therefore, will have some records containing a student's personal data and records containing data about the many classes he or she attends. You use two records, each of different lengths. Figure 3.8 contains the DATA DIVISION description for a variable-length record.

You read STUDENT-CLASS-FILE and check TYPE-OF-RECORD-1 and TYPE-OF-RECORD-2 to determine which type record was loaded by the system. Then the record is processed using normal COBOL logic. The system loads any record it finds between two end-of-record (EOR) markers.

COBOL also allows you a second method of handling variable-length records. Figure 3.9 shows the same data as in Figure 3.8, but in a different record format.

All of the data about a student, including his or her classes, is in one record. CLASS-DATA can be repeated from 0 to 10 times, depending on the value in CLASS-VARIABLE-INDICATOR. You read such a record in the normal fashion. To process such a record, use normal COBOL logic to handle the part of the record defined by STUDENT-DATA (known as the constant portion of the record); however, to handle the data defined by CLASS-DATA (known as the variable portion of the record), you must loop through the code the number of times specified by CLASS-VARIABLE-INDICATOR (known as the variable indicator of the record). Figure 3.10 shows one method of doing this.

This method of storing variable-length data has some disadvantages. First, it generally uses more storage and more CPU time than the "record-type" method. Second, it requires you to set a maximum on the number of times the variable portion can occur in a record, for example, 10. The main advantage of variable-length data is that all of the data for one student including his or her classes, for example, is held in one record. In some cases, this can make processing of the data easier.

RECORD INCOMPATIBILITY

Each record in a file has hidden codes that tell the accessing method the location of the EOR marker (Figure 3.11). This marker is apparent when you create the following:

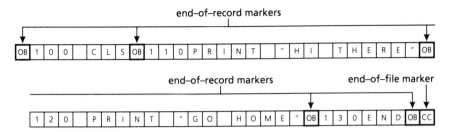

FIGURE 3.11 *Part of a record showing the EOR and EOF markers. OB is the one-byte hexadecimal code for the EOR marker and CC is the one-byte hexadecimal code for the EOF marker.*

- PC files using the EDLIN or COPY CON: commands
- Text files using a mainframe text editor
- Program code where one line of code represents one record

In each of these cases, you write one line of data and press the return key to load that line into the file. After you press the return key, the system places a one-byte hexadecimal code at the end of that line for that record's (EOR) marker. Later, when you print or display the file containing your text or program, the output program locates each EOR marker and displays the data between each EOR on one line of screen or one line of paper.

The output program (TYPE or PRINT for PCs or ISPFs, utility menu options for mainframe text files) must have these codes in the file so that the software can properly perform its function or task. To see what happens when these hex codes are missing, you can TYPE one of the COM files that are on a PCs DOS disk. On a PC enter the command:

a)TYPE FORMAT.COM

The screen presents an unusual display. Funny symbols and beeps produce a glamorous display resembling fireworks at a holiday celebration. The TYPE program is trying to locate ASCII text and EOR markers, but the load module contains instructions in a different format. The machine version of the FORMAT.COM program is a load module (an executable file) and contains commands and codes that only the JOB MANAGER can read and interpret. The equivalent of EOR and EOF markers in load modules are different from their counterparts in other system programs.

Because each software package creates hex codes for EOR, EOF, and other functions or their equivalence, software from one vendor might be incompatible with software from another vendor. That means records and files created by one software package might not contain the same hex codes for EOR and EOF that another software package reads and uses. Therefore, if you want to use records or files created by one vendor's software on another vendor's software package, you will need to use a utility program to translate from one format to another. This problem will become more apparent later when you try to convert classical files to database files or try to transfer PC files to the mainframe or vice versa. Each of these tasks requires the use of a utility program to massage the data to make it readable by the appropriate software product.

Disk Labels

Mainframe disks and the data sets they contain have various configurations of information, known as labels, associated with them. Disks have what are known as volume labels, which contain information about the volume serial number (which is used in JCL to refer to the volume), the volume's security restrictions (which determines who can access the volume), and pointers to the volume's VTOC.

Data sets can have two types of label: The first is the Data Set Control Block (DSCB), which we will discuss shortly; the second is the user label, which is optional. If there is a user label, the systems programming team writes programs to interface the user label to the operating system. Recall, the systems team's main responsibility is to maintain the operating system and its component parts. The content of the user labels also is largely determined by the systems team.

The format of user labels is shown in Figure 3.12. User labels consist of 80 bytes of data and contain the following data:

- The first three bytes contain a label identifier (UHL, UTL, etc.)
- The next byte consists of a label number, which is incremented for each label (1, 2, ..., 8)
- The remaining 76 bytes of data can be whatever the systems programming team has specified

User labels can fall into one of two groups, user-header labels and user-trailer labels. Header labels precede the data set, and trailer labels follow it;

Label identifier	Label number	User–specified data
UHL	1	XXXXXXXXXXXX
UHL	2	XXXXXXXXXXXX
•	•	•
•	•	•
•	•	•
UHL	8	XXXXXXXXXXXX
UTL	1	XXXXXXXXXXXX
UTL	2	XXXXXXXXXXXX
•	•	•
•	•	•
•	•	•
UTL	8	XXXXXXXXXXXX

FIGURE 3.12   *User data set labels. There can be up to eight user-header labels and user-trailer labels.*

there can be up to eight of each. The operating system will write these labels automatically when it creates the data set.

FILE STRUCTURES

Linked Lists

An array forms a listing of data where each cell has a corresponding index used to access elements of that array. Some arrays include both an index and a pointer. The index refers to the cell's physical location and the pointer identifies the logical relationship between the cells. Let's look at a listing of six names and place them logically in alphabetical order. We will physically store the array in the following sequence:

Index	Name
1	Mary
2	Sue
3	Steve
4	Bob
5	Tony
6	Karen

The array has six cells: NAME(1), NAME(2), NAME(3), NAME(4), NAME(5), and NAME(6) and contains names in unsorted order. We will use pointer values in a second array (called pointer), which indicates the logical order of the alphabetical listing. The name and pointer arrays will contain the following data:

Index	Name	Pointer
1	Mary	3
2	Sue	5
3	Steve	2
4	Bob	6
5	Tony	NULL
6	Karen	1
7	empty	•••

START	4
Next available cell is 7	

To find the list of names in sorted order, begin with a START value. In this case the start value is 4 because Bob is in the 4th cell and is logically the first name in the alphabetized list. Search the list using the pointer value to find the next name in the list. The technique to access the list becomes:

1. Use the value in START to access the list (4). The first name, therefore, is Bob because Bob is in cell 4. Bob's pointer contains the number 6. We now access the 6th cell (NAME(6)) to get the next name in the sequence.

2. NAME(6) is the next name in the sorted list, in this case Karen. Karen's pointer contains the number 1.

3. NAME(1) is the next name in the sorted list. It contains the name Mary and pointer value 3.

4. NAME(3) contains the name Steve and the pointer value 2.

5. NAME(2) contains the name Sue and the pointer value 5.

6. NAME(5) contains the name Tony and has a null character as its pointer value. This is the end of the list.

You have not physically rearranged the order of the NAME array. Instead you simply use the array's pointer value to access the next cell in the array. The use of a list and a series of pointers is called a **linked list.** Linked lists are used frequently in databases to arrange data in some logical order without physically rearranging the data in the list.

To process a linked list you must have three pieces of data before you can proceed with your search through the list. First, you must have a beginning value or START value. This value logically points to the beginning of the list. Second, you must have a null value in the pointer of the cell that will be the last logical cell. Whenever you access this null value, you have found the end of the linked list. This value is called the ENDING value. Third, you must have the index value of the next available empty cell so you can add more cells to the list. In the previous example, this value would be 7 because the 7th cell is the next physical location where you can store data.

Suppose you wanted to add another name to the linked list. There are three possible cases you must consider before you can add any name to the list.

Case 1. The added name will become the first logical name in the list. That is, by adding the name, you create a new START value.

Case 2. The added name will become the last logical name in the list. That is, by adding the name you create a new ENDING value.

Case 3. The added name will fall somewhere between the first logical name (START) and the last logical name (ENDING). In this case you must create a pointer value for this name and you must adjust a pointer of another name so that the other name points to the added name.

Let's look at each of these cases in detail. For Case 1, let's add the name Andrew to the list. Now the list looks like this (see next page).

Index	Name	Pointer
1	Mary	3
2	Sue	5
3	Steve	2
4	Bob	6
5	Tony	NULL
6	Karen	1
7	Andrew	
8	empty	•••

START | 4
Next available cell is 8

Because Andrew is the new beginning of the list, his pointer takes on the value of START (4) and START becomes the index value of Andrew's cell (7). The list now becomes:

Index	Name	Pointer
1	Mary	3
2	Sue	5
3	Steve	2
4	Bob	6
5	Tony	NULL
6	Karen	1
7	Andrew	4
8	empty	•••

START | 7
Next available cell is 8

For Case 2, let's add the name Veronica. Here you have a new last cell in the list. Now place Veronica's index number (8) into Tony's pointer and set Veronica's pointer to null. The list becomes:

Index	Name	Pointer
1	Mary	3
2	Sue	5
3	Steve	2
4	Bob	6
5	Tony	8
6	Karen	1
7	Andrew	4
8	Veronica	NULL
9	empty	•••

START | 7

Next available cell is 9

For Case 3, add the name Nancy. Place the name in the next available cell. Not only do you increment the cell counter to 10, but you also must search through the list and logically place the name in alphabetical order within the list. In particular, you search through the names Andrew, Bob, Karen, Mary, and Steve. After you access the cell containing the name Steve, you know the new name logically follows Mary in the list. Now you move the value in Mary's pointer (3) to Nancy's pointer and reset Mary's pointer to Nancy's index location (9). The list becomes:

Index	Name	Pointer
1	Mary	9
2	Sue	5
3	Steve	2
4	Bob	6
5	Tony	8
6	Karen	1
7	Andrew	4
8	Veronica	NULL
9	Nancy	3
10	empty	•••

START | 7

Next available cell is 10

You can continue adding names to the list by placing a name in the next available empty cell. Then search the list to identify the new name's logical location within the list.

Instead of placing null values in the last logical cell's pointer, you could use as its pointer the value that identifies the beginning of the list. Now you create a list that forms a **ring** or **circular list.** In a ring, you can start anywhere in the list and sequentially access all its records stopping only when you return to the place where you started. For example, the linked list in the last example becomes a ring when you set Veronica's pointer to the START value. The ring then looks like:

Index	Name	Pointer
1	Mary	9
2	Sue	5
3	Steve	2
4	Bob	6
5	Tony	8
6	Karen	1
7	Andrew	4
8	Veronica	7
9	Nancy	3
10	empty	•••

Next available cell is 10

Now it doesn't matter where you start; you can search through the list and access each and every record in it, stopping only when you arrive back at where you started.

One major problem with this linked list is that it is unidirectional—you can only go in the forward direction. Suppose you needed to access the records in a backward direction. Surely not every list demands that it read only in ascending alphabetical order. Recreating the list in reverse order would certainly take valuable time. Because you want the capabilities of reading the list in a backward direction, all you need is backward pointers. The linked list with both forward and backward pointers looks like this:

Index	Name	Forward pointer	Backward pointer
1	Mary	9	6
2	Sue	5	3
3	Steve	2	9
4	Bob	6	7
5	Tony	8	2
6	Karen	1	4
7	Andrew	4	8
8	Veronica	7	5
9	Nancy	3	1
10	empty		

Next available cell is 10

A linked list that can be followed only in one direction is known as a **single-threaded** linked list; a linked list that can be followed in both directions is known as a **double-threaded** linked list. Following a linked list is known as **traversing** it.

Obviously, you will spend considerable time establishing the backward and forward pointers in a double-threaded linked list. In addition, the logic to add or delete records in the list becomes more complex. However, linked lists provide an excellent technique to establish the relationship between the many members in an owner-member system or between the children in a parent-children system. In fact, many database systems use pointers to identify and locate records within the database.

Trees

You use trees to represent a hierarchical relationship between objects. Each cell in the tree is called a **node** and the lines connecting the nodes are known as the tree's **branches** (Figure 3.13). Most of us are already familiar with tree structures because many of us construct a family tree to depict our ancestral lineage. In a tree structure, one object (a parent node) usually precedes a group of other objects (children nodes). In a family tree, the parents are placed above their children. The children in turn become parents and have children. Each level in the tree represents a generation within the family. We continue the tree structure until we have satisfied some criteria for establishing the tree, for example, until we have determined who Aunt Bessie's great-great grandchildren are.

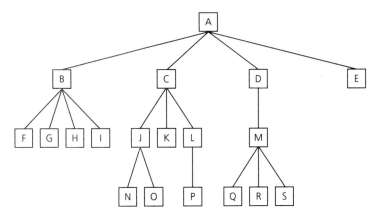

FIGURE 3.13   *Example of a tree structure.*

A typical family tree is given in Figure 3.14. Grandma Bessie has four children (Mary, Sue, William, and Robert). Mary has two children (Jim and Nancy), Sue has one (Sally), William has two (Karen and Darlene), and Robert has one (Mike).

Each person in Figure 3.14 is a node of the tree and we can represent its structure symbolically as:

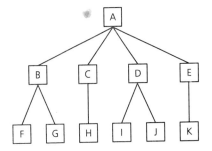

The single node at the top of a tree is called the **root** of the tree (A). A tree has only one root node and that root node has no parent. The bottom-most nodes are the **leaves** of the tree (F, G, H, I, J, and K). The leaves of a tree are those nodes that have no children. In fact, not all the leaves in a tree structure need to be at the bottom-most layer of the structure. The tree structure in Figure 3.15 has leaves at various layers within the structure (E, F, G, and H at layer 3, and I and J at layer 4).

The root node branches out to other nodes creating a parent-child relationship within the tree. The parent is an **ancestor** of its children and the children are **descendants** of the parent. You can form some unusual trees. A tree with no nodes is called an **empty tree** and a tree with one node is still a tree.

Each parent forms a layer within the tree. Also, the leaves at the bottom

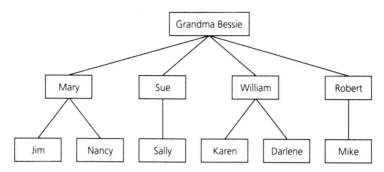

FIGURE 3.14   *A family tree.*

of the tree, even though they are not parents, are considered a layer within the tree. The height of a tree is the maximum number of layers within the tree. For example, the heights of the trees in Figures 3.14 and 3.15 are 3 and 4, respectively.

Binary Trees A **binary tree** is a special type of tree where each parent can have a maximum of only two children, a left child and a right child. In particular, each parent in a binary tree can have no children, one child, or two children. By convention, and obviously by reference to its name, the left and right child are placed below and to the left or right, respectively, of the parent. Figure 3.16 shows a binary tree composed of records with keys R, D, E, S, X, U, A, T, and C. The records were added to the tree in that order.

The following facts about Figure 3.16 illustrate some of these concepts:

- Node R is the root node
- A node that is larger than its parent is always the right child of the parent, while a node that is smaller than its parent is always the left child

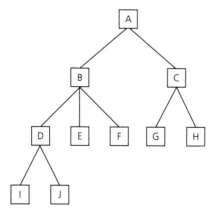

FIGURE 3.15   *Tree structure showing its root and leaves.*

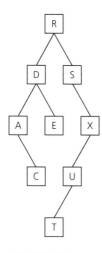

- Descendants on the left side of their ancestor are always smaller than the ancestor, while descendants on the right side of their ancestor are always larger
- Nodes E, C, and T are leaf nodes
- Nodes D and S are the left and right child of the parent node R, respectively
- Nodes A and E are the left and right child of the parent node D, respectively
- The height of the tree is 5

You can store trees on the computer system as lists. The binary tree in Figure 3.16 could have the list structure:

Cell	Key	Pointer 1	Pointer 2
1	R	2	4
2	D	7	3
3	E	NULL	NULL
4	S	NULL	5
5	X	6	NULL
6	U	8	NULL
7	A	NULL	9
8	T	NULL	NULL
9	C	NULL	NULL

FIGURE 3.16
A binary tree.

A set of two pointers indicates the location of the next child of each parent Null values in both pointers indicate that the child is a leaf. That is, a null value in a pointer terminates that traversal of that branch of the tree.

FILES AND ACCESS METHODS

VTOC

In Chapter 2 we briefly discussed mainframe DASD units and their corresponding VTOCs. Let's now go into more detail on how the system stores and accesses files or data sets.

Each volume of DASD contains a VTOC. When you want to OPEN a data set for possible usage, the Data Manager accesses data in the VTOC using the parameters you supply in a JCL statement. The JCL statement contains the name of the data set, the name of the volume where the data set resides, and other information about the data set, such as its structure, size, and disposition. The Data Manager verifies that the data set is available for processing by querying the VTOC of the indicated volume.

Each data set has a data set label, the DSCB, containing the data set's name, its physical attributes, and its boundaries on DASD. The VTOC contains the DSCB's of all data sets on that particular volume (Figure 3.17). The VTOC also has a DSCB. When you try to list all the data sets on the volume using

DASD volume

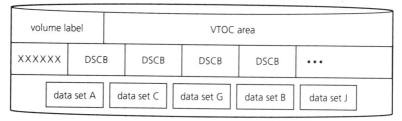

FIGURE 3.17   *A DASD volume's VTOC and data set storage layout.*

a utility program, the operating system locks the VTOC until the listing is completed. Other users of the system who require disk I/Os to that volume must wait until the system unlocks the VTOC's DSCB.

When you attempt to access a data set, the operating system accesses the volume containing the data set and searches the VTOC looking for the data set's DSCB. The operating system then uses the data in the DSCB, along with other information, to verify that you can use the data set. A few of the reasons you might not be able to access the data set include:

- It is not resident on that DASD volume
- There is no data in the data set
- Someone else could be using the data set and it is locked until that person is finished with it
- You do not have authorization to use the data set
- The data set organization is of a different type (i.e., it could be a sequential data set and you are trying to access it as a VSAM data set)
- The record length and blocking factor of its records on DASD do not match the record length and blocking factor indicated in your program

This list is just a partial list of what can go wrong when you try to access a data set. If you fail to access the data set, the operating system usually will indicate the reason for the failure in an error message and terminate the processing of the job. IBM's list of error messages consumes several large manuals containing hundreds of pages. In some cases, for example, if someone else has locked the data set, the operating system will wait for a predetermined length of time for the data set to become available. If the dataset does not become available in that length of time, the job will abend.

If everything in the DSCB matches the declarations in the JCL statement, the Data Manager moves the read/write head to the data set's location. If the job indicates that the system is to read the data, the Data Manager performs a disk input and copies data from the data set into a buffer area for usage by a program. If the job indicates that the system is to write the data, the Data Manager performs a disk output and copies data from some predefined buffer onto the data set and updates the DSCB for that data set (Figure 3.18).

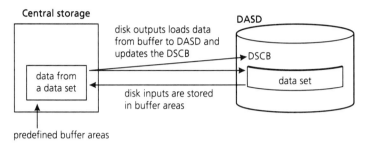

FIGURE 3.18   *Using buffer areas for disk I/Os.*

Note what is happening on the system. When you attempt to access data on DASD, the system first must verify that you can actually use the data set by querying the VTOC. The data in the VTOC contains the needed information for the operating system to perform the work that you require of it. You indicate to the operating system what work you want performed by placing instructions or commands in multiple JCL statements. If you cannot write JCL, some experienced programmer will have to write the JCL for you. Remember, all jobs on IBM mainframes require some series of JCL statements before those jobs can execute.

All input and output data must pass through some buffer area. Using buffer areas enables the machine to process data quickly and efficiently without having to wait for a slow hardware device. Don't forget, the Data Manager is that part of the operating system that handles all I/O to DASD. This includes handling the buffers, accessing and updating the VTOC, verifying security, allocating and deallocating data sets, and all reading of DASD and writing to DASD.

The VTOC is a very active area of the disk. The operating system must first check the VTOC before any disk I/Os take place. All data set allocations must use the VTOC to find vacant space on the volume. Any deallocation of a data set forces an entry into the VTOC's list of available space on that volume. The OPENing and CLOSEing of files via programs require accessing the data set's DSCBs that are in the VTOC. The Data Manager part of the operating system must resolve all disk contention problems on the volume, and this includes the activity in the VTOC.

If you store files on a PC rather than on a mainframe, you must perform a similar ritual. You will have to instruct the PC via some DOS command on what work you want performed. Writing a DOS statement serves the same function as the writing of a JCL statement. Certain sections of the DOS operating system handles all disk activity much like the Data Manager handles it on a mainframe. Instead of a VTOC on a volume, the PC uses a File Allocation Table (FAT) to store data about the files on a disk. A PC's disk access follows a similar logical procedure as a disk access on the mainframe, except on a much smaller and simpler scale.

Blocked and Unblocked Files

You rarely transfer records from central storage to secondary storage one record at a time. First, a one-record transfer is very time consuming, especially if hundreds of thousands of records need processing. Second, a disk access on a DASD unit does not include the reading and writing of just a single record. The disk head is not designed to move to a certain cylinder and read only a few bytes from a track. Rather, the disk head passes over the track, reads a large section of the disk, and stores it in a buffer area. It is in this buffer area that the system electronically segregates the data into the desired record. The system then transfers that record to central storage using an electronic-memory to electronic-memory transfer. Multiple records are resident in this electronic-memory area, called a buffer. Rather than making another disk access, the system, if told to do so, can segregate other records in the buffer area and process them as individual records. This simulates a disk I/O occurring multiple times because multiple records already exist in the buffer area. Now the system uses records it already procured, thereby saving a disk I/O.

The system tries to avoid mechanical work whenever possible. The mechanical movement of read/write heads and the mechanical rotation of the disk platter significantly slows the processing cycle, if the system had to wait for the mechanical movement. Using a buffer area permits the channel programs to access the mechanical devices and store the data in electronic memory while the CPU is processing some other work. When you instruct the system to perform a disk I/O, the operating system establishes a channel program to perform the work and creates an interrupt of the CPU. The CPU performs some other work as the channel program instructs the Data Manager to perform the necessary mechanical accessing of the file. After the data is placed in a buffer, the Data Manager issues an interrupt to the CPU. The CPU then can use the data in the buffer and continue processing the job. Remember, the system can perform an electronic transfer of data much faster than a mechanical transfer of data.

Fixed versus Variable Blocking

There are basically two different types of blocked records with a variation on each type. The two basic types are **fixed-blocked records** and **variable-blocked records.** The variation has to do with what are known as spanned records, which gives rise to two other types, **fixed-blocked spanned records** and **variable-blocked spanned records.** We will examine each type below.

Fixed-blocked Records Let's look at how the system handles fixed blocks. To see how blocking works, let's assume the following:

1. The disk device you wish to use resides on an IBM mainframe and has a track size of 47,476 bytes
2. You want to store 144 records with a fixed length of 500 bytes

3. You want to use half-track blocking (i.e., you want to cause the operating system to read one-half of a track at a time)

If you use fixed-blocked records, the records would be stored on disk in the format shown in Figure 3.19.

You can fit 47 500-byte records on each block. Because the block size is one-half of a 47,476-byte track (23,738 bytes), we divide 23,738 by 500 (the length of each record) to obtain a result of 47.476. You must drop the fractional portion, because you can only store a whole number of records in each block. The result is 47 and is your blocking factor. Thus, you can store 47 records per block, and your block size is 500 (the record length) multiplied by 47 (the blocking factor) or 23,500. Because you are using half-track blocking (two blocks per track), you will store 94 records per track. If you divide the total number of records you want to store (144) by 94, you obtain approximately 1.5319. Round up to the nearest integer because you cannot allocate less than a track on an IBM mainframe disk device. You will need two tracks to contain your data.

Variable-blocked Records Assume now that you want to store the same records on the same device with the same blocking scheme, but that they are variable-length records with an average record length of 500 bytes. Some records might be 300 bytes while others could be 700 bytes, but the average would be 500 bytes. This variable-blocked format is shown in Figure 3.20.

The operating system adds two extra fields to a variable blocked file. The block descriptor word (BDW) is a four-byte field at the beginning of each block that contains the length of the block. The record descriptor word (RDW) is a four-byte field at the beginning of each record that contains the length of the record. Thus, you must subtract four bytes from your block size of 23,500 to determine the amount of usable space in the block (23,496 bytes). To determine the blocking factor, add four bytes to the average record length of 500, which is 504. Dividing your block size, 23,496, by 504 is 46.992. Again, drop the fraction. Therefore, you can store 46 records per block. But is this really the blocking factor?

```
TRACK: 1
  BLOCK: 1
    RECORDS:    1,      2,      3,    ...,   47
  BLOCK: 2
    RECORDS:   48,     49,     50,    ...,   94

TRACK: 2
  BLOCK: 3
    RECORDS:   95,     96,     97,    ...,  141
  BLOCK: 4
    RECORDS:  142,    143,    144
```

FIGURE 3.19   *Fixed-blocked records. It would take two tracks to store 144 500-block records using half-track blocking.*

Note that Figure 3.20 shows 47 records in the first block, not 46. How did you get the extra record? Remember you are dealing with variable-length records and 504 is your average record length. If you had some records that are less than 504 bytes in the first block, there easily might be enough room for extra records in any block. Thus, 46 is not an absolute blocking factor for this file, but is your average blocking factor. By determining the minimum and maximum record sizes that are possible, you can perform the same math as above and determine your maximum and minimum blocking factors. Before creating a variable blocked file, it is frequently useful to run a program or utility against the input data to compute the minimum, maximum, and average record lengths.

There is a problem with both fixed-blocked and variable-blocked files. In both cases, you wished to use half-track blocking. That is, you wanted to fit as many records as possible into 23,738 bytes. However, because you cannot store a fractional part of a record, your block size only could be 23,500. Therefore, you must waste 238 bytes on each half of a track. Spanned records allow you to solve this problem by storing part of a record on one block and the rest of the record on the next block. In other words, the records can span two different blocks. This would allow you to specify a block size of 23,738 for your fixed-blocked and variable-blocked files. Your fixed-blocked spanned file would then look very much like Figure 3.19, except that the first 238 bytes of record 48 would be on the first block and the last 262 bytes would be on the second block. The other blocks also could have partial records on them. Similarly, your variable-blocked spanned file would look like Figure 3.20, except that there also could be partial records on each block.

One final note before we leave the subject of blocked and unblocked files. How do you determine an appropriate block size? In the previous examples, you were given half-track blocking as the goal. However, in practice, programmers and analysts are typically also given target block sizes for different disk devices and types of files by the Systems Programming Team. Determining a desirable block size involves balancing such factors as I/O efficiency, available buffer space, CPU load, availability to process large blocks, and so

```
TRACK: 1
┌──────────────────────────────────────────────────────────┐
│ BLOCK: BDW 1                                               │
│    RECORDS:    RDW   1,    RDW   2,    RDW   3,   ...,   RDW   47 │
│ BLOCK: BDW 2                                               │
│    RECORDS:    RDW  48,    RDW  49,    RDW  50,   ...,   RDW   93 │
└──────────────────────────────────────────────────────────┘

TRACK: 2
┌──────────────────────────────────────────────────────────┐
│ BLOCK: BDW 3                                               │
│    RECORDS:    RDW  94,    RDW  95,    RDW  96,   ...,   RDW  140 │
│ BLOCK: BDW 4                                               │
│    RECORDS:    RDW 141,    RDW 142,    RDW 143,         RDW  144 │
└──────────────────────────────────────────────────────────┘
```

FIGURE 3.20   *Variable-blocked records. The operating system adds block descriptor words (BDW) and record descriptor words (RDW).*

forth. Typically, the Systems Programming Team will run benchmark tests to determine the relative efficiency of different block sizes. The type of file processing also can affect what is considered to be an optimal block size. Files that you intend to process primarily via sequential access should have larger block sizes because you presumably will be processing all of the records in a given block. On the other hand, files that you intend to process primarily via direct access should have smaller block sizes because you will normally process only one record in a given block.

Sequential Files and Logical Merging

Sequential files are not typically used for databases, though they still play important roles in database management. Most database products include utilities to create sequential files. These files can be used for backup purposes, for transferring data from one database product to another, or for purposes that do not need up-to-the-minute data, such as reports designed to show long-term trends. Most database products also include utilities to load a database from a sequential file. There is also a very powerful technique for manipulating sequential files, known as a logical merge.

Keys in Files

Before you examine the logical merge, you need to consider keys for sequential files. Although keys are not required for sequential files, they are very useful. In fact, the logical merge technique requires them. Keys in sequential files are not used to access records, but to indicate a record's identity, that is, to "name" the record. Keys can be unique or nonunique.

Unique keys exist when no two records can have the same key. Nonunique keys exist when multiple records can have the same key. An example of a unique key would be a person's Social Security Number in a personnel file because no two people have the same number. An example of a nonunique key in a personnel file would be a person's name. In these files there could be multiple people named John Robert Smith, for example.

The logical merge technique can be made to work with nonunique keys, but it works best with unique keys. In addition, unique keys are conceptually more consistent with the idea of a key as an identifier. The logical merge technique is used to merge two sequential files into one. It is called a "logical" merge because the two files need not be in the same format. In fact, the classic example is updating a master file from a transaction file. The transaction file usually has a different format from the master file. Typically, the transaction records in the transaction file has three parts (Figure 3.21). First, each record has a key field that has the same value as some master file's record key. Second, it has a transaction-type field, which is an indicator of the operation to be performed on the master file, for example, add a master record,

```
01 TRANSACTION-RECORD.
      05 TRANS-KEY-FIELD    PIC...
      05 TRANS-TYPE         PIC...
    * 05 REST-OF-RECORD.
        10...
        10...
          •
          •
          •
```

FIGURE 3.21   *Three main parts of a transaction record.*

delete a master record, or update a master record. Third, it has other fields that contain the data necessary to perform the operation.

The inputs to a logical merge are a sequential master file and a sequential transaction file. The outputs of a logical merge are a new master file and an error report. The old master file usually is archived as a historical file. The logical merge pseudocode is in Figure 3.22.

For the logical merge to work properly, you first must sort both files to the same order. You can now read records from both input files and take action based on how the keys compare. If the keys are equal, you can update or delete. If the transaction file key is less than the master file key, you can add. If the transaction file key is greater than the master file key, you must write the current master file record to the output file and then read another master file record. Any other relationship between the keys is an error.

You delete a master record simply by not writing it to the output file. You add a record by writing the transaction file data to the output file in master file format. A record is updated by changing the master file record as specified in the transaction record. If you reach end-of-file on the master file before you reach end-of-file on the transaction file, the only valid transaction is to add a record. When you have exhausted all master file records before exhausting all transaction file records, all remaining keys in the transaction file will be greater than the last key in the master file. Here, you can add records to the end of the master file, but you cannot update or delete records that do not exist.

BATCH PROCESSING OF DATABASE RECORDS

Why do we consider the logical merge so powerful? For one thing, it is the only update technique that allows us to maintain a database on tape instead of disk. For years, before technological advances made disk units relatively cheap, databases were stored on tape. Even today, tape units are considerably less costly than disk units. This is particularly true if database updates are to be made via batch processing. Remember, batch processing at nonpeak hours can be cheaper and more efficient. You can use sequential processing to update

```
SORT MASTER FILE INTO ASCENDING ORDER BY KEY
SORT TRANSACTION FILE INTO ASCENDING ORDER BY KEY

READ MASTER FILE RECORD

IF END OF MASTER FILE
   PERFORM PREMATURE-MASTER-END-ROUTINE
   TERMINATE PROGRAM

DO UNTIL END OF TRANSACTION FILE
   DO UNTIL TRANSACTION FILE RECORD IS IN PROPER FORMAT
      READ TRANSACTION FILE RECORD
      EDIT CHECK TRANSACTION FILE RECORD
      IF TRANSACTION FILE RECORD IS NOT IN PROPER FORMAT
         WRITE "INVALID TRANSACTION RECORD" TO ERROR REPORT
         WRITE TRANSACTION FILE RECORD TO ERROR REPORT

   IF TRANSACTION TYPE IS ADD
      DO UNTIL TRANSACTION KEY IS LESS THAN OR EQUAL TO MASTER KEY
         IF TRANSACTION KEY IS LESS THAN MASTER KEY
            FORMAT TRANSACTION FILE RECORD INTO MASTER FILE FORMAT
            WRITE TRANSACTION FILE RECORD TO OUTPUT FILE
         IF TRANSACTION KEY IS EQUAL TO MASTER KEY
            WRITE "CANNOT ADD -- MASTER KEY ALREADY EXISTS" TO ERROR REPORT
            WRITE TRANSACTION RECORD TO ERROR REPORT
         IF TRANSACTION KEY IS GREATER THAN MASTER KEY
            WRITE MASTER FILE RECORD TO OUTPUT FILE
            READ MASTER FILE RECORD
            IF END OF MASTER FILE
               PERFORM PREMATURE-MASTER-END-ROUTINE
               TERMINATE PROGRAM

   IF TRANSACTION TYPE IS UPDATE
      DO UNTIL TRANSACTION KEY IS LESS THAN OR EQUAL TO MASTER KEY
         IF TRANSACTION KEY IS LESS THAN MASTER KEY
            WRITE "CANNOT UPDATE -- MASTER KEY DOES NOT EXIST" TO ERROR REPORT
            WRITE TRANSACTION RECORD TO ERROR REPORT
```

FIGURE 3.22   *Algorithm for logical merge. Both files must be sorted to the same order.*

a database by running a utility to create a sequential file, performing a logical merge on the sequential file, and running a utility to reload the database from the new sequential file. A typical example of this is a bank that updates its account databases from payroll tapes sent by companies that have payroll accounts with the bank.

Hashing and Direct Access Files

Unlike sequential files, direct access files frequently are used by database products as part of the database structure. IMS, for example, uses a form of direct access files for certain types of hierarchical database.

Remember that direct access files access records via a hashing function, which is a program that takes a record's key as input and returns a pointer to that record's location in the file. Keys are required when you use direct

```
                 IF TRANSACTION KEY IS EQUAL TO MASTER KEY
                    FORMAT UPDATED MASTER RECORD
                    WRITE MASTER RECORD TO OUTPUT FILE
                 IF TRANSACTION KEY IS GREATER THAN MASTER KEY
                    WRITE MASTER FILE RECORD TO OUTPUT FILE
                    READ MASTER FILE RECORD
                    IF END OF MASTER FILE
                       PERFORM PREMATURE-MASTER-END-ROUTINE
                       TERMINATE PROGRAM
              IF TRANSACTION TYPE IS DELETE
                 DO UNTIL TRANSACTION KEY IS LESS THAN OR EQUAL TO MASTER KEY
                    IF TRANSACTION KEY IS LESS THAN MASTER KEY
                       WRITE "CANNOT DELETE -- MASTER KEY DOES NOT EXIST" TO ERROR REPORT
                       WRITE TRANSACTION RECORD TO ERROR REPORT
                    IF TRANSACTION KEY IS EQUAL TO MASTER KEY
                       FORMAT UPDATED MASTER RECORD
                       WRITE MASTER RECORD TO OUTPUT FILE
                    IF TRANSACTION KEY IS GREATER THAN MASTER KEY
                       WRITE MASTER FILE RECORD TO OUTPUT FILE
                       READ MASTER FILE RECORD
                       IF END OF MASTER FILE
                          PERFORM PREMATURE-MASTER-END-ROUTINE
                          TERMINATE PROGRAM

        PREMATURE-MASTER-END-ROUTINE
              READ TRANSACTION FILE RECORD
              IF END OF TRANSACTION FILE
                 TERMINATE PROGRAM

              IF TRANSACTION TYPE IS ADD
                 FORMAT TRANSACTION FILE RECORD INTO MASTER FILE FORMAT
                 WRITE TRANSACTION FILE RECORD TO OUTPUT FILE
              ELSE
                 WRITE "CANNOT PROCESS -- PREMATURE MASTER END" TO ERROR REPORT
                 WRITE TRANSACTION RECORD TO ERROR REPORT
```

FIGURE 3.22 *(Continued.)*

access files. The pointer can be an absolute cylinder and track address, but it is typically a relative pointer to the block that contains the record. For example, if a record with a key of X9043 is located in the first block, the randomizer might return 1. However, if the record is located in the 95th block, the randomizer might return 95.

Alternate Randomizations

An alternative method would be 0 in the first case and 94 in the second. Now you can use offsets from the first block, rather than actual block numbers. In either case, the data set would be known as a **relative block direct access file.** Unblocked files can be accessed as **relative record direct access files.** In this latter case, the pointer refers to the actual record location in the file. The advantage of using relative pointers rather than absolute addresses is that the database software can let the operating system keep track of where the file is physically located on the disk. In other words, the software works independently of the physical disk organization.

The hashing function is sometimes known as a **randomizer.** Its purpose is to return a set of pointers for a given group of record keys so that the pointers are more or less evenly distributed over the entire space that is allocated to the file. This is done to minimize overflow. In addition, you do not want a large number of records to "clump" close together in a few blocks. It is more advantageous to have them spread out more evenly.

RANDOMIZING METHODS

Remainder Method

There are several methods of randomizing. One of the most frequently used is the **remainder method,** usually with an enhancement. Assume that you want to randomize the key A1587X3, which is stored in EBCDIC on an IBM mainframe, and that you have a total of 20 blocks allocated to your file. To use the remainder method, you would do the following:

1. Consider the field as an unsigned binary number. In hexadecimal this would be 00C1 F1F5 F8F9 E7F3, or 54,590,709,251,565,555 in decimal.
2. Divide the number by the total number of blocks (i.e., 20). This gives a quotient of 2,729,536,462,578,277 with a remainder of 15.
3. Ignore the quotient; the remainder is the relative block offset. You will store the record in block 16.

Folding Method

The remainder method works reasonably well if the keys are themselves fairly evenly distributed. However, in cases where the keys tend to clump together in groups, you can enhance the remainder method by **folding** the number before using the remainder method. To do this you:

1. Consider the key as an unsigned binary number, but pad the number to the right with zeroes until you have a number of bytes that is evenly divisible by eight. In this case, you would have C1F1 F5F8 F9E7 F300.
2. Split the number into groups of eight bytes, C1F1 F5F8 and F9E7 F300.
3. Add the groups

    $$
    \begin{array}{r}
    \text{C1F1 \quad F5F8} \\
    + \quad \text{F9E7 \quad F300} \\
    \hline
    \text{1 \quad BBD9 \quad E8F8}
    \end{array}
    $$

4. Add any carry digits (e.g., the leftmost 1) back in without padding

    $$
    \begin{array}{r}
    \text{BBD9 E8F8} \\
    + \qquad\qquad 1 \\
    \hline
    \text{BBD9 E8F9}
    \end{array}
    $$

5. At this point, you have BBD9 E8F9, or 3,151,620,345 as a folded key; now apply the remainder method. Divide by the number of blocks (20), and you get 157,581,017 for a quotient with a remainder of 5. Store the record in block 6.

OVERFLOWS

With direct access files, it is necessary to contend with overflow. This occurs when more records randomize to a given block than there is room to store them. Let's look at the case where the following occurs:

- You have 20 blocks in which to store records
- You are using fixed-blocked records with a blocking factor of five
- You are using the remainder method to randomize keys
- You have records with keys which, when considered as binary numbers, have values including 20, 40, 80, 100, 120, and 140

In this case, six keys will randomize to a relative block offset of zero. But, because you can store only five records per block, you have overflowed the block. Obviously, you will need to store one of them in some other block.

One method of managing overflow is to store the record in any other block you can find, within limits. You must set some limits; otherwise, your database software will not "know" when to stop searching for a place to add the record and report a "database too full" error message.

Numeric Limits

One way of imposing a limit is to just set a numeric limit. In this case, you will search the next ten or twenty blocks until you either find a block with enough space, or until you exceed the limit. A question that occurs here is: Which way do I search, forward or backward? The answer is: Either way will suffice, as long as you are willing to "wrap around" the database. For example, suppose you wish to search for 10 blocks forward in a database that holds 100 blocks. You have no problem unless you start at block 92 or higher— then you could not search 10 blocks without running out of blocks to search. Similarly, you would have problems searching backward for 10 blocks if you started at block 9 or lower. The solution is to wrap around to the beginning (or end). That is, whenever you have searched less than 10 blocks and are at the end (or beginning) of the database, you continue with the first (or last) block and continue searching until you have searched 10 blocks.

Limits Using Hardware

Another way of imposing a limit is to search whatever blocks are contained in the same cylinder as the one the key randomized to. Note that disk packs with multiple read/write heads can read one cylinder without moving the heads, which gives you a reasonably efficient way of searching for extra blocks. You pay the price of becoming device dependent, because your software must now be able to determine which blocks are on which cylinders, but you gain in I/O efficiency.

Prime Blocks

Another method of managing overflow that can be used in place of or in conjunction with storing records in any block you can find within certain limits is to allocate specific blocks for overflow purposes. These blocks are known as **overflow blocks.** The blocks in which you initially attempt to store records (which we have been referring to thus far as simply "blocks") are called **prime blocks.**

Assume that you have a database with 25 blocks—of these, 20 are prime blocks, and 5 are overflow blocks. You can store five records per block. Using the remainder method, you want to store records with keys of 20, 21, 40, 41, 80, 81, 100, 101, 120, 141, and 121, in that order. After storing these records, your database would look like Figure 3.23.

You were able to store the first ten records without any problems. There was room for records with keys from 20 through 141 in their prime blocks. However, the eleventh record (121) would have been the sixth record to be stored in the second block, and there was no more room in that block. Note, however, that each block has been allocated with space for an overflow block pointer. To store record 121, place the number of the next available overflow block in the overflow pointer of the second block and place record 121 in that block.

Blocks with null overflow pointers have no more records that randomize to them than the number of records that they can contain. This allows your database software to "know" when to stop searching for a given record and report a "record not found" error message.

Block number	Records in block					Overflow pointer
1	20,	40,	80,	100,	120	NULL
2	21,	41,	81,	101,	141	21
•		•		•		•
•		•		•		•
•		•		•		•
21	121					NULL
22						NULL
23						NULL
24						NULL
25						NULL

FIGURE 3.23   *A direct access file with overflow blocks. The overflow pointer points to the next block containing records that randomized to a given prime block.*

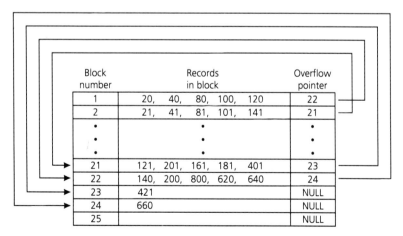

FIGURE 3.24 *Adding a record to a direct access file. You can add record 140 to the direct access file in Figure 3.23. Overflow blocks are used sequentially.*

Also, when you store a record from one prime block in a given overflow block, you do not store any records from any other prime blocks in it. Instead, you store them in the next available overflow block. For example, if you now attempted to store a record with a key of 140, your database would look like Figure 3.24.

Once you determine the proper prime block to search, you can "chain" from that prime block to its first overflow block, then its next overflow block, and so on. You do this by using the overflow pointer in the overflow block to point to the next block when the overflow block itself overflows. In other words, you can process overflow blocks in the same manner as a linked list. Figure 3.25 shows your database after adding records with keys of 200, 201, 161, 181, 401, 800, 620, 640, 660, and 421.

Block number	Records in block					Overflow pointer
1	20,	40,	80,	100,	120	22
2	21,	41,	81,	101,	141	21
•			•			•
•			•			•
•			•			•
21	121,	201,	161,	181,	401	23
22	140,	200,	800,	620,	640	24
23	421					NULL
24	660					NULL
25						NULL

FIGURE 3.25 *Adding a record. The direct access file in Figure 3.24 with several additional records added. Overflow blocks also can use overflow pointers.*

INDEXED FILES

Like direct access files, indexed files are frequently used to implement databases, particularly on microcomputers, where the machine's architecture lends itself to this sort of file structure more readily than does a mainframe. Remember, database files on a microcomputer tend to be smaller than on a mainframe. You can, therefore, keep the low-level index in main memory. We will discuss this in more detail in the next section.

Sequential Indexes

There are many methods of indexing a file; one of the simplest is a sequential index. Figure 3.26 shows such a file structure.

In this figure, the indexed file consists of two components, a data component and an index component. The data component is simply a sequential file with five records per block. The data component is also, in this example, a sequential file, though with ten records per block. Figure 3.26 shows only the record keys of the data records. You do not know, from this figure, what data the records contain or how long they are. Presumably, they are much longer than the index records. Figure 3.26 does show the data contained in the index records. Each record contains the key of a record in the data component and a pointer to the block where that record is located.

To find a record, search the index sequentially. Start with the first record and end when you reach a record whose key matches the one you want or when you reach end-of-file (EOF) on the index. When you reach the EOF on the index, you must report a "record not found" error message. To add a record, you simply write a record at the end of the data component and write an index record at the end of the index component.

However, you can considerably improve the performance of this indexing scheme. Remember that on a microcomputer, the data component is probably small enough to maintain the index in memory, which allows you to do a sequential search, that is, start at the beginning and read each block in turn. On a mainframe, however, the index might be too large to retain in memory. In addition, the extra overhead of performing several I/O operations to the index can be prohibitive, particularly in an online system.

Sorted Indexes and Binary Searches

One method of improving your indexing would be to sort the index. Figure 3.27 shows the indexed file with a sorted index. A sorted index speeds up search time in two ways.

First, you can now use a binary search instead of a sequential search. Second, you can reduce search time by using high-level indexes. The complete algorithm for a binary search is fairly complex, but we can distill the main points here.

DATA COMPONENT

Block number	Records in block
1	20, 40, 80, 100, 120
2	21, 41, 81, 101, 141
3	151, 82, 83, 147, 192
4	1, 2, 3, 4, 5
5	61, 76, 210, 45

INDEX COMPONENT

BLOCK: 1

Record number	Key	Block pointer
1	20	1
2	40	1
3	80	1
4	100	1
5	120	1
6	21	2
7	41	2
8	81	2
9	101	2
10	141	2

BLOCK: 2

Record number	Key	Block pointer
11	151	3
12	82	3
13	83	3
14	147	3
15	192	3
16	1	4
17	2	4
18	3	4
19	4	4
20	5	4

BLOCK: 3

Record number	Key	Block pointer
21	61	5
22	76	5
23	210	5
24	45	5

FIGURE 3.26   *An indexed file with a simple sequential index. Adding records is easy, but searching can be time consuming.*

DATA COMPONENT

Block number	Records in block				
1	20,	40,	80,	100,	120
2	21,	41,	81,	101,	141
3	151,	82,	83,	147,	192
4	1,	2,	3,	4,	5
5	61,	76,	210,	45	

INDEX COMPONENT

BLOCK: 1

Record number	Key	Block pointer
1	1	4
2	2	4
3	3	4
4	4	4
5	5	4
6	20	1
7	21	2
8	40	1
9	41	2
10	45	5

BLOCK: 2

Record number	Key	Block pointer
11	61	5
12	76	5
13	80	1
14	81	2
15	82	3
16	83	3
17	100	1
18	101	2
19	120	1
20	141	2

BLOCK: 3

Record number	Key	Block pointer
21	147	3
22	151	3
23	192	3
24	210	5

FIGURE 3.27 *An indexed file with a sorted index. Now, searching is quicker, but adding records is difficult.*

Suppose you wanted to find the block containing the record with a key of 81. Because you have 24 index records, you would divide that number in half and examine record number 12. The key is 76, which is less than 81. You now know that there is no point in searching records 1 through 11, because they also must contain keys that are less than 81. There are 12 remaining records, those from 13 through 24. Dividing 12 in half gives a quotient of 6, which you add to 13 to get 19. Examining the record number 19, you find that the key is 120, which is greater than 81. You now know that you need not examine records 20 through 24. There are 7 records between records 13 and 19. Divide 7 in half and get a quotient of 3. (Ignore the remainder.) When you subtract 3 from 19, you get 16. Record 16 has a key of 83, which is larger than 81, so you know you need not search records 16 through 18. There are 3 records between records 13 and 19, so you divide 3 in half and get a quotient of 1. Adding 1 to 13, you search record 14, which has a key of 81. The search is now ended.

Note that, using a binary search, you had to examine records 12, 19, 16, and 14. Had you used a sequential search, you would have had to examine records 1 through 14. In other words, you examined four records with a binary search as compared with 14 records with a sequential search. Binary searches are quicker and more efficient than sequential searches because each time you examine a record using binary searching, you in effect discard half of the remaining records. Remember, in a sequential search, you must examine each record in turn until you reach your goal.

High-level Indexes

You can reduce search time by using high-level indexes. If your database were large enough to keep the index in secondary storage, you might use the indexing scheme shown in Figure 3.28.

Typically, the high-level index is much smaller than the low-level index, so you might be able to keep it in storage. The block pointers in the high-level index point to blocks in the low-level index and the keys indicate the largest record key found in that block. For example, to find record 81, you search the high-level index until you find a key that is greater than or equal to the key you are searching (i.e., 141 in record 2). Then you examine the block pointer, which tells you to read block 2 of the low-level index. There you find record number 14, which tells you that the desired record is in the second block of the data component.

Of course, as the database grows, the high-level index will also grow, perhaps to the point where you can no longer keep it in main memory. At this point, you can construct another high-level index with block pointers to the first high-level index. In fact, you can have as many high-level indexes as you need, each pointing to the index below it. Obviously, at some point, a large number of high-level indexes will cause I/O time to rise to an unacceptable level because the computer will need to perform several read op-

DATA COMPONENT

Block number	Records in block				
1	20,	40,	80,	100,	120
2	21,	41,	81,	101,	141
3	151,	82,	83,	147,	192
4	1,	2,	3,	4,	5
5	61,	76,	210,	45	

LOW-LEVEL INDEX

BLOCK: 1

Record number	Key	Block pointer
1	1	4
2	2	4
3	3	4
4	4	4
5	5	4
6	20	1
7	21	2
8	40	1
9	41	2
10	45	5

BLOCK: 2

Record number	Key	Block pointer
11	61	5
12	76	5
13	80	1
14	81	2
15	82	3
16	83	3
17	100	1
18	101	2
19	120	1
20	141	2

BLOCK: 3

Record number	Key	Block pointer
21	147	3
22	151	3
23	192	3
24	210	5

HIGH-LEVEL INDEX

BLOCK: 1

Record number	Key	Block pointer
1	45	1
2	141	2
3	210	3

FIGURE 3.28 *An indexed file with a high-level index. Searching is even quicker, but adding records is even more difficult.*

erations against the indexes to find a record. For this reason, direct access files typically give better performance than indexed files for databases with a large number of records.

Another type of indexing scheme that gives better performance than those we have discussed so far requires that the records in the data component be sorted. The low-level index then can be in high-level index format. That is, instead of having a record for each record in the data component, the index can have a record for each block in the data component and contain the largest key found in that block. Again, you can construct high-level indexes as needed, but you will not need as many of them.

The problem, though, with either a sorted index or a sorted data component, is that adding records becomes more difficult. When you try to add a record, you also must add to the index the necessary data in the proper places to maintain the sorted order. This can involve considerable overhead, especially where high-level indexes are used, because they also might have to be adjusted.

Consider, for example, the relatively simple task of adding a record with a key of 211 to the indexed file in Figure 3.28. You must not only add an additional index record to block 3 of the low-level index, but you also must change the last record in the high-level index to reflect the fact that the highest key is now 211 rather than 210. Adding records becomes even more complex if you are adding records that should go into the middle of the range of keys rather than at the end.

Tree Formats for Indexes

There are several ways of minimizing this problem, such as using overflow management schemes similar to those used with direct access files. A better method, however, is to change the index structure from a sequential format or a sorted sequential format to a tree format.

Remember that one of the reasons you sorted the index was to be able to use a binary search technique. Also remember that a binary search is more efficient than a sequential search because you are able to discard half of the remaining records each time you examine a record. You can do the same thing when you search a binary tree.

Let's look at the binary tree in Figure 3.29, which has had records D, A, X, H, B, F, C, Y, and E added to it, in that order.

To find record H, you traverse the tree, beginning at the root, which is D. Recall that a binary tree is constructed so that the left child of a node always has a key that is smaller than that of its parent, and that a right child always has a key that is larger. Thus, comparing H with D, you find that you must continue down the right side of the tree. Then access node X and compare H to X. This time you must continue down the left side of the tree, where you find the record you want.

To add a record to a binary tree, simply follow the tree structure until you find a node that has a null pointer on the proper side to contain the

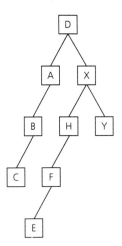

FIGURE 3.29   *A binary tree.*

record. For example, to add record R to the tree in Figure 3.29, start at the root and compare keys. In this case, R is greater than D, so examine the right child of D, which is X. Because R is less than X, you continue down the left side to H. Here, R is greater than H, so you continue down the right side and find a null pointer. This is where you place the R node (Figure 3.30).

Binary trees also can have problems, however. Depending on what keys are added and in what order they are added, binary trees can become unbalanced. This occurs when records tend to clump on one side of the tree. For this reason, sometimes **B-trees** are used for indexes. A B-tree is a tree structure that allows you to add records in such a way that the tree is always

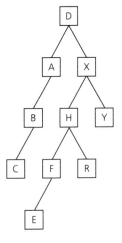

FIGURE 3.30   *Binary tree with added node.*

in balance. DB2, IBM's relational database system, uses B-trees. A refinement of the B-tree is known as the **B+-tree.** (The third character is a hyphen, not a minus sign, so the term is pronounced "bee plus tree.") A B+-tree maintains pointers among the nodes in sequential, as well as hierarchical, order. This allows the data indexed by a B+-tree to be accessed sequentially as well as directly. VSAM, which is discussed next, uses B+-trees.

VSAM

Virtual storage access method (VSAM) is an IBM file storage method that allows considerable flexibility in creating file structures while maintaining quick data access. IBM's DB2 and IMS database products make use of VSAM file structures.

A typical VSAM file is shown in Figure 3.31. In this case, blocks of memory are known as control areas, and records are contained in control intervals within each control area.

Overflow is managed by allocating free space within the file itself, within control areas, and within control intervals. Did you notice that the second control interval in the control area at the left in Figure 3.31 has no free space? The control interval in Figure 3.31 that is on the right also has no free space. Figure 3.32 shows what will happen if you attempt to add a record to the full control interval and to one of the control intervals in the full control area.

When you attempt to add a record to the full control interval, an activity known as a control interval split takes place. Half of the records in the control interval are written to a new control interval in the same control area. Now, both the old and the new control intervals have free space that can accommodate new records. The free space in the control area has decreased, because some of it was used to create the new control interval.

What happens when there is no free space in the control area? When a

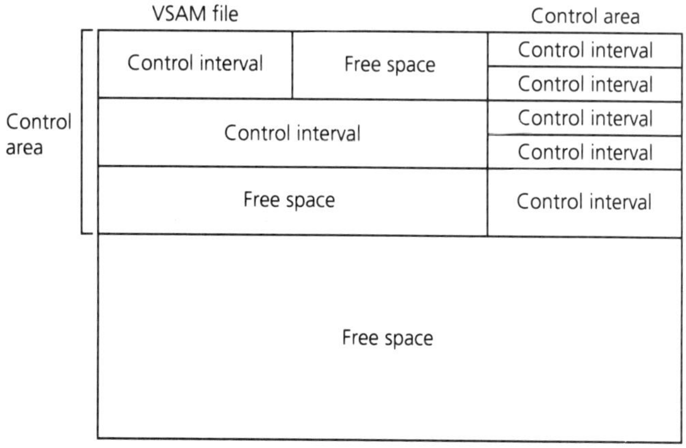

FIGURE 3.31 *A typical VSAM file.*

VSAM file   Control area

Control interval	Free space	Control interval
Control interval	Free space	Control interval
Control interval	Free space	Control interval / Free space

Control area

Free space	Free space

Control interval	
Control interval	
Control interval / Free space	Free space
Free space	

Control area

FIGURE 3.32   *The VSAM file in Figure 3.31 after a control interval split and a control area split. Note that the old and new control intervals and control areas now have free space.*

control interval split is attempted and fails, a control area split takes place. That is, some of the free space belonging to the entire data set is used to create a new control area, which then receives half of the control intervals in the old control area. Now, both control areas have sufficient free space to allow the control interval split.

Kinds of VSAM Data Sets

Remember that VSAM allows considerable flexibility. You can create three different kinds of VSAM data sets: relative record data set (RRDS), entry sequenced data set (ESDS), or a key sequenced data set (KSDS). An RRDS usually is processed in the same manner as a sequential file. An ESDS also is processed as a sequential file, although you have the capability of updating a record in place, that is, reading a record, changing it, and writing it back out over the old record. A KSDS gives the most capability, allowing you to process it as either a sequential file or a direct access file, or a combination. That means you can perform a direct read to access a record with a given key, and then read sequentially from that point. A KSDS also allows you to search on a partial key. For example if your file contains records with keys such as A100, A103, B298, B385, and B876, you can access the first record with a key that begins with B.

SUMMARY   Numeric data is stored in the computer either in binary form, in unpacked form using EBCDIC or ASCII codes, in packed form, or in floating point form. Integers are stored in binary form in either a byte, a halfword, or a fullword. Signed integers are stored using the two's complement form. Most data entered via a program is stored in unpacked (display) form. These numbers must be packed before they partake in any arithmetic operations. High-level languages perform this task automatically. The largest packed number is a function of the machine language instruction set, which varies from computer to computer. Usage of real numbers in computations also is handled by the high-level language used for the application.

Data can be grouped into cells called arrays, which contain an index identifying the data's position in the array. These arrays sometimes are called subscripted variables. A single-indexed array is called a linear or one-dimensional array. Most computers have restrictions on the number of indexes that can be used in a multiple indexed or multidimensioned array.

Although variable-length fields can save DASD space, they are difficult to program and use. However, most DBMS products have an automatic function called VARCHAR that creates and manages variable-length alphanumeric data. Fixed-length fields are accessed using the function CHAR.

All records and files on the system contain an end-of-record (EOR) and an end-of-file (EOF) marker. The hex codes used to represent the EOR and EOF vary among the software products and computer systems making many files incompatible with each other. Users must access a utility program to transfer files between different software products.

A linked list is an array containing pointers logically linking the cells within the array. A circular list or ring is a linked list where each and every pointer points to some other cell within the list. A single-threaded linked list can be followed only in one direction, while a double-threaded linked list can be followed in both directions.

Hierarchical relationships can be represented using a tree. Each cell on the tree is called a node and the lines connecting these nodes are called branches. A single node at the top of a tree is called the root of the tree. The bottom-most nodes are the leaves of the tree. A tree with no nodes is called an empty tree. The branching from one node to another node creates a parent-child relationship within the tree. The parent is an ancestor of its children and the children are descendants of the parent. Each parent forms a layer within a tree. The leaves at the bottom of the tree also form a layer within the tree. The height of the tree is the maximum number of layers within the tree. A binary tree is a tree where each parent can have either 0, 1, or 2 children. Children in a binary tree are called the left child and the right child. Trees are stored in computer systems in a list structure.

Each data set on DASD has a data set label, the DSCB, that contains the data set's name, its physical attributes, and its boundaries on DASD. A volume's VTOC contains the DSCB of all the data sets on that volume. The system first will access a data set's DSCB in the VTOC before it attempts to access the data set. Parameters in the DD section of the JCL requesting the access must match the values in the data set's DSCB before access to the data set is granted by the system.

Records are moved from DASD to central storage via a buffer area. The number of records that the system moves into a buffer area is determined by the file's blocking factor. The blocking factor determines how many records are stored in each block. Each disk I/O then loads the appropriate number of records into storage when indicated by some program. Records can be either of fixed length or variable length. Blocks can be of fixed length or of variable length. When programs use a variable-length block, the system places the length of the block in a four-byte block descriptor word (BDW) and adds it to the beginning of each block. When variable-length records are used, the system places the length of the record in a four-byte record descriptor word (RDW) and adds it to the beginning of each record. The blocking factor programmers use in their computer code is determined by benchmark programs executed by the installation's systems team.

Data is stored either in a direct file using a key or in a sequential file. The system uses a specialized random number generator on the value in the key field to create a pointer for the location of the record on DASD. This pointer identifies which logical block the record resides in on DASD. After the initial loading of the file, the storage of additional records into an already record-filled block forces the system to store the additional records in an overflow area. An overflow pointer for each block identifies the location of the block containing the overflow for that block area.

When records contain an index, the system stores the record number, the key value, and the block pointer in the index. The index can be a sequential index, a sorted index or a tree index. When the system uses a sequential index, it sequentially searches the index using the key value to find the record's block location. When the index is sorted, the system uses a binary search to find the location of the record via its key. When the index has a binary tree format, the system uses a tree search to locate the record.

QUESTIONS

1. Describe the differences between fixed-blocked, variable-blocked, fixed-blocked spanned, and variable-blocked spanned files.
2. Which blocking technique uses space most efficiently?
3. Which blocking technique do you think uses the least CPU and channel program resources?
4. Which blocking technique do you think would be easiest to use in a program?
5. Why do we sort the files in a logical merge?
6. Describe the function of a randomizer.
7. What are some methods of implementing a randomizer? Which one is most likely to work the best?
8. What is the difference between overflow and prime blocks?
9. What factors would you consider in determining how many overflow blocks to allocate?
10. Why are trees a good index structure?
11. What is a control interval split? What is a control area split?
12. Convert the number 463 to hexadecimal. How is the number stored in EBCDIC code? In packed format? In two's complement format?
13. What is the difference between fixed point and floating point?

14. What is an array? Give an example of a real world use of a five-dimensional array.
15. You have a Lotus 1-2-3 data file on a PC floppy diskette. What problems will you encounter in trying to upload that file to a mainframe?
16. Why do disks have labels and volume names?
17. What is the difference between a single-threaded and double-threaded linked list?
18. What is the difference between a tree, a binary tree, and a B+-tree?
19. Why are not all files blocked?
20. What are some of the advantages of using fixed blocking over variable blocking?

CASE STUDY

Programs R Us, Inc., a software vendor, wants to develop and market a mainframe product that would implement microcomputer-type directories for mainframe disk volumes. They know that most products on the market treat a mainframe VTOC like a sequential file that contains data concerning, among other things, file names and file types (e.g., VSAM or sequential). This means that VTOC data usually appears to mainframe users like this:

FILE NAME	FILE TYPE
ACCOUNTS.PAYABLE.MASTER	VSAM
ACCOUNTS.PAYABLE.TRANSACT	SEQUENTIAL
ACCOUNTS.RECEIVE.MASTER	VSAM
ACCOUNTS.RECEIVE.TRANSACT	SEQUENTIAL
BUDGET.ACTUAL	SEQUENTIAL
BUDGET.PLANNED	SEQUENTIAL
BUDGET.VARIANCE	SEQUENTIAL
PAYROLL.MASTER	VSAM
PAYROLL.PRINT	SEQUENTIAL
PERSONNEL.CURRENT	VSAM
PERSONNEL.PLANNED	VSAM

Programs R Us has decided that this system will operate by maintaining a file that contains the data concerning the subdirectories and the names of the files that they (logically) contain. Users will be able to list the file as shown above and also will be able to list the files or subdirectories under a given subdirectory. They will also be able to add or delete subdirectories and to add files to or delete files from a given subdirectory.

Questions

1. What kind of data structure would be appropriate for the file that Programs R Us wants the system to maintain?
2. What kind of access method would be appropriate to store the file?
3. Describe how subdirectories would be added to the file. How would they be deleted? Would renaming a subdirectory cause any special problems?
4. Describe how files would be added to or deleted from a given subdirectory.

4 *Database Management Systems*

DBMS COMPONENTS AND FUNCTIONS

A DBMS has several components, and different DBMS have different components. Still, it is possible to classify the different components of all databases by function. All databases must do basically the same things, regardless of how they do it. Viewed this way, a DBMS can be said to be composed of a data interface, a user interface, and a programmer interface. Figure 4.1 depicts the relationships among these interfaces.

The Data Interface

The data interface is a set of low-level routines that implement the database using one or more of the file and data structures discussed in the preceding chapter. Typically, on IBM mainframes, VSAM is chosen as an underlying file structure, perhaps with additional indexes along with those that VSAM maintains. On microcomputers, direct access or indexed files are more likely to be used. As Figure 4.1 indicates, all I/O to the actual data is performed by the data interface. Here, I/O efficiency is the responsibility of the data interface; how the files are accessed and the file structures will be determined by the data interface. For this reason, the system programmer team's evaluation of the database as a whole most likely will be strongly effected by how well the data interface performs its function.

The User Interface

The user interface interacts with the end user. It presents a simple, user-friendly method for the user to make queries of the database, processes the queries as needed for edit checking and formatting for use by the data interface, and presents the results of the queries to the user. The user interface must communicate with the data interface to access the data. The user interface itself is the series of menus, data-entry panels, and report screens that the user sees.

138

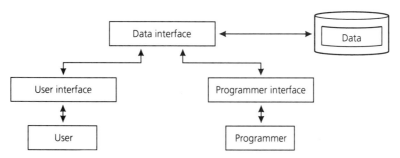

FIGURE 4.1   *DBMS components and the relationships among them. Components can communicate with entities external to the database and with each other.*

The user interface might be the only contact the end user will have with the database. For this reason, the end user's evaluation of the database probably will be determined primarily by the user interface.

The Programmer Interface

The programmer interface interacts with the programmer. It might be a database command language such as DB2's SQL or IMS's DL/I that is embedded in another programming language such as COBOL, PL/I, or FORTRAN. Also, it can be a programming language in itself, such as dBASE IV's programming language. It also can include utilities for exporting or importing data to or from other databases or file structures. The function of the programmer interface is to accept the commands from the programmer, edit check them as necessary, and pass them on to the data interface. It is the data interface that actually accesses the data and passes it back to the programmer interface, which in turn formats it for the programmer's use in the form of program variables.

The programmer's evaluation of the database will be affected most strongly by the operation of the programmer interface. The operation of the data interface probably also will play a part, because programmers usually are conscious of I/O overhead. In fact, it is frequently taken into account as a criterion of program design.

USING A DATABASE MANAGEMENT SYSTEM

The Database Designer

In many corporations, upper management's decision to proceed with a new product line or to revamp an existing service or product initiates the need for additional software systems. A manager of a user department within the company might request an enhancement to an existing system. The manager also might initiate dialog with the software developers to create a totally new software system to solve some problem within that user department. The request could be as simple as an informal phone call to a member of the software development team or as complex as a formal document stating the need and desire for programming services. Whatever the method a company uses to communicate the need for computer software generation, some member of the software development team must perform a study based on this communication. This systems study varies in length from a day to many months, depending on the services needed and the complexity of the problem. The study is done by a systems analyst from the software development team. He or she has the training to perform this detailed study and has the experience and expertise to make the necessary recommendations for either the new system or the enhancement to an older system.

After the systems analyst performs the study, he or she then must make a prototype of the potential system and begin the preliminary design of it. Most companies have a database designer whose main job function is to design the database records and files for a particular DBMS. If the company has three different DBMS installed on its computer systems, the company might have three different database designers, one for each database product. These individuals have special training from the vendor of the DBMS and have the skills necessary to design efficient and effective database structures within their assigned DBMS.

The database designer might not have that specific job title within the company. He or she might be a senior systems analyst, a project manager, or a database administrator (Figure 4.2). In any of these cases, the job function remains the same. The database designer must create an efficient design of the database records and files so that the DBMS product runs efficiently and the necessary information can be extracted with little or no difficulty. Databases can be huge. Many application software systems contain millions of lines of COBOL code that can access hundreds of database files. These massive systems also can contain hundreds of different computer screens or menus within the application. In these large systems, only an experienced and highly trained individual can create an efficient, integrated file structure for the data involved in the application.

The designer's first problem is to identify all the data stores within the application. These data stores are logical lists of the data within the application that identify each field's name and general characteristics about it. The data stores are in the Analysis Data Flow Diagram, called the Analysis DFD. The systems analyst creates the Analysis DFD during the analysis phase of the systems study. The systems analyst diagrams the user's needs using structured analysis techniques. Once the systems analyst fully understands the user's needs, he or she then finalizes the documentation of the analysis phase. This final step in the analysis phase of the study requires the systems analyst to identify the fields and document their characteristics for each of the data stores within the Analysis DFD. An example of an analysis DFD can be seen in Figure 4.3.

Remember, these data stores were created in the initial systems study performed by the systems analyst, who also might be the designer for the

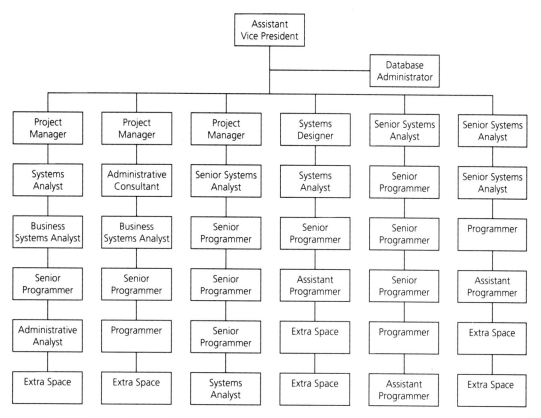

FIGURE 4.2   *Organizational chart for information systems.*

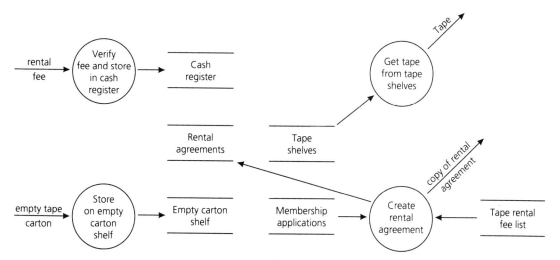

FIGURE 4.3   *Section of data flow diagram for video tape rental shop. Circles represent processes, parallel lines represent data stores, and the lines connecting processes to data stores represent the flow of data.*

system. For the fields within each data store the designer needs to know such things as the following:

- What is the size of each field?
- Whether the fields contain alphanumeric or numeric data
- Which fields are required fields?
- What restrictions are on the data within each field?
- The number of occurrences of the field
- Whether the field is a primary key, foreign key, or a nonkey field
- Whether the key field will contain unique keys or nonunique keys

A foreign key is some key field in a record of one data set referencing one or more records in another data set.

In addition to looking at all the data stores found by analyzing the system, the designer must investigate each prototype screen and identify the data fields on each of them. A prototype is a series of screens either the designer or the systems analyst paints or creates in cooperation with the end user of the application (Figure 4.4). These screens will become the screens for the new application or are the enhanced screens for the modification to the existing system. They are created as part of the initial systems study and represent the first step in the designing of the application.

The software tool used to generate the prototype could be a 4GL product (TELON), a CASE tool (Excellerator), or part of the DBMS (IDMS/R's Automatic Mapping Facility). In all these cases, the designer must be proficient in the use of the respective prototyping tool.

After the designer has compiled a list of all the fields within the application, he or she now must design the logical configuration of the database for the new application or modify the existing logical database's structure if the new system is an enhancement. After the designer becomes satisfied with the logical design, he or she can begin the physical design of the database. The physical design is loaded into the computer system using some facility of the DBMS (Table 4.1).

The actual details of the logical and physical design are in Chapters 6, 7, and 8 within this text. After the designer creates the physical design, he or

TABLE 4.1   *Facilities within selected DBMS*

DBMS Product	Facility to Load the Physical Design
DB2	Data Definition Language
IMS	Database Definition Generation (DBDGEN)
IDMS/R	Integrated Data Dictionary and the SCHEMA Compiler
dBASE IV	Control Center Data Panel

```
                    VIDEO RENTAL SYSTEM
                 MEMBERSHIP APPLICATION SCREEN

   CUSTOMER NAME:          JEAN C. SCHWAB
   CUSTOMER ADDRESS:       5905 WOODS DR
                           CHATTANOOGA, TN 37409

   MEMBERSHIP APPLICATION DATE:   04/09/87

   CREDIT RATING:    GOOD
```

```
                    VIDEO RENTAL SYSTEM
                    TAPE RENTAL FEE LIST

   TAPE                                    RENTAL FEE

   BACK WITH THE WIND                         5.00
   JAWS XIX                                   3.00
   MORE ALIENS                                3.00
   WALKING MISS PETUNIA                       3.00
   STILL MORE ALIENS                          2.00
   RAMBO IV:  NO MORE MR. NICE GUY            3.00
   THE BURMESE PIGEON                         5.00
   ONLY ONE OR TWO MORE ALIENS LEFT NOW       3.00

   ENTER "M" FOR MORE TAPES OR "Q" TO QUIT: _
```

FIGURE 4.4   *Sample screens in a prototype.*

she then writes the program specifications for each module of the new system or the enhancement of the old system.

The Database Programmer

The database programmer uses the program specifications produced in the design phase to write computer code for the application. A sample program specification can be seen in Figure 4.5. Depending on the DBMS software system he or she will use, the database programmer uses the language of the specific DBMS to access database records and display, update, or delete them as necessary. Because each DBMS product has its own language to access its database records, the database programmer must be proficient in that lan-

PROGRAM SPECIFICATIONS

Program name: PREMCALC

Program function: Calculate premium for insurance policy.

Inputs: Policy Type
        Insured's Age
        Indemnity Amount
        Policy Term
        Premium Table (PREMTABL)

Outputs: Term Premium

Return Codes: 0 - No errors detected
               12 - Erroneous User input

Processing:

```
GET POLICY TYPE, INSURED'S AGE, INDEMNITY AMOUNT, AND POLICY TERM FROM USER
IF INSURED'S AGE > 69
    DISPLAY ERROR MESSAGE
    EXIT WITH RETURN CODE OF 12
IF INDEMNITY AMOUNT > 50,000
    DISPLAY ERROR MESSAGE
    EXIT WITH RETURN CODE OF 12
IF POLICY TERM NOT ANNUAL, SEMI-ANNUAL, QUARTERLY OR MONTHLY
    DISPLAY ERROR MESSAGE
    EXIT WITH RETURN CODE OF 12
READ PREMIUM TABLE WITH POLICY TYPE AND INSURED'S AGE TO GET PREMIUM RATE
IF RECORD NOT FOUND
    DISPLAY ERROR MESSAGE
    EXIT WITH RETURN CODE OF 12
COMPUTE ANNUAL PREMIUM = (INDEMNITY AMOUNT / 100) * PREMIUM RATE
CASE OF POLICY TERM
    ANNUAL
        COMPUTE PREMIUM = ANNUAL PREMIUM
    SEMI-ANNUAL
        COMPUTE PREMIUM = ANNUAL PREMIUM / 2
    QUARTERLY
        COMPUTE PREMIUM = ANNUAL PREMIUM / 4
    MONTHLY
        COMPUTE PREMIUM = ANNUAL PREMIUM / 12
DISPLAY PREMIUM
EXIT WITH RETURN CODE OF 0
```

FIGURE 4.5   *Sample program specification.*

guage. Note that for DB2 and IMS, the database programmer probably will be using COBOL as the main language and will write specific DB2 or IMS statements within the COBOL code. For IDMS/R databases, the database programmer will write dialogs to access the database records. An IDMS/R dialog resembles COBOL code. However, it is a specific language designed by Computer Associates that the database programmer must learn and master.

Programming in IMS Databases If the database product is IMS, the system designer will communicate the database design to the systems programming team, who will create the physical database, typically using VSAM file structures. The systems programmers then will define the database structure to IMS by running a database definition generation (DBDGEN).

The system designer also must communicate certain information about the programs that will use the database to the systems programming team. This information includes the following:

- The name of each program that will access the database
- How the programs will access the database, that is, through batch, online, or as batch message processing (BMP) programs
- Which segments of the database the program is sensitive to, that is, which segments it will be allowed to access

This information is used to define the program to IMS by running a Program Specification Block Generation (PSBGEN).

The programmer uses IMS calls and the DL/I language to access the data within the IMS database. DL/I is used by coding calls to the DL/I interface from COBOL. Database records can be read sequentially, directly, or in various combinations of sequential and direct access.

Programming in DB2 or SQL/DS Databases If the database product is DB2 or SQL/DS, the company's DB2 Systems Administrator (SYSADM) creates one or more Database Administrators (DBADM) for the application. SYSADM controls all aspects of DB2 within the company and usually is a member of the systems team. Members of the systems team are experts in the function and use of the systems software that is on the mainframe. Their main function is to manage the computer's resources to guarantee a smooth-running system.

Each DBADM is assigned to a specific database. In fact, every database on the system needs a DBADM to monitor and control the accessing of a particular database. Hence, there are multiple DBADM in the company and each DBADM could be a DBADM of multiple databases. Normally the DBADM is the project manager or the senior systems analyst for some user department. Programmers assigned to the DBADM will embed SQL instructions within their COBOL code and interface that code to DB2 or SQL/DS. The programmers must be proficient in writing SQL instructions, JCL statements, and COBOL code.

Programming in IDMS/R If the database product is IDMS/R, the database programmer writes dialogs to access records within the database. Unlike IMS and DB2 which uses the programmer's existing knowledge of COBOL and JCL, IDMS/R requires the database programmer to know a series of software products specifically designed by Computer Associates. These products include:

- *Integrated Data Dictionary* (IDD) to store database records, screens (called maps in IDMS/R terminology), dialogs, and other IDMS/R entities
- *Online Mapping Facility* (OLM) to generate the screens and prototypes

- *Application Development System/Application* (ADS/A) to link screens, dialogs, and database records to each other
- *Application Development System/Generation* (ADS/G) to compile the dialogs and create executable load modules
- *Logical Record Facility* (LRF) to program the accessing strategy for the extraction of records from the IDMS/R database.

IDMS/R is not just a database product. It is also a systems development product that permits you to create entire systems using one product or tool.

Programming in dBASE IV If the database product is dBASE IV, the systems analyst or programmer can create the database by either coding a program in dBASE programming language, by entering dBASE commands into dBASE IV, or by using the control center, which is a menu-driven interface to dBASE commands. The programmer then can create programs that can be run under dBASE IV to access the data.

In addition to dBASE programming language, the programmer can also use SQL to access the database. SQL is a database language by IBM and adapted for use with DB2, but it has quickly become an industry standard; many non-IBM products, such as dBASE IV, can perform SQL commands.

THE DATABASE ADMINISTRATOR

The Database Administrator (DBA) is a person who manages the database on the system. If the company has multiple DBMS products, it can have multiple DBAs; probably at least one for each DBMS product. The main function or duties of the DBA are the following:

- Managing the database
- Providing security for the database
- Monitoring system performance
- Planning backup and recovery
- Maintaining skills

Managing the Database

The DBA works with the database designers and the database programmers during the logical and physical design phases of the application's development. By being part of the design phase, the DBA can foresee any unusual problems that can dynamically affect the database's future performance. All problems, modifications, and corrections to the DBMS software product are given to the DBA. The DBA works closely with the vendor's performance programmers to correct problems in the DBMS software. He or she makes recommendations for future enhancements to the product and installs all updates or enhancements to the DBMS software product as they are released.

Providing Security for the Database

The DBA designs and enforces security procedures for the database. Anyone wanting access to a database must formally request accessing privileges from the DBA. The DBA gives that user the right to access records in the database by creating a subschema (for IDMS/R databases), a view (for DB2 databases), or a multiple logical database structure for IMS databases.

Generally, the security procedures have been approved by management and become part of the corporate procedures and standards guidelines for all employees. A view, a subschema, and a logical database structure all identify which files, records, and fields a database user can access.

Monitoring System Performance

The DBA constantly monitors the DBMS's performance, including monitoring the response time of the system during peak loads. When the system's performance begins to degrade, the DBA must respond with preplanned action to ensure the efficient operating of the system. This requires the DBA to work closely with the capacity planners to guarantee the current hardware configuration can handle the capacity placed on it by the users. In addition, the DBA works with the systems team in designing detailed plans for the future upgrading of the hardware system due to the impact of the database on the system.

Planning Backup and Recovery

The DBA provides the guidelines, procedures, and standards for the normal backup of database files. These procedures are implemented by the operations team who actually performs the backing up of all data on the system. If the database system crashes, it is the DBA's responsibility to recover from the crash. In these instances the DBA must work closely with members of the systems team to ensure all database users are placed back online and their data salvaged. The DBA either creates or participates in the Disaster Recovery Plan so recovery of the system will be orderly in case of a major disaster.

Maintaining Skills

It is crucial for the DBA to remain current about developments in database technology because new products and enhancements to existing products can dramatically affect the productivity of the programming staff. Because the DBA is the main contact the company has with the vendor supplier, that DBA must remain knowledgeable about the product. Most vendor products have a user support group. These groups meet on a regular basis and exchange information about the vendor product.

At these meetings, the DBA can learn different approaches to solving a problem and, in turn, share his or her solutions to problems with other users of the DBMS. These meetings feature representatives from the DBMS vendor who give lectures and presentations on how to use their product more effectively. The DBA will learn from roundtable discussions and other group sessions. It is at these conferences the DBA will first hear of new releases of the DBMS and when they will be implemented.

THE END USER

Role in System Development and Database Design

Obviously, the end user is, or should be, an expert in his or her job function. When the systems analyst performs the systems study, the analyst must interview the end user to understand the user's problem and the user's need for a systems change. If the end user is uncooperative, either deliberately or unknowingly, the systems analyst cannot accurately analyze and design a correct system.

The end user must, within a short period of time, teach the systems analyst as much as possible as soon as possible. This requires a great deal of cooperation between the analyst and the end user. If the analyst does not fully understand the problems of the end user, he or she cannot design the system the user wants or needs. This is particularly true when large databases are involved. Because the database designer will be using the data stores to design the many integrated files within the database structure, any omission of fact by the end user can have serious ramifications on the design of the database. Omitting a field could mean the redesign of the major sections of the database structure if that field will be a crucial component in the database.

The real problem the end user faces is identifying what he or she wants and needs. The end user should have some vague idea of what is needed, but might not know how to implement it. Or, as happens in many cases, the need for computer services depends on the company's ability to bid on contracts. Fortunately, many end user departments are dynamic in nature and must respond to the needs of the customer or client, in what seems to be an instantaneous time frame. Market conditions might not wait for the completion of a systems study before the end user department must react in a decisive manner. The user department might bid on contracts and commit the company to a major contract without knowing how that contract impacts the existing database system. The merger or takeover of another business can involve top secret negotiations among only upper management personnel. The acquisition of another business dynamically changes the current system. The DBA and the end users must redesign systems and database structures to accommodate the new business entity.

The user must make sure that the systems the user departments get are the systems the user departments want and need. The user must set goals and objectives for the database designers to meet. The end user is the ultimate manager of the project and should dictate to the development team the type of system the end user wants.

Role in Accessing the Database

One of the main disadvantages of network and hierarchical databases is that the end user depends on the programming staff to create reports for the user departments. Typically, the end user must request a change in a report and wait for the change to be implemented by the very busy programming staff. Sometimes this process consumes days and even weeks. On occasion, modifying a report can take so long that the change is no longer wanted or needed. However, for more technically oriented end users, several products are available that permit the end user to access data in the database without programmer intervention. One such product is Easytrieve Plus from Computer Associates. This product is a report generator that can access classical files, VSAM data sets, IDMS/R records, and DB2 records. In fact, many programmers use Easytrieve Plus to create reports, because the product can access both database records and VSAM records in the same program.

One of the main advantages of relational databases is the availability of SQL for users. SQL is an easy-to-use and easy-to-learn product that accesses relational databases. Because most commands in SQL are standardized, once the end user learns how to write SQL statements, he or she can use that knowledge on a wide variety of products, such as DB2, dBASE IV/SQL, and OS2/SQL. DB2 contains a separately priced product called Query Management Facility (QMF), which uses SQL to access the DB2 database. The product is user friendly and users can generate their own reports without programmer intervention.

Although QMF is relatively easy to use, some training is needed to successfully use the product. An End User Support Center (EUSC) can provide the training to the user departments on QMF. Most companies have an EUSC to train the employees on the use of PCs and can expand their training to include classes on QMF.

SUMMARY

Database management systems contain routines and modules that interface user and programmer requests with the stored database on DASD. Data interfaces handle all I/O to the database and are specifically designed for a particular database structure. User interfaces handle all I/O to the user. Programmers use the database's command language either directly or embedded in a high-level language to manipulate the data for the users.

A database designer implements a user's request by first performing a system study. One product of this study is the identification of all the data stores required for the application. Using the data stores, the designer can identify the data relationships and establish the logical configuration for the database. After the logical design is completed, the designer can begin the physical design of either the new database or the modifications to the current database. The physical design is loaded into the system using modules within the DBMS. The designer issues program specifications for the programming staff, who then write the needed programs for the user's request.

The Database Administrator (DBA) manages the DBMS and its databases. In addition, the DBA handles all security for the databases including the establishing of procedures and standards for its use. The DBA constantly monitors both the operating system's performance and the performance of the DBMS. The DBA modifies both the operating system and the DBMS to create a reliable and efficient system. Another duty of the DBA is the planning of both the backup and recovery of the database and the creating of a disaster recovery plan in case of major disaster.

QUESTIONS

1. What relationship does the database designer have with the end user?
2. What are some of the skills the database designer must have to successfully design systems for end users?
3. What steps can end users take to ensure the system they receive is the system they want?
4. What are some of the skills a Database Administrator must have to be successful in his or her job function?
5. Who resolves conflicts between the database designer and the end user?
6. What specific skills must a database programmer have to perform his or her job?
7. If one company merges with another company and each has a different database system, what are some of the problems they will have in merging the two possibly incompatible systems?
8. Why does the DBA work so closely with the systems team? Would he or she be more productive working for the end user departments?
9. If the database designer and end user department are jointly in conflict with the procedures and standards the DBA enforces, who resolves these conflicts?

5

DBMS Concepts and Architecture

In Chapter 1 we briefly described some of the key terms in database architecture. We gave examples of one-to-one, one-to-many, and many-to-many relationships and outlined their relationship to hierarchical, network, and relational database structures. We defined the terms parent and child and briefly discussed how we use them in hierarchical databases. We also introduced the concept of owner and member as they are used in network databases. At the conclusion of the chapter, we defined the relational database entities of tables, rows, and columns. In this chapter we will elaborate on all these concepts and show how the DBMS accesses and stores data in the database.

Before we look at each of the three database structures, let's look at how DBMS products store data in databases.

ACCESSING RECORDS ON THE DATABASE

Remember, you create records within the database and establish keys for selected fields within the records. You use these keys to extract data from the database. First, you place a value in the key field. Next, you use some specialized command to access the database based on that key value. The DBMS then extracts the data based on the key value from the database and places it in a buffer for your use. In Figure 5.1, for example, you would:

1. Place the value 123456789 in the key field.
2. The database system accesses an index containing the key value.
3. The database locates the page number and its relative location on the page (page 14, RID value 5).
4. The system extracts the page from DASD.
5. The system places the page into memory.
6. The system then scans memory and locates the record and moves it to a special buffer area for processing.

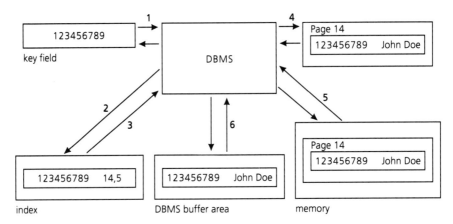

(1) Place the value 123456789 in the key field. (2) The database system accesses an index containing the key value and (3) locates the page number and its relative location on the page (page 14, RID value 5). (4) The system then extracts the page from DASD and (5) places it into memory. (6) It then scans memory and locates the record and moves it to a special buffer area for processing.

FIGURE 5.1   *Accessing a single record from a database.*

Remember, the mainframe's operating system stores everything on the system in 4K pages. The DBMS must store and retrieve records on 4K pages if it is to use the virtual memory facility, which is part of the operating system. Therefore, when you place records on DASD using a key field, you have several techniques you can use.

Using an Index to Store Records

The first technique is to place the records one after another onto a page and keep their location in an index. The index will contain the key value for the record, the identity of the page where the record resides, and its relative location on the page. As in Figure 5.2, each record is stored on DASD in sequential order, beginning with the first row on the first page. The algorithm for the record placement places a new record in the first available slot on DASD. It updates the index by placing the record's key value in sorted order within the index. If the next record is 4000, for example, it would be stored in the 6th slot on Page 2. The index entry 4000 2,6 will appear in the index between the key values 3891 and 4054.

When you want to access the record, you search the index for the key value using some efficient algorithm. Once you find the location of the record, you can read the page it resides on and extract the data for the record. When you use this technique, you can use demand allocation of DASD space. That means you tell the system how large the database will be and the system will allocate the spaces as records are loaded onto DASD (Figure 5.3). Space on

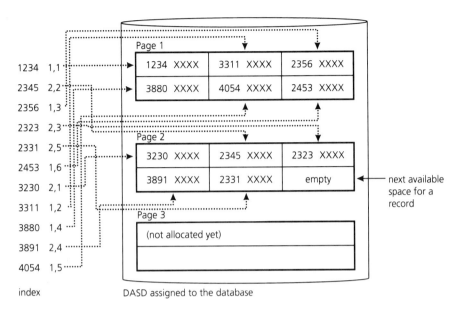

FIGURE 5.2   *Using a page index to access records.*

DASD is conserved because you only appropriate the space as you need it and not based on some future need for it. One disadvantage to this technique is that because many records are grouped together on the same page, disk contention problems can slow the system.

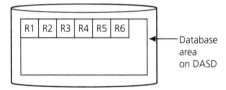

Records R1, R2, R3, R4, R5, and R6 placed in sequential order on DASD pages.

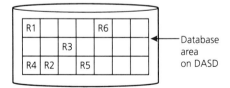

Records R1, R2, R3, R4, R5, and R6 placed in random order on DASD pages.

FIGURE 5.3   *Demand allocation of DASD space versus total allocation of DASD.*

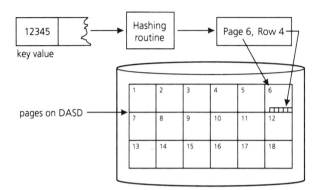

FIGURE 5.4   *Using a hashing technique to store and access database records.*

Using a Hashing Routine to Store Pages

The second technique is to use a hashing routine and place the record on some random page (Figure 5.4). With this technique you have to allocate the entire DASD space assigned to the database. Because you will be randomly using pages anywhere within the database region, you cannot conserve DASD space as with the first technique. However, because the database records are randomly distributed over the entire database, disk contention problems are greatly reduced.

Makeup of a Database Page

A database page has three main parts: a header area, a Record ID (RID) value area, and a storage area (Figure 5.5). The header area has basic information the system needs to properly access the page. This includes such information as the page's ID, its protection codes, and various pointers. The RID area contains RID values, which are pointers to the location of the record on the

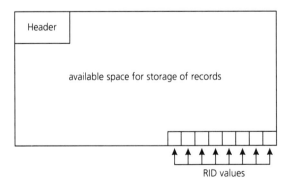

FIGURE 5.5   *Format of a page.*

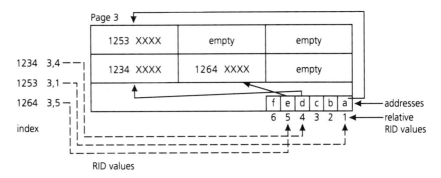

FIGURE 5.6   *Using RID values to access a database record.*

page (Figure 5.6). Whenever the system attempts to access a record, it searches the index to find the page ID and RID value for that record. The system then loads the page into memory and uses the RID value to find the physical address of the record on the page. The system then loads the record into a buffer area for processing.

Keys and Indexes

You create indexes on key fields to increase the efficiency of the database system. Usually you identify a field as a key field if you are going to use that field for sorting or accessing the database. When you try to access a record without using a key field and its associated index, the database system will have to sequentially search every record on every page within the database, which is very time consuming. It is a better idea to make the fields you use in queries key fields or indexed fields.

When the system stores a record using an index, it stores the record on the database and places its address and the record's key value in an index (Figure 5.7). Whenever you access the record using the primary key and index, the system first accesses the index's root page to find the leaf page containing the key value. The root page only contains a range of key values and a leaf page's ID for keys within that range.

The system then searches the leaf page containing the key value to find the page number and RID value for the record (Figure 5.8). Finally, the system accesses the record using the record's page number and RID value.

Because you might want to query the database using a field different from the primary key, you can create an index on that field to speed the record search. When you create an index on a secondary field, you call that field a secondary key. The system stores the address of the record and its secondary key value in an index. When using the secondary index in a query, the system extracts the location of the record from the secondary index and uses that data to access the record (Figure 5.9). In this figure, the secondary

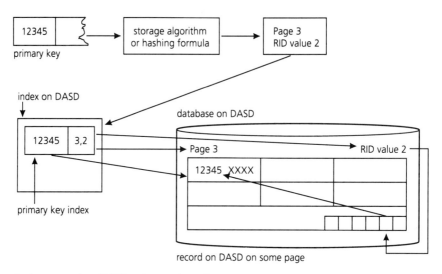

FIGURE 5.7   *Storing a record on DASD using a primary key.*

index contains nonunique keys for the last name. The page location and RID value indicates the record's location on DASD. To access all the Smiths, the system searches the index until it finds the first entry for Smith. It extracts the record from DASD using the page and RID values. It continues searching the index for additional Smiths until it exhausts the list for that value.

NUMBER OF RECORDS ACCESSED CONSIDERATIONS

Types of Relationships

The three types of databases rely on the relationships between data. We will summarize briefly these relationships. Recall the three commonly occurring relationships between data include:

- *One-to-one relationship.* If each record in file A has one and only one record in file B and each record in file B has one and only one record in file A, then the relationship is a one-to-one relationship.
- *One-to-many relationship.* If each record in file A has one or more records in file B and each record in file B has one and only one record in file A, then the relationship is a one-to-many relationship.
- *Many-to-many relationship.* If each record in file A has one or more records in file B and each record in file B has one or more records in file A, then the relationship is a many-to-many relationship.

These relationships are illustrated in Figure 5.10. Remember, each of the three types of databases (hierarchical, network, and relational) uses some

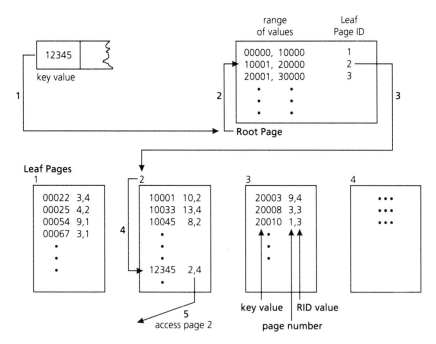

(1) The system uses the key value and searches the root page. (2) It locates which range of values the key value falls between and extracts that range's leaf page ID. (3) It accesses the leaf page and (4) finds the key value. (5) It extracts the page number and RID value for the record corresponding to the key value. It accesses the page containing the record and uses the RID value to find the record.

FIGURE 5.8 *Root pages and leaf pages.*

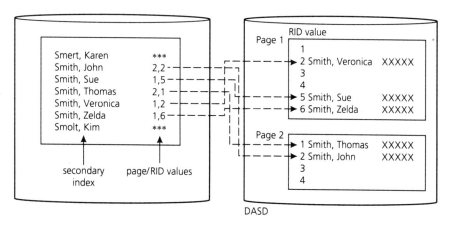

FIGURE 5.9 *Accessing an index using a secondary key.*

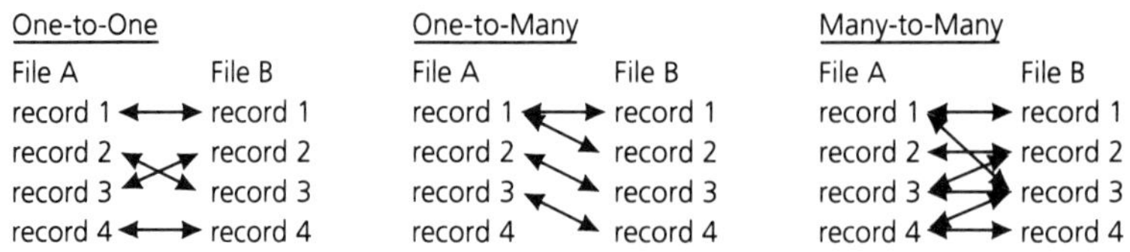

One-to-One   One-to-Many   Many-to-Many

File A   File B   File A   File B   File A   File B
record 1 ←→ record 1   record 1 ←   record 1   record 1 ←→   record 1
record 2 ↘↗ record 2   record 2 ↖↘   record 2   record 2 ←↘↗ record 2
record 3 ↗↘ record 3   record 3 ↙↘   record 3   record 3 ←↗↘ record 3
record 4 ←→ record 4   record 4   record 4   record 4 ←→   record 4

FIGURE 5.10   *One-to-one, one-to-many, and many-to-many relationships.*

form of these relationships to define their respective structures. And each
relationship returns a different number of records from the database.

Coding Logic in One-to-One and One-to-Many Relationships

Obviously, in a one-to-one relationship, the DBMS only accesses a single record
and sends it to the buffer area (see Figure 5.1). Therefore, the database system
will display one record, either as a single line or as a single record report.
For example, in DB2, the software tool SQL returns a single line, while the
software tool QMF returns a report screen. If you accessed a single record
using a computer program, the COBOL code uses the data and process it like
it does any single disk or tape record (Figure 5.11).

But what happens when the system returns multiple records in a one-
to-many relationship (Figure 5.12)? Here, the buffer contains more than one
record because there is more than one record on DASD for the key you used.
That is, multiple pages were accessed and multiple records now reside in the
buffer area for the program to process. Here, the logic in your COBOL code

```
01    DATABASE-RECORD.
      03 IN-EMPL-ID      PIC X(9).
      03 IN-EMPL-NAME  PIC X(20).
      03 IN-ADDRESS     PIC X(20).
       •
       •
       •

EXEC SQL
SELECT EMPLID, EMPLNAME, EMPLADDR
    INTO :IN-EMPL-ID
         :IN-EMPL-NAME
         :IN-ADDRESS
    FROM EMPLOYEE
    WHERE EMPLID = '123456789'
END-EXEC.
PERFORM PROCESS-DATABASE-RECORD.
```

FIGURE 5.11   *Example of a COBOL process of a one-to-one relationship. The database system loads one record
into a buffer. The COBOL program accesses the buffer and places the data in an 01 group level
variable. The program then processes that one record.*

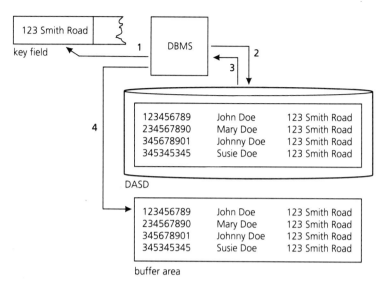

FIGURE 5.12 *Accessing records from a database for a one-to-many relationship. The key value "123 Smith Road" is used to access the database. The DBMS software extracts multiple records from DASD and places them in a buffer area. Because there are multiple members of the Doe family living at the same address, the key field is nonunique.*

must include techniques for accessing these multiple records. Remember, COBOL processes one record at a time. Therefore, you must use a looping mechanism within COBOL (e.g., PERFORM) so you can repeat the processing of a single record, multiple times.

Obviously, you cannot place all the multiple records in a single 01 or 03 group level variable. Even subscripted variables or tables would not help because you have no idea how many records could be loaded into the buffer at any one time. Clearly, the COBOL code you use for a one-to-one access is inadequate for a one-to-many access. You must change the logic and the way the system handles the data. The DBMS you use must have facilities to handle these cases—which they do. In DB2, you will use the concept of a cursor or pointer and read the buffer area, one record at a time. In DB2 you process each record from the buffer much in the same way as you process records from a sequential tape or disk file (Figure 5.13). The only skill necessary is to learn DB2's technique and its language commands. We will discuss these commands in Chapter 12 when we elaborate on the programming of relational databases.

This is what happens in Figure 5.13: The database system accesses the records and places them in a buffer. The COBOL code reads one record at a time from the buffer and places it in predescribed COBOL variable names. The code then processes the record and loops to read additional records from the buffer until all the records are processed.

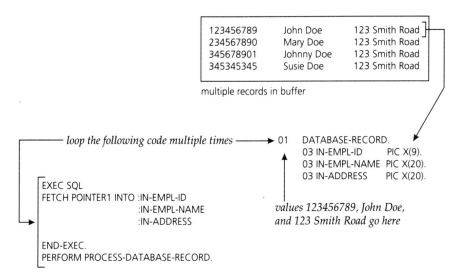

FIGURE 5.13   *Accessing multiple records from a one-to-many or a many-to-many relationship.*

USING FOREIGN KEYS

Accessing a One-to-Many Relationship Using Indexes

Foreign keys play a vital role in relational databases. Because a network is the only type database that can handle many-to-many relationships directly, you need foreign keys to use this relationship in relational databases. Remember, a foreign key in file A is a primary or secondary key of file B. That means foreign keys cross-reference data in one file with data in another file.

Let's look at an example of a one-to-many relationship and the use of foreign keys by investigating the inventory of a college classroom building. Buildings contain many classrooms with multiple furniture items in each classroom. We identify each classroom by its building code and classroom number. Within each classroom is furniture including desks for students, a table and chair at the front of the room for the instructor, and a variety of other furnishings. Each piece of furniture has an identification tag affixed to it containing a unique ITEM-ID number. We will create two files, one called ROOMS and the other called FURNITURE. They are illustrated in Figures 5.14A and 5.14B.

In Figure 5.14A, room number contains code for building name and room location within the building. ITEM-ID is a unique serial number assigned to each item in inventory. Each room has multiple items, but each item has a unique ITEM-ID. Room number is a nonunique primary key and ITEM-ID is a foreign key. Now look at Figure 5.14B. The file contains an ITEM-ID, the item's

ROOMS

ROOM NUMBER	ITEM ID
HUN123	C12344
HUN123	C12345
HUN123	D12322
HUN123	D12323
HUN123	D12324
HUN123	D12325
HUN125	C12346
HUN125	D12345
HUN125	D12347

FIGURE 5.14A
ROOMS file for classroom buildings.

name, a code for the supplier, the item's cost, and the date it was purchased. Each ITEM-ID is unique with multiple items coming from the same supplier. ITEM-ID is a unique primary key and Supplier-Code is a nonunique foreign key.

You can extract information from these database files by placing a value in the primary key field. For instance, if you wanted to list all the furnishings in Room HUN125, place HUN125 into the variable for Room Number and access the database file called ROOMS. In this case you get the values C12346 and D12345 (which are foreign keys in ROOMS but primary keys in FURNITURE). Now access the database file FURNITURE to extract further information about the furnishings. Here, place the value C12346 into the variable for ITEM-ID and access the database file called FURNITURE. You get the following record:

C12346	CHAIR	W122	120.00	1/23/79

Remember, the value W122 is a foreign key in FURNITURE and a primary key in the file SUPPLIERS (which is not listed here).

Next, place the value D12345 into the variable for ITEM-ID and again access the database file FURNITURE. You get this record:

D12345	DESK	P056	89.00	3/23/80

To identify the name and address of the supplier of the furniture, you have to access a third file, called SUPPLIERS. Remember the procedure you had to follow. You always must include some value in your key field because the DBMS will use that value to query the database. It extracts the data and places it in a buffer. Then it makes it available to whoever is entering the instructions into the computer. The foreign keys in one file are used as primary

FURNITURE

ITEM ID	ITEM NAME	SUPPLIER CODE	COST	DATE PURCHASED
C12344	CHAIR	W122	120.00	1/23/79
C12345	CHAIR	W122	120.00	1/23/79
D12322	DESK	P056	89.00	3/20/80
D12323	DESK	P056	89.00	3/20/80
D12324	DESK	P056	89.00	3/20/80
D12325	DESK	R008	86.00	4/10/80
C12346	CHAIR	W122	120.00	1/23/79
D12345	DESK	P056	89.00	3/23/80

FIGURE 5.14B   *FURNITURE file for classroom buildings inventory.*

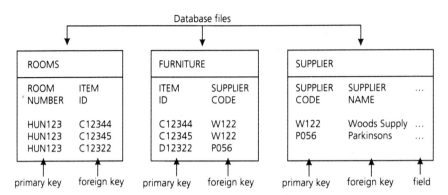

FIGURE 5.15   *Using foreign keys to cross-reference files within the database.*

keys for another file, cross-linking the data among the various files within the database (Figure 5.15).

Many-to-Many Relationships

Many-to-many relationships have special problems in using foreign keys. Occasionally you will have to create a special file containing only keys to other files. Because this type of file associates one file to another file, it is called an **association file**.

We will again use the college campus to illustrate many-to-many relationships and the use of foreign keys to form an association file. A college offers classes in which students enroll. A CLASSES file will have a listing of classes available, where each class is a unique item in the listing. A STUDENT-

CLASSES

CLASS ID	CLASS NAME	INSTRUCTOR ID	LOCATION CODE	SEMESTER HOURS
MATH10101	ALGEBRA	123456789	HUN103	4
MATH10102	ALGEBRA	123456789	HUN223	4
MATH10103	ALGEBRA	123456789	HUN105	4
MATH15001	CALCULUS I	232323232	HUN211	5
MATH15101	CALCULUS II	232323232	HUN311	5
CHEM30101	ORGANIC I	454545454	RUH003	4
CHEM30102	ORGANIC I	454545454	RUH003	4
CHEM30103	ORGANIC I	363636363	RUH004	4
CHEM30501	PHYS CHEM I	363636363	RUH005	4
CHEM30502	PHYS CHEM I	565656565	RUH004	4
CHEM31501	PHYS CHEM II	565656565	RUH004	4
ENGL10101	ENGLISH I	121212121	WEN122	3
ENGL10102	ENGLISH I	424242424	WEN325	3
ENGL20101	ENGLISH LIT	439439439	WEN351	3

FIGURE 5.16A   *CLASSES record layout with one-to-many relationship. CLASS ID is a unique primary key and INSTRUCTOR ID and LOCATION CODE are nonunique foreign keys.*

STUDENT-ROSTER

STUDENT ID	CLASS CODE
112112112	MATH15001
112112112	CHEM30101
112112112	ENGL20101
112112112	HIST11003
213213213	ENGL20101
213213213	MATH30101
213213213	BIOL12502
213213213	HIST11003
345345345	ENGL20101
345345345	MATH30101
345345345	BIOL12502
345345345	HIST11003

FIGURE 5.16B   *STUDENT-ROSTER record layout with many-to-many relationship.*

ROSTER file will contain the student's ID and the class codes for the classes each student has enrolled in (Figures 5.16A, 5.16B, and 5.16C).

In Figure 5.16B, both STUDENT ID and CLASS CODE are nonunique keys. Multiple occurrences of the same student in the STUDENT-ID column and multiple occurrences of classes in the CLASS CODE field make this relationship a many-to-many relationship. In this case, STUDENT-ROSTER is an association file because it contains only keys to other files.

You can list all the students in the Calculus I class by placing the value MATH15001 into the CLASS CODE variable. Then you can access the database file STUDENT-ROSTER using that variable as the primary key. The DBMS will search the database file looking for that value in the primary key field. Once it finds a match for the value, it will place a copy of the record satisfying the value into a buffer area (Figure 5.17). You can access the STUDENT file to find the students' names associated with the student IDs. You can print a listing of the student names for each class.

You do this by extracting the data from the buffer area using some software tool, such as a COBOL program, QMF, or EASYTRIEVE PLUS, to produce your report.

Notice that STUDENT-ROSTER contains only keys from other files. You will have to access these other files to get more detailed information about the value in the key. This is an example of an association file. By itself, it produces unusable reports. However, when used in conjunction with other files, it

STUDENT

STUDENT ID	STUDENT NAME
112112112	John Doe
213213213	Jane Doe
345345345	Patty Schwab

FIGURE 5.16C   *STUDENT record that contains information that can be referenced via the foreign keys in STUDENT-ROSTER. This table will be used to format the report in Figure 5.17.*

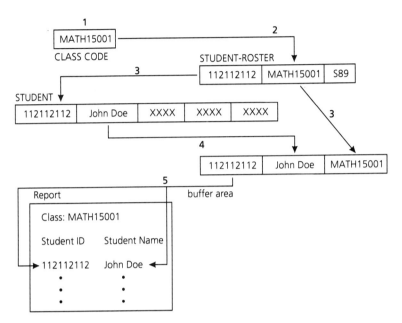

FIGURE 5.17   *Using an association file. (1) Place the CLASS ID into the CLASS CODE variable. (2) Access the association file STUDENT-ROSTER and extract all STUDENT IDs for all class values having a match with the CLASS CODE (MATH15001). These are foreign keys in STUDENT-ROSTER, but primary keys in STUDENT. (3) Place the record in a buffer and use the STUDENT ID key value to (4) access the student's name in the STUDENT file and (5) print a report.*

becomes a powerful tool in setting up relationships between numerous seemingly unrelated files.

DATA MODELS

Hierarchical Models

Hierarchical models contain data in groups of parent records and child records having a one-to-one or a one-to-many entity relationship. That means a parent record can have one or more child records, but each child record can have one and only one parent (Figure 5.18). In the hierarchical model, each record is called a segment. So you have a root segment corresponding to the root node in the hierarchical tree structure, and dependent segments corresponding to the child nodes. The access path to any dependent segment must contain the identity of all nodes between the root segment and the desired dependent segment. For example, in Figure 5.19, if you want to access the dependent segment CUSTOMER, you must include in the access path the segments CITY and BRANCH.

The principal database system incorporating the hierarchical model is IBM's

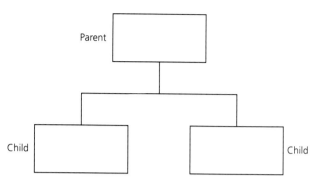

FIGURE 5.18   *Hierarchical entity-to-entity relationships.*

IMS. Chapter 15 describes in detail how IMS manipulates and uses data in the hierarchical structure.

Network Models

Network databases have the ability to handle one-to-one, one-to-many, and many-to-many data relationships. The most popular network database is Computer Associates' IDMS/R, which is covered in detail in Chapter 13. However, we need to describe some basic concepts and ideas before we can begin looking at how network databases are implemented on computer systems. Whereas the hierarchical database uses a parent-child relationship to define its structure, a network database uses the owner-member principle for its structure. An owner is similar to a parent and a member is similar to a child. The principal difference between the two structures is that members can have multiple owners, but a child can have but one parent (Figure 5.20).

Network databases create pointer files to hold the structure and the lo-

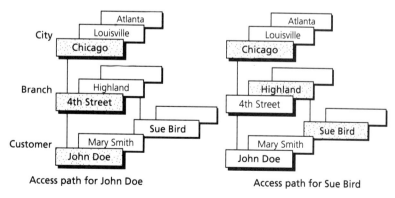

FIGURE 5.19   *Access path in the hierarchical structure.*

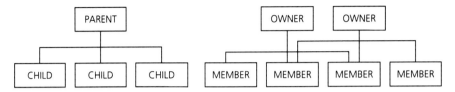

FIGURE 5.20   *Representation of the difference between parent-child and owner-member.*

cation of members. These pointer files are linked lists or rings, depending on the DBMS product. Let's look at an example to see how network databases are constructed. Again, we will use the academic world for our example. The following structure contains four files: SCHOOL, DEPARTMENT, FACULTY, and STUDENT.

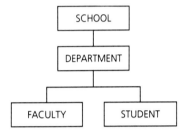

These four owner-member combinations have the following relationship:

DEPARTMENT is the owner of FACULTY and STUDENT
SCHOOL is the owner of DEPARTMENT

The records in SCHOOL might include

School of Business	School of Science
School of Medicine	School of Engineering
School of Education	School of Arts and Humanities
School of Nursing	School of Information Science
School of Dentistry	School of Music

and a sample of the records in DEPARTMENT might include

Mathematics	Chemistry
English	Physics
History	Marketing
Art	Accounting
Political Science	Management

In this case, each department is a member of some school and each faculty member is a member of some department. Also, each student is assigned to a department within the school.

The record layout for this structure is given in Figure 5.21.

SCHOOL

School's name	PIC X(30)
Dean's name	PIC X(20), PIC X(20), PIC X(45)
Building location	PIC X(15)
Secretary	PIC X(20), PIC X(20), PIC X(45)
Dean's office location	PIC X(7)
Dean's phone	PIC X(7)
Degrees granted	PIC X(5), PIC X(5), PIC X(5), PIC X(5)

DEPARTMENT

Department's name	PIC X(15)
Building location	PIC X(15)
Secretary	PIC X(20), PIC X(20), PIC X(45)
Phone	PIC X(7)
Chairman's name	PIC X(20), PIC X(20), PIC X(45)
Chairman's phone	PIC X(7)
Office location	PIC X(7)

FACULTY

Faculty's ID	PIC X(9)
Faculty's name	PIC X(20), PIC X(20), PIC X
Office location	PIC X(7)
Phone	PIC X(7)
Highest degree	PIC X(5)
Date of degree	PIC 9(6)
Faculty address	PIC X(30), PIC X(30), PIC X(2), PIC X(5)

STUDENT

Student's ID	PIC X(9)
Student's address	PIC X(30), PIC X(30), PIC X(2), PIC X(5)
Student's status	PIC X
Student's major	PIC X(15)
Credit hours passed	PIC 999
GPA	PIC 9V99

FIGURE 5.21   *Record layout for SCHOOL, DEPARTMENT, FACULTY, and STUDENT.*

Using Occurrence Diagrams Figure 5.22 shows the relationship between the records and how they occur within the database structure using an occurrence diagram.

In addition, you can create forward, backward, and owner pointers on all the records within the structure. This means each record will have pointers via a linked list. The linked list contains the location of the next record and the prior record in the list. In addition, each record will have a pointer identifying its owner. The group of records in Figure 5.23 illustrates this concept.

When you add a new record to the list in Figure 5.23, where do you want to place it? Obviously, you have the choice of placing it in alphabetical order within the list, because the list already is alphabetized. But, you might not need the list alphabetized, so, you could place any new record in one of the following locations within the list (Figure 5.24):

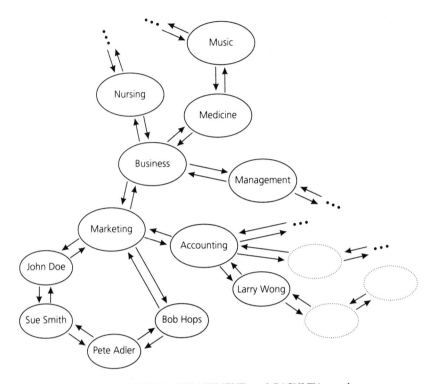

FIGURE 5.22   *Occurrence diagram for SCHOOL, DEPARTMENT, and FACULTY records.*

- In alphabetical or sorted order
- At the beginning of the list
- At the end of the list
- After the last record you accessed in the list
- Before the last record you accessed in the list

For example, to insert the record Ben Franklin in Figure 5.24, you can place the record at (A) the beginning of the list; (B) the end of the list; (C) after the last record you accessed; (D) before the last record you accessed; or (E) in sorted order.

Location pointer	Faculty name	Forward pointer	Backward pointer	Owner pointer
1	Doe, John	2	-	MATH
2	Evers, Mary	6	1	MATH
3	Keller, Sue	4	7	MATH
4	Martinez, Dorothy	5	3	MATH
5	Mueller, Mike	-	4	MATH
6	Faxxon, Bob	7	2	MATH
7	Gregory, Tom	3	6	MATH

FIGURE 5.23   *Forward, backward, and owner pointers for faculty records.*

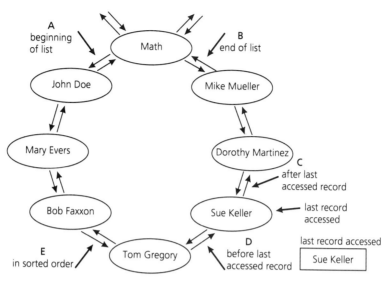

FIGURE 5.24 *Options for insertion of a record.*

Remember, you have some choices in where you insert new records. You also have some choices in what you do with the record when you delete it from the database. You can either expunge the record from the database or move the record from one owner to another owner.

To see how to use this process, let's look at a typical manufacturing case where a customer sends an order to the manufacturer. The manufacturer will place the order into an Order file for processing against an Inventory file. If the item is not in inventory, the ordering system must initiate a work order to manufacture the item. If the item is in inventory, the ordering system issues an invoice and packing slip and authorizes the shipment of the merchandise. Once the order is shipped, what do you do with the data in the Order file? Surely, you want to retain it by placing it into a History file to create an audit trail of all orders that are processed. You want to keep track of all the filled orders; therefore, you do not want to erase the record from the database. You just want to move a record from one file to another file without erasing it. In this case, you detach the record from the Order file and attach it to the History file (see Figure 5.25).

Relational Models

The relational model is the easiest of the three models to use and understand. Instead of creating files, records, owners, members, parents, or children, you create a table (file) containing rows (records) and columns (fields). You design each table to eliminate redundancy and link them together using foreign keys. A typical table is given in Figure 5.26.

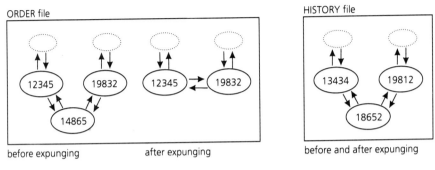

Expunging of Record 14865 from ORDER File.

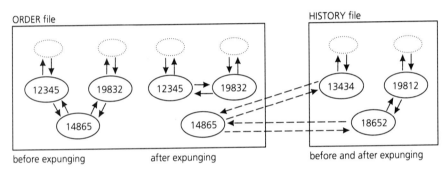

Deleting without erasing from ORDER. Record 14865 is disconnected from ORDER and manually attached to HISTORY. Pointers of HISTORY are adjusted to handle the new entry 14865.

FIGURE 5.25   *Expunging versus moving a record.*

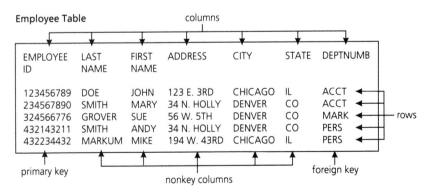

FIGURE 5.26   *Employee table with a primary and a foreign key. The column DEPTNUMB is a primary key in the Department table and logically links these two tables together.*

Department Table

DEPTNUMB	NAME	MANAGER ID	ASSISTANT MANAGER ID
ACCT	Accounting	123456789	346565432
MARK	Marketing	902902902	898989898
PERS	Personnel	432143211	453453453

FIGURE 5.27   *Department table.*

In this example, the table has seven columns and five rows. Other information about each employee is located in additional tables (Figure 5.27). You place a foreign key in a table (i.e., DEPTNUMB in Employee table) to logically link that table to another table (i.e., Department table). Similarly, we can create an association table equivalent to an association file.

Design Advantages   You design tables to eliminate data redundancy. By placing data in tables so it appears only once, you not only save disk space, you also maintain data integrity. Remember, two of the main advantages of using databases were to eliminate redundancy and to maintain data integrity. Because the data will appear only once in the database, any change to it will be reflected in all future use of it. Now you have a preferred system over classical file structure.

Disadvantages of Network and Hierarchical Designs

When you define the structure of networks and hierarchical databases to the system, that structure must exist before you load any data into the databases. And once that structure is defined, it is difficult to modify or change it. There are two reasons for this.

First, the creation of owners–members or parents–children requires a great deal of planning and sophisticated design skills because these arrangements are so complex. Once the design is created, the structure depends on the entire configuration integrating properly. This makes modifications to the final structure difficult, if not impossible. With these two databases, the relationships between the data must be defined before you load data into the files.

Second, the language to create the structure in network and hierarchical databases is difficult to learn and use. IMS, a popular hierarchical database, requires the Database Administrator to have a command of JCL and assembler macro instructions. Most end users do not have that skill. As a matter of fact, many programmers don't have it either. IDMS/R, a popular network database, requires the Database Administrator to be skilled in the language of the Integrated Data Dictionary and the schema and subschema compilers. In fact, in this DBMS product only the DBA has access to the schema and subschema compilers. Therefore, end users cannot even attempt to implement their own design of network databases even if they know these complicated and advanced products.

Advantages of Relational Designs

The situation with relational databases is different. End users can constantly add columns to the tables, create indexes, generate views, and perform other functions on the database after it is created. In relational databases, the relation between the files is defined after data is loaded into the files. This lets you change the relationships between data any time you find it necessary.

In relational databases, Data Definition Language (DDL) permits this varied use of the database's systems resources. And DDL is easy to use and understand. Once the end user has the necessary training from his or her End User Support Group (EUSG), that user can implement simple and effective relational databases.

This does not mean that anyone can create and design relational databases. Some training is necessary to effectively design a group of tables and create the proper indexes for an efficient system. Therefore, the designer of relational tables should have some experience, especially if complicated and multiple tables are involved. It is always wise to show your design to an experienced database designer before you implement that design on the system. This is true for both experienced and inexperienced designers. The cost is small and the savings in time and computer resources can be substantial, especially if the alternate design improves the performance of the computer. This becomes more apparent when a design has inferior relationships or improper keying and indexing.

SCHEMA, SUBSCHEMA, AND DMCL

The Schema and Subschema

After you design the database's structure and identify the records, fields, and other characteristics of the data, you must define the database to the DBMS. You do this by creating a **schema**. A schema is the complete description of the content and structure of the fields, records, and data relationships for the database. Each database has one and only one schema to define that database. You must have a test schema for the test database and a production schema for the production database (Figure 5.28). Remember, very few organizations give their program developers the power to experiment in the production environment. Such factors as security, response time, and both internal and external auditing standards prohibit using the production databases except for pretested and preapproved programs.

For network databases you can use a form of the DDL to create the description of the database. You must describe the following entities and their respective relationships to the system:

production
enviroment

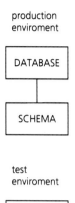

test
enviroment

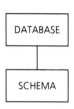

FIGURE 5.28
A production and test schema.

- The database name
- The name of all files within the database
- The DASD volumes where the database will reside
- The size of the database and each file within it
- The logical name of the areas on DASD where the files will reside
- The record and field names
- A description of each file, record, and field
- The name of the owners and members and how they are related
- The name of all key fields, both primary and secondary
- The name of the indexes and which fields have them
- The relationships between the files, records, and fields
- The technique to insert and delete records
- The name of all special edit and validation routines that will be attached to a database file

First you enter the entire configuration of the database into the system. Then you must use the schema compiler to link the schema description to the database. The results of the schema's compile are placed in the system's data dictionary. The schema's compiler checks for syntax in all the statements within the schema and verifies that the system can create the database you described. All misspellings, typographical errors, and duplicate or incorrect names are flagged by the compiler for future resolution. The compiler also identifies the following errors: lack of disk space, conflicts with system resources, impossible structures, and any other problems. After you get a clean compile, you can proceed with the next step in identifying the database to the system. A clean compile refers to getting error-free results from the compile. A sample schema description for an IDMS/R database is given in Figure 5.29.

For security reasons, only the DBA has access to the schema and subschema compilers and the Device Media Control Language (DMCL). Before you can use the facilities of the DBMS on a particular database, the DBA must define the database structure and its components. If someone wants to practice using the database system, that user must be assigned to a database. Vendors equip their product with several dummy databases that contain files and data that can be used in a training session. New users of a database system usually are assigned to the dummy database during their training period.

Keep in mind that the schema only describes the database to the system. It does not place data into the database. That will come much later, after other entities are created and programs are written.

The DMCL

The Device Media Control Language (DMCL) is part of the database's DDL on several vendors' database systems. Its main function is to map the file and

```
ADD SCHEMA NAME IS DEPTSCHM VERSION 10
ADD FILE NAME IS DEPT001 ASSIGN TO DEPT001
ADD FILE NAME IS ...
        •
        •
        •

ADD AREA NAME IS DEPT-REGION
        RANGE IS 100200 THRU 100300
        WITHIN FILE DEPT001 1 THRU 50
ADD AREA NAME IS ...
        •
        •
        •

ADD RECORD NAME IS DEPARTMENT
        SHARE STRUCTURE OF RECORD DEPARTMENT
        RECORD ID IS DEPT1
        LOCATION MODE IS CALC
        DEPT-FACULTY SET
        WITHIN AREA DEPT-REGION
        02  DEPT-NUMB        PIC X(05) USAGE IS DISPLAY.
        02  DEPT-NAME        PIC X(15) USAGE IS DISPLAY.
        02  DEPT-CHAIRMAN-ID PIC X(05) USAGE IS DISPLAY.
        02  DEPT-LOCATION    PIC X(03) USAGE IS DISPLAY.
        03  DEPT-COST-CODE   PIC 9(05) USAGE IS DISPLAY.

ADD RECORD NAME IS FACULTY
        •
        •
        •

ADD SET NAME IS DEPT-FACULTY
        ORDER IS FIRST
MODE IS CHAIN LINKED TO PRIOR
        OWNER IS DEPARTMENT   NEXT DBKEY IS AUTO
                              PRIOR DBKEY IS AUTO
        MEMBER IS FACULTY     NEXT DBKEY IS AUTO
                              PRIOR DBKEY IS AUTO
                              LINKED TO OWNER
                              OWNER DBKEY POSITION IS AUTO
        DUPLICATES NOT ALLOWED
        OPTIONAL MANUAL.

ADD SET NAME IS ...
        •
        •
        •
VALIDATE.
```

FIGURE 5.29   *Example of a schema description.*

record areas you defined in the schema to the physical DASD units. The DMCL links the database description to the system's load library so you can use the database. The result of the DMCL's compile and link-edit is a load module that you store in the system's load library or core-image library (Figure 5.30).

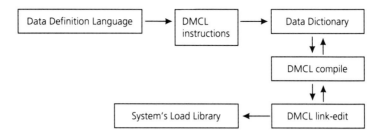

FIGURE 5.30 *Example of using the DMCL compiler.*

Load Libraries

A load library is any partitioned data set specifically created to contain load modules. You generate a load module every time you get a successful compile and link-edit of your COBOL or other language programs. When you compile a program, you must tell the operating system the following information:

- *The name of the source library for the code.* This partitioned data set is where you stored the source code for the program.
- *The name of the load library where the load module will reside.* Usually this is a special systems PDS created by the systems team.

After you get a clean compile and link-edit, the system stores the resultant load module in the load library. When you want to execute the load module, you tell the system the name of the program you want executed and in which load library it resides. The system accesses the load library, finds the load module, copies it to central storage, and executes it (Figure 5.31).

The Subschema

The subschema is your view of the database. That means the subschema contains a list of all the entities within the database a particular user can

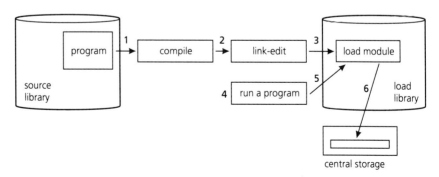

FIGURE 5.31 *Using a source and load library.*

```
ADD SUBSCHEMA NAME IS USER1
     OF SCHEMA NAME IS DEPTSCHM
     DMCL NAME IS DEPTDMCL.
ADD AREA NAME IS DEPT-REGION.
ADD AREA NAME IS FACULTY-REGION.
ADD RECORD NAME IS DEPARTMENT.
ADD RECORD NAME IS FACULTY.
ADD RECORD NAME IS CLASSES.
ADD SET NAME IS DEPT-FACULTY.
ADD SET NAME IS FAC-CLASSES.
VALIDATE.
```

FIGURE 5.32   *An example of a subschema description. A database will have one such subschema for each user of the database.*

access and use. The list includes all the files, records, fields, and DML statements a particular user can use within the database (Figure 5.32). An item that is not listed in the subschema becomes unavailable to that user. The subschema is the security mechanism the database system uses to control access to entities within the database. When you assign user accounts to a particular database, each user account must have a subschema for that database. Keep in mind that each database has only one schema, but it can have hundreds—or thousands—of subschemas depending on the number of users of that database (Figure 5.33).

A database is a permanent description of a series of files, records, and fields, and their associated relationships. You can have multiple databases on the system, each designed to hold certain data to accomplish a certain task. When a user wants to access multiple databases, that user must have multiple subschemas—one for each database (see Figure 5.34). No subschema can access more than one schema and the subschema only protects those items within a particular database. In other words, if hundreds of users need to access multiple databases, then the DBA must create multiple groups of hundreds of subschemas to accommodate these users.

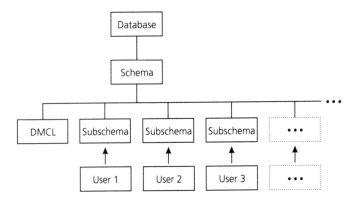

FIGURE 5.33   *The database and its schema, DMCL, and multiple subschemas.*

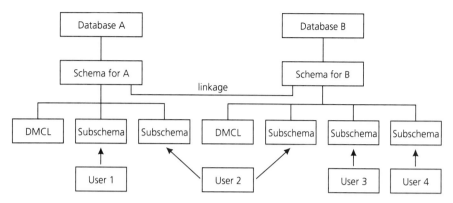

FIGURE 5.34   *Multiple databases and their associated schema, DMCL, and multiple subschemas.*

DBMS CATALOGS AND THEIR DATA DICTIONARIES

The previous discussion showed how to create the schema, subschema, and load modules for the DMCL. The source code for each of these items resides on DASD volumes dedicated to a particular vendor's database product. Figure 5.35 illustrates the hardware configuration for a system containing an operating system, some vendor's DBMS product, and user files.

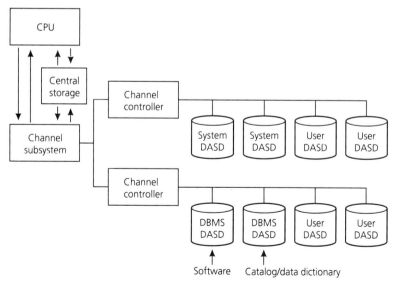

FIGURE 5.35   *DASD configuration with DBMS product. In this example, volumes contain systems software for the operating system. Two other DASD volumes contain the DBMS software and DBMS files and tables to manage the databases and their entities.*

The DBMS software is a series of programs written by a vendor that creates, manages, and accesses databases and their entities. When you create a database, the schema, subschema, and database entities (files, records, fields, relationships, etc.) are all stored in the DBMS's data dictionary or catalog. For the sake of this discussion, we will use the term data dictionary to represent either the DBMS's data dictionary or the DBMS's catalog. Computer Associates' IDMS/R uses the term data dictionary, while IBM's DB2 uses the term DB2 catalog to describe that region of DASD that holds database structure data. In both of these cases, each of these items holds the description of the database entities, their associated characteristics (the schema), and security criteria (the subschemas).

Whenever you attempt to access data in the database, the DBMS software must confirm the existence of the structure using data in the DBMS data dictionary. When you create entities (files, records, etc.), the DBMS software stores their descriptions and definitions in files within this dictionary. In fact, all activity on the database must be authorized by the DBMS software, which uses its data dictionary to obtain information about the database. Therefore, the data dictionary is an active dictionary constantly accessing and updating entries in these software files. If the system is divided into two separate environments (production and test), the DBA will have to maintain two separate data dictionaries. Obviously, the DBA will place more restrictions on the use of the production database because it contains live data and is the lifeblood of the company.

The DBA controls access to these data dictionaries and is the only one who has automatic access to data in their files. It is the DBA's responsibility to restrict access to certain database commands that access the dictionary so unauthorized individuals cannot peruse the data dictionary. It is important to remember that if the data in the data dictionary is destroyed or damaged, the database structures of some or all the databases can be lost or damaged. This can result in the reloading of thousands of files from backup copies in an attempt to salvage the databases' structures and entity characteristics. The DBA must maintain the integrity of the DBMS product and its supporting files. It is mandatory for management to establish corporate policies that allow the DBA the power and authority to manage the database system on a company-wide basis.

DATABASE LANGUAGES

DL/I

The most widely known hierarchical database product is IBM's IMS. Figure 5.36 shows the elements of DL/I used to manipulate an IMS database, as well as the tools used to create an IMS database. The database creation tools—the DBDGEN and the PSBGEN—are not properly part of DL/I. In this case, DL/I assumes that the database already has been defined to IMS. The DBA does this using these tools.

```
DATABASE CREATION
        DBDGEN -- DATABASE DEFINITION
        PSBGEN -- PROGRAM DEFINITION

ADDING RECORDS TO THE DATABASE
        ISRT  -- INSERT

READING THE DATABASE
        GU   -- GET UNIQUE
        GN   -- GET NEXT
        GNP  -- GET NEXT WITHIN PARENT

UPDATING THE DATABASE
        GHU  -- GET HOLD UNIQUE
        GHN  -- GET HOLD NEXT
        GHNP -- GET HOLD NEXT WITHIN PARENT
        REPL -- REPLACE

DELETING RECORDS FROM THE DATABASE
        DLET -- DELETE
```

FIGURE 5.36   *DL/I database language.*

The remainder of the DL/I elements shown in Figure 5.36 are almost exclusively used by programmers. Unlike DB2, dBASE IV, and most other relational database products, IMS does not have an end-user tool for querying a database. Instead, programmers create online systems for end users using standard programming languages such as COBOL, FORTRAN, PL/I, and so on. Programmers embed calls to DL/I in their code and pass parameters to DL/I to request different types of database access.

Creating the Database To create an IMS database, the DBA runs a DBDGEN to generate the Database Description. Then the DBA runs a PSBGEN to generate a Program Specification Block for each program that will use the database. DBDGENs and PSBGENs are assembler macros that define control blocks that IMS uses to define the schema and subschema for the database.

Adding Records to the Database Once the database has been defined, programmers can use a utility to add records from a sequential file, or they can write programs that use the ISRT DL/I call. To use the ISRT call, the program moves the data into variables that comprise an I/O area. The ISRT call then causes these data to be written to the database.

Reading the Database To read the database, the program issues the GU, GN, or GNP call. Get Unique (GU) does direct access I/O. The program places a value into the key field of the I/O area and then issues the call. Get Next (GN) does sequential I/O; the next segment is read, regardless of the value in the key field. Get Next within Parent (GNP) is used to retrieve multiple child segments; typically, the program loops through some code that contains the GNP call until the return code indicates that there are no more child segments under the current parent.

Regardless of which call is made, after the call, the I/O area contains the values read from the database.

Updating the Database Updating the database is a two-step process. First, the program must read the record that is to be updated, using Get Hold Unique (GHU), Get Hold Next (GHN), or Get Hold Next within Parent (GHNP). These calls correspond to the GU, GN, and GNP calls, respectively. But, they have one difference: As "hold" suggests, these calls make the record unavailable to other programs accessing the database.

You place "holds" on your records for data integrity. Obviously, you would not want several programs trying to update the same record simultaneously. If this were allowed, you would have partial updates from each program, because, just as one program would be in the process of updating the record, another would begin its update. Instead, IMS forces each program to read and update the record in turn. This is done by ensuring that, when one program is in the process of updating the record, other programs cannot begin the process.

Once the program has read the record using one of the hold calls, the data is copied into the I/O area, just as with any read operation. The program then can modify the data and use the REPL call to replace the record with the new data.

Deleting Records from the Database To delete a record from the database, the program must use the key. A value for the key of the record to be deleted is placed in the key field of the I/O area. The DLET call is issued, which causes the record to be deleted.

Structured Query Language

Data Definition Language Structured Query Language (SQL) has three components (Figure 5.37) with each performing a specific function. The first component is Data Definition Language (DDL), which creates the schema for the database. It contains three statements: CREATE, ALTER, and DROP. You use CREATE to define database entities. The major database entities you must

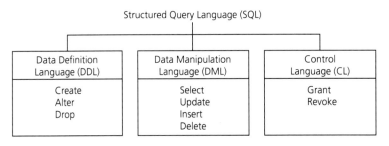

FIGURE 5.37 *Structured Query Language's three components.*

define using CREATE are: STORAGE GROUP, DATABASE, TABLESPACE, TABLE, INDEX, and VIEW.

A storage group is the set of DASD volumes that will contain the database. Remember, in mainframe environments, databases are huge and can span two or more DASD packs. You must tell both the DBMS software and the operating system the location of the databases and on what volumes they will reside. Unlike network databases, which require a schema and its associated schema compile, you use the CREATE statement multiple times to define the entities of the database. In addition, you do not have to use DMCL as you did in network databases. The CREATE statement forces the DBMS software to interact with the operating system to reserve secondary storage.

The ALTER statement lets you change the configuration of certain database entities. For example, you can alter a table and add additional columns to it. In addition, you can alter a storage group and remove and add volumes for the database.

The DROP statement expunges a database entity from the system. DDL defines the structure of the entities, not the data within them. Therefore, you can destroy a table's structure by DROPping it.

Data Manipulation Language The second component of SQL is the Data Manipulation Language (DML). DML contains the statements SELECT, UPDATE, INSERT, and DELETE. The SELECT statement reads rows from tables and has certain parameters included to identify the exact rows you want. The UPDATE statement allows you to modify certain rows, and the DELETE statement allows you to erase or expunge a row or series of rows from a table. The INSERT statement allows you to add a row or rows to a table. Each of these commands work with data by adding, modifying, erasing, or reading rows of data in a table. Whereas DDL performs operations on the structure of the database's entities, DML performs operations on the data within those structures.

Control Language The third component of SQL is Control Language (CL). CL has the two statements GRANT and REVOKE. The GRANT statement is used to give users access to the database product, entities, and language statements. Everyone on the database system must be GRANTed authority to use a particular database, tablespace, table, and columns within that table. In addition, each user is GRANTed the privilege of using either selected SQL statements or all of them. You can restrict a user to SELECTing only certain columns in a table. In this case, that is the only activity that user can perform on the DBMS. You could, however, restrict a user to accessing (SELECT) and modifying (UPDATE) all the rows but only certain columns within a table. The REVOKE statement abolishes a privilege that a GRANT had given. An IBM saying states "Whatever the GRANT giveth, the REVOKE taketh away."

CL serves the same function as the subschema in network databases. It is the security mechanism that protects the entire product and is independent of the protection mechanism for files that is available on the operating system.

Unlike the subschema in network databases, you do not have to perform a subschema compile.

THE DATABASE ENVIRONMENT

The DB2 and SQL/DS Environment

Database 2 (DB2) is a relational database system from IBM. It contains many facilities including:

- SQL for defining the structure and security of the entities and for manipulating data within those entities.
- Query Management Facility (QMF) for creating and formatting reports; QMF is a user-friendly facility that lets users generate reports using SQL or Query By Example (QBE)
- Data Extract (DXT) for converting non-DB2 data to DB2 data
- DBEDIT for creating screens so end users can quickly access data

DB2 is a product that runs on MVS/XA or MVS/ESA operating systems. For non-MVS systems, you need to use SQL's Data Systems (SQL/DS). SQL/DS and DB2 are basically identical because virtually all statements and procedures that work in DB2 also work in SQL/DS.

The IDMS/R Environment

Computer Associates' IDMS/R is a popular network database and systems generation product. IDMS/R is not only a database product, it also is a systems development tool that lets you create entire systems quickly. The following list is a summary of a few of the facilities in IDMS/R:

- Online Query (OLQ), which is a query language that allows you to access table records within the database.
- Online Mapping (OLM) for generating screens and relating data on the screens to database records and fields. It also can be used as a prototyping tool.
- Advanced Development Systems Online (ADS/O) is the system you use to generate an entire application. It includes ADS/A and ADS/G for creating applications and compiling them into load modules.
- IDD for creating and editing code, and storing description of entities.
- UC/DCF operating system to provide communications between the user and the system.

There are other facilities available in IDMS/R, but this list represents the major tools available in the product. IDMS/R runs under Cullinet's UC/DCF operating system. Therefore, in the mainframe environment, you have an operating system (UC/DCF) running under another operating system (MVS on

IBM). Here, the UC/DCF handles all communications between the terminals and the application programs and the database and the application programs.

The IMS Environment

IMS is the oldest of the mainframe products covered in this chapter. It predates both IDMS/R and DB2 by several years. To a certain extent, it is more primitive than these other products, meaning it does not have as many "bells and whistles" in the form of prototyping and end-user tools. Instead, what IBM has done is to integrate IMS into its other database strategies. As such, IMS is more of the "workhorse" of IBM databases. Primarily, it is programmers, creating sophisticated applications for end users, who will be dealing most closely with IMS.

For example, the IMS teleprocessing manager is the most frequently used online environment for programs that access DB2 databases. Another example of IMS's interfacing with newer technology is that DB2's DXT product can process DL/I databases. Finally, DL/I itself can be used with other teleprocessing managers, such as CICS.

The PC Environment

There are many database products available on the PC. These products include INGRES, ORACLE, FOCUS, and dBASE IV. In fact, there are hundreds of database products ranging from freeware products to products costing thousands of dollars. Two popular products that are available on both PCs and mainframes are ORACLE and FOCUS. With these products you can create databases on the PC and transfer them to the mainframe or vice versa. You only need to learn one set of commands when using these products and that set works for both the PC and mainframe version. In addition, the ORACLE version of SQL is DB2 and SQL/DS compatible. When you learn SQL in ORACLE you also can use the same commands and statements when you use IBM's DB2 and SQL/DS.

However, before you go out and buy these products, you need to know that there are some restrictions on their use. To use INGRES on your PC, you must have at least a 5M hard disk system and 640K of main memory. The PC version of ORACLE also requires your PC to have at least 5M of hard disk and 1M of main memory. Before you purchase either of these products, check your system's configuration to see if the product will fit into your system. Remember, the 5M of available memory is a minimum configuration. You still need additional disk space on the hard disk to be able to store the database and its associated indexes.

Another popular PC database package is dBASE IV. dBASE IV consists of a database manager that may be accessed through an end-user interface, a high-level programming language, or SQL.

There also is an application generator that can be used to create customized end-user applications. These features make dBASE IV popular with both pro-grammers and end users. In addition, because the programming language is quite powerful, a considerable number of vendors have marketed database systems written in dBASE language and designed to run under dBASE.

As is the case with the other products mentioned in this section, dBASE IV requires a fair amount of machine capacity—640K of RAM and 3.7M of hard disk space are required.

SUMMARY

Database management systems extract records from the database using a key value in some primary key field. The data with its key value resides on a 4K page within the database structure. This data can be placed in a random page within the database or in the first available space starting at the first page in the database. Each database page contains a header, an area to store the data, and a series of RID values identifying where on the page the data resides. If an index is created for the data, the index contains the key field value, the page ID, and the RID value. When instructed, the system uses the index for fast accessing of database records. When an index is used, the system first searches the index's root page and finds the leaf page containing the key value. The system then searches the leaf page to extract the data's page number and RID value. Finally, the system accesses the designated page and, using the address in the RID value, extracts the requested data from the page.

Database systems use buffers to temporarily hold data before and after database I/O operations. After an I/O operation on a database, the buffer also contains the status codes representing the outcome of the I/O operation. Programs accessing the database must contain the necessary logic to identify the status codes and handle the potential output created by a query. If output exists, it is found in the database buffer.

A database record can contain both primary keys and foreign keys. A foreign key is a field in a record or file that is a primary key field in another record or file. Primary keys can contain either unique or nonunique values. An association file containing multiple foreign keys is used to extract data in many-to-many relationships.

In network models, programmers use occurrence diagrams to aid them in coding the navigation of the database. The occurrence diagram indicates the existence of forward, backward, and owner pointers along with owner and member relationships. The schema and subschema compilers define the database structure and relationship of data within the structure to the DBMS. A schema is a complete description of the content and structure of the fields, records, and data relationships for the database. The DMCL maps the logical structure of the database to the physical DASD units. The subschema provides the security framework for users accessing data in the database because it contains each user's view of the database. Only the DBA has access to the schema, subschema, and DMCL.

In relational databases, tables contain rows and columns representing records and fields, respectively. Unlike hierarchical and network models, relational models permit the creation of a relationship between entities after the data is loaded into the database. DDL defines the structure of network entities to the DBMS.

The DBMS catalog contains the descriptions of the database entities as defined by the schema and subschema. In IDMS/R, the catalog is called the Data Dictionary. For relational databases, the catalog contains the database entity descriptions as they are defined by DDL. The DB2 catalog is an active catalog that verifies the security and the existence of the query parameters and entities.

IMS is the most popular hierarchical database. The DBDGEN and PSBGEN define the database structure to IMS. DL/I language embedded in COBOL accesses IMS data. Programmers write GET, ISRT, and DLET calls to read the data, insert data, and delete data, respectively.

Structured Query Language (SQL) has three components: Data Definition Language (DDL), Data Manipulation Language (DML), and Control Language (CL). DDL has the commands of CREATE, ALTER, and DROP to define database entities, modify them, and delete them, respectively. DML has the commands SELECT to read, UPDATE to change, INSERT to add, and DELETE to erase data from the database. In CL the GRANT command authorizes a user access to DB2 entities. The REVOKE command removes a user's authorization to access an entity.

DB2 has many facilities including SQL, QMF, DXT, and DBEDIT. QMF is a report and query writing facility that gives end users easy access to data in the database. DXT converts non-DB2 files to DB2 data and DBEDIT is an automatic screen generation facility. DB2 only runs under MVS/XA and MVS/ESA.

QUESTIONS

1. What are the three kinds of relationships that are possible between data items? How are they handled by hierarchical, network, and relational databases?
2. What is an association table? How is it used?
3. What are some of the advantages of relational databases over hierarchical and network databases?
4. What is a schema? What is a subschema?
5. What is a load library?
6. Describe the process of updating a record in an IMS database. Why is it done this way?
7. What are DDL, DML, and CL?
8. How do we provide for security when using SQL?
9. What are the advantages of using a database like ORACLE or FOCUS? What are the advantages of using dBASE IV?
10. What is DL/I?
11. What are some of the advantages of a PC-based database over a mainframe database?
12. What is the difference between a primary key, a secondary key, and a foreign key? Give an example of each.

13. What is a RID value, a leaf page, and a root page? Explain in detail how each is used in a mainframe environment.
14. What is an index? How is it used in a database environment?
15. What is a key? How is it used in a database environment?
16. What is the difference between a key and an index?
17. How does the system use an index to find a record? Elaborate.
18. What are the major advantages of creating an index? Of not creating an index?
19. What is meant by hashing? Why do we not create all files as hash files?
20. How do we determine which fields to use for the primary key in indexed files?
21. How do we determine which fields to use for the secondary key in indexed files?
22. What is the difference between a load library and a source library? What exactly is a library?
23. A company currently uses a network database and expects only modest growth over the next five years. Is there any major justification for them to switch to a relational database within the next two years?
24. What are some of the major considerations for switching from a network or hierarchical database to a relational database?
25. A company has non-IBM hardware and wants to investigate the possibilities of using IBM's DB2. List some of the problems a task force must investigate before it can recommend or not recommend the conversion.

CASE STUDY

An Information Systems Department in a large corporation consists of two sections. The first section, an Application Development Section, consists of programmers, analysts, and project managers who develop computer systems for the corporation's end users. The second section, an Application Support Section, consists of a project manager, programmers, and analysts who develop computer systems for the Information Systems Department. The Application Development Section consists of 150 employees; the Application Support Section consists of 10 employees.

When a request for a system comes from an end-user department, a project manager is assigned to the project. Depending on the complexity of the project, a certain number of programmers and analysts are also assigned to the project. Each project manager (and the programmers and analysts assigned to him) only works on one project at a time. Programmers and analysts are assigned to projects based on the completion of continuing education classes: For example, if a project requires five programmers who know dBASE, those programmers will be selected from a group of programmers who have completed a dBASE class.

This organization is flexible, but the department experiences a lot of change: For example, when a project is completed, the project manager, programmers, and analysts are reassigned to other projects. Also, programmers and analysts are periodically scheduled for continuing education classes to develop new skills.

The Application Support Section has been asked to create a database system to keep track of personnel assignments in the Information Systems Department. Management wishes to be able to keep track of which project a project manager is assigned to, which programmers and analysts are assigned to a given project, and which programmers and analysts have completed a given continuing education class. Typical uses of the database would be:

- Update the database when a project is completed (freeing personnel for new projects) or when personnel are assigned to a new project.
- Update the database when an employee completes a class.
- Obtain a report showing all programmers and analysts assigned to a given project.
- Obtain a report showing all programmers and analysts who are not currently assigned to a project and who have completed a given class.

Questions

1. What kind of database (hierarchical, network, or relational) would best suit this application?
2. How will you express the relationship between programmers and analysts and classes completed?
3. Describe the coding logic needed to produce the report showing all programmers and analysts assigned to a given project.
4. Assuming that the Application Development Section personnel will update the database and obtain their own reports, what training will be required for them to use the database?

6

Conceptual Database Design

The next three chapters will examine the process of database design. Regardless of which kind of database you are designing, you use basically the same process. First, you create a conceptual design, which is a logical model of the database. Then you create a physical design, which is a model of how the database actually will be implemented.

Proceeding from conceptual to physical design is primarily a matter of fine-tuning the database design, taking into account various trade-offs, to produce a database that will meet the user's needs in a cost-efficient manner. If you are designing a relational database, you will **normalize** the database as well. Normalizing a database means you apply certain rules which, if followed, produces a design that matches the relational model, on which relational database theory is based. These discussions will focus on the design of relational databases, because this is the most recent database technology and the trend of database software.

Before considering the design of a database, however, it is necessary to become familiar with the entire system development process, because database design is only a part of system development and must mesh with the other parts.

OVERVIEW OF SYSTEM DEVELOPMENT

All systems for processing data, whether manual, automated, or both, do basically three things: input, process, and output. Obviously, the data to be processed must be input into the system. This data can be in several forms, for example, invoices, receipts, or canceled checks for a manual system; or tapes, floppy diskettes, or telecommunications lines for an automated system. In this context, data is simply information. Anything that contains information, such as paper, computer media, or a spoken message, can be data that can be input into a system. Processing of data is using it or transforming it in some fashion. Processing can include the following:

- Selecting data you want to keep, for example, purging old records from a file
- Using data to create new data, for example, summarizing accounting information to determine credit balances and comparing them to credit limits
- Transforming data, for example, merging a transaction file with a master file to update the master file records

The new or transformed data must be output in a form that can be used by other systems or by end users. Printed reports, computer media, and teleprocessing screens are examples of output.

You can derive two key elements of system development from this scenario. First, your design of a computer system usually can be based on an existing manual system. The classic example begins with a system that is done manually. For example, an accounting system might have accounting documents, such as invoices and receipts, which are sent to bookkeepers who enter the figures into journals. Junior accountants then organize the data in journals into ledgers, and senior accountants prepare balance sheets, income statements, and other reports for company management (see Figure 6.1). The example continues when management decides to automate the system. After this is done, data-entry clerks enter the data from accounting documents into teleprocessing screens on computer terminals. The computer then processes the data and outputs the reports on request or according to some predetermined schedule (see Figure 6.2). In this case, the final system is not fully automated. Data entry is still done manually, and on-request reports very well can be triggered by verbal or written requests from management to

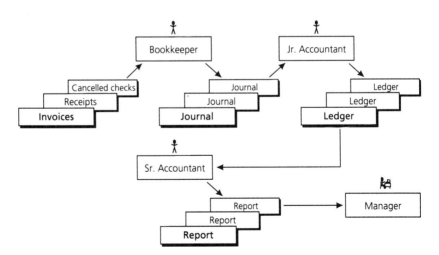

FIGURE 6.1 *A fully manual accounting system. Data from accounting documents are entered manually into journals. Data from journals are sorted manually into ledgers. Data from ledgers are used to prepare management reports.*

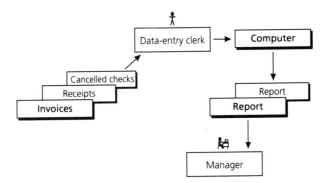

FIGURE 6.2   *A partially automated accounting system. Data from accounting documents are inputted manually into the computer, which produces management reports.*

personnel in the accounting department. In a fully automated system, data might be input from computer media or telecommunications lines, and managers might have terminals in their offices that they use to request reports from the system (see Figure 6.3).

Although this example is classic, it does not represent the most frequent case encountered in the real world. Usually we do not create an automated system from scratch by computerizing a fully manual system. Most programmers spend the large majority of their time changing an existing automated system with some manual elements. Remember, the marketplace is dynamic. As changes occur, successful businesses must change their activities to meet them, and computer systems must change to support the changing business activities.

The second key element of system development is output because it is the most important part of a system. In fact, the sole purpose of input and processing is to support output. Without output, there is no reason for the other activities of the system. Moreover, output usually is the only part of

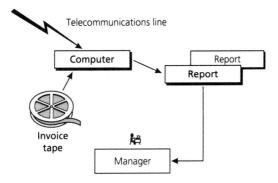

FIGURE 6.3   *A fully automated accounting system. Data from accounting documents are received in computer-readable form. The computer then produces management reports.*

the system that users ever see. The reason users request, authorize, and pay for system development is because of their need for output.

A System Development Methodology

These elements suggest that system development should begin by analyzing and understanding the current system and that the focus throughout the development process should be on the outputs. In fact, in those rare situations where there is no current system, system development can be approached by concisely defining the outputs required, and working back to the processes and inputs that will be necessary to create them. Keeping these points in mind, we can now examine the specifics of the system development process. System development consists of a series of activities that can be grouped into phases. Each phase produces outputs that are input into the following phase. Although many system development methodologies have been developed, most consist of the following phases:

1. Feasibility Study
2. Preliminary Plan
3. System Analysis
4. System Design
5. System Implementation

Table 6.1 lists these phases. Each phase has its outputs, which become inputs to the next phase.

The Feasibility Study Phase In the Feasibility Study phase, you identify the requirements of the new system. Make sure these requirements include both the existing system requirements, whether manual or automated, and any other requirements desired by management that are not currently being met.

TABLE 6.1 *A system development methodology*

Phase	Outputs
Feasibility Study	Requirements List
	Cost Estimate
	Agreed Solution
Preliminary Plan	Implementation Schedule
	Context Data Flow Diagram
System Analysis	Model Data Flow Diagram
System Design	Conceptual Database Design
	Physical Database Design
	System Structure Chart
	Program Specifications
System Implementation	Installed System
	Documentation

These requirements usually will be outputs, but they also might include operational requirements, such as user friendliness or machine efficiency. The outputs are a "laundry list" of requirements, an estimate of the gross cost of the system, and a solution that is agreed upon by the application development department and the end-user department. Typical decisions include:

- Which kind of database to use, such as relational, network, or hierarchical
- Which database software to use, for example DB2, dBASE, or IMS
- Which machine you will run the system on, for instance microcomputer, minicomputer, or mainframe

The Preliminary Plan Phase In the Preliminary Plan phase, you divide the system development into "doable" tasks. The outputs are a schedule for implementation that lists each task with an expected completion date and a Context Data Flow Diagram (DFD). A DFD is a method of representing the flow of data in any system—manual, automated, or both. DFDs will be covered in detail in a later section of this chapter. For now, all you need to know is that the Context DFD identifies the inputs and outputs of the system that come from or go to points outside of the system.

Figure 6.4 is a Context DFD for the manual accounting system in Figure 6.1. The Context DFD establishes the boundaries of the system or the scope of the project. The system must be able to accept accounting documents as inputs from other operating departments of the company as well as requests from corporate management for reports. The system also must be able to create reports as output to management, both on a regular schedule (e.g., quarterly) and on request. How the system processes data is not yet defined.

The System Analysis Phase In the System Analysis phase, you determine the processing of the current system by analyzing it and creating an Analysis DFD. The Analysis DFD shows the internal data flows of the system—it essentially is a more detailed view of the system. Figure 6.5 shows an Analysis DFD for the accounting system shown in Figure 6.1.

The Analysis DFD is not the main output of the System Analysis phase. In fact, the primary usefulness of the Analysis DFD is in the process of creating it. Diagramming the data flows of the existing system forces a methodical analysis and the eventual understanding of the existing system. The Analysis DFD also is used as a tool to create the Model DFD. The Model DFD is the

FIGURE 6.4 *A Context DFD for an accounting system. The system must accept accounting documents from other operating departments and requests for reports from management, and must generate reports for management.*

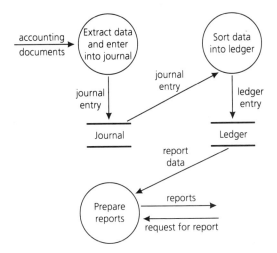

FIGURE 6.5   *An Analysis DFD for an accounting system. The Analysis DFD shows the internal data flows of the system.*

output from the System Analysis phase and shows the data flows of the new system. In this case, the flow becomes:

$$\text{Context DFD} \xrightarrow{\text{generates}} \text{Analysis DFD} \xrightarrow{\text{generates}} \text{Model DFD}$$

When creating the Model DFD, first create a Context DFD for the new system. The context of the new system will consist of two elements: a subset (which can be the entire set) of the context of the existing system; and any new external data flows necessitated by requirements of the new system that are not being met by the existing system. The first element is considered to be a subset because some requirements that the current system meets might become obsolete. If this happens, these requirements, and any associated external data flows, will be omitted from the context of the new system. When data flows for any additional requirements are added, you can create the Context DFD for the new system. After this is done, you expand the context DFD into the Model DFD, just as you expanded the Context DFD for the existing system into the Analysis DFD. System development, therefore, becomes the following equation:

the current system + modifications to the current system + new requirements = the new system

The System Design Phase   The System Design phase consists of Process Design and Database Design. The outputs of Process Design are the System Structure Chart and the Program Specifications. The System Structure Chart shows all of the programs of the new system and the hierarchy of control among them (see Figure 6.6). The Program Specifications describe the input, processing, and output for each program in the new system.

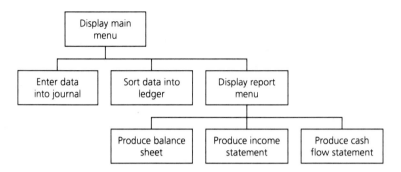

FIGURE 6.6   *A system structure chart for a hypothetical accounting system. Each box represents a program. Programs that are connected by lines to a program above them are called by that program.*

The output of Database Design are the Conceptual Database Design and the Physical Database Design. The Conceptual Database Design is a logical model of the database. The Physical Database Design is a translation of the Conceptual Database Design into a "real world" design, taking into account constraints such as machine efficiency, availability of DASD space, and so forth. Creating the Conceptual Database Design ensures that when you change the theoretical design to create the Physical Database Design, you can make intelligent choices in accommodating real constraints. The result is a practical database design that is firmly grounded in valid theory. Physical Database Design will be covered in detail in Chapter 8.

At this point, it is a good idea to consider the dynamics of Process Design versus Database Design. Although we have considered them separately, in practice it is almost impossible to separate them, and they typically proceed concurrently. The reason is that Process Design affects Database Design and Database Design affects Process Design. That means the way you must process your data affects the way you package it, and the way you package your data affects the way you process it. In practice, the System Design phase usually consists of an iterative process. Database Design proceeds until you reach a point where a portion of Process Design must be redone. Process design proceeds until you reach a point where a portion of Database Design must be redone. This process of "two steps forward and one step backward" continues until you have a tight, integrated design of both processes and data.

It might seem that this process of redoing earlier design is wasteful. However, don't forget that one of the primary goals of the system development methodology presented here is to discover and correct design errors in the most cost-efficient manner possible. Design errors are cheapest to correct during the earlier phases of development, that is, before System Implementation, when the new system exists primarily on paper. Errors are more expensive to correct during System Implementation, when program code will have to be changed. Errors are the most expensive to correct after System

Implementation, when data will have to be "backed out" of the system, corrected, and reentered into the system. In fact, in the worst cases, such errors cannot be corrected short of redeveloping the entire system. For this reason, whenever your Process Design leads to discovery of an error in the Database Design (or vice versa), you are able to correct the error in the most cost-effective manner possible. In other words, the system development methodology is working as it should.

The System Implementation Phase The System Implementation phase consists of Structured Coding, Structured Testing, Structured Installation, and Documentation. Structured Coding is a programming methodology that tends to produce systems that consist of separate modules, each of which performs a separate, distinct, and single function. This not only makes the code more readable and understandable, but also facilitates Structured Testing. Structured Testing is testing and debugging each module as it is created, rather than testing the entire system at once. This makes it easier to isolate and correct errors and facilitates Structured Installation, which is making the most critically needed portions of the system available to users first, before other portions of the system are even developed. Finally, Documentation primarily consists of gathering together outputs from the system development process, for example, the Model DFD, the System Structure Chart, the Program Specifications, and so on.

RELATIONSHIPS IN CONCEPTUAL DATABASES

Now that we have a framework of system development methodology to serve as a base, we will examine Conceptual Database Design in more detail. We will begin by considering the elements of any kind of database design (i.e., relational, network, or hierarchical), data, and relationships between data.

We have already noted that data is simply information. Data can be classified in several ways, but for our purposes here, the most useful classification is to say that data can consist of **data entities, data elements,** or **relationships** between data entities. A data entity is a discrete piece of information. A person's name, a part number, or a product color are all examples of data entities. A data element is a data entity that cannot be meaningfully broken down into other data elements. One example is a person's name, "Mr. Joe Smith, Jr." Although the name can be further broken down into title, first name, last name, and suffix, in most cases, this subdivision of a name is not useful. In such cases, the name is a data element. On the other hand, if it is necessary for a system to be able to process a name both in first name/last name order (for mailing labels) and in last name/first name order (for alphabetized lists), then the parts of the name become relevant and the name is not a data element, but a group of data elements. Thus, whether a given piece of information is a data element depends on what we want to do with it.

EMPLOYEE NUMBER	DEPARTMENT	FLOOR	VICE PRESIDENT
111-22-3333	Personnel	First	Wong Soo
999-88-7777	Supply	Third	Mary Brown
444-55-6666	Data Processing	Second	Dorothy Martinez
777-88-9999	Accounting	Second	Dave Smith
555-66-7777	Supply	Fourth	Mary Brown
111-33-2222	Accounting	Second	Dave Smith
222-33-4444	Data Processing	Second	Dorothy Martinez
333-44-5555	Personnel	First	Wong Soo

FIGURE 6.7   *Some data from an employee database. Each row shows the employee's number, the employee's department, the department's floor, and the vice president of the department.*

Relationships between data entities also can be thought of as data. Relationships between data entities can be one-to-one, one-to-many, and many-to-many relationships. Consider Figure 6.7, which shows some of the information that might be kept in an employee database.

Each row in Figure 6.7 shows the employee's number, the department the employee works in, the floor the department is located on, and the vice president of the department. The relationship between DEPARTMENT and VICE PRESIDENT is an example of a one-to-one relationship. Each department has only one vice president and each person is vice president of only one department. The relationship between DEPARTMENT and EMPLOYEE NUMBER is an example of a one-to-many relationship. A department can have many employees, but an employee can work in only one department. Finally, the relationship between DEPARTMENT and FLOOR is an example of a many-to-many relationship. A department (Supply) can be on more than one floor (Third and Fourth), and a floor (Second) can have more than one department (Accounting and Data Processing).

Some methodologies treat a one-to-one relationship as a special case of the one-to-many relationship. We will treat the two separately, however. A relationship between two data entities can be determined by asking a "has" question, for example, how many employees can a department have, how many departments can a vice president have, and so on.

Parent-Children versus Owner-Members versus Tables

Although there are basically three kinds of relationships among data entities, different kinds of database structures treat them differently. We will examine how the hierarchical, network, and relational database structures might treat the relationships between the data elements in Figure 6.7. We are dealing with data elements here for simplicity. In a real database, we would be dealing with nonelemental data entities. For example, even though EMPLOYEE NUMBER appears by itself in the discussion below, in a real database it probably would be stored along with date of employment, date of birth, and other pertinent data related to the employee.

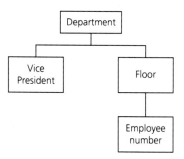

FIGURE 6.8 *Data arranged in a hierarchical structure. Data segments have parent-child relationships.*

The simplest treatment is found in hierarchical databases. Figure 6.8 shows a sample hierarchical structure for the data in Figure 6.7. In a hierarchical database structure, one-to-many and one-to-one relationships are called parent-children or parent-child relationships. DEPARTMENT is the parent of VICE PRESIDENT and FLOOR, while FLOOR is the parent of EMPLOYEE NUMBER. VICE PRESIDENT and FLOOR are the children of DEPARTMENT, and EMPLOYEE NUMBER is a child of FLOOR.

In a network database structure, relationships between data entities are called sets. Each set has an owner and consists of its owner and one or more members. Figure 6.9 shows a sample network structure for the data in Figure 6.7. The relationship between DEPARTMENT and VICE PRESIDENT is a set, as are the relationships between DEPARTMENT and EMPLOYEE NUMBER, DEPARTMENT and FLOOR, and FLOOR and EMPLOYEE NUMBER. DEPARTMENT and FLOOR are owners of their sets, and VICE PRESIDENT, EMPLOYEE NUMBER, and FLOOR are members of sets.

In a relational database structure, relationships between data entities are known as relations. In most relational database managers, relations are called tables. Figure 6.10 shows a set of tables for the data in Figure 6.7. Notice that many-to-many relationships are dealt with directly by treating the relationship itself as a data entity and storing it in a table. This is what is done in

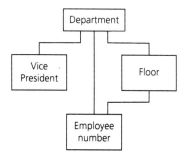

FIGURE 6.9 *Data arranged in a network structure. Data segments have owner-member relationships.*

Employee Table

EMPLOYEE NUMBER	DEPARTMENT
111-22-3333	Personnel
999-88-7777	Supply
444-55-6666	Data Processing
777-88-9999	Accounting
555-66-7777	Supply
111-33-2222	Accounting
222-33-4444	Data Processing
333-44-5555	Personnel

Department Table

DEPARTMENT	FLOOR
Personnel	First
Supply	Third
Data Processing	Second
Accounting	Second
Supply	Fourth

Vice President Table

VICE PRESIDENT	DEPARTMENT
Wong Soo	Personnel
Mary Brown	Supply
Dorothy Martinez	Data Processing
Dave Smith	Accounting

FIGURE 6.10   *Data arranged in a relational structure. Relationships are expressed as tables.*

DEPARTMENT TABLE. This table consists only of the data elements DEPARTMENT and FLOOR. It expresses the many-to-many relationship between them. Although hierarchical databases cannot express a many-to-many relationship, and network databases express them through a set of pointers used internally by the database manager, relational databases consider relations as data and express them as foreign keys in a table.

DATABASE DESIGN TOOLS

Before we examine in detail the method of creating a Conceptual Database Design, it is a good idea to become familiar with the tools available to help in this process.

Data Flow Diagrams

We already have examined several types of Data Flow Diagrams: Context DFDs, Analysis DFDs, and Model DFDs. All of these depict data flows between processes. The main difference is which processes we depict and the detail of the depiction. DFDs are composed of four symbols, which are shown in Figure 6.11. A **terminator** is represented by a rectangle, a **process** is represented by a circle, a **data flow** is represented by a line with an arrow showing the direction of the flow, and a **data store** is represented by two parallel lines. Different kinds of DFDs use different subsets of these symbols. Context DFDs use terminators, data flows, and processes; Analysis DFDs and Model DFDs use data flows, processes, and data stores. This is because different types of DFDs are intended to depict different elements of a system.

Context DFDs are used to show the boundaries of a new or existing system. Terminators are used to show sources of inputs and targets of outputs. Data flows are used to show inputs from, and outputs to, terminators. All inputs and outputs go to or from a process, which represents the system we are diagramming. At this point, the system is a "black box," represented by a single process. We will break it down to the detail level in the Analysis DFD. We never show data flows between terminators, because they are outside the scope of the system. If any data flows between terminators were within the scope of the system, we would logically move them into the process at the center of the diagram, that is, we would not show them on the context DFD. (See Figure 6.4 for an example of a Context DFD.)

Analysis DFDs and Model DFDs are used to show the details of the existing or current system. We do not use terminators in these DFDs because we are now "inside" the process in the Model DFD. Instead, we show the external data flows coming into the processes that use or produce them. Figure 6.5 is an example of an Analysis DFD. (A Model DFD would look the same.) Note that ACCOUNTING DOCUMENTS, REPORTS, and REQUESTS FOR REPORTS from the Context DFD are shown on this DFD. An Analysis DFD or a Model DFD also will show internal data stores. A data store is any place where data is stored between processes. Examples of data stores are computer media, filing cabinets, and a desk drawer.

The DFD shown in Figure 6.5 is a top-level DFD. When you construct DFDs, you use a top-down, structured approach, meaning you move from the general to the specific. Each process in the DFD can be broken down further into another, lower-level DFD that shows the process in more detail. This is known as **leveling** a DFD. For example, the PREPARE REPORTS process in Figure 6.5 can be leveled as shown in Figure 6.12.

You practice **conservation of data flows** when you level a DFD, that is,

terminator   process   data flow   data store

FIGURE 6.11   *Symbols used in DFDs. Different kinds of DFDs use different subsets of these symbols.*

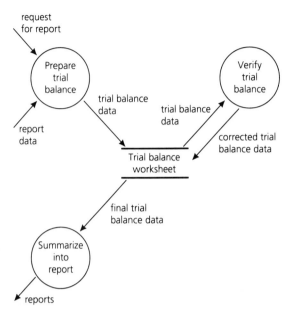

FIGURE 6.12   *A lower level of the PREPARE REPORTS process. You level a DFD until you understand the system it depicts.*

when you show all data flows into or out of the process you are leveling. In Figure 6.12, REQUEST FOR REPORT, REPORT DATA, and REPORTS are shown on the lower-level DFD. Also shown are data flows, processes, and data stores that are internal to the process you are leveling. Leveling is a technique to use to understand the system you are studying. You need only level your DFDs to the point where you understand the system. Typically, two or three levels are sufficient.

Data Dictionaries

Data Dictionaries are used to document the data entities in a system. A good data dictionary will help answer questions such as:

- "What data entities are needed to create this report?"
- "What processes must change if we begin using a nine-digit zip code?"
- "What data entities are used to calculate annualized premium?"

In short, a data dictionary documents data entities in data stores that are used by processes.

There are several automated data dictionaries on the market. All will allow the inputting of information about the following:

- The data entities

- The data stores that contain them
- The processes that use them

Most data dictionaries will produce reports from the information in the dictionary or permit users to run queries on the data in them. Some will also analyze programming code and automatically input data into the dictionary from the code.

Of course, it is also possible to create a data dictionary using a text editor. Using the simple sequential or flat file created by the text editor, you can create simple programs to access these files, as needed. Although creating a data dictionary manually is time consuming, it is almost always worth the time spent.

Data Hierarchy Charts

Hierarchy Charts are used when designing hierarchical databases. They show parent-child relationships between data entities. You create a Conceptual Data Hierarchy Chart during Conceptual Database Design and a Physical Data Hierarchy Chart to document the Physical Database Design. The Physical Data Hierarchy Chart typically is given to the DBA or someone else on the systems programming team to use in defining the database to the database management software. Figure 6.8 shows a Data Hierarchy Chart.

Entity-Relation Diagrams

Entity-Relation Diagrams are used in relational database design and show relationships between data entities. Figure 6.13 shows an Entity-Relation Diagram for the data entities in Figure 6.7. We show data entities as boxes and relationships between them as lines with arrows. The number of arrows at the end of a line is significant. A single arrow denotes a "one" relationship and a double arrow denotes a "many" relationship. Thus, there is a one-

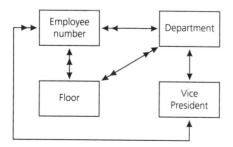

FIGURE 6.13   *An Entity-Relation Diagram. Relationships between data entities are shown by lines with arrows.*

to-many relationship between DEPARTMENT and EMPLOYEE NUMBER, a
one-to-one relationship between DEPARTMENT and VICE PRESIDENT, and a
many-to-many relationship between DEPARTMENT and FLOOR. We will
examine the use of Entity-Relation Diagrams in detail in a later section in
this chapter.

CASE Tools

Computer-Assisted Software Engineering (CASE) consists of a wide range of
products that automate the various phases of System Development. Products
that create data dictionaries were already mentioned. There also are graphics
products that assist the analyst in drawing DFDs, making it easy to create or
change a DFD and produce an attractive, easily read hardcopy on a printer.
Other helpful products include code generators, which generate stand-alone
program code to perform certain tasks according to programmers' specifications. Testing and debugging tools, which allow programmers to quickly
generate test data for their programs and isolate and examine portions of their
programming code as they operate on the data, also are handy to have. Finally,
there are prototyping tools, which allow programmers and analysts to quickly
create a working model of a new system to demonstrate how the system will
look to end users.

Fourth-Generation Languages (4GLs) are powerful and easy-to-use programming languages. The easiest way to define 4GLs is to examine the evo-
lution of programming languages. The first computers were programmed in
Machine Language, which consists solely of binary numbers. Machine Language is known as a First-Generation Language. Assemblers came next. They
translated alphanumeric mnemonics into Machine Language. This allowed
programmers to code, for example, "MVC" for a "move character" instruction
instead of the binary Machine Language instruction. Assembler Language is
known as a Second-Generation Language. Then Third-Generation Languages,
or High-Level Languages, were developed, which allowed programmers to
code a single instruction that would be translated into several Machine Language instructions. The popular programming languages COBOL, BASIC, FOR-
TRAN, and PL/I are examples of Third-Generation Languages.

All three of these languages are also known as Procedural Languages.
The programmer must not only tell the computer what to do, but how to do
it. 4GLs are Nonprocedural Languages. That means the programmer simply
tells the computer what to do, not how to do it. For example, SQL allows a
programmer to find the first row in a table where STATE is equal to "TN" by
coding:

```
SELECT * FROM MYTABLE WHERE STATE = 'TN'
```

The equivalent code in COBOL to access such a record from a file would
be:

```
        OPEN INPUT MYTABLE.
READ-LOOP.
        READ MYTABLE.
        IF STATE NOT = 'TN' GO TO READ-LOOP.
```

This COBOL code is not a good example of how to code COBOL. The example is simply intended as the shortest way to approximate the function of the SQL example. In the SQL example, you do not need to prepare the file for access (OPEN INPUT . . .), nor do you need the IF statement, which directs the program to return to the READ statement if your record does not match the selection criteria. SQL takes care of all of this for you.

Lower-generation languages also can be classified as Imperative Languages, that is, you must tell the computer what to do and, in some cases, how to do it. Fifth-Generation Languages are Declarative Languages, that is, Nonimperative Languages. In such languages as PROLOG or LISP, you only have to state a goal to be reached and the rules that the computer must follow to reach the goal. The compiler then generates code that causes the computer to apply and reapply, as necessary, the rules you stated. The results (whether the goal could be reached) are returned by the computer. Fifth-Generation Languages frequently are used to program expert systems and other artificial intelligence applications.

An interesting example of CASE is the recently announced IBM system development framework, Application Development/Cycle (AD/Cycle). AD/Cycle is a framework of integrated CASE and artificial intelligence tools developed by IBM and other vendors who have agreements with IBM that will allow IBM to market their products. IBM anticipates that program development using AD/Cycle primarily will be done by using PS/2 microcomputers with mainframe attachments. The PS/2s will be able to access a DB2 database, known as a **Repository,** on the mainframe. It will contain source code, analysis and design output, and other system development information.

AD/Cycle will follow the guidelines of Systems Application Architecture (SAA), which is a set of programming standards. These standards allow programmers to use the CUA standards to create different applications that will tend to look and "feel" alike to end users, thus simplifying training for end users who use several applications. At some time in the future these standards will allow programmers to use the Common Programming Interface (CPI) to create single applications that can run, unchanged, on microcomputers, mini-computers, or mainframes. AD/Cycle is the most ambitious and far-reaching CASE direction on the market today.

DESIGNING A RELATIONAL DATABASE

It is time to examine in detail a methodology of Conceptual Database Design, focusing on relational databases. The methodology we will examine here is known as the Entity-Relation methodology. In the next chapter, we will examine normalization as a design methodology. Normalization consists of applying a set of rules while organizing data into tables. That means, if the rules are followed, the tables will be in the format prescribed by relational database theory. In the Entity-Relation methodology, normalization is used primarily to check the design that is generated by other steps and verify that it is a proper relational design. However, it is possible to design a relational database simply by normalizing the data it is to contain.

Conceptual Database Design for a relational database consists of three steps:

1. Defining the data entities of the database
2. Defining the relationships between the data entities
3. Translating the relationships into tables

We will examine these steps in detail by considering a hypothetical application, a billing system for Professional Computer Consultants, a computer consulting firm. Although such an application probably would be implemented on a microcomputer (unless the company were larger than the average consulting firm), it makes no difference whether we are designing a microcomputer database or a mainframe database. The underlying design methodology is the same in either case.

The primary output of the billing system is a bill, such as the one shown in Figure 6.14. The bill in Figure 6.14 is known as a "paragraph" bill. Instead of itemizing each charge, billable services are grouped into paragraphs. Each paragraph summarizes the services performed pursuant to a given project— LAN installation, maintenance fees, and custom software development.

A Context DFD for the billing system as it currently exists is shown in Figure 6.15. Currently, billing is done manually. As consultants who work for Professional Computer Consultants perform various billable services for customers, they fill out slips of paper (service slips) and give them to the person who is responsible for billing. The output from the system is a monthly bill.

You can learn more about how the bill is produced by examining the Analysis DFD shown in Figure 6.16. As the Analysis DFD shows, service slips are first sorted into alphabetical order. Conversations with the user indicate that this is done manually by simply putting each slip in one of twenty-six stacks on a table. Remember to keep in contact with the user during any system development project. We will be illustrating close contact with the user throughout our design of this hypothetical system. Typically, we maintain contact with the user to get information about his or her needs, and get feedback concerning proposed elements of the new system.

As you can see from the Analysis DFD, service slips are again sorted by customer. Then they are summarized and become part of the bill. Other information that becomes a part of the bill, such as customer name and billing address, are extracted from contracts for each project.

Professional Computer Consultants
3/8/90

Jack Customer
1919 This ST
Somewhere, TN 99999

For Services Rendered:

LAN Project: Procuring LAN Hardware and
        Software, Hardware installation,
        Software installation, System testing:
        10 Hr. @ $45.00/Hr. 450.00

Desktop Publishing Project: Maintenance on
        Hardware and Software 01/01/90 –
        03/31/90 .... 200.00

Client Database Project: Feasibility Study,
        Preliminary Plan, System Analysis,
        System Design, System Implementation 1,000.00

Total 1,650.00

FIGURE 6.14   *Sample bill from Professional Computer Consultants. This is what is known as a "paragraph" bill.*

Conversations with the user identify the three different types of fees that are charged. One type is a simple hourly fee, such as the fee for the LAN Project in Figure 6.14. Another is a maintenance fee charged to provide on-request service and free software upgrades, such as the fee for the Desktop Publishing Project. Finally, there is a "set" fee charged to provide all services necessary for a given project, such as the fee charged for the Client Database Project. The type of fee charged depends on contract negotiations between the user and his customer at the beginning of a project. For this reason, the type of fee charged can differ from project to project and from customer to customer. A given project can even have more than one kind of fee charged for it, depending on the contract.

Figure 6.17 shows a Context DFD for the new system. There are some added input and output because of user requirements. The management of the consulting firm would like for the new system to be able to keep track of a customer's payments to be able to compute an account balance. Thus, the customer's payments must be input into the system and the balance must be output to management.

FIGURE 6.15   *A Context DFD for the current billing system. This is a manual system.*

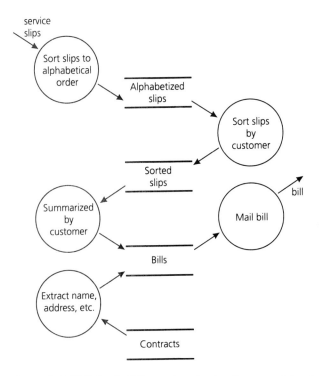

FIGURE 6.16   *An Analysis DFD for the billing system. Service slips are sorted and summarized. Then they become part of the bill.*

Figure 6.18 shows a Model DFD for the new system. The processing is similar to the existing system, with two exceptions. First, the two sorts (alphabetically and by customer) have been combined. Although it might be easier to have separate sorts when processing manually, there is no need for this when processing electronically. Second, processing has been added to handle account balances. Payments are received and posted to a payment file, which can be compared to the bill file to calculate a customer's balance.

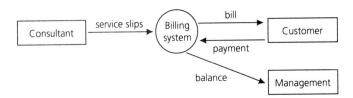

FIGURE 6.17   *A Context DFD for the new billing system. New inputs and outputs have been added because of user requirements.*

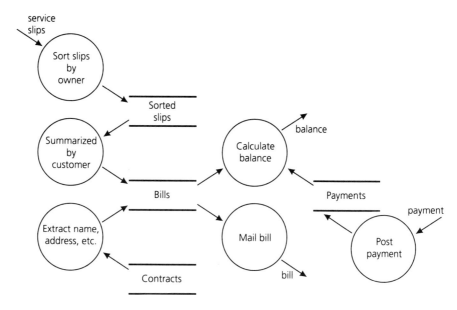

FIGURE 6.18   *A Model DFD for the new billing system. Some of the processing has been simplified, and additional processing has been added to handle account balances.*

Now that you have a basic understanding of the operation of the new system, we can proceed to design the database.

Defining the Data Entities of the Database

The best way to define the data entities of the database is to begin by examining the Model DFD in conjunction with the outputs of the system. Then list the contents of each data store. For the Billing Systems, these contents would include the data entities in Figure 6.19.

Be sure to notice the difference between a data store in the Model DFD and the data in a database. Each data store might be a separate table; then again, it might not. It is more proper to consider each data store as a view, that is, a list that indicates what data the processes accessing the data store require. Where the data actually exists is irrelevant. The four data stores in Figure 6.19 do not guarantee there will be four files or tables in the database.

For this reason, you must examine the list of items from the data stores and extract those items that are logically independent of the data store under which they are listed. For example, a service slip represents a service performed. The description of the service and the date of the service have no meaning outside of the context of the service itself. On the other hand, project names, customer names, and billing addresses do have meaning outside of the context of the bill. These items are listed under more than one data store.

SERVICE SLIP   PAYMENT
    DESCRIPTION OF SERVICE   DATE OF PAYMENT
    DATE OF SERVICE   CUSTOMER NAME
                                   AMOUNT PAID

BILL
    DATE OF BILL   CONTRACT
    HOURLY FEE   CUSTOMER NAME
    SET FEE   BILLING ADDRESS
    MAINTENANCE FEE   PROJECT NAME
    PROJECT NAME   SET FEE
    SUBTOTALS BY PROJECT   HOURLY FEE
    TOTAL AMOUNT   MAINTENANCE FEE
    CUSTOMER NAME
    BILLING ADDRESS

FIGURE 6.19   *A preliminary list of four data items for the billing system. This list is obtained by listing the contents of each data store. Each of the four data items contain a list of fields for the data item.*

Any time we see a redundant data item, there is a good chance that it is an independent data element. Similarly, an hourly fee, a set fee, and a maintenance fee represent billable items regardless of whether they have been billed yet.

After extracting those data items under each data store that have a logically independent existence and adding them to the list as nonsubordinate data items, you have the list in Figure 6.20.

We are now beginning to see the logical structure of the database. The data items listed as headings will become, after further manipulation, tables in the database. The data items listed as subordinate data items will become, again after further manipulation, columns in various tables.

Defining the Relationships between Data Entities

Having defined the data entities of the database, it is time to define the relationships between the entities. This is done by creating an Entity-Relation Diagram and then simplifying it. Figure 6.21 shows an initial Entity-Relation Diagram for the Billing System.

An Entity-Relation Diagram shows relationships between data entities. Each data entity is shown inside of a box. Relationships between data entities are shown by lines between boxes terminating in arrows. A single arrow designates a "one" relationship, while a double arrow designates a "many" relationship. For example, each CONTRACT specifies one BILLING ADDRESS. However, each BILLING ADDRESS can be found in many CONTRACTs. The diagram in Figure 6.21 shows that there is a one-to-many relationship between CONTRACTs and BILLING ADDRESSes. This is shown in Figure 6.21 symbolically as

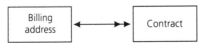

SERVICE SLIP
    DESCRIPTION OF SERVICE
    DATE OF SERVICE

PAYMENT
    DATE OF PAYMENT
    AMOUNT PAID

BILL
    BILLING DATE
    SUBTOTALS BY PROJECT
    TOTAL AMOUNT
    PROJECT NAME
    CUSTOMER NAME
    BILLING ADDRESS

CONTRACT
    HOURLY FEE
    SET FEE
    MAINTENANCE FEE

FIGURE 6.20 *A revised list of data items for the billing system. Logically independent entities have been added as nonsubordinate data items. This list contains seven independent items.*

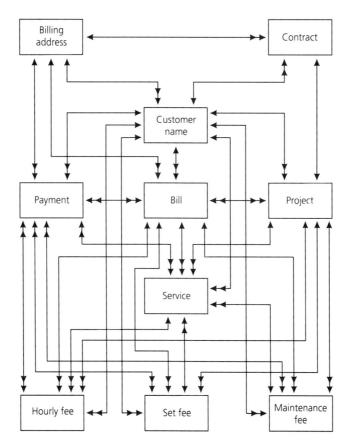

FIGURE 6.21 *An Entity-Relation Diagram for the billing system. A "one" relationship is shown by a single arrow. A "many" relationship is shown by double arrows.*

To create an Entity-Relation Diagram, begin by drawing a box for each entity. Then consider the first box and determine the relationships you need to show between it and all of the other boxes. For example, there is only one BILLING ADDRESS per CONTRACT, while there can be many CONTRACTs with the same BILLING ADDRESS. Similarly, each customer is billed at one address, though many customers might be billed at the same address. You determine the relationships by questioning the user. Relationships between data entities can be determined by asking a generic type of "has" question. A sample dialogue between an analyst and a user would be the following:

Analyst: "How many billing addresses can a contract have?"
User: "One."
Analyst: "How many contracts can a billing address have?"
User: "Several."

Now you know that you have a one-to-many relationship between contracts and billing addresses.

Sometimes the relationship is obvious. You know, for example, that many customers could be billed at one address, say a post office box. Of course, you should verify such "obvious" facts with the user. Regardless of how you determine the relationship, however, you repeat the process with each data entity until you have shown all meaningful relationships between them.

At this point, we are in a position to take the next step, which is to simplify the Entity-Relation Diagram. Figure 6.22 shows a simplified version of the Entity-Relation Diagram shown in Figure 6.21.

There are no standard rules for simplifying an Entity-Relation Diagram. It's a good idea to follow some guidelines. The first guideline is to remove unneeded or redundant relationships. An example of unneeded relationships are the relationships between CONTRACT and BILLING ADDRESS and CUSTOMER NAME. Even though BILLING ADDRESS and CUSTOMER NAME are derived from the contract, you have decided already that they probably will be separate tables of their own. In addition, consider the process of billing. You doubtless will be scanning the SERVICE table for services to bill as of a given date and matching services with projects from the PROJECT table. Once you know the project, you can determine the customer name, and once you know the customer name, you can determine the billing address. So you really do not need to express the relations between the contract and these entities.

An example of redundant relationships are the relationships between PROJECT and SET FEE, HOURLY FEE and MAINTENANCE FEE. These relationships are redundant because you also express relationships between SERVICE and the three types of fee. Because you express a relationship between PROJECT and SERVICE, you can associate any project with the fees it generated without having to express direct relationships between it and the fees.

Figure 6.23 shows the Entity-Relation Diagram after we have eliminated all unneeded and redundant relationships. This is an intermediate stage of the diagram somewhere between the initial stage (Figure 6.21) and the final stage (Figure 6.22).

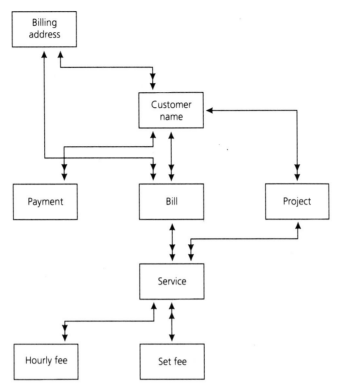

FIGURE 6.22 *A simplified version of an Entity-Relation Diagram. There are no hard-and-fast rules for simplifying an Entity-Relation Diagram.*

Another guideline for simplifying an Entity-Relation Diagram is to combine data entities when one is logically a subset of another. An example is MAINTENANCE FEE. Through conversations with the user, you learn that a maintenance fee is simply another type of set fee—there is no real reason to keep them separate. SET FEE and MAINTENANCE FEE both have the same relationships to other data entities in Figure 6.21. Although this does not always indicate that the two data entities should be combined, it is a clue that suggests that you should reexamine them to determine whether they are really different logical entities.

A final guideline is to consider combining data entities that have a one-to-one relationship when one of the data entities has no relationships to any other data entities. An example is CONTRACT. It has a one-to-one relationship with PROJECT and no other relationships with any other data entities. Sometimes it is useful to keep data entities separate in such circumstances, but in this case, there is no reason not to combine the data entities. CONTRACT is a physical document from which you have already extracted the major data elements (such as name and address) into tables of their own. Also, although it is useful to maintain a pointer to where the physical document can be

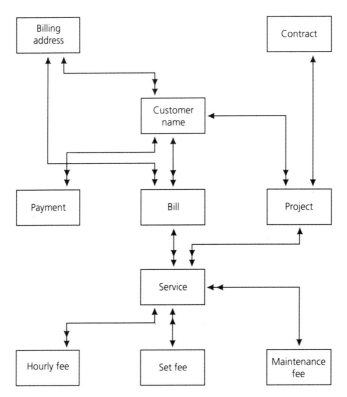

FIGURE 6.23 *The Entity-Relation Diagram after unneeded and redundant relationships have been deleted. This is an intermediate stage of the diagram.*

located (which filing cabinet drawer it is kept in), this is probably all that you will keep in this table. For these reasons, you can combine the contents of CONTRACT with those of PROJECT.

Translating the Relationships into Tables

Having defined the data entities of the database and the relationships between them, it is time to translate the relationships into tables. This is done by performing the following three steps:

1. Defining primary keys for each data entity
2. Translating relationships into foreign keys
3. Normalizing the database

   Normalizing a database can be used as a database design methodology in its own right. For this reason, we will defer consideration of normalization techniques until the next chapter. For now, you only need remember that the last step in the Entity-Relation methodology is to normalize the database as a means of verifying that you have created a valid relational database structure. The Entity-Relation methodology tends to produce normalized databases in any event. However, you normalize the database just for verification.

The next step is to define primary keys for each data entity. In formal relational theory, a primary key is not just a method of accessing a given row; it is a unique identifier for a given data entity. Some relational database managers, such as DB2, allow you to create nonunique primary keys. DB2, does, however, allow you to enforce uniqueness among primary keys by creating a unique index on a primary key. Because relational theory considers a primary key to be an identifier rather than an access path, however, primary keys must be unique. Recall that one of the goals of a relational database is to eliminate data redundancy—you don't want to allow duplicate occurrences of the same data entity. Because the primary key is the identifier of the data entity, if data entities can occur only once, their keys also must be unique.

There are two kinds of primary keys in relational theory, simple and combined. A **simple key** is a key that is composed of one and only one data element. An example would be a social security number as a key for a table containing information about students. A **combined key** is a key that is composed of more than one data element. An example would be a table containing information about dormitory rooms. To uniquely identify a room, use a key that consists of both room number and dormitory name.

From a practical standpoint, there are many ways to create a key for a table row. If a unique identifier already exists among the data entities you have decided to store in a row, you can use it. For example, suppose an insurance company needs to store the social security number of policy holders for purposes of meeting IRS reporting requirements for claim payments. In this case, the social security number also can be used as the key for a policy holder table.

However, when no unique identifier exists, you need to generate a key. An example is the customer name in your billing table. You cannot use the name itself as the key because you cannot guarantee uniqueness. It is quite possible that your user could have several different customers named "John Richard Smith." We are not storing social security numbers. Indeed, because you do not have any legal requirements to store social security numbers, a customer might be reluctant to divulge his or her number. In this case, you will simply generate a unique number for the customer. This can be done by determining the largest number of customers you expect the table to hold and creating a column large enough to hold that maximum number. For example, if you never expect to have more than 10,000,000 customers over the life of the billing system, you can create a key column large enough to hold the number 10,000,000. Then, whenever you add a new customer, you simply find the largest customer number that currently exists and add one to it to create a key for the new customer.

After defining keys for each data entity, we have the tables in Figure 6.24.

```
SERVICE SLIP                      BILLING ADDRESS
    SERVICE KEY                       ADDRESS KEY
    SERVICE DESCRIPTION               ADDRESS
    SERVICE DATE
                                  PAYMENT
BILL                                  PAYMENT KEY
    BILL KEY                          PAYMENT DATE
    BILLING DATE                      AMOUNT PAID
    SUBTOTALS BY PROJECT
    TOTAL AMOUNT                  HOURLY FEE
                                      HOURLY FEE KEY
PROJECT NAME                          HOURLY FEE
    PROJECT KEY
    PROJECT NAME                  SET FEE
    CONTRACT NUMBER                   SET FEE KEY
                                      SET FEE
CUSTOMER NAME
    CUSTOMER KEY
    CUSTOMER NAME
```

FIGURE 6.24   *Tables for the billing system with keys assigned. Each table contains fields or columns that will be stored in the table.*

You must now translate the relationships between the tables into foreign keys. Relational databases are different from other types of databases because relationships between data entities are themselves considered to be data. Therefore, unlike network or hierarchical databases, which express relationships as pointers that are kept external to the data, relational databases internalize relationships into the data structure. This is done via foreign keys.

There are two types of relationships in the database: one-to-many and many-to-many. For these purposes, a one-to-one relationship can be treated as a special type of one-to-many relationship because they are handled in the same manner. One-to-many relationships are handled by adding the key of the table on the "one" side of the relationship to the table on the "many" side of the relationship. For example, the key of BILLING ADDRESS should be added to both CUSTOMER NAME and BILL. After repeating this process for all one-to-many relationships, we have the tables in Figure 6.25.

Many-to-many relationships are handled by creating a separate table that expresses only the relationship between two other tables. This table is called an **association table.** The association table expresses relationships via foreign keys. Therefore, you create the following table (called SERVICE BILL) to express the many-to-many relationship between SERVICE and BILL:

```
SERVICE BILL
    SERVICE KEY
    BILL KEY
```

The table SERVICE BILL consists of nothing other than the keys from the two tables it associates. Because this table represents nothing other than a relationship, its primary key is the combined key consisting of the two foreign keys.

Our final database design consists of the tables in Figure 6.26.

SERVICE SLIP
    SERVICE KEY
    SERVICE DESCRIPTION
    SERVICE DATE
    PROJECT KEY
    SET FEE KEY

BILL
    BILL KEY
    BILLING DATE
    SUBTOTALS BY PROJECT
    TOTAL AMOUNT
    ADDRESS KEY
    CUSTOMER KEY

PROJECT NAME
    PROJECT KEY
    PROJECT NAME
    CONTRACT NUMBER
    CUSTOMER KEY

CUSTOMER NAME
    CUSTOMER KEY
    CUSTOMER NAME
    ADDRESS KEY

BILLING ADDRESS
    ADDRESS KEY
    ADDRESS

PAYMENT
    PAYMENT KEY
    PAYMENT DATE
    AMOUNT PAID
    CUSTOMER KEY

HOURLY FEE
    HOURLY FEE KEY
    HOURLY FEE
    SERVICE KEY

SET FEE
    SET FEE KEY
    SET FEE

FIGURE 6.25 *Tables for the billing system with one-to-many relationships shown. This is done by using foreign keys.*

SERVICE SLIP
    SERVICE KEY
    SERVICE DESCRIPTION
    SERVICE DATE
    PROJECT KEY
    SET FEE KEY

BILL
    BILL KEY
    BILLING DATE
    SUBTOTALS BY PROJECT
    TOTAL AMOUNT
    ADDRESS KEY
    CUSTOMER KEY

PROJECT NAME
    PROJECT KEY
    PROJECT NAME
    CONTRACT NUMBER
    CUSTOMER KEY

CUSTOMER NAME
    CUSTOMER KEY
    CUSTOMER NAME
    ADDRESS KEY

BILLING ADDRESS
    ADDRESS KEY
    ADDRESS

PAYMENT
    PAYMENT KEY
    PAYMENT DATE
    AMOUNT PAID
    CUSTOMER KEY

HOURLY FEE
    HOURLY FEE KEY
    HOURLY FEE
    SERVICE KEY

SET FEE
    SET FEE KEY
    SET FEE

SERVICE BILL
    SERVICE KEY
    BILL KEY

FIGURE 6.26 *The final database design for the billing system.*

The final step is to normalize the database, which will be covered in the next chapter. Keep in mind, however, the importance of this verification step. In the database in Figure 6.26, we have committed one normalization error that we will correct when we normalize the database.

SUMMARY

All computer systems do basically three things: input, process, and output. Usually, some part of this is done manually. Keep in mind that, from the user's standpoint, the output is the most important part of the system.

A typical system development methodology consists of a Feasibility Study, a Preliminary Plan, System Analysis, System Design, and System Implementation. Each phase has outputs that are input to the next phase. During System Design, you create the Conceptual Database Design. Process Design and Database Design each affect the other.

In a relational system, data consists of data entities, data elements, and relationships. Relationships can be one-to-one, one-to-many, or many-to-many. Hierarchical databases express one-to-one or one-to-many relationships as parent-child relationships. Network databases express all relationships as owner-member relationships. Relational databases express all relationships as tables.

There are many database design tools. Data Flow Diagrams show data stores and processes and the data flows between them. Data Dictionaries show what data entities are required for certain processes. Data Hierarchy Charts show parent-child relationships. Entity-Relation Diagrams show data entities and the relationships between them.

There are also many CASE tools. Fourth-Generation Languages relieve us of the necessity of telling the computer how to perform tasks. Fifth-Generation Languages relieve us of the necessity of telling the computer in which order to perform tasks. Perhaps the most ambitious CASE direction today is IBM's AD/Cycle.

Designing a conceptual database consists of defining the data entities of the database, defining the relationships between the data entities, and translating the relationships into tables. The Entity-Relation methodology uses Entity-Relation diagrams to do this. We first create an Entity-Relation Diagram, and then we simplify it. Then, after defining primary keys for each data entity, we translate the relationships into foreign keys and normalize the database. Many-to-many relationships are expressed via an association table.

QUESTIONS

1. All systems for processing data do basically three things. What are they?
2. Does system development typically involve automating a completely manual system?

3. What are the five phases of a typical system development methodology?
4. In what phase does database design take place?
5. What is a Context DFD? An Analysis DFD? A Model DFD?
6. What kinds of relationships can exist between data entities?
7. How are relationships handled in hierarchical databases? Network databases? Relational databases?
8. Describe the symbols used in DFDs and their meanings.
9. What is leveling?
10. What is an Entity-Relation Diagram?
11. Describe some types of CASE tools.
12. What is a 4GL?
13. What is a Fifth-Generation Language?
14. List the steps we take to design a relational database.
15. How do we simplify an Entity-Relation Diagram?
16. Why does relational theory only deal with unique primary keys?
17. What is a simple key? A combined key?
18. What is an association table? What is its primary key?
19. A DP Director of a medium-size firm wants to promote one of its programmers to a Systems Analyst position. So that the new Analyst will have the necessary skills to perform his or her new job functions, the Director wants to send the new Analyst to Yourdon's Systems Analysis and Design classes. Each class (one in Analysis and one in Design) lasts for a week. Each class will be offered next month in New York, San Francisco, and Miami. The tuition for the two one-week classes is $1,400 per class. Construct a travel budget for traveling to one of these cities for the two classes. What is the total cost for this training? What is the real cost to the company for this training?

CASE STUDY   Acme University (AU) has a class scheduling system that they would like to rewrite as a relational database system. Currently, all data for class scheduling resides in a sequential master file with the following format:

```
01  CLASS-SCHEDULE
    03  CLASS-ID.
        05  CLASS-DEPARTMENT        PIC X(20).
        05  CLASS-NUMBER            PIC X(3).
    03  CLASS-DESCRIPTION           PIC X(20).
    03  CLASS-INSTRUCTORS
        05  CLASS-PROFESSOR         PIC X(20).
        05  CLASS-GRAD-ASSISTANT    OCCURS 3 TIMES
                                    PIC X(20).
    03  CLASS-ROOM                  PIC X(3).
    03  CLASS-BUILDING              PIC X(20).
    03  CLASS-DAY-TIME              OCCURS 5 TIMES.
        05  CLASS-DAY               PIC X.
        05  CLASS-TIME              PIC X(4).
    03  NUMBER-OF-ENROLLMENTS       PIC 999.
```

There is one record for each class in the catalog, for example, Information Systems 101. Each class has one description (e.g., "Fundamentals of Programming"), and is taught by one instructor and up to three graduate assistants. Each class is taught in one room of one building. The room can be scheduled for the class up to five times per week. The number of students enrolled in the class is also stored.

Question

1. Design a relational database to handle and contain the above data using the Entity-Relation methodology.

7 *Normalization*

We will now examine normalization, both as a design tool and as a design methodology. Normalization is a tool used in other design methodologies, for example, the Entity-Relation methodology presented in Chapter 6. However, we also will present the techniques of normalization here in the context of a design methodology. In this chapter we will design the Billing System of Chapter 6 in a way that relies almost exclusively on normalization.

So far we have examined design techniques in a nonrigorous fashion. Instead of concerning ourselves with the details of relational design theory, we have instead aimed for a more intuitive understanding of their practical application. This is, in fact, the standpoint from which most systems analysts and systems designers approach system development. Understanding normalization will require that we probe somewhat more deeply into theoretical aspects. Normalization is strongly based on relational database theory, which is in turn based on the mathematical theory of relations. However, our focus still will be on a practical understanding, which we will attempt to reconcile with theoretical aspects.

With this in mind, you should be aware that the normalization "rules" that will be covered later in this chapter are really only guidelines. Relational databases are rarely fully normalized. In fact, one of the phases of Physical Database Design is to determine whether to "unnormalize" our Conceptual Database Design to some extent, taking into account the dynamics of how our particular application will use the database as well as the environment under which our application will execute with its processing and storage constraints. These matters will be more fully discussed in Chapter 8.

OVERVIEW OF NORMALIZATION: THEORY VERSUS PRACTICE

When examining the details of normalization, consider the following:

- The purpose of normalization
- The role of keys in normalization

- The concept of functional dependence in normalization
- The terminology of normalization

Let's look at some of these aspects with regard to both theoretical and practical considerations.

One of the purposes of normalization is to reduce data redundancy because data redundancy can lead to data inconsistency. For example, consider the unnormalized table of employees, companies, and company addresses in Figure 7.1.

If a company listed in the table should move to a new location, several rows in the table would have to be updated with the new address. If any row is not updated for some reason, such as human error, the table would contain inconsistent data. A normalized database design would use two tables to contain this information. Such tables are given in Figure 7.2. Now, with the data selectively split between two tables, when a company changes location, only one row needs to be updated.

In this example, we have implicitly assumed that the columns EMPLOYEE and COMPANY are keys for their respective tables. Keys are integral to normalization—most normalization rules are based on keys. Remember that **primary keys** are considered identifiers of a row in relational theory, **foreign keys** are columns in a table that are keys to another table and that express relationships. **Combined keys** are keys that are made up of data from more than one column. Relational database theory includes the concept of two other kinds of key—candidate keys and alternate keys.

Candidate keys are columns (or combinations of columns) that uniquely identify their row. Typically, these are the columns we choose as primary keys. **Alternate keys** are candidate keys that we have not chosen as primary keys.

Consider the table of tax data for self-employed people who own one and only one business in Figure 7.3. All of the first three columns in Figure 7.3 are candidate keys. Remember, given these assumptions concerning the data in the table, there can only be one social security number, tax ID, or business license number for any particular person. If you choose SOCIAL SECURITY NUMBER as a primary key, FEDERAL TAX ID and BUSINESS LICENSE NUMBER become alternate keys.

In relational database theory, there always must be at least one candidate key for every table. Recall, however, that in practice you do not always find

EMPLOYEE TABLE

EMPLOYEE	COMPANY	COMPANY ADDRESS
JOHN DOE	ABC COMPANY	123 ANY STREET
JANE DOE	XYZ COMPANY	456 SOME AVENUE
JOHN Q. PUBLIC	ABC COMPANY	123 ANY STREET
SAM SMITH	XYZ COMPANY	456 SOME AVENUE
SALLY SMITH	XYZ COMPANY	456 SOME AVENUE

FIGURE 7.1   *An unnormalized table of employees, companies, and company addresses.*

EMPLOYEE TABLE

EMPLOYEE	COMPANY
JOHN DOE	ABC COMPANY
JANE DOE	XYZ COMPANY
JOHN Q. PUBLIC	ABC COMPANY
SAM SMITH	XYZ COMPANY
SALLY SMITH	XYZ COMPANY

COMPANY TABLE

COMPANY	COMPANY ADDRESS
ABC COMPANY	123 ANY STREET
XYZ COMPANY	456 SOME AVENUE

FIGURE 7.2   *A partially normalized table of employees, companies, and company addresses with data redundancy eliminated.*

a candidate key among the data entities that you can store. Sometimes you must allow the system to generate a key, which might be just a sequential number. There are two viewpoints from which this seeming discrepancy between theory and practice can be resolved.

First, from the viewpoint of relational database theory, it does not really matter whether the data you store has any relationship to the "real world" you are attempting to "data-fy." Relational theory concerns itself instead with the relationships between the data entities you do store. In fact, relational theory allows you to meet the requirement of at least one candidate key per table by considering the entire row to be a combined key. Because no two rows will be exactly identical across all columns, you have a unique key. (Generally this is considered to be a trivial solution.) In other words, a bill number that a system generates for a key is considered to be as "valid" a candidate key as a bill number that actually appears on the bill.

Second, from a practical standpoint, you frequently find that some candidate key, such as a bill number, an invoice number, or a check number actually is printed on the document you wish to data-fy. Such a key also is used frequently to manually retrieve a copy of the document, prepare reports about the document, and identify the document in correspondence. In such cases, you obviously have a valid candidate key. Of course, the small billing system we designed in the previous chapter did not have such a key printed on the actual bill. This would tend to indicate that the system processes a relatively small volume of data. This is usually the case when you automate

SOCIAL SECURITY NUMBER	FEDERAL TAX ID	BUSINESS LICENSE NUMBER	DEDUCTIBLE BUSINESS EXPENSES
123456789	1234567890	1234567	1234.56
234567890	2345678901	2345678	2345.67
345678901	3456789012	3456789	1234.56

FIGURE 7.3   *A table of tax data for self-employed persons who own one and only one business. The first three columns are candidate keys.*

an existing manual system. However, as the business grows and more and more bills are printed, users probably will find it necessary to print some identifying number on each bill. Because the number is used to identify the bill in correspondence and reports, the number serves the same purpose in practice that it does in theory.

In relational database theory, the relationship between a primary key column and other columns in a row is based on the concept of **functional dependence.** In theory,

> *Column B is functionally dependent on column A if and only if for each value of column A there can be only one value of column B at any particular time.*

For example, in a table showing family relationships, the column MOTHER is functionally dependent on the column CHILD, because each child has only one mother. When two children have the same mother, MOTHER is still functionally dependent on CHILD. In practice, we tend to say that:

> *Column B is functionally dependent on column A if and only if column B represents a fact about column A that has only one value which is true for an occurrence of column A at any one time.*

For example, if the value of CHILD is John, the value of MOTHER always will be Sue at any one time. The phrase "at any one time" is significant. Sue can die and John can be adopted by Elaine. However, MOTHER is still functionally dependent on CHILD.

Is there a discrepancy between theory and practice? The answer is "no." The practical definition has essentially added an extra constraint to the theoretical definition. Not only must there be a one-to-one or a one-to-many relationship between column B and column A, but column B must also be a fact about column A. This tends naturally to result because you tend to keep facts about the same thing grouped together when designing any kind of database or file system. For example, you would not store a university's class scheduling data in a student dormitory file.

We already have dealt with several terms of relational theory—candidate keys, alternate keys, and functional dependence. Now we will consider some terms that are specific to normalization.

Normalization rules are stated in terms of normal forms. A **normal form** is a description of the rules that a database at a certain level of normalization must follow. There are several levels of normalization including:

- First Normal Form (1NF)
- Second Normal Form (2NF)
- Third Normal Form (3NF)
- Fourth Normal Form (4NF)
- Fifth Normal Form (5NF)

We will focus here on the first three because 4NF and 5NF are based on rather complicated theoretical considerations and are rarely used in practice. Each level of normalization imposes additional constraints on the level below

COURSE INSTRUCTOR TABLE

CLASS CODE	PROFESSOR	GRADUATE ASSISTANT	GRADUATE ASSISTANT	GRADUATE ASSISTANT
IS101	J. DOE	J. PUBLIC	S. SMITH	J. JONES
MIS101	S. SNEED			
MIS213	J. DOE	A. SNYDER		
IS301	R. JONES	J. SMITH	A. JONES	

FIGURE 7.4 *A table that is not in 1NF. There is a variable number of graduate assistants for each class.*

it. That is, a database in 2NF also must be in 1NF, and a database in 3NF also must be in 2NF.

THE NORMAL FORMS

A table is in 1NF if and only if each row contains the same number of columns (i.e., there are no repeating columns). For example, the table in Figure 7.4, which contains names of instructors and graduate assistants for classes, is not in 1NF.

A given class can have a variable number of graduate assistants, which violates 1NF. To normalize such a table with regard to 1NF, you must construct a second table to contain the repeating data. This has been done in Figure 7.5.

In Figure 7.5 the repeating data has been extracted to the second table. The relationship between the second table and the first has been expressed via the foreign key CLASS CODE.

A table is in 2NF if and only if the table is in 1NF and every column that is not a part of the key is functionally dependent on the whole key. This

COURSE INSTRUCTOR TABLE

CLASS CODE	PROFESSOR
IS101	J. DOE
MIS101	S. SNEED
MIS213	J. DOE
IS301	R. JONES

GRADUATE ASSISTANT TABLE

GRADUATE ASSISTANT	CLASS CODE
J. PUBLIC	IS101
S. SMITH	IS101
J. JONES	IS101
A. SNYDER	MIS213
J. SMITH	IS301
A. JONES	IS301

FIGURE 7.5 *Data in 1NF. The repeating data has been extracted to a second table, which is related to the first via a foreign key.*

CLASSROOM TABLE

BUILDING	ROOM	SEATING CAPACITY	NUMBER OF FLOORS
JOHNSON HALL	101	30	3
JOHNSON HALL	203	200	3
ART BUILDING	201	45	2
GEOLOGY BUILDING	101	120	1

FIGURE 7.6   *A CLASSROOM table that violates 2NF. A combined key (BUILDING and ROOM) is used.*

CLASSROOM TABLE

BUILDING	ROOM	SEATING CAPACITY
JOHNSON HALL	101	30
JOHNSON HALL	203	200
ART BUILDING	201	45
GEOLOGY BUILDING	101	120

BUILDING TABLE

BUILDING	NUMBER OF FLOORS
JOHNSON HALL	3
ART BUILDING	2
GEOLOGY BUILDING	1

FIGURE 7.7   *The data from Figure 7.6 in a normalized structure with regard to 2NF. Again, we have extracted data into a second table.*

CLASS TABLE

CLASS	INSTRUCTOR	INSTRUCTOR'S OFFICE ADDRESS
IS101	J. JONES	101 HOOPER HALL
GEO201	S. SMITH	201 GEOLOGY BUILDING
MIS102	J. SMITH	301 MIS BUILDING
IS203	J. JONES	101 HOOPER HALL

FIGURE 7.8   *A table of classes with instructor data. This table violates 3NF.*

CLASS TABLE

CLASS	INSTRUCTOR
IS101	J. JONES
GEO201	S. SMITH
MIS102	J. SMITH
IS203	J. JONES

INSTRUCTOR TABLE

INSTRUCTOR	INSTRUCTOR'S OFFICE ADDRESS
J. JONES	101 HOOPER HALL
S. SMITH	201 GEOLOGY BUILDING
J. SMITH	301 MIS BUILDING

FIGURE 7.9   *Data normalized using 3NF. We extracted data from one table to form a second table.*

definition imposes two additional constraints on 1NF: nonkey columns must be functionally dependent on the key, and nonkey columns must not be functionally dependent on only part of the key. Of course, the second constraint is automatically fulfilled if you do not have a combined key.

Figure 7.6 shows a table of classrooms that violates 2NF. The table has a combined key (BUILDING and ROOM). In this example, SEATING CAPACITY is functionally dependent on the whole key. NUMBER OF FLOORS, however, is functionally dependent on BUILDING but not ROOM. To remedy this, you must again extract data into a second table, as in Figure 7.7.

A table is in 3NF if and only if the table is in 2NF and every column that is not a part of the key is functionally dependent only on the key (i.e., is not functionally dependent on another nonkey column). Figure 7.8 shows a table of classes with data concerning instructors for each class.

In the example, if CLASS is the key, the table violates 3NF because INSTRUCTOR'S OFFICE ADDRESS is functionally dependent on a nonkey field (i.e., INSTRUCTOR). To remedy this, you again extract data into a second table, as in Figure 7.9.

─────── **NORMALIZATION AS A DESIGN METHODOLOGY**

Normalization can be used both as part of a design methodology, such as the Entity-Relation methodology, and as a methodology in its own right. In this section, we will examine both uses of normalization.

The Entity-Relation methodology relies on normalization as a final check on the design. In Chapter 6, you developed a final design with the tables (Figures 7.10 and 6.26).

It is time to normalize the database. To begin, check the tables for any repeating columns. Check for violations of 1NF. There is only one table that violates this constraint, BILL. Obviously, the "column" SUBTOTALS BY PROJECT conceals a repeating column because there are many such subtotals per bill. (See Figure 6.14.) Therefore, you must extract the subtotals data into a second table:

BILL
     BILL KEY
     BILLING DATE
     TOTAL AMOUNT
     ADDRESS KEY
     CUSTOMER KEY

PROJECT SUBTOTAL
     PROJECT KEY
     BILL KEY
     AMOUNT

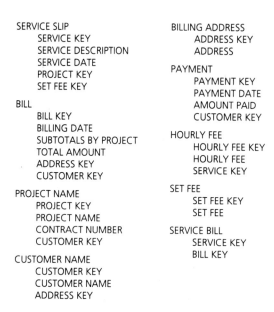

SERVICE SLIP
   SERVICE KEY
   SERVICE DESCRIPTION
   SERVICE DATE
   PROJECT KEY
   SET FEE KEY

BILL
   BILL KEY
   BILLING DATE
   SUBTOTALS BY PROJECT
   TOTAL AMOUNT
   ADDRESS KEY
   CUSTOMER KEY

PROJECT NAME
   PROJECT KEY
   PROJECT NAME
   CONTRACT NUMBER
   CUSTOMER KEY

CUSTOMER NAME
   CUSTOMER KEY
   CUSTOMER NAME
   ADDRESS KEY

BILLING ADDRESS
   ADDRESS KEY
   ADDRESS

PAYMENT
   PAYMENT KEY
   PAYMENT DATE
   AMOUNT PAID
   CUSTOMER KEY

HOURLY FEE
   HOURLY FEE KEY
   HOURLY FEE
   SERVICE KEY

SET FEE
   SET FEE KEY
   SET FEE

SERVICE BILL
   SERVICE KEY
   BILL KEY

FIGURE 7.10   *The final database design for the billing system before normalization.*

The PROJECT SUBTOTAL table has a combined key that consists of two foreign keys, PROJECT KEY and BILL KEY. The reason is that a subtotal by project is related to both the bill in which it is included and the project that it references. You have corrected a very basic design error. When you began designing a database, you really did not have a clear understanding of what was meant by SUBTOTALS BY PROJECT. Recall that one of the purposes of applying the rules of normalization is to check your design. In other words, you want to detect and correct errors before the design becomes finalized. You now have the database design as shown in Figure 7.11.

Now check the tables for violations of 2NF and 3NF. All nonkey fields must be functionally dependent on the whole key and only the whole key. There are no such violations in the tables we have, so the final conceptual database design is as shown in Figure 7.11. In this case you need only check tables with combined keys for violations of 2NF. Recall that the Entity-Relation methodology tends to produce a normalized design. The violation of 1NF that we corrected earlier was not so much a failure of the methodology as a failure to properly understand and define the data entities.

Now we will examine normalization as a design methodology of its own. This use of normalization best lends itself to cases where the data is already identified and organized into some logical order. A typical example is when you convert a nonrelational database system to a relational database system. It also can be used when automating a manual system, such as the billing system.

SERVICE SLIP
    SERVICE KEY
    SERVICE DESCRIPTION
    SERVICE DATE
    PROJECT KEY
    SET FEE KEY

BILL
    BILL KEY
    BILLING DATE
    TOTAL AMOUNT
    ADDRESS KEY
    CUSTOMER KEY

PROJECT NAME
    PROJECT KEY
    PROJECT NAME
    CONTRACT NUMBER
    CUSTOMER KEY

CUSTOMER NAME
    CUSTOMER KEY
    CUSTOMER NAME
    ADDRESS KEY

BILLING ADDRESS
    ADDRESS KEY
    ADDRESS

PAYMENT
    PAYMENT KEY
    PAYMENT DATE
    AMOUNT PAID
    CUSTOMER KEY

HOURLY FEE
    HOURLY FEE KEY
    HOURLY FEE
    SERVICE KEY

SET FEE
    SET FEE KEY
    SET FEE

SERVICE BILL
    SERVICE KEY
    BILL KEY

PROJECT SUBTOTAL
    PROJECT KEY
    BILL KEY
    AMOUNT

FIGURE 7.11   *The database design after the first step of normalization. The database is now in 1NF.*

Begin with the list of data entities created by listing the contents of the data stores on the Model DFD. (See Figures 7.12 and 6.20.)

Now examine the data entities in light of the required outputs from the system. In this case, the main output is a bill, so you begin with a preliminary BILL table with data entities grouped under it, as shown in Figure 7.13. This is the table that you will normalize.

Before you normalize this table, you must choose a key for it. Typically, you will do this with every table you create as you go through the process of normalization. You will create a key for the table, and call it BILL KEY. The table now appears as shown in Figure 7.14.

SERVICE SLIP
    DESCRIPTION OF SERVICE
    DATE OF SERVICE

BILL
    BILLING DATE
    HOURLY FEE
    SET FEE
    MAINTENANCE FEE
    SUBTOTALS BY PROJECT
    TOTAL AMOUNT
    PROJECT NAME
    CUSTOMER NAME
    BILLING ADDRESS

PAYMENT
    DATE OF PAYMENT
    CUSTOMER NAME
    AMOUNT PAID

CONTRACT
    CUSTOMER NAME
    BILLING ADDRESS
    PROJECT NAME
    HOURLY FEE
    SET FEE
    MAINTENANCE FEE

FIGURE 7.12   *A preliminary list of data items for the billing system.*

```
BILL                                         SUBTOTALS BY PROJECT
      HOURLY FEE                             TOTAL AMOUNT
      SET FEE                                CUSTOMER NAME
      MAINTENANCE FEE                        BILLING ADDRESS
      DATE OF BILL                           SERVICE SLIP
      CONTRACT                                    DESCRIPTION OF SERVICE
            HOURLY FEE                             DATE OF SERVICE
            SET FEE                          PAYMENT
            MAINTENANCE FEE                        DATE OF PAYMENT
            CUSTOMER NAME                          AMOUNT PAID
            BILLING ADDRESS                        CUSTOMER NAME
            PROJECT NAME
```

FIGURE 7.13   *Unnormalized BILL table for billing system. You will normalize this table.*

Now check the table for violations of 1NF (i.e., repeating groups). The following columns are such violations in the BILL table:

HOURLY FEE
SET FEE
MAINTENANCE FEE
PROJECT NAME
SUBTOTALS BY PROJECT
SERVICE SLIP
PAYMENT
CONTRACT

None of these are functionally dependent on BILL; there could be several of each for any one bill. Some of these data entities are listed more than once. This is the case for the following:

HOURLY FEE
SET FEE
MAINTENANCE FEE
PROJECT NAME

```
BILL                                         PROJECT NAME
      BILL KEY ◄─────── The key              SUBTOTALS BY PROJECT
      HOURLY FEE                             TOTAL AMOUNT
      SET FEE                                CUSTOMER NAME
      MAINTENANCE FEE                        BILLING ADDRESS
      DATE OF BILL                           SERVICE SLIP
      CONTRACT                                    DESCRIPTION OF SERVICE
            HOURLY FEE                             DATE OF SERVICE
            SET FEE                          PAYMENT
            MAINTENANCE FEE                        DATE OF PAYMENT
            CUSTOMER NAME                          AMOUNT PAID
            BILLING ADDRESS                        CUSTOMER NAME
```

FIGURE 7.14   *The BILL table with the addition of a key. The system will generate values for the key.*

There also are other data entities that are listed more than once. This includes CUSTOMER NAME and BILLING ADDRESS.

Data entities that are listed more than once also are repeating groups. These are redundant repeating groups, and are also violations of 1NF. Logically, all of these redundant repeating groups have more to do with the contract than the bill or, in the case of CUSTOMER NAME, the payment. The contract would contain the values for these items that are appropriate for bills pursuant to that contract, and the bills to a given customer would generate payments pursuant to the contract. We will therefore list these data items under CONTRACT only, and extract CONTRACT into a table of its own. In addition, SUBTOTALS BY PROJECT, SERVICE SLIP, and PAYMENT also will be extracted into tables of their own.

Whenever you extract one or more columns into another table, you must determine the relationship between the two tables. For example, one bill can cover many contracts, and one contract can generate many bills, so there is a many-to-many relationship between BILL and CONTRACT. Therefore, an association table (BILL CONTRACT) is necessary to express the relationship between BILL and CONTRACT.

Similarly, there is a many-to-many relationship between BILL and PAYMENT. That is, a bill can generate many payments, and a payment can cover many bills. In addition, there is a many-to-many relationship between CONTRACT and PAYMENT. For example, a contract can specify that many payments will be made, and a payment can be made that covers several contracts. There are one-to-many relationships between BILL and SUBTOTALS BY PROJECT and between BILL and SERVICE SLIP.

Therefore, SUBTOTALS BY PROJECT and SERVICE SLIP will both contain BILL KEY as a foreign key.

There are also some other relationships regarding SERVICE SLIP and SUBTOTALS BY PROJECT. There is a one-to-many relationship between PROJECT and each of these data entities. Because PROJECT is contained in the CONTRACT table, we will let CONTRACT KEY be a foreign key in SERVICE SLIP and SUBTOTALS BY PROJECT.

The database design now consists of the tables in Figure 7.15. There are no tables with combined keys, so there are no violations of 2NF. Examining the tables, you also find no violations of 3NF. Therefore, Figure 7.15 represents the final database design using the normalization methodology.

Fourth and Fifth Normal Forms

So far our discussions have included only the first three normal forms. An experienced systems analyst will intuitively use them in the design of files and records because the forms follow a common-sense approach to database design. Obviously, repetitive fields in the same record and variable length records are difficult to maintain and update. Also, redundant or repetitive

BILL
    BILL KEY
    DATE OF BILL
    TOTAL AMOUNT

CONTRACT
    CONTRACT KEY
    CUSTOMER NAME
    BILLING ADDRESS
    PROJECT NAME
    SET FEE
    HOURLY FEE
    MAINTENANCE FEE

BILL CONTRACT
    BILL KEY
    CONTRACT KEY

SERVICE SLIP
    SERVICE KEY
    DESCRIPTION OF SERVICE
    DATE OF SERVICE
    CONTRACT KEY
    BILL KEY

PAYMENT
    PAYMENT KEY
    DATE OF PAYMENT
    CUSTOMER NAME
    AMOUNT PAID

BILL PAYMENT
    BILL KEY
    PAYMENT KEY

CONTRACT PAYMENT
    CONTRACT KEY
    PAYMENT KEY

SUBTOTAL
    PROJECT SUBTOTAL KEY
    AMOUNT
    CONTRACT KEY
    BILL KEY

FIGURE 7.15   *The database for the billing system with repeating data extracted into a separate table. Association tables (BILL CONTRACT) relate tables with many-to-many relationships. In addition, each table has a key.*

data in the database produces inconsistencies during the updating process. Databases are constructed so that data occurs only once in the database. For instance, a person's address is in only one record and other records have keys or pointers to it. In addition, each row in a database table contains data based only on the key for that row. A quick way to determine if the design satisfies this criteria is to ask yourself "If I delete the row, will I lose valuable information that I need to keep?" If the answer is "yes," then you must remove the valuable information, place it in another table and use a foreign key to point to it.

In each of these cases, we try to construct a database so that each row of data in a table contains facts based solely on the primary key for that row and use foreign keys to point to other facts in other tables. These rows contain data about single-valued facts.

But what if a row contains multivalued facts? This is when you refer to Fourth and Fifth Normal Forms. Both Fourth and Fifth Normal Forms deal with many-to-many relationships. Recall, only network databases handle many-to-many relationships directly. In hierarchical and relational databases, you must split the many-to-many relationship into multiple one-to-many or many-to-one relationships. Fourth and Fifth Normal Forms contain the rules for this splitting process.

Fourth Normal Form The Fourth Normal Form (4NF) states that a record should not contain two or more independent multivalued facts about an entity. For facts to be independent of each other there must be no direct connection

PUBLICATIONS

Author ID	Author Name	Title of Publication	Bookstore Location	Number of Copies Ordered	Price Per Copy

FIGURE 7.16   *A record in violation of fourth normal form. Multiple authors can have multiple works and these multiple works can appear in multiple bookstores. This one record containing two multivalued facts must be divided into two different record entities to satisfy 4NF.*

between them. For example, a book publishing company can have multiple authors producing multiple published works (a many-to-many relationship) and at the same time these works can appear in multiple bookstores (another many-to-many relationship) (see Figure 7.16). A record containing the authors and their published works should not contain the list of published works and the list of bookstores that sell them. Fourth Normal Form dictates that these facts must be separated into two records (see Figure 7.17).

Fifth Normal Form   Fourth Normal Form eliminates multivalued independent facts in the same row of a table. But when a table contains redundant data, you need to eliminate the redundancy by decomposing the table into multiple tables. The Fifth Normal Form states that a table is in 5NF when its data can no longer be decomposed into smaller tables without each row in the smaller tables having the same primary key.

Let's look at an example of normalizing a table using 5NF. Suppose a local independent insurance office has several agents, each licensed to sell only certain types of insurance such as automobile, health, or home. Each agent is committed to a certain insurance company or underwriter and can only sell insurance for that underwriter. Figure 7.18 lists the salespersons for this office,

PUBLICATIONS

Author ID	Author Name	Title of Publication	Publication ID Number

SALES

Publication ID Number	Bookstore Location Code	Number of Copies Ordered	Price per Copy

FIGURE 7.17   *Records subdivided to satisfy fourth normal form. The foreign key Publication ID Number links the data together.*

Salesperson	Type of Insurance he/she can sell	Underwriter
John Doe	Life, Health	Allnation
Wong Soo	Accident, Boat	United Insurers
Karen Miller	Car, Home	City Farm
Bob Helms	Life, Accident	United Mutual
Mike Harpe	Car, Home	United Insurers

FIGURE 7.18   *Salesperson, type of insurance, and underwriters for a small insurance sales office.*

SALESMEN

Salesperson	Type of Insurance he/she can sell	Underwriter
John Doe	Life	Allnation
John Doe	Health	Allnation
Wong Soo	Accident	United Insurers
Wong Soo	Boat	United Insurers
Karen Miller	Car	City Farm
Karen Miller	Home	City Farm
Bob Helms	Life	United Mutual
Bob Helms	Accident	United Mutual
Mike Harpe	Car	United Insurers
Mike Harpe	Home	United Insurers

FIGURE 7.19 *Unnormalized table for a small insurance office. This table has several many-to-many relationships in it. Redundant data can be eliminated using 5NF.*

SALESMEN_TYPE

Salesperson	Type of Insurance he/she can sell
John Doe	Life
John Doe	Health
Wong Soo	Accident
Wong Soo	Boat
Karen Miller	Car
Karen Miller	Home
Bob Helms	Life
Bob Helms	Accident
Mike Harpe	Car
Mike Harpe	Home

TYPE_UNDERWRITER

Type Insurance	Underwriter
Accident	United Insurers
Accident	United Mutual
Boat	United Insurers
Car	City Farm
Car	United Insurers
Health	Allnation
Home	City Farm
Home	United Insurers
Life	Allnation
Life	United Mutual

SALESMEN_UNDERWRITER

Salesperson	Underwriter
John Doe	Allnation
Wong Soo	United Insurers
Karen Miller	City Farm
Bob Helms	United Mutual
Mike Harpe	United Insurers

FIGURE 7.20 *The insurance office normalized to 5NF. Redundant data is eliminated and only one-to-many relationships exist within the tables. Each table has nonunique primary keys.*

the types of insurance they can sell, and their respective insurance company or underwriter.

Because this firm has a successful ongoing business, it has several agents that can sell the same type of insurance—but for a different insurance company. Here, both Miller and Harpe can sell car and home insurance protection, but each can only sell for his or her specific company, City Farm and United Insurers, respectively.

Figure 7.19 contains a table representing the data. Notice the many-to-many relationships between the salespersons, the types of insurance they sell, and their underwriters. The many-to-many relationships within one table produce a large amount of redundant data within it. You can normalize this table to 5NF by splitting the unnormalized table into smaller tables containing one-to-many relationships and cross-referencing the data using foreign keys. This decomposition produces the three tables: SALESMEN_TYPE, TYPE_UNDER-WRITER, and SALESMEN_UNDERWRITER (see Figure 7.20).

SUMMARY

Normalization is a tool that can be used both as a primary design methodology and as a part of some other design methodology. Normalization is based on relational database theory. The main purpose of normalization is to reduce data redundancy.

Normalization deals with keys and functional dependence. Candidate keys are columns that uniquely identify the row and could be used as primary keys. Alternate keys are candidate keys that are not used as primary keys. Column B is functionally dependent on Column A if, for every occurrence of Column A, there can be only one occurrence of Column B.

The rules of normalization are expressed as normal forms. A table is in First Normal Form (1NF) if and only if each row contains the same number of columns. A table is in Second Normal Form (2NF) if and only if the table is in 1NF and every column that is not part of the key is functionally dependent on the whole key. A table is in Third Normal Form (3NF) if and only if the table is in 2NF and every column that is not part of the key is functionally dependent only on the key. A table is in Fourth Normal Form (4NF) if it does not contain two or more independent multivalued facts about an entity. Facts are independent if there is no direct connection between them. A table is in Fifth Normal Form (5NF) when its data can no longer be decomposed into smaller tables without each row in the smaller table having the same primary key.

QUESTIONS

1. Are normalization "rules" really rules?
2. What is the purpose of normalization?
3. Why is data redundancy undesirable?
4. What are candidate keys? Alternate keys?
5. What is functional dependence?

6. What is a normal form?
7. Define the first three normal forms.
8. What is the purpose of normalization in the Entity-Relation methodology?
9. What must you do whenever you extract a data entity from one table and create a new table?
10. State the first normal form and briefly explain what it means.
11. State the second normal form and briefly explain what it means.
12. Compare and contrast the second and third normal forms.
13. Briefly describe the third normal form and how it is used to normalize a design.
14. Explain how the fourth normal form is used to normalize a design.
15. What is the difference between the fourth and fifth normal forms? Elaborate.
16. What are the steps in normalizing a table?

CASE STUDY
*Normalization
Minilab*

Do the Case Study at the end of Chapter 6 using the normalization methodology.

Questions

Compare the designs you developed using the Entity-Relation methodology and the normalization methodology.

1. Which is the better design?
2. What are the strengths and weaknesses of each methodology?

The Ajax Service Company of Louisville, Kentucky specializes in servicing household appliances. For an annual membership fee of $200 the company will service and repair all major appliances in the home. When a customer subscribes to the service, an Ajax salesperson visits the customer's home and inventories all the appliances that are to be covered by the service. A maximum of 20 appliances can be covered by one service subscription.

Ajax currently has a manual system for its operation. This system includes the Customer's Inventory List, the Customer's Repair Service Record, and a Daily Journal of Repairs.

The Customer's Inventory List contains the customer's name and address and a list of the customer's appliances along with each estimated purchase date.

The Customer's Repair Service Record keeps track of the repairs to each customer's appliances covered by the subscription. It identifies the customer's name and address and contains a list of all repairs made at the customer's residence. Also, the record includes the name of the repairman who fixed the appliance.

When a repairman fixes an applicance for a customer, he or she logs both the customer's number and the repaired appliance number onto a Repair Log Sheet. The last four numbers of the customer's phone number serve as the customer's number and the appliance number is the number assigned to the appliance on the Customer's Inventory List.

At the end of each day, a clerk records the daily repairs from each repairman's Repair Log Sheet onto the Daily Journal of Repairs. Each line of this Journal

CUSTOMER'S INVENTORY LIST

CUSTOMER'S NAME: John Doe   DATE: January 15, 1991
CUSTOMER'S ADDRESS: 123 Holzer
CITY: Louisville
STATE: KY
ZIP: 40390

PHONE NUMBER: 234-555-3444

LIST OF APPLIANCES COVERED BY SERVICE:

NUMBER OF APPLIANCE	APPLIANCE NAME	APPROXIMATE YEAR PURCHASED
01	TV set	1987
02	Washer	1978
03	Dryer	1982
04	Freezer	1991
05	CD player	1990
•		
•		
•		
20		

SALESPERSON'S NAME: Mary Jones

CUSTOMER'S REPAIR SERVICE RECORD

CUSTOMER'S NAME: John Doe
CUSTOMER'S ADDRESS: 123 Holzer
CITY: Louisville
STATE: KY
ZIP: 40390

PHONE NUMBER: 234-555-3444

NUMBER OF APPLIANCE	APPLIANCE NAME	DATE REPAIRED	REPAIRMAN
01	TV set	02/11	J. Smith
01	TV set	04/21	D. Martinez
05	CD Player	05/09	J. Smith
03	Dryer	11/03	W. Jones

DAILY JOURNAL OF REPAIRS

DATE: February 11

REPAIRMAN NUMBER	REPAIRMAN NAME	CUST NUMB	UNIT REP.	CUST NUMB	UNIT REP.	CUST NUMB	UNIT REP.
16131	J. Smith	3444	01	3544	04	9844	11
16131	J. Smith	8740	18	8700	05	4118	08
16134	W. Jones	4544	19	3422	09	9877	05
89333	D. Martinez	8733	09	7211	13	9888	06
89333	D. Martinez	7655	10	9855	09	5438	03

FIGURE 7.21   *Three main documents for the Ajax Service Company.*

contains the repairman's number, the repairman's name, and data about three repairs made that day. If a repairman has logged more than three repairs for the day, multiple lines are used.

Given the above data, do the following:

1. Construct a series of relational tables equivalent to this manual system.
2. Construct any Association Tables, if needed.
3. Normalize all the tables.

Three of the main documents for the company are shown in Figure 7.21 on page 235.

8 *Physical Database Design*

Once you have created the Conceptual Database Design, by whatever method, you must convert it into a Physical Database Design. Here is where you define the details of the database that are necessary to create it. Use whatever tools are available, depending on the DBMS you have chosen: SQL for DB2, DBDGENs for IMS, and so on. It is impossible to give hard-and-fast rules for Physical Database Design, because appropriate physical design depends on the specific DBMS chosen and the machine environment in which the database will be implemented. Instead, we will examine general guidelines for Physical Database Design. Again, we will emphasize relational database design.

We will begin the chapter by discussing considerations that must be kept in mind throughout the physical design process. Remember, there will be trade-offs between minimal data redundancy and systems performance. Also, we must remember to provide for what is known as referential integrity. That is, we must ensure consistency between tables that reference each other via any foreign keys. Finally, we will examine some specific techniques for converting a Conceptual Database Design to a Physical Database Design.

TRADE-OFFS BETWEEN MINIMAL DATA REDUNDANCY AND PERFORMANCE

When creating the Physical Database Design, you should be concerned with trade-offs between reducing data redundancy and providing acceptable performance. These trade-offs become more complicated when you have either of the following:

- Large amounts of data to store, which makes minimal data redundancy more critical
- Large numbers of users accessing the data, which makes optimum performance more critical

Frequently, you must deal with both situations at once.

Figure 8.1 illustrates some of the trade-offs involved in minimizing data redundancy. There are two sets of employee and company data. The first set, consisting of the EMPLOYEE COMPANY table, is unnormalized and contains redundant data—COMPANY ADDRESS. The second set, consisting of the EMPLOYEE and COMPANY tables, has been normalized to remove the redundant data. Let's consider the effects of selecting, inserting, updating, and deleting rows from these tables on data integrity and performance.

When you select a row from EMPLOYEE COMPANY, you get all of the data concerning both the employee and his company. If you have a normalized design, two table I/Os are necessary to do this, one for EMPLOYEE and one for COMPANY. Normalization has doubled the number of I/Os. This could be extremely significant in cases where millions of select operations are performed each day. Data integrity does not suffer directly from selecting a row from an unnormalized table, though there can be an indirect effect. Insofar as insert, update, or delete operations result in a loss of data integrity, this will impact the validity of data retrieved via select operations.

When you insert a row into EMPLOYEE COMPANY, only one I/O is necessary. If you have a normalized design, two I/Os are necessary if you add an employee who works for a new company. In that case, it is necessary to add

Unnormalized design

EMPLOYEE COMPANY TABLE

EMPLOYEE	COMPANY	COMPANY ADDRESS
JANE DOE	XYZ COMPANY	456 SOME AVENUE
JOHN DOE	ABC COMPANY	123 ANY STREET
JOHN Q. PUBLIC	ABC COMPANY	123 ANY STREET
SAM SMITH	XYZ COMPANY	456 SOME AVENUE
SALLY SMITH	XYZ COMPANY	456 SOME AVENUE

Normalized design

EMPLOYEE TABLE

EMPLOYEE	COMPANY
JANE DOE	XYZ COMPANY
JOHN DOE	ABC COMPANY
JOHN Q. PUBLIC	ABC COMPANY
SAM SMITH	XYZ COMPANY
SALLY SMITH	XYZ COMPANY

COMPANY TABLE

COMPANY	COMPANY ADDRESS
ABC COMPANY	123 ANY STREET
XYZ COMPANY	456 SOME AVENUE

FIGURE 8.1   *Unnormalized and normalized versions of employee and company data. Minimizing data redundancy can result in less than optimal performance.*

both the employee to EMPLOYEE and the company to COMPANY. On the other hand, if you add an employee who works for an existing company, only one I/O is necessary. Without some information concerning the typical use of the database, that is, how many employees are added who work for new companies as opposed to how many employees are added who work for existing companies, it is impossible to determine the effects of normalization on performance.

However, data integrity can be impaired within an unnormalized design in two ways. First, if you add an employee who works for an existing company, there is no clear-cut method of ensuring that COMPANY ADDRESS is valid. If you have a normalized design, you can check the COMPANY table to verify that the foreign key COMPANY exists. Second, because EMPLOYEE is the key to EMPLOYEE COMPANY, you cannot add a new company that does not have any employees. For example, suppose that the database contains employee data for a parent company that owns various subsidiaries. If management decides to form a new corporation with personnel (to be assigned later) from various existing companies, it might be useful to add the company data before adding employee data. The unnormalized design does not allow this.

When you update a row in EMPLOYEE COMPANY to change company data—for example, the address of a company—you must update all rows where that company is found, which results in many I/Os against the table. With a normalized design, however, only one I/O is necessary. You must update one row in the COMPANY table. The need to make multiple I/Os in an unnormalized database not only impairs performance, but can impair data integrity. If, through some error, you do not update all of the necessary rows in EMPLOYEE COMPANY, the table will contain inconsistent data.

When you delete a row in EMPLOYEE COMPANY, there is little difference in performance than when you delete a row from EMPLOYEE. Data integrity can be impaired, however, if you delete the last employee from a given company. In that case, you lose all data concerning that company, which might not be what you intended.

You can see that normalization tends to impair performance on select operations and some insert operations, while denormalization tends to impair performance on some update operations. On the other hand, overriding normalization tends to impair data integrity on some select operations, insert operations, some update operations, and some delete operations.

It is impossible to determine whether to override normalization rules without having some idea as to the type of I/O operations that will be performed. For this reason, always attempt to determine how many select, insert, update, and delete operations will be performed against the database, as well as which columns of which tables will be affected by each type of I/O operation. Also attempt to determine the environment in which I/O operations will execute. For example, many performance problems encountered in on-line processing can be reduced in batch processing. Most companies schedule batch processing after normal working hours when users are no longer ac-

STUDENT TABLE

STUDENT NUMBER	STUDENT NAME	DEPARTMENT KEY
101109876	EINSTEIN, ALBERT	M01
209393828	SARTRE, JEAN PAUL	P01
302938483	VESPUCCI, AMERIGO	G01
403949382	FORD, HENRY	B01
803939283	VAN GOGH, VINCENT	F01

DEPARTMENT TABLE

DEPARTMENT KEY	DEPARTMENT NAME
B01	BUSINESS ADMINISTRATION
F01	FINE ARTS
G01	GEOGRAPHY
M01	MATHEMATICS
P01	PHILOSOPHY

FIGURE 8.2 *Two normalized tables that require maintenance of referential integrity. DEPARTMENT table is a parent table and STUDENT table is a dependent table.*

cessing the database. At these times, I/O and CPU contention can be considerably reduced, resulting in performance gains.

REFERENTIAL INTEGRITY

Thus far, we have discussed data integrity primarily in terms of ensuring the validity of the data within a table. **Referential Integrity** deals with ensuring the validity of data between tables. Recall that relationships between data entities are treated as data in a relational database and are expressed as foreign keys. That means tables in a relational database reference each other via foreign keys. Referential Integrity deals with the validity of foreign keys in a table.

The details of maintaining Referential Integrity are dealt with in a later chapter. At this point, we will simply discuss the general concepts with regard to Physical Database Design.

Figure 8.2 shows two normalized tables. The STUDENT table contains student numbers (the key), student names, and each student's major department, which is a foreign key to DEPARTMENT table. The DEPARTMENT table contains department keys and department names. DEPARTMENT table, which is referenced via a foreign key, is known as a **parent table.** STUDENT table, which references another table via a foreign key, is known as a **dependent table.**

Suppose you now add the following row to the STUDENT table:

STUDENT NUMBER	STUDENT NAME	MAJOR DEPARTMENT KEY
839093939	DOE, JANE	Z01

Now you have a foreign key (Z01) that does not reference a valid key in the parent table. You have created a violation of referential integrity by an insert operation on a dependent table. Remember, you also can create such a violation by a delete operation on a parent table. For example, suppose you delete the following row from DEPARTMENT TABLE:

DEPARTMENT KEY	DEPARTMENT NAME
M01	MATHEMATICS

Again, you have a foreign key (M01 in the STUDENT table) that no longer references a valid key in the parent table. You must keep in mind that operations on either dependent tables or parent tables can affect referential integrity. Therefore, you also must be aware of relationships between tables during Physical Database Design.

CONVERTING CONCEPTUAL DATABASE DESIGN TO PHYSICAL DATABASE DESIGN

Converting Conceptual Database Design to Physical Database Design can be approached in the following sequence of activities:

- Define all columns of all tables
- Determine whether (and where) to override normalization
- Define Referential Integrity requirements
- Define essential views
- Define essential indexes

Defining All Columns of All Tables

To define all columns of all tables, you must determine each column's type, size, number of occurrences, validity of nulls, and I/O frequency by type of I/O. For example, the CONTRACT table from the system we designed in Chapter 6 (and modified in Chapter 7) might have the column definitions shown in Figure 8.3.

In this case, we have assumed that the database manager will be DB2. We have defined each column's type (SMALLINT, VARCHAR, etc.), as well as the number of bytes each column will use. For variable-length columns, we have given the average column size.

We also have specified whether nulls are valid as a value for the column, that is, whether the column is required or optional. In addition, we also specified the number of rows in the table, which is also the number of occurrences of each column in the row (10,000). I/O frequencies are specified by type of I/O.

Some of the data you specify concerning the number of occurrences and

CONTRACT   *Column Definitions*

COLUMN	TYPE	SIZE (BYTES)	NULLS VALID
CONTRACT KEY	SMALLINT	2	NO
CUSTOMER NAME	VARCHAR(40)	18	NO
BILLING ADDRESS	VARCHAR(160)	45	NO
PROJECT NAME	VARCHAR(80)	44	NO
SET FEE	DECIMAL(7,2)	7	YES
HOURLY FEE	DECIMAL(5,2)	5	YES
MAINTENANCE FEE	DECIMAL(6,2)	6	YES

CONTRACT   *I/O Frequency*

NUMBER OF ROWS IN TABLE: 10,000

COLUMN	SELECT	DELETE	UPDATE	INSERT
CONTRACT KEY	10,000	2000	50	8000
CUSTOMER NAME	10,000	2000	100	8000
BILLING ADDRESS	10,000	2000	300	8000
PROJECT NAME	10,000	2000	50	8000
SET FEE	10,000	2000	50	2000
HOURLY FEE	10,000	2000	50	6000
MAINTENANCE FEE	10,000	2000	50	3000

FIGURE 8.3   *A hypothetical set of column definitions and I/O frequencies for the CONTRACT table of the billing system. The I/O frequencies can be estimates.*

the I/O frequencies might be estimates. In fact, it is rare that you will have exact statistics for all columns. There are, however, ways to get information on which to base reasonable estimates. Recall that the most frequent system development scenario involves replacing a partially automated existing system. Insofar as the existing system is automated, audit or log files might exist showing I/O activity. Also, once the data flows of the existing system are understood, determining the number of records in master and transaction files can give important information.

For activities that are performed manually, end users frequently can give accurate estimates of activity. For example, they could count the number of bills sent in an average month, the number of times billing addresses change and have to be updated, and so forth. It is worth noting that, when soliciting such information from end users, you should contact not only the managers or supervisors with whom you have been dealing to define system requirements, but also the clerks who actually use the system on a routine basis. On occasion, you will find that you get different information from different sources.

Determining Whether (and Where) to Override Normalization

To determine whether (and where) to override normalization, you use the I/O frequency data that you have accumulated while defining the columns.

Using this data, you can override normalization when you find that you will derive a performance benefit that justifies any adverse effects on data integrity. Avoid overriding normalization unless the amount of redundant data is small and relatively stable. This occurs when the I/O frequencies of insert, update, and delete operations are small. The effects of overriding normalization on data integrity are lessened when there is only a small amount of redundant data which is stable.

Defining Referential Integrity Requirements

To define Referential Integrity requirements, you must understand the parent-dependent relationships between the tables in your Conceptual Database Design. One way to do this is to create a diagram such as the one in Figure 8.4.

Figure 8.4 shows the parent-dependent relationships between the tables in the billing system. BILL has the following four dependent tables: SUBTOTAL, BILL CONTRACT, BILL PAYMENT, and SERVICE SLIP. CONTRACT PAYMENT is a dependent table with two parent tables, PAYMENT and CONTRACT. Such a diagram is useful in determining how to ensure Referential Integrity within our database. The specifics of doing this will be covered in a later chapter.

Defining Essential Views

To define essential views, you must look to the processing requirements and the data flows of the system you are developing. This can be done most easily by examining the Model Data Flow Diagram for the system. Figure 6.18 shows the Model DFD for the billing system, repeated here as Figure 8.5.

For example, consider the process CALCULATE BALANCE. What view would be needed for this process? You can see from the DFD that data about bills and payments is needed. Now you must investigate the details of the process

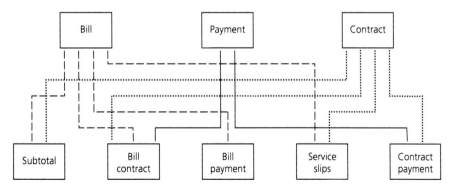

FIGURE 8.4   *Parent-dependent relationships between the tables in the billing system. Parent tables are shown above their dependent tables with lines connecting them.*

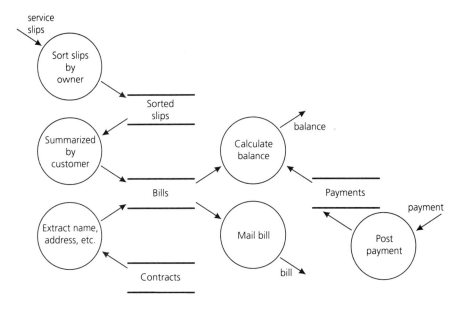

FIGURE 8.5   *The Model DFD for the billing system.*

of computing a balance. To compute a balance for a given customer on a given date, you must:

1. Search the CONTRACT table for all contracts for the customer.
2. Search the BILL CONTRACT table to determine all bills for each contract.
3. Add up the amounts of all bills billed as of the date you are interested in from the BILL table.
4. Search the CONTRACT PAYMENT table to determine all payments for each contract.
5. Add up the amounts of all payments paid as of the date you are interested in from the PAYMENT table.
6. Subtract the computed amount of payments from the computed amount of bills.

Obviously, you need the following data in the view:

CUSTOMER NAME	from CONTRACT table
DATE OF BILL	from BILL table
TOTAL AMOUNT	from BILL table
DATE OF PAYMENT	from PAYMENT table
AMOUNT PAID	from PAYMENT table

The following data, although not explicitly in the view, will be used to join the three tables:

CONTRACT KEY	from CONTRACT table
CONTRACT KEY	from BILL CONTRACT table

BILL KEY	from BILL CONTRACT table
BILL KEY	from BILL table
CONTRACT KEY	from CONTRACT PAYMENT table
PAYMENT KEY	from CONTRACT PAYMENT table
PAYMENT KEY	from PAYMENT table

You must determine any needed views for all processes.

Defining Essential Indexes

To define essential indexes, you first must consider the purpose of an index. An index can serve two different functions. The first is to ensure a unique key. In most relational database systems, you do this by defining a unique index on the key. Recall that, according to relational database theory, every table should have a unique key. In the "real world," you will find that you are typically storing data about unique entities, for example, a contract, a bill, a payment, and so on. Unless there are strong reasons not to, it usually is best to define unique indexes on primary keys.

The second function of an index is to speed up performance. Here again, you must take your processing requirements into consideration. It is usually desirable to create indexes on any columns used as search arguments in a table, as well as any columns that are used to join separate tables. It also can be useful to create indexes on any columns used to sort or summarize data.

SUMMARY

Physical Database Design takes place after Conceptual Database Design. General guidelines exist that must be applied to specific situations. The specific DBMS as well as the specific machine environment will affect the application of the guidelines.

There are trade-offs between minimal data redundancy, that is, normalization and performance. Frequently, you deal with large amounts of data that are accessed by many users, making the trade-offs more complicated to handle. Normalization can impair performance for select and certain insert operations. Overriding normalization can impair data integrity on certain select, insert, update, and delete operations. To properly assess the impact of normalization versus overriding normalization, you must determine the I/O frequency on each column by I/O operation.

Referential Integrity deals with data integrity as it applies to relationships between tables, which are shown via foreign keys. Parent tables are referenced by dependent tables via foreign keys. I/O operations on either type of table can impair Referential Integrity.

To convert Conceptual Database Design to Physical Database Design, you must define all columns of all tables, determine whether (and where) to override normalization, define Referential Integrity requirements, define essential views, and define essential indexes.

QUESTIONS
1. What kind of trade-offs are involved in Physical Database Design? What complications can arise?
2. Why does the environment in which I/O operations execute affect data integrity and performance?
3. List the ways that data integrity can be impaired during insert operations on an unnormalized design.
4. What is Referential Integrity?
5. List the activities involved in converting Conceptual Database Design to Physical Database Design.
6. What information do you need to define all columns of all tables?
7. What guidelines can you follow to determine whether to override normalization?
8. What do you need to understand to define Referential Integrity requirements? How do you diagram this information?
9. What must you consider to define needed views and indexes?
10. Suppose you have normalized several tables. Under what conditions would you want to override normalization?

CASE STUDY
Using the Conceptual Database Design you created in the Case Study from either Chapter 6 or Chapter 7, perform the steps detailed in this chapter for converting Conceptual Database Design to Physical Database Design. Make any assumptions that you find necessary.

Questions

1. List the assumptions that you found necessary to complete this Case Study.
2. In a "real world" business environment, for each assumption, how would you obtain the information necessary to derive an answer (or form a good estimate for the answer) to each question underlying the assumption? (Hint: Begin by determining the question underlying each assumption.)

9

Relational Databases and SQL

There are numerous relational databases on the market. Some are available only on a mainframe, some are available only on a PC, and still others work on both a PC and a mainframe. In this chapter we will look at two mainframe relational databases, DB2 and SQL/DS, both from IBM. DB2 runs on IBM's MVS/XA and MVS/ESA operating systems. SQL/Data Systems (SQL/DS) runs on IBM's non-MVS operating systems (VM/CMS). For all practical purposes, these two databases are essentially the same.

Both DB2 and SQL/DS use the nonprocedural language Structured Query Language (SQL), which is the main Database Manipulation Language for the products. Many database vendors (for example, ORACLE Corp.) have adopted IBM's version of SQL and are therefore DB2–SQL compatible. This is particularly handy for users of these products because users will not have to relearn the commands and idiosyncrasies of the language if and when they decide to migrate to DB2. Since IBM introduced DB2 in the early 1980s, most of the IMS database installations also have installed DB2. Therefore, in this chapter we will discuss DB2's treatment of relational databases and its version of SQL.

THE RELATIONAL MODEL

Data is stored in relational databases in tables containing rows and columns. The relationship between the two tables in Figure 9.1 is not explicitly defined as it must be in network and hierarchical databases. The relationship between these tables is implicitly defined via the relationship between the column DEPTNUMB, which is in both tables. One way to establish the relationship between tables is to use the primary key of one table as a foreign key of another table. This establishes the potential for a relationship between the two tables. You reveal the relationship between the tables whenever you attempt to use the data in them via DML. Only when you attempt to access the data will SQL create the relationship between tables and construct the navigation of the database for that relationship.

EMPLOYEE

EMPLOYEE ID	LAST NAME	FIRST NAME	ADDRESS	CITY	STATE	SEX	DEPTNUMB
123456789	DOE	JOHN	123 E. 3RD	CHICAGO	IL	M	ACCT
234567890	SMITH	MARY	34 N. HOLLY	DENVER	CO	F	ACCT
324566776	GROVER	SUE	56 W. 5TH	DENVER	CO	F	MARK
432143211	SMITH	ANDY	34 N. HOLLY	DENVER	CO	M	PERS
432234432	MARKUM	MIKE	194 W. 43RD	CHICAGO	IL	M	PERS

DEPARTMENT

DEPTNUMB	NAME	MANAGER ID	ASSISTANT MANAGER ID
ACCT	Accounting	123456789	346565432
MARK	Marketing	902902902	898989898
PERS	Personnel	432143211	453453453
AUDT	Auditing	848484848	122221122
TRNG	Training	980980980	878767777

FIGURE 9.1   *EMPLOYEE and DEPARTMENT tables. These two tables are linked by the relationship between DEPTNUMB in the EMPLOYEE table and DEPTNUMB in the DEPARTMENT table.*

USING DATA DEFINITION LANGUAGE

Creating Entities

Recall, in nonrelational systems, one-to-one and one-to-many relationships had to be defined using DL/I or a schema for hierarchical and network databases, respectively. These relationships had to be hard coded into the system before you could load data into the database and access that data. With SQL, you identify the table columns by designing tables in such a way that data redundancy is eliminated or greatly reduced. You then normalize the tables in an effort to perfect the design. Once you are satisfied with the design of the tables, you can load their structure into the database using the Data Definition Language (DDL). You then use DML to establish the relations between multiple tables and access this relation. These tables on DASD are called base tables.

Creating Databases and Tablespaces

Before you can load the table's structure into the system, the DBA must create the databases and tablespace to hold the tables. The DBA responsible for the SQL product is the Systems Administrator (SYSADM). SYSADM must do the following:

- *Create the storage group for the database*—This identifies to SQL the DASD volumes allocated for the database.
- *Create the database and tablespaces*—This includes the specific volumes that will be used and the size of the database. You store your tables in the tablespaces.

- *Grant you the right to use the database and tablespace*
- *Grant you the right to create tables and use either all the SQL statements or a subset of them*

In these steps, SYSADM allocated space for the tables and gave you the privilege of using that space. That is, SYSADM could use the statement:

```
CREATE STOGROUP PAY001
    VOLUMES (MONPAY1, MONPAY2, MONPAY3)
```

to group the three DASD volumes MONPAY1, MONPAY2, and MONPAY3 into a logical storage group called PAY001. SYSADM then can assign a database name to this DASD grouping using:

```
CREATE DATABASE PAYROLL
    STOGROUP PAY001
```

At this point, SYSADM has several options available. SYSADM now could create the tablespaces to hold the tables and, for that matter, create the tables. However, because the main function of SYSADM is to manage the database product and not the entities created within the product, most SYSADMs give the power to create tablespaces and tables to some member of the application support team. SYSADM does this by creating a DBADM for that team using the statement:

```
GRANT DBADM ON DATABASE PAYROLL
    TO STEVEN
```

where STEVEN is some TSO account for the team.

Before you can create tables in the database, either SYSADM or a DBADM must create a tablespace to hold the tables and grant you the right to create tables within the database. These instructions are:

```
CREATE TABLESPACE PAYTBL1
    IN PAYROLL
    USING STOGROUP PAY001
    PRIQTY 60
    SECQTY 20;
GRANT USE OF TABLESPACE PAYTBL1 TO KAREN;
GRANT CREATETAB ON DATABASE PAYROLL TO KAREN;
```

These commands create a 60KB tablespace called PAYTBL1 and give the account KAREN the right to use the tablespace and create tables within the database PAYROLL. (A more detailed discussion of the GRANT statement is given later in this chapter.)

When KAREN fills the original 60KB of DASD with data, the system will automatically allocate an additional 20KB of DASD space for his or her usage. The system will continually allocate 20KB of DASD memory on the volumes MONPAY1, MONPAY2, and MONPAY3 for a maximum of fifteen additional allocations.

Note that unlike hierarchical and network databases, SYSADM generally does not create any table structures or relationships. It is up to the user or programmer to define the configuration of the tables and place them correctly in the database's allocated space. However, this does not mean that SYSADM cannot create tables. In fact, SYSADM has complete power within DB2 or SQL/DS.

Creating Tables

You use the CREATE statement of DDL to define tables within tablespaces that are in a database area. You define the EMPLOYEE and DEPARTMENT tables in Figure 9.1 using the CREATE statements in Figure 9.2.

SQL creates the tables EMPLOYEE and DEPARTMENT in tablespace PAYTBL1 within database PAYROLL. The NOT NULL option indicates that columns EMPLOYEE_ID, LASTNAME, FIRSTNAME, DEPTNO, SEX, and DEPTNAME are required fields. Required fields are those fields that must contain a value whenever you place data in the tables. In this case, when you load a row into the table DEPARTMENT, the columns DEPTNUMB and DEPTNAME must contain values, while the columns MANAGER_ID and ASSISTANT_ID might or might not have values.

The CREATE statement is similar to defining the schema in network databases. When you enter a CREATE statement and execute it, SQL checks the statement for syntax errors. If none exist, SQL queries its catalog to see if the database and tablespace exist and if the table name is not a duplicate of one already in the tablespace. Finally, SQL checks the security tables in its catalog to see if you are authorized to create tables in the tablespace. If no errors exist for any of these conditions, SQL adds the table description and its associated column definitions to the SQL catalog.

Remember, the structure and definition of each table you defined in the design phase of application development must be entered into the system. Typically, you place the CREATE statements in a large batch file within one

```
CREATE TABLE EMPLOYEE
        (EMPLOYEE_ID  CHAR(9)        NOT NULL,
        LASTNAME      VARCHAR(20)    NOT NULL,
        FIRSTNAME     VARCHAR(20)    NOT NULL,
        ADDRESS       VARCHAR(25),
        CITY          VARCHAR(25),
        STATE         CHAR(2),
        SEX           CHAR(1)        NOT NULL,
        DEPTNO        CHAR(4)        NOT NULL)
        IN PAYROLL.PAYTBL1

CREATE TABLE DEPARTMENT
        (DEPTNUMB     CHAR(4)        NOT NULL,
        DEPTNAME      VARCHAR(20)    NOT NULL,
        MANAGER_ID    CHAR(9),
        ASSISTANT_ID  CHAR(9))
        IN PAYROLL.PAYTBL1
```

FIGURE 9.2   *CREATE statement for EMPLOYEE and DEPARTMENT tables.*

of the SQL menus. You visually check it for errors and then execute the batch file. Remember, if problems arise at a later date that force you to DROP, or remove, the tablespace or database, you might need this batch file to recover the structure of the tables within your database.

To remove or erase a table, use the SQL statement:

DROP TABLE DEPARTMENT

This removes the definition of the table from the DB2 catalog, that is, it removes the table's existence as far as DB2 is concerned.

The CREATE statement does not place data into tables and the DROP statement does not take data out of tables. The CREATE statement simply adds the structure's definition to the SQL catalog. Similarly, the DROP statement removes structure definitions from the SQL catalog. Obviously, if the system does not have the structure for the table, it cannot access it. Therefore, you must backup the data in the database in a timely manner and maintain a current batch file of all DDL and CL statements you used to create the database and all its entities.

Don't forget, a tablespace is divided into pages, not tables. The pages contain rows from a single table if you created a single table in the tablespace — or they contain rows from multiple tables if you created multiple tables within the tablespace. The table itself does not exist in the tablespace as a set of contiguous rows that you can access as a group or entity. Instead, the table exists as separate rows scattered throughout the tablespace and can be interspersed with other rows from other tables.

When you access a table the system does not access all the rows in one cluster. Instead it treats the table as a collection of multiple rows and it extracts them from the tablespace one row at a time. The SQL catalog, the index, and the RID values are all used to identify which rows on which pages belong to a particular table. It is this integration of data within the DBMS software that forbids anyone from singularly DELETEing entries in the SQL catalog. You must DROP or CREATE structures of database entities. That means you can never DELETE or INSERT items into the SQL catalog.

Defining Columns

Data in columns either can be alphanumeric (CHAR or VARCHAR) or numeric (INTEGER, SMALLINT, DECIMAL, or FLOAT). You use VARCHAR to define alphanumeric fields that vary in length (i.e., last name, first name, address) and CHAR to define alphanumeric fields that will contain values of a fixed length (i.e., FICA number, state, ZIP code). Numeric fields can be any one of the following four types:

- SMALLINT—an integer value between -32768 and $+32767$
- INTEGER—an integer value between $-2,147,483,648$ and $+2,147,483,647$
- FLOAT—a double precision real number or floating-point number

- DECIMAL (L,R)—a decimal number with "L" digits and "R" digits to the right of the decimal point; L (length) cannot be larger than 15

You add additional columns to the table using the ALTER statement. That is, the statement:

```
ALTER TABLE EMPLOYEE
ADD HOURLY_WAGE DECIMAL (5,2)
```

adds the column HOURLY_WAGE to the table EMPLOYEE. In the EMPLOYEE table the added column HOURLY_WAGE becomes the right-most column in the table. In this example, values in HOURLY_WAGE can be up to five digits long with two digits to the right of the decimal point. For the EMPLOYEE table in Figure 9.1, if data already exists in the table when you add a column to it via the ALTER statement, SQL loads null values in that column for all the already existing rows. In this case, you would have to load some hourly wage values into each row using a program or other software device.

Creating Unique Indexes

You create unique indexes on the EMPLOYEE and DEPARTMENT tables using:

```
CREATE UNIQUE INDEX EMPLNDX1
ON EMPLOYEE (EMPLOYEE_ID)
STOGROUP RT1001 PRIQTY 20 SECQTY 5

CREATE UNIQUE INDEX DEPTNDX1
ON DEPARTMENT (DEPTNUMB)
STOGROUP RT1001 PRIQTY 20 SECQTY 5
```

In this case, SQL creates a unique index on EMPLOYEE_ID and DEPTNUMB and places the indexes with their associated Root and Leaf Pages in the indexspaces EMPLNDX1 and DEPTNDX1, respectively. An indexspace has all the properties of a tablespace except SQL creates and manages it. You do not use the CREATE statement to define an indexspace. SQL automatically creates the indexspace when it CREATEs the index. In this case, the indexspace and its index will use the storage group RT1001 and allocate 20KB of DASD for the initial storage of the index. When the system exhausts this first primary quantity of 20KB (i.e., PRIQTY 20), the system will allocate secondary quantities of DASD memory in units of 5KB, as needed (Figure 9.3).

DASD Usage by User Departments

In the previous CREATE INDEX example, storage group RT1001 is some user volume either entirely or partially assigned to hold SQL entities (databases, tablespaces, tables, etc.). Remember, the SQL software and its corresponding catalog reside on some designated volume or volumes. All user files are stored on some preassigned volume for that user's department (Figure 9.4). That is, a DASD volume is assigned to a user department based on the user's needs

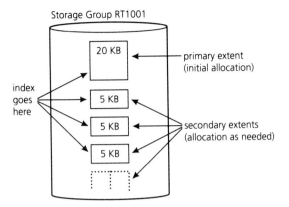

FIGURE 9.3   *Index and indexspace on DASD.*

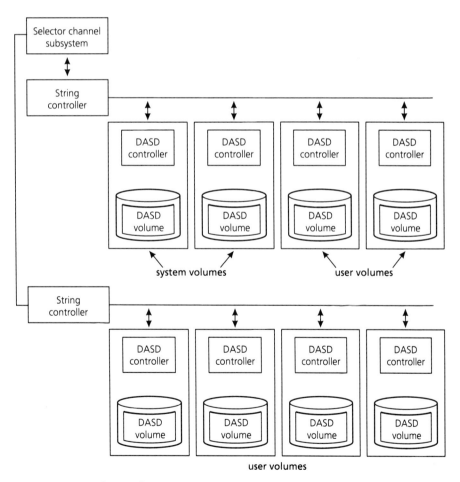

FIGURE 9.4   *System volumes and user volumes.*

and its cost is charged back to that department as part of the budgetary cycle within the company. Most companies require all files that a user creates to be stored on that user's DASD volume. Each user department manager receives detailed weekly or monthly reports on the utilization of that department's DASD volumes and its associated cost. The cost then is charged against that department's budget and the appropriate bookkeeping entries automatically logged into the Accounting Department's files.

Creating Nonunique Indexes

If you do not want unique keys, you can create nonunique indexes by eliminating the word UNIQUE in the CREATE statement. That is, the statements:

```
CREATE INDEX EMPLNDX2
ON EMPLOYEE (LASTNAME)
STOGROUP RT1001 PRIQTY 20 SECQTY 5
```

and

```
CREATE INDEX DEPTNDX2
ON DEPARTMENT (DEPTNUMB, DEPTNAME)
STOGROUP RT1001 PRIQTY 20 SECQTY 5
```

create indexes on the column LASTNAME of table EMPLOYEE and on columns DEPTNUMB, and DEPTNAME of table DEPARTMENT.

If the table already contains data when you create the index, the database system will create the index immediately. That is, it will lock the tablespace containing the table and generate the index. If the table does not contain data when you create the index, then each time you add a row to the table, the system will use the index keys and page location for the new row to create the index entry for that row (Figure 9.5). Remember, the system loads the page location and RID value for the stored row into a Leaf Page in the index.

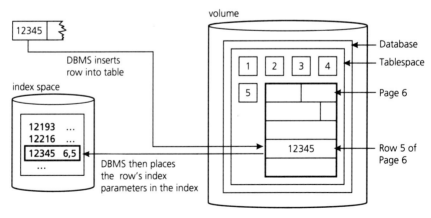

FIGURE 9.5   *Creation of an index.*

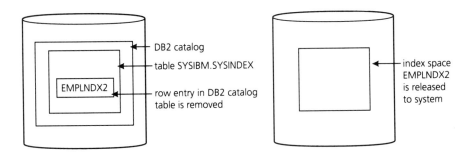

DB2 catalog

table SYSIBM.SYSINDEX

EMPLNDX2

row entry in DB2 catalog
table is removed

index space
EMPLNDX2
is released
to system

FIGURE 9.6 *DROP and the SQL catalog. When the indexspace EMPLNDX2's is DROPped, the DASD space on the user's volume it occupied is released to the system for future usage by it. The row in the DB2 catalog table SYSIBM.SYSINDEX containing the data about the index is deleted.*

Be careful when creating an index on a table containing a large amount of data. Obviously, if a table contains a million rows of data, the creating of an index at 10 AM on a busy workday can cause havoc with a user department trying to access that table. Because SQL will lock the tablespace and index space of the table when it tries to create the index, the table will not be available to the user department during this creation. Depending on the size of the table, the creation of the index might take minutes or hours. Therefore, schedule index creation for off-hours processing or place it in a batch job for execution during second and third shifts.

To change or eliminate an index, simply DROP the index. The statement:

DROP INDEX EMPLNDX2

destroys the indexes in EMPLNDX2 that were associated with LASTNAME (Figure 9.6). Again, be careful in dropping an index because the loss of an index can affect other entities in the SQL catalog. This is particularly true if you wrote computer programs based on a table having an index. These computer programs might not function properly when you drop an index used by them. We will discuss this topic in more detail when we get to the section on BINDing a program in a later chapter.

USING DATA MANIPULATION LANGUAGE

The Data Manipulation Language (DML) has the following four statements:

- SELECT—to read rows and columns in a table
- INSERT—to add rows to a table
- DELETE—to erase a row or group of rows from a table
- UPDATE—to modify or change data in a table

Unlike the statements in DDL that define the structure of database entities, each of the DML statements works with the data in tables.

The SELECT Statement

The SELECT statement reads rows from one or more tables. You include in the SELECT statement the table's name and a list of the columns you want extracted from it. The column names must be separated by a comma. The general form of the SELECT statement is:

```
SELECT list of column names
FROM table name
```

That is, the statement:

```
SELECT EMPLOYEE_ID, LASTNAME, FIRSTNAME
FROM EMPLOYEE
```

requests SQL to extract the data in the EMPLOYEE_ID, LASTNAME, and FIRST-NAME columns of table EMPLOYEE. Because there are no other restrictions on the query, SQL will copy all the data from the requested columns of every row within the table and load it into a buffer area. SQL then displays this buffer area on the screen. Figure 9.7 contains the results of this query.

Notice the arrangement of the data in the output. The columns you list in the SELECT statement will be the only columns SQL displays. In addition, the order in which you place a column's name in SELECT will be the order the data appears in the output. Rearranging the order of the column names in SELECT rearranges the order of the output columns. For example:

```
SELECT LASTNAME, FIRSTNAME, EMPLOYEE_ID
FROM EMPLOYEE
```

displays the same data that appears in Figure 9.7, but with a different column order. SQL places the name of the column above the data for each column in the results. SQL uses a free-form format for writing the SQL statements where the keywords can be anywhere on a line or multiple lines and each keyword must be separated by a blank or space. That is, the statements:

```
SELECT EMPLOYEE_ID, LASTNAME, FIRSTNAME FROM EMPLOYEE
```

and

```
SELECT
EMPLOYEE_ID,
LASTNAME,
FIRSTNAME
FROM
EMPLOYEE
```

are valid statements and are equivalent.

You do not have to list columns in the SELECT statement if you use the wildcard symbol *. That is, the statement:

```
SELECT *
FROM EMPLOYEE
```

EMPLOYEE_ID	LASTNAME	FIRSTNAME
123456789	DOE	JOHN
234567890	SMITH	MARY
324566776	GROVER	SUE
432143211	SMITH	ANDY
432234432	MARKUM	MIKE

FIGURE 9.7   *Sample results from an SQL query.*

lists all rows in the EMPLOYEE table. SQL accesses the columns as they were defined in the table's CREATE statement and later added to the table using the ALTER statement. Remember, when you alter a table and add a new column, that column becomes the right-most column in the table (Figure 9.8). For the previous SELECT you get the display in Figure 9.9.

Using the WHERE Clause   Fortunately, most queries will only require a subset of the rows in the table instead of every row within it. You restrict the number of rows extracted from the database by using the keyword WHERE in the SELECT statement. The statement:

```
SELECT EMPLOYEE_ID, LASTNAME, FIRSTNAME
FROM EMPLOYEE
WHERE   CITY = 'DENVER'
```

produces the display:

EMPLOYEE_ID	LASTNAME	FIRSTNAME
234567890	SMITH	MARY
324566776	GROVER	SUE
432143211	SMITH	ANDY

The column name in WHERE does not have to appear in the listing of column names after SELECT. Valid operators in the WHERE clause are listed in Figure 9.10.

EMPLOYEE table

EMPLOYEE ID	LAST NAME	FIRST NAME	ADDRESS	CITY	ST	SEX	DEPT NUMB	HR WAGE	HR WK

original table

configuration of the table after altering it by adding the column HOURLY_WAGE.

configuration of the table after altering it by first adding the column HOURLY_WAGE and then the column HOURS_WEEK.

FIGURE 9.8   *Creating and altering a table. When adding a column to a table using the ALTER command it becomes the right-most column in the table.*

EMPLOYEE ID	LAST NAME	FIRST NAME	ADDRESS	CITY	ST	S	DEPT NUMB	HR WAGE	HR WK
123456789	DOE	JOHN	123 E. 3RD	CHICAGO	IL	M	ACCT	12.00	45
234567890	SMITH	MARY	34 N. HOLLY	DENVER	CO	F	ACCT	10.55	30
324566776	GROVER	SUE	56 W. 5TH	DENVER	CO	F	MARK	9.55	40
432143211	SMITH	ANDY	34 N. HOLLY	DENVER	CO	M	PERS	8.00	45
432234432	MARKUM	MIKE	194 W. 43RD	CHICAGO	IL	M	PERS	15.00	45

FIGURE 9.9 *Results of the SELECT * FROM EMPLOYEE query.*

The query:

```
SELECT EMPLOYEE_ID, LASTNAME, FIRSTNAME
FROM EMPLOYEE
WHERE HOURLY_WAGE NOT > 5.00
```

will display only those employees who are making $5 or less as an hourly wage. Numeric constants in the WHERE clause do not have a delimiter. However, alphanumeric constants must have an apostrophe as a delimiter. That is, the statement:

```
SELECT EMPLOYEE_ID, LASTNAME, FIRSTNAME
FROM EMPLOYEE
WHERE SEX = 'M'
```

lists the names of all the males in the table EMPLOYEE. In this case, SQL searches the rows in the table for a capital M in the SEX column. Don't forget, lower case m and upper case M have different EBCDIC codes and are not equal.

Using the AND, OR, and NOT Keywords You also can use the keywords AND, OR, and NOT in the WHERE clause. The query:

```
SELECT EMPLOYEE_ID, LASTNAME, FIRSTNAME, DEPTNUMB
FROM EMPLOYEE
WHERE DEPTNUMB = 'ACCT' OR DEPTNUMB = 'MARK'
```

lists only those employees in Accounting or Marketing. The results of this query are:

EMPLOYEE_ID	LASTNAME	FIRSTNAME	DEPTNUMB
123456789	DOE	JOHN	ACCT
234567890	SMITH	MARY	ACCT
324566776	GROVER	SUE	MARK

When using the AND and OR clause, you must repeat the column name in the second half of the WHERE statement. For example, the statement:

```
SELECT EMPLOYEE_ID, LASTNAME, FIRSTNAME, DEPTNUMB
FROM EMPLOYEE
WHERE DEPTNUMB = 'ACCT' OR 'MARK'
```

=	equal to	NOT =	not equal to
<	less than	NOT <	not less than
>	greater than	NOT >	not greater than
<=	less than or equal to	NOT <=	not less than or equal to
>=	greater than or equal to	NOT >=	not greater than or equal to

FIGURE 9.10 *Valid operators in WHERE.*

produces an error message. In this case, SQL will display one of the hundreds of error messages that are possible in SQL. You will have to refer to an SQL error messages manual to decipher the meaning of any error message you receive. However, it might be quicker first to visually check the SQL statement to see if the error is easy to spot. If it is not, then you might have to search the manuals to get a clue so you can solve the problem.

Similarly, if you want all the employees who are not in the marketing department, use the query:

```
SELECT EMPLOYEE_ID, LASTNAME, FIRSTNAME, DEPTNUMB
FROM EMPLOYEE
WHERE DEPTNUMB NOT = 'MARK'
```

Be sure to take care in using the correct logic in the WHERE clause, especially when intermixing the keywords NOT, AND, and OR. Remember, NOT is the negation of a condition and you must use the proper Boolean Algebra in an operation containing NOT, AND, or OR. That is, the opposite of the operation "A or B" using Boolean Algebra is:

$$\sim(A \text{ or } B) = \sim A \text{ and } \sim B$$

and the opposite of the operation "A and B" becomes:

$$\sim(A \text{ and } B) = \sim A \text{ or } \sim B$$

Therefore, the negation of "A OR B" is "NOT A AND NOT B" and the negation of "A AND B" is "NOT A OR NOT B."

For example, if you want all the employees who are not in either the Accounting or Marketing departments, the query becomes

```
SELECT EMPLOYEE_ID, LASTNAME, FIRSTNAME, DEPTNUMB
FROM EMPLOYEE
WHERE DEPTNUMB NOT = 'ACCT' AND DEPTNUMB NOT = 'MARK'
```

Checking for Data Entry Errors One way to check the accuracy of the data in the table is to check for errors in the data. The query:

```
SELECT EMPLOYEE_ID, SEX
FROM EMPLOYEE
WHERE SEX NOT = 'M' AND SEX NOT = 'F'
```

should display no rows. In this case, you want to get a null answer, which means the system has not found a row matching the condition in the WHERE clause. Because you made the SEX column a required field by creating it as NOT NULL, whoever entered data into the database had to enter some value for the SEX column in each row. You are checking that data entry operation to verify that all the data in SEX is valid, that is, M or F.

Similarly, you might want to verify that the column for the employee's social security number (EMPLOYEE_ID) has numbers for every person. The statement:

```
SELECT EMPLOYEE_ID
FROM EMPLOYEE
WHERE EMPLOYEE_ID = '
```

checks the EMPLOYEE_ID column for nine spaces. If a row is found, SQL will display it. You will not be able to see it because the display of nine spaces cannot be seen on the screen. Therefore, you can change the last query to:

```
SELECT EMPLOYEE_ID, 'HERE IS A BLANK LINE'
FROM EMPLOYEE
WHERE EMPLOYEE_ID = '
```

Now if SQL finds nine spaces in EMPLOYEE_ID, it displays it along with the message "HERE IS A BLANK LINE." Now you can visually see the results of the query.

But why are you checking for space values in the EMPLOYEE_ID field? When you created the table, you created it as a required field by using NOT NULL in CREATE for that column. In addition, you created a unique index on the EMPLOYEE_ID column. SQL could store one row having spaces in this unique column because spaces are valid characters. Here, you are checking for a data entry error where someone might have inadvertently loaded a blank row into the database. If such a row does exist in the table, you probably would never see it. Later, if you attempt to count the number of rows in a column for some statistical work, this extra invisible row could change the accuracy of the results.

The IN Keyword SELECT has many keywords you can use to extract selected data from the database. The general form of the SELECT statement having the IN keyword is:

```
SELECT list of columns
FROM table name
WHERE column name IN (list)
```

Let's write the query to extract all the rows from the EMPLOYEE table containing the codes TN, KY, or KS in the STATE column. It becomes:

```
SELECT EMPLOYEE_ID, CITY, STATE
```

```
FROM EMPLOYEE
WHERE STATE = 'TN' OR STATE = 'KY' OR STATE = 'KS'
```

We could rewrite this query, however, using the IN keyword in the WHERE clause. The rewritten query becomes:

```
SELECT EMPLOYEE_ID, CITY, STATE
FROM EMPLOYEE
WHERE STATE IN ('TN', 'KY', 'KS')
```

You need to use a comma to separate all data within the parentheses. You also need to use the apostrophe delimiter in the search argument because the column contains alphanumeric data.

SQL searches the column for all items listed in the IN clause. For the last query, if an index on STATE exists, SQL searches the index and extracts the data using the page number and RID values found in the index. If, however, STATE does not have an index, SQL locks the tablespace containing all the rows for the logical table EMPLOYEE and searches each row on each page until it exhausts the data in the tablespace.

The list within the parentheses for the IN clause does not have to contain unique values. That is, the query:

```
SELECT EMPLOYEE_ID, CITY, STATE
FROM EMPLOYEE
WHERE STATE IN ('TN', 'KY', 'TN', 'KS', 'KY')
```

is a valid statement. If you executed this above query and no rows fulfilled the query requirements for the IN clause, SQL would return a null row.

The BETWEEN Keyword   On occasion you might want to extract data that has a value between two numbers. For example, to find all the employees who make between $5 and $9.99 (inclusive) per hour you could write either of the following queries:

```
SELECT EMPLOYEE_ID, LASTNAME, FIRSTNAME, HOURLY_RATE
FROM EMPLOYEE
WHERE HOURLY_RATE >= 5.00 AND HOURLY_RATE < 10.00
```

or

```
SELECT EMPLOYEE_ID, LASTNAME, FIRSTNAME, HOURLY_RATE
FROM EMPLOYEE
WHERE HOURLY_RATE BETWEEN 5.00 AND 9.99
```

The LIKE Keyword   You can use the underscore character ("_") as a one character wildcard in a column search using the LIKE keyword in WHERE. The statement:

```
SELECT STATE
```

```
FROM EMPLOYEE
WHERE STATE LIKE 'I_'
```

displays all rows where the first character in the STATE column begins with the letter "I." A sample output would include the following states:

```
STATE

IN
IO
```

In this case, the underscore is a wildcard for any single alphanumeric character. The column you search using the wildcard, however, must contain only alphanumeric data (defined as CHAR or VARCHAR).

On the other hand, if you want to search the data for a three-character code where the first character must be a D, you would use

```
WHERE DEPARTMENT_CODE LIKE 'D__'
```

as the search parameter. Here, the two underscored wildcard characters guarantee that the results will contain three characters in the selected field.

If you are unsure as to the length of the data in the column, you can use the wildcard "%" to represent from zero to 254 characters. That means the query:

```
SELECT LASTNAME, FIRSTNAME
FROM EMPLOYEE
WHERE LASTNAME LIKE 'S%'
```

lists every name in the table that begins with the letter "S." The results of this query could look like this:

LASTNAME	FIRSTNAME
SMITH	SUE
STREEP	MIKE
S	LIN
SOO	WONG
SOTHERLAND	RICHARD

In addition, you can place these wildcard characters anywhere within the search argument. That is, the query:

```
SELECT LASTNAME, FIRSTNAME
FROM EMPLOYEE
WHERE LASTNAME LIKE 'SM%' AND FIRSTNAME LIKE 'D__' AND
      SEX = 'M' AND STATE IN ('OH', 'IL')
```

lists all employees who are males from either Ohio or Illinois and whose last name begins with the two letters SM and whose first name is a three character name beginning with the letter D.

Using Parentheses as a Separator You must look to Boolean Algebra when placing AND and OR keywords in the same query search argument. The rule is: use parentheses to separate the statements by treating as a group the parameters on either side of the AND or OR keyword. So, the query:

```
SELECT LASTNAME, FIRSTNAME
FROM EMPLOYEE
WHERE (SEX = 'M' AND STATE IN ('IN', 'IL'))
    OR (SEX = 'F' AND STATE IN ('FL', 'GA'))
```

displays the names of all the male employees who live in Indiana or Illinois. In addition, it displays the names of all the females who live in Florida or Georgia. Note that all the parameters on the left side of OR are enclosed in parentheses, as are those on the right side.

The NULL and NOT NULL Keyword Because null values could exist in the data, you might need to identify which columns actually contain them. Remember, when you CREATE a table and do not make the column a required column (i.e., by using NOT NULL), the column could contain nulls. To check for null characters in the WHERE clause of SELECT, you must use either the phrase:

```
IS NULL
```

or

```
IS NOT NULL
```

as the search parameter. That is, the query:

```
SELECT EMPLOYEE_ID, LASTNAME, FIRSTNAME
FROM EMPLOYEE
WHERE PHONE IS NULL
```

lists all the employees having a null value in their PHONE column. The phrase:

```
WHERE PHONE = NULL
```

will generate an error message.

After loading data into the database, check all columns for null values. For the EMPLOYEE table, someone might have failed to answer a question on some employment form and the data entry operator will have to bypass that column when he or she enters the data into the database. Obviously, if you CREATE a column as NOT NULLs, the data entry operator will be forced to place a value in that column when he or she INSERTs it into the database. If you CREATE the column as a NULL column, however, then SQL permits nulls to be loaded as a valid data value. In certain queries, these null values can cause problems by generating incorrect counts when you tabulate the number of rows in a column. Also, some averages might be incorrect when you use certain functions on a column containing nulls. You can resolve the null columns by systematically entering queries identifying those rows that contain null values.

Arithmetic Operations You can use the arithmetic operators of $+$, $-$, $/$, and $*$ anywhere in the SELECT criteria. For example, the query:

```
SELECT EMPLOYEE_ID, LASTNAME, FIRSTNAME, HOURLY_WAGE * 1.1
FROM EMPLOYEE
WHERE DEPTNUMB = 'ACCT'
```

produces the results in Figure 9.11.

When you place an arithmetic operation in the list of selected columns for display, SQL does not place the column name as a heading above that column.

In addition, you can use arithmetic operations in the WHERE clause. The query:

```
SELECT EMPLOYEE_ID, LASTNAME, FIRSTNAME,
        HOURLY_WAGE * HOURS_WEEK
FROM EMPLOYEE
WHERE HOURLY_WAGE * HOURS_WEEK < 100.00
```

lists all employees whose base wage for the week was less than $100. Sample results would look like this:

EMPLOYEE_ID	LASTNAME	FIRSTNAME	
117878788	SMITH	ADAM	72.87
123456789	DOE	JOHN	98.33
656565656	JEFFERSON	TOM	34.50
989898989	LINCOLN	ABE	56.93

Clearly, the statements

```
WHERE 100 > HOURLY_WAGE * HOURS_WEEK
```

and

```
WHERE HOURLY_WAGE * HOURS_WEEK < 100.00
```

are equivalent. However, be careful in writing queries containing inequalities because their use must conform to algebraic rules.

The results in Figure 9.11 are sorted by EMPLOYEE_ID. Remember, you placed an index on EMPLOYEE_ID and SQL extracted the rows from the database using that index. Because the index keys in the index are in sorted order, the results are extracted from the pages in the tablespace in that sorted order.

EMPLOYEE_ID	LASTNAME	FIRSTNAME	
123456789	DOE	JOHN	4.95
234567890	SMITH	MARY	9.85
342234432	JOHNSON	KAREN	8.31
351010101	STEVENS	HARRY	7.21
410210210	ANDREWS	JOHN	9.75

FIGURE 9.11   *Results of a query containing an arithmetic expression.*

But what if you wanted to sort the results based on some nonkey field or some other criteria? You need a technique or keyword that performs automatic sorts on the results.

The ORDER BY Keyword One disadvantage to queries is that the results could appear in any order. That means the results are not necessarily presorted in ascending or descending order. You can force SQL to sort the results by placing the keyword ORDER BY in the query. The query:

```
SELECT EMPLOYEE_ID, LASTNAME, FIRSTNAME,
       HOURLY_WAGE * HOURS_WEEK
FROM EMPLOYEE
WHERE HOURLY_WAGE * HOURS_WEEK < 100.00
ORDER BY LASTNAME
```

sorts the results using the column LASTNAME as the key for sorting. Now the output looks like:

EMPLOYEE_ID	LASTNAME	FIRSTNAME	
123456789	DOE	JOHN	98.33
656565656	JEFFERSON	TOM	34.50
989898989	LINCOLN	ABE	56.93
117878788	SMITH	ADAM	72.87

SQL still uses the index to extract the data from the tablespace. But, because we used the keyword ORDER BY, SQL places the extracted data into a buffer area in central memory and sorts the results using a second buffer area. After the memory sort is completed, SQL displays the sorted results of this second buffer area.

You can rearrange the list and place the results in descending sorted order by using the keyword DESC in ORDER BY. That is, the query:

```
SELECT EMPLOYEE_ID, LASTNAME, FIRSTNAME,
       HOURLY_WAGE * HOURS_WEEK
FROM EMPLOYEE
WHERE HOURLY_WAGE * HOURS_WEEK < 100.00
ORDER BY LASTNAME DESC
```

produces the following results:

EMPLOYEE_ID	LASTNAME	FIRSTNAME	
117878788	SMITH	ADAM	72.87
989898989	LINCOLN	ABE	56.93
656565656	JEFFERSON	TOM	34.50
123456789	DOE	JOHN	98.33

Obviously, if SQL performs a memory sort when you use ORDER BY, you need to place certain restrictions on the number of rows you sort. As a general rule, you do not sort more than 1000 rows using ORDER BY because the time it takes to sort and the amount of memory available makes larger sorts inappropriate. For larger sorts, use a system's utility, a system's sort, or some other routine to accomplish the task. Whereas the ORDER BY sort algorithms are primitive, the system's sort utility typically uses advanced algorithms to sort the data and is very efficient in its use of systems resources.

The previous data still presents you with a problem. Suppose you want to sort the data based on the weekly salary each employee receives. SQL, however, does not permit the use of a numeric computation in the ORDER BY clause. So, you can only sort using the column name from the original table. In this case, you must use the relative location of the column as it appears in the SELECT statement's list of columns. To sort the data based on the employee's weekly wage, use:

```
SELECT EMPLOYEE_ID, LASTNAME, FIRSTNAME,
       HOURLY_WAGE * HOURS_WEEK
FROM EMPLOYEE
WHERE HOURLY_WAGE * HOURS_WEEK < 100.00
ORDER BY 4
```

Use the statement:

```
ORDER BY 4
```

because the column HOURLY_WAGE * HOURS_WEEK appears in the fourth column of the selected data. The results now become:

EMPLOYEE_ID	LASTNAME	FIRSTNAME	
656565656	JEFFERSON	TOM	34.50
989898989	LINCOLN	ABE	56.93
117878788	SMITH	ADAM	72.87
123456789	DOE	JOHN	98.33

Conversely, you can use:

```
ORDER BY 4 DESC:
```

if you want to rearrange the results in descending order.

You can perform multiple sorts within a sort, a process called **subsorting**. In a subsort, you place the columns to be subsorted in the ORDER BY clause in the order in which you want them sorted. Suppose you want a listing of all employees who are from Illinois. In addition, you want this list alphabetized by city. And finally, if multiple employees live in the same city, you want the listing to sort the employees' names in alphabetical order. For this example, you would use the query:

```
SELECT STATE, CITY, LASTNAME
FROM EMPLOYEE
WHERE STATE = 'IL'
ORDER BY CITY, LASTNAME
```

In this case, when SQL extracts the data from the database, it first sorts it by city and, for any data having the same city name, it sorts that data by last name. A sample listing might look like this:

IL	CHICAGO	BRUDER
IL	CHICAGO	FRATER
IL	CHICAGO	SYSTUR
IL	CLARKSVILLE	KITER
IL	CLARKSVILLE	LAMBERS
IL	PEORIA	MATHEWS
IL	PEORIA	NOTHAM
IL	RASTER	SMITH
IL	TOMSVILLE	JONES

Summary Functions Like many other software products, SQL has some built-in functions. These include:

MIN	SUM
MAX	COUNT(*)
AVG	COUNT(DISTINCT)

Each of these functions returns a single value. For example, to find the smallest hourly wage in the EMPLOYEE table, use:

```
SELECT MIN(HOURLY_WAGE)
FROM EMPLOYEE
```

which returns the single summary value: 4.95. You also can find the average hourly wage in the EMPLOYEE table using the query:

```
SELECT AVG(HOURLY_WAGE)
FROM EMPLOYEE
```

This query returns the value: 7.85. Notice the absence of headings above the data in the results. For summary functions, SQL eliminates the column name above the data it extracts.

You can place multiple summary functions in the same SELECT statement. The query:

```
SELECT COUNT(*), MIN(HOURLY_WAGE), AVG(HOURLY_WAGE)
FROM EMPLOYEE
```

returns the three values: 59, 4.95, 7.85. For this query, there are 59 rows matching the query conditions (i.e., COUNT(*)). In addition, the smallest hourly wage in the table is $4.95 and the average of all the hourly wages is $7.85.

You could restrict the query further by placing conditions in the WHERE clause. That is, to find the minimum hourly wage, the average hourly wage, and the number of males in the EMPLOYEE table we use the query:

```
SELECT COUNT(*), MIN(HOURLY_WAGE), AVG(HOURLY_WAGE)
FROM EMPLOYEE
WHERE SEX = 'M'
```

Now the results appear as: **33, 4.95, 8.88**. This translates to 33 males making an average hourly wage of $8.88 with the smallest wage being $4.95.

The option COUNT DISTINCT finds the number of different entries existing in any one column. The query:

```
SELECT COUNT(DISTINCT SEX)
```

should give the value 2 as a result because only M or F are possible. Obviously if the result of this query is 1, then the data in the database is about a single sex, either M or F. If the query produces an answer higher than 2, however, then the data contains contamination somewhere in the column for SEX. If this occurred, you then would query the data further to identify the rows that do not contain an F or M in the SEX column. You can later make the necessary corrections.

You can find out how many different departments exist in the EMPLOYEE table by using the query:

```
SELECT COUNT(DISTINCT DEPTNUMB)
FROM EMPLOYEE
```

The result of **5** indicates that five different department numbers exist in the data of the DEPTNUMB column.

The GROUP BY Keyword You can summarize data into groupings based on data in a table's column. Although the query:

```
SELECT COUNT(DISTINCT DEPTNUMB)
FROM EMPLOYEE
```

gives the number of distinct entries in the column DEPTNUMB, it tells you little about the makeup of that data. However, the query:

```
SELECT DEPTNUMB, COUNT(*)
FROM EMPLOYEE
GROUP BY DEPTNUMB
ORDER BY DEPTNUMB
```

gives the following results:

```
DEPTNUMB

ACCT        12
AUDT         5
MARK        11
PERS         4
TRNG         3
```

Now you know there are 12 people in Accounting, 5 in Auditing, and so on. Whenever you use the GROUP BY clause, the column used to group the data also must appear in the column listing after the SELECT keyword. That is, the query:

```
SELECT COUNT(*)
FROM EMPLOYEE
GROUP BY DEPTNUMB
ORDER BY DEPTNUMB
```

produces an error message and will not work because it did not contain the grouping column name (DEPTNUMB) in the list of columns after the SELECT keyword.

Also, the columns you list in SELECT containing a GROUP BY must be summary data. GROUP BY is a summary function and produces a single value for items in that grouping. Because SQL produces a single value for the grouping, it only reserves one line for its results. Obviously, you cannot use this procedure to list the names of the employees in the grouping. The query:

```
SELECT DEPTNUMB, LASTNAME
FROM EMPLOYEE
GROUP BY DEPTNUMB
```

produces an error message. In this case LASTNAME is not a summary value, which causes the query to fail. Remember, if only one line displays for each grouping, you cannot place data that potentially contains more than one piece of data in the column listing.

You can, however, place restrictions in the WHERE clause. For example, the query:

```
SELECT DEPTNUMB, COUNT(*)
FROM EMPLOYEE
WHERE SEX = 'F'
GROUP BY DEPTNUMB
ORDER BY DEPTNUMB
```

lists the number of females in each department. The results appear in Figure 9.12.

The WHERE clause restricts SQL so it selects only those rows from the database that match the search criteria in WHERE. SQL uses several buffer areas to handle the varying criteria within the query. In the last query, SQL creates a buffer to hold the data from WHERE. It then summarizes this data using a second buffer. Finally, SQL uses a third buffer to sort the results for display (Figure 9.13).

DEPTNUMB	
ACCT	10
AUDT	2
MARK	6
PERS	2
TRNG	1

FIGURE 9.12
Results from a GROUP BY query.

The HAVING Keyword Suppose for the results in Figure 9.12 you want to view only certain selected data from the third buffer. You might want to display only those departments that have more than five females. In this case, you cannot use WHERE because you have not summarized the data (it's in the first buffer). Remember, WHERE restricts SQL in the extraction of certain data from the database. It does not participate in the summarization, grouping, or sorting of it. In this case, it isn't until you already have grouped the data that you want to restrict the results.

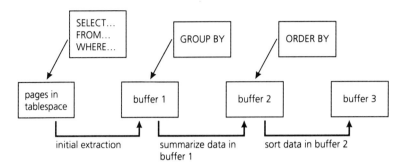

FIGURE 9.13   *Using buffers to create correct results.*

The keyword HAVING is similar to the WHERE keyword but only restricts the summary results produced from a GROUP BY. The query:

```
SELECT DEPTNUMB, COUNT(*)
FROM EMPLOYEE
WHERE SEX = 'F'
GROUP BY DEPTNUMB
HAVING COUNT(*) > 5
ORDER BY DEPTNUMB
```

lists the departments having more than five female employees. Remember, the data in Figure 9.12 is the result of a GROUP BY and, therefore, can be restricted by HAVING. The final results of this query are:

DEPTNUMB

ACCT	10
MARK	6

In effect, you have summarized the summary data.

Notice the order in which the keywords appear in the query. The order you must use is:

```
SELECT . . .
FROM . . .
WHERE . . .
GROUP BY . . .
HAVING . . .
ORDER BY . . .
```

SQL requires all queries to follow this arrangement of keywords. You can eliminate the WHERE, the GROUP BY, the GROUP BY and HAVING, or the ORDER BY, but you must place whatever you use in the above pattern. Obviously, you must have the keywords SELECT and FROM in every query and you cannot use HAVING without GROUP BY in any query.

The INSERT Statement

You use the INSERT statement to load data into the database. INSERT places a row into the first available row on a page in a tablespace. SQL uses the tablespace you identified in the CREATE statement when you created the table definition.

To load the row in Figure 9.14, you use one of three versions of the INSERT statement.

The first version identifies the column names and the data that will go into them. For the row in Figure 9.14, the INSERT statement becomes:

```
INSERT INTO EMPLOYEE
    (EMPLOYEE_ID, LASTNAME, FIRSTNAME, ADDRESS, CITY, STATE,
    SEX, DEPTNUMB)
VALUES
    ('123456789', 'DOE', 'JOHN', '123 E. 3RD', 'CHICAGO', 'IL',
    'M','ACCT')
```

In this INSERT version, SQL uses a one-to-one correspondence between the column names preceding the VALUES keyword and the data following the VALUES keyword. You could use either the above statement or the statement:

```
INSERT INTO EMPLOYEE
    (LASTNAME, FIRSTNAME, ADDRESS, CITY, STATE,
    DEPTNUMB, EMPLOYEE_ID, SEX)
VALUES
    ('DOE', 'JOHN', '123 E. 3RD', 'CHICAGO', 'IL',
    'ACCT', '123456789', 'M')
```

because they are equivalent. In both cases, the data following the VALUES keyword must match up with the column names preceding the VALUES keyword. And this matchup must be a one-to-one matchup.

Because ADDRESS, CITY, and STATE are not required columns, you could alternately use:

```
INSERT INTO EMPLOYEE
    (EMPLOYEE_ID, LASTNAME, FIRSTNAME, SEX, DEPTNUMB)
    VALUES
    ('123456789', 'DOE', 'JOHN', 'M', 'ACCT')
```

In this case, SQL places null values in the nonlisted columns of INSERT.

The second version, however, only identifies the data that will go into

EMPLOYEE ID	LAST NAME	FIRST NAME	ADDRESS	CITY	STATE	SEX	DEPTNUMB
123456789	DOE	JOHN	123 E. 3RD	CHICAGO	IL	M	ACCT

FIGURE 9.14 *A row of the EMPLOYEE table.*

the columns of the table. This form uses the table definition from the CREATE statement to place the data in the row. Again, for the row in Figure 9.14, the INSERT statement becomes:

```
INSERT INTO EMPLOYEE
    VALUES ('123456789', 'DOE', 'JOHN', '123 E. 3RD', 'CHICAGO', 'IL',
        'M', 'ACCT')
```

In this case, the data in the INSERT statement must match up with SQL's catalog description of the table. One obvious disadvantage to this form is that the end user might not know the table definition as it was CREATEd and later ALTEREd. In addition, in the second version's INSERT, you must list all the data for each column. That is, if you want to place data only in the required columns, you would need to use:

```
INSERT INTO EMPLOYEE
    VALUES ('123456789', 'DOE', 'JOHN', ' ', ' ', ' ', 'M', 'ACCT')
```

because EMPLOYEE_ID, LASTNAME, FIRSTNAME, SEX, and DEPTNUMB are the only columns you created as NOT NULL. In this version, you have to use three values containing spaces to correspond to ADDRESS, CITY, and STATE. Because the table definition contains these three columns, they must be included in this version of the INSERT statement and their values (i.e., a space) must be properly placed in INSERT to correspond to their relative location in the table.

A third version of the INSERT statement allows you to capture multiple rows from one table and place them into another table. It has the general form:

```
INSERT INTO tablename
    SELECT list of columns
    FROM tablename
    WHERE condition
```

This third version of INSERT is particularly handy if you want to create copies of existing tables for use by the various user departments without their actually accessing the original base table in real time.

Suppose that a user department wants to create reports based on the company's previous day's business activity. If the table holding yesterday's activity is called BUSINESS, you can create a second table called YESTERDAY that will have the same column format as BUSINESS. You then can load the prior day's business activity into this temporary user-department's table using:

```
DELETE FROM YESTERDAY;
INSERT INTO YESTERDAY
    SELECT *
    FROM BUSINESS
```

The user department then can write reports and modify the data using YESTERDAY without touching the original base table BUSINESS. You execute the DELETE and INSERT statements in a batch file during the third shift of your data processing operations. First you DELETE all data from YESTERDAY so that it will contain only the prior day's business activity. Obviously, you could list the individual column names and place conditions on the data using the WHERE option. The statement:

```
DELETE FROM TODAY;
INSERT INTO TODAY
    SELECT CUSTNAME, CUSTID, ITEMSOLD, AMOUNTSOLD
    FROM BUSINESS
    WHERE DEPTNUMB IN ('HOUSEHOLDS', 'APPLIANCES', 'GARDEN')
```

copies selected data from the table BUSINESS and places it in the table TODAY. In this case, be certain that the column descriptions in the CREATE statement for the TODAY table match the column descriptions for CUSTNAME, CUSTID, ITEMSOLD, and AMOUNTSOLD of BUSINESS.

Using Synonyms and Views

You do not have to use the fully qualified name for the table names in the SELECTs. If the table EMPLOYEE_HISTORY was created by #QWERT, its fully qualified name is #QWERT.EMPLOYEE_HISTORY. If #QWERT gives us permission to use his or her table, he or she would have to use CL to indicate that fact to SQL. After you have been GRANTed authority to use the table, you would have to use the fully qualified name each time you wanted to access data in it.

When you access #QWERT's table you could use:

```
SELECT *
FROM #QWERT.EMPLOYEE_HISTORY
```

Rather than use the fully qualified name of a table, you can create a synonym for it and use the synonym name in SELECT. You could create a synonym for #QWERT's table using:

```
CREATE SYNONYM HISTORY
FOR #QWERT.EMPLOYEE_HISTORY
```

and use:

```
SELECT *
FROM HISTORY
```

to extract data from it. This might be more convenient than using the fully qualified name.

However, suppose #QWERT does not want you to access all the rows within his or her table. He or she could create a view of it using the statement:

```
CREATE VIEW HISTORY_VIEW
```

AS SELECT EMPLOYEE_ID, LASTNAME, FIRSTNAME
    FROM EMPLOYEE_HISTORY

In this case, when #QWERT gives other users authority to use the view, these other users have access to only the EMPLOYEE_ID, LASTNAME, and FIRSTNAME columns of the EMPLOYEE_HISTORY table. Once these other users have authority to access the view, they can create a synonym for it if they wish. As far as SQL is concerned, it does not care if the name in an SQL statement is a table, view, or synonym.

Once you create a view or synonym you cannot ALTER it. If for some reason you want to change a view, you must DROP the view and then re-CREATE it. You must be careful, however, when you drop SQL structures. If user #QWERT gives you a view of a table and you in turn give someone else a view of your view (i.e., a view of a view), when #QWERT drops your view, all other SQL structures based on that view are lost. In this case, #QWERT's dropping of a view might severely hinder other users.

In the corporate world, a DBADM or a member of the systems development team will create views for the user departments. Remember, the actual table design is dependent on the structure of the data, not on a particular user department's wants and needs. Hence, a single table might contain only a few columns that an individual user department wants or needs. The user's view then must link multiple tables containing multiple columns so the user can access the data he or she needs. Although the user's view is a composite of multiple tables, it is transparent to him or her. The user really does not know (or care) whether the table he or she is accessing is a base table, a view, or a synonym—as long as it works. You need to be careful in dropping structures because that action might cascade throughout the database and affect other entities the users need.

The DELETE Statement

You can erase one or more rows from logical tables using the DELETE statement. It has the general form:

DELETE FROM name
WHERE condition

The "name" can be a table name, a synonym, or a view. For example, you can erase all rows in the logical table EMPLOYEE using:

DELETE FROM EMPLOYEE

When you execute this statement, SQL erases all the rows on all pages in the tablespace containing the logical table EMPLOYEE. When you erase data from tables using DELETE without the WHERE keyword, you must be careful because all the data in the table disappears. If you inadvertently make a mistake, you can regenerate the destroyed data using a backup of it—if it exists. It is crucial for the data center's computer operators to backup the tablespaces in a timely manner. Failure to do so might result in a tremendous loss of data, especially if inexperienced users have access to the DELETE command.

You can put a condition clause after the WHERE keyword to restrict the rows SQL erases. The statement:

```
DELETE FROM EMPLOYEE
WHERE EMPLOYEE_ID = '123456789'
```

erases all the data in the row having 123456789 as the employee number. In this case, because EMPLOYEE_ID has unique keys, SQL will erase only one row. Similarly, if you use the statement:

```
DELETE FROM EMPLOYEE
WHERE SEX = 'M' AND STATE = 'IL'
```

SQL will erase all the rows containing data on the males from Illinois. The condition clause in the DELETE's WHERE clause can be any SQL condition similar to the SELECT's WHERE clause.

When using the DROP statement, you erase the structure of an entity. When you use the DELETE statement, however, you simply erase data within some structure—the structure remains, the data does not. Also, you must be careful in using someone else's table via a view. If you delete rows from the view, those rows are deleted from the base table. Similarly, if you INSERT or UPDATE on a view, SQL INSERTs and UPDATEs the base table.

The UPDATE Statement

You modify data in the rows of a logical table using the UPDATE statement. Its general form is:

```
UPDATE name
SET column name #1 = value,
    column name #2 = value,
    .
    .
    .
WHERE condition
```

You must use a comma to separate the modifications to multiple columns in the same UPDATE statement. The statement:

```
UPDATE EMPLOYEE
SET LASTNAME = 'MACKEY',
    ADDRESS = '8456 FELLOW ST.'
WHERE EMPLOYEE_ID = '910910910'
```

changes the last name and street address of the employee whose ID number is 910910910.

Not only can you set different columns to specific values, you also can put algebraic operators in the WHERE condition. So, if you want to give every female a 10% increase in her hourly wage, you use:

```
UPDATE EMPLOYEE
SET HOURLY_RATE = HOURLY_RATE * 1.1
WHERE SEX = 'F'
```

To verify that the modifications actually occurred, enter:

```
SELECT SEX, HOURLY_RATE, EMPLOYEE_ID
FROM EMPLOYEE
WHERE SEX = 'F'
```

both before and after you enter the UPDATE statement and compare the results.

Commercial Usage

For many users, the tables they access are in reality views of other tables. These views were created either by the DBADM or a member of the systems development staff. Obviously, if the view contains columns that really do not exist in a base table, SQL cannot change the data in it, delete it, or insert new values into it. How do you get columns that are composites of other columns and exist logically, but not physically in some row in the tablespace? Remember, a view can include such things as:

- Summary data (i.e., AVG(GRADE1 + GRADE2))
- Computations (i.e., HOURS_WORKED * RATE_PAY)
- GROUP BY (i.e., GROUP BY DEPTNUMB)

In each of these cases, the data in the view's columns resides in a buffer area and not in a row on some DASD page. Because the data is not on a page on DASD, SQL cannot modify, delete, or insert values into it.

Joining Multiple Tables

You can use data from more than one table by joining the tables containing the data. You logically link two tables together by doing the following:

- Listing the desired columns in SELECT
- Listing the table names in FROM
- Coupling in the WHERE clause a secondary or foreign key of one table with a key of the second table

Suppose you want to display the last name, first name, and department name of all the female employees. Both the first and last name of the employees are in the EMPLOYEE table and the department name is in the DE-PARTMENT table. Remember, when you designed these tables, you created a

EMPLOYEE table

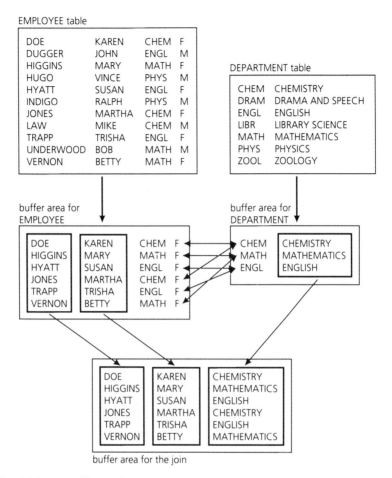

FIGURE 9.15 *Joining two tables together.*

common linkage via the DEPTNUMB column in EMPLOYEE and DEPTNO column in DEPARTMENT. The query statement to logically link these tables becomes:

SELECT LASTNAME, FIRSTNAME, DEPTNAME ◄——— list of columns from both tables
FROM EMPLOYEE, DEPARTMENT ◄——
WHERE SEX ='F' AND the table names for the join
    DEPTNO = DEPTNUMB ◄——
ORDER BY LAST NAME the joining criteria

In this case, SQL accesses the tables and places the query's data in buffer areas (Figure 9.15). The results become:

LASTNAME	FIRSTNAME	DEPTNAME
DOE	KAREN	CHEMISTRY
HIGGINS	MARY	MATHEMATICS
HYATT	SUSAN	ENGLISH

JONES	MARTHA	CHEMISTRY
TRAPP	TRISHA	ENGLISH
VERNON	BETTY	MATHEMATICS

You can link more than two tables together by placing additional joining criteria in the WHERE clause and listing the multiple tables in FROM. The query:

```
SELECT LASTNAME, FIRSTNAME, DEPTNAME, SCHOOLNAME
FROM EMPLOYEE, DEPARTMENT, SCHOOL
WHERE DEPTNO = DEPTNUMB AND
      SCHOOLNUMB = SCHOOLNO AND
      SEX = 'F'
ORDER BY LASTNAME
```

logically joins the three tables EMPLOYEE, DEPARTMENT, and SCHOOL and produces the following results:

LASTNAME	FIRSTNAME	DEPTNAME	SCHOOLNAME
DOE	KAREN	CHEMISTRY	APPLIED SCIENCE
HIGGINS	MARY	MATHEMATICS	ARTS & SCIENCE
HYATT	SUSAN	ENGLISH	ARTS & SCIENCE
JONES	MARTHA	CHEMISTRY	APPLIED SCIENCE
TRAPP	TRISHA	ENGLISH	ARTS & SCIENCE
VERNON	BETTY	MATHEMATICS	ARTS & SCIENCE

In each of these cases, the key columns in the joining criteria (i.e., DEPT-NUMB = DEPTNO) had different names. If they have the same name in each table, you have to use their fully qualified column names. So for the last query, if both tables had DEPTNUMB as a column name, you would use:

```
SELECT LASTNAME, FIRSTNAME, DEPTNAME, SCHOOLNAME
FROM EMPLOYEE, DEPARTMENT, SCHOOL
WHERE EMPLOYEE.DEPTNUMB = DEPARTMENT.DEPTNUMB AND
      DEPARTMENT.SCHOOLNUMB = SCHOOL.SCHOOLNUMB AND
      SEX = 'F'
ORDER BY LASTNAME
```

This query uses the fully qualified column names of EMPLOYEE.DEPTNUMB, DEPARTMENT.DEPTNUMB, DEPARTMENT.SCHOOLNUMB, and SCHOOL.SCHOOL-NUMB.

Remember, when you join two or more tables, you logically create a larger table (see Figure 9.16) that will physically reside in some buffer area of memory.

Subselects

Suppose you want a list of all employees who make more than the average hourly wage of the company. You would have to run two queries: one to

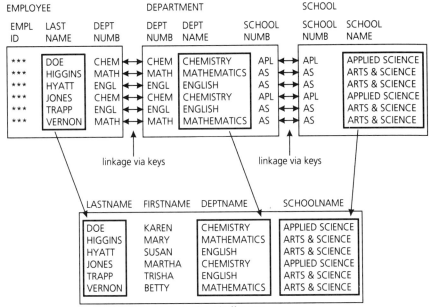

FIGURE 9.16 *Buffer area for a join.*

find the average hourly wage, and one to list the desired employees using this value. In this case, you would run the query:

```
SELECT AVG(HOURLY_WAGE)
FROM EMPLOYEE
```

to get the answer 7.32. Then you would use that value in WHERE and run the following query:

```
SELECT EMPLOYEE_ID, LASTNAME, FIRSTNAME, HOURLY_WAGE
FROM EMPLOYEE
WHERE HOURLY_WAGE > 7.32
```

Rather than splitting the problem into two (or more) queries, you can combine them into one SQL statement using the concept of a subselect. In a subselect you place one query inside another query using parentheses as a separator. The combination of the last two queries into a subselect becomes:

```
SELECT EMPLOYEE_ID, LASTNAME, FIRSTNAME, HOURLY_WAGE
FROM EMPLOYEE
WHERE HOURLY_WAGE > (SELECT AVG(HOURLY_WAGE)
                     FROM EMPLOYEE)
```

For subselects, SQL first executes the innermost query (i.e., SELECT AVG(HOURLY_WAGE) FROM EMPLOYEE). It then uses that value and executes the next outermost query. When you use a subselect in an arithmetic expression, you must always guarantee that only a single value is returned from the query. When you use summary functions in subselects, it is generally a part of an algebraic expression. The summary function guarantees only one number will return from the innermost query of the subselect.

You also can use subselects to generate a list of items for the IN keyword of SELECT. If you wanted to list all the department names that have no female employees, you could use:

```
SELECT DEPTNUMB
FROM EMPLOYEE
WHERE SEX NOT = 'F'
```

in one query to get PHIL, SOCO, and RELI. Then you could place these values in the query:

```
SELECT DEPTNAME, COUNT(*)
FROM DEPARTMENT
WHERE DEPTNUMB IN ('PHIL', 'SOCO', 'RELI')
```

to get your answer. Rather than using two independent queries to solve the task or problem, however, you could place the first query into the second query as a subselect to create the following single SELECT statement:

```
SELECT DEPTNAME, COUNT(*)
FROM DEPARTMENT
WHERE DEPTNUMB NOT IN (SELECT DEPTNUMB
                       FROM EMPLOYEE
                       WHERE SEX = 'F')
```

SQL works the innermost query first, extracts the data about the female employees, and places it into the IN selection list. SQL then works the outer SELECT statement and displays the results.

Typically you use subselects whenever you have to read the table more than once to obtain information for another query. In this case, you could execute the query:

```
SELECT DEPTNUMB
FROM EMPLOYEE
WHERE SEX = 'F'
```

and place the answers:

```
PHIL
SOCO
RELI
```

into the query:

```
SELECT DEPTNAME, COUNT(*)
FROM DEPARTMENT
WHERE DEPTNUMB IN ('PHIL', 'SOCO', 'RELI')
```

to obtain the needed results. However, running one query after another is not always practical because the results generated by the first query might include hundreds or even thousands of values. Surely, you would not want to reenter thousands of answers into the IN clause's list of values! For short queries on small tables, it might be best to forgo writing subselects and simply run one query after another using the answers of one query as parameters in the next query. If you are simply testing the query for future embedding into COBOL code, however, you must use subselects.

CONTROL LANGUAGE

In a mainframe environment, a user must log onto the system via TSO, CICS, or IMS. This logon process provides a first level of security by restricting access to SQL and its databases to only authorized users of the system. Once a user logs onto the system, he or she then can access an SQL menu screen. But unless that user has been GRANTed authorization to perform tasks within SQL, he or she can not proceed past viewing this initial SQL menu screen.

Control Language (CL) is the facility within SQL that provides the security for the database and the authorization to use SQL. Everything within SQL is protected and users must be given explicit authority to do the following:

- Access the entities within the database (i.e., database, tablespace, tables, views, etc.)
- Access the SQL language (i.e., DDL, DML, and CL statements)
- Perform other tasks within SQL (run programs, etc.)

The GRANT Keyword

In most cases, SYSADM creates a DBADM for a database and that DBADM then assigns authorizations to the various users of that database. SYSADM creates DBADMs using the command:

```
GRANT DBADM
ON DATABASE name
TO userid
```

In this case, "name" is the database name and "userid" is the user's logon ID. If a user is a DBADM, he or she can create tablespaces, tables, views, and other items within SQL. Obviously, SYSADM does not give such power to any end user. Typically, the DBADMs are project managers, senior systems analysts, other DBAs, and the directors of the educational facilities (including the Director of Technical Education and the Director of the End User Support Center).

SYSADM is responsible for maintaining the integrity of SQL and is generally not concerned with the day-to-day management of end-user applications. In most organizations, it is the DBADM's responsibility to control the user's access to SQL and to monitor his or her applications and the problems associated with them. Therefore, the end users are GRANTed authorization to use a particular database from the DBADM of that database. For the first-time SQL users KAREN, MIKE, and BILL, DBADM must use the commands:

```
GRANT USE OF TABLESPACE XYZ
TO KAREN, MIKE, BILL
```

```
GRANT CREATETAB
ON DATABASE DBXYZ
TO KAREN, MIKE, BILL
```

These statements give KAREN, MIKE, and BILL the authorization to access tablespace XYZ and to create tables within the databases DBXYZ. Here the general form of the GRANT statement is:

```
GRANT authority
ON entity
TO user id's
```

where "authority" is some SQL authority, "entity" is a database, tablespace, etc., and "user id's" are TSO, CICS, or IMS logon ID's.

Not only must DBADM grant users the authorization to use tablespace and create tables, he or she also must grant users the authorization to use the DML commands of SELECT, UPDATE, DELETE, and INSERT. The statement:

```
GRANT SELECT
ON EMPLOYEE
TO WANDA, TONY, MIKE
```

gives users WANDA, TONY, and MIKE the authorization to use only the SELECT statement when accessing the EMPLOYEE table. In addition, the statement:

```
GRANT UPDATE (LASTNAME, ADDRESS, CITY, STATE), INSERT, SELECT
ON EMPLOYEE
TO VALERY
```

restricts VALERY to only inserting new rows, viewing all rows, and updating columns LASTNAME, ADDRESS, CITY, and STATE of the EMPLOYEE table. Here, the GRANT statement specifies the exact columns VALERY can update. The less restrictive statement:

```
GRANT ALL
ON EMPLOYEE
TO VALERY
```

permits VALERY to use all the DML statements on the table EMPLOYEE.

When granting authorization to a particular user, only that user has the authorization. You can, however, give a user the authorization to GRANT to other users certain powers by using the phrase WITH GRANT OPTION in your GRANT statement. The statement:

```
GRANT UPDATE, INSERT
```

ON EMPLOYEE
TO VALERY
WITH GRANT OPTION

gives VALERY the right to modify all columns and add new rows to the table EMPLOYEE. In addition, she has the power to pass along this same authorization to another user (i.e., BOB) by issuing the statement:

GRANT UPDATE
ON EMPLOYEE
TO BOB

Now BOB can modify any column in the EMPLOYEE table.

In the business environment, DBADM gives the manager of a user department certain authorizations on the many tables assigned to that user department. By giving the manager of the department the GRANT OPTION authorization, he or she then can assign staff members within the department certain tasks and responsibilities on the database. DBADM issues the statement:

GRANT ALL
ON EMPLOYEE, DEPARTMENT, OFFICE, REGION
TO BIGGY
WITH GRANT OPTION

The manager "BIGGY" can reassign the SELECT, DELETE, UPDATE, and INSERT authorizations to selected individuals within his or her department. In this way, the division of labor permeates downward from the systems administrator (SYSADM) to the database administrator (DBADM) to the manager of the user department (BIGGY) and, finally, to the worker (WANDA, SUSAN, etc.).

The REVOKE Keyword

While GRANT gives users the authorization to use entities and SQL statements, the REVOKE statement removes authorizations from the user. The statement:

REVOKE UPDATE
ON EMPLOYEE
FROM BOB

removes BOB's authorization to modify the table EMPLOYEE. On the other hand, the statement:

REVOKE ALL
ON EMPLOYEE
FROM VALERY

destroys all DML privileges VALERY had on the table EMPLOYEE.

When you give someone the authorization to UPDATE on selected columns, however, you cannot selectively remove their authorization to update some of those columns. So the statement:

```
GRANT UPDATE (LASTNAME, SALARY)
ON PAYROLL
TO JOHN
```

gives JOHN the authority to modify the LASTNAME and SALARY columns of
PAYROLL. If you wanted to revoke his authorization to modify just the SALARY
column, you would have to revoke his entire UPDATE authorization using:

```
REVOKE UPDATE
ON PAYROLL
FROM JOHN
```

and reissue the selective update on LASTNAME using:

```
GRANT UPDATE (LASTNAME)
ON PAYROLL
TO JOHN
```

Be careful when revoking authorizations, especially if you gave a user
the WITH GRANT OPTION privilege. In this case, when you revoke the authorization containing WITH GRANT OPTION, a cascading effect occurs. When
you use the command:

```
GRANT ALL
ON EMPLOYEE
TO MANAGER
WITH GRANT OPTION
```

MANAGER has the power to give other users the right to access the EMPLOYEE
table. If and when you revoke MANAGER's authorization on the EMPLOYEE
table, you automatically revoke the authority of all users that were given
authority by MANAGER for that table via GRANT OPTION. If MANAGER uses:

```
GRANT ALL
ON EMPLOYEE
TO CHARLES, BETTY
```

and you revoke MANAGER's authority, SQL will automatically revoke CHARLES's
and BETTY's authorization. This becomes particularly troublesome when you
authorize a manager of a user department the power to access a large number
of tables and that department has a large staff. In these cases, the manager
might have assigned numerous individuals a wide variety of authorizations
to efficiently run the department. If that manager is promoted, retires, resigns,
or in some other way leaves that position, the authorizations given that manager will have to be revoked. The DBADM who originally gave the manager
the authorizations might have to spend a considerable amount of time and
effort to identify the users of the tables and what powers and privileges they
had. After DBADM revokes the former manager's privileges, DBADM must
reconstruct the authorizations to the members of that user department. Remember, the cascading of a revoke affects all authorizations that were based
on the original WITH GRANT OPTION statement.

In many companies, granting an authorization is not given to a user's individual account, but instead given to a special account. In this case, a manager is given a special account on the system in which to access SQL and the databases. When the manager allocates resources to the personnel in his or her department, it is via this special account. When you need to revoke the manager's privileges, you simply change the password on the special account. This in effect takes that manager off the system and protects the databases.

Suppose this manager is moved to a position of power within the company. Although he or she was once the manager of a department, certain security procedures must be followed. These procedures must have the support of upper management to allow things to run smoothly. By designing standards and procedures and having them approved by upper management and both internal and external auditing, you can produce a system of orderly transferring of power within the organization as the needs of the company change.

Automatic Authorizations

One of the features within SQL is the automatic authorization facility to creators of entities. When you are given CREATETAB authority to create tables, you do not need authorization to access the table. Once you create a table, you have automatic authorization to SELECT, DELETE, UPDATE, and INSERT on that table. You also have the automatic authorization to use WITH GRANT OPTION and assign other users the authorization to access the tables you create. You can create views and GRANT other users the authorization to use that view of your table.

In other words, if you create a table, you own that table and have certain automatic authorizations for that table. These authorizations are irrevocable. In fact, even SYSADM cannot revoke your automatic rights to tables you create. In particular, SYSADM cannot drop the tables you create nor access the table without your GRANTing authorization to do so. This does not mean that SYSADM is powerless. SYSADM (or DBADM, if authorized) always can drop the database or tablespace containing your table. This, in effect, destroys the structure of your table from the SQL catalog.

SUMMARY

Relational databases store data in tables containing rows (records) and columns (fields). The first tasks of the Systems Administrator (SYSADM) are to create a storage group identifying the volumes that will contain the data and create the database's name. He or she does this using the Data Definition Language (DDL) command CREATE. Next, SYSADM uses the Control Language (CL) command of GRANT to create a Database Administrator (DBADM) for each of the databases. DBADM, in turn will CREATE tablespaces and GRANT users the power to create tables in the tablespaces.

The CREATE TABLE statement stores a table's structure in the database's catalog. It identifies the column names, the type and size (VARCHAR, CHAR, INTEGER, SMALLINT, DECIMAL) of the data, and the column's code (NOT NULL, blank) for required/not required columns. In addition the CREATE TABLE statement identifies the table's name and the tablespace containing it.

The CREATE INDEX statement establishes an index for the table. In particular, it identifies the index's name, the indexed table's name, the index key's column name, and the name of the storage group that will hold the indexes. The CREATE UNIQUE INDEX statement creates a unique index. The description of the index is stored in the catalog and the index itself resides in an indexspace. The system manages the indexspace without programmer intervention.

Users can CREATE, ALTER, and DROP selected database entities. In addition, they can access data in the database using the Data Manipulation Language (DML) commands of SELECT, UPDATE, DELETE, and INSERT. SELECT reads database rows, UPDATE changes data in rows, DELETE erases rows from a table, and INSERT adds rows to a table.

Numerous options exist for the SELECT statement. These options include FROM, WHERE, GROUP BY, HAVING, ORDER BY, and UNION. In addition, when using the WHERE and HAVING option, the keywords AND, OR, NOT, IN, LIKE, BETWEEN, and IS NULL are available. The option ORDER BY sorts the data while GROUP BY summarizes data into groupings. Summary functions summarize data. These functions include MIN (minimum), MAX (maximum), COUNT (count), AVG (average), and SUM (sum). These functions appear either as an item in SELECT's list of columns or as a parameter in WHERE or HAVING. The guide in Figure 9.17 illustrates the required syntax for a variety of SELECT statements.

The INSERT statement loads data into tables. The data entries in INSERT form a one-to-one relationship between the column names and the values assigned to a row. The DELETE statement erases rows from a table. The UPDATE statement modifies or changes one or more rows in a table.

A view is established for one or more tables using the CREATE VIEW statement. It identifies the view's name and the rows and columns for the view via an embedded SELECT statement. A synonym is an alternate name for a table or view name. The CREATE SYNONYM statement establishes the synonym for a table or view. Once a view or synonym exists, it appears in the FROM statement in place of the table's name.

A SELECT statement can access multiple tables by a process of joining the tables together. The process requires the table names to be listed in FROM and the joining criteria to be established in WHERE. The joining criteria establishes the relationship between the tables by linking the keys of one table to the keys of another table.

Subselects extract data from a table and that data is used as a parametric value in the WHERE or HAVING clause of another SELECT. A SELECT statement can contain multinested subselects. The system uses a set of buffers to hold intermediate data while it systematically executes each subselect.

Guide to DML Statements

```
SELECT * FROM TEMP

SELECT A,B,C,D FROM TEMP
    WHERE E='XXX'
    ORDER BY A,B DESC

SELECT A,B,C,(A+B)/22 FROM TEMP
    ORDER BY 4

SELECT A,B,C FROM TEMP
    WHERE D BETWEEN 3 AND 9

SELECT A,B,C,D FROM TEMP
    WHERE B IN ('TN', 'GA', 'CA')

SELECT A,B,C FROM TEMP
    WHERE C LIKE 'W%' AND D LIKE '__R'

SELECT A,B,C FROM TEMP
    WHERE A IS NULL AND D IS NOT NULL AND E < = 23.33

SELECT A,B,C,D FROM TEMP
    DISTINCT

SELECT AVG(A), MIN(B), SUM(C) FROM TEMP

SELECT COUNT(*) FROM TEMP

SELECT COUNT(DISTINCT A) FROM TEMP
    WHERE C = 'XXX'

SELECT SUM(A),B,COUNT(*) FROM TEMP
    WHERE A LIKE 'D%'
    GROUP BY B

SELECT A,B,MIN(C),AVG(D) FROM TEMP
    WHERE E > 45
    GROUP BY A
    HAVING COUNT(*) > 23
    ORDER BY A

SELECT A,B,C,D FROM TEMP
    WHERE A IN (SELECT E FROM TEMP2
    WHERE F>10)

SELECT A,B,C,D FROM TEMP, TEMP2
    WHERE A=AA

SELECT A,B,C FROM TEMP, TEMP2
    WHERE TEMP.A = TEMP2.A

SELECT A,B,C,D FROM TEMP, TEMP2
    WHERE A=AA AND (B>21 OR C IN ('NY', 'CA'))

INSERT INTO TEMP
    (A,B,C,D) VALUES (122, 'CAT', 12.22, NULL)

INSERT INTO TEMP
    VALUES (12.22, 122, NULL, 'CAT', 12.22, ' ', NULL)

INSERT INTO TEMP
    SELECT AA,BB,CC,DD FROM TEMP2 WHERE AA>100

DELETE FROM TEMP

DELETE FROM TEMP WHERE A IN ('AR', 'KS', 'IN')

UPDATE TEMP
    SET A = 'QWERT',
        B = 23.33,
        C = 2*C
    WHERE D = '12345'
```

FIGURE 9.17   *Sample DML statements illustrating syntax.*

Control Language (CL) contains the two commands—GRANT and REVOKE. GRANT authorizes the use of a database entity or SQL command, and REVOKE cancels the authorization. If a user creates an entity, that user has certain inherent rights to that entity requiring no further authorization.

QUESTIONS

Given the following SALARY, DEPARTMENT, and JOB tables:

SALARY TABLE

EMPL ID	LAST NAME	FIRST NAME	SALARY	RACE	SEX	BIRTH DATE	JOB TITLE	DEPT
12000	MASDER	MARY	54000	W	F	431211	MGR	ACCT
12345	DOE	JOHN	32000	W	M	671110	SA	BUDG
23456	SMITH	MARY	35500	W	F	620103	SSA	BUDG
32456	GROVER	SUE	28000	W	F	651118	SP	ACCT
43000	GRIT	TRIB	51000	W	F	410903	MGR	PERS
43214	SMITH	ANDY	28500	B	M	610922	SP	PERS
43223	MARKUM	MIKE	30000	W	M	560717	SSA	PERS
45000	HERTS	FRED	56000	W	M	400916	MGR	BUDG
53211	BIRDY	KAREN	27500	W	F	651212	P	PERS
54322	KROSS	WM	23000	W	M	651109	AP	ACCT
55678	SMITH	BETTY	24000	B	F	660405	P	ACCT
56789	LOMB	LARRY	35000	W	M	540212	SSA	ACCT
59800	KRITTE	MARY	35000	W	F	590918	SSA	PERS
60311	JONES	LARRY	20000	W	M	630817	P	BUDG
61110	LAPLER	GIG	23900	W	F	610901	P	BUDG

DEPARTMENT TABLE

DEPTNUMB	NAME	MANAGER ID
ACCT	ACCOUNTING	12000
PERS	PERSONNEL	43000
BUDG	BUDGET	45000

JOB TABLE

JOB TITLE	JOB NAME
MGR	MANAGER
SSA	SENIOR SYSTEMS ANALYST
SA	SYSTEMS ANALYST
SP	SENIOR PROGRAMMER
P	PROGRAMMER
AP	ASSISTANT PROGRAMMER

Write the SQL statement to:

1. Create the SALARY table.
2. Create the DEPARTMENT table.
3. Create a unique index on DEPTNUMB and EMPLID.
4. Create a secondary index on job title and DEPT.
5. Find all the females making more than $30,000.
6. List all the managers.
7. List all the males.
8. List the last name and first name of all programmers and assistant programmers.
9. List all the female senior systems analysts.
10. List all females over 40 years old.
11. List all the males who are between 30 and 40 years old.

For the following set of questions exclude all the managers in the results. Write the SQL statement to:

12. List all the males in sorted order.
13. List all the females sorted by salary, the smallest salary first.
14. List all the employees who are not assigned to Accounting. List the data in sorted order by department.
15. Find the average salary of all employees; of the males; and of the females.
16. Find the average salary per department. List the data in sorted order by department.
17. Find the number of whites and blacks per department. List the data by department and by race per department.
18. Find the average salary by job title. List the data by department with the highest average salary listed first.
19. Find the sum of the salaries per department. List the data so the department with the largest payroll appears first.
20. Find the number of different job titles and the number of different departments.
21. List the smallest salary, the largest salary, and the average salary per department.
22. List the smallest salary, the largest salary, and the sum of all the salaries per job title.
23. List the average salary of all the males and females per job title.
24. List all the job titles having more than 3 females.
25. List all the departments having fewer than 5 employees.
26. Insert three more males into the EMPLOYEE table. Design the data so that it is consistent with the existing data.
27. Give all females a 10% raise.
28. Give all males who are not senior systems analysts or systems analysts a 9% raise.
29. Change JOHN DOE's employee number to 11234.
30. Delete MARY SMITH from the table.

Using either a join or a subselect, write the SQL statement to:

31. List all the females and the name of their work department.

32. List all employees, their job title name, and the name of their work department.
33. List the managers' names and the name of each respective work department.
34. List all employees making more than the average of all the females.
35. List the average salary for all job titles per department. The list is to include the full name of both the job title and the department.
36. List the average salary per department of all employees who are not managers and who are at least 30 years old.

For the following, write the CL statement to

37. Authorize WANDA, STEVE, and MIKE to SELECT and UPDATE the table SALARY.
38. Authorize FRED to use tablespace SCHOOLTST in database BUSINESS. Also, give him the authorization to create tables within the database.
39. Revoke STEVE's authorization on table PAYROLL.
40. Authorize SUSAN to update only the last name, first name, and job title in the SALARY table.
41. Give MARK and JAN the authorization to access and change the SALARY, DEPARTMENT, and JOB tables.

SPECIAL PROJECT
Minilab Assignment

Using either SQL/DS or DB2, perform the following mini-lab assignment:

1. Log onto SQL/DS or DB2.
2. Create the two tables EMPLOYEE and DEPARTMENT.
3. Have a friend log onto SQL/DS and also create these two tables in his or her account.
4. Write the INSERT statements to insert data into your tables—make up the data as you enter it.
5. Write a CL command to allow the friend to access your two tables.
6. Have the friend create a synonym in his or her account for your tables.
7. Have the friend load the data from your account into his or her account using the third version of the INSERT statement.
8. Have the friend grant you authorization to access his or her tables.
9. Write an SQL statement to create a view for the friend. Give the friend a view of only the ID and first and last names of the EMPLOYEE table.
10. Have the friend access the data via the view using the fully-qualified name of your table; then, using a synonym for your table.
11. Delete your friend's data in his or her EMPLOYEE table.
12. Make a backup copy of your EMPLOYEE data by creating a third table and using the third version of the INSERT statement.
13. Have your friend delete your data in the EMPLOYEE table from his or her account.
14. Revoke your friend's authorizations for your tables.
15. Reload the EMPLOYEE data using your backup copy of it. (Hint: use the third version of the INSERT statement).
16. Verify that the data is properly loaded into your table.
17. Logoff SQL/DS or DB2.

CASE STUDY

The XYZ Company has a staff of 135 data processing professionals. Their job titles include Assistant Programmer, Programmer, Senior Programmer, Systems Analyst, and Senior Systems Analyst. Each member of the DP staff is assigned to a team which is responsible for a particular user department. There are five teams corresponding to the five major departments within the company. The members of the team include one or more of each of the job titles listed above. Each team is composed of 25 to 35 staff members.

Each team has a manager who is responsible for the hiring, firing, and other activities within the team. In addition, each manager is responsible for the software product development and the maintenance of existing software programs for his or her corresponding user department. Each team manager works with the manager of his or her corresponding user department in coordinating the needs of the user department with the personnel resources of the team members. All conflicts are resolved jointly by the company's Vice President of Information Services and Vice President of Production. The Vice President of Production oversees the five user departments.

On a yearly basis, each team manager evaluates the employees within his or her team and recommends a merit raise based on that employee's performance for the preceding year. The Personnel Director, Mr. Tophat, wants to ensure that equality within the workplace relative to salaries is a fact within the company. To ensure this principle, Mr. Tophat wants a series of reports to identify the salary histories within each team, job title, sex, and race.

Questions

1. What entities and authorizations does Mr. Tophat need to accomplish his mission?
2. What specific reports must Mr. Tophat have to ensure that discrimination based on sex and race does not exist within the DP team structure relative to salaries? (We do not have to look at age discrimination since the oldest member of the DP staff is 47 years old.)
3. What columns in a view would Mr. Tophat need in order to fulfill his mission?
4. After the reports are identified, what SQL queries do we need to generate the reports? Write these queries.
5. What queries do we need to identify the team managers who may be biased toward a group based on race and/or sex?
6. How do we determine if a manager is biased toward a group? Can our reports show that certain groups may lack experience and expertise and consequently have lower yearly salaries than other groups?
7. How can the DBA help Mr. Tophat perform his mission?

10 *Relational Database Implementations*

When you access a database you want to be confident that its data is accurate and reflects the company's current business posture. Don't forget, one advantage of using a relational database is the ability of end users to access the database and change its data to ensure its accuracy. At the same time this becomes one of its main disadvantages.

This chapter looks at the ramifications of deleting, inserting, and updating data and how that activity affects already existing data in other rows in the database. Next, we will look at how to load data into the database using both the INSERT statement and the LOAD utility. Finally, we will look at the structure of the tablespaces and indexspaces and discuss how database entities are stored physically on DASD and logically in the DB2 Catalog.

REFERENTIAL INTEGRITY

Suppose a company reorganizes its various departments and, in the process, eliminates one of the departments. If employee and department data appear in EMPLOYEE and DEPARTMENT relational tables, respectively, you can easily DELETE data on the eliminated department "ACCOUNTING" from the DEPARTMENT table using:

```
DELETE FROM DEPARTMENT
WHERE DEPTNUMB = 'ACCT'
```

But once you do that, you logically affect the employee data in the EMPLOYEE table. In this case, those employees who worked in accounting will now have foreign keys that point to a nonexistent department (see Figure 10.1). The DEPARTMENT table contained data that the EMPLOYEE table needs. In this case, the DEPARTMENT table is called a parent table and the EMPLOYEE table is called a dependent table. When you eliminate data in the parent table DEPARTMENT, you also must update the data in all of the parent's dependent tables (i.e., EMPLOYEE) to ensure the reliability and integrity of the data in the database.

FIGURE 10.1   *Deleting a row from a parent table. The ACCT key no longer exists in DEPARTMENT. Therefore, rows in EMPLOYEE have no reference value for their foreign key "ACCT."*

Referential integrity, therefore, is a set of rules or procedures for preserving the reliability of the data in a database. Unless you specifically instruct SQL to maintain referential integrity within the databases, SQL will not place constraints on your ability to insert, delete, or update rows in tables. This could cause some tables to have values in key fields that have no corresponding value in their referenced table.

You can force SQL to maintain a set of referential integrity rules when you CREATE or ALTER a table. This is accomplished by specifically stating in the CREATE TABLE statement the fact that you want SQL to abide by a certain referential integrity rule. If the table already exists, you can use the ALTER statement to establish one of the referential integrity rules. Either way, using a referential integrity rule is entirely optional. If you do not place the rule into a table definition, SQL will not follow it. Remember, we created all the tables in Chapter 9 without using the concept of referential integrity.

PARENT AND DEPENDENT TABLES

The three referential integrity rules available in SQL are CASCADE, SET NULL, and RESTRICT. These rules affect the parent table and the dependent table in different ways, so you have two cases: parent table rules and dependent table rules.

Parent Table Rules

For Insertions   When you INSERT rows in a parent table, you can do so without regard to any referential integrity rules. Obviously, a company can create a department without first hiring the employees for it. Similarly, if the EMPLOYEE table is a parent table to the OFFICELOCATION table, you might want the option of hiring an employee without first preassigning that person to an office location. Therefore, INSERTs into parent tables do not have to abide by any referential integrity rule structure.

For Deletions When you DELETE a row from a parent table, you might want to enforce a set of rules so that you do not delete data in the parent table that affects other data in its dependent tables as was the case with Figure 10.1. When you attempt to DELETE a row in DEPARTMENT, you probably want SQL to do one of the following:

1. Delete all rows in dependent tables that reference the parent table's deleted row. In other words, delete all employees who were in the deleted department. This option is called CASCADE.
2. Set the corresponding foreign keys in the dependent table to null values. That is, set the values in column EMPLOYEE.DEPTNUMB to nulls for all those employees who referenced the deleted department ACCT. This option is called SET NULL.
3. Inhibit the deletion of that DEPARTMENT row. That means do not delete rows from the parent table if there are rows that reference them in a dependent table. This option is called RESTRICT.

For Updates Because it is possible to change a key value in a parent table that could be a foreign key in some dependent table, you might violate referential integrity's requirements when you UPDATE. So, you also control UPDATEs using the options CASCADE, SET NULLS, and RESTRICT. Any update that affects a key in the parent table might:

- Change all rows in the dependent table to the updated value (CASCADE)
- Change all the rows in the dependent table to nulls (SET NULL)
- Inhibit the update in the parent table (RESTRICT)

Dependent Table Rules

For Deletions You can delete any row in a dependent table without violating the referential integrity guidelines. For example, you can delete an employee from the EMPLOYEE table without regard to which department he or she works for.

For Insertions You can insert a row into a dependent table only if the referential integrity rules (CASCADE, SET NULLS, or RESTRICT) allow it. When you insert an employee into the EMPLOYEE table, the value in EMPLOYEE.DEPTNUMB must be either a null value or an already existing value in DEPART-MENT.DEPTNUMB. In this latter case, you are inserting an employee into a department that already exists. Logically this makes sense. Companies typically do not hire employees without assigning them to some department. In the case when management hires an employee for an undefined job function, you can set that employee's department code to nulls until the employee's job function and department are decided.

For Updates As with inserts, you cannot change data in dependent tables that reference data in parent tables without following one of the three referential integrity rules. In particular, you could not change the value in EMPLOYEE.DEPTNUMB to a nonexistent department. You must either set the value to an already existing department or to a null value.

Initiating Referential Integrity

Referential integrity rules are not initiated automatically by SQL. You need to select the rule and load it into SQL using either the CREATE or ALTER statements. Only after you define the rule to SQL will SQL follow that rule when it INSERTs, UPDATEs, and DELETEs data from tables. Remember, one of the major benefits of using a DBMS is its ability to perform services and routines automatically without you having to hard code that logic into the system. Obviously, you could design tables, restrict end users, and write code to guarantee the referential integrity of tables. But that defeats the purpose of having a DBMS.

IMPLEMENTING REFERENTIAL INTEGRITY USING DDL

Using the CREATE Statement

You can create a table without using any referential integrity guidelines. You did this quite successfully in the last chapter when you created tables using the CREATE statement. You used the two statements in Figure 10.3 to create the tables DEPARTMENT and EMPLOYEE given in Figure 10.2.

After executing the table definitions in Figure 10.3, you can add, erase, or change any row regardless of the data's logical relevance to other values in another table. You can add employees to the EMPLOYEE table and assign them any department number. You do not have to worry about the fact that the values loaded into the EMPLOYEE table logically have to make sense. The system does not check to see if the department codes loaded into the EMPLOYEE table actually exist as a code in the DEPARTMENT table. All checking for logical compatibility must be done manually by you. It is up to you to visually check the data in all the tables to see if it is both logical and consistent with the other data in the database. For small tables, this might not be such a chore. For databases with hundreds of tables and thousands of rows in each table, however, this manual checking for consistency between the tables becomes an enormous task.

You can modify the CREATE statements in Figure 10.3 to include a referential integrity rule by adding one of these options:

EMPLOYEE   table

EMPLOYEE ID	LAST NAME	FIRST NAME	ADDRESS	CITY	STATE	SEX	DEPTNUMB
123456789	DOE	JOHN	123 E. 3RD	CHICAGO	IL	M	ACCT
234567890	SMITH	MARY	34 N. HOLLY	DENVER	CO	F	ACCT
324566776	GROVER	SUE	56 W. 5TH	DENVER	CO	F	MARK
432143211	SMITH	ANDY	34 N. HOLLY	DENVER	CO	M	PERS
432234432	MARKUM	MIKE	194 W. 43RD	CHICAGO	IL	M	PERS

DEPARTMENT table

DEPTNUMB	NAME	MANAGER ID	ASSISTANT MANAGER ID
ACCT	Accounting	123456789	346565432
MARK	Marketing	902902902	898989898
PERS	Personnel	432143211	453453453
AUDT	Auditing	848484848	122221122
TRNG	Training	980980980	878767777

FIGURE 10.2   *EMPLOYEE and DEPARTMENT tables. These two tables are linked by the relationship between EMPLOYEE.DEPTNUMB and DEPARTMENT.DEPTNUMB.*

```
CREATE TABLE DEPARTMENT
    (DEPTNUMB     CHAR(4)       NOT NULL,
    DEPTNAME      VARCHAR(20)   NOT NULL,
    MANAGER_ID    CHAR(9),
    ASSISTANT_ID  CHAR(9))
    IN PAYROLL.PAYTBL1

CREATE TABLE EMPLOYEE
    (EMPLOYEE_ID  CHAR(9)       NOT NULL,
    LASTNAME      VARCHAR(20)   NOT NULL,
    FIRSTNAME     VARCHAR(20)   NOT NULL,
    ADDRESS       VARCHAR(25),
    CITY          VARCHAR(25),
    STATE         CHAR(2),
    SEX           CHAR(1)       NOT NULL,
    DEPTNUMB      CHAR(4)       NOT NULL)
    INPAYROLL.PAYTBL1
```

FIGURE 10.3   *CREATEing two tables, DEPARTMENT and EMPLOYEE, without referential integrity rules.*

```
ON DELETE CASCADE
ON DELETE SET NULL
ON DELETE RESTRICT
```

By using one of these options, SQL will enforce the respective referential integrity rule.

For example, to establish the rule RESTRICT on the department numbers of the two tables, you define the parent table DEPARTMENT using:

parent table

```
CREATE TABLE DEPARTMENT
        (DEPTNUMB     CHAR(4)       NOT NULL,
        DEPTNAME      VARCHAR(20)   NOT NULL,
        MANAGER_ID    CHAR(9),
        ASSISTANT_ID  CHAR(9),
        PRIMARY KEY  (DEPTNUMB))
        IN PAYROLL.PAYTBL1
```

and you define the dependent table EMPLOYEE using:

dependent table

```
CREATE TABLE EMPLOYEE
        (EMPLOYEE_ID  CHAR(9)       NOT NULL,
        LASTNAME      VARCHAR(20)   NOT NULL,
        FIRSTNAME     VARCHAR(20)   NOT NULL,
        ADDRESS       VARCHAR(25),
        CITY          VARCHAR(25),
        STATE         CHAR(2),
        SEX           CHAR(1)       NOT NULL,
        DEPTNUMB      CHAR(4)       NOT NULL,
        FOREIGN KEY   (DEPTNUMB)
            REFERENCES DEPARTMENT
            ON DELETE RESTRICT)
        IN PAYROLL.PAYTBL1
```

This tells SQL that you want it to enforce the referential integrity rule RESTRICT on the primary key DEPARTMENT.DEPTNUMB and foreign key EMPLOYEE.DEPTNUMB. Now, when you attempt to INSERT, DELETE, or UPDATE on these two tables, SQL first will check the rule using the RESTRICT enforcement logic.

If the EMPLOYEE table is to be a parent table to another dependent table (i.e., MEDICALCOVERAGE), you can establish the PRIMARY KEY in EMPLOYEE using:

```
PRIMARY KEY (EMPLOYEE_ID)
FOREIGN KEY  (DEPTNUMB)
    REFERENCES DEPARTMENT
    ON DELETE RESTRICT)
IN PAYROLL.PAYTBL1
```

Now, EMPLOYEE can be a parent table to other tables while also being a dependent table to DEPARTMENT. Once you establish the primary key EMPLOYEE_ID in EMPLOYEE for referential integrity usage, you can use it as a foreign key in other tables that need to reference it. The statement:

```
CREATE TABLE MEDICALCOVERAGE
        (EMPLOYEE_ID        CHAR(9)    NOT NULL,
        COVERAGE_CODE       CHAR(10)   NOT NULL,
        PRIMARY_PHYSICIAN   CHAR(9),
        HEALTH_CARE_PLAN    CHAR(15),
```

```
SINGLE_FAMILY        CHAR(1),
MONTHLYPREMIUM    DECIMAL(5,2),
FOREIGN KEY (EMPLOYEE_ID)
    REFERENCES EMPLOYEE
    ON DELETE RESTRICT)
IN PAYROLL.PAYTBL1
```

creates a MEDICALCOVERAGE table that references EMPLOYEE_ID of the EM-
PLOYEE table. The DEPARTMENT table is a parent table with the EMPLOYEE
table as its dependent table. The EMPLOYEE table is a parent table having the
MEDICALCOVERAGE table as its dependent table (see Figure 10.4).

Using the ALTER Statement

If the table definition already exists, you can add a referential integrity rule
to the table using the ALTER statement. First, establish the primary key for
the parent table using:

```
ALTER TABLE DEPARTMENT
PRIMARY KEY (DEPTNUMB)
```

Second, establish the rule on the dependent table using:

```
ALTER TABLE EMPLOYEE
FOREIGN KEY (DEPTNUMB)
    REFERENCES DEPARTMENT
    ON DELETE RESTRICT
```

Before you create the PRIMARY KEY for a table, remember that the table
must have a unique index for that column.

You have to be careful whenever you create the FOREIGN KEY rule on the
dependent table. If data already exist in the table that violates the rule you
establish—CASCADE, SET NULL, or RESTRICT—the table is placed in a CHECK
PENDING STATUS. When this occurs, SQL freezes the data in the table and
makes it unusable. You then must purge the offending data from the table
using a utility program called CHECK.

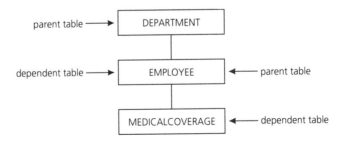

FIGURE 10.4   *Parent and dependent tables.*

ELIMINATING REFERENTIAL INTEGRITY FROM TABLES

The checking process for a referential integrity rule can be eliminated by using the DROP option in ALTER. Use the statement:

```
ALTER TABLE DEPARTMENT
DROP PRIMARY KEY
```

or the statement:

```
ALTER TABLE EMPLOYEE
DROP FOREIGN KEY DEPTNUMB
```

to eliminate the relationship between a dependent table and its parent table.

When you use DROP PRIMARY KEY, you eliminate all references between the parent table and all its dependent tables. When you use DROP FOREIGN KEY, you eliminate only the relationship between the one dependent table and its parent table. In both these cases, you must have ALTER authority before using the statement.

Loading Data into a Relational Database

In Chapter 9 we used the INSERT statement to load values into tables. The INSERT statement had the following three versions:

```
1) INSERT INTO tablename
     VALUES (list of values)
```

```
2) INSERT INTO tablename
       (list of column names)
     VALUES (list of values)
```

```
3) INSERT INTO tablename
       SELECT list of column names
       FROM tablename
       WHERE condition
```

Obviously, it would be very tedious to use either of the first two versions to load large amounts of data into tables. The best solution in this case is to place either of these statements in COBOL code and load the data using some add or update screen. Data entry personnel then can use the program to load the data, delete it, or update it, as needed. We will discuss how to embed SQL statements in higher-level languages in more detail in Chapter 13.

The third version of the INSERT statement is used to load data from one relational table to another relational table. Typically, you will use this version to back up the table so end users can query the data using the backup. Usually the operations team runs a Procedure (PROC) containing this version of INSERT during third-shift operations. At the beginning of the next business day, the end users have a copy of all the data of the prior day's activity for report-generation activities.

Suppose the data you want resides on a nonrelational database or is contained in a VSAM dataset or some other file, either on DASD or magnetic tape. You need a way of converting nonrelational files to relational tables. You can use the following tools to convert the nonsequential file to a sequential file:

- DXT
- An in-house written program
- third-party vendor software (e.g., EASYTRIEVE PLUS from Computer Associates)

If you are using DB2, an IBM relational database, you can use IBM's Data Extractor product, called DXT. DXT massages existing VSAM or IMS data sets and converts them to sequential data sets. Once you have a sequential data set, you can use a utility program within DB2 to load that data set into one or more DB2 tables. This utility program is appropriately called the LOAD utility.

You need a sequential data set to use the LOAD utility within DB2. Once you have the sequential data set, you can begin the loading of that data into a table. But still you are faced with a problem. What if your target table already contains existing data? Do you want to intermingle this new data with the existing data in the table or do you want to overwrite the existing data with the new data? You need to be specific when telling the LOAD utility what to do.

You must describe the parameters of your activity to the software product that you are running so that it can perform the desired task. Typically, most users of computer systems struggle with defining the parameters of the problem and with telling the software system what those parameters are.

Using the LOAD Utility

Suppose you want to load the data in Figure 10.5 into the table EMPLOYEE in account $HARRY. You would use the statement in Figure 10.6.

In this example, the LOAD DATA statement relates the byte location of the data (i.e., POSITION) in the sequential file to the table's column name and column type (VARCHAR, CHAR, DECIMAL, INTEGER, SMALLINT, etc.) If you are intermingling the data in the sequential file with the already existing data in the table $HARRY.EMPLOYEE, you use the keyword RESUME YES. If you want to overwrite the data in the existing table $HARRY.EMPLOYEE with the new data in the sequential file, you would use the keyword RESUME NO.

You enter the LOAD DATA statement into the system using either TSO, MVS, VM, or some other system editor. That means you create a data set containing the above LOAD DATA statement in some PDS using any name of columns

0 1	0 9 1 0		2 4 2 5	4 0 4 1		6 0 6 1		7 6 7 7 7 8 7 8 9 0	8 3
1	23456789 D	OE	J	OHN	1	23 E. 3RD	C	HICAGO	I L M A CC T
2	3456789 0 S	MITH	M	ARY	3	4 N. HOLLY	D	ENVER	C O F A CC T
3	2456677 6 G	ROVER	S	UE	5	6 W. 5TH	D	ENVER	C O F M AR K
4	3214321 1 S	MITH	A	NDY	3	4 N. HOLLY	D	ENVER	C O M P ER S
4	3223443 2 M	ARKUM	M	IKE	1	94 W. 43RD	C	HICAGO	I L M P ER S

FIGURE 10.5   *Sequential data set with 83 bytes of data per record.*

your choosing via the system's editor—just as if you were writing a COBOL program or a set of JCL statements.

But how does the system know the location of the sequential data set containing the data you want to load into a table and the location of the data set containing the LOAD DATA statement? Remember, the LOAD DATA statement simply defines the structure of the data. You must tell the system a few more details. Data sets reside on DASD volumes and have a data set name. When you use the LOAD utility, it will provide a set of questions to answer. These questions will extract from you the name of the volume containing the sequential data set, the sequential data set name, and the name of the data set containing your LOAD statement.

Once you enter all the required information into the LOAD utility, you can execute it. The utility will load the data from the sequential data set into the desired table. But now you must be aware of still another problem. When is the best time to execute the LOAD utility? Keep in mind, if the sequential data set is very large, DB2 or SQL/DS will lock the tablespace and indexspace during the loading process. You surely do not want to lock vital tablespaces during peak hours. Not only are system resources the most costly during this time, but the locking of tablespaces and indexspaces might cause the user departments productivity problems. Therefore, you should write a PROC containing all the instructions for the load and execute the PROC in batch mode during nonpeak hours.

```
LOAD DATA
RESUME YES
INTO TABLE $HARRY.EMPLOYEE
(EMPLID      POSITION (1)    CHAR(9),
LASTNAME     POSITION (10)   VARCHAR(15),
FIRSTNAME    POSITION (25)   VARCHAR(16),
ADDRESS      POSITION (41)   VARCHAR(20),
CITY         POSITION (61)   VARCHAR(16),
STATE        POSITION (77)   CHAR(2),
SEX          POSITION (79)   CHAR(1),
DEPTNUMB     POSITION (80)   CHAR(4))
```

FIGURE 10.6   *The LOAD DATA statement as part of the LOAD utility.*

The LOAD DATA statement in Figure 10.6 defines the loading of data from a sequential data set into a single table. If you wanted to load data into multiple tables, you would use:

```
LOAD DATA
RESUME NO
INTO TABLE $HARRY.EMPLOYEE
INTO TABLE $HARRY.PAYSALARY
(EMPLID          POSITION (1)    CHAR(9),
 LASTNAME        POSITION (10)   VARCHAR(15),
  .
  .
  .
```

The LOAD utility will overwrite the existing data currently in tables EM-PLOYEE and PAYSALARY of account $HARRY with the new data found in some sequential data set.

The LOAD utility is a specific option of the relational database DB2. Suppose you don't have DB2 installed on your system. How do you accomplish the same task? In this case, your installation must either write an in-house systems routine that performs the same function as the LOAD utility, or it must purchase a third-party software product that performs the identical task.

Remember, regardless of the product you use for the load, you must define the structure of the target tables to the system via some statement similar to the LOAD DATA statement. Next, you must massage the pointers that exist on the current VSAM, IMS, IDMS/R, or other file to eliminate those pointers. In addition, you must either write a PROC or use some JCL statement to identify the locations of source data, target data, and the table defini-tion/conversion statement. In most cases, you will need to secure the proper manuals describing the software product you will use. Then you will have to study the manuals to understand the product and learn how to use it effectively.

PHYSICAL STRUCTURE AND CHARACTERISTICS

A Look at DB2

The major function of DDL is to define the structure of database entities to the system. These entities include:

- Storage Group
- Database
- Tablespace
- Index (and its corresponding Indexspace)
- Table
- View
- Synonym

Tablespace Structure

Some of these entities exist physically as objects on DASD and others are logical representations of the already existing objects. For example, a view and a synonym are logical entities. When you create either of them, DB2 makes an entry into one or more tables in the DB2 catalog and uses that information whenever you attempt to use the view or synonym.

When you define a storage group or a database in DB2, however, DB2 keeps track of that information by again making entries in the appropriate DB2 catalog tables. DB2 does not immediately allocate storage on the DASD units. Remember, you do not define the amount of DASD storage needed for your database until you create the tablespace. Only when you execute the CREATE TABLESPACE statement does the system allocate DASD space based on the value in the PRIQTY option. That means the statements:

```
CREATE STOGROUP PAY001
      VOLUMES (MONPAY1);
CREATE DATABASE PAYROLL
      STOGROUP PAY001;
```

identify where the database will reside and the statement:

```
CREATE TABLESPACE PAYTBL1
    IN PAYROLL
    USING STOGROUP PAY001
    PRIQTY 60
    SECQTY 20;
```

physically allocates 60KB of secondary memory on DASD volume MONPAY1 (see Figure 10.7).

When you insert a row into a table, DB2 places the row on a page within

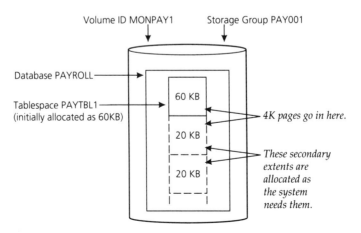

FIGURE 10.7 *Storage group, database, tablespace, and pages within the tablespace.*

the tablespace. Each page occupies 4K of memory. No row can extend beyond a page, meaning a row cannot cross the page boundary. Therefore, the maximum size of a row is 4K. In actuality, the row is somewhat smaller than 4K because each page contains a header label including the page number and other page codes.

Remember, tables are nothing more than a collection of rows logically grouped together on some tablespace. The statement:

```
CREATE TABLE DEPARTMENT
      (DEPTNUMB    CHAR(4)        NOT NULL,
       DEPTNAME    VARCHAR(20)   NOT NULL,
       MANAGER_ID  CHAR(9),
       ASSISTANT_ID  CHAR(9))
       IN PAYROLL.PAYTBL1
```

assigns the table DEPARTMENT to the tablespace PAYTBL1 within the database PAYROLL. It is the CREATE TABLE statement that identifies the tablespace and it is on the pages of that defined tablespace that DB2 stores the rows for the table (see Figure 10.8).

If you create another table and assign it to the same tablespace, the rows of both tables then will be intermingled throughout the pages of the tablespace. So, if you also define the table EMPLOYEE on tablespace PAYTBL1 using the statement:

```
CREATE TABLE EMPLOYEE
      (EMPLOYEE_ID  CHAR(9)        NOT NULL,
       LASTNAME    VARCHAR(20)   NOT NULL,
       FIRSTNAME   VARCHAR(20)   NOT NULL,
       ADDRESS     VARCHAR(25),
       CITY        VARCHAR(25),
       STATE       CHAR(2),
       SEX         CHAR(1)        NOT NULL,
       DEPTNUMB    CHAR(4)        NOT NULL)
       IN PAYROLL.PAYTBL1
```

DB2 will load the rows for the tables EMPLOYEE and DEPARTMENT into the first available page area in the tablespace PAYTBL1. When you load the four rows in Figure 10.9, the tablespace PAYTBL1 will have the configuration given in Figure 10.10.

Types of Tablespaces

In fact, in DB2 you can have three kinds of tablespaces—simple, shared, and partitioned. A **simple tablespace** contains a single table within a single tablespace. A **shared tablespace** contains multiple tables within a single tablespace. A **partitioned tablespace** contains a single table in a single tablespace, but the tablespace resides on multiple areas of DASD.

Partitioned Tablespaces A partitioned tablespace is created using the keyword NUMBPARTS in the CREATE TABLESPACE statement. That means you can par-

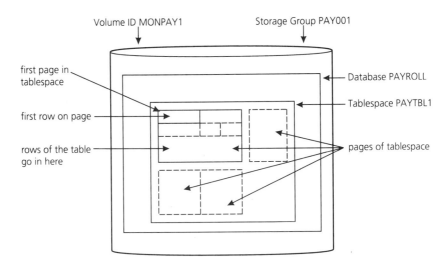

FIGURE 10.8 *Storing data on pages in tablespaces. DB2 stores a row in the first available area beginning with the first page of the tablespace.*

```
INSERT INTO EMPLOYEE
VALUES ('123456789','DOE','JOHN','123 E. 3RD','CHICAGO','IL',
       'M','ACCT');

INSERT INTO DEPARTMENT
VALUES ('ACCT','ACCOUNTING','666666666','787878787');

INSERT INTO EMPLOYEE
VALUES ('987654321','SMITH','MARY','322 W. 9TH','ELMS','IL',
       'F','MARK');

INSERT INTO DEPARTMENT
VALUES ('PERS','PERSONNEL','090909090','333333333');
```

FIGURE 10.9 *INSERTing multiple rows for multiple tables in the same tablespace area.*

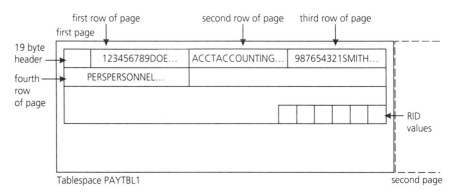

FIGURE 10.10 *The structure of tablespace PAYTBL1 after loading four rows into two tables. Here, the rows of one table intermingle with rows of another table.*

tition the tablespace PAYTBL1 into four parts, with the first part residing on
DASD volume MONPAY2 and the three remaining parts residing on DASD volume MONPAY1 (see Figure 10.11). The statements to accomplish this become:

```
CREATE STOGROUP PAY001
        VOLUMES (MONPAY1);
CREATE STOGROUP PAY002
        VOLUMES (MONPAY2);
CREATE DATABASE PAYROLL
        STOGROUP PAY001, PAY002;
CREATE TABLESPACE PAYTBL1
    IN PAYROLL
    USING STOGROUP PAY001
    PRIQTY 60
    SECQTY 20
NUMBPARTS 4
        (PART 1 USING STOGROUP PAY002
            PRIQTY 60
            SECQTY 20);
```

After the tablespace is partitioned, how do you get the data to reside in
the various partitions? The INSERT statement does not direct the row to any
particular tablespace DASD area. You need to rely on the index to properly
place the rows in the various partitions of the tablespace. This is done by
partitioning the index into clusters. Because the tablespace has four partitions,
you must direct the index keys to the desired partition. The statement:

```
CREATE INDEX PAYNDX1
ON EMPLOYEE (EMPLID)
USING STOGROUP PAY002
        PRIQTY 10
        SECQTY 4
        CLUSTER (PART 1 VALUES ('199999999'),
                PART 2 VALUES ('499999999'),
                PART 3 VALUES ('799999999'),
                PART 4 VALUES ('999999999'))
```

assigns all employees with EMPLID values between:

000000000 and 199999999 to the first partition,
200000000 and 499999999 to the second partition,
500000000 and 799999999 to the third partition, and
800000000 and 999999999 to the fourth partition of the tablespace.

After partitioning the tablespace and loading data into it, you can use
system utility programs to backup the multiple volumes at different time
periods. Because the data is scattered over multiple DASD units, the entire
database does not have to be shut down to back up the database. Operations
can lock one DASD volume, perform the backup, and then unlock the unit

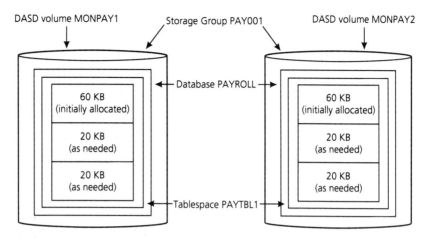

DASD volume MONPAY1 · Storage Group PAY001 · DASD volume MONPAY2

Database PAYROLL

60 KB (initially allocated) · 20 KB (as needed) · 20 KB (as needed)

Tablespace PAYTBL1

FIGURE 10.11 *Partitioning a tablespace using multiple volumes. Both database PAYROLL and tablespace PAYTBL1 span two volumes.*

with only minor inconvenience to the user departments. In fact, many user departments are unaware of the temporary logical shutdown of a DASD device.

For example, if you partitioned your customer tables into four parts, you could assign the different parts of the tablespace to different geographical regions of the nation. The first partition could be for your West Coast customers and the remaining partitions for the rest of your customers. This allows you to perform the backup of the West Coast data sometime in the early morning while keeping the database online for the processing of the East Coast and Midwest customer activity. In the late afternoon when the East Coast and Midwest end their business day, you can backup the remaining three partitions while keeping the West Coast customers online.

It is important for a DBMS to have certain features to handle typical business functions. For small databases, the problem of backups and recoveries does not involve a lot of work or planning. If the database has millions of rows of data in one table, however, you have to resort to more sophisticated algorithms and structures to handle the large amount of data. Remember, the routines and procedures you use for small amounts of data have to be dynamically changed and modified to handle the enormous amounts of data in very large databases. This is obvious when you try to sort records. The algorithm to perform a sort of 50,000,000 records is dynamically different and more complicated than the algorithm to sort 50 records.

Indexspace Structures Each page within a tablespace is divided into three areas: a 19-byte header area, an area to hold row data, and an area for RID values. These RID values are pointers to the relative location of the row on the page (see Figure 10.12).

When you insert a row into a table that has an index assigned to it, DB2 stores the page number, the RID value for the row, and the index key for that row in the index. Figure 10.13 is a logical representation of the structure of an index with four index keys.

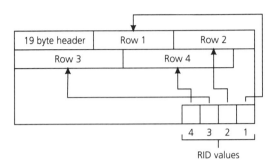

FIGURE 10.12 *Rows and RID values on pages. The first RID value contains the relative address of row 1, the second RID value contains the relative address of row 2, and so on.*

DB2 uses the RID value as a relative pointer to the row on a page (see Figure 10.14). By using relative addresses to store rows, DB2 can reorganize the pages to increase the amount of free space available for row storage. Because each page is an independent unit, DB2 does not have to refer to the index when it rearranges the row on a page. DB2 simply has to maintain each row's relative position in the RID values and adjust the memory addresses that the RID values contain. This reorganization of the pages normally is done on a routine basis or after a large number of row deletions occurs in the tablespace. Either the DBADM or some member of the operations staff initiates the necessary utility programs to accomplish this reorganization.

In Figure 10.14, DB2 searches the index for the index key 123456789. Using the index, DB2 extracts the page number (102) and RID value (4) for that key. Next, it accesses page 102 and finds the actual address of the row in RID location 4. DB2 then extracts the row from the page and places it in a buffer area for later processing.

Each index you create resides in a tablespace on some DASD unit in an area called an indexspace. DB2 creates this indexspace when you execute the CREATE INDEX statement. DB2 manages and maintains the index without your intervention. When you drop the index, DB2 drops the indexspace containing that index. For all practical purposes, the indexspace is transparent to most users because everything is managed by the DB2 software.

index key	page, RID value
123456789	102,4
323232323	104,2
350900998	101,8
376665566	105,2

FIGURE 10.13 *Logical structure of an index. The row with index key "123456789" is located on page 102. The actual address of the row on that page is located in the fourth RID value of that page. Similarly, the row with index key "323232323" is on page 104 and you use the address in the second RID value to find it on the page.*

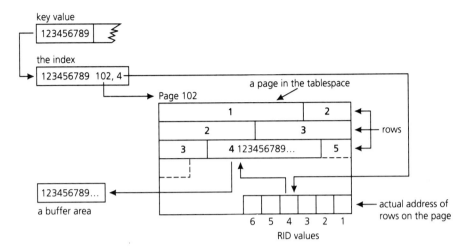

FIGURE 10.14 *Extracting a row from a tablespace using an index.*

Root and Leaf Pages Each indexspace contains two kinds of pages—root pages and leaf pages. When you attempt to access a row in a tablespace, DB2 will search the root page to find what leaf page contains the index key. Then DB2 searches the leaf page until it finds the index key and the row's page location and RID value (see Figure 10.15).

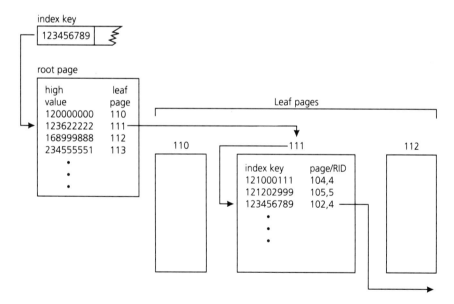

FIGURE 10.15 *Using root and leaf pages in the index. DB2 searches the root page to locate the leaf page (111) containing the key 123456789. It accesses leaf page 111 and searches that page until it finds the index key 123456789. Then it uses the tablespace's page number 102 and RID value 4 to access the row.*

━━━━━━━━━━ ## THE DB2 CATALOG

The DB2 catalog contains approximately 28 to 32 tables that contain information about all the entities created within DB2. Table 10.1 contains several of the tables found within DB2. Notice that the DB2 catalog contains all the descriptions about the structure of each database, tablespace, table, column, and any other object that is created within DB2. Each time someone executes a DDL or CL statement, DB2 makes an appropriate entry into one or more DB2 catalog tables. Each time someone attempts to access a DB2 entity (e.g., table, view, column) using DML, DB2 first accesses the DB2 catalog to find a description of the entity. In addition, DB2 checks its various authorization tables within the catalog to see if the account accessing the entity is authorized to obtain data from a particular table, view, and so on.

The DB2 catalog is a dynamic catalog. It is constantly in use to:

- Validate authorizations for accessing the entities of table, column, and so on
- Identify which columns have indexes
- Update authorization tables when someone executes a GRANT or REVOKE statement or issues a CREATE TABLE statement
- Update entity definition tables when someone executes a CREATE, ALTER, or DROP statement
- Update statistical information on the structure of the data within its pages, tables, and tablespaces whenever someone inserts or deletes rows

Accessing the DB2 Catalog

The SELECT statement is used to view the data within DB2 catalog tables. For example, the statement:

```
SELECT NAME, CREATOR, DBNAME, TSNAME
FROM SYSIBM.SYSTABLES
WHERE TYPE = 'T'
```

will list all the tables defined within DB2. In this case, DB2 will list the table name, the ID of whoever created it, and the database and tablespace name where the table resides. Table 10.2 is a partial list of some of the columns found in SYSIBM.SYSTABLES.

When you execute the SELECT statement in Table 10.2, you might get a security violation code and the query could fail. In many installations, SYSADM restricts access to the DB2 catalog. The first thing to do when getting a security violation, is check with the DBADM of your database or with SYSADM to identify the corporate policy toward accessing the DB2 catalog. Typically, SYSADM gives the many DBADMs the power to control who has access to particular database information resident in the DB2 catalog. Generally, users of a particular database can query the DB2 catalog concerning the entities within their database. In addition, some corporate policies dictate that an owner of a DB2 entity (i.e.,

TABLE 10.1 *Selected DB2 catalog tables*

SYSIBM.SYSSYNONYMS
SYSIBM.SYSVIEWS
SYSIBM.SYSTABLES
SYSIBM.SYSTABLESPACES
SYSIBM.SYSDATABASE
SYSIBM.SYSCOLUMNS
SYSIBM.SYSTABAUTH
SYSIBM.SYSDBAUTH
SYSIBM.SYSUSERAUTH

table, synonym) can query the DB2 catalog and extract information about that entity.

Corporate policy dictates who can access the DB2 catalog. This policy can be mandated by SYSADM or could be part of an overall policy and procedures guideline established by upper management. Don't forget, a database is not just software installed on hardware. A DBMS includes procedures and standards established by management that dictate how the software is used and who can access the information contained within it. It is this corporate policy that protects the data within the database from unauthorized access. These guidelines protect both the individual and the corporation from someone who is not authorized to access sensitive information resident within the database. It is SYSADM's responsibility to ensure the integrity of the databases and this includes keeping curious people out of the DB2 catalog.

Accessing Specific DB2 Catalog Tables

Having access to the data in the DB2 catalog means you can extract valuable information about the entities within it. Suppose you want to list all the synonyms you created in your account. You would use the query:

TABLE 10.2 *Selected column names in SYSIBM.SYSTABLES*

NAME	table or view name
CREATOR	ID of table or view creator
DBNAME	name of database containing the table or view
TSNAME	name of tablespace containing the table or view
COLCOUNT	number of columns in the table or view
CARD	number of rows within the table
NPAGES	number of active pages containing rows
EDPROC	name of the EDITPROC for the table
VALPROC	name of the VALIDPROC for the table
TYPE	a one-character code where T = table and V = view

TABLE 10.3   *Selected column names in*
SYSIBM.SYSSYNONYMS

NAME	name of synonym for table or view
TBNAME	name of table or view
CREATOR	ID of creator of synonym

```
SELECT NAME, TBNAME
FROM SYSIBM.SYSSYNONYMS
WHERE CREATOR = 'myaccount'
```

NAME is the synonym name for the table or view, TBNAME is the name of the table or view, and CREATOR is the ID of the creator of the synonym (Table 10.3).

You can find certain statistical data about your tablespace by querying SYSIBM.SYSTABLESPACE (Table 10.4). The query:

```
SELECT NTABLES, NACTIVE
FROM SYSIBM.SYSTABLESPACE
WHERE NAME = 'PAYTBL1'
```

lists both the number of tables defined in the tablespace PAYTBL1 and the number of pages active within it. In this case, an active page is any page in the tablespace that contains (or has contained) rows for a table.

You can extract more specific information about the number of rows and active pages for a particular table by using the query:

```
SELECT CARD, NPAGES
FROM SYSIBM.SYSTABLES
WHERE NAME = 'PAYROLL'
```

Suppose you are unsure of the name and number of tables you have created in your account. You could use the query:

```
SELECT NAME, TSNAME, DBNAME, COLCOUNT
FROM SYSIBM.SYSTABLES
WHERE TYPE = 'T' AND
      CREATOR = 'myaccount'
```

TABLE 10.4   *Selected column names for*
SYSIBM.SYSTABLESPACE

NAME	tablespace name
CREATOR	ID of tablespace creator
DBNAME	database name containing tablespace
NTABLES	number of tables in tablespace
NACTIVE	number of active pages in tablespace

TABLE 10.5 *Selected columns for SYSIBM.SYSCOLUMNS*

NAME	column name
TBNAME	table or view name containing column
COLNO	relative location of column in table
COLTYPE	column type (SMALLINT, INTEGER, DECIMAL, CHAR)
LENGTH	length of column
NULLS	Y or N for nulls allowed in column
TBCREATOR	ID of table or view creator

In this example, 'myaccount' is a TSO, IMS, or CICS systems account number. Once you know the name of the table, you can list its column names and their respective characteristics by querying SYSIBM.SYSCOLUMNS (Table 10.5). For example, the query to list all the columns in table $HARRY.EMPLOYEE becomes:

```
SELECT COLNO, NAME, COLTYPE, LENGTH, NULLS
FROM SYSIBM.SYSCOLUMNS
WHERE TBNAME = 'EMPLOYEE' AND
      TBCREATOR = '$HARRY'
```

The results of this query list the column's relative location in the table, the column's name, its column type and length, and a Y or N code to indicate if nulls are allowed in that column. The length value will be 2 for SMALLINT, 4 for INTEGER, n for DECIMAL (depending on the number of digits in it), and 1 to 254 for CHAR and VARCHAR. These numbers represent the number of bytes each of the respective column types requires for storing values. Remember, for both CHAR and VARCHAR columns, the first byte of the value in the column determines if it is a null or not null value and the second byte indicates the length of the alphanumeric data in that column.

For a more detailed description of all the DB2 catalog tables, consult IBM's DB2 manuals. The IBM manual, *IBM Database 2 SQL Reference Manual*, contains a complete list of all the DB2 catalog tables, their column names, and a brief description of their meaning. Other DB2 manuals available from IBM are given in Table 10.6.

TABLE 10.6 *A selected list of DB2 reference manuals*

IBM Database 2 SQL Reference
IBM Database 2 Command and Utility Reference
IBM Database 2 SQL Learner's Guide
IBM Database 2 Application Programming Guide
IBM Database 2 Advanced Application Programming Guide
IBM Database 2 Database Planning and Administration Guide
IBM Data Extractor User's Guide
IBM Database Edit Facility (DBEDIT) User's Guide

SYSTEMS INTERFACING

DB2 has been designed by IBM to operate under various other database and terminal management systems, such as TSO, IMS, and CICS. Traditionally, TSO has been a programmer's development environment, while IMS and CICS have been end-user application environments. That means programmers write programs that make use of IMS's or CICS's terminal-I/O facilities and some sort of database-I/O facility, for example, IMS DL/I or COBOL's VSAM capability. These programs then are utilized by end users to access the database. With DB2, however, you not only have the capability to write IMS or CICS programs in the traditional manner, but you also have end-user facilities under TSO.

DB2 and TSO

DB2 is closely tied to TSO. Under TSO, there is a programmer's DB2 development facility, SPUFI, as well as an end-user facility, QMF. Both of these are interactive facilities. It is possible, however, to execute SQL in batch as well. To do this, your batch job must execute the TSO Terminal Monitor Program (TMP). The TMP is what normally provides an interactive TSO session and uses some system terminal I/O program, such as Virtual Terminal Access Method (VTAM), to interface with the user's terminal. The TMP can recognize, however, when it has been invoked by a batch program, and then will direct I/O to files instead of a terminal. In this way, you can execute SQL statements in a noninteractive batch mode. Either way, you will use TSO.

DB2 and IMS or CICS

Although DB2 under TSO includes an end-user facility, QMF, you might not want your users to be forced to rely on QMF as their sole database tool. One reason is that you do not want your users to have to undertake the training necessary to be able to use QMF. Another reason is that you might not want your users to have access to all of the capability that QMF can give them. For example, under QMF, users can execute any SELECT statement that they are authorized to use; you might want to exercise more control under some circumstances. To do this, you would write a program that gets user input, edit checks it for appropriateness, and then forms and executes an SQL statement for them.

You can write such programs under TSO, but IMS and CICS usually make more efficient use of machine resources than TSO does. Traditionally, IMS programs use IMS's database facility, DL/I, while CICS programs use COBOL's VSAM facilities. Both IMS and CICS also have terminal-I/O facilities. To write a DB2 program that executes under IMS or CICS, you use the available terminal-I/O facilities of whichever of the two subsystems under which you want your program to execute. Instead of using the usual database-I/O facilities, however, you simply use embedded SQL. Of course, the systems programming area in charge of IMS or CICS must define your program to the subsystem as one that uses DB2.

SUMMARY

Referential integrity is the process of maintaining the integrity of data by selectively inhibiting the insertion, deletion, and modification of rows and columns based on some preestablished criteria. Tables that contain data that other tables need are called parent tables. Tables that require data from other tables are called dependent tables. SQL has the three referential integrity rules of CASCADE, SET NULL, and RESTRICT.

For parent tables, insertions are unrestricted. However, when a row is deleted from a parent, the CASCADE rule forces SQL to delete all rows in dependent tables that reference the parent table's deleted row, the SET NULLS rule sets the corresponding foreign keys in the dependent table to nulls, and the RESTRICT rule inhibits the deletion of the parent row.

When a row is updated in a parent table and a key field is affected, the CASCADE rule changes all rows in the dependent table to the updated value, the SET NULLS rule changes the corresponding foreign keys in the dependent table to nulls and the RESTRICT rule inhibits the update in the parent table.

For dependent tables, deletions are unrestricted. But when a row is inserted into a dependent table, all values in the foreign keys of that row either must be null values or they must already exist in the corresponding parent table. For updates on dependent tables, the updated value either must be a null value or already exist in a corresponding parent table row.

To establish a referential integrity rule between a parent table and a dependent table, the CREATE statement (or ALTER if the tables already exist) must contain the option ON DELETE CASCADE, ON DELETE SET NULL, or ON DELETE RESTRICT. In addition, the CREATE statement also must identify the PRIMARY KEY and FOREIGN KEY columns of the parent and dependent tables. The ALTER...DROP statement eliminates a referential integrity rule from a table.

In addition to using various forms of the INSERT statement to load data into databases, programmers can use specialized software to perform the load. Because DB2 contains a LOAD utility that loads data from a sequential file into tables, the programmer must convert nonsequential files into sequential ones. For those files that already exist in an IMS database or for those that are a VSAM data set, IBM's Data Extractor product converts these nonsequential files into sequential ones. If preexisting software is not available, the programmer must write code to convert a nonsequential data set into a corresponding sequential data set. In either case, the programmer uses the LOAD utility to input preexisting data into tables.

Data in databases resides on pages within tablespaces. The tablespace can be a simple tablespace containing a single table or a shared tablespace containing multiple tables interspersed among the tablespace's pages. A partitioned tablespace contains a single table but the tablespace resides on multiple areas of DASD. Partitioned tablespaces are created using the keyword NUMB-

PARTS in the CREATE TABLESPACE statement. Indexes then reference the multiple tablespace partitions. The CLUSTER option in the CREATE INDEX statement establishes the criteria for placing data into partitioned tablespaces.

Each CREATE INDEX statement creates an index that resides in an indexspace. The index contains a row's index key and the row's location in the tablespace. The row's location includes the number of the page containing the row and the row's relative location on the page called its RID value. When using the index to access a row, the system searches the root page in the index to find on which leaf page the index resides. This root page contains a range of values for keys found on the leaf pages. Once the system locates the leaf page containing the key value, it accesses the leaf page and finds the index value, the row's page location, and its RID value. The system then uses the page number to access the page containing the row. It uses the RID value to find the physical address of the row on the page.

The DB2 catalog contains a series of tables containing database entity descriptions and their structures. Authorized users can query the catalog using the SELECT statement.

DB2 is designed to operate under TSO; there are programmer and end-user facilities under TSO, and there is the capability of running DB2 programs under TSO. The TSO TMP is used to execute DB2 batch programs. If you wish to create interactive end-user programs to access a DB2 database, however, you can run them under IMS or CICS. To do this, you make use of either IMS's or CICS's terminal-I/O facilities and use embedded SQL for database access.

QUESTIONS

1. What is the difference between a dependent table and a parent table? How is this concept similar to parent-child and owner-member for hierarchical and network databases, respectively?
2. Suppose you created the EMPLOYEE table using the options:

   FOREIGN KEY (DEPTNUMB)
   ON DELETE CASCADE

   How does this change affect insertions, deletions, updates, and selections?
3. Why must you create an index on a primary key when you use the PRIMARY KEY option in CREATE?
4. Assume you altered the EMPLOYEE table using:

   ALTER TABLE EMPLOYEE
   FOREIGN KEY (DEPTNUMB)
       REFERENCES DEPARTMENT
       ON DELETE SET NULLS

   If you attempt to insert a row into the employee table containing the department number 'SECU' for the SECURITY Department, does a row in DEPARTMENT.DEPTNUMB have to contain the value 'SECU'? Explain what happens to the data in the EMPLOYEE table when you try to update DEPARTMENT using:

```
UPDATE DEPARTMENT
SET DEPTNUMB = 'INFR'
WHERE DEPTNUMB = 'SECU'
```

5. Your company, which has DB2, has acquired another company that has IDMS/R. You want to move all the database data from the acquired company to DB2. Discuss some of the problems you will encounter in this conversion. Discuss some possible solutions to these problems.

6. Your company, which has DB2, has acquired a smaller company that has approximately 250 sequential and VSAM files on its system. Discuss the time frame, the amount of work needed, and the number of people needed to convert all of the acquired company's files to DB2.

7. In problems 5 and 6 above, how do we go about estimating the true cost of such a conversion?

8. For a small database having under 100,000 total rows in its only tablespace, what are the advantages and disadvantages of partitioning the tablespace into four or more parts?

9. Write the SQL statement to list all the tables created by $WANDA.

10. Write the SQL statement to list all the views created by $WANDA.

11. Write the SQL statement to list all the tables having column name EMPLOYEE_ID.

12. Write the SQL statement to list all the views having column name ADDRESS.

13. Write the SQL statement to list all the tablespaces in database PAYROLL.

14. Write the SQL statement to list all the tables in database PAYROLL.

15. Write the SQL statement to list all the users who created tables in database PAYROLL.

16. Write the SQL statement to list the tables having column names LASTNAME, FIRSTNAME, and ADDRESS. List the data by the creator's ID in ascending order.

17. Write the SQL statement to list all tables that have column lengths greater than 15 and are defined as CHAR rather than VARCHAR.

18. Write the SQL statement to list all the columns and the tables as they appear in database PAYROLL.

19. Write the SQL statement to find the average number of rows for all the tables in tablespace SPRING01.

20. Write the SQL statement to find the table having the greatest number of rows in database PAYROLL.

11

Microcomputer Relational Database Implementations

One of the more widely used microcomputer **relational database management systems** (RDBMS) is Ashton-Tate's dBASE. Not only are there thousands of microcomputer database systems written by purchasers of dBASE, but also there are numerous preprogrammed systems available that are specifically designed to run under dBASE. Also, dBASE is a good example of a typical microcomputer RDBMS because other major microcomputer RDBMSs, such as Borland's Paradox, are similar in concept to dBASE.

In this chapter, we will examine the two major versions of dBASE—dBASE III PLUS and dBASE IV. Throughout the chapter we will use the nomenclature "dBASE III PLUS" and "dBASE IV" when referring to the specific product and "dBASE" when referring generically to both. Because there are more systems using dBASE III PLUS than there are using dBASE IV, the focus of this chapter will be on the earlier product. We will examine dBASE IV primarily from the viewpoint of noting its differences from dBASE III PLUS.

Both versions of dBASE consist of an end-user interface, which also can be used by programmers for such tasks as defining databases and views, and a high-level programming language. In this chapter, we will examine the end-user interface briefly, but will focus on an introduction to dBASE programming because most serious work with dBASE is done by using the programming language.

dBASE OVERVIEW

In dBASE, instead of tables, rows, and columns, databases, records, and fields are used. When dBASE first appeared on the market, many nonrelational databases for microcomputers that used these terms existed. To maximize user friendliness, dBASE used terminology that was familiar to many potential users of the product.

Both dBASE III PLUS and dBASE IV primarily consist of two components, an end-user interface and an interpreted programming language. The end-user interface is known as **ASSIST** in dBASE III PLUS and the **Control Center** in dBASE IV. The change in names is appropriate, because dBASE IV's Control Center is quite different from dBASE III PLUS's ASSIST. However, both perform many of the same functions.

dBASE's programming language is an interpreted language. That is, each command is compiled into machine language as it is executed. dBASE compilers are available for a nominal cost from numerous vendors.

dBASE IV has added several features to those of dBASE III PLUS, most notably an SQL interface and programming language enhancements. With the SQL interface, you can access a database using Structured Query Language. dBASE IV's version of SQL is similar to that of IBM's mainframe product, DB2. (It should be noted that at the time of this writing, there have been some problems reported with the reliability of dBASE IV's SQL; an upgrade, however, soon will be available to alleviate this situation.)

In addition to the SQL interface, dBASE IV adds several programming language enhancements. Some of these enhancements, such as pop-up windows, are available with dBASE III PLUS only by calling a program written in some other language, such as C or Assembler. Other enhancements, such as support for arrays, are difficult, if not impossible, to implement outside of dBASE IV.

THE dBASE END-USER INTERFACE

The dBASE end-user interface consists of two parts: a menu-driven part known as ASSIST (dBASE III PLUS) or the Control Center (dBASE IV), and a command-driven part known as the **dot prompt.** The dot prompt takes its name from the fact that dBASE prompts you to enter a command by printing the dot (".") symbol. Dot prompt commands have the same functionality as does ASSIST and the Control Center.

Rather than using a dot prompt command, you can access ASSIST and the Control Center via a series of pull-down menus or pop-up windows. In these windows or menus, you can execute commands or specify parameters for them.

ASSIST in dBASE III PLUS

When first invoking dBASE III PLUS, you see the ASSIST screen shown in Figure 11.1. This initial screen contains pull-down menus that we use to select options within dBASE III PLUS.

When you first enter the screen in Figure 11.1, the system displays the menu for the first option (SET UP). You can use this option to select an entity for use, such as a database, a screen format, or a query.

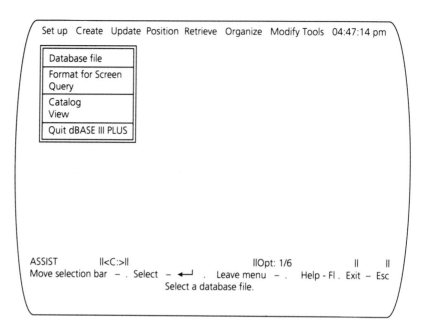

FIGURE 11.1   *The ASSIST screen. ASSIST uses pull-down menus.*

CREATING AN ENTITY

If you have not as yet created an entity to select, you must create one. To do this, move the cursor to the right and select the CREATE menu by pressing the Enter key. The CREATE Menu allows you to create various entities, such as databases, screen formats, views, and reports.

Creating a Database

To create a database, identify the disk drive on which to create the database. dBASE III PLUS will present a menu of all drives defined to DOS. To select a drive, position the cursor over the desired drive and press Enter. You will be asked to enter the name of the database file. For example, you could enter the word EMPLOYEE to create an EMPLOYEE database on the disk.

Creating the Field Description for the Database

After you specify a name for the database, the system displays a screen to define the fields for the database. For each field, we enter the name, type, width, and, if the field is numeric, number of decimal points.

For example, you might create an EMPLOYEE database with the field definitions shown in Figure 11.2.

FIELD NAME	FIELD TYPE	FIELD WIDTH	NUMBER OF DECIMALS
EMPLNUM	CHARACTER	9	0
NAME	CHARACTER	40	0
OFFICENUM	CHARACTER	3	0

FIGURE 11.2 *Field definitions for the EMPLOYEE database. Although all of the fields in this database are of type CHARACTER, you can define other types of fields as needed.*

In Figure 11.2 all of the fields are CHARACTER fields. In dBASE, the following fields are available:

Character: Any printable alphanumeric character
Numeric: Any numeric value, including a decimal point and a sign
Logical: A Boolean value of true or false
Date: A Gregorian date
Memo: A variable-length field that stores text data that can span several screen lines

After you enter the field descriptions, dBASE III PLUS creates the database file. This database file is stored on disk with the name you specified followed by a .DBF qualifier. Therefore, the EMPLOYEE database is named EMPLOYEE.DBF.

USING THE DATABASE

Placing Data in the Database

After defining the database and its field descriptions, you can begin adding records to the database. There are two options available for entering data. First, you can select a default screen format that simply lists each field name down the left side of the screen. Each field name is followed by a space for entering the value for that field. Second, you can select the CREATE menu option and create a screen format. To do this, specify a drive and a name for the format. dBASE III PLUS will display the default screen and allow you to modify it by changing field names, moving fields, adding or deleting fields, drawing boxes, and so on. After you have created a screen format, you can select it by using the SET UP menu. Regardless of which screen format you use, you can enter the data for as many records as you wish.

Because dBASE is a relational database manager, you will want to store the data in several normalized databases (or tables) that are related by foreign keys. For example, you can use the EMPLOYEE database as part of an employee office system. To do this, you can define the following OFFICE database by following the same steps you took to define the EMPLOYEE database. The structure of the OFFICE database is shown in Figure 11.3.

In Figure 11.3 the OFFICENUM field in the EMPLOYEE database is a foreign key that logically links the two databases.

FIELD NAME	FIELD TYPE	FIELD WIDTH	NUMBER OF DECIMALS
OFFICENUM	CHARACTER	3	0
PHONE	CHARACTER	4	0
SIZE	CHARACTER	5	0

FIGURE 11.3   *Field definitions for the OFFICE database. OFFICENUM also is stored in the EMPLOYEE database as a foreign key.*

Manipulating Data in the Database

After you create a database and enter some data into it, you can use ASSIST to manipulate the database using the UPDATE menu. So, you can use the APPEND option to add records using either the default screen format or one that you have created. In addition, you can use the EDIT option to change selected records and use the BROWSE option to list the records. When you browse records, the system again uses a default screen format. Under this format, each field is listed across the screen for as many fields as will fit on the screen and each record is listed down the screen for as many records as will fit on the screen. You then scroll right and left to view all the fields, and up and down to see all the records.

Deleting and Recalling a Record

When editing a record, you can specify that you want to DELETE that record. The record is not physically deleted from the database, but is marked for deletion. After the record is marked, you need to use the PACK option of the UPDATE menu to physically delete the record from the database. To unmark a record that was previously DELETEd, use the RECALL option of the UPDATE menu. You can RECALL a record only if the database has not yet been PACKed.

Creating Indexes

By using the ORGANIZE menu, you can create one or more indexes for a database. dBASE uses an index in much the same way as DB2. That is, when searching for a record, dBASE searches the index instead of searching the entire database. As with DB2, a dBASE index contains pointers to the location of the record in the database. Unlike DB2, dBASE allows each user to specify whether an index is to be used at execution time.

THE dBASE IV CONTROL CENTER

The first thing you see when you invoke dBASE IV, is the Control Center screen shown in Figure 11.4.

Notice that the Control Center is organized differently from ASSIST. Where

```
┌─────────────────────────────────────────────────────────────────┐
│  Catalog  Tools  Exit                                 8:35:41 pm  │
│                    dBASE IV CONTROL CENTER                        │
│             CATALOG: C:\DBASE\SAMPLES\SAMPLES.CAT                  │
│                                                                   │
│      Data      Queries     Forms     Reports    Labels  Applications │
│   ┌──────────┬──────────┬──────────┬──────────┬──────────┬──────────┐ │
│   │<create>  │<create>  │<create>  │<create>  │<create>  │<create>  │ │
│   ├──────────┤          │          │          │          │          │ │
│   │EMPLOYEE  │          │          │          │          │          │ │
│   │OFFICE    │          │          │          │          │          │ │
│   │          │          │          │          │          │          │ │
│   │          │          │          │          │          │          │ │
│   │          │          │          │          │          │          │ │
│   └──────────┴──────────┴──────────┴──────────┴──────────┴──────────┘ │
│                                                                   │
│                                                                   │
│   File:        New file                                           │
│   Description: Press ENTER on <create> to create a new file       │
│                                                                   │
│   Help: FL  Use: ◄─┘  Data: F2  Design: Shift-F2  Quick Report: Shift-F9  Menus: F10 │
└─────────────────────────────────────────────────────────────────┘
```

FIGURE 11.4 *The dBASE IV Control Center. Unlike ASSIST, the Control Center is organized by object, not function.*

ASSIST is organized by function (e.g., setting up a database or screen format, creating a database or screen format, etc.), the Control Center is organized by object. Some of the objects available are:

- DATA (a database)
- FORMS (a screen format)
- APPLICATIONS (a program)

First choose an object to manipulate and then choose the way to manipulate it (create it, update it, etc.).

The organization of the Control Center probably is more logical than that of ASSIST, at least from the end user's viewpoint. When training an end user, you must of course define for him or her the objects that he or she will need to be able to manipulate, and explain their use. This is true regardless of which version of dBASE you are using. With dBASE IV, however, there is a natural transition from the user's knowledge of objects to a discussion of using the Control Center. With dBASE III PLUS, you must first train the user on objects and then on functions, before you can introduce ASSIST in a meaningful way.

Each object category lists the objects that already have been defined under it, for example, the EMPLOYEE and OFFICE databases listed under DATA. To select one of these objects, move the cursor to it and press Enter. To create an object, move the cursor to the ⟨CREATE⟩ function under an object category and press Enter.

dBASE PROGRAMMING

One of the most powerful features of dBASE is its programming language. Not only do end users have a tool to allow them to manipulate databases—ASSIST or the Control Center—but programmers also can use the language to create applications for end users. Typically, this is done when you need more flexibility than is available with ASSIST or Control Center. Also, if end users are unwilling to learn to use these software tools, programmers must use the programming language to implement the user's application. Remember, one of the reasons for dBASE's large share of the microcomputer DBMS market is the fact that several vendors have produced "canned" systems written in dBASE programming language to support various business functions. These functions cover a wide variety of applications including general ledger accounting, inventory control, and payroll administration. With these prewritten applications, users can implement an application with little or no knowledge of programming.

A Simple Application

In this section, we will examine a simple application. Although dBASE IV's programming language is more powerful than that of dBASE III PLUS, the application we will write will not take advantage of dBASE IV's language extensions. Instead, as an introduction to dBASE programming, we will examine simple code that will run under both versions of dBASE.

THE APPLICATION'S DESIGN

Our application will allow a user to manipulate data in the EMPLOYEE and OFFICE databases that we created earlier. The user will invoke the application by issuing the command:

    DO MAINMENU

at the dot prompt. The user then will be presented with the Employee Office System Menu shown in Figure 11.5. This is the primary menu of the system. In this main menu, the user can choose the option:

- A to work with the EMPLOYEE database
- B to work with the OFFICE database
- C to produce a phone directory which uses both
- Q to quit

Option A—The Employee Database Selection

If the user chooses option "A" in the main menu, he or she sees the submenu called the Employee Menu. This submenu is shown in Figure 11.6.

```
mainmenu.prg
```

Employee Office System Menu

Option	Action
A	Work with Employee File
B	Work with Office File
C	List Phone Directory
Q	Quit

Enter one of the options above

FIGURE 11.5 *The primary menu of the Employee Office System Menu. The user can select an option to work with either the EMPLOYEE or the OFFICE databases or to produce a phone directory, which uses both.*

In this Employee Menu, users can add (A), delete (B), change (C), or list (D) records in the EMPLOYEE database. This is done by making a selection from the options listed on the screen (i.e., options A, B, C, D, or Q). If the user chooses option "A," a data entry add screen appears so he or she can enter values for the fields in the record (see Figure 11.7). If the user chooses either option "B" (to delete a record) or option "C" (to change a record) from the Employee Menu, a box will appear to prompt him or her for the employee number (EMPLNUM) of the record to delete (Figure 11.8). If the record cannot be found in the database, an error message appears in the box (Figure 11.9). If the user chooses option Q, the application returns to the main menu.

If the record specified by the user is found in the database, the program's next action depends on which option the user chooses. If the user chooses option "B" (to delete a record), then the record is deleted and the Employee Menu is reshown. If the user chooses option "C" (to change a record), he or she is presented again with the Employee Screen. This time, however, the screen does not contain blank values for its data, but has the data filled in for the requested record. The user now can change any of the fields he or she desires (see Figure 11.10).

If the user chooses option "D" (to list records) from the Employee Menu, he or she is presented with dBASE's default BROWSE screen as shown in Figure 11.11.

```
emplmenu.prg
```

Employee Menu

Option	Action
A	Add employee record
B	Delete employee record
C	Change employee record
D	List employee records
Q	Return to Employee Office System Menu

Enter one of the options above

FIGURE 11.6 *The Employee Menu. The user can select an option to add, delete, change, or list employee records.*

emplfmt.fmt

    Employee Screen
Employee Number:
Employee Name:
Office Number:

FIGURE 11.7   *The Employee Screen. The user can enter the data for the record he or she wishes to add.*

emplmenu.prg

    Employee Menu

Option   Action

  A   Add employee record
  B   Delete employee record
  C   Change employee record
  D   List employee records

  Q   Return to Employee Office System Menu

Enter one of the options above   c
| Enter employee number: |

FIGURE 11.8   *The Employee Menu with a prompt for the employee number. The system then scans the database for the record with the entered number.*

emplmenu.prg

    Employee Menu

Option   Action

  A   Add employee record
  B   Delete employee record
  C   Change employee record
  D   List employee records

  Q   Return to Employee Office System Menu

Enter one of the options above   c
| Employee 111111111 not found. |
Press any key to continue...

FIGURE 11.9   *The Employee Menu with an error message. Here, the requested record could not be found.*

emplfmt.fmt

    Employee Screen
Employee Number: 799127272
Employee Name: Two, D. B.
Office Number: B03

FIGURE 11.10   *The result of choosing option "C" (to edit records) from the Employee Menu. The user can change any of the fields in the record.*

```
EMPLNUM-- NAME-------------------------OFFICENUM
837422773 DOE, JOHN              A02
123443243 PUBLIC, JOHN Q.        A05
902323421 WHIZ, P. C.            B01
799127272 TWO, D. B.             B03
488737999 ESS, I. M.             B01
```

FIGURE 11.11   *The result of choosing option "D" (to list records) from the Employee Menu. Here, the user is presented with dBASE's BROWSE screen.*

```
Record  name              officenum   office->phone
     1  DOE, JOHN         A02         2543
     2  PUBLIC, JOHN Q.   A05         9876
     3  WHIZ, P. C.       B01         7632
     4  TWO, D. B.        B03         2876
     5  ESS, I. M.        B01         7632
```

FIGURE 11.12   *The phone directory produced by choosing option "C" on the Employee Office System Menu. This option uses both databases.*

Remember, option "Q" in the Employee submenu returns the user to the main Employee Office System Menu.

Option B—The Office Database Selection

In the main Employee Office System Menu (Figure 11.5), option "B" allows the user to perform the same functions as option "A," except that the user will manipulate the OFFICE database instead of the EMPLOYEE database.

Option C—List Phone Directory Selection

Option "C" of the main Employee Office System Menu, however, lists data from both databases, as shown in Figure 11.12.

WRITING CODE IN dBASE

It is time to examine the programs that produced the screens in Figures 11.5 through 11.11. The user invokes a program by entering the statement:

    DO programname

at the dot prompt. dBASE then searches for a program with the specified name followed by ".PRG" as an extension. Because the user started the system by entering:

    DO MAINMENU

the name of the first program is MAINMENU.PRG.

Using dBASE's Program Editor

You can create a program using dBASE's program editor. To invoke the editor, use the statement:

```
MODIFY COMMAND programname
```

where "programname" is the name of the program you wish to write. That is, the statement:

```
MODIFY COMMAND MAINMENU
```

invokes the editor and establishes "MAINMENU" as the name of the program you will write.

You are not restricted to using dBASE's system editor. You can create a program using any editor or word processor as long as it creates an ASCII file.

Once in the editor, you can write a program and save it. Figure 11.13 illustrates a sample program. When you execute this program, you get the menu in Figure 11.5.

A DESCRIPTION OF THE EMPLOYEE MAIN MENU PROGRAM

Using Comments and Documenting the Program

The program in Figure 11.13 begins with the following comments to identify it:

```
*File name:  mainmenu.prg
*System name:  Employee Office System
*Module name:  Main Menu
```

Any line that begins with an asterisk is considered to be a comment by dBASE. Of course, you are not required to use comments, although they are strongly recommended to enhance program readability.

The SET Command

The next section of code uses a pair of SET commands to establish the environment for the program. These commands are:

```
* establish environment:
set talk off
set echo off
```

When you use ASSIST or the Control Center, the commands in the program display on the screen when they execute. In addition, certain other messages display as the program executes. The command SET ECHO OFF suppresses the

```
* File name:  mainmenu.prg
* System name:  Employee Office System
* Module name:  Main Menu

* establish environment:
set talk off
set echo off

* initialize memory variables:
store " " to mchoice

* display menu:
do while .t.
   clear
   ? "mainmenu.prg"
   ?
   ? "              Employee Office System Menu"
   ?
   ? "   Option    Action"
   ? "   --------   --------"
   ? "     A        Work with Employee File"
   ? "     B        Work with Office File"
   ? "     C        List Phone Directory"
   ?
   ? "     Q        Quit"
* get user's choice:
   @ 12,00 say " "
   wait "     Enter one of the options above  " to mchoice
* process user's choice:
   do case
       case upper(mchoice)="A"
           use employee
           do emplmenu
           use
       case upper(mchoice)="B"
           use office index office
           do offcmenu
           use
       case upper(mchoice)="C"
           select 1
           use employee
           select 2
           use office index office
           select 1
           set relation to officenum into office
           clear
           list name, officenum, office->phone
           wait
           close all
       case upper(mchoice)="Q"
           return
   endcase
enddo
```

FIGURE 11.13   *The MAINMENU program. This program displays the Employee Office System menu shown in Figure 11.5.*

displaying of the commands as they execute in the program, while the SET TALK OFF command suppresses the displaying of system messages. Consequently, when you want to display the program's commands for debugging purposes, you must use SET TALK ON in the program. SET TALK OFF is the system's default.

Another factor to consider is that this system consists of more than one program. The main program calls other programs that return control to it. If one of the other programs sets the option to TALK ON, program commands will continue to display after control is returned to MAINMENU. Therefore, use SET TALK OFF in the main menu program.

The STORE Command

Next you initialize any memory variables that will be used by the program by entering the following STORE command:

```
* initialize memory variables:
store " " to mchoice
```

dBASE supports two kinds of variables in a program. One type is a database variable. Don't forget that you defined three fields for the EMPLOYEE database—EMPLNUM, NAME, and OFFICENUM. When accessing a record from the database, you access the data fields by using variables with the same names as the field names. Any other type of variable is a memory variable. Both types of variables can be initialized using the general statement:

```
STORE value TO variablename
```

In this case, "mchoice" is a memory variable that stores the user's menu selection and you initialize it as a one-character blank.

Note that "mchoice" is not a variable in any of the databases. It is simply an arbitrary name created to handle a specific need. The names of memory variables typically begin with "m" to enhance program readability. This way, memory variables can be identified easily because they begin with an "m."

The DO WHILE Command

Next, the program displays the main menu using the statements:

```
* display menu:
do while .t.
   clear
   ? "mainmenu.prg"
   ?
   ? "                        Employee Office System Menu"
   ?
   ? "        Option            Action"
```

```
? "
    ? "          A              Work with Employee File"
    ? "          B              Work with Office File"
    ? "          C              List Phone Directory"
    ?
    ? "          Q              Quit"
```

This section of code begins with a DO WHILE loop because you will continue to display the menu, get the user's choice, and process the choice until the user chooses the "Q" (quit) option. The DO WHILE loop has the general form:

```
DO WHILE condition
        executable statements
ENDDO
```

The loop executes as long as the condition is true. In the program, we have chosen a condition of ".t.," which is a Boolean constant whose value is true. In other words, we will execute the loop forever. Of course, as you will see later, there is a way you can break out of the loop when the user chooses the "Q" option.

The CLEAR, PRINT, SAY, and WAIT Commands

The next statement in the program clears the screen using the CLEAR command. A list of the main menu selections available is displayed. There are several ways in dBASE to display information on the screen. The first way is to use the "?" command, which acts very much like the "?" (or PRINT) command in BASIC. In this case, the

```
? "expression"
```

statement prints the expression onto the screen. In this way, you print the program name, a blank line, the screen title, a blank line, and the options and their associated actions. In addition to the "?" command, there is another way to display data on the screen. Suppose, for example, that you wished to display a copyright notice at the bottom of the screen, just above the status bar. To do this, you could use the second method of displaying information on the screen, the @...SAY command. The @...SAY command takes the form:

```
@ row,column SAY expression
```

The @...SAY command would cause the expression in quotes (the copyright notice) to display starting in the column and row specified.

The next lines of code now get the user's choice:

```
* get user's choice:
    @ 12,00 say " "
    wait "Enter one of the options above " to mchoice
```

The @...SAY command is simply used to position the cursor. The WAIT command is used to display a prompt to the user. The WAIT command then will pause the program until the user presses a key. The value of the key then will be stored in the variable "mchoice."

Processing the User's Choice

You must now process the user input using the following series of instructions:

```
* process user's choice:
  do case
      case upper(mchoice) = "A"
         use employee
         do emplmenu
         use
      case upper(mchoice) = "B"
         use office index office
         do offcmenu
         use
      case upper(mchoice) = "C"
         select 1
         use employee
         select 2
         use office index office
         select 1
         set relation to officenum into office
         clear
         list name, officenum, office-)phone
         wait
         close all
      case upper(mchoice) = "Q"
         return
   endcase
enddo
```

The DO CASE Command

You use a DO CASE command to process the user's choice, which is in the variable "mchoice." The general format of the DO CASE command is:

```
DO CASE
      CASE condition
            executable statements
      CASE condition
            executable statements
ENDCASE
```

In this example, if the first "condition" is true, the first set of executable statements executes. Alternately, if the first "condition" is false, the second "condition" is evaluated. If this second "condition" is true, then the second set of executable statements executes. You can have as many CASE statements with conditions and executable statements as you need.

In the program, you check variable "mchoice" for values of "A," "B," "C," and "Q," which are the valid menu choices from the user. The UPPER function is used to translate the value of "mchoice" to upper case, just in the event the user entered a lower-case letter. This saves you from having to check for "a," "b," "c," and "q" as well as for their upper-case equivalents.

The RETURN and USE Commands

If the user enters "Q," you execute the RETURN command, which breaks out of the DO WHILE loop and terminates the program, returning control to the dot prompt. If the user enters "A," you open the EMPLOYEE database with the USE command. Then you execute another program, EMPLMENU, with the DO command. EMPLMENU will return control to MAINMENU at the statement following the DO command, which is another USE command. Because you do not specify a database name, this USE command closes the current database (EMPLOYEE).

Much the same happens if the user enters "B," except that OFFCMENU is executed instead of EMPLMENU and you use the OFFICE database instead of the EMPLOYEE database. If the user enters "C," you execute commands that logically join the two databases. We will defer our discussion of processing multiple databases, however, until we have examined the single-database processing in EMPLMENU. Because OFFCMENU is virtually identical to EMPLMENU, we will not examine that program.

A Description of the Employee Submenu Program

Remember dBASE will expect the program EMPLMENU to reside in a file called EMPLMENU.PRG. This program is shown in Figure 11.14 and produces the menu shown in Figure 11.6.

The SET PROCEDURE Command

The program begins with some identifying comments. Some SET commands are issued to establish the environment. This time, however, you also execute the following command:

```
set procedure to emplmenu
```

The SET PROCEDURE command changes where dBASE looks for programs when a DO command is encountered. Normally, dBASE looks for an external file. However, the above command causes dBASE to look first in

```
* File name: emplmenu.prg                                    do errormsg with mempl
* System name: Employee Office System                  else
* Module name: Employee Menu                              delete next 1
                                                          pack
* establish environment:                              endif
set talk off                                      case upper(mchoice)="C"
set echo off                                          store "        " to mempl
set procedure to emplmenu                             do getempl with mempl
                                                      goto top
* initialize memory variables:                        locate for emplnum = mempl
store " " to mchoice                                  if eof()
                                                          do errormsg with mempl
* display menu:                                       else
do while .t.                                              set format to emplfmt
   clear                                                  edit
   ? "emplmenu.prg"                                       set format to
   ?                                                  endif
   ? "              Employee Menu"                 case upper(mchoice)="D"
   ?                                                   browse
   ? "     Option     Action"                     case upper(mchoice)="Q"
   ? "     ---------  -------"                         set procedure to
   ? "       A        Add employee record"            return
   ? "       B        Delete employee record"    endcase
   ? "       C        Change employee record"  enddo
   ? "       D        List employee records"
   ?                                            * get employee number:
   ? "       Q        Return to Employee Office System Menu"  procedure getempl
                                                      parameters mempl
* get user's choice:                                  @ 16,08 to 18,44
   @ 14,00 say " "                                    @ 17,10 say "Enter employee number:  "
   wait "    Enter one of the options above  " to mchoice  @ 17,34 get mempl
                                                      read
* process user's choice:                          return
   do case
      case upper(mchoice)="A"                     * display error message:
         set format to emplfmt                    procedure errormsg
         append                                       parameters mempl
         set format to                               @ 16,08 clear to 18,44
      case upper(mchoice)="B"                       @ 16,08 to 18,40
         store "        " to mempl                   @ 17,10 say "Employee "+mempl+" not found."
         do getempl with mempl                       ?
         goto top                                    wait
         locate for emplnum = mempl              return
         if eof()
```

FIGURE 11.14   *The EMPLMENU program. This program displays the Employee Menu shown in Figure 11.6.*

EMPLMENU.PRG, which is the currently executing program. You will see later
how this is used in conjunction with DO commands.

Next you initialize memory variables, display a menu, and get the user's
input in the same fashion as in the MAINMENU program. You process the
user's input with a CASE statement, just as in the MAINMENU program.

The SET FORMAT and APPEND Commands

If the user chooses option "A" (to add records), you execute the following
code to display the screen shown in Figure 11.7:

```
case upper(mchoice) = "A"
  set format to emplfmt
  append
  set format to
```

Notice that the APPEND command, which invokes the APPEND function as if we had chosen the option from ASSIST, was used. You do not, however, see the dBASE default screen format. Instead, you have selected a format that you have created. This was done with the command:

```
set format to emplfmt
```

which causes the form stored in EMPLFMT.FMT to be used. After issuing the APPEND command, issue the command:

```
set format to
```

Because you do not specify the format name, this command resets the format to the default format.

You already have seen that you can create formats using ASSIST or the Control Center. If you examine the file EMPLFMT.FMT, shown in Figure 11.15, you will see another way to create a form.

Figure 11.15 shows a way to create a format other than using ASSIST or the Control Center. The format begins with some comments, a command to clear the screen, and some @...SAY commands to display the titles of the fields. The @...GET commands cause input fields to be created on the screen for the user to enter the values for the fields in the database. In this instance you use the field names as variables. When you set the format to EMPLFMT with the SET FORMAT command, dBASE will use that format when you issue the APPEND command.

Some Logical Considerations

If the user chooses option "B" (to delete a record), the code on page 336 is executed and displays the screens shown in Figure 11.8 and Figure 11.9:

```
* File name: emplfmt.fmt
* System name: Employee Office System
* Module name: Employee Screen

clear

@ 01,01 say "emplfmt.fmt"
@ 03,25 say "Employee Screen"
@ 05,10 say "Employee Number:"
@ 06,10 say "Employee Name:"
@ 07,10 say "Office Number:"

@ 05,27 get emplnum
@ 06,27 get name
@ 07,27 get officenum
```

FIGURE 11.15   *The EMPLFMT format.*

```
case upper(mchoice) = "B"
   store "              " to mempl
   do getempl with mempl
   goto top
   locate for emplnum = mempl
   if eof()
      do errormsg with mempl
   else
      delete next 1
      pack
   endif
```

In this section of code you first initialize the memory variable "mempl." An obvious question then is "Why do we initialize it here instead of at the beginning of the program?" Remember, this part of the program is in a loop controlled by a DO WHILE statement; the menu will be displayed repeatedly until the user chooses the "Q" option (to quit). You want the variable "mempl" to be reinitialized every time the user chooses the "B" option. For this reason, you need to put the STORE command at this point in the program.

Using a Procedure

The next statements in the code use a DO command. Normally, this would transfer control to the external program GETEMPL.PRG. Recall, however, that you issued the command:

```
set procedure to emplmenu
```

This command causes dBASE to search for any procedures referenced by a DO command in the file EMPLMENU.PRG (i.e., the current program file). What dBASE will search for is a PROCEDURE statement with an identifier of GETEMPL. This procedure is found toward the end of the program and is as follows:

```
* get employee number:
procedure getempl
   parameters mempl
   @ 16,08 to 18,44
   @ 17,10 say "Enter employee number:   "
   @ 17,34 get mempl
   read
return
```

When you issue the DO GETEMPL command, control is transferred to this procedure. Note that the command you actually executed was:

```
do getempl with mempl
```

and don't forget that the variable "mempl" is a memory variable.

Identifying Parameters

After the PROCEDURE statement in GETEMPL, you have the command:

```
parameters mempl
```

This command, along with the WITH clause on the DO command, cause the value in "mempl" to be passed to GETEMPL as a parameter. The procedure then can modify the value in "mempl" whose new value can be available for use by the calling procedure.

The @... Commands

Note that we have used a screen display command that you have not seen before. This command has the form @ n TO m and appears in the code as @ 16,08 to 18,44. The @...TO command draws a box with upper left and lower right corners at the coordinates you specify, for example, row 16, column 8 and row 18, column 44. Rows and columns are numbered starting with zero.

After an @...SAY command to prompt the user for the employee number, you issue an @...GET command to get the user's input value for "mempl" using:

```
@ 17,34 get mempl
```

Note that the @...GET command does not take effect immediately; it merely defines an input field on the screen. You need to issue the READ command (as you do in the next program line) to cause dBASE to wait to receive the user's input. You then end the procedure with a RETURN command, causing the program to proceed with the next statement after the DO command that called the GETEMPL procedure.

The GOTO and LOCATE Commands

The next two statements attempt to locate the employee number entered by the user. These are:

```
goto top
locate for emplnum = mempl
```

The GOTO statement causes dBASE to begin any search for a record at the top of the database. This can be important if the user repeatedly executes one of the options that search the database (such as the current option "B"). When a search is successful, the database is "positioned" at the record that was found. Later you will see where the database is positioned when the search is unsuccessful. If another search takes place, the search will begin at the current position, that is, the last record found. To make certain that you search the entire database each time, you have to position the database at the beginning before each search. The LOCATE command causes dBASE to search the database for the record with a value in EMPLNUM that equals that in the variable "mempl."

The IF Command

In the code you use an IF command to determine whether the requested record was found. The statements include:

```
if eof()
   do errormsg with mempl
else
   delete next 1
   pack
endif
```

Here, the IF command has the general format:

```
IF condition
   action
ELSE
   action
ENDIF
```

If the specified condition is true, the action under the IF statement executes. If the condition is not true, the action under the ELSE statement executes instead. You can code as many actions under either statement as necessary. In the EMPLMENU program, the EOF() condition is true if the database is positioned at the end. This will happen if a database search is unsuccessful. In this case, we call the ERRORMSG procedure, which we will discuss below.

If the EOF() condition is not true, then the search performed by the LOCATE command was successful, meaning the record specified by the user was found. In this case, the actions under the ELSE statement execute. The DELETE statement deletes the specified record (i.e., the NEXT 1 record starting with the current position). Then you issue the PACK command so you can physically delete the records from the database.

Handling Error Messages

The procedure ERRORMSG is invoked when a record the user specifies cannot be found. Executing the following code produces the display shown in Figure 11.9 on page 326:

```
* display error message:
procedure errormsg
   parameters mempl
   @ 16,08 clear to 18,44
   @ 16,08 to 18,40
   @ 17,10 say "Employee " + mempl + " not found."
```

```
    ?
    wait
return
```

Remember that we called this procedure with the command:

```
do errormsg with mempl
```

The @...CLEAR Command

Procedure ERRORMSG contains the statement:

```
parameters mempl
```

This means that you are passing data in "mempl" as a parameter to
ERRORMSG. As the name suggests, ERRORMSG displays an error message when
the specified record cannot be found in the database. This error message will
be displayed over the box that contained the prompt for the employee number.
To do this, first clear the area of the screen occupied by the box with the
following @...CLEAR command:

```
@ 16,08 clear to 18,44
```

This command clears the screen in a rectangular area from the upper left
corner of row 16, column 8 to row 18, column 44. Recall that the CLEAR
command clears the entire screen. The @...CLEAR command clears only a
portion of the screen.

Concatenating Alphanumeric Strings

To display an error message with the @...SAY command, draw a box with
an @...TO command. You can concatenate alphanumeric strings with the "+"
operator. In this case, you concatenate a literal ("Employee "), a variable
(mempl), and another literal (" not found.") to create the error message:

```
@ 17,10 say "Employee "+mempl+" not found."
```

The WAIT Command

Now issue a "?" command to position the cursor at the beginning of the next
screen row. Then issue a WAIT command without any parameters. Earlier,
you issued a WAIT command to display a prompt and get input from the
user. Here, because you do not specify a message with the WAIT command,
dBASE will automatically display the message:

```
"Press any key to continue..."
```

and wait for the user to press a key. This is done to give the user time to
read the error message. Then you RETURN to the part of the program that
displays the Employee Menu.

Code for Changing a Record

If the user chooses the "C" option, to change a record, the following code executes and produces the display shown in Figure 11.10, as well as displays very similar to those in Figure 11.8 and Figure 11.9 (page 326):

```
case upper(mchoice) = "C"
    store "          " to mempl
    do getempl with mempl
    goto top
    locate for emplnum = mempl
    if eof()
        do errormsg with mempl
    else
        set format to emplfmt
        edit
        set format to
    endif
```

This code is almost identical to the code that executes when the user chooses the "B" option to delete a record. The only difference is that, when the requested record is found, the dBASE EDIT function is invoked—with the EMPLFMT format—to allow the record to be changed. This produces the display shown in Figure 11.10.

Using Data from Two Databases

We have now examined all of the options on the Employee Menu displayed by the EMPLMENU program. Recall however, that we deferred consideration of one of the options on the Employee Office System Menu displayed by the MAINMENU program. This was the "C" option, which uses both the OFFICE database and the EMPLOYEE database. This is because we wish to list the employee name (which is in the EMPLOYEE database), the office number (which is in both databases), and the phone number (which is in the OFFICE database). The two databases are related through the office number. This relationship must be used to extract the information needed. This can be done by the following code:

```
case upper(mchoice) = "C"
    select 1
    use employee
    select 2
    use office index office
    select 1
    set relation to officenum into office
    clear
    list name, officenum, office-)phone
```

```
wait
close all
```

You employ the USE statement to select and open a database. When you do this, dBASE allocates a set of buffers for the database known as a **workarea.** When you operate on only one database, you typically use a default workarea and are mostly oblivious to its presence. When you perform multidatabase operations, however, you need to manage multiple work areas because dBASE allows only one database to be opened (via the USE command) per workarea.

The SELECT and USE Commands

In the previous example, you select a workarea (workarea number 1) with the following SELECT statement:

```
select 1
```

You then open the EMPLOYEE database in workarea 1 with the following USE statement:

```
use employee
```

Now you select a second workarea and open the OFFICE database using the statements:

```
select 2
use office index office
```

The USE command specifies that you want to use the index that you created for the office file with ASSIST or the Control Center. When you use the statement:

```
INDEX OFFICE
```

dBASE searches for the file OFFICE.NDX.

Whenever you SELECT a workarea, the fields in the database that is open in that workarea are available to you and can be referenced by name. Fields in other databases are not directly available—although you will see how, by using the SET RELATION command, you can make them available. For this reason, it is important to issue another SELECT command. This statement becomes:

```
select 1
```

and makes the EMPLOYEE database available.

The SET RELATION Command

The next command is a SET RELATION command. This command, in effect, relates two databases via a common field, just as joining two tables does in DB2. Also, as with DB2, a third "database" (or "table") is created by dBASE in a buffer area with data from both databases (or tables). You effect this join by issuing the following statement:

set relation to officenum into office

This command causes data from records in both databases with equal values for OFFICENUM to be available simultaneously. The databases that supply the data are the database that is open in the currently SELECTed workarea, number 1 (i.e., the EMPLOYEE database), and the database that is specified in the SET RELATION command (i.e., the OFFICE table). There are several conditions to meet for you to successfully use this version of the SET RELATION command:

1. Both databases must have a field (e.g., OFFICENUM) of the same length and type and of the same name
2. Both databases must be open in separate workareas
3. You must have SELECTed a workarea in which one of the databases (e.g., EMPLOYEE) is open
4. The database (e.g., OFFICE) in the workarea that you have not SELECTed must be indexed

The LIST Command

Now you can clear the screen and issue a LIST command to produce the display shown in Figure 11.12. The LIST command becomes:

list name, officenum, office→phone

You can access the fields from the database open in the currently SELECTed workarea (e.g., NAME and OFFICENUM) by name. However, you need to access the fields in the related database (open in another workarea) by specifying the database name and the "→" operator (e.g., OFFICE→PHONE).

Both dBASE III PLUS and dBASE IV allow much more sophisticated programming techniques than we have examined here. These examples illustrate, however, how easily you can create a useful program with a minimum of code.

dBASE IV AND SQL

dBASE IV's use of SQL is similar in many ways to DB2's. The syntax is virtually identical to that of DB2, which is described in earlier chapters. Like DB2, dBASE IV allows you to create tables and indexes using CREATE, INSERT rows, and SELECT rows. There is also a LOAD command that parallels DB2's LOAD utility in that it allows the importing of data from other types of files, such as files produced by other database managers, files produced by spreadsheets, or files produced as ASCII files. dBASE IV also maintains tables very much like those in the DB2 catalog, such as SYSVIEWS and SYSTABL.

There are, however, some differences. The SQL interface for end users and programmers, which is described shortly, is different from that of DB2. In addition, dBASE IV has several special function commands (e.g., UPPER) that can be used in an SQL statement. Finally, the tables that are accessed via SQL under dBASE IV are not physically organized like DB2 tables, but instead are dBASE IV databases.

Accessing SQL via the SET SQL Command

To use SQL from within dBASE IV, use SET SQL ON to turn SQL mode on. dBASE IV now will recognize SQL commands. Use SET SQL OFF to return to the normal dBASE IV mode where only non-SQL dBASE IV commands are recognized.

You issue the SET SQL command from either the dot prompt or from within a program. When issuing the SET SQL command at the dot prompt, the system displays the prompt "SQL" followed by a dot. When issuing the SET SQL command from within a program, you can embed SQL statements within the program. Each SQL statement is delimited by a semicolon. For example, if you wish to access a certain record in the EMPLOYEE database whose employee number is equal to the value in the memory variable MEMPL, you could code:

```
SELECT *
    FROM EMPLOYEE
    WHERE EMPLNUM = MEMPL;
```

This is equivalent to the non-SQL statement:

```
LOCATE FOR EMPLNUM = MEMPL
```

which you would use if SQL mode were set to OFF. This SQL statement would be expected to return only one row. The LOCATE statement does return only one row. If multiple rows might be returned, then the program must declare and open a cursor, just as with DB2.

SUMMARY

Ashton-Tate's dBASE is the most widely used microcomputer RDBMS, partly due to the number of prewritten systems written by third-party vendors. dBASE III PLUS and dBASE IV are the major versions of the product.

Both versions of dBASE consist of an end-user interface and a programming language. The end-user interface consists of a menu-driven component, known as ASSIST (dBASE III PLUS) or the Control Center (dBASE IV), and a command-level component, known as the dot prompt. ASSIST is organized by function, while the Control Center is organized by object.

dBASE includes a very powerful programming language. It can be used to display multiple menus, get and process input from users, and issue dBASE database manipulation commands such as DELETE, EDIT, and APPEND. Structured programming is facilitated by such statements as CASE, DO WHILE, and

IF-ELSE, as well as by support for procedures. dBASE IV adds even more capability to the language.

Multiple databases can be manipulated by opening them in separate workareas. You can relate these databases by use of the RELATE statement. Both databases must have a common field of the same name, length, and type. In addition, one of the databases must be indexed.

dBASE IV includes an SQL interface that uses a version of SQL that is very similar to that of DB2. You can use SQL either from the dot prompt or from within a program by using the SET SQL command.

QUESTIONS

1. Name the components of dBASE.
2. What are the differences between dBASE III PLUS and dBASE IV?
3. How is dBASE terminology different from that of other relational databases?
4. What is the dot prompt?
5. Why would we want to write a dBASE program?
6. What kinds of variables can be used in a dBASE program?
7. What is the function of the following commands?
   A. @...SAY
   B. @...GET
   C. @...TO
   D. @...CLEAR
8. How does the CASE command work?
9. What steps must we follow to relate two databases?
10. How do we embed SQL in a dBASE IV program?
11. What is the SQL prompt?

12

End Users and Relational Databases

I n this chapter we discuss how end users access a relational database. This discussion will center around the relational databases DB2 and SQL/DS, because they are the predominant relational databases on mainframes. DB2 is a specific product for MVS/XA or MVS/ESA operating systems, and SQL/DS is used on machines having the VM operating system. Both DB2 and SQL/DS are database management systems that control and manage the actual data in the database. An ancillary product to DB2 and SQL/DS is the Query Management Facility or QMF. This product is the main vehicle that end-user departments use to access the data in the database. Because the majority of businesses have IBM mainframes and these installations have DB2 or SQL/DS that end users must access via QMF, this chapter will discuss QMF in detail. End users access QMF via a screen option in DB2 or the command SQLQMF in SQL/DS.

ACCESSING DATABASES

You log onto a mainframe computer system by logging onto one of its operating system's subsystems. On IBM mainframes, this subsystem usually is TSO, IMS, or CICS. There is no formal process or ritual for logging onto the DB2 subsystem. That is, one of the security features of DB2 requires the user to first logon to TSO using that subsystem's user's account ID and password (see Figure 12.1). The User's ID of that subsystem (i.e., the TSO's User ID) becomes DB2's User ID. If the system is not an MVS/XA or MVS/ESA system, the installation can use the product SQL/DS, which is similar to DB2.

Once a user connects to the TSO subsystem, he or she can access DB2 software either by executing a PROC or by selecting an option in the main TSO menu. Although users can view the DB2's main menu, they will not be able to access any of its products until either SYSADM or DBADM gives them the proper authorization to do so. Remember, everything within DB2 is protected and each user must be GRANTed authority to access an entity or a DB2 software product.

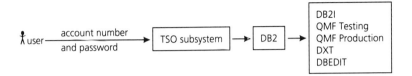

FIGURE 12.1   *Accessing DB2 products via TSO. User logs onto TSO subsystem. After user is granted authorization to use DB2's database subsystem by SYSADM or DBADM, he or she can access specific products using a menu system or PROC.*

DB2 AND ITS ASSOCIATED PRODUCTS

The DB2 related products available from IBM include the following:

- DB2I (Database 2 Interactive) contains the main menu screen for accessing the database, executing queries, and performing other functions within DB2. Typically, the programming staff is the main group authorized to use DB2I to test SQL queries before embedding them in COBOL.
- QMF (Query Management Facility) contains a series of menus so end users can query the database and produce reports. Most installations have two versions of QMF. The production version accesses the production database and the testing version accesses the test database. QMF is a separately priced product and, therefore, is not automatically included in the purchase of DB2.
- DXT (Data Extractor) is a software product the programming staff uses to convert certain non-DB2 files to sequential files. These sequential files later can be loaded into DB2 using the LOAD option in DB2I. DXT is also a separately priced product.
- DBEDIT (Database Edit) is a software product that automatically generates screens for inserting, deleting, selecting, and updating data in DB2 tables. DBEDIT is also a separately priced product.

Because different products are available for accessing DB2 databases, each class of users will have a different access screen. That is, SYSADM (or corporate policy) might dictate that end users cannot have access to DB2I, DXT, and DBEDIT software, while the programming staff might be allowed to access all the products referencing DB2 databases. This is particularly true of DBEDIT. Because DBEDIT does not have an audit trail facility, its use for production databases can be severely limited by internal and external auditing guidelines. However, DBEDIT is an excellent tool that lets the programming staff create test databases for the testing and debugging of code that accesses DB2 databases.

If SYSADM restricts end users to particular software products, he or she will typically create a different set of product selection menus: one for the restricted end user and another for the remaining users. Remember, each company has its own standards and procedures for the creation of system-accessing screens; and the screens each user sees can vary from department to department and company to company.

DB2I

Because end users typically do not access DB2I, we will discuss this product in more detail in Chapter 13.

QMF

Overview

QMF is a separately priced end-user product from IBM. Nonprogrammers use QMF to query databases and produce reports. In fact, one of the many reasons to convert to a relational database is to have end users access the database without programmer intervention.

QMF is divided into two main screens: the Query Screen and the Forms Screen. You write a query in the Query Screen using either SQL or QBE. You then execute this query:

- By entering the statement RUN QUERY on the Command line of the Query Screen
- By pressing the PF2 key (see Figure 12.2).

You use the Forms Screen to format the data generated by the query. In this screen you can create headings and footers, generate control breaks, and

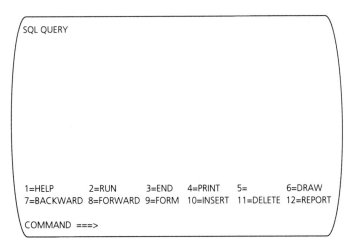

```
SQL QUERY




















1=HELP        2=RUN       3=END    4=PRINT    5=         6=DRAW
7=BACKWARD  8=FORWARD  9=FORM   10=INSERT  11=DELETE  12=REPORT

COMMAND ===>
```

FIGURE 12.2   *The Query Screen in QMF. You write a query in this screen and execute it using the PF2 key (2 = RUN). To print the screen, you press the PF4 key and to exit use the PF3 key. The PF9 key displays the Forms Screen while the PF12 key displays the results of the previous query, which is in the Report Screen.*

add page numbers and a date to a report. You can save these formats for later use. It is this ability to save both the forms and queries that give end users their ability to create multiple reports and process them at different time intervals.

End Users and QMF

By using QMF, the end user can create queries and format data into reports. They can save the formats and queries for later recall and usage. If the end user is not capable of writing queries or if the query becomes too involved or complicated, a member of the programming staff or a member of the EUSC can write it. It is vital that proper communications between the end users and the technical support staff exist. Because many end users are computer neophytes, a help desk or help center can aid these users. These novices might feel intimidated by the machine, and their lack of computer knowledge should not be a handicap to the departments in which they work. Don't forget, implementing a database requires management's dedication and commitment to the proper training of the end users.

In fact, because QMF is user friendly, the personnel in the various user departments can learn how to use QMF to access the database within days of QMF's installation and database creation. After QMF is installed by the computer center, one of the major tasks of the EUSC will be to train the company's nontechnical staff on how to use QMF. After they are properly trained, these end users can generate their own reports whenever they need them, rather than wait for the programming staff to respond to their requests.

It is this ability of the end users to directly access the database that gives relational databases their true power. Obviously, an improperly trained staff will create havoc and lead to frustration within the user departments. Because the users now will be responsible for their own data and report generation, it is the responsibility of the technical staff, in coordination with the EUSC, to see that these users know what they are doing. The technical staff must realize that by using a relational database, the end users will be thrust into a new world previously reserved for the highly technical computer whiz.

Remember, prior to using QMF, most end users relied entirely on the technical staff for maintaining the integrity of the database and for creating the reports. When these neophytes first attempt to use QMF, they will be like baby birds yet to fly their first flight. They will make mistakes and perhaps fail several times before they grasp and comprehend their limits and powers. Like most baby birds, however, these end users will attain their goals and become successful in their task.

Keep in mind that it is the responsibility of the technical staff to aid these end users during this quest for learning. Although many mistakes will be made in the process, the technical staff's expertise must provide an environment for the end user's successful transition from dependent users of databases to independent users of databases. Historically, the data center had the primary responsibility of creating reports and ensuring the integrity that produced them. By using a relational database, however, the corporation can transfer the report creation responsibilities from the data center to the end-user departments. This basic transferring of power is traumatic for both the end-user departments and the programming staff. By using QMF, the end-user departments become responsible for their own reports and the accuracy of the data within them. And this might be the first time that they are exposed to this type of responsibility.

QMF does not solve all of the end user's report-creation problems. Although QMF is quite versatile, it does have a fixed structure. Even though QMF can handle the bulk of creating reports for the user departments, it cannot create all of the specialized reports the various end users want and need. Therefore, the programming staff still will need to write code and create files based on the end user's requirements. QMF accesses only DB2 databases. A user might need data from multiple sources that resides in tables within DB2 and within files in IDMS/R, CICS, or IMS (Figure 12.3). In these cases, the programming staff will need to write computer programs to access these multiple database structures.

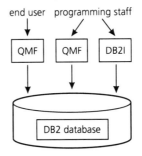

End users access database via QMF while programming staff access it via either QMF or DB2I.

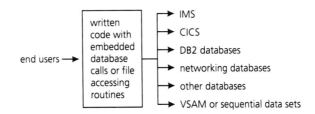

End users access multiple database types using computer programs written by programmers. The programming staff must know the accessing language of each of the database types which the code must access (i.e., DL/I, SQL, etc.). In addition, the programmer must write the JCL to access the databases and nondatabase data sets.

FIGURE 12.3   *Accessing databases by the end user or the programmer.*

In addition, a user department's data can span multiple databases. A database of one department might contain data another department wants and needs. Typically, a DBADM is responsible for only a particular database and there might be many databases on the system. Consequently these multiple databases will require multiple DBADMs to control and monitor the data for the different databases.

What happens when, due to politics within the organization, one department finds it difficult to share its data with another department? Who becomes the final arbitrator of conflicts between the various DBADMs on the system? In fact, even if corporate politics were not involved, who will be responsible for coordinating the data and views, and the granting and revoking of privileges when data resides within databases in different departments or different divisions within the company? You don't want the corporate structure and the conflicts between the various department heads and upper management personnel to hinder the cooperative spirit of the database users.

Prior to this new age of distribution of computer resources to the end users, the data center had complete authority over who accessed the database and what information he or she could capture from it. In today's corporate world, database accessing rights are given to the end-user departments via QMF and other end-user tools. As in any human endeavor, conflicts between the end users will arise. Any conflicts that do occur, therefore, must be resolved to the satisfaction of all the parties involved. This requires a task force to establish a unified corporate policy concerning the accessing of the databases. Obviously, there are no simple solutions to many conflicts and it becomes the responsibility of management to identify possible sources of conflict and provide remedies that will benefit all parties.

When conflicts do occur, it is the responsibility of SYSADM to find out who is involved and suggest remedies. If this initial contact fails to resolve the dispute, SYSADM must initiate communication with management. In this case, preplanning by SYSADM and working with upper management in defining the scope and power of SYSADM probably will resolve most disputes. SYSADM must identify areas of possible dispute and establish procedures and standards before the conflicts occur. In fact, with proper planning by SYSADM, major systems can create and use databases without conflicts ever occurring.

Using QMF

Most systems contain two identical versions of QMF: a test version for accessing testing databases and a production version for accessing production databases (see Figure 12.4). After selecting the appropriate version of QMF in a selection menu, the system displays the QMF Home Screen. It is from this Home Screen that you enter either the Query Screen or the Forms Screen (Figure 12.5). If you want to execute a query upon entering QMF, select the Query Screen option in the QMF's Home Screen.

SOFTWARE OPTION LIST FOR DB2

0 DB2I
1 QMF Testing
2 QMF Production
3 DXT
4 DBEDIT
X EXIT--RETURN TO MAIN MENU

SELECTION PLEASE? _

FIGURE 12.4   *Typical selection menu for DB2-related software.*

The Query Screen

To execute a query in the Query Screen, first move the cursor to the top of the screen and enter the query (Figure 12.6).

After you are satisfied that the query is entered correctly (i.e., it has no misspellings or typographical errors), execute the query by either pressing the PF2 key or by moving the cursor to the beginning of the COMMAND line and typing the statement RUN QUERY. The menu at the bottom of the screen provides a clue to the options within each of the QMF screens. In this case, 2=RUN in Figure 12.6 tells you to press the PF2 key to RUN the query.

The Query Screen contains four regions or areas including:

1. A query writing area for entering a single query statement.
2. A menu selection area listing 11 options available for the screen. These options refer to the PF keys that activate the desired selection.
3. A one-line COMMAND area to enter a command or statement.
4. A one-line message area between the COMMAND line and the last line of the menu selection area. It is on this message line that QMF displays any error messages that occur when it executes a query.

The results of a query appear in a Report Screen (Figure 12.7). The data in the Report Screen is formatted using a default format found in the Forms Screen. In Figure 12.7, the column name EMPLID is truncated because the original column was defined as CHAR(5) and only five spaces are allocated for its column heading.

The results in Figure 12.7 conform to the column definitions that were in the CREATE statement for the table. The table's column definitions, there-

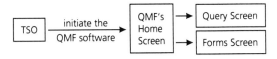

FIGURE 12.5   *Accessing the QMF software system via TSO.*

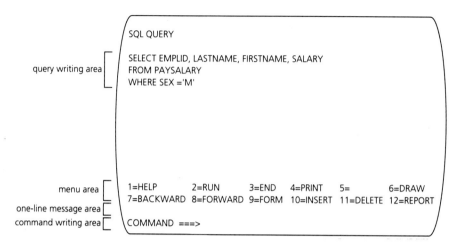

FIGURE 12.6 *A query entered into the Query Screen. After writing a query, you execute it by pressing the PF2 key.*

fore, make up the default format of the data whenever a query executes. In this case, EMPLID, LASTNAME, FIRSTNAME, and SALARY were defined as CHAR(5), VARCHAR(20), VARCHAR(20), and DECIMAL(8,2), respectively.

USING AND SAVING QUERIES AND FORMS

Using Queries, Data, and Forms

QMF uses several buffers to hold the query, the form, and the data (Figure 12.8). When you write a query, QMF stores the query in a query buffer. If you have not presaved a form for the data, QMF uses the query's table description from the DB2 catalog and places that formatting structure in the forms buffer. When you execute a query, the data is extracted from the database and stored in the data buffer. The query, data, and forms buffers can be saved using a version of the SAVE QUERY, SAVE DATA, and SAVE FORM statements, respectively. The query buffer contains the current query. The data buffer contains the data that was extracted from the database after a

EMPLI	LASTNAME	FIRSTNAME	SALARY
12345	DOE	JOHN	$32,000.00
43214	SMITH	ANDY	$28,500.00
43223	MARKUM	MIKE	$30,000.00
45000	HERTS	FRED	$56,000.00
54322	KROSS	WM	$23,000.00
56789	LOMB	LARRY	$35,000.00
60311	JONES	LARRY	$20,000.00

FIGURE 12.7 *The Report Screen containing results of a query. If a presaved form is not used when you execute a query, QMF uses a default form.*

```
┌──────────────┐                          ┌──────────────┐
│ Query Buffer │                          │ Forms Buffer │
└──────────────┘                          └──────────────┘
```

The query goes here.   ┌──────────────┐   *The formatting criteria*
                              │ Data Buffer │   *for the data goes here.*
                              └──────────────┘

The data from the query
goes here.

FIGURE 12.8   *Three buffers to hold the query, the data, and the form.*

query executes. The forms buffer contains either a presaved form or a default form. You run a query in the Query Screen by pressing the PF2 key or by entering RUN QUERY on the Command line.

After you type a query into the Query Screen, you can press the PF2 key to see the results of the query, or move the cursor to the command line and enter the command RUN QUERY. In either case, the results of the query automatically appear in the Report Screen.

When you do not indicate the name of a presaved form on the COMMAND line, QMF places a default form in the forms buffer and uses it to format the data in the Report Screen. To use a presaved form to format the data, place a presaved form in the form buffer. The statement:

RUN QUERY (FORM = PAYROLF1

on the COMMAND line of the Query Screen loads the form PAYROLF1 into the forms buffer and RUNs the query in the query buffer. PAYROLF1 is the name of the presaved form. Alternately, you can enter the statement:

(FORM = PAYROLF1

on the COMMAND line and press the PF2 key. PF2 serves the save function as RUN QUERY. You can omit the right-hand parenthesis when entering the statement. The statement:

RUN QUERY PAYROLQ1

executes a presaved query. QMF:

1. Loads the presaved query PAYROLQ1 into the query buffer
2. Loads its default form into the form's buffer
3. Executes the query by accessing the tables in the query
4. Loads the data generated by the query into the data buffer
5. Displays the results in the Report Screen

Finally, the statement:

RUN QUERY PAYROLQ1 (FORM = PAYROLF1

executes the presaved query PAYROLQ1 and formats its results using the presaved form PAYROLF1. The results appear in the Report Screen.

Remember, when a query executes, QMF uses either the default form or a presaved form to format the data every time a query executes. You need to take care in executing queries. Suppose you spent considerable time in the Forms Screen to format the report. If for some reason you want to modify the query, you must go to the Query Screen to make the necessary change. If you forget to save the form in the Forms Screen before you execute the modified query, QMF destroys the unsaved form and uses a new default form for the modified query.

Starting Over

Suppose you run a query and decide that you want to write another query in the Query Screen. How do you erase the existing query from the Query Screen and its subsequent version in the query buffer? You can start with a fresh screen (and query buffer) by entering the statement:

RESET QUERY

in the COMMAND line and then press RETURN. Similarly, you can erase the form in the form buffer by entering the statement:

RESET FORM

on the COMMAND line and then press RETURN.

Saving a Query, Its Data, and Form

You can save the query in the Query Screen (which is also in the query buffer) by entering the command:

SAVE QUERY AS queryname

where "queryname" is some name assigned to the saved query. You save the form in the form's buffer and the data in the data's buffer by entering:

SAVE FORM AS formname

and

SAVE DATA AS dataname

respectively. Again, "formname" and "dataname" are some names we assign to the form and data, respectively.

Deleting Presaved Queries, Forms, and Data

Once a query, data, or form is saved, QMF keeps a copy of the saved item on some DASD device. You can list these saved items using an option in QMF's

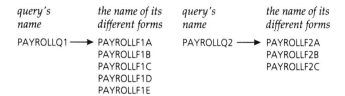

query's name | the name of its different forms | query's name | the name of its different forms

PAYROLLQ1 ⟶ PAYROLLF1A
                    PAYROLLF1B
                    PAYROLLF1C
                    PAYROLLF1D
                    PAYROLLF1E

PAYROLLQ2 ⟶ PAYROLLF2A
                    PAYROLLF2B
                    PAYROLLF2C

FIGURE 12.9 *Sample naming standard for a query with multiple forms. The query PAYROLLQ1 has five different forms for the same query. The query PAYROLLQ2 has three different forms for the query.*

Home Screen. Similarly, you can erase a presaved item by entering the statement:

> ERASE itemname

on the COMMAND line. "Itemname" can be the name of a saved query, data, or form. For example, the statement:

> ERASE DOGGY

deletes the item named DOGGY, whether that item is a saved query, saved data, or a saved form.

Naming Conventions of Saved Items

Obviously, if you are going to perform a large number of queries and create a correspondingly large number of forms for these queries, you have to establish some criteria for naming these items. The convention of assigning a name to the query followed by the letter Q (for query) and a number (for version) could be a solution to the problem. Using this convention, you save a query about the payroll using the name PAYROLLQ1 and save its associated form using the name PAYROLLF1A. Variations of this form then could be saved as PAYROLLF1B, PAYROLLF1C, and so on. Subsequently, you might want to save similar queries about the payroll as PAYROLLQ2, PAYROLLQ3, and their respective forms as PAYROLLF2A, PAYROLLF3A. The names in Figure 12.9 illustrate how to name queries and forms where one query has multiple forms assigned to it.

The name of a saved query, data, or form can be from one to eighteen characters long. The first character of the name must be an alphabetic character, a through z. The remaining characters in the name can be either alphabetic (a through z), numeric (0 through 9), an underscore (_), or the special characters $, @, or #.

Error Messages

When you make an error in writing a query and executing it, an error message appears in the Report Screen, not in the Query Screen. To correct the error, you must return to the Query Screen, correct it, and re-RUN the query. When SQL issues an error, it identifies the error by displaying a negative number followed by a short message. Although the error message might give some hint as to the reason for the error, the error message's number (always a negative integer) can aid in identifying the exact nature of the problem. Refer to one of IBM's many QMF manuals to find the error message's number and its reason for issuance. An easier and sometimes quicker way to solve the problem is to return to the Query Screen and carefully look at the query. The most common errors are typographical errors, followed by misspelled column or table names. If you still cannot identify the error, refer to one of the reference manuals for help.

THE REPORT SCREEN

When you run a query, the results appear in the Report Screen. One way to execute a query is to press the PF2 key in the Query Screen. In fact, QMF makes extensive use of PF keys to make migrating from screen to screen easier. Figure 12.10 lists the main PF keys available to navigate between the numerous QMF screens.

For example, when you execute a query such as the one in Figure 12.6, the results will appear in a Report Screen similar to Figure 12.11. After viewing the results, you can return to the Query Screen (using PF6) and make any needed changes in the query. If an error occurs because an incorrectly written query fails to process, that error message appears in the one-line message line of the Report Screen.

If you did not use a presaved form when executing the query, you can go to the Forms Screen using PF9 (i.e., 9 = FORM) and format the data in the report.

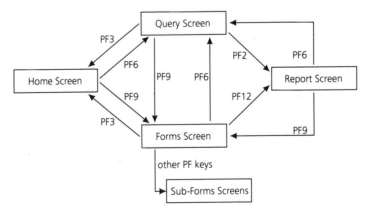

FIGURE 12.10   *Using PF keys to navigate the screens within QMF.*

EMPLI	LASTNAME	FIRSTNAME	SALARY
12345	DOE	JOHN	$32,000.00
43214	SMITH	ANDY	$28,500.00
43223	MARKUM	MIKE	$30,000.00
45000	HERTS	FRED	$56,000.00
54322	KROSS	WM	$23,000.00
56789	LOMB	LARRY	$35,000.00
60311	JONES	LARRY	$20,000.00

```
1=HELP        2=           3=END     4=PRINT    5=         6=QUERY
7=BACKWARD    8=FORWARD    9=FORM    10=LEFT    11=RIGHT   12=
Ok, this is the report from your RUN
COMMAND ===>
```

FIGURE 12.11   *Results of a query in the Report Screen. PF6 returns you to the Query Screen and PF9 returns you to the Forms Screen. In addition, you can write statements on the COMMAND line. Successful queries produce an "Ok, ..." message on the message line of the Report Screen.*

THE FORMS SCREEN

The Main Forms Screen

The Forms Screen is used to format a report. When you first enter the Forms Screen, QMF places either a copy of the default form or a presaved form into the forms buffer. You can modify this information and save it for future use. For example, the default form in Figure 12.12 was generated from the query:

```
SELECT EMPLID, LASTNAME, FIRSTNAME, SALARY
FROM PAYSALARY
WHERE SEX ='M'
```

When you RUN this query without indicating a presaved form, QMF uses the table definition's description of the columns to initially format the data in the Report Screen. You can modify the format of the resultant report by

```
FORM    MAIN COLUMNS:
NUM     COLUMN HEADINGS          USAGE   INDENT   WIDTH   EDIT

 1      EMPLID                             2        5      C
 2      LASTNAME                           2       20      C
 3      FIRSTNAME                          2       20      C
 4      SALARY                             2        8      L2

PAGE:        HEADING ==>
             FOOTING ==>

CONTROL BREAK TEXT:

1=HELP        2=           3=END     4=COLUMNS  5=OPTIONS   6=QUERY
7=BACKWARD    8=FORWARD    9=PAGE    10=FINAL   11=BREAK1   12=REPORT

COMMAND ===>
```

FIGURE 12.12   *Sample default form. This default form uses the table PAYSALARY's column definitions to format the data. It extracts the parameters for this form from the DB2 catalog.*

modifying the information in the Forms Screen. For example, you can change the column headings in Figure 12.11 from:

| EMPLI | LASTNAME | FIRSTNAME | SALARY |

to

| EMPL | LAST | FIRST | YEARLY |
| ID | NAME | NAME | SALARY |

by changing the values under COLUMN HEADINGS in the Forms Screen (Figure 12.12). These changes are given in Figure 12.13.

Displaying Headings on Multiple Rows

The original default form uses the table definition's column names as the headings for the columns in the report. You can change the headings by rewording the values in COLUMN HEADINGS. The underscore (_) in Figure 12.13 indicates the heading is to appear on two lines. Two underscores in a single COLUMN HEADING's value would force the column heading to appear on three lines. The values under NUM in Figures 12.12 and 12.13 refer to the relative position of the column names in the query. So, 1 refers to the first column in the query (EMPLID) and 4 refers to the fourth column in the query (SALARY). To rearrange the order of the columns in the report, rearrange the columns in the query and re-RUN it.

Sometimes a report includes too many spaces between the employee's first and last name. To shorten this space, change the values in the WIDTH column (i.e., WIDTH = 15 for both LASTNAME and FIRSTNAME). In addition, you can add a heading and a footer to the report (Figure 12.14). After making these changes in the Forms Screen, we view their impact on the report by transferring to the Report Screen (Figure 12.15).

Edit and Width Codes

The two columns, USAGE and EDIT, in the Forms Screen provide the capabilities of further editing the data within the report. By using a code in the EDIT column, you can format numeric data by:

- Providing a comma for thousands separation
- Displaying a negative sign when one exists in the column
- Displaying leading zeros
- Displaying "n" decimal places in the number
- Providing a "$" symbol for monetary values
- Inserting a "%" symbol for percent

The options available in the EDIT column are given in Table 12.1. Be careful when using these codes because the selection must be consistent with the other parameters on the screen. That is, when formatting a number using an EDIT code, you must modify the value in WIDTH to allow for this editing. For

NUM	COLUMN HEADINGS	USAGE	INDENT	WIDTH	EDIT
1	EMPL_ID		2	5	C
2	LAST_NAME		2	20	C
3	FIRST_NAME		2	20	C
4	YEARLY_SALARY		2	8	L2

FIGURE 12.13 *Changing the Forms Screen by modifying the column headings in COLUMN HEADINGS.*

NUM	COLUMN HEADINGS	USAGE	INDENT	WIDTH	EDIT
1	EMPL_ID		2	5	C
2	LAST_NAME		2	15	C
3	FIRST_NAME		2	15	C
4	YEARLY_SALARY		2	8	L2

PAGE: HEADING ==> EMPLOYEE SALARY REPORT
             FOOTING ==> CC: ALL MANAGERS

CONTROL BREAK TEXT:

```
1=HELP         2=           3=END      4=COLUMNS  5=OPTIONS   6=QUERY
7=BACKWARD     8=FORWARD    9=PAGE     10=FINAL   11=BREAK1   12=REPORT
COMMAND ===>
```

FIGURE 12.14 *Revised Forms Screen. Changing the values in WIDTH from 20 to 15 shortens the displayed fields LASTNAME and FIRSTNAME from 20 columns to 15 columns. You can view the results of these changes by pressing PF12.*

```
                EMPLOYEE SALARY REPORT

    EMPL    LAST       FIRST    YEARLY
    ID      NAME       NAME     SALARY

    12345   DOE        JOHN     32000.00
    43214   SMITH      ANDY     28500.00
    43223   MARKUM     MIKE     30000.00
    45000   HERTS      FRED     56000.00
    54322   KROSS      WM       23000.00
    56789   LOMB       LARRY    35000.00
    60311   JONES      LARRY    20000.00

              CC: ALL MANAGERS

1=HELP         2=           3=END      4=PRINT    5=          6=QUERY
7=BACKWARD     8=FORWARD    9=FORM     10=LEFT    11=RIGHT    12=
COMMAND ===>
```

FIGURE 12.15 *Report Screen after modifying the Forms Screen. Report contains a one-line header and footer.*

√ **TABLE 12.1**   *Options for numeric data under EDIT in Forms Screen. "Sign/no sign" option indicates that the symbol "−" will/will not display on the report*

Edit Codes	Code Description
Ln	number with no leading zeros, sign, and no commas. Contains "n" digits to right of decimal (i.e., L2 displays number as 9012.34, .34, and −3.45).
Kn	number with no leading zeros, sign, and commas. Contains "n" digits to right of decimal (i.e., K2 displays number as 9,012.34, .34, and −3.45).
Jn	number with leading zeros, no sign, and no commas. Contains "n" digits to right of decimal (i.e., J2 displays number as 9012.34, 000.34, and 003.45).
In	number with leading zeros, sign, and no commas. Contains "n" digits to right of decimal (i.e., I2 displays number as 9012.34, 000.34, and −03.45).
Pn	number with percent sign, sign, commas as needed, and no leading zeros. Contains "n" digits to right of decimal (i.e., P5 displays number as 9,012.34%, .34%, −3.45%).
Dn	number with "$" symbol, sign, commas as needed, and no leading zeros. Contains "n" digits to right of decimal (i.e., D2 displays number as $9,012.34).

example, the values for the 4th column (SALARY) in Figure 12.14 are:

NUM	COLUMN HEADINGS	USAGE	INDENT	WIDTH	EDIT
4	YEARLY_SALARY		2	8	L2

The formatted number in SALARY must fit in the size field indicated by the WIDTH value (i.e., 8). That means, if you change the code under EDIT to D2, the edited number must fit in 8 print positions. In this case, a salary of 32000.00 will look like $32,000.00 on the report. Because this edited number requires 10 print positions, QMF will generate a nonfatal error. That is, any resultant error due to mismatching of EDIT and WIDTH forces QMF to place a series of asterisks in the number field. Instead of displaying the properly edited value, QMF will instead display "**********" in the YEARLY SALARY column of the report. When this occurs, you must return to the Forms Screen and increase the value in WIDTH to accommodate the edited number. In this case, you have to increase the value in WIDTH to 10. The values for the fourth column in the Forms Screen in Figure 12.14 then become

NUM	COLUMN HEADINGS	USAGE	INDENT	WIDTH	EDIT
4	YEARLY_SALARY		2	10	D2

This change produces the report in Figure 12.16.

Usage Codes

Because many reports contain intermediate, major, and minor totals, QMF must have a way to sum the values in selected columns. In addition, many

```
                    EMPLOYEE SALARY REPORT

           EMPL    LAST       FIRST    YEARLY
           ID      NAME       NAME     SALARY

           12345   DOE        JOHN     $32,000.00
           43214   SMITH      ANDY     $28,500.00
           43223   MARKUM     MIKE     $30,000.00
           45000   HERTS      FRED     $56,000.00
           54322   KROSS      WM       $23,000.00
           56789   LOMB       LARRY    $35,000.00
           60311   JONES      LARRY    $20,000.00

                    CC: ALL MANAGERS
```

FIGURE 12.16   *Report using D2 in the EDIT column of the Forms Screen.*

TABLE 12.2   *USAGE codes in the Forms Screen*

Usage Codes	Code's Description
SUM	Find the sum of all the values in the column
AVE	Find the average of all the values in the column
COUNT	Find the count of all the not-null values in the column
MAX	Find the maximum value in the column
MIN	Find the minimum value in the column
BREAKn or BRn	Perform a control break on the column ("n" is a number from 1 to 6)
OMIT	Omit displaying the column
STDEV	Find the standard deviation of the values in the column
GROUP	Group the data in the column

reports contain control breaks, averages for a column, the number of entries in a particular column, and other grouped values. Placing a code in the USAGE column in the Forms Screen further formats the report. Table 12.2 lists some of the codes available in the USAGE column.

You can provide totals for the YEARLY SALARY column in the report in Figure 12.16 by using the code "SUM" in the USAGE column of the Forms Screen. QMF automatically handles the formatting of the totals at the bottom of the report. Here, because option SUM appears in the SALARY column, QMF uses the same format given in EDIT for that column (i.e., D2) and uses as many display positions as it needs to display the number. You do not have to readjust the WIDTH value in SALARY to handle the totals—QMF handles the final SUM's width separately. The Forms Screen to SUM the totals for SALARY is given in Figure 12.17 and produces the report in Figure 12.18.

This Main Forms Screen can access several other subforms, including COLUMNS, OPTIONS, PAGE, FINAL, and BREAK1 (see Figure 12.17).

Other Screens for Formatting the Report

The Main Form Screen has several Subform Screens including:

- Form.Columns   (PF4)

NUM	COLUMN HEADINGS	USAGE	INDENT	WIDTH	EDIT
1	EMPL_ID		2	5	C
2	LAST_NAME		2	15	C
3	FIRST_NAME	OMIT	2	15	C
4	YEARLY_SALARY	SUM	2	10	D2

PAGE: HEADING ==> EMPLOYEE SALARY REPORT
             FOOTING ==> CC: ALL MANAGERS

CONTROL BREAK TEXT:

1=HELP   2=   3=END   4=COLUMNS   5=OPTIONS   6=QUERY
7=BACKWARD   8=FORWARD   9=PAGE   10=FINAL   11=BREAK1   12=REPORT

COMMAND ===>

FIGURE 12.17 *Using the SUM, OMIT, and D2 codes in the Forms Screen. OMIT prohibits the displaying of data in column 3 of the query (FIRSTNAME). The code SUM totals the SALARY column. The code D2 formats the data using the standard currency format. The value 10 in the WIDTH column tells QMF to use 10 print positions for the formatted data in column 4 of the report.*

- Form.Options   (PF5)
- Form.Page   (PF9)
- Form.Final   (PF10)
- Form.Break1   (PF11)

Each of these screens provide a set of options to further improve the report. Although the Main Form Screen provides a quick and easy way of formatting the data, you might need to use one or more of these subscreens to finalize the format of the report. The only subscreen we will discuss is the PAGE Subscreen.

The Page Subscreen

One of the main disadvantages of the Main Forms Screen is its inability to allow for multiple headings at the top of the report. Most corporate reports require three or four lines and these lines indicate the report's name, the current date, and the page number of the report. The Page Screen is used to

EMPLOYEE SALARY REPORT

EMPL ID	LAST NAME	YEARLY SALARY
12345	DOE	$32,000.00
43214	SMITH	$28,500.00
43223	MARKUM	$30,000.00
45000	HERTS	$56,000.00
54322	KROSS	$23,000.00
56789	LOMB	$35,000.00
60311	JONES	$20,000.00
		$224,500.00

CC: ALL MANAGERS

FIGURE 12.18 *A report using USAGE and EDIT options.*

place multiple headings and footers, page numbers, and the current date on the report. Figure 12.19 gives a sample heading layout for a typical payroll report.

The Page subscreen provides room for five lines for headings and five lines for a footing. In addition, you can use the keywords CENTER, RIGHT, or LEFT to center, right justify, or left justify the text, respectively. To place the text at a particular column location, you could place the column location in ALIGN. The text area of the screen holds the verbiage for the heading and the codes &PAGE, &TIME, and &DATE to force QMF to print the page number, the current time, and the current date.

After writing the headings and footer for the report, you can view the finished report in the Report Screen (Figure 12.20). When you enter the Report Screen, QMF places the Page Subscreen into the forms buffer. Now when you press the PF9 key in the Report Screen to return to the Forms Screen, QMF displays the Page Subscreen. If you want the Main Forms Screen, you have to select the appropriate PF key in the Page Subscreen.

QMF has only limited options for headings. If you want more than 5 lines for a heading or are dissatisfied with the layout structure for the forms, you must resort to programming to remedy the problem. Unless the structure of the report is vital to the company, QMF can handle the bulk of the simple reports most end users need and want. QMF is not designed to access multiple-database types. It cannot, for instance, access IMS databases. Nor can it print payroll checks. Although QMF is a powerful tool for the end user, specialized report generation still must come from the programming staff.

```
FORM.PAGE

Blank Lines Before Heading   2

LINE      ALIGN        TEXT
────      ─────        ─────────────────────────────────────────────
 1        LEFT         &DATE
 2        CENTER       TONY'S GOLD MINE COMPANY
 3        CENTER       PAYROLL REGISTER
 4        CENTER       DECEMBER PAYROLL
 5        CENTER

Blank Lines Before Footer   2

LINE      ALIGN        TEXT
────      ─────        ─────────────────────────────────────────────
 1        LEFT         COPIES TO:      MIKE
 2        LEFT                         WANDA
 3        LEFT                         TONY
 4        LEFT
 5        18           &PAGE

1=HELP         2=          3=END       4=COLUMNS    5=OPTIONS    6=QUERY
7=BACKWARD     8=FORWARD   9=MAIN      10=FINAL     11=BREAK1    12=REPORT

COMMAND  ===>
```

FIGURE 12.19 *The Page Subscreen for forms.*

```
12/23/98
              TONY'S GOLD MINE COMPANY
              PAYROLL REGISTER
              DECEMBER PAYROLL

EMPL      LAST        YEARLY
ID        NAME        SALARY

12345     DOE         $32,000.00
43214     SMITH       $28,500.00
43223     MARKUM      $30,000.00
45000     HERTS       $56,000.00
54322     KROSS       $23,000.00
56789     LOMB        $35,000.00
60311     JONES       $20,000.00
                      --------------
                      $224,500.00

COPIES TO:  MIKE
            WANDA
            TONY

            1
1=HELP          2=              3=END     4=PRINT    5=         6=QUERY
7=BACKWARD      8=FORWARD       9=FORM    10=LEFT    11=RIGHT   12=

COMMAND ===>
```

FIGURE 12.20 *Report with multiple headings, date, and page number in the Report Screen.*

```
                        CUSTOMER ORDER REPORT

ITEM       ITEM      CUSTOMER    AMOUNT     WHOLESALE    SHIPPING
NUMBER     NAME      NAME        ORDERED    PRICE        COST

12345      SHOVELS   KMART       100        4.50         34.55
12345      SHOVELS   WALMART     225        4.50         44.90
12345      SHOVELS   SEARS       400        4.50         66.70

           TOTAL FOR 12345       725                     146.15

23450      HOES      KMART       100        3.20         34.55
23450      HOES      WALGREENS    15        3.50         23.20
23450      HOES      SEARS       300        3.20         66.70

           TOTAL FOR 23450       415                     124.45

                                 1240                    270.60
```

FIGURE 12.21 *Shipping report containing a control break on ITEMNUMB.*

```
ITEM       ITEM      CUSTOMER    AMOUNT     WHOLESALE    SHIPPING
NUMBER     NAME      NAME        ORDERED    PRICE        COST

12345      SHOVELS   KMART       100        4.50         34.55
12345      SHOVELS   WALMART     225        4.50         44.90
12345      SHOVELS   SEARS       400        4.50         66.70
23450      HOES      KMART       100        3.20         34.55
23450      HOES      WALGREENS    15        3.50         23.20
23450      HOES      SEARS       300        3.20         66.70
```

FIGURE 12.22 *Shipping report without a control break.*

Performing Control Breaks

A control break is a predefined splitting of the data into sections based on a change in value in some key field. The report in Figure 12.21 contains a control break based on ITEMNUMB. The data is split into a section each time the value in ITEMNUMB changes (i.e., from 12345 to 23450). Obviously, for a control break to work effectively, the data must be in sorted order.

The query to extract data for the report in Figure 12.22 is:

```
SELECT ITEMNUMB, ITEMNAME, CUSTNAME, ORDERAMT, WHOLEPRICE,
       SHIPCOST
FROM INVENTORY,CUSTOMER
WHERE CUSTOMER.ORDERNUMBER = INVENTORY.ITEMNUMB
ORDER BY ITEMNUMB
```

The report has neither totals nor control breaks. To format this data, you need to select the Forms Screen and make modifications to the default form. To create totals and a control break on ITEMNUMB, place the codes BREAK1 and SUM in the USAGE column as indicated in Figure 12.23.

To save the modifications to the Forms Screen, enter the statement:

```
SAVE FORM AS ORDERF1
```

on the COMMAND line and press RETURN. The saved form ORDERF1 contains the Forms Screen and all its subscreens. This saved form can be used later when executing a query. That is, the statement:

```
RUN QUERY (FORM = ORDERF1
```

executes the query in the query screen and formats the resultant data using the codes in the ORDERF1 presaved form.

NUM	COLUMN HEADINGS	USAGE	INDENT	WIDTH	EDIT
1	ITEM_NUMBER	BREAK1	2	5	C
2	ITEM_NAME		2	15	C
3	CUSTOMER_NAME		2	15	C
4	AMOUNT_ORDERED	SUM	2	10	L2
5	WHOLESALE_PRICE		2	10	L2
6	SHIPPING_COST	SUM	2	10	L2

```
PAGE:      HEADING ==> CUSTOMER ORDER REPORT
           FOOTING ==>

CONTROL BREAK TEXT: TOTAL FOR &1

1=HELP        2=          3=END        4=COLUMNS    5=OPTIONS    6=QUERY
7=BACKWARD    8=FORWARD   9=PAGE       10=FINAL     11=BREAK1    12=REPORT

COMMAND ===>
```

FIGURE 12.23   *Forms Screen using control break options. The text for each control break is defined on the "CONTROL BREAK TEXT" line. The '&1" is a wild-card that tells QMF to print the value found in column 1 (ITEMNUMB) at each control break.*

PROCEDURES

QMF's Home Screen contains options to enter the Forms Screen and the Query Screen. In addition, QMF's Home Screen has an option to enter the PROCs Screen. You write a PROC by selecting the PROC option in QMF's Home Screen. In this screen, you list the series of steps (or procedures) that QMF is to perform. For example, to execute the queries SALARYQ1 and ORDERQ1 using the presaved forms SALARYF3 and ORDERF1, respectively, and print the resultant reports on the system's printer, enter the statements:

```
RUN SALARYQ1 (FORM = SALARYF3
PRINT REPORT
RUN ORDERQ1 (FORM = ORDERF1
PRINT REPORT
```

into the PROC Screen. You save a procedure using the statement:

```
SAVE PROC AS PROC123
```

You execute the PROC using the statement:

```
RUN PROC123
```

in the COMMAND line.

Using the PROC Screen, the programming staff can create multiple PROCs for the end-user department and save them in the department's account. Whenever someone in that department wishes to generate a series of reports, he or she can run the appropriate PROC.

All printing via QMF screens occurs at some printer defined by SYSADM. If end-user departments want their printing to occur at a local printer within that department, some member of the systems team must write the necessary systems commands (JCL) to direct the printing to the nonsystem printer. The manager of the user department must make a request through normal corporate channels for computer services. If, on the other hand, the user department does not have a local printer, the department's manager must requisition a printer via normal corporate procedures. In this case, the department manager would first contact his or her computer center liaison and work closely with that liaison in its purchase and installation. Remember, adding hardware to a system often involves buying additional hardware in the form of controllers, modems, and lines.

SUMMARY

DB2 has a variety of supporting products including DB2I, QMF, DXT, and DBEDIT. DB2I, DXT, and DBEDIT typically are used by the programming staff, while QMF typically is used by end users. DB2I allows programmers to work with DB2 interactively (see Chapter 9). DBEDIT is a facility that creates screens for the updating, deleting, inserting, and selecting of data in DB2 databases. DXT converts non-DB2 files and databases into sequential data sets. These sequential data sets later can be loaded into DB2 via the LOAD utility. QMF is a report generator that accesses DB2 and creates reports based on a written query and a formatted form.

QMF has the two primary screens (Query and Forms) and one secondary screen (PROC). The Query Screen contains the query, and the Forms Screen contains codes for the formatting of the data extracted by the query. The PROC Screen contains a list of instructions that can be executed later.

QMF runs under ISPF either under TSO or VM. The test version of QMF accesses a testing database, and the production version of QMF accesses a production database. Authorized users enter QMF via a series of screens defined by SYSADM.

After RUNning a query in the Query Screen, the results display in the Report Screen. Users access QMF's screens by either entering a statement on the COMMAND line (i.e., SAVE, RESET, RUN, ERASE) or by pressing a specific PF key.

The SAVE QUERY AS QUERYNAME statement, when entered on the COMMAND line, saves the query currently in the Query Screen under the name QUERYNAME. Similarly, the statement SAVE FORM AS FORMNAME saves the form currently in the Forms Screen under the name FORMNAME.

The statement RUN QUERYNAME executes the presaved query QUERYNAME. The statement RUN QUERY (FORM = FORMNAME) executes the query in the Query Screen and formats the extracted data using the form FORMNAME. The statement RUN QUERYNAME (FORM = FORMNAME) executes the presaved query QUERYNAME and formats the extracted data using codes in the presaved form FORMNAME.

The statement ERASE WHATNAME deletes the presaved query or form called WHATNAME. The statement RESET QUERY erases the current query from the Query Screen, while the statement RESET FORM erases the current form in the Forms Screen.

When executing a query without indicating a presaved form, QMF uses the column's DB2 Catalog Definition to format the results of the query. Users can enter codes in the Forms Screen to override these preestablished default values. These codes appear as options in the COLUMN HEADINGS, USAGE, WIDTH, and EDIT columns of the Forms Screen, and in the many subscreens of the Form Screen.

Valid codes for USAGE include SUM, AVE, COUNT, MAX, MIN, BREAKn, OMIT, STDEV, and GROUP. Many of these codes are similar to the summary functions for SELECT (see Chapter 9). Valid codes for EDIT include L, K, J, I, P, and D. These codes indicate if numeric data is to have leading zeros, a sign, commas, and other editing features.

The Forms Screen contains multiple subscreens. One of these subscreens, the Page Subscreen, has a facility to include up to five lines each for a footer and a header. This screen has options for placing the date and page number onto a report.

QUESTIONS

1. What is the difference between using a GROUP BY in a SELECT statement and using the GROUP code in the USAGE column in the Forms Screen?
2. Do all users need authorization to use QMF?
3. Can SYSADM restrict the use of QMF to only the programming staff? What are some advantages and disadvantages for this restriction?
4. What are some considerations a department manager must include in his or her decision to purchase a local printer for the printing of QMF reports?
5. If a user wants the order of the columns in a report changed, do the presaved forms for that report also need to be changed?
6. Can QMF access non-DB2 databases?
7. Suppose a user has a non-DB2 database. Is it possible for that user to use QMF to generate reports? If so, what steps must the development team take for the data to be accessible to QMF?
8. List two types of reports that QMF cannot produce.
9. Suppose a member of a user department is incapable of writing SQL queries, but still wants to use QMF. What remedies does he or she have?
10. Should members of end-user departments and members of the programming staff both be trained in the same class?
11. Who should be responsible for the training in QMF?
12. A user department of 220 employees will be using a newly designed DB2 database application. Each of the employees in the department will be responsible for accessing data on the database using QMF. The two-member EUSC staff has been assigned the task of training these end users in QMF. Estimate the time and total cost associated with the training of these end users if each class takes three full days. What resources are needed for the EUSC to perform this task? What is the cost associated with this training?
13. For problem 12, assume management wants the end users trained in a one-month time period. What additional resources would the EUSC need?
14. For the above EUSC, what procedures must the EUSC staff establish to ensure each end user was properly trained? What additional training (and at what cost) must the EUSC perform to continue the training and provide support to this user department?
15. Suppose the user department in problem 12 finds that several employees have extreme difficulty in grasping the concepts of QMF. What is the next step the manager of that user department should take?
16. Management determines that certain controls are needed on the data entry department's production rate. It assigns a programmer to write a program to monitor the keystrokes of each data entry operator and tabulate the number of errors each data entry clerk makes in a period of a day. The programmer determines that the ultimate purpose of this program is to fire nonproductive data entry clerks who do not meet certain production rates. Discuss the ethics of a programmer accepting such an assignment.
17. An employee on an assembly line posts for a position in data entry and receives that position. The employee is trained for two weeks and works at the position for one month. At the end of the month, management determines that the employee's production rate is unacceptable and fires him or her, as per company policy. Discuss the ethics of this action.

CASE STUDY

Hopkins Enterprises owns a group of department stores, each with an identical floor plan and store merchandise location. Each department store is divided into ten sales departments. All sales are electronically recorded as they are entered into a point-of-sale terminal. The resultant data is loaded into a DB2 database via in-house written code. The data that is captured includes the retail cost of the item and the item's ID number found on a bar code on each item. This data is merged with another file that contains the item's name, its wholesale cost, the manufacturer or supplier of the item, the date it was placed in inventory, and the department that stocks the item in each store.

The company wants a series of reports that indicates the profit for each item, the profit for each department, and the number of items in inventory and its total cost.

Questions

1. Using only the above information, design a series of reports to submit to management for their consideration.
2. Because management's time is extremely valuable and because they do not want to personally generate QMF reports, who should be responsible for creating these reports?
3. For the reports proposed in question 1, write the SELECT statements to create the data for them.

MINILAB

The ABC Shopping Emporium stocks merchandise for mail order and telemarketing only. Customers either write in or call to order merchandise. If the customer has preapproved credit or has a commercial account with Purchase Order approval, the merchandise is shipped immediately. All other customers must wait for the Credit Department to approve the order. For credit card orders, the approval generally takes about a minute. The following five tables compose the customer database for the company:

CUSTOMER table

NUMB	NAME	CREDIT RATING	TOTAL SALES	CREDIT LIMIT
12345	KMART	P	123456	100000
23456	SEARS	P	34567	100000
34567	WALMART	P	434343	100000
65656	KRAMERS	C	5600	4000
78787	PHILS	A	0000	1000

ORDER table

ORDER NUMBER	PO NUMBER	DATE RECEIVED	PREFERRED SHIPPING CODE
A2322Z	WE3212DE	901211	TRUCK
A2323Z	EDFR454ED	901211	UPS
A2324Z	23445D	901211	AIR

ORDER-CUSTOMER association table

ORDER NUMBER	CUSTOMER NUMBER
A2322Z	12345
A2354Z	12345
A2323Z	78787
A2324Z	43434

ORDER-ITEM association table

ORDER NUMBER	ITEM NUMBER	QTY ORDERED	DATE SHIPPED	ACTUAL SHIPPING METHOD
A2322Z	3456	45	901213	LAND
A2322Z	4343	10	901213	LAND
A2322Z	4545	100	901213	LAND
A2323Z	0100	200	901212	LAND
A2323Z	0101	200	901212	LAND

ITEM table

ITEM NUMBER	ITEM NAME	UNIT COST
3456	HOE	10.00
4343	SHOVEL	12.34
4545	RAKE	9.90
0100	HAMMER	5.90
0101	AX	6.70

For the CUSTOMER table, the credit rating "A" represents approved credit (for billing and/or checks), "P" represents authorized for Purchase Orders, and "C" represents cash only customers. For the ORDER and the ORDER-ITEM tables, the shipping codes are AIR, UPS, MAIL, TRUCK, and RAIL.

Questions

Log onto QMF and do the following:

1. Write the DDL to create each of these tables. Which columns need indexes? Which need unique indexes? Create the appropriate indexes on each column.
2. Write the INSERT statements to create the data for each of the five tables. If QMF with the data update version is available on your system, use QMF to load the data into the tables.
3. Write the DDL statement to create a view so that a data entry clerk can list all the items a customer orders.
4. Write the DDL statement to create a view so that a data entry clerk can list the customer's number and name, and the items the customer ordered.
5. Write the DML statement to list the customer name, the order numbers, and PO numbers for that customer. Use QMF and create a report containing this information.

6. Write the DML statement to list all the items in inventory and the customers that ordered those items. Use QMF and create a report containing this information. Include proper headings with data and page numbers for each page.

7. Write the DML statement to list all the orders and the items for each order. Include in this listing the total cost of each order. Use QMF and create a report containing this information. Include a control break for each order.

8. Design referential integrity guidelines for the five tables in the database. Implement the guidelines.

13 *SQL and the Programmer*

I n prior chapters, we discussed how to use SQL either in DB2I or QMF. Systems developers (the programmers) use DB2I to test SQL queries and to manage the database. On the other hand, the nontechnical staff writes queries and generates reports using QMF. Because many end users need specialized reports that QMF is incapable of producing, the system developers must write computer programs to generate them. In addition, these developers will need to embed SQL statements in programs to bypass the cumbersome DB2I screens. This is particularly evident in the daily data processing needs of a large company or corporation. Most on-line systems require fast and efficient programs to insert, delete, and update records in the many databases on the system. These programs will require embedded SQL statements to access the relational databases.

In this chapter, we will discuss the procedures systems developers must follow to embed SQL statements in COBOL code. In addition, we will discuss the logic and syntax these developers must use to access the relational database DB2 using COBOL. Although FORTRAN, PL/I, assembler, and other languages also support embedded SQL, in this chapter we will discuss using only COBOL because it is the principal language of most large companies.

COBOL AND EMBEDDED SQL

Program Preparation

Obviously, programmers cannot place the SQL statement:

```
SELECT LASTNAME, FIRSTNAME
FROM CUSTOMER
```

directly into a COBOL program because the COBOL compiler will flag it as a non-COBOL entity and generates a fatal error. Even if the COBOL compiler accepted this statement, database security would surely be compromised if the system let just anyone access data in a database via COBOL code. The system needs two different procedures to handle embedded SQL.

The first procedure must convert all embedded SQL statements to valid COBOL commands acceptable to the COBOL compiler. This procedure is called a **precompile.** During a precompile, the system scans the COBOL program line by line looking for SQL keywords and phrases. Once an SQL keyword or phrase is located, the precompiler must convert it to its COBOL-language equivalent or to a CALL to some external system modules.

The second procedure to handle embedded SQL must perform database housekeeping chores, such as verifying the authorizations for each of the embedded SQL statements, validating the existence of the database entities, and constructing the navigation of the database. This second procedure is called a **bind.** The binding process creates a **plan,** which contains all the logic the system needs to navigate the database and an authorization list for each of the SQL statements in the code. Figure 13.1 illustrates the steps a systems developer must follow when he or she uses embedded SQL statements.

The Precompiler

The primary function of the precompiler is to identify all SQL statements in the code and convert them to something the COBOL compiler can translate into machine code. The precompiler's secondary function is to flag all the SQL statements for later input into the binding process. During the precompile, the precompiler creates the source code with translated SQL statements, and it creates a Database Request Module (DBRM) that the binder uses as an input file for the BIND (Figure 13.2). The DBRM is a sequential file containing a list of all the SQL statements found in the code.

To precompile SQL-embedded COBOL, the programmer accesses DB2I and selects the PRECOMPILE option. It is in this option that the programmer must identify the library containing the source code (the library will contain the massaged source code) and the library that will contain the resultant DBRM. Because you are using libraries outside of DB2's software product, DB2 does

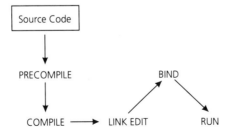

FIGURE 13.1 *Steps for processing code containing embedded SQL statements.*

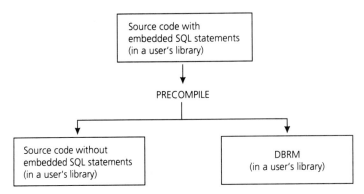

FIGURE 13.2   *Steps in a precompile.*

not have to be on line or active to precompile, compile, and link edit. However, because the BIND accesses the DB2 catalog, DB2 must be on line when you perform the BIND on the DBRM.

Delimiters for Embedded SQL

Before embedding SQL statements into a COBOL program, first enter the DB2I screen and verify that the statement works in DB2. After you are satisfied the SQL statement produces the desired results, the statement then can be inserted into COBOL. So that the precompiler can identify each SQL statement, you need to place a delimiter before and after each embedded SQL statement. For COBOL programs the delimiters EXEC SQL and END-EXEC appear before and after each SQL statement, respectively. The statement:

```
DELETE FROM CUSTOMER
```

becomes the embedded statement:

```
EXEC SQL
DELETE FROM CUSTOMER
END-EXEC.
```

The precompiler locates each delimiter, converts the SQL statement to equivalent COBOL code, transforms the original embedded statement to a COBOL comment, and uses the statement to create an entry in the program's DBRM. There must be a delimiter before and after each and every SQL statement in the program. That is, consecutive SQL statements require delimiters around each SQL statement. For example, the two statements:

```
DELETE FROM CUSTOMER;
DELETE FROM DEPARTMENT;
```

become the embedded statements:

```
EXEC SQL
DELETE FROM CUSTOMER
END-EXEC.
EXEC SQL
DELETE FROM DEPARTMENT
END-EXEC.
```

in a COBOL program.

When the precompiler locates each embedded SQL statement, it does not validate the existence of the database entities (i.e., table name, column names, and so on). The precompiler only translates the SQL statement and converts it to COBOL—it does not access the DB2 catalog to verify the existence of the columns, names, views, or other database items. The statement:

```
EXEC SQL
DELETE FROM DEPURTMENT
END-EXEC.
```

is a valid statement to the precompiler even though DEPURTMENT might not exist in the database.

THE BIND AND PLAN

Before BINDing a program's DBRM, you have to be either a SYSADM or have been given BIND authority from a SYSADM. Once authorized to perform a BIND, you enter the DB2I menu and select the BIND option. Remember, the DBRM resides in a user library and is one of the products of the precompile.

The BINDer reads each record in the DBRM and does the following:

1. Checks the DB2 catalog to verify the existence of the database entities given in the SQL statement
2. Validates the authorization for each statement
3. Constructs the navigation of the database based on the SQL statement and the physical characteristics of the database
4. Establishes the locking strategy (tablespace or page lock)
5. Compares the DB2 catalog description of the variables in the SQL statements with their PIC clauses in COBOL (i.e., a column name defined as CHAR(5) must be defined as PIC X(5))

If an error exists at BIND time, you must correct it and redo the BIND. After all errors are resolved and a successful BIND occurs, the system produces a **valid plan** and a **Processed DBRM.** The valid plan contains all the instructions the system needs to access the database for each of the embedded SQL statements. When you run the program's load module, the system will access the plan whenever a database activity occurs in the load module.

The Processed DBRM is a copy of the DBRM that created the plan. Both

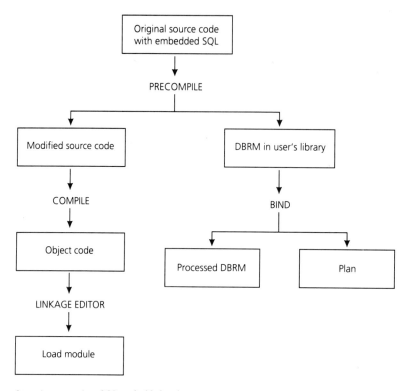

FIGURE 13.3   *Steps in processing SQL embedded code.*

the plan and the Processed DBRM reside in the DB2 catalog and are protected and managed by the DB2 software. The original DBRM is in a user library and therefore is protected only by the operating system—not by DB2 (see Figure 13.3).

DB2I contains the three BIND options: BIND ADD, BIND REPLACE, and RE-BIND. BIND ADD is used to initially name a plan and place it into the DB2 catalog. Later, when you make changes to the COBOL program and need to redo the BIND, you use the BIND REPLACE option because the plan's name already exists in the DB2 catalog. Here, you must again precompile, compile, and link edit before you select the BIND REPLACE option in DB2I (see Figures 13.4A, 13.4B, and 13.4C).

If someone destroys an entity in the DB2 catalog that was referenced by one or more plans, DB2 invalidates all the plans that referenced the destroyed entity. For example, if someone drops an index, table, or view, then all plans referencing that index, table, or view are set as **invalid.** For invalid plans, you need to resupply the missing resource and REBIND the Processed DBRM. When a load module accesses an invalid plan, the system will perform a REBIND immediately, that is, during run time. If during this REBIND the system fails to produce a valid plan, the program ABENDs.

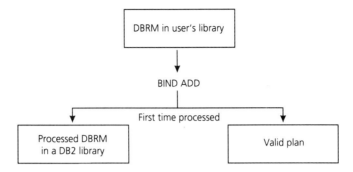

FIGURE 13.4A   *Using BIND ADD to initially process a DBRM.*

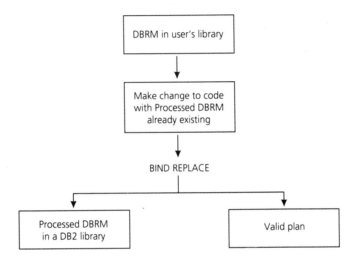

FIGURE 13.4B   *Using BIND REPLACE with an already existing processed DBRM.*

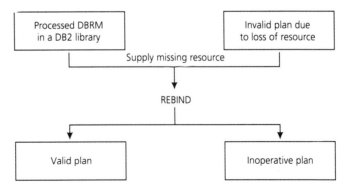

FIGURE 13.4C   *Using REBIND on the Processed DBRM in a DB2 library to create a valid plan. Some user DROPped a resource and, consequently, DB2 invalidated all the plans based on that resource. A REBIND produces either a valid plan or an inoperative one.*

When the system attempts to REBIND the Processed DBRM and still fails to generate a valid plan, the plan is said to be **inoperative.** In the case of a dropped index, when you REBIND the plan without reCREATEing a new index, the system will create a valid plan with a different locking procedure (e.g., a tablespace lock) and database navigation strategy. In the case of a dropped table or view, you must resupply the missing resource before the system will produce another valid plan.

Before dropping a database entity, query the DB2 Catalog and identify all plans that use that entity. Then create a PROC to drop the entity and REBIND all plans that used the entity. Remember, the binding and rebinding process can consume significant systems resources in addition to being time consuming. This PROC can be executed during second or third shift operations when end users typically are not using the system. Because a load module only calls on the plan when it has to process a database activity, you do not want the system to perform a REBIND during run time. Binding during run time not only consumes valuable time and resources during peak computer-usage time, but there also exists a chance that the program will ABEND during run time. Remember, end users get upset when their program either appears to stop for no apparent reason, such as during a run-time rebind, or when their on-line program ABENDs, such as when the system cannot find the resource during the rebind.

The option FREE in the DB2I menu screen deletes the plan and Processed DBRM. In this case, DB2 drops both the plan and Processed DBRM from its catalog. The original DBRM in the user's library, however, still is available because that library is beyond the control of DB2.

AUTHORIZATIONS

SYSADM is the only person automatically authorized to perform a BIND. He or she must GRANT individual users the authorization to BIND on a plan. The statement:

```
GRANT BIND ON PLAN PAYBND1
TO $WANDA
```

gives $WANDA the authority to BIND ADD, BIND REPLACE, REBIND, and FREE only on plan PAYBND1. However, the statement:

```
GRANT BIND, BINDADD, EXECUTE
TO PUBLIC
```

gives all users the authority to perform the above four functions on any plan.

Whoever BINDs must have the authorization to perform all the SQL statements in the code that is bound. That is, if $WANDA is to BIND code containing the SQL statements:

```
DROP INDEX . . .
CREATE TABLE . . .
SELECT . . .
```

she would need SELECT, CREATETAB, DROP, and BIND authorizations. The person who BINDs also owns and has automatic EXECUTE authority on the code.

Time Stamps

When the precompiler creates the DBRM and places the modified source code in a user's library, it puts a time stamp on both modules. At each subsequent stage of processing the embedded code, the system maintains the original time stamp on each product it creates (see Figure 13.5). When the load module accesses its corresponding plan during run time, DB2 compares the time stamp of the load module with the time stamp on the plan. If there is a mismatch, DB2 will perform an on-line REBIND. This procedure guarantees that the COBOL code that created the load module is the same code that generated the plan.

You are faced with two problems. First, suppose you precompile on one CPU and BIND on another CPU. The time stamps will be different because the CPU's clocks are not exactly synchronized. Second, suppose you make a mod-

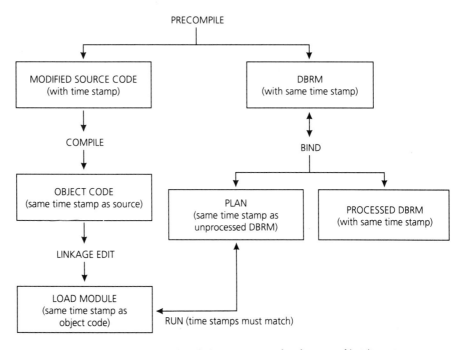

FIGURE 13.5   *Using time stamps. System copies original time stamp to each subsequent object it creates.*

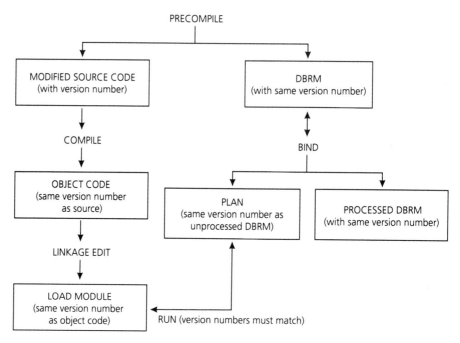

FIGURE 13.6 *Using version numbers instead of time stamps. The system copies the version number of the module to each subsequent object it creates.*

ification to the original code without changing any of the SQL statements in it. Suppose you simply want to move a heading on a report over one space. Do you really need to perform another BIND because the DBRM is still the same? If you select the time stamp option in both of these cases, you must perform a BIND REPLACE to make the time stamps of the load module and the plan compatible. You can alleviate this problem, however, by abandoning time stamps and using version numbers instead. Now, when you create the load module, you assign it the same version number as the plan. Because the version number on the plan matches the version number on the load module, the program works without doing another BIND (see Figure 13.6). The option to use a time stamp or version number is one of the options available in the BIND screen.

EMBEDDED SQL

Now that you know how to process embedded SQL statements in COBOL, we need to discuss the syntax and logistics of placing SQL in COBOL code. Only two areas in COBOL have any significance relative to embedded SQL; the WORKING-STORAGE SECTION and the PROCEDURE DIVISION.

Working-Storage Considerations

Most programs containing embedded SQL statements will have one or more of the following items defined in WORKING-STORAGE:

- SQLCA area
- DECLARE or DCLGEN entry
- definition of the host variables

The SQL Communications Area (SQLCA) So that database programmers can determine the status of a database activity, DB2 sets certain status codes in predefined variables in the SQL Communications Area (SQLCA). One of these variables is SQLCODE that either can be positive, negative, or zero. If a database activity was unsuccessful, SQLCODE is set to a negative number. If the activity was successful, SQLCODE is set to either zero or a positive number. You determine the exact error condition by comparing the value in SQLCODE with the list of possible error codes found in IBM's "Messages and Codes" manual.

Other variables in the SQLCA provide additional information about the activity performed on the database. For example, the variable SQLERRD(3) contains a value representing the number of rows updated, inserted, or deleted by DB2 after an UPDATE, INSERT, or DELETE, respectively.

All the SQLCA variables are loaded into a COBOL program by placing the statement:

```
EXEC SQL
      INCLUDE SQLCA
END-EXEC.
```

in WORKING-STORAGE. Every program must have an INCLUDE SQLCA statement so that DB2 can communicate with the program. Failure to place it in the COBOL program results in a fatal error at precompile time.

The DCLGEN

When you precompile a COBOL program, the precompiler does not check the DB2 catalog to verify the existence and structure of the database entities as they appear in the embedded code. Only at BIND time does the system access the DB2 catalog and resolve any inconsistencies between the SQL variables in the code and the actual structure of the data in the database. Because the BINDer is not a compiler, a single error at BIND time terminates the BIND. For example, the seemingly valid SQL statement:

```
EXEC SQL
      DELETE FROM DEPURTMENT
END-EXEC.
```

will not be flagged as an erroneous SQL statement by the precompiler. If

DEPURTMENT is not a valid table, view, or synonym in the DB2 catalog, however, it will be flagged as an error by the BIND.

Errors at BIND time might necessitate the need to correct the error in the code and re-precompile, re-compile, re-link edit, and re-BIND ADD or re-BIND REPLACE. Obviously, it would be simpler to check the variables in the COBOL program with the structure of the database (as it is defined in the DB2 catalog) at precompile time, not at BIND time. To do this, however, you need a snapshot of the structure of the database entities as they appear in the DB2 catalog. We do this by performing a **DCLGEN**.

The DCLGEN is an option in the DB2I menu. Typically, only SYSADM or an authorized DBADM performs a DCLGEN on a database table. When SYSADM performs a DCLGEN, DB2 accesses its catalog for the indicated table and translates that table's database description into a COBOL description. The results are placed in an Include Library (Figure 13.7). You load the table description produced by the DCLGEN into code by placing the statement:

```
EXEC SQL
      INCLUDE dclgenname
END-EXEC.
```

in WORKING-STORAGE. In this example, "dclgenname" is some name given to the results of a DCLGEN on a particular table.

During a DCLGEN, DB2 uses the criteria in Table 13.1 to convert the table's DB2 catalog description into COBOL PICTURE clauses. Typically, SYSADM will DCLGEN the more frequently accessed tables.

The programming staff then places in WORKING-STORAGE an INCLUDE statement for each table the code accesses. For example, the statements:

```
WORKING-STORAGE SECTION.
      EXEC SQL    INCLUDE SQLCA       END-EXEC.
      EXEC SQL    INCLUDE TABLEONE    END-EXEC.
      EXEC SQL    INCLUDE TABLETWO    END-EXEC.
```

load the SQLCA area and the COBOL description for tables TABLEONE and TABLETWO into WORKING-STORAGE.

The DECLARE Statement

Rather than DCLGEN a table to produce its COBOL description, you can define the description using the DECLARE statement. For example, suppose the table PAYROLL was created using the following DDL statement:

```
CREATE TABLE PAYROLL
      (EMPLOYEEID    CHAR(5)         NOT NULL,
      LASTNAME       VARCHAR(20) NOT NULL,
      FIRSTNAME      VARCHAR(20) NOT NULL,
      HOURSWORKED    DECIMAL(4,1)         ,
      RATEOFPAY      DECIMAL(5,2)         ,
```

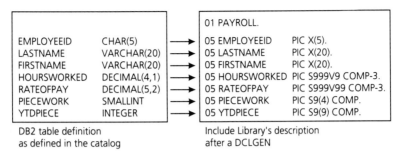

01 PAYROLL.	
EMPLOYEEID CHAR(5)	05 EMPLOYEEID PIC X(5).
LASTNAME VARCHAR(20)	05 LASTNAME PIC X(20).
FIRSTNAME VARCHAR(20)	05 FIRSTNAME PIC X(20).
HOURSWORKED DECIMAL(4,1)	05 HOURSWORKED PIC S999V9 COMP-3.
RATEOFPAY DECIMAL(5,2)	05 RATEOFPAY PIC S999V99 COMP-3.
PIECEWORK SMALLINT	05 PIECEWORK PIC S9(4) COMP.
YTDPIECE INTEGER	05 YTDPIECE PIC S9(9) COMP.

DB2 table definition
as defined in the catalog

Include Library's description
after a DCLGEN

FIGURE 13.7 *The results of a DCLGEN on the table PAYROLL as it appears in the Include Library.*

```
        PIECEWORK      SMALLINT             ,
        YTDPIECE       INTEGER              )
    IN PRODBASE.MONEYTS1
```

You can define this table in WORKING-STORAGE using the following DE-CLARE statement:

```
EXEC SQL
    DECLARE PAYROLL TABLE
        (EMPLOYEEID     CHAR(5),
        LASTNAME       VARCHAR(20),
        FIRSTNAME      VARCHAR(20),
        HOURSWORKED    DECIMAL(4,1),
        RATEOFPAY      DECIMAL(5,2),
        PIECEWORK      SMALLINT,
        YTDPIECE       INTEGER)
END-EXEC.
```

When the precompiler checks a program containing a DECLARE statement, it checks the column names, the table names, and the column's data types of the embedded SQL statement against those in the DECLARE statement. Any inconsistency is flagged and listed when the precompile finishes. Then you can reedit the code and make the necessary corrections. After all errors have

TABLE 13.1 *Conversion criteria for converting DB2 definitions into COBOL descriptions*

Database Data Types	The COBOL Equivalent
INTEGER	PIC S9(9) COMP
SMALLINT	PIC S9(4) COMP
DECIMAL(N,M)	PIC S9(N-M)V9(M) COMP-3
VARCHAR(A)	PIC X(A)
CHAR(A)	PIC X(A)

been resolved, the code can be compiled and link edited. The BIND on the resultant DBRM should produce a valid plan on the first pass.

Obviously, there are a few disadvantages of using the DECLARE statement rather than performing a DCLGEN. First, the DCLGEN places a copy of the COBOL description in an Include Library that can be accessed by all programs. When a change occurs to a table description, SYSADM (or some other authorized user) can perform a DCLGEN on the modified table. This produces a new COBOL description of the table's columns in the Include Library. Now you can precompile, compile, link edit, and BIND REPLACE all programs accessing that table. This process usually is done in batch mode during second or third shift operations.

If a system contains hundreds of tables, DCLGENing every table is not a trivial amount of work, even if they were run in batch mode. Because SYSADM typically does not work with individual databases, he or she will have to give someone, typically each DBADM, the authorization to perform the DCLGEN.

Typically, when a table is modified, programs containing the DECLARE statement for the altered table must be changed manually to reflect the new table description. This might not be too problematic because a change in the table description can force some changes to other COBOL variables accessing the modified table. You probably will have to edit each program anyway to readjust the code for the modified table (i.e., move headings, add columns, etc.).

One major disadvantage of using the DECLARE statement is that the programmer could make the same mistake in the DECLARE statement as he or she made in the embedded SQL statement. That is, the programmer could have misspelled DEPURTMENT in both statements, thereby producing an error at BIND time. Remember, one reason for using the DCLGEN and/or DECLARE is to eliminate typing and other errors that will abort the BIND.

Using Host Variables

Obviously, you cannot simply place the statement:

```
EXEC SQL
    SELECT LASTNAME, FIRSTNAME, RATEOFPAY
    FROM PAYROLL
    WHERE STATE = 'IN' AND RATEOFPAY )20.00
END-EXEC.
```

in COBOL code because the data that returns from the database is in table form and there are no COBOL variables to hold the returned values. In this case, you will have to introduce **host variables** to serve as an interface between the data returning from the database and the COBOL program. Using host variables, the last SELECT statement becomes the embedded SQL statement:

```
EXEC SQL
    SELECT LASTNAME, FIRSTNAME, RATEOFPAY
```

```
            INTO :LAST-NAME-TBL, :FIRST-NAME-TBL, :RATE-PAY-TBL
            FROM PAYROLL
            WHERE EMPLOYEEID = :EMPLOYEE-ID
        END-EXEC.
```

) may not need - see version

For this SELECT statement, you need to define four host variables in WORKING-STORAGE. These become:

```
01 PAYROLL-TABLE-AREA.
        05 LAST-NAME-TBL        PIC X(20).
        05 FIRST-NAME-TBL       PIC X(20).
        05 RATE-PAY-TBL         PIC S9(3)V99 COMP-3.
        .
        .
        .

01 INPUT-RECORD.
        05 EMPLOYEE-ID          PIC X(5).
        .
        .
        .
```

The host variable in each embedded SQL statement is preceded by a colon. These variables must be defined as COBOL variables (but without the colon) in WORKING-STORAGE. The precompiler checks the data type of each host variable with the data type of its corresponding column from the table. If there is any discrepancy, it will be flagged and later printed out in an error listing. The precompiler also checks all the database column and table names with those defined in the DECLARE statement or those brought into the code by the INCLUDE statement. Again, all inconsistencies are to be flagged as errors.

Obviously, for this SELECT to work, the program must have some value in EMPLOYEE-ID. In an on-line system, this value would be entered via some screen routine. The inputted value would be edited and then MOVEd to EMPLOYEE-ID before accessing the database via the SELECT.

When using host variables outside the EXEC SQL and END-EXEC delimiters, you omit the colon preceding the host variable. For example, the statement:

```
MOVE FIXED-VALUE TO EMPLOYEE-ID.
```

moves the value in FIXED-VALUE to the variable EMPLOYEE-ID.

In this SELECT statement, the system will extract data for LASTNAME, FIRSTNAME, and RATEOFPAY from the table PAYROLL and place the values in the COBOL variables LAST-NAME-TBL, FIRST-NAME-TBL, and RATE-PAY-TBL, respectively. Alternately, we could use:

```
EXEC SQL
        SELECT LASTNAME, FIRSTNAME, RATEOFPAY
        INTO :PAYROLL-TABLE-AREA
        FROM PAYROLL
```

```
          WHERE EMPLOYEEID = :EMPLOYEE-ID
     END-EXEC.
```

In this case, the use of the SELECT statement is similar to the COBOL statement:

```
READ FILE-A INTO RECORD-A.
```

Using Cursors

For the last SELECT statement to work satisfactorily, the table PAYROLL must have a unique index on EMPLOYEEID. This requirement guarantees that only a single row returns from DB2. Remember, in the SELECT you place the data from the database in the 01 group level PAYROLL-TABLE-AREA. What happens when multiple rows return from the database? Surely they all cannot fit in this one group level. When DB2 accesses the database, one of three possibilities will occur:

- No rows are returned
- A single row is returned
- Multiple rows are·returned

No Rows Returned Only the SELECT statement returns a row to the calling program. However, all of the DML statements (SELECT, UPDATE, DELETE, INSERT) can use host variables. For example, the embedded SQL statement to update the table PAYROLL using an update program would be:

```
EXEC SQL
     UPDATE PAYROLL
     SET  LASTNAME      = :LAST-NAME-IN,
          FIRSTNAME     = :FIRST-NAME-IN,
          HOURSWORKED   = :HOURS-WORKED-IN,
          RATEOFPAY     = :RATE-OF-PAY-IN,
          PIECEWORK     = :PIECE-WORK-IN,
          YTDPIECE      = :YTD-PIECE-WORK-IN
     WHERE EMPLOYEEID = :EMPLOYEE-ID-IN
END-EXEC.
```

In this example, no row is returned from DB2 and values in host variables update a row in the table for some value in EMPLOYEE-ID-IN. Don't forget, in an on-line system, all values for the host variables (i.e., those preceded by a colon) will be captured via some input-screen routine. This routine, in addition to capturing the data from some data-entry clerk, also must edit the input data and reject those values that are invalid (e.g., -20 for hours worked or 63,&* for rate of pay).

One Row Returned When you use the SELECT statement on a table and extract data based on a unique key, either no row or one row will return from the database. In either case, you have no problem because the column values from a single row returning match the COBOL 01 Group Level variable area given in the INTO option of SELECT. This occurred in:

```
SELECT LASTNAME, FIRSTNAME, RATEOFPAY
INTO :PAYROLL-TABLE-AREA
FROM PAYROLL
WHERE EMPLOYEEID = :EMPLOYEE-ID
```

where PAYROLL-TABLE-AREA is defined in WORKING-STORAGE and contains three fields. DB2 extracts the data from the tablespace, places it into a buffer, and then moves it to the group level variable PAYROLL-TABLE-AREA.

Multiple Rows Returned When DB2 extracts multiple rows from the tablespace in the database, these rows load into a buffer area, you logically process these rows in the buffer in the same way you logically process any sequential file. In particular, to process these multiple rows, you must:

- Place the SELECT statement in a DECLARE CURSOR statement to establish a multiple record buffer area
- Use an OPEN statement to extract data from the database using the SELECT in DECLARE to place the data in the buffer
- Place a FETCH in a looping routine to read each row from the buffer sequentially
- Use a CLOSE statement to end the processing of the buffer

The general form of the DECLARE CURSOR statement is:

```
DECLARE cursorname CURSOR FOR
    SELECT statement
```

where "cursorname" is an arbitrary name assigned to a pointer and "SELECT statement" is any valid SELECT statement. For example, the statement:

```
EXEC SQL
    DECLARE CURSOR1 CURSOR FOR
        SELECT LASTNAME, FIRSTNAME, RATEOFPAY
        FROM PAYROLL
        WHERE RATEOFPAY ) :RATE-OF-PAY-IN
END-EXEC
```

defines the pointer CURSOR1 for the given SELECT statement. The DECLARE. . .CURSOR statement is placed in WORKING-STORAGE and notifies DB2 that multiple rows possibly could be returned during a SELECT extraction from the database. If you fail to use a cursor for an embedded SELECT and more than one row is extracted by DB2, the program ABENDs.

In the PROCEDURE DIVISION, you place the logic to use the cursor. This logic is similar to the logic you use to process a sequential tape file. In this case, however, rather than reading a tape drive using COBOL's READ statement, you will read the buffer area that is holding the table's data using the FETCH statement.

13. SQL and the Programmer

But how do we get the data into the buffer? The DECLARE statement is in WORKING-STORAGE (which contains nonexecutable code) and not in the PROCEDURE DIVISION (which contains executable code). DB2 executes the SQL statement whenever you OPEN the given "cursorname." In the previous example, before DB2 executes the SELECT statement, the host variable RATE-OF-PAY-IN must contain a value for the database extraction to work properly. For example, you could use the statement:

MOVE RATE-OF-PAY-SCREEN TO RATE-OF-PAY-IN.

to move a value extracted from some screen routine to RATE-OF-PAY-IN. Now, the statement:

```
EXEC SQL
        OPEN CURSOR1
END-EXEC.
```

tells DB2 to execute the SQL statement assigned to CURSOR1 and places the data in a special buffer. Once the data resides in the buffer, DB2 creates a pointer that points to the first row in the buffer. You read a row from the buffer using:

```
EXEC SQL
        FETCH CURSOR1
                INTO :PAYROLL-TABLE-AREA          ) may need to list variables in COBOL
END-EXEC.
```

Now you can process the buffer much like you process any sequential tape or disk file. Each time the program FETCHes a row from the buffer, DB2 moves the pointer to the next row in the buffer. You process the extracted row and continue to FETCH rows from the buffer area until you exhaust all rows resident in the buffer (Figure 13.8).

You need a way to indicate when all the rows are read from the buffer. Place the statement:

```
IF SQLCODE = 100
        MOVE 'YES' TO FINISHED-PROCESSING
ELSE
        PERFORM 300-PROCESS-BUFFER.
```

immediately after the embedded FETCH statement to determine when all rows are read from the buffer area. You test the variable SQLCODE (found in the SQLCA region) for the value 100. Recall, the SQLCA area contains the status codes created by DB2 for each activity on the database. The code of 100 in SQLCODE indicates that no further data is in the buffer area created for that particular cursor (i.e., CURSOR1). The possible values SQLCODE are given in Table 13.2. After all rows have been processed, you CLOSE the cursor using

```
EXEC SQL
```

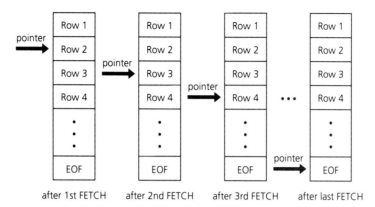

after 1st FETCH   after 2nd FETCH   after 3rd FETCH   after last FETCH

FIGURE 13.8   *Using a cursor to read multiple rows in a buffer. Each time a row is FETCHed from the buffer, DB2 moves the cursor to point to the next row. When a program tries to FETCH past the last row in the buffer, DB2 returns a status code of 100 to the SQLCA region. This value is stored in the variable SQLCODE.*

```
        CLOSE CURSOR1
    END-EXEC.
```

The complete routine to access multiple rows in the database is given in Figure 13.9. The routine extracts only three columns per table row—LAST-NAME, FIRSTNAME, and RATEOFPAY. So you defined only three COBOL variables in the target area—LAST-NAME-TBL, FIRST-NAME-TBL, and RATE-PAY-TBL. If you wanted to extract all the columns from the PAYROLL table, you would use:

```
EXEC SQL
    DECLARE CURSOR1 CURSOR FOR
        SELECT LASTNAME, FIRSTNAME, RATEOFPAY, HOURSWORKED,
            PIECEWORK, YTDPIECE
        FROM PAYROLL
        WHERE RATEOFPAY ) :RATE-OF-PAY-IN
END-EXEC.
```

Commit changes— will close all cursors

and include in WORKING-STORAGE the description (see page 390, bottom):

TABLE 13.2   *Valid codes for SQLCODE*

SQLCODE Value	Meaning of Value
0	statement executed successfully
100	no data exists
a	indicates an error occurred when "a" is some negative integer

```
WORKING-STORAGE SECTION.
    01 PAYROLL-TABLE-AREA.
        05 LAST-NAME-TBL      PIC X(20).
        05 FIRST-NAME-TBL     PIC X(20).
        05 RATE-PAY-TBL       PIC S9(3)V99 COMP-3.
*
    01 INPUT-RECORD.
        05 RATE-OF-PAY-IN     PIC 9(3)V99.
*
    EXEC SQL
        INCLUDE SQLCA
    END-EXEC.
*
    EXEC SQL
        DECLARE CURSOR1 CURSOR FOR
            SELECT LASTNAME, FIRSTNAME, RATEOFPAY
            FROM PAYROLL
            WHERE RATEOFPAY > :RATE-OF-PAY-IN
    END-EXEC
PROCEDURE DIVISION.
*
100-USING-CURSOR-ROUTINE.
    EXEC SQL
        OPEN CURSOR1
    END-EXEC.
    PERFORM 110-PROCESS-CURSOR-ROUTINE
        UNTIL FINISHED-PROCESSING = 'YES'.
    EXEC SQL
        CLOSE CURSOR1
    END-EXEC.
    STOP RUN.
*
110-PROCESS-CURSOR-ROUTINE.
    PERFORM 200-EXTRACT-SCREEN-DATA.
    EXEC SQL
        FETCH CURSOR1
            INTO :PAYROLL-TABLE-AREA
    END-EXEC.
    IF SQLCODE = 100
        MOVE 'YES' TO FINISHED-PROCESSING
    ELSE
        PERFORM 300-PROCESS-BUFFER.
110-PROCESS-COMPLETE. EXIT.
*
```

FIGURE 13.9   *Routine to extract multiple rows from a database using a cursor. The OPEN CURSOR1 statement extracts data from the tablespace and places it in a buffer. The FETCH statement reads the buffer and places one row in the COBOL group level variable PAYROLL-TABLE-AREA. When SQLCODE equals 100, all rows in the buffer have been read. A PERFORM. . .UNTIL routine creates a loop for multiple FETCHes of the buffer area.*

```
01 PAYROLL-TABLE-AREA.
    05 LAST-NAME-TBL          PIC X(20).
    05 FIRST-NAME-TBL         PIC X(20).
    05 HOURS-WORKED-TBL       PIC S9(2)V9   COMP-3.
    05 RATE-PAY-TBL           PIC S9(3)V99  COMP-3.
```

```
05 PIECE-WORKED-TBL        PIC S9(4)     COMP.
05 YTD-PIECE-WORK-TBL      PIC S9(9)     COMP.
```

Note several things about the DECLARE and its corresponding WORKING-STORAGE layout:

- Column names in SELECT do not have to be in the same order in which they were created
- Column names in SELECT must be valid column names as defined in the table's CREATE statement (and ALTERed statement if altered)
- WORKING-STORAGE description of the host variables must follow the guidelines of Table 13.1 (i.e., SMALLINT column types must have a PIC 9(4) COMP description and INTEGER column types must have a PIC 9(9) COMP description)

The statement:

```
EXEC SQL   INCLUDE dclgenname END-EXEC.
```

(where "dclgenname" is the product of the DCLGEN for the table) should be included in the code. With the inclusion, the precompiler can cross-check the table's description with the variable description in the COBOL code.

Updating Using a Cursor

Data in database rows is modified via the embedded UPDATE statement. The program must establish the proper communication between the program, the database table, and the buffer area containing the data. This is done by using the following steps:

1. Use DECLARE with the FOR UPDATE OF option
2. OPEN the cursor
3. FETCH the desired row from the database
4. Use UPDATE with the WHERE CURRENT OF option
5. CLOSE the cursor

To update using a cursor, use the following general form of DECLARE:

```
EXEC SQL
     DECLARE cursorname CURSOR FOR
         some SELECT statement
     FOR UPDATE OF list of updatable columns
END-EXEC.
```

The option FOR UPDATE OF tells DB2 that an update is to occur that forces DB2 to generate special pointers and routines to handle the modifications of the table.

If you wanted potentially to update all the rows in the PAYROLL table, you would use:

```
EXEC SQL
    DECLARE CURSOR1 CURSOR FOR
        SELECT LASTNAME, FIRSTNAME, RATEOFPAY, HOURSWORKED,
            PIECEWORK, YTDPIECE
        FROM PAYROLL
        WHERE EMPLOYEEID = :EMPLOYEE-ID-IN
    FOR UPDATE OF LASTNAME, FIRSTNAME, RATEOFPAY,
            HOURSWORKED, PIECEWORK, YTDPIECE
END-EXEC.
```

In this case, you exclude the potential to modify column EMPLOYEEID because it is the primary key for the PAYROLL table.

After you FETCH the row that is to be modified, you display the row's data to the user. He or she then can decide what values in the row are to be modified. Figure 13.10 illustrates what a data-entry clerk would typically see in an update screen for the PAYROLL table.

The screen in Figure 13.10 is an option of a Main Menu. First, you enter a value for Employee ID and press PF4. If the employee is not on the database, you can enter appropriate data and press PF6. If the employee is on the database, you can change the data and press PF5. To query the database on another employee, you press PF2 and enter another Employee ID value. If display of data for a single employee requires multiple screens, you press PF7 and PF8 to scroll to these screens. The COMMAND line allows you to enter specialized commands or instructions. This screen is one of three screens containing data on the employee. PAY006 is an assigned name for the screen to aid in problem resolution.

```
PAY006                                      SCREEN 1 OF 3
                    PAYROLL UPDATE SCREEN

EMPLOYEE'S ID _____

LAST NAME: _____

FIRST NAME: _____

RATE OF PAY (XXX.XX): ___.__

HOURS WORKED (XX.X): __._

AMOUNT OF PIECEWORK (0000 THRU 9999): ____

ENTER CORRECTIONS AS NEEDED AND PRESS

                        PF5  UPDATE THIS EMPLOYEE
PF2  CLEAR SCREEN VALUES   PF6  ADD THIS EMPLOYEE
PF3  RETURN TO MAIN MENU   PF7  NEXT SCREEN
PF4  DISPLAY EMPLOYEE DATA  PF8  PRIOR SCREEN

COMMAND==>
```

FIGURE 13.10   *Typical update screen as seen by data entry clerk.*

After the data clerk enters the modified data, the program then must update the buffer's data using:

```
EXEC SQL
UPDATE PAYROLL
        SET  LASTNAME       = :LASTNAME-SCREEN-IN,
             FIRSTNAME      = :FIRSTNAME-SCREEN-IN,
             RATEOFPAY      = :RATE-OF-PAY-SCREEN-IN,
             HOURSWORKED  = :HOURS-WORKED-SCREEN-IN,
             PIECEWORK      = :PIECE-WORK-SCREEN-IN,
             YTDPIECE       = :YTD-PIECE-WORK-SCREEN-IN
        WHERE CURRENT OF CURSOR1
END-EXEC.
```

The complete routine to update a row in the database is given in Figure 13.11. In the routine you FETCH the row that is to be updated using the row's key field (i.e., EMPLOYEEID). Then you display that row to the data-entry clerk using some screen routine. In the screen routine the clerk makes the necessary changes to the data (i.e., in PAYROLL-TABLE-AREA). After the clerk makes the changes on the screen, the clerk selects the option to physically update the database.

The COBOL code in Figure 13.11 does not contain any COBOL instructions to perform the screen's interaction with the data-entry clerk. Typically, the code to create this interaction is generated by some 4GL product, such as TELON, or some other screen-generation product and is omitted here.

Saving Work

Only when you close the cursor will the system permanently save your work. This process is called a **COMMIT.** COMMIT is a technique DB2 uses to permanently write the program's buffer areas to the tablespace. Prior to a COMMIT, DB2 saves all the changes to the database in some log file. This log file is created automatically by DB2 and is part of the audit-trail mechanism built into DB2. If for some reason, the system ABENDs or encounters an error before DB2 performs a COMMIT, all the changes made to the database since the last COMMIT will be erased. That means the database's log journal will undo or back-out all the changes made to the database since the last COMMIT. This backing out process is called a **ROLLBACK.** Whenever an error condition occurs, DB2 automatically issues a ROLLBACK command to recreate the database to some prior state before the error condition arose. These implicit COMMITS and ROLLBACKS are dependent on the various operations and error conditions that occur within DB2.

You can issue the COMMIT and ROLLBACK commands explicitly using

```
EXEC SQL COMMIT END-EXEC.
```

```
WORKING-STORAGE SECTION.
    01 PAYROLL-TABLE-AREA.
            05 LAST-NAME-TBL          PIC X(20).
            05 FIRST-NAME-TBL         PIC X(20).
            05 HOURS-WORKED-TBL       PIC S9(2)V9  COMP-3.
            05 RATE-PAY-TBL           PIC S9(3)V99 COMP-3.
            05 PIECE-WORKED-TBL       PIC S9(4)    COMP.
            05 YTD-PIECE-WORK-TBL     PIC S9(9)    COMP.
*
    01 INPUT-RECORD.
        05 RATE-OF-PAY-IN            PIC 9(3)V99.
*
    EXEC SQL
        INCLUDE SQLCA
    END- EXEC.
*
    EXEC SQL
        DECLARE CURSOR1 CURSOR FOR
            SELECT LASTNAME, FIRSTNAME, RATEOFPAY, HOURSWORKED,
                    PIECEWORK, YTDPIECE
            FROM PAYROLL
            WHERE EMPLOYEEID = :EMPLOYEE-ID-IN
        FOR UPDATE OF LASTNAME, FIRSTNAME, RATEOFPAY,
                    HOURSWORKED, PIECEWORK, YTDPIECE
    END-EXEC.
*
PROCEDURE DIVISION.
*
100-USING-CURSOR-ROUTINE.
    EXEC SQL
        OPEN CURSOR1
    END-EXEC.
    PERFORM 110-PROCESS-CURSOR-ROUTINE
        UNTIL FINISHED-PROCESSING = 'YES'.
    EXEC SQL
        CLOSE CURSOR1
    END-EXEC.
    STOP RUN.
*
110-PROCESS-CURSOR-ROUTINE.
    EXEC SQL
      FETCH CURSOR1
        INTO :PAYROLL-TABLE-AREA
    END-EXEC.
    IF SQLCODE = 100
        MOVE 'YES' TO FINISHED-PROCESSING
        GO TO 110-PROCESS-COMPLETE.
    PERFORM 300-DISPLAY-SCREEN-ROUTINE.
    IF UPDATE-THE-ROW = 'YES'
        EXEC SQL
            UPDATE PAYROLL
                SET  LASTNAME       = :LASTNAME-SCREEN-IN,
                    FIRSTNAME      = :FIRSTNAME-SCREEN-IN,
                    RATEOFPAY      = :RATE-OF-PAY-SCREEN-IN,
                    HOURSWORKED = :HOURS-WORKED-SCREEN-IN,
                    PIECEWORK      = :PIECE-WORK-SCREEN-IN,
                    YTDPIECE       = :YTD-PIECE-WORK-SCREEN-IN
                WHERE CURRENT OF CURSOR1
        END-EXEC.
110-PROCESS-COMPLETE. EXIT.
```

FIGURE 13.11   *Routine to update a database row using a cursor.*

or

EXEC SQL ROLLBACK END-EXEC.

You can explicitly force DB2 to perform a COMMIT or ROLLBACK.

You can open multiple cursors at the same time and a COMMIT automatically closes all of these cursors. So if you want to permanently save all the changes made to the database, you must issue a COMMIT. By doing so, however, DB2 closes the cursors and destroys the pointers in the buffer areas. You need to again issue an OPEN statement to reestablish the data in the buffers and create pointers to the rows in them. This can adversely affect the program, especially if you are sequentially processing data in the buffer and need to COMMIT.

Don't forget, any error produces an automatic ROLLBACK and you lose all the changes made to the database since the last COMMIT. Obviously, you don't want to require a data-entry clerk to reenter massive amounts of data because of a system error causing an automatic rollback of his or her work. You therefore must force DB2 to COMMIT at certain intervals, for example, every fifth update, every tenth insert, and so forth. You have to decide whether to save the data permanently at some predefined interval and lose your place in the buffers, or keep your place in the buffers and not save your work until all processing is complete.

Deleting Using a Cursor

Deleting a Single Row Rows are deleted from tables using a modification of DELETE in an embedded SQL statement. The rows you delete are established by a DECLARE CURSOR statement in WORKING-STORAGE. The statement:

```
EXEC SQL
    DECLARE CURSOR1 CURSOR FOR
        SELECT LASTNAME, FIRSTNAME, RATEOFPAY, HOURSWORKED,
            PIECEWORK, YTDPIECE
        FROM PAYROLL
        WHERE EMPLOYEEID = :EMPLOYEE-ID-IN
END-EXEC.
```

in WORKING-STORAGE identifies a single row in the database for some EMPLOYEE-ID-IN value. In the PROCEDURE DIVISION you must move some value to EMPLOYEE-ID-IN and then open the cursor CURSOR1 using:

EXEC SQL OPEN CURSOR1 END-EXEC.

Now, DB2 extracts a row from the database using the value in EMPLOYEE-ID-IN as a key and places that row in a buffer area. When you later use the statement:

```
EXEC SQL
    DELETE FROM PAYROLL
```

```
          WHERE CURRENT OF CURSOR1
     END-EXEC.
```

DB2 deletes the row in the database. Here, the general form of the embedded DELETE statement is:

```
EXEC SQL
     DELETE FROM tablename
     WHERE CURRENT OF cursorname
END-EXEC.
```

Then you close the cursor using:

```
EXEC SQL    CLOSE CURSOR1    END-EXEC.
```

When the DECLARE statement contains a SELECT statement that accesses multiple rows, you can selectively delete a single row by placing an embedded FETCH statement in a looping routine and displaying multiple rows to the user. When the user selects the row to be deleted, use a DELETE FROM. . .WHERE CURRENT OF statement to delete the row to which the cursor is pointing. For example, a deletion routine is given in Figure 13.12.

Deleting Multiple Rows The statement:

```
EXEC SQL
     DELETE FROM tablename
     WHERE condition
END-EXEC.
```

deletes multiple rows from a table. In an on-line system, when a user attempts to delete multiple rows from a table, as a precaution, you would first display those rows followed by the message "Are you sure?" If the user answers yes, DB2 would be allowed to delete the rows.

The program in Figure 13.13 contains a routine to delete all the employees who work less than 40 hours in the week.

Inserting Rows via a Program

You can INSERT rows into a table using an embedded INSERT statement. There are three versions of INSERT:

- Version 1
  INSERT INTO tablename
  VALUES (list)
- Version 2
  INSERT INTO tablename
       (columnname list)
  VALUES (list)
- Version 3
  INSERT INTO tablename
       SELECT query statement

```
WORKING-STORAGE SECTION.
*
    EXEC SQL
        DECLARE CURSOR1 CURSOR FOR
            SELECT LASTNAME, FIRSTNAME, RATEOFPAY, HOURSWORKED,
                PIECEWORK, YTDPIECE
            FROM PAYROLL
        END-EXEC.
*
PROCEDURE DIVISION.
*
    MOVE 'NO' TO DONE-LOOP.
    EXEC SQL   OPEN CURSOR1   END-EXEC.
    PERFORM 100-LOOPING-ROUTINE
        UNTIL DONE-LOOP = 'YES'
    EXEC SQL   CLOSE CURSOR1   END-EXEC.
    STOP RUN.
*
100-LOOPING-ROUTINE.
    EXEC SQL
        FETCH CURSOR1 INTO :RECORDA
    END-EXEC.
    IF SQLCODE = 100
        MOVE 'YES' TO DONE-LOOP
        GO TO 100-DONE-ROUTINE.
    PERFORM 200-DISPLAY-RECORD-ROUTINE.
    IF USER-FINISHED = 'YES'
        MOVE 'YES' TO DONE-LOOP
        GO TO 100-DONE-ROUTINE.
    IF DELETE-ROW = 'YES'
        EXEC SQL
            DELETE FROM PAYROLL
            WHERE CURRENT OF CURSOR1
        END-EXEC.
100-DONE-ROUTINE. EXIT.
*
200-DISPLAY-RECORD-ROUTINE.
```

FIGURE 13.12   *Routine to delete one row using FETCH.*

Typically, you would not embed version 1 into code because it is dependent on DB2's table description. Remember, when you insert data using version 1, the values you place in the "list" must match one to one with the column's location as it appears in the DB2 catalog. Suppose a user ALTERed the table and added several more columns to it. Now the program's description does not match the table's description and problems could arise. To avoid unnecessary problems, use version 2 of INSERT and list the column names and their respective values. For example, the statement:

```
EXEC SQL
    INSERT INTO PAYROLL
        (LASTNAME, FIRSTNAME, RATEOFPAY,
          HOURSWORKED, PIECEWORK, YTDPIECE)
    VALUES
        (:LAST-NAME-IN, :FIRST-NAME-IN, :RATE-PAY-IN,
```

```
*
*
    EXEC SQL
        DECLARE CURSOR2 CURSOR FOR
            SELECT LASTNAME, FIRSTNAME, RATEOFPAY, HOURSWORKED,
                PIECEWORK, YTDPIECE
            FROM PAYROLL
            WHERE HOURSWORKED > :HOURS-IN
    END-EXEC.
*
PROCEDURE DIVISION.
*
    MOVE 40 TO HOURS-IN.
    MOVE 'NO' TO DONE-LOOP.
    EXEC SQL   OPEN CURSOR2   END-EXEC.
    PERFORM 100-READ-TABLE-ROUTINE
        UNTIL DONE-LOOP = 'YES'
    PERFORM 200-QUERY-USER-ROUTINE.
    IF SURE-DELETE-ROWS = 'YES'
        EXEC SQL
            DELETE FROM PAYROLL
            WHERE HOURSWORKED > :HOURS-IN
        END-EXEC.
    EXEC SQL   CLOSE CURSOR2   END-EXEC.
    STOP RUN.
*
100-READ-TABLE-ROUTINE.
    EXEC SQL
        FETCH CURSOR2 INTO :RECORDA
    END-EXEC.
    IF SQLCODE = 100
        MOVE 'YES' TO DONE-LOOP
    ELSE
        PERFORM 300-DISPLAY-ROW-ROUTINE.
100-DONE-READING. EXIT.
```

FIGURE 13.13   *Routine to delete multiple rows using FETCH.*

```
                        :HOURS-WORKED-IN, :PIECE-WORK-IN, :YTD-PIECE-IN)
            END-EXEC.
```

in an ADD program loads data into the table PAYROLL. In this program, you would display a screen similar to the one in Figure 13.10. The values the user enters then would be placed in host variables listed in the VALUES clause. Remember, the arrangement of the columns in this version of INSERT does not have to match one to one with the arrangement of the columns in the CREATE TABLE statement. That is, the statement

```
EXEC SQL
    INSERT INTO PAYROLL
        (HOURSWORKED, PIECEWORK, YTDPIECE,
        LASTNAME, FIRSTNAME, RATEOFPAY)
    VALUES
        (:HOURS-WORKED-IN, :PIECE-WORK-IN, :YTD-PIECE-IN,
```

```
                         :LAST-NAME-IN, :FIRST-NAME-IN, :RATE-PAY-IN)
      END-EXEC.
```

also correctly inserts data into the table PAYROLL. The values in VALUES must match up one for one with their respective column names in the column listing (i.e., LASTNAME and :LAST-NAME-IN are in the same relative position in the statement).

Similarly, the statements:

```
MOVE 39.9 TO HOURS-IN.
EXEC SQL
      INSERT INTO PAYROLLTEMP
            SELECT LASTNAME, FIRSTNAME, RATEOFPAY, HOURSWORKED,
                  PIECEWORK, YTDPIECE
            FROM PAYROLL
            WHERE HOURSWORKED ⟩ :HOURS-IN
END-EXEC.
```

load data into the temporary table PAYROLLTEMP. Here, only data about employees who work 40 hours or more loads into the table.

Typically, PAYROLLTEMP is created independently of code (i.e., via DB2I or QMF). To guarantee that no other data exists in this temporary table, place the statement:

```
EXEC SQL
      DELETE FROM PAYROLLTEMP
END-EXEC.
```

immediately before the INSERT statement.

EXECUTION OF EMBEDDED-SQL COBOL PROGRAMS

DB2 can interface with other parts of the mainframe environment, such as TSO, IMS, or CICS. This gives you several ways to execute an embedded-SQL COBOL program.

The simplest way to execute a DB2 program is under TSO, using the RUN option of DB2I (see Figure 13.14). This allows programmers to quickly test a noninteractive program. After testing and debugging the program, it could be executed as a regularly scheduled production program in batch. To do this, the programmer would code JCL to execute the program. This would entail coding the JCL in such a way as to invoke the TSO TMP. The TMP could be given commands through a data file to cause it to execute your program.

If you wanted to execute an interactive, on-line program, you would probably use the terminal-I/O facilities of IMS or CICS. To do this, the programmer would code an IMS or CICS program that would display screens, get user input, validate the input, display error messages, and so on. This part

```
                        DB2I PRIMARY OPTION MENU
===>

Select one of the following DB2 functions and press ENTER.

1 SPUFI                         (Process SQL statements)
2 DCLGEN                        (Generate source language declarations)
3 PROGRAM PREPARATION           (Prepare an application program to run)
4 PRECOMPILE                    (Invoke DB2 precompiler)
5 BIND/REBIND/FREE              (BIND, REBIND, or FREE application plans)
6 RUN                           (RUN an SQL program)
7 DB2 COMMANDS                  (Issue DB2 commands)
8 UTILITIES                     (Invoke DB2 utilities)
X EXIT                          (Leave DB2I)
```

FIGURE 13.14   *Initial selection list to use a DB2 product.*

of the program would look like a standard IMS or CICS program; however, instead of using the database facilities of IMS or COBOL's VSAM capabilities for CICS, embedded SQL would be used for database access.

━━━━━━━ DB2I

IBM's DB2 product runs under MVS/XA and MVS/ESA. Any installation that wants to use DB2 also must have IBM's TSO/ISPF product. Once DB2 is installed, some member of the systems team will modify the ISPF's selection screen to include an option for DB2. If a programmer or user wants to access DB2, he or she does so by accessing the DB2 option in the ISPF screen. Because IBM has multiple products to support DB2 (to enhance its use), most installations include a secondary menu that lets programmers and users select the product they want. Figure 13.15 illustrates a typical DB2 Product Selection Menu.

Because most end users are not programmers, the end-user departments will have only the QMF selections as options on their DB2 Product Selection Menu screen. Programmers and other system developers need to access all the DB2 products, so their screen typically looks like the one in Figure 13.15. In this screen, the programmer will select DB2I in the DB2 Product Selection Screen and then SPUFI in the DB2I Primary Option Menu screen (see Figure 13.14) when he or she wants to test SQL statements against DB2 databases.

```
DB2 PRODUCT SELECTION LIST

    1 DB2I
    2 QMF PRODUCTION
    3 QMF TEST
    4 DBEDIT
    5 DXT
    X EXIT

==>
```

FIGURE 13.15   *The DB2I menu selection screen.*

DB2I is a menu-driven product that accesses the various DB2 panels that are essential to doing program preparation. Before selecting any option in this screen, SYSADM must give authorization for its use. Typically, only SYSADM or selected DBADMs perform DCLGENs. In addition, the use of DB2 Commands is reserved for the systems team to monitor and control the DB2 environment. The result is that programmers generally are denied access to these two options.

Each option in the DB2I screen has secondary screens. It is in these secondary screens that you supply the names of the various libraries and members that access DB2 entities. For example, in the SPUFI screen you must identify the library that contains the SQL instructions for the queries. In addition, you must identify the library that will hold the results of a query. The names of these libraries are controlled by either SYSADM or some member of the systems team. Most installations use:

    $userid.SQL.CNTL

and

    $userid.SQL.OUT

as the libraries to hold each user's SQL queries and the query's results, respectively. To write an SQL query, select the SPUFI option of DB2I. Then you identify the location of the query library (i.e., SQL.CNTL) and the data set that will contain the SQL query (i.e., LAB1 in Figure 13.16). Then you write the query into the data set (Figure 13.17).

You execute the query by pressing the PF3 key. DB2 performs a dynamic BIND on the query and places the results in the indicated output data set (SQL.OUT) for later browsing. Multiple queries can be written in SPUFI's Query Screen when each query is separated by a semicolon.

```
                         SPUFI
===>

Enter the Input data set name:

      1 DATA SET NAME ........ ===> SQL.CNTL(LAB1)
      2 VOLUME SERIAL ......... ===>
      3 DATA SET PASSWORD ===>

Enter the Output data set name:

      4 DATA SET NAME ........ ===> SQL.OUT

Specify processing options:

      5 CHANGE DEFAULTS ....===> YES
      6 EDIT INPUT ................. ===> YES
      7 EXECUTE .................... ===> YES
      8 AUTOCOMMIT ........... ===> YES
      9 BROWSE OUTPUT .......===> YES
```

FIGURE 13.16 *Typical SPUFI screen. This screen creates the data set LAB1 in the library SQL.CNTL and the data set SQL.OUT. If only the library name is listed in line 1, all the member names resident in the library will be listed.*

```
SQL.CNTL(LAB1)
SELECT LASTNAME, FIRSTNAME, RATEOFPAY, HOURSWORKED,
       PIECEWORK, YTDPIECE
FROM PAYROLL
WHERE HOURSWORKED > 40;
SELECT *
FROM DEPARTMENT;
SELECT *
FROM STORE;
```

FIGURE 13.17   *Typical SQL query screen containing three queries.*

CONVERTING NONRELATIONAL FILES TO RELATIONAL TABLES

Most files can be converted to relational or DB2 tables. Obviously, programmers can write a program to access a VSAM file, an IMS database, or some other nonsequential file and create a sequential file containing the data that is needed. The load utility loads data into a DB2 table only if the data resides in a sequential data set. Because programming requires considerable resources, most companies prefer to purchase preprogrammed facilities or utility programs to perform the conversion. When IBM programmers introduced DB2, they created a conversion facility, DXT, which converts existing non-DB2 files to DB2 tables.

DXT is used to convert VSAM data sets, random disk files, and DLI database records (IMS segments) to sequential files (Figure 13.18). Because DXT is an IBM vendor product for files created by its software, DXT generally will not work on files created by other vendor software, such as Computer Associates' IDMS/R network records. In these cases, you must either program the conversion to a sequential file or purchase some third-party product to perform the needed task.

CONVERTING MICROCOMPUTER DATABASES TO MAINFRAME DATABASES

Converting microcomputer databases to mainframe databases necessitates an additional step in the conversion process. This step requires the conversion of the microcomputer file to a mainframe sequential file. Then you can use the methods previously described to convert the sequential file to a relational database. This additional step involves two activities. The first activity involves the conversion of the file from microcomputer to mainframe format. The second activity involves the uploading of the file from the microcomputer to the mainframe.

These activities can be performed in either order, meaning you can upload the file and convert it on the mainframe, or you can convert the file on the microcomputer and then upload it. Either way, you must at some point convert

FIGURE 13.18   *Converting nonrelational files to DB2 tables using Data Extract or (DXT).*

the file. There are two major differences between microcomputer data storage and mainframe data storage. The first is alphanumeric data representation. Although virtually all microcomputers store alphanumeric data in ASCII format, most mainframes in use in business—IBM mainframes—store alphanumeric data in EBCDIC. Fortunately, this usually is a trivial problem, because most upload utilities automatically convert ASCII data to EBCDIC data.

The second difference between microcomputer data storage and mainframe data storage is numeric data representation. Microcomputers typically store integer data in low-byte/high-byte binary format, whereas mainframes typically use packed format. This problem is not as easily solved. In most cases, a program must be written to either convert the microcomputer format to the mainframe format, or to convert the microcomputer numeric format to an alphanumeric format, that is, ASCII, which then can be translated by the upload utility.

CONVERTING MAINFRAME DATABASES TO MICROCOMPUTER DATABASES

Converting mainframe databases to microcomputer databases presents the same problems as noted in the last section. Again, you need to translate the data between the two formats and you must download the data to the microcomputer. You can perform the conversion on either machine—either before or after the download—and most download utilities automatically translate from EBCDIC to ASCII. You probably will need to write a program to perform some conversion.

SUMMARY   SQL statements can be embedded in COBOL code by placing the SQL statement between the delimiters EXEC SQL and END-EXEC. Because SQL statements are not valid COBOL commands, a precompile converts the SQL statement between the delimiters into COBOL language or a CALL with parameters to an external system module.

A compile on the resultant source code converts it into object code. A link edit of the object code produces a load module. The precompiler also produces a DBRM. The DBRM is a sequential data set containing a listing of all the SQL statements found in the code. A BIND on the DBRM produces a plan and a Processed DBRM. The plan contains the accessing strategies and an authorizations list for the database.

BIND ADD places an initial copy of the DBRM into the DB2 Catalog. Further BINDs on the DBRM must occur using the BIND REPLACE option. A REBIND uses the Processed DBRM to create a new plan. The result of a successful BIND is a valid plan. If the BIND fails to produce a plan due to an error, the error must be resolved and another BIND REPLACE initiated. A dropped resource invalidates all plans based on that resource, thereby making them invalid plans. REBINDing of these invalid plans (after supplying the needed resource) converts the invalid plans to valid plans. Plans that are still invalid after a REBIND are said to be inoperative plans.

DB2 places either a time stamp or a version number on the products of the precompile. The system maintains the time stamp or version number throughout the various stages of program preparation. When running the load module, the system accesses the plan for that load module to extract the strategy for accessing the database and the authorization criteria. If the plan and the load module have different time stamps or different version numbers, the system will perform an on-line REBIND. If this REBIND fails to produce a valid plan, the system ABENDs the program.

A COBOL program that contains an embedded SQL statement must have an INCLUDE SQLCA statement in its WORKING-STORAGE area. The SQLCA area contains status codes in its variables that programmers can use to monitor the activity between the program and the DB2 database. Values in host variables provide a vehicle to link COBOL data and variables to database data and column names. The host variable's PICTURE description must conform to certain standards dictated by DB2.

A cursor is a technique to establish pointers to the row data that reside in a buffer area. The DECLARE CURSOR statement establishes a buffer to hold database data and contains the SELECT statement that eventually will read the database. The OPEN "cursorname" statement forces DB2 to read the database using the SELECT in DECLARE CURSOR and place the data in a buffer. The FETCH statement in a looping routine reads the data from the buffer and places it in some COBOL variable. Logic in the program then processes the data in the COBOL variable. The CLOSE "cursorname" statement erases the buffer area and terminates the cursor. When DB2 returns more than one row when using a SELECT, the system ABENDs if no cursor exists for that SELECT.

A COMMIT permanently saves all the changes to the database. If an error occurs during database processing, DB2 will ROLLBACK or erase all the changes made to the database since the last COMMIT. Certain activities in DB2 generate an automatic COMMIT. COBOL programs can contain the explicit statements COMMIT and ROLLBACK.

Converting data from relational to nonrelational format, or vice versa, can be simply accomplished via the use of various utilities. Problems of numeric format conversion arise when you wish to transport data between mainframes and microcomputers. Usually, some special program coding must be done to accomplish this.

DB2I is a menu-driven product that runs under TSO/ISPF. The options within DB2I allow users and system developers to access the numerous DB2 products. It is in the SPUFI menu that programmers test SQL queries to the database. DB2I also contains options to perform the BIND, REBIND, FREE, PRE-COMPILE, COMPILE, LINK EDIT, DCLGEN, and RUN. In addition, DB2I contains an option to access the DB2 Utilities.

QUESTIONS

1. Explain the difference between a BIND ADD, a BIND REPLACE, and a REBIND.
2. What is the difference between the DBRM in a user library and the Processed DBRM in the DB2 Catalog?
3. What are the advantages and disadvantages of a time stamp and a version number?
4. What is a DCLGEN?
5. What is a cursor?
6. How does a COMMIT affect the cursors and buffers in a COBOL program?
7. Write the module to insert multiple rows containing ITEMID, ITEMNAME, NUMBERINSTOCK, and ITEMCOST into a table called PRODUCT. What would the CREATE TABLE statement look like?
8. For the table in question 7, define the COBOL WORKING-STORAGE SECTION for all the variables.
9. For the PRODUCT table in question 7, write the embedded SQL statements to update the table PRODUCT.
10. For the PRODUCT table in question 7, write the embedded SQL statements to DELETE the products with ITEMID of '1234', '3456', and '7890'.
11. For the PRODUCT table in question 7, write the embedded SQL statements to print all the rows to paper.

CASE STUDY
A Compre-hensive Lab Exercise

Using the following SALARY, DEPARTMENT, and JOB tables on page 406, do the following exercises.

1. Write the DDL statements to create each table.
2. Write the DDL statements to include referential integrity options that will RESTRICT the inserting, updating, and deleting of rows.
3. Create unique indexes on all three tables. What other columns in the three tables need indexes? Create nonunique indexes on these columns.
4. Using a series of INSERT statements, load the above data into the tables.
5. Verify the integrity of the tables by executing SELECT * statements on all three tables. Perform this function in both DB2I and in QMF. When using QMF, place proper headings along with date and page numbers on the reports.
6. Write a COBOL program to read the SALARY table and DISPLAY it to the screen (use COBOL's ACCEPT and DISPLAY verbs).
7. Write a COBOL program to ACCEPT an Employee ID. FETCH the row from the table and display it to the screen.
8. Write a COBOL program to ACCEPT an Employee ID. Using a series of DISPLAYs and ACCEPTs, change the last name, salary, and job title of MIKE MARKUM and KAREN BIRDY.

SALARY TABLE

EMPL ID	LAST NAME	FIRST NAME	SALARY	RACE	SEX	BIRTH DATE	JOB TITLE	DEPT
12000	MASDER	MARY	54000	W	F	431211	MGR	ACCT
12345	DOE	JOHN	32000	W	M	671110	SA	BUDG
23456	SMITH	MARY	35500	W	F	620103	SSA	BUDG
32456	GROVER	SUE	28000	W	F	651118	SP	ACCT
43000	GRIT	TRIB	51000	W	F	410903	MGR	PERS
43214	SMITH	ANDY	28500	B	M	610922	SP	PERS
43223	MARKUM	MIKE	30000	W	M	560717	SSA	PERS
45000	HERTS	FRED	56000	W	M	400916	MGR	BUDG
53211	BIRDY	KAREN	27500	W	F	651212	P	PERS
54322	KROSS	WM	23000	W	M	651109	AP	ACCT
55678	SMITH	BETTY	24000	B	F	660405	P	ACCT
56789	LOMB	LARRY	35000	W	M	540212	SSA	ACCT
59800	KRITTE	MARY	35000	W	F	590918	SSA	PERS
60311	JONES	LARRY	20000	W	M	630817	P	BUDG
61110	LAPLER	GIG	23900	W	F	610901	P	BUDG

DEPARTMENT TABLE

DEPTNUMB	NAME	MANAGERID
ACCT	ACCOUNTING	12000
PERS	PERSONNEL	43000
BUDG	BUDGET	45000

JOB TABLE

JOB TITLE	JOB NAME
MGR	MANAGER
SSA	SENIOR SYSTEMS ANALYST
SA	SYSTEMS ANALYST
SP	SENIOR PROGRAMMER
P	PROGRAMMER
AP	ASSISTANT PROGRAMMER

9. Using the updating program in question 8, verify the referential integrity option RESTRICT by changing the Department code of GIG LAPLER to BUS.
10. Write a COBOL program to ACCEPT an Employee ID. Display the row to the screen. Using the message "DO YOU WANT TO DELETE THIS EMPLOYEE?" delete three employees from the SALARY TABLE.
11. Write a COBOL program to ACCEPT an employee ID and INSERT or add three employees to the SALARY table.
12. Create a backup copy of each table using the INSERT INTO...SELECT * statement.

13. Using QMF, verify all the changes made to the three tables using the SELECT * statement. Place proper headings along with date and page numbers on the reports.

14. GRANT a fellow student the authorization to UPDATE the SALARY table. Have him or her make modifications to your table. Have this fellow student GRANT you the same authorization on his or her table. Verify that you have this authorization by updating two rows in his or her account.

15. Create a view for a fellow student. This view should give them only SELECT and UPDATE authorization on EMPLOYEE ID, LASTNAME, FIRSTNAME, and SALARY. Have them verify this authorization by having them list all the males in the table. Have them list everyone in the table. Have them UPDATE one employee in the table.

16. For 14 and 15 above, swap roles with this fellow student. That is, have him or her grant you the indicated authorization on his or her tables. Now, perform the same verifications as he or she did.

17. Access the DB2 Catalog and list all the tables in your account. List all the rows in these tables. List all the views created on your tables. List all the authorizations granted on your tables.

14 *Network Databases*

I n 1971, the Conference on Data Systems Languages (CODASYL) issued a proposal for three distinct database languages. These languages were

- A schema Data Description Language (a schema DDL)
- A subschema Data Description Language (a subschema DDL)
- A Data Manipulation Language (DML)

Several database systems were designed using the CODASYL proposal, the most popular being Computer Associates' Integrated Database Management System (IDMS). This chapter discusses IDMS and its related product, IDMS/R, because they represent one of the more popular network databases available today.

NETWORK STRUCTURE

Relational databases store data in rows and columns within a table structure. Hierarchical databases store data in a parent or child segment. Network databases store data either in a parent record, called an **owner,** or a child record, called a **member.** Because network databases can handle many-to-many relationships, owners can have multiple members and members can have multiple owners (see Figure 14.1).

The structure chart for a small network system is given in Figure 14.2.

Typically, in an owner-member relationship, you first access an owner record and then access the members' records associated with the owner. You navigate through the database accessing the members via their owners using some navigational language, such as DML and, in some cases, a search criteria. For example, one way of finding the record for Dr. Gross within the database illustrated by Figure 14.3 requires:

- Finding the first record in DEPARTMENT (MATH)
- Finding the next record in DEPARTMENT (ENGLISH)

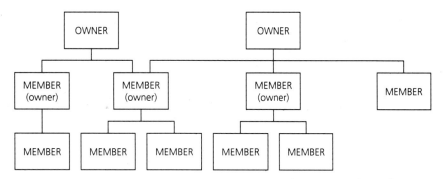

FIGURE 14.1 *Owner-member relationships. An owner can have several members. These members can, in turn, be owners of other members. Members can have multiple owners.*

- Finding the first record in FACULTY (Dr. Pent)
- Finding the next record in FACULTY (Dr. Gross)

In addition to navigating the database by accessing selected owner-member combinations, you can create indexes on both the owners and members and extract data via the index. When using indexed entities, the DBMS extracts a record from the database using an indexed key value as part of some search criteria.

OCCURRENCE DIAGRAMS

You use an **occurrence diagram** to illustrate the distribution of owner and member records. The diagram in Figure 14.3 lists the records in the owner DEPARTMENT (MATH, ENGLISH, and PHYSICS). Each DEPARTMENT record has FACULTY members assigned to it. In this case, MATH has three members (Drs. Smith, Brown, and Yan), ENGLISH has four members (Drs. Pent, Gross, McIntosh, and Walker), and PHYSICS has two members (Drs. Wilson and Mathews).

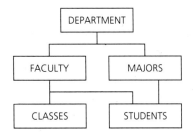

FIGURE 14.2 *Sample network structure chart. The owner DEPARTMENT has members FACULTY and MAJORS. FACULTY is the owner of the members CLASSES and STUDENTS. MAJORS also is the owner of the member STUDENTS.*

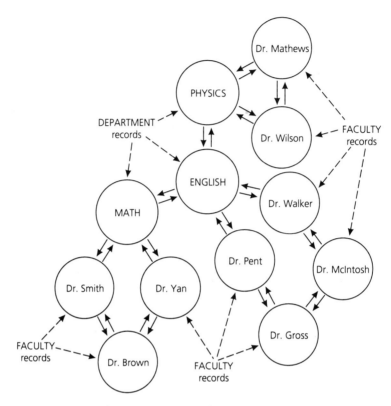

FIGURE 14.3   *Occurrence diagram for DEPARTMENT and FACULTY.*

The occurrence diagram in Figure 14.3 can be expanded further to include additional relationships between other owners and members. For example, the diagram in Figure 14.4 lists the classes each of the faculty members in Physics and English teach next term.

As you can see in Figure 14.4, ENGLISH and PHYSICS have four and two faculty members, respectively. In Physics, Dr. Wilson teaches three classes (PHY20101, PHY20201, PHY32101) while Dr. Mathews teaches two classes (PHY12001 and PHY12101). In English, Dr. Pent teaches three classes (ENG10101, ENG10104, and ENG10121), Dr. Gross teaches three classes (ENG20101, ENG34501, and ENG40201), Dr. McIntosh teaches two classes (ENG50001 and ENG50101), and Dr. Walker teaches one class (ENG62101).

Occurrence diagrams help in establishing the navigation of the database. They are particularly helpful when you must search the database sequentially without the aid of an index. In these cases, the occurrence diagram serves as a road map to the records within the database. You can see how the diagram is used by looking at how to find the classes Dr. Pent teaches next term using a sequential search. Using Figure 14.3 as a reference, the process is as follows:

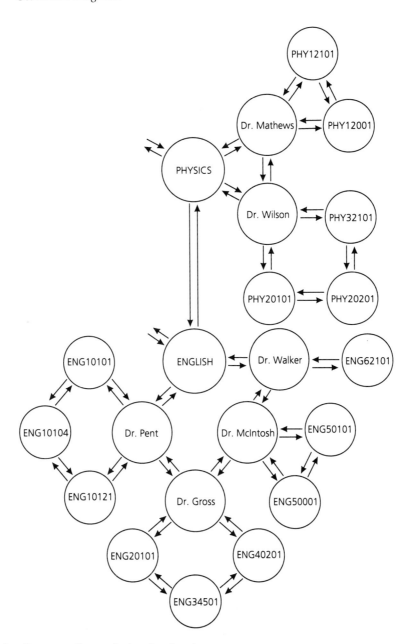

FIGURE 14.4 *Occurrence diagram for two departments.*

1. Read the first owner record of DEPARTMENT (MATH).
2. Read the first member record of that owner (Dr. Smith).
   - If the name Dr. Pent is found, discontinue the search.
   - If the name Dr. Pent is not found, continue the sequential reading of

```
      GET FIRST DEPARTMENT
      PERFORM FIRST-LOOP
          UNTIL READ ALL DEPARTMENTS OR
          UNTIL HAVE FOUND DESIRED RECORD
      STOP PROCESSING

FIRST-LOOP:
      GET FIRST FACULTY WITHIN DEPARTMENT
      PERFORM SECOND-LOOP
          UNTIL LAST RECORD OF GIVEN DEPARTMENT IS READ OR
          UNTIL FOUND DESIRED RECORD
      GET NEXT DEPARTMENT
      IF END-OF-DEPARTMENTS = 'YES'
          DISPLAY 'RECORD NOT FOUND'
END-FIRST-LOOP:

SECOND-LOOP:
      IF FACULTY-NAME = SEARCH-CRITERIA
          DISCONTINUE SEARCHING
      ELSE
          GET NEXT FACULTY WITHIN DEPARTMENT
END-SECOND-LOOP:
```

FIGURE 14.5   *Pseudo-code for the sequential search of a network database.*

the next member of that owner until all members of the owner have
been read or until Dr. Pent's name is found (read Drs. Brown and
Yen of MATH).

- If the name Dr. Pent is not found in any member record of the given
  owner, read the next owner record of DEPARTMENT (ENGLISH) and go
  to step 2 above (begin reading the records of ENGLISH).
- If no record exists in the database containing the name Dr. Pent, indicate that fact using some return code.

You can program this process using the pseudo-code of Figure 14.5. Such
a program is called a **dialog** and most DBMS products have their own language
to create a dialog.

Obviously, you could establish an index on the Faculty name field and
use the index to search for Dr. Pent. In this case, the pseudo-code is greatly
simplified to the following two pseudo-code instructions:

```
MOVE 'DR. PENT' TO FACULTY-NAME-INDEX
GET FACULTY USING FACULTY-NAME-INDEX
```

Note that, as in both hierarchical and relational databases, network databases permit the location of records within the database using both sequential
and random accessing modes.

THE SCHEMA

Establishing an index and determining the owner-member relationships are
defined in the schema. Typically, the DBA uses a special language to define

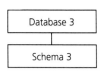

FIGURE 14.6
Databases and schemas. Each database has only one schema.

the record descriptions and the relationships between owners and members. This language is dependent on the DBMS product purchased and is called the **Schema Compiler Language.** The schema for the database contains the following:

- The record descriptions for each type record in the database
- The set definition (described below)
- The index description
- The size and configuration of the database
- Other entities that define the database

Each database has only one schema that defines all the characteristics and records of that database (see Figure 14.6).

The Set Definition

The linkage between the owner and a member is defined in the **set definition.** A set definition, or set, is the list of pertinent facts that defines the relationship between an owner and its member records. Typically, the set definition describes the following relationships, called set options:

- Establishment of pointers (next, owner, prior)
- Insertion criteria (first, last, next, prior, sorted)
- Disconnect/connect criteria (MA, MM, OA, OM)
- Duplicates allowed criteria (first, last, not)
- Location mode (CALC, VIA)
- Name of owner
- Name of member

These seven facts must be defined to the system by the DBA via some schema compiler language. After describing these facts, the DBA compiles them into a module. The DBMS software references this module before any activity is allowed to occur on the database.

Next, Owner, and Prior Pointers (NOP) The first set option establishes the type of pointers the system uses to access the records within the owner or member. A typical database query can navigate the database beginning with the first owner record and then can systematically search all member records of the owner. This type query is typical of most display and listing screens. For the query to work successfully, the network DBMS must have a series of pointers linking all the records within the database. That is, it must establish a series of linked lists that the DBMS must navigate to find the appropriate data. Each record can have forward pointers, backward pointers, and owner pointers that enable the software to find records in the list. The diagrams in Figures 14.7A and 14.7B show how such a linked list would work.

Recall, if the software structure maintains forward, backward, and owner pointers for each record, the speed of processing increases because the system

A. The DEPARTMENT linked list

DEPARTMENT

record location	record name	location of next record in DEPARTMENT	location of first member in FACULTY
1	MATH	2	6
2	ENGLISH	3	5
3	PHYSICS	-	8

B. The FACULTY linked list

FACULTY

record location	record name	location of next record	location of owner record in DEPARTMENT
1	Dr. Brown	9	1
2	Dr. Gross	4	2
3	Dr. Mathews	-	3
4	Dr. McIntosh	7	2
5	Dr. Pent	2	2
6	Dr. Smith	1	1
7	Dr. Walker	-	2
8	Dr. Wilson	3	3
9	Dr. Yan	-	1

FIGURE 14.7A   *The DEPARTMENT linked list. Record 1 (MATH) points to record 2 (ENGLISH). Record 2 (ENGLISH) points to record 3 (PHYSICS). Record 3 is the end of the list because its next record location is a null value (i.e., "–"). The first record of MATH's member is found at record 6 of FACULTY. The first record of ENGLISH's member is found at record 5 of FACULTY. The first record of PHYSICS's member is found at record 8 of FACULTY.*

FIGURE 14.7B   *The FACULTY linked list. The MATH owner record points to Smith of FACULTY. Smith points to Brown and Brown points to Yan. Yan is the last member record for this owner since it has a null pointer. The ENGLISH owner record points to Pent of FACULTY. Pent points to Gross, Gross points to McIntosh, and McIntosh points to Walker. Walker is the last member record for this owner because it has a null pointer. The PHYSICS owner record points to Wilson of FACULTY. Wilson points to Mathews. Mathews is the last record for this owner because it has a null pointer.*

can traverse the database in either direction. Forward and backward pointers are sometimes referred to as **next** and **prior** pointers, respectively.

Insertion Criteria   The second set option defines where new records are to be inserted. Remember, when adding a new record to a network database, you have several options as to where the new record will be inserted. For example, if the Chairman of the English Department gave Dr. Gross the additional class ENG30101 to teach, this extra class could be inserted in any of the following places:

- The first position after owner
- The last position after owner
- The next position after the pointer
- The prior position preceding the pointer
- Sorted order or indexed order (either ascending or descending)

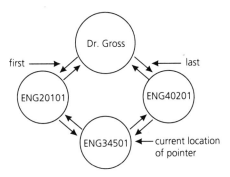

FIGURE 14.8 *Order option for insertions where current pointer location is at ENG34501. The class ENG30101 can be inserted first (before ENG20101 and after owner Dr. Gross), last (after ENG40201 and before owner Dr. Gross), next (after ENG34501 and before ENG40201), prior (before ENG34501 and after ENG20101), or in ascending sorted order (after ENG20101 and before ENG34501).*

Figure 14.8 illustrates the order options for insertions.

Disconnect and Connect Criteria The third set option identifies how records are detached and attached to the database. When attempting to delete a record from the database, you might or might not want to lose the information that is stored in that record. That is, rather than deleting the record, you might want to disconnect it from the database and reconnect it to some other owner within the database. Obviously, if a Department Chairman wants to reassign a class from Dr. Pent to Dr. Gross, he or she does not want to delete the record. Rather, the Chairman wants to disconnect the record from Dr. Pent (the current owner) and reassign it to Dr. Gross (who will be the new owner).

To accomplish this, the DBMS software needs parameters defined in the schema to prohibit users from erasing certain records. That is, if the DBA, along with management, determines that certain classes of records cannot be deleted from the database, then that fact must be coded into the schema. The DBA for the database, therefore, must establish a disconnect/connect option for the deleting and inserting of records. The two disconnect options are:

- *Mandatory*—all records when disconnected from an owner are automatically erased and the data expunged.
- *Optional*—all records when disconnected are placed in a buffer and later must be erased manually from the buffer or reconnected to a new owner via an operator command.

The two connect options are:

- *Automatic*—all new records are automatically connected to an owner.
- *Manual*—all new records are placed in a buffer area and later must be connected manually to an owner via an operator command.

These four options defining how disconnections and connections occur within the database can be coded into the schema as:

- MA for Mandatory/Automatic
- MM for Mandatory/Manual
- OA for Optional/Automatic
- OM for Optional/Manual

The disconnect option is given first; followed by the connect option.

Duplicate Records The fourth set option defines how the system handles duplicate records. Suppose someone wants to add a duplicate record to the database. Obviously, you do not want to prevent the database from adding multiple customers whose last name begin with Smith or Jones. But you probably do want to restrict the database to unique FICA numbers or unique customer numbers. Here, you need to tell the database software that duplicates will or will not be allowed for certain types of records. Again, there are three options. When permitting the insertion of an additional record with the same key, the newly added record can be loaded prior to its duplicate (**duplicate first**) or after its duplicate (**duplicate last**). The option **duplicates not allowed** denies the insertion of a record containing a duplicate key.

Location Mode The fifth set option defines the physical placement of the records with the database pages on DASD. There are two major options, called **location modes,** available for placing records on DASD—the CALC and VIA location modes. The CALC location mode places the record on a random page within a predefined database area (see Figure 14.9). The VIA location mode

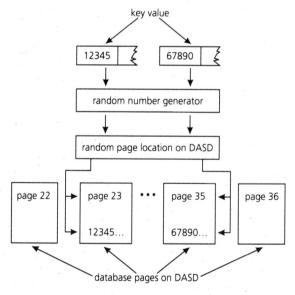

FIGURE 14.9   *The CALC location mode. A random number generator creates a unique location ID based on the CALC key value. Here, the record with key value 12345 is randomly assigned to page 23 while the record with key value 67890 is assigned to page 35. This scheme randomly distributes database records throughout the database's assigned disk area.*

places the record on or near the page containing the record's owner (see Figure 14.10).

Recall, in DB2 the system placed the records (rows) on DASD beginning in the first available space on the first available page. Therefore, in DB2 all database records tend to reside on the beginning pages of the database. Also, DASD was conserved because DB2 did not allocate the actual DASD space until it was needed. As a result, processing speed was increased because the system did not have to scan empty pages. This increased speed, however, was counteracted by contention problems. Because all the records are clumped together, users have a higher probability of accessing two different records, each residing on the same page. In these cases, the first user to access the page locks it, which prohibits the other user from gaining access to that page. In this case, the second user must wait until the first user finishes with the page and it is released back to the system.

In a network system using a CALC key, the database records are randomly distributed throughout the database area. Here, DASD space for the entire database is allocated immediately by the system. Although this type system has less contention problems relative to DB2 due to the random distribution of database records, the system consumes time searching the many linked lists to find the record's location. Obviously, you can create indexes on all key search fields to speed the accessing time. The creation of an index and the readjustment of both prior and next pointers consume time, however, especially for inserts and deletions. Therefore, for random searches, the records should have indexes and for sequential searches, the records do not need indexes.

A sample IDMS/R schema is given in Figure 14.11.

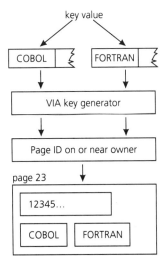

FIGURE 14.10 *The VIA location mode. The VIA key generator creates a page ID which is the same page ID as the owner of the record. In this example, the language skills of COBOL and FORTRAN are placed on the same page as their owner (employee ID 12345).*

```
ADD SCHEMA NAME IS DEPTSCHM VERSION 10
ADD FILE NAME IS DEPT001 ASSIGN TO DEPT001
ADD FILE NAME IS ...
    •
    •
    •
ADD AREA NAME IS DEPT-REGION
        RANGE IS 100200 THRU 100300
        WITHIN FILE DEPT001 1 THRU 50
ADD AREA NAME IS...
    •
    •
    •
ADD RECORD NAME IS DEPARTMENT
        SHARE STRUCTURE OF RECORD DEPARTMENT
        RECORD ID IS DEPT1
        LOCATION MODE IS CALC
        DEPT-FACULTY SET
        WITHIN AREA DEPT-REGION
        02 DEPT-NUMB         PIC X(05) USAGE IS DISPLAY.
        02 DEPT-NAME         PIC X(15) USAGE IS DISPLAY.
        02 DEPT-CHAIRMAN-ID  PIC X(05) USAGE IS DISPLAY.
        02 DEPT-LOCATION     PIC X(03) USAGE IS DISPLAY.
        03 DEPT-COST-CODE    PIC 9(05) USAGE IS DISPLAY.
ADD RECORD NAME IS FACULTY
    •
    •
    •
ADD SET NAME IS DEPT-FACULTY
        ORDER IS FIRST
        MODE IS CHAIN LINKED TO PRIOR
        OWNER IS DEPARTMENT NEXT DBKEY IS AUTO
                            PRIOR DBKEY IS AUTO
        MEMBER IS FACULTY    NEXT DBKEY IS AUTO
                            PRIOR DBKEY IS AUTO
                            LINKED TO OWNER
                            OWNER DBKEY POSITION IS AUTO
        DUPLICATES NOT ALLOWED
        OPTIONAL MANUAL.
ADD SET NAME IS...
    •
    •
    •
VALIDATE.
```

FIGURE 14.11   *A sample IDMS/R schema description. The schema identifies the files and their logical DASD location, the records, and the sets for the database. This description is then compiled using the Schema Compiler.*

THE SUBSCHEMA

While the schema defines the database to the DBMS, the subschema defines the user's view of the database. Every user must have a subschema before he or she can access the database. Although a database will have only one schema, it will have numerous subschemas—one for each user (see Figure 14.12). A sample subschema is given in Figure 14.13.

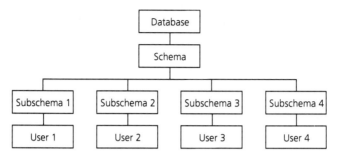

FIGURE 14.12 *Database with one schema and multiple subschemas. A user without a subschema cannot access the database.*

```
ADD SUBSCHEMA NAME IS USER1
       OF SCHEMA NAME IS DEPTSCHM
       DMCL NAME IS DEPTDMCL.
ADD AREA NAME IS DEPT-REGION.
ADD AREA NAME IS FACULTY-REGION.
ADD RECORD NAME IS DEPARTMENT.
ADD RECORD NAME IS FACULTY.
ADD RECORD NAME IS CLASSES.
ADD SET NAME IS DEPT-FACULTY.
ADD SET NAME IS FAC-CLASSES.
VALIDATE.
```

FIGURE 14.13 *A sample IDMS/R subschema for one user. A database will have one such subschema for each user of the database.*

The DBA enters the subschema commands into the system in the same way he or she enters the schema commands—by using a schema/subschema compiler language and the IDD editor. After entering each subschema, the DBA compiles it using the Subschema Compiler. The resultant compiled module, therefore, contains the security criteria for a particular user's access to the database. Each time the user accesses the database via a query, the system checks that user's subschema to verify his or her authorization to the database entity. Unauthorized accesses results in the system issuing a security violation error message. For authorized accesses, the system then uses parameters in the schema to perform the query or database call.

A LOOK AT IDMS/R

One of the more popular network database products on mainframes is IDMS from Computer Associates (formerly Cullinet Software, Inc.). IDMS, and its companion, IDMS/R, is a complete applications development tool. Unlike DB2 and IMS, IDMS/R does not rely on the existence of other software tools being on the system (i.e., COBOL, system's editors, etc.). When using IDMS/R to implement an application, the only software an installation needs is the basic operating system (i.e., MVS/XA) and the IDMS/R subsystem.

Some major components of IDMS/R include the following:

- IDD—*Integrated Data Dictionary*. The IDD is the main dictionary containing all the definitions and entities created by IDMS.
- OLM—*Online Mapping*. Programmers use OLM to generate screens and application prototypes.
- ADS/O—*Application Development System/Online*. An application development tool that quickly and easily develops and executes online applications that interact with a database.
- ADS/A—*Application Development System/Applications*. A facility that links responses and functions together. It also provides the communications link between screens.
- ADS/G—*Application Development System/Generation*. A facility that links dialogs, screens, and other entities to the database data and creates the application structure.
- OLQ—*Online Query*. A query language to access database records.

Designing an Application Using IDMS/R

One of the main advantages of IDMS/R is its ability to create applications quickly. The first step in creating an IDMS/R application is to create the schema for the database and several subschemas for its users. The DBA enters the schema and subschema statements via the IDD editor and compiles them using the schema and subschema compilers. The resultant modules are stored in the IDD. The IDD is an active dictionary. That is, because it contains all the modules for all the entities created within IDMS/R, it is constantly being accessed by the users and by the system.

After the database is defined by the DBA, the remaining tasks for creating an application are left to the application development team. These tasks include the:

- Generating of the screens for the user's application (a process called **painting** the screen)
- Identifying of the valid responses for each of these screens
- Writing of the code (in the form of a dialog) to access database records, perform calculations, and other activities

OLM

The programmer's first step in creating a user application is to use OLM to define the screens' layout. OLM is a menu-driven product that allows programmers to paint screens, assign variable names to data items on those screens, and designate other parameters for screens. These screens later can be linked together to form a prototype for the application. Figure 14.14 contains a chart outlining the major steps in using OLM. A name is assigned to the

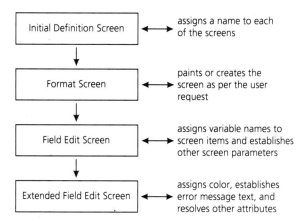

FIGURE 14.14 *Four major options within OLM.*

screen using the initial definition option. Then you paint or format the screen using the format screen option. After the screen is painted, you assign variable names to items on it using the field edit option. Other screen formatting options are available in the extended field edit option.

After formatting or painting each of the screens for the application, they are linked together using a combination of ADS/A and ADS/G (see Figure 14.15).

ADS/A and ADS/G

ADS/A is a **menu-driven product** that links screens together and establishes a network of communications between them. The three main facilities within ADS/A are:

- The response definition screen
- The function definition screen
- The valid response screen

Before using ADS/A, you have to identify all the valid responses available for all the screens within the application. You need to list all the possible valid responses per screen. Then you must compile a list of the programs

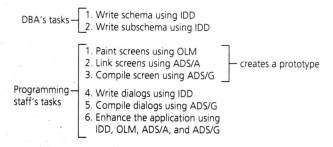

FIGURE 14.15 *Steps in creating an IDMS/R application.*

(called functions) each response initiates. For example, you might determine that the response of entering the statement "ADD" and pressing the return key will transfer control to the program ADD001.

After identifying all the responses, you code them into the system using the response definition screen. Next, you select the function definition screen and identify the names of functions that will later be associated with these responses. In this case, a function includes the screen definition, the records associated with the screen, and the dialogs for accessing the database. Finally, you select the valid response screen and tag each of the functions to a specific response (for example, the response "ADD" activates the function "FADD01").

In this initial creation of the screens, the programs or dialogs are dummy programs or dialogs. IDMS/R generates skeleton code so that this part of the application works without the writing of code.

After you load all the functions and responses and identify their interrelationships, you use ADS/G to identify the main calling program or screen and compile the application. The resultant module is a load module executable only in IDMS/R's operating environment. Then you execute the main calling program (usually a main menu) and test the application and the linkage between the screens.

All you have created so far is a prototype of the application. Because you have not written any code to date, the system will not make any calls to the database. You can, however, test each of the responses per screen to determine if that response transfers control to the correct program or screen. Here, because ADS/A establishes the communication linkage between the screens, you are verifying that the linkage you created is the correct linkage for the application. In addition, this prototype enables the user department to verify the initial design of the screens and the fluidity of the application.

IDD

The final step in developing the application is to write the code or dialogs for each of the screens. You use the editor of IDD to write the dialogs to access the database. IDD is the main dictionary containing all the definitions and entities created by IDMS. All data and the application definitions created by the DBA and yourself are stored in the IDD.

After you write the dialogs using IDD, use ADS/G to recompile the modules within the application. Then test the entire application and make any corrections using the OLM, IDD, ADS/A, and ADS/G facilities.

SUMMARY

Network databases contain owner and member records. Unlike relational and hierarchical databases, in a network an owner can have multiple members and a member can have multiple owners. An occurrence diagram illustrates the arrangement of owner and member records within the database. The diagram aids programmers in writing the code for the navigation of the database. The code that accesses the database is called a dialog.

The schema defines the database's record description, the owner-member relationships, and the set descriptions. The set description identifies the type of pointers the system uses when accessing a record. The three types of pointers are forward pointers (next), backward pointers (prior), and owner pointers. The set description also identifies where new records are inserted (first, last, next, prior, and sorted), how they are connected (automatic or manual) and disconnected (mandatory, optional), how they are physically stored on DASD (CALC or VIA), and how duplicates are handled (duplicates first, duplicates last, duplicates not allowed).

A subschema is a security mechanism that identifies the files, records, and sets a particular user can access on the database. Each database must have one schema to define the physical characteristics of the database. In addition, the database will have multiple subschemas, one for each user. The DBA enters the schema and subschemas into the system using the database editor. He or she then must compile them using the schema and subschema compilers.

IDMS/R is a popular network DBMS and contains a series of products that enable systems to be developed quickly and efficiently. The IDD contains all the components of IDMS/R along with the description and structure of all the entities for the database. The OLM facility lets programmers generate application screens. The ADS/A facility links screens and establishes the communications network between them. The ADS/G facility is the main compiler that links screens, database entities, and programs together.

QUESTIONS

1. What is the difference between an owner-member relationship and a parent-child relationship?
2. A user wants to access data in two separate databases. How do we authorize that user to access data in these databases?
3. What are some of the advantages of using next, prior, and owner pointers? What are some of the disadvantages?
4. Under what conditions could you eliminate the need for prior and owner pointers?
5. Network databases have a disconnect and connect option. Is there an equivalent function in DB2?
6. IDMS/R has the option duplicates not allowed. How do you accomplish the same task in DB2?
7. What are some of the benefits to using a VIA key?
8. Conceptually, what are some of the differences between the IDD and the DB2 catalog?
9. Figure 14.15 lists the steps in creating an IDMS/R application. Design a similar list for creating a non-IDMS/R application using VSAM files. Design a similar list for creating a DB2 application.
10. How is security implemented in IDMS/R?
11. What is a set? How does IDMS/R implement set definitions? Who defines the structure of a set?
12. What advantages do network databases have over relational databases?

15 *Hierarchical Databases*

As a model of hierarchical databases, we will examine one of the most widely used hierarchical databases, IBM's Information Management System (IMS). In this discussion of IMS, we will first examine conceptual models of hierarchical databases, followed by physical implementations of hierarchical databases. Next, we will discuss how to define an IMS database to the system via the creating of the schema and subschema for the database. Finally, we will examine methods of manipulating the database using DL/I in batch and on-line systems.

But why study an antiquated database structure? The answer is simple. IBM's IMS is *the* prominent hierarchical database used by most large mainframe installations. Although the concept and principles of hierarchical databases might be archaic by today's standards, most large database shops have a significant investment in IMS and its supporting software code. Therefore, we cannot neglect hierarchical relationships because billions of lines of code in millions of programs exist using the hierarchical structure. And these programs will not disappear anytime in the near future. Most database programmers and designers, therefore, will need a working knowledge of IMS to access already existing data resident in IMS databases.

Remember, in a production environment, it might not be economical, or even feasible, to convert existing hierarchical databases into the more convenient relational structure. Even state-of-the-art shops with the best relational software and technology probably will have to upload or download data to and from the already existing IMS databases.

In addition, IMS is more than 17 years old and most, if not all, of its idiosyncrasies are well documented. It is a mature product that works—and works very well. Remember, in a production environment, the number of transactions per second often is a significant factor in deciding which database product (and structure) to use. IMS can handle about 65 transactions per second, while DB2 (a popular mainframe relational database) can handle only 35 to 45 transactions per second. When an installation must process millions of transactions per day, that installation might have no other choice than to implement IMS as its preferred database and that decision might be based solely on performance considerations.

OVERVIEW OF IMS

IMS has two components, a database (DB) component and a data communications (DC) component. The DB component manages database I/O, and the DC component manages terminal I/O. You can run other types of database managers under the IMS DC component (e.g., DB2). Also, you can run the IMS DB component under other types of communications managers, such as CICS.

In this chapter, we will focus on the DB component and only briefly cover the DC component. The DB component consists of the database language, DL/I, which is used in conjunction with some other programming language, such as COBOL, PL/I, FORTRAN, or Assembler Language. Again, we will use COBOL descriptions to define the data characteristics of an IMS database. Appendix B contains a short discussion on how to implement an IMS application program using COBOL.

BASIC DEFINITIONS FOR HIERARCHICAL DATABASES

Hierarchical databases contain segments arranged in a tree or hierarchical structure. The topmost segment in the hierarchy is called the **root segment** and the remaining segments are called **dependent segments.** Each dependent segment is the parent of the segment(s) immediately under it or is a child of the segment immediately above it. Child segments also can be parent segments if dependent segments exist under the child. If a parent has more than one child, then those children are called **siblings.** If there are multiple occurrences of a segment in a parent or child, those occurrences are called **twins** (see Figure 15.1).

The structure of a hierarchical database requires the segments to have a one-to-one or a one-to-many relationship with other segments in the structure. That means a parent can have one child (a one-to-one relationship) or many children (a one-to-many relationship). Each child, however, can have only one parent, which means many-to-many relationships are not allowed.

THE HIERARCHICAL MODEL

Figure 15.2 shows a typical database structure for an insurance company. We will identify the database as POLICY to IMS. This example is a conceptual model of the database. It bears no direct relationship to the physical structure of the database nor does it fully detail the logical database structure that the programmer will use. Typically, a systems analyst creates such a diagram as

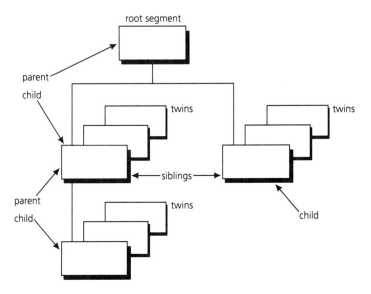

FIGURE 15.1   *Parent, child, twins, and siblings in hierarchical structure.*

a part of the database design process. The diagram is known as a **hierarchy chart.**

Remember, Figure 15.2 shows the hierarchical relationships betweeen the segments as well as the segment names. The name of the segment is used in defining the database to the IMS software and serves the same function as a record name in IDMS/R or a table name in DB2. Each segment name can be from one to eight alphanumeric characters in length.

The root segment (PLCYHLDR) in Figure 15.2 contains data about the policyholder. It has one child (PLCY) that contains data about the policies owned by a policyholder. The policy segment has the three children CLAIM, BILL, and PAYMENT that contain data about claims filed under the policy, bills for premiums sent to the policyholder, and premium payments made by the policyholder, respectively.

Figure 15.3 shows a COBOL description of each segment and details the data each segment contains.

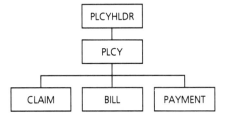

FIGURE 15.2   *The POLICY database structure. A systems analyst created this conceptual model. It bears no relationship to the physical structure of the database.*

```
01 PLCYHLDR-SEGMENT
      03 PLCYHLDR-SOC-SEC-NO        PIC 9(9).
      03 PLCYHLDR-NAME.
          05 PLCYHLDR-NAME-FIRST    PIC X(20).
          05 PLCYHLDR-NAME-MIDDLE   PIC X(20).
          05 PLCYHLDR-NAME-LAST     PIC X(20).
      03 PLCYHLDR-ADDR.
          05 PLCYHLDR-ADDR-STREET.
              07 PLCYHLDR-ADDR-STREET-1  PIC X(40).
              07 PLCYHLDR-ADDR-STREET-2  PIC X(40).
              07 PLCYHLDR-ADDR-STREET-3  PIC X(40).
          05 PLCYHLDR-CITY          PIC X(20).
          05 PLCYHLDR-STATE         PIC X(2).
          05 PLCYHLDR-ZIP           PIC 9(5).
      03 PLCYHLDR-BIRTH-DATE.
          05 PLCYHLDR-BIRTH-DATE-YEAR   PIC 9(2).
          05 PLCYHLDR-BIRTH-DATE-MONTH  PIC 9(2).
          05 PLCYHLDR-BIRTH-DATE-DAY    PIC 9(2).

01 PLCY-SEGMENT.
      03 PLCY-NO                    PIC 9(10).
      03 PLCY-TERM                  PIC 99.
      03 PLCY-PREMIUM               PIC 9(4)V99.
      03 PLCY-DATE-SIGNED
          05 PLCY-DATE-SIGNED-YEAR  PIC 9(2).
          05 PLCY-DATE-SIGNED-MONTH PIC 9(2).
          05 PLCY-DATE-SIGNED-DAY   PIC 9(2).
      03 PLCY-STATE-SIGNED          PIC XX.
      03 PLCY-BENEFIT-LIMIT         PIC 9(5)V99.

01 CLAIM-SEGMENT.
      03 CLAIM-NO                   PIC 9(10).
      03 CLAIM-AMOUNT               PIC 9(5)V99.
      03 CLAIM-DISPOSITION          PIC 9.
      03 CLAIM-PAID-DATE.
          05 CLAIM-PAID-DATE-YEAR   PIC 9(2).
          05 CLAIM-PAID-DATE-MONTH  PIC 9(2).
          05 CLAIM-PAID-DATE-DAY    PIC 9(2).

01 BILL-SEGMENT.
      03 BILL-NO                    PIC 9(10).
      03 BILL-DATE.
          05 BILL-DATE-YEAR         PIC 9(2).
          05 BILL-DATE-MONTH        PIC 9(2).
          05 BILL-DATE-DAY          PIC 9(2).

01 PAYMENT-SEGMENT.
      03 PAYMENT-NO                 PIC 9(10).
      03 PAYMENT-DATE.
          05 PAYMENT-DATE-YEAR      PIC 9(2).
          05 PAYMENT-DATE-MONTH     PIC 9(2).
          05 PAYMENT-DATE-DAY       PIC 9(2).
```

FIGURE 15.3 *A COBOL description of the segments in the POLICY database. The COBOL data definitions, combined with the database's hierarchy chart, comprise the programmer's view of the database.*

In Figure 15.3, the policyholder segment (PLCYHLDR) contains the:

- Policyholder's social security number (which is the key of the segment)
- Name
- Address
- Date of birth

The policy segment (PLCY) contains the:

- Policy number (the key)
- Policy term (the basis on which the policy comes up for renewal)
- Premium for the policy
- Date the policy was signed
- State where the policy was signed
- Maximum benefit payable under the policy.

The claim segment (CLAIM) contains the:

- Claim number (the key)
- Amount the claim was filed for
- Disposition of the claim (whether the insurance company accepted and paid the claim or instead contested the claim as being outside the coverage of the policy)
- Date the claim was paid or zeroes if it has not been paid

The bill segment (BILL) contains the:

- Bill number (the key)
- Date payment is due on the bill

The payment segment (PAYMENT) contains:

- An arbitrarily assigned payment number (the key)
- The date payment was received

The COBOL data descriptions, combined with the hierarchy chart, comprise the programmer's view of the database.

Each segment in the above example has a key. Although keys are not necessary, they allow the accessing of segments via direct access, for example, by using the GU DL/I function. If a segment does not have a key, you must access it sequentially, by using the GN function. All these functions will be discussed later.

Figure 15.4 shows another example of a typical database, called AGENTDB, that the insurance company might maintain. This database contains data on commissions paid to the insurance company's agents. The root segment (AGENT) contains data on the agent, while its children contain data on the policies that are serviced by an agent (PLCY) and on commission payments made to that agent (COMMPMT).

Figure 15.5 shows the COBOL data definitions for the segments in the agent database. In this figure the agent segment contains the agent's social

FIGURE 15.4   *The AGENTDB database. This database contains data on commissions paid to the insurance company's agents.*

security number (the key) and his or her name and address. The policy segment contains policy number (the key), which is the same as the policy number in the POLICY database, the commission rate paid to the agent for servicing the policy, and the base amount on which the commission is figured. The commission payment segment contains the payment number (the key) and the date that each payment was made.

Both of the previous examples illustrate how easily a hierarchical structure can handle one-to-many relationships. In the POLICY database, for example, each policyholder can have several policies, while each policy can have many claims on it, can generate many billings, and have many payments. Similarly, in the AGENTDB database, an agent can have many policies that he or she serves and can have many commission payments made to him or her.

```
01 AGENT-SEGMENT
    03 AGENT-SOC-SEC-NO              PIC 9(9).
    03 AGENT-NAME.
        05  AGENT-NAME-FIRST         PIC X(20).
        05  AGENT-NAME-MIDDLE        PIC X(20).
        05  AGENT-NAME-LAST          PIC X(20).
    03 AGENT-ADDR.
        05  AGENT-ADDR-STREET.
            07  AGENT-ADDR-STREET-1  PIC X(40).
            07  AGENT-ADDR-STREET-2  PIC X(40).
            07  AGENT-ADDR-STREET-3  PIC X(40).
        05 AGENT-CITY                PIC X(20).
        05 AGENT-STATE               PIC X(2).
        05 AGENT-ZIP                 PIC 9(5).

01 PLCY-SEGMENT.
    03 PLCY-NO                       PIC 9(10).
    03 PLCY-COMMISSION.
        05 PLCY-COMMISSION-RATE      PIC V999.
        05 PLCY-COMMISSION-BASE      PIC 9(5)V99.

01 COMMPMT-SEGMENT.
    03 COMMPMT-NO                    PIC 9(10).
    03 COMMPMT-DATE.
        05 COMMPMT-DATE-YEAR         PIC 9(2).
        05 COMMPMT-DATE-MONTH        PIC 9(2).
        05 COMMPMT-DATE-DAY          PIC 9(2).
```

FIGURE 15.5   *COBOL data definitions for the AGENTDB database. This figure shows in detail the data in each segment.*

THE IMS DATABASE

The Logical Database

The POLICY and AGENTDB databases use hierarchy charts and detail definitions of the fields in each segment. The hierarchy charts give a conceptual view of the database that shows the parent-child relationships. In particular, the hierarchy charts in conjunction with the field definitions describe the programmer's view of the databases. These do not define the physical storage structures of the databases. For now, we will assume that these are two independent and separate physical databases. Let's now consider how they can be processed.

The POLICY database maintains data on policies owned by a policyholder. It also maintains data on claims, billing, and payments. You can, for example, query this database to determine a policyholder's payment history to determine how promptly he or she pays premiums. In addition, you can analyze the policyholder's claims and premium payments to determine whether he or she is a good risk.

The AGENTDB database maintains data on agents, the policies they sell and service, and the commissions paid to them.

What if someone wants data from both databases? For example, suppose a field sales manager wants a report that analyzes claim and premium data on policies sold by each agent to determine the quality of the business that an agent typically solicits? You could do this with the current database structures because the policy number is kept in both databases. A program could, for example, read the AGENTDB database sequentially to access each agent. Then, for each agent, it could read the policy segments sequentially to access the policies he or she sold. Then, for each policy, it could read the POLICY database directly to access the premium and claim data.

This method of processing, however, requires the program to keep track of two databases. An easier method is to create a **logical database** that uses data from both physical databases. Creating the logical database is typically done by the DBA.

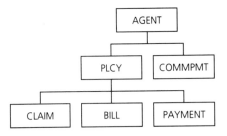

FIGURE 15.6   *The AGPOLICY database. This is a logical database that allows you to conveniently access data from two physical databases.*

Figure 15.6 shows a logical database known as AGPOLICY that contains data from POLICY and AGENTDB.

The AGENT, PLCY, and COMMPMT segments are physically stored in the AGENTDB database, while the CLAIM, BILL, and PAYMENT segments are physically stored in the POLICY database. To a program, however, AGPOLICY appears to be a physical database that contains all of these segments.

Now the processing logic is much simpler. You can write a program, for example, to read the AGPOLICY database sequentially to access each agent. For each agent, it can read the policy segments sequentially to access the policies he or she sold. For each policy, it can sequentially read the premium and claim data. Here, you avoid having to do any direct I/O because sequential I/O consumes less resources than direct I/O.

The Secondary Index

A feature that is closely related to logical databases is secondary indexing. A program can access the POLICY database directly if it has the policyholder's social security number. Many times, however, you might want to access the database without using the social security number. For example, on mail correspondence, the policyholder might fail to give his or her social security number, but might give, for example, a policy number. In this case, it would be very convenient to be able to access the database via the PLCY segment rather than the root segment.

Because the PLCY segment has a key (the policy number), it is possible to do this with the current database structure. Later we will discuss using a Segment Search Argument (SSA) to search for a given policy. For now, however, it is sufficient to know that an SSA can be used to qualify the search by giving IMS a specific policy ID number. This can produce a large overhead in time and DASD space because, in some cases, IMS must search the database sequentially from the beginning to find the segment. But the root segment has an index while other segments do not.

You (or the DBA), however, can define a secondary index on a nonroot segment (e.g., the PLCY segment). The database would appear to a program as shown in Figure 15.7.

The segments above the segment with the secondary index appear in reverse hierarchical order, for example, the parent of PLCY (PLCYHLDR) be-

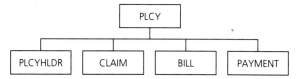

FIGURE 15.7   *The POLICY database with a secondary index on PLCY, as it appears to a program. The segments above the segment with a secondary index appear in reverse hierarchical order.*

comes its child. If the PLCYHLDR segment had parents, they would become its children. The program can now directly access the PLCY segment in an efficient manner. Also, because you no longer need to code an SSA, the program can access the PLCY segment in a somewhat simpler manner.

Schema and Subschema: The DBDGEN and the PSBGEN

The schema for a database is its complete description including all fields in the database, while its subschema is a description of the database as seen by an application program. IMS does not necessarily contain a full definition of schema and subschema for any particular database; some elements of both might be located only in programs or external documentation. The tools that the DBA uses to define various elements of schema and subschema are the DBDGEN and the PSBGEN.

The DBDGEN uses a set of assembler macro statements to define a database. Figure 15.8 shows what some of the DBDGEN statements might look like for the POLICY database. Note that Figure 15.8 does not show all of the DBDGEN statements that are possible, or even necessary, to describe the database. Instead, the major components are abstracted.

The DBDGEN statements begin with the DBD macro that specifies the name of the database. It also specifies the physical access method for this database, which is HDAM implemented with VSAM. Because we have not yet discussed the physical database structure, it is only important to know, for now, that

```
DBD        NAME=POLICY,ACCESS=(HDAM,VSAM)

SEGM       NAME=PLCYHLDR,PARENT=0,BYTES=222
FIELD      NAME=(PLCYHSSN,SEQ),START=1,BYTES=9,
           TYPE=Z

SEGM       NAME=PLCY,PARENT=PLCYHLDR,BYTES=32
FIELD      NAME=(PLCYNO,SEQ),START=1,BYTES=10,
           TYPE=Z

SEGM       NAME=CLAIM,PARENT=PLCY,BYTES=24
FIELD      NAME=(CLAIMNO,SEQ),START=1,BYTES=10,
           TYPE=Z
FIELD      NAME=CLAIMDAT,START=18,BYTES=6,TYPE=Z

SEGM       NAME=BILL,PARENT=PLCY,BYTES=16
FIELD      NAME=(BILLNO,SEQ),START=1,BYTES=10,
           TYPE=Z
FIELD      NAME=BILLDAT,START=11,BYTES=6,TYPE=Z

SEGM       NAME=PAYMENT,PARENT=PLCY,BYTES=16
FIELD      NAME=(PAYMTNO,SEQ),START=1,BYTES=10,
           TYPE=Z
FIELD      NAME=PAYMTDAT,START=11,BYTES=6,TYPE=Z

DBDGEN
```

FIGURE 15.8 *A DBDGEN for the POLICY database. This is not a complete DBDGEN.*

ACCESS = (HDAM, VSAM) indicates that this is a physical database (as opposed to a logical database).

The DBD macro is followed by a series of SEGM macros, which define the segments of the database. Each SEGM macro is followed by one or more FIELD macros, which define certain fields in each segment.

The first SEGM macro in Figure 15.8 defines the root segment as PLCYHLDR (PARENT = 0). Note that the other segments, which are all child segments, specify the actual name of the parent segment. In addition, these dependent segments contain a code for the total number of bytes in the segment (BYTES =).

Each SEGM macro has one or more FIELD macros following it. These macros define certain fields in the database. You can define all fields in the database, but it is not required. Instead, you can define only those fields that are key fields or that you intend to use in SSAs. This is why IMS might not contain a complete schema for a database, because the DBA might elect not to define all the fields. In this example, we have chosen to define only key fields and date fields in some segments. This allows you to code SSAs for a specific database search (for instance, to find all claims after a given date).

Each FIELD macro specifies the name of the field, the beginning location of the field in the segment, the length of the field in bytes, and the field type. There are several different types of fields that you can specify, corresponding basically to the different data storage formats on an IBM mainframe. In this case we have chosen "Z" for zoned decimal, which is basically numeric data in EBCDIC format. In addition to the data in Figure 15.8, field statements for key fields specify the field name in parentheses followed by a comma and "SEQ." "SEQ" indicates that the field is a sequence field (i.e., a key field). Names for fields are used in SSAs and can be up to eight alphanumeric characters in length.

The final macro used in the DBDGEN is the DBDGEN macro. This macro is used to mark the end of the DBDGEN statements. Figure 15.9 shows the DBDGEN code for the AGENTDB database.

Part of the subschema for a database also can be found in the DBDGEN.

```
DBD        NAME=AGENTDB,ACCESS=(HDAM,VSAM)

SEGM       NAME=AGAGENT,PARENT=0,BYTES=216
FIELD      NAME=(AGENTSSN,SEQ),START=1,BYTES=9,
           TYPE=Z

SEGM       NAME=AGPLCY,PARENT=AGAGENT,BYTES=20
FIELD      NAME=(AGPLCYNO,SEQ),START=1,BYTES=10,
           TYPE=Z

SEGM       NAME=AGCOMM,PARENT=AGAGENT,BYTES=16
FIELD      NAME=(AGCOMNO,SEQ),START=1,BYTES=10
FIELD      NAME=AGCOMDAT,START=11,BYTES=6,TYPE=Z

DBDGEN
```

FIGURE 15.9 *A DBDGEN for the AGENTDB database. The DBDGEN macros serve the same function as those used in Figure 15.8.*

Don't forget that there are two types of logical "views" on an IMS database that a program can have and that bear no relationship to the physical database structure. These are a logical database description and a secondary index.

To create a logical database, you need to run a DBDGEN for the physical databases involved as well as the logical database itself. Figure 15.10 shows the DBDGEN statements for the AGPOLICY database.

Like any DBDGEN, you begin with a DBD macro that specifies the name of the database and identifies this database as a logical database via the ACCESS=LOGICAL parameter. SEGM macros are coded the same way as when defining a physical database. You code NAME and PARENT parameters to define the parent-child relationships, but you do not code a BYTES parameter, nor do you code any FIELD macros. Instead, you point to the segment from a physical database via the SOURCE statement. The physical databases must already have been DBDGENed before you can define a logical database that uses them.

To define a secondary index on a database, first define the physical database itself. This time you will do this somewhat differently than you have done so far. As you will see when you examine physical database structure, a secondary index on a database is itself a physical database, though this is transparent to the application program. Figure 15.11 shows the DBDGEN statements for the POLICY database that are needed to support a secondary index.

Notice that we have added two macros to the database definition—an LCHILD macro and an XDFLD macro. Both macros define part of the PLCY segment, which is the segment you will index. The LCHILD macro defines the index database segment that will be used to index the PLCY segment, in this case, the PLCYIX segment from the PLCYIXDB database, which we have yet to define. The XDFLD macro defines the logical field that is to be indexed (i.e.,

```
DBD         NAME=AGPOLICY,ACCESS=LOGICAL
SEGM        NAME=APAGENT,PARENT=0,
            SOURCE=((AGAGENT,,AGENTDB))
SEGM        NAME=APPLCY,PARENT=APAGENT,
            SOURCE=((AGPLCY,,AGENTDB))
SEGM        NAME=APCOMMPM,PARENT=APAGENT,
            SOURCE=((PLCY,,POLICY))
SEGM        NAME=APCLAIM,PARENT=APPLCY,
            SOURCE=((CLAIM,,POLICY))
SEGM        NAME=APBILL,PARENT=APPLCY,
            SOURCE=((BILL,,POLICY))
SEGM        NAME=APPAYMT,PARENT=APPLCY,
            SOURCE=((BILL,,POLICY))
DBDGEN
```

FIGURE 15.10   *A DBDGEN for the AGPLCY database. This is a logical database composed of data from two physical databases.*

```
DBD            NAME=POLICY,ACCESS=(HDAM,VSAM)

SEGM           NAME=PLCYHLDR,PARENT=0,BYTES=222
FIELD          NAME=(PLCYHSSN,SEQ),START=1,BYTES=9,
               TYPE=Z

SEGM           NAME=PLCY,PARENT=PLCYHLDR,BYTES=32
LCHILD         NAME=(PLCYIX,PLCYIXDB),POINTER=INDX
FIELD          NAME=(PLCYNO,SEQ),START=1,BYTES=10,
               TYPE=Z
XDFLD          NAME=PLCYNOIX,SRCH=PLCYNO

SEGM           NAME=CLAIM,PARENT=PLCY,BYTES=24
FIELD          NAME=(CLAIMNO,SEQ),START=1,BYTES=10,
               TYPE=Z
FIELD          NAME=CLAIMDAT,START=18,BYTES=6,TYPE=Z

SEGM           NAME=BILL,PARENT=PLCY,BYTES=16
FIELD          NAME=(BILLNO,SEQ),START=1,BYTES=10,
               TYPE=Z
FIELD          NAME=BILLDAT,START=11,BYTES=6,TYPE=Z

SEGM           NAME=PAYMENT,PARENT=PLCY,BYTES=16
FIELD          NAME=(PAYMTNO,SEQ),START=1,BYTES=10,
               TYPE=Z
FIELD          NAME=PAYMTDAT,START=11,BYTES=6,TYPE=Z

DBDGEN
```

FIGURE 15.11   *A DBDGEN for the POLICY database with a secondary index on the PLCY segment. Note that LCHILD and XDFLD macros have been added for the PLCY segment.*

PLCYNOIX). Then you code a SRCH parameter to indicate that this field is to be used to index the field PLCYNO.

Figure 15.12 shows the DBDGEN statements for the index database. In this figure a DBD statement defines the name of the database and identifies it as an index database via the ACCESS parameter. The single SEGM statement with the LCHILD parameter indicates the segment to index (i.e., the PLCY segment in the POLICY database). The INDEX parameter specifies the indexed field (i.e., PLCYNOIX). This is a logical field that was specified by the XDFLD macro in the DBDGEN for the POLICY database. The physical field, PLCYIXN2, contains the index data and is identified as a key field for this database via the SEQ parameter.

The remainder of the subschema is defined by the PSBGEN. The PSBGEN creates a Program Specification Block (PSB) for a program. Each program that

```
DBD            NAME=PLCYIXDB,ACCESS=INDEX

SEGM           NAME=PLCYIX,PARENT=0,BYTES=10
LCHILD         NAME=(PLCY,POLICY),INDEX=PLCYNOIX
FIELD          NAME=(PLCYIXN2,SEQ),START=1,BYTES=10,
               TYPE=Z

DBDGEN
```

FIGURE 15.12   *A DBDGEN for the secondary index database for the POLICY database. A secondary index requires a second physical database that is transparent to the application program.*

is to access an IMS database must have a PSB defined for each database it is
to access. The PSB defines the program's view of the database, that is, which
segments or fields the program can access and how it can access them. For
example, assume that the program PLCYRPT is to print reports from the data
in the POLICY database. A set of PSBGEN statements for such a program is
shown in Figure 15.13.

A Program Communications Block (PCB) macro identifies the database
that the program will access. The TYPE parameter indicates that this is a
database PCB. For this example, IMS's DC component requires the PCBs to be
coded for terminals. The DBDNAME parameter gives the name of the database
as it was defined in the DBDGEN.

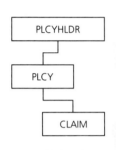

The KEYLEN parameter is used to define the maximum length of all keys
for any possible hierarchical path that the program might use to access a
segment. For example, suppose that you want to access data about a claim
on a given policy for a given policyholder. The CLAIM segment is a child of
the PLCY segment, which is in turn a child of the PLCYHLDR segment. The
hierarchical path to the desired segment is shown in the diagram at the left

Hierarchical path.

Notice that PLCYHLDR has a key that is nine bytes long, while PLCY and
CLAIM each have keys that are 10 bytes long. Thus, 29 bytes would be needed
to contain all keys that would be used to access a given CLAIM segment. In
fact, 29 bytes is the maximum size of all keys needed to reach any segment
(not just the CLAIM segment), so we use the code KEYLEN=29 in the PCB
macro. Two additional matters are of interest here. First, the reason we must
define this key length is because IMS will use this information to construct a
buffer that it uses when accessing the database. Second, as a matter of terminology, the 29-byte sequence consisting of the nine-byte PLCYHLDR key
followed by the ten-byte PLCY key followed by the ten-byte CLAIM key is
known as a **concatenated key.**

The final parameter in the PCB macro is the Processing Options (PROCOPT)
parameter. This parameter determines how the program can access the data
in the database, that is, whether it can read, update, or add data. In this case,
you have limited the program to reading data by specifying G (Get) as the
only processing option. You could add other options, if needed, to allow the
program to update data, delete data, load data into an empty database, etc.

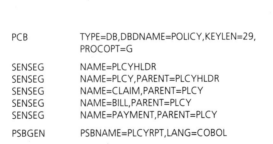

FIGURE 15.13   *A possible PSBGEN for the POLICY database. This PSBGEN defines segment-level sensitivity.*

The PROCOPT parameter defines the processing options for the entire database. In addition, a PROCOPT parameter in the SENSEG macros can define the different processing options for each segment in the database.

After you finish the previous procedure, the SENSEG macros now define the segments that the program is sensitive to, that is, that it can access. This is known as **segment-level sensitivity.** Segment-level sensitivity implies that a program can access all of the data in one or more segments. You also can define **field-level sensitivity,** however, so that a program can access only certain fields within certain segments. In this case, you have only defined segment-level sensitivity, and you have used SENSEG macros to give the program sensitivity to all segments in the POLICY database. The segment names are those names that are coded in the DBDGEN.

The final macro is the PSBGEN macro, which names the PSB and specifies, via the LANG parameter, the programming language that will be used in this program, here COBOL.

A PSBGEN for a logical database would be very similar to one for a physical database. Although, for the PCB and SENSEG macros, you would reference the database and field names in the logical database DBDGEN rather than in the physical database DBDGENs. A PSBGEN for a database with a secondary index is coded somewhat differently, however. Figure 15.14 shows a PSBGEN for the POLICY database that uses the secondary index on the PLCY segment.

The first difference is in the PCB macro, where the code KEYLEN=20 appears instead of the code KEYLEN=29. Recall from Figure 15.7 that a database has a different hierarchical structure when using a secondary index. Basically, the indexed segment (PLCY) becomes the logical root segment, and the other segments are subordinate to it. This explains why the KEYLEN parameter on the PCB macro now has a different value. Because you now have a two-level hierarchical design, and because no segment has a key field that is longer than ten bytes, the maximum length for a concatenated key is twenty bytes.

Another difference in the PCB macro is the addition of the processing sequence (PROCSEQ) parameter. In this case you specify the name of the index database, as defined in its DBDGEN. If you do not specify a processing sequence, IMS will access a database specified in a PSBGEN via the root segment rather than the segment with the secondary index.

```
PCB        TYPE=DB,DBDNAME=POLICY,KEYLEN=20,
           PROCOPT=G,PROCSEQ=PLCYIXDB

SENSEG     NAME=PLCY
SENSEG     NAME=PLCYHLDR,PARENT=PLCY
SENSEG     NAME=CLAIM,PARENT=PLCY
SENSEG     NAME=BILL,PARENT=PLCY
SENSEG     NAME=PAYMENT,PARENT=PLCY

PSBGEN     PSBNAME=PLCYRPTX,LANG=COBOL
```

FIGURE 15.14   *Another PSBGEN for the POLICY database. This PSBGEN makes use of the secondary index on the PLCY segment.*

Because the hierarchical structure is different, the SENSEG macros are rearranged and coded differently to reflect the new database structure.

Finally, you give the PSB a new name in the PSBGEN macro. Having two PSBs will allow a program to access the database through both the root segment as well as the segment with the secondary index.

PHYSICAL DATABASE STRUCTURE

Thus far, we have examined hierarchical databases as they might be viewed by system designers and application programmers. The DBA also must concern himself or herself with how the databases are physically stored. In this section we will examine the major types of physical database structure, although there are some other types that are seldom used. Also, recall that the most recent version of IMS, designed to run under the MVS/ESA operating system, can use hiperspace for certain data structures. In other words, while we will assume that databases reside on secondary storage (tape or disk), it is possible that certain data will reside in an area of main memory that is treated like secondary storage but that has much faster access rates.

IMS has two major types of database structure—sequential and direct. Each type has two variations, giving a total of four major IMS database structures. There are other structures, but they are not used frequently. Table 15.1 lists each structure with notes on common ways of pronouncing the acronyms. (The emphasis is on the italic syllables.)

The sequential database structures, HSAM and HISAM, store data in what is known as hierarchical sequence. Hierarchical sequence involves storing each segment in order by its key, followed by each of its children, also in order.

TABLE 15.1 *The four major IMS database structures*

Sequential Access Structures	
HSAM	hierarchical sequential access method pronounced "huh-*sam*" or "*aitch*-sam"
HISAM	hierarchical indexed sequential access method pronounced "*high*-sam"
Direct Access Structures	
HDAM	hierarchical direct access method pronounced "huh-*dam*" or "*aitch*-dam"
HIDAM	hierarchical indexed direct access method pronounced "*high*-dam"

```
PLCYHLDR: 000000001
    PLCY: 0000000001
            CLAIM: 0000000001
            CLAIM: 0000000002
            BILL: 0000000001
            BILL: 0000000002
            PAYMENT: 0000000001
            PAYMENT: 0000000002
    PLCY: 0000000002
            CLAIM: 0000000003
            CLAIM: 0000000004
            BILL: 0000000003
            BILL: 0000000004
            PAYMENT: 0000000003
            PAYMENT: 0000000004

PLCYHLDR: 000000002
    PLCY: 0000000003

PLCYHLDR: 000000003
    PLCY: 0000000004
            BILL: 0000000005
            PAYMENT: 0000000005
    PLCY: 0000000005
            CLAIM: 0000000005
            BILL: 0000000006
            PAYMENT: 0000000006
```

FIGURE 15.15   *Sample data for the POLICY database. Only the keys are shown.*

Figure 15.15 shows some data for the POLICY database, arranged in hierarchical sequence. In this example, only the keys are shown for brevity.

In Figure 15.15 only three policyholders exist in the database. The first has two policies, each with two claims, two bills, and two payments. The second has only one policy with no claims, no bills, and no payments. (Presumably, this is a new policy.) The third has two policies, each with one bill and one payment; one has no claims and one has one claim. To list these segments in hierarchical sequence, we list, for each policyholder, all policies he or she owns along with all claims, bills, and payments for each policy.

HSAM Databases

HSAM databases are the simplest of the four types of IMS database structures. They are simply sequential files that contain the database's segments in hierarchical sequence. To access a given root segment, for example, policyholder 000000003, it is necessary to scan all of the root segments from the beginning of the database. You cannot delete or add segments to the database without copying it from one storage area to another. In fact, when the DBA performs a DBDGEN for a HSAM database, he or she must define two physical databases, one for input and one for output. Deleting, modifying, or adding segments is performed by using the logical merge algorithm described in Chapter 2. HSAM databases do have one advantage over the other types. Because they are always processed sequentially, they can be stored on tape as well as disk; all of the other types must be stored on disk.

Figure 15.16 shows how the data in Table 15.1 might be physically stored on tape or disk in a HSAM database. The segments shown would be stored sequentially.

Remember, there is no relationship between the data set's records and the database's root segments. Some records contain only one root, while others contain several roots or no root. If all of a root's dependent segments will not fit in a given record, the excess data is simply placed in the next record. Figure 15.16 shows the record numbers in parentheses to illustrate this, but these data are not actually carried in the database.

Here, each segment is prefaced by a two-byte segment prefix. The first byte identifies the segment type—01 is a root segment. The other segments are numbered in hierarchical sequence. In this case, PLCY would be segment type 02, CLAIM would be segment type 03, BILL would be segment type 04, and PAYMENT would be segment type 05.

The second byte of the segment prefix is what is known as a **delete byte.** In some types of database structure, the delete byte is set to a nonzero value to indicate that a particular segment has been deleted. A zero value indicates that the segment still contains data. In HSAM databases, however, the delete

RECORD NUMBER	SEGMENT PREFIX	SEGMENT DATA
(1)	001 000	000000001
	002 000	0000000001
	003 000	0000000001
	003 000	0000000002
	004 000	0000000001
	004 000	0000000002
	005 000	0000000001
(2)	005 000	0000000002
	001 000	000000002
	002 000	0000000003
	002 000	0000000004
	003 000	0000000003
	003 000	0000000004
	004 000	0000000003
(3)	004 000	0000000004
	001 000	000000002
	002 000	0000000003
	001 000	000000003
	002 000	0000000004
	004 000	0000000005
	005 000	0000000005
(4)	002 000	0000000005
	003 000	0000000005
	004 000	0000000006
	005 000	0000000006

FIGURE 15.16 *Data physically stored in a HSAM database. Only keys are shown.*

byte is not used because a new copy of the database must be created to delete a segment. The delete byte exists in HSAM databases simply to provide a consistent segment prefix format across all database types.

What follows the segment prefix is the data contained in the segment. Here, we have only shown the key values, again for brevity, but other data, as defined in Figure 15.3, would normally follow the key values. By comparing Figure 15.16 with Figure 15.15, you can see that the database consists of segments in hierarchical sequence, each with a segment prefix.

HISAM Databases

HISAM databases are processed very much like HSAM databases; however, an index on the root segment allows direct access to the database. Each HISAM database is made up of two physical databases, a primary database and an overflow database. There are two methods of implementing a HISAM database.

The first method is to use an Indexed Sequential Access Method (ISAM) file for the primary database and an Overflow Sequential Access Method (OSAM) file for the overflow database. An ISAM file is simply an indexed file as described in Chapter 2. An OSAM file is a type of direct access file, also as described in Chapter 2, which is used for IMS databases.

The second method of implementing a HISAM database is to use a VSAM Key Sequenced Data Set (KSDS) for the primary database and a VSAM Entry Sequenced Data Set (ESDS) for the overflow database. Both types of VSAM files are described in Chapter 2.

Figure 15.17 shows how the data in Figure 15.15 might be physically stored on disk in a HISAM database. In the figure the segments are stored in hierarchical sequence in the primary database, just as with a HSAM database. Unlike a HSAM database, however, each record in the primary database contains one and only one root segment. Again, the record numbers are shown even though they are not carried in the database. If there is not enough room in a record in the primary database for the root and all of its dependent segments (e.g., records 1 and 4), the excess data is placed in the overflow data set.

Each record in the primary database begins with a four-byte overflow pointer (shown in decimal in Figure 15.17), which has a value of zero if the overflow database was not used for that root segment. If the overflow database was used, however, then the overflow pointer contains the relative byte address of the excess data in the overflow database. The relative byte address is simply the position, in bytes, of the excess data. For example, the excess data for record 1 in the primary database begins at the 500th byte in the overflow database. The relative byte addresses are shown in parentheses in the overflow database in Figure 15.17, but these data are not actually carried in the database. Note also that the addresses used in this example are not necessarily the actual addresses that would be used by IMS; they were chosen at random for illustrative purposes only.

PRIMARY DATABASE

RECORD NUMBER	OVERFLOW POINTER	SEGMENT PREFIX	SEGMENT DATA
(1)	0000000500	001 000	000000001
		002 000	0000000001
		003 000	0000000001
		003 000	0000000002
		004 000	0000000001
		004 000	0000000002
		005 000	0000000001
(2)	0000000000	001 000	000000002
		002 000	0000000003
		002 000	0000000004
		003 000	0000000003
		003 000	0000000004
		004 000	0000000003
		004 000	0000000004
(3)	0000000000	001 000	000000002
		002 000	0000000003
(4)	0000000600	001 000	000000003
		002 000	0000000004
		004 000	0000000005
		005 000	0000000005
		002 000	0000000005
		003 000	0000000005
		004 000	0000000006

OVERFLOW DATABASE

RELATIVE BYTE ADDRESS	OVERFLOW POINTER	SEGMENT PREFIX	SEGMENT DATA
(500)	0000000000	005 000	0000000002
(600)	0000000000	005 000	0000000006

FIGURE 15.17   *Data physically stored in a HISAM database. Only keys are shown.*

Each record in the overflow database also begins with an overflow pointer. If there is not sufficient room in the overflow database record to store all of the excess data, then another overflow database record is used and the overflow pointer in the first overflow database record contains the relative byte address of the other overflow database record. In Figure 15.17, both overflow pointers have a value of zero, indicating that another overflow record was not used.

The direct access database structures, HDAM and HIDAM, are required for certain kinds of logical databases. Secondary indexes also require either a HDAM or a HIDAM structure.

HDAM Databases

A HDAM database consists of a single physical database, which can be implemented via an OSAM data set or a VSAM ESDSs. In either case, data is stored via a randomizing algorithm which, given the key of a root segment, returns the relative byte address of the location of the data. For this reason, root segments in an HDAM database cannot be processed efficiently in hierarchical sequence. Remember, HDAM is designed for databases with segments that will be processed primarily via random access.

Figure 15.18 shows how the data in Figure 15.15 would be physically stored on disk in a HDAM database. As with the other examples, values in parentheses are not actually carried in the database, but are provided for reference.

A HDAM database is divided into two parts, a root addressable area and an overflow area. Unlike a HISAM database, these are not two physical data sets, but are combined into one data set. The root addressable area is used to store root segments and as many of a root's dependent segments as will fit in a record. The overflow area is used to store segments that will not fit in the record.

The first record in the root addressable area contains only information about available free space in the data set, that is, the space that is available to store more database segments. The record begins with a Free Space Element Anchor Point (FSEAP); this field indicates what free space is available in this particular record. In record 1, the value of the FSEAP is zero, indicating that there is no more space in this record. In fact, all of this record is devoted to free space information. The next field is a record type field that identifies this record as one with no segment data in it. Records with segment data have a record type with a value of zero, while records with only free space data have a record type with a value of one.

The next field is a Root Anchor Point (RAP). One or more RAPs are found in all records in the root addressable area. The DBA can specify the number of RAPs per record at DBDGEN time. RAPs are used to point to the relative byte address of root segments with keys that randomize to that record. In this case, you have no root segments for this record, so the RAP contains a value of zero. If a root segment were to contain a key that randomizes to the first record, the RAP would point to one of the other records, because there is no free space in the first record.

The final field in record 1 is the bit map. This is a series of binary data (shown here in decimal) that shows the locations of records with free space. In the bit map, there is one bit for each record. If the bit has a value of 0, there is no free space in that record. If the bit has a value of 1, there is some free space. The first byte has a value of 23 in decimal, which is 0001 0111 in binary. The FSEAPs for all of the first five records except record 4 contain values of zero, indicating that those records with numbers that correspond to the bit positions with zero values are in fact full. The bit map data for the records after the first five (which are not shown) indicate that free space exists.

Record 2 is the first record that actually contains database segments, as the record type (which has a value of zero) indicates. The FSEAP indicates that there is no free space in the record. The RAP contains the relative byte address of the root segment, which is eight.

ROOT ADDRESSABLE AREA

RECORD NUMBER: (1)

FREE SPACE ELEMENT ANCHOR POINT	RECORD TYPE	ROOT ANCHOR POINT	BIT MAP
00000	00001	0000000000	023 255 255 255

RECORD NUMBER: (2)

RELATIVE BYTE ADDRESS	FREE SPACE ELEMENT ANCHOR POINT	RECORD TYPE	ROOT ANCHOR POINT
(050)	00000	00000	0000000008

RELATIVE BYTE ADDRESS	SEGMENT PREFIX				SEGMENT DATA
(058)	001 000	0000000070			000000001
(070)	002 000	0000000080	0000000090	0000000100	
		0000000608			0000000001
(080)	003 000				0000000001
	003 000				0000000002
(090)	004 000				0000000001
	004 000				0000000002
(100)	005 000				0000000001

RECORD NUMBER: (3)

RELATIVE BYTE ADDRESS	FREE SPACE ELEMENT ANCHOR POINT	RECORD TYPE	ROOT ANCHOR POINT
(150)	00000	00000	0000000158

RELATIVE BYTE ADDRESS	SEGMENT PREFIX			SEGMENT DATA
(158)	001 000	0000000120		000000002
(170)	002 000	0000000210	0000000240	0000000003
	002 000			0000000004
(210)	003 000			0000000003
	003 000			0000000004
(240)	004 000			0000000003
	004 000			0000000004

FIGURE 15.18   *Data physically stored in a HDAM database. Only keys are shown.*

The segment prefix contains more data than in HSAM or HISAM databases. In addition to the segment type identifier and the delete byte, there is a set of pointers that contains the relative byte addresses of the first occurrence of each child of a parent segment. For example, the root segment has one dependent, the second segment, which is located at a relative byte address of

RECORD NUMBER: (4)

RELATIVE BYTE ADDRESS	FREE SPACE ELEMENT ANCHOR POINT	RECORD TYPE	ROOT ANCHOR POINT
(300)	00340	00000	0000000308

RELATIVE BYTE ADDRESS	SEGMENT PREFIX		SEGMENT DATA
(308)	001 000	0000000320	000000002
(320)	002 000		0000000003

RECORD NUMBER: (5)

RELATIVE BYTE ADDRESS	FREE SPACE ELEMENT ANCHOR POINT	RECORD TYPE	ROOT ANCHOR POINT
(400)	00000	00000	0000000408

RELATIVE BYTE ADDRESS	SEGMENT PREFIX				SEGMENT DATA
(408)	001 000	0000000420	0000000480		000000003
(420)	002 000	0000000440	0000000460		0000000004
(440)	004 000				0000000005
(460)	005 000				0000000005
(480)	002 000	0000000500	0000000520	0000000700	0000000005
(500)	003 000				0000000005
(520)	004 000				0000000006

OVERFLOW AREA

RELATIVE BYTE ADDRESS	FREE SPACE ELEMENT ANCHOR POINT
(600)	0000000800

RELATIVE BYTE ADDRESS	SEGMENT PREFIX	SEGMENT DATA
(608)	005 000	0000000002
(700)	005 000	0000000006

FIGURE 15.18 *Continued.*

70. The second segment has child occurrences of the third, fourth, and fifth segments at relative byte addresses of 80, 90, and 100. Note that there is not enough space to hold the last segment, the second occurrence of the fifth segment, so there is also a pointer into the overflow area at a relative byte address of 608. Each segment prefix is followed by the segment's data.

There are several different kinds of pointers that can occur in a HDAM database's segment prefixes. The pointer type used in these examples is a physical child first pointer which, as the name implies, contains the relative byte address of the first child of a parent segment. This type of pointer is required in HDAM databases. Optionally, the DBA can specify other types of pointers. The different types of pointers are noted in Table 15.2.

Record 4 is different from the records we have examined so far: It has free space. The FSEAP contains the relative byte address of the free space (which is not shown) at the end of the second segment.

HIDAM Databases

HIDAM databases have an advantage over HDAM databases. They can be processed efficiently in sequential order. Like HDAM databases, they also can be processed via direct access. The sequential access capabilities come from the fact that, like HISAM databases, HIDAM databases consist of two physical data sets. One data set contains the segment data, while the other is an index keyed on the key fields of the root segments. Also like HISAM databases, HIDAM databases can be implemented via OSAM data sets or VSAM data sets. If OSAM is chosen, then the database with the segment data is an OSAM data set, while the index database will be an ISAM data set. On the other hand, if VSAM is chosen, the database with the segment data is an ESDS, while the index database is a KSDS. ISAM data sets and VSAM KSDSs are more fully described in Chapter 2.

HIDAM databases are very similar to HDAM databases in physical structure. For this reason, we will not examine HIDAM databases in as much detail as

TABLE 15.2 *Types of pointers used in HDAM databases*

Child/Twin Pointers

  Physical child first: Points from parent segment to first occurrence of child segment. Only physical child first pointers are required in HDAM.

  Physical child last: Points from parent to last occurrence of child segment.

  Physical twin forward: Points from one twin segment to the next twin.

  Physical twin backward: Points from one twin segment to the previous twin.

Hierarchical Pointers

  Hierarchical forward: Points from one segment to the next in hierarchical sequence.

  Hierarchical backward: Points from one segment to the previous in hierarchical sequence.

we have the other types of database. Instead, we will simply focus on the differences between HIDAM and HDAM databases.

We have already mentioned one of the differences: HIDAM databases consist of two data sets—one that contains the segment data and one that serves as an index to that database. The segment data data set is virtually identical to the root addressable area of a HDAM data set; however, there are no RAPs in a HIDAM database: The index database is used to locate all root segments.

Each record in the index data set consists of a key that is the key of a given root segment in the segment data data set. The data portion of each record in the index data set is the relative byte address of the root segment in the segment data data set.

MANIPULATING THE DATABASE USING DL/I

Elements of DL/I

DL/I is used by the application programmer to manipulate an IMS database. The program must call the DL/I program as a subroutine and pass it parameters that make up the DL/I functions to retrieve, add, update, or delete segments in the database. For this discussion we will focus on the DL/I functions themselves. Keep in mind, however, that the format in which the DL/I functions are presented in this section is somewhat different from the format in which they are coded in an application program. The format here is designed to give a clearer picture of what the application code is trying to accomplish. The format of the DL/I functions as they appear in application programs is discussed in Appendix B.

At its most basic level, DL/I consists of a group of function codes that specify the type of operation you wish to perform in a given DL/I call. Parameters that follow the function code specify the method of performing the operation. The major DL/I functions are summarized in Figure 15.19.

Simple sequential read operations are fairly straightforward. For example, to read the first root segment in the database, you can use the DL/I call GN.

Then you can process the segment in some way. For example, you can create a report line from it. To read the first child of the first root segment, you issue the GN function again. You can continue to issue GN functions to read each segment in the database, in hierarchical sequence. Probably, you would code the GN function in a loop. When you reach the end of the database, a return code from IMS known as a **status code** will indicate that no more segments exist.

The GNP and GU functions are less straightforward, as they require what is known as a Segment Search Argument (SSA) to be really useful. (SSAs also can be used with the GN command.) We will discuss SSAs more fully later. The basic purpose of the GNP function is to retrieve the next (or first) segment under a parent that was previously retrieved with a GN or GU command. Just

READ OPERATIONS

    GN (GET NEXT) .... SEQUENTIAL READ
    GNP (GET NEXT WITHIN PARENT) .... SEQUENTIAL READ
    GU (GET UNIQUE) .... DIRECT READ

UPDATE OPERATIONS

    GHN (GET HOLD NEXT) .... SEQUENTIAL READ FOR UPDATE
    GHNP (GET HOLD NEXT WITHIN PARENT) .. SEQUENTIAL READ FOR UPDATE
    GHU (GET HOLD UNIQUE) .... RANDOM READ FOR UPDATE
    REPL (REPLACE) .... UPDATE

DELETE OPERATIONS

    DLET (DELETE) .... DELETE

ADD OPERATIONS

    ISRT (INSERT) .... ADD

FIGURE 15.19   *DL/I function codes. These codes are used from within an application program.*

as the GN function generates a status code at the end of the database, the GNP call generates a status code at the end of the group of child segments under the parent. The specific child segment to access is specified by the SSA.

The GU function is used to perform a direct read. An SSA is used to specify the value of key of the segment you want to read. If a GU function is used to read a given segment, the GN function will access the next segment following the one just read. In this way, a combination of GU and GN functions can be used to perform sequential I/O beginning at some point other than the first segment in the database.

The first three update functions, GHN, GHNP, and GHU, operate just as their counterparts GN, GNP, and GU do, with one exception. These functions inform IMS that you intend to update the segment just read. The data in the segment then can be modified and written back out to the database with a REPL function. But if any other function is issued after one of the "hold" functions, the REPL function will fail. A REPL function must be preceded immediately by a GHN, GHNP, or GHU function.

To delete a segment, use the DLET function. The DLET function also requires a GHN, GHNP, or GHU function to immediately precede it. The DLET function can then be used to delete the segment just read.

To add a segment, use the ISRT function. You create the data you want to add to the data set in a buffer, and you issue the ISRT function to add the contents of the buffer to the database.

So far, we have been dealing with DL/I calls without SSAs; such a call is known as an **unqualified call.** However, one or more SSAs can be used to indicate the segment you want to access; such a call is known as a **qualified call.** Suppose you want to prepare a report from the POLICY database (described at the beginning of this chapter) that lists the number of policies by various categories of benefit amount. That is, you want to list the number of policies with benefit amounts less than $1000, the number of policies with benefit amounts between $1001 and $2000, the number of policies with benefit amounts between $2001 and $3000, and so on.

The data you need are contained in the PLCY segment. You could use the GN function to process the database sequentially. This function will retrieve all segments, however, not just the PLCY segment. To retrieve just the PLCY segments, you would issue the DL/I call:

```
GN    PLCY
```

In this case, you suffix the DL/I function with the name (as defined in the DBDGEN) of the segment. This causes the DL/I function to only operate on the segment that you specify in the SSA—we have not specified any particular segment occurrence. The GN function will read the next PLCY segment, whichever one it might be. This is known as an **unqualified SSA.**

You also can code a **qualified SSA.** A qualified SSA allows you to specify exactly which segment occurrence you want to access. Suppose you wanted to create an on-line system that allows the operator to enter a given policyholder via a social security number (e.g., 593-22-9876), and view all policies owned by that policyholder. Obviously, it would be extremely inefficient to sequentially search the database for the desired policyholder. Instead, you need to be able to directly access the database. This could be accomplished with the DL/I call:

```
GU    PLCYHLDR(PLCYHSSN = 593229876)
```

For a qualified SSA, you suffix the segment name as defined in the DBDGEN with a parenthetical statement. For an unqualified SSA, you suffix the segment name with a blank. The parenthetical statement consists of a field name (as defined in the DBDGEN), a two-character-long relational operator, and a value.

Embedded spaces are not allowed in these statements. In the last GU example, the relational operator includes a space at the beginning because the relational operator must be two characters long. Some relational operators (e.g., ">=", "<=", etc.) contain exactly two characters and do not need an embedded space. The embedded space in the relational operator can be either the first or second character. In addition, all relational operators can be coded using either mathematical symbols or alphabetic characters. All of the following DL/I calls, then, are equivalent:

```
GU    PLCYHLDR(PLCYHSSN = 593229876)
GU    PLCYHLDR(PLCYHSSN= 593229876)
GU    PLCYHLDR(PLCYHSSNEQ593229876)
```

Table 15.3 shows the valid relational operators for qualified SSAs. Each relational operator is two characters long with a space as the first or second character if needed.

To view all policies for this policyholder, you would issue the following two DL/I calls:

TABLE 15.3   *Valid relational operators for qualified SSAs*

Relational Operators	Meaning
= , =,EQ	equal to
⌐=,=⌐,NE	not equal to
> , >,GT	greater than
>=,=>,GE	greater than or equal to
< , <,LT	less than
<=,=<,LE	less than or equal to

```
GU     PLCYHLDR(PLCYHSSN =593229876)
GNP    PLCY
```

You probably would place the GNP function in a loop that would exit after you receive a status code that indicates that there are no more PLCY segments under this parent. You use an unqualified SSA with the GNP function. If you had used an unqualified call (without an SSA), the loop of GNP functions would have accessed all children under the PLCYHLDR segment, including the CLAIM, BILL, and PAYMENT segments. By using a qualified call, you limit retrieval to only the PLCY segment.

Command Codes

You can further modify the effect of an SSA by using a **command code.** To use a command code, you embed an asterisk after the segment name in the SSA and follow it with the one-byte command code. For example, to use the command code "L," you would issue the DL/I call:

```
GU     PLCYHLDR*L(PLCYHSSN =593229876)
```

There are several command codes, some of which perform functions that are fairly esoteric. For illustrative purposes, however, we will discuss some of the more useful command codes, which are listed in Table 15.4. These codes are used to further modify the effect of SSAs.

The "concatenated key" command code can be used to reduce the number of SSAs you must use. For example, suppose you wanted to read a given

TABLE 15.4   *List of selected command codes*

Command Code	Effect
C	uses concatenated key
D	creates pathcall
L	accesses last occurrence
-	null—does nothing

policy belonging to a given policyholder. You could use two SSAs and issue the DL/I call:

```
GU    PLCYHLDR(PLCYHSSN = 593229876)
      PLCY(PLCYNO = 2349874569)
```

This DL/I call would either return the data from the PLCY segment where the key has a value of 2349874569 and which is a child of the PLCYHLDR segment where the key has a value of 593229876, or it would return a status code indicating that the segment you specified does not exist. You can code more than one SSA on a DL/I call. You could, however, simplify the call somewhat by using the "C" command code and specifying a concatenated key:

```
GU    PLCY*C(5932298762349874569)
```

Here, you do not code either a field name or a relational operator. The field name is assumed to be the key field of each segment in the hierarchical path from the root segment down to the segment you specify (e.g., the PLCY segment). The relational operators are all assumed to be "equal to."

The "pathcall" command code is similar in concept to the "concatenated key" command code, although its purpose is different. When using either of the previous methods of accessing the PLCY segment (with two SSAs and with the concatenated key command code), only the data from the PLCY segment is returned. What if you wanted to access the data from both the PLCYHLDR and the PLCY segments? One way to do this would be to use two DL/I calls, e.g.:

```
GU    PLCYHLDR(PLCYHSSN = 593229876)
GNP   PLCY(PLCYNO = 2349874569)
```

Each call would return the data from the requested segment. You can, however, use the "D" command code to reduce the number of DL/I calls:

```
GU    PLCYHLDR*D(PLCYHSSN = 593229876)
      PLCY(PLCYNO = 2349874569)
```

Thus, the "D" command code causes the data to be returned from each segment specified that is followed by the command code. DL/I always returns the data from the lowest level segment specified, such as the PLCY segment in the last example.

The "last" command code is primarily useful when you have nonunique fields on which you wish to search. Normally, DL/I returns the first segment that matches the value you specify in a qualified SSA. The "L" command code causes DL/I to return the last segment instead. Suppose that you need to determine the key of the last claim filed by a given policyholder on a given policy on a given date. You could determine this data by coding the following DL/I call:

```
GU    PLCYHLDR(PLCYHSSN = 593229876)
```

```
PLCY(PLCYNO = 2349874569)
CLAIM*L(CLAIMDAT = 900105)
```

This would return the data from the last CLAIM segment filed on 1/5/90, which would include the key of the segment.

The usefulness of the "null" command code becomes more apparent when you code DL/I calls in an application program (see Appendix B). The null command code allows you to create a set of SSAs in storage with space for command codes. Then, when you want to use a command code, you can embed it in the proper place. Otherwise, you can fill that place with "-". For example, the previous DL/I call could be coded as:

```
GU     PLCYHLDR*-(PLCYHSSN = 593229876)
       PLCY*-(PLCYNO = 2349874569)
       CLAIM*L(CLAIMDAT = 900105)
```

This would have the same effect as the first example. If you wanted to issue this call a second time as, for example, a pathcall, you simply could replace the hyphens with "D"s:

```
GU     PLCYHLDR*D(PLCYHSSN = 593229876)
       PLCY*D(PLCYNO = 2349874569)
       CLAIM*L(CLAIMDAT = 900105)
```

Writing IMS Programs in COBOL

Appendix B contains a detailed description of a typical IMS application written in COBOL.

EXECUTING IMS PROGRAMS

Thus far, we have examined IMS database manipulation without regard to the environment under which a program that issues DL/I calls will execute. There are three types of IMS programs, each of which executes under a different environment:

- DL/I Batch Programs
- Message Process Programs (MPPs)
- Batch Message Processing (BMPs)

Coding DL/I Batch Programs

DL/I Batch Programs are the simplest of the three types of IMS programs. They execute under the normal environment under which any batch program executes. Specifically, they do not execute under the control of IMS.

Because they run under the normal batch environment, DL/I Batch Programs can access any type of file—sequential, direct access, or VSAM. They also can access IMS databases by making DL/I calls. The primary difference between DL/I Batch Programs and other types of IMS programs is that DL/I Batch Programs, instead of executing under the control of IMS, simply make use of certain IMS services, such as DL/I.

Before a DL/I Batch Program can access any databases, you need to issue a Database Release (DBR) IMS command. This is because IMS normally is set up so that it has exclusive control of its databases. That means it does not share any kind of database access (not even read-only access) with any non-IMS systems or programs. This is necessary because IMS must be able to enforce "hold" calls against a database and ensure that, while one program is updating a segment, no other programs are attempting to update that segment. The DBR command removes a database from the control of IMS and allows other programs, such as DL/I Batch Programs, to manipulate it. When you issue a DBR command for a given database, IMS can no longer access the database. In this case, you must issue another IMS command, the Restart Database command, to return control of the database (and the ability to access it) to IMS.

From the programmer's viewpoint, there are no special requirements, other than the need to issue the DBR command, for accessing a database from a DL/I Batch Program. We simply use DL/I calls as described earlier in this chapter and in Appendix B.

Coding MPPs

Unlike DL/I Batch Programs, MPPs run under the control of IMS. Also, they cannot access anything except IMS databases and the IMS message queue. The message queue is used for two purposes. First, it is used to store data that later can be accessed by a BMP. Second, it is used to send and receive data to and from a terminal.

This capability to access a terminal allows MPPs to interact with a user. In fact, MPPs typically are used to implement on-line systems that allow users to enter data on a terminal to add records to a database, change records in a database, and read records from a database. On-line systems make use of the DC component of IMS.

When working with the DC component of IMS, you manage database access by using the DL/I calls that have been presented throughout this chapter. One way to manage terminal access, however, is by using Message Formatting Service (MFS). Suppose you wanted to present the user with a screen containing the data from the CLAIM segment from the POLICY database in the format shown in Figure 15.20.

To do this, you first would code MFS macros similar to those in Figure 15.21. This is not a complete set of MFS macros—only the major components have been shown. This set of MFS macros consists of three parts:

```
CLAIM DATA FOR CLAIM NUMBER:  1234567890

AMOUNT OF CLAIM        : 12345.67
DISPOSITION OF CLAIM   : ACCEPTED
DATE OF CLAIM PAYMENT : 02/20/90
```

FIGURE 15.20   *A typical terminal screen showing the data from the CLAIM segment of the POLICY database. MFS would be used to format the screen.*

- The Message Input Descriptor (MID)
- The Message Output Descriptor (MOD)
- The Device Input Format/Device Output Format (DIF/DOF)

These parts are labeled CLAIMI, CLAIMO, and CLAIM, respectively, at the left of each section. The MID and the MOD control the transfer of data between the terminal and the program. The DIF/DOF controls the physical placement of data on the screen.

The MID begins with a MSG macro that specifies that you are defining the transfer of data from the screen to the program (TYPE=INPUT). You also specify the DIF/DOF that is associated with this MID (SOR=CLAIM) and the MOD that is associated with this MID (NEXT=CLAIMO). Then you specify a series of MFLD macros to define each field that your program will receive and the lengths of those fields. The MSGEND macro indicates the end of the MID.

Similarly, the MOD begins with a MSG macro that specifies that you are defining the transfer of data from the program to the screen, the name of the DIF/DOF, and the name of the MID. Again, a series of MFLD macros list the

```
CLAIMI    MSG       TYPE=INPUT,SOR=CLAIM,NXT=CLAIMO
          MFLD      NUMBER,LTH=10
          MFLD      AMOUNT,LTH=8
          MFLD      DISP,LTH=8
          MFLD      DATE,LTH=8
          MSGEND
CLAIMO    MSG       TYPE=OUTPUT,SOR=CLAIM,NXT=CLAIMI
          MFLD      NUMBER,LTH=10
          MFLD      AMOUNT,LTH=8
          MFLD      DISP,LTH=8
          MFLD      DATE,LTH=8
          MSGEND
CLAIM     FMT       TYPE=(3270,2)
          DFLD      'CLAIM DATA FOR CLAIM NUMBER:',POS=(1,9)
NUMBER    DFLD      POS=(1,39),LTH=10
          DFLD      'AMOUNT OF CLAIM        :',POS=(3,1)
AMOUNT    DFLD      POS=(3,25),LTH=8
          DFLD      'DISPOSITION OF CLAIM   :',POS=(4,1)
DISP      DFLD      POS=(4,25),LTH=8
          DFLD      'DATE OF CLAIM PAYMENT:',POS=(5,1)
DATE      DFLD      POS=(5,25),LTH=8
          FMTEND
          END
```

FIGURE 15.21   *A typical set of MFS macros. Macros similar to these could be used to create the screen shown in Figure 15.20.*

fields that your program will send to the screen, and a MSGEND macro ends the MOD.

The DIF/DOF begins with a FMT macro that specifies the type of terminal you will be sending the data to, for example, an IBM 3270 Model 2. Next, you specify a series of DFLD macros to indicate the placement of various fields on the screen. In fact, there are two kinds of fields: constant, or literal, fields; and variable fields. Literal fields are fields such as screen titles and variable labels. Variable fields are variables that take on different values according to how the program initializes them.

The first DFLD specifies a literal field, the screen title ("CLAIM DATA FOR CLAIM NUMBER:"). To specify a literal field, list the literal in single quotes, followed by the position of the first character of the field, here, the ninth column of the first line (1,9). The second DFLD specifies a variable field. To specify a variable field, begin with a label that references the MFLDs in the MID and the MOD that define the data that will be placed in this field (NUMBER). Then specify the position on the screen of the first byte of the field, in this case, the 39th column of the first line (1,39). Then specify the length of the field (LTH = 10).

The lengths of the fields (as specified in the MFLD and DFLD macros) do not necessarily match the lengths of the fields in the database (refer to Figure 15.3). For example, the claim amount has a length of seven in the database, but a length of eight on the screen. Similarly, the payment date has a length of six in the database, but a length of eight on the screen. Finally, the claim disposition has a length of one in the database, but a length of eight on the screen. The reason for this is that the formats of the various data items are different between the screen and the database. For example, you have added a decimal point to the claim amount, you have added two slashes to the date, and you have translated a value of zero in the claim disposition field to "ACCEPTED" on the screen. It is important to note that the program must do any such reformatting of data between the screen and the database. MFS, however, allows you to do such reformatting.

Once you have created an MFS screen definition, you can use it in a program to transfer data to and from the terminal. However, the DBA first must run a PSBGEN for the program, allowing you to access the terminal. Then you can perform terminal I/O with DL/I calls. To send a screen to the terminal, initialize an output buffer within the program with data for the variables you want to display. Then use the ISRT call and specify the output buffer, the MOD name, and a PCB Mask (see Appendix B) that indicates that the terminal is the target of the call. To retrieve a screen from the terminal, use the GU call and specify an input buffer, the MID name, and the terminal PCB Mask. The data will be placed into the input buffer.

When using MFS to send and receive data to and from a terminal, you do not actually access the terminal directly. Instead, you access the **message queue**, which is an internal buffer used by IMS. IMS manages the transfer of data between the message queue and the physical terminal. An alternate use of the message queue is to store data for use by another program (e.g., a BMP). To use the message queue in this way, the DBA must run a PSBGEN that specifies the name of the BMP that will receive the data. The MPP then references a PCB Mask for the message queue in a DL/I call that specifies the ISRT function to place data into the message queue from an output buffer that the program initializes. MFS is not used in this process.

Coding BMPs

Recall that BMPs are "hybrid" programs. Like DL/I Batch Programs, they can access both IMS databases and other types of files or databases. In addition, they also can access the message queue. Because they run under the control of IMS, there is no need to issue the DBR command to make a database accessible to a BMP.

An IMS database is accessed using DL/I calls just as in a DL/I Batch Program. To access the message queue, you reference a PCB Mask for the message queue with a DL/I call that specifies the GU function. Don't forget that the PSBGEN for the MPP that writes data to the message queue must specify the name of the BMP that will read it. This ensures that IMS will only return to the BMP the data that was intended for it by one or more MPPs.

DESIGNING A HIERARCHICAL DATABASE

Database design was examined in Chapter 6. Although we focused on relational database design, most of the material in that chapter also applies to hierarchical database design. You still divide the development process into the Feasibility Study, Preliminary Plan, System Analysis, System Design, and System Implementation phases. You still use data flow diagrams and other tools to diagram the existing system and the new system. And you still divide database design into Conceptual Database Design and Physical Database Design. In fact, the major differences between hierarchical database design and relational database design are:

- Instead of creating an entity relation diagram, you create a hierarchy chart
- Instead of normalizing your design, you focus on developing the subschema for the database
- Instead of fine tuning the database during the physical design phase, you determine what kind of database structure (HDAM, HISAM, etc.) will best meet the needs of the application

The physical design and, sometimes, the development of subschema, typically are done by the DBA rather than the programmer/analyst.

You already have seen several examples of hierarchy charts (see Figures 15.2, 15.4, 15.6, and 15.7). We replace the entity relation diagram of relational database design with the hierarchy chart. Instead of showing one-to-one, one-to-many, and many-to-many relationships, we show parent-child relationships. We do this simply by determining which data items are logically subordinate to others.

Remember that normalization can be used to check and refine a conceptual relational database design. When designing a hierarchical database, however, instead of normalizing, you begin developing the subschema of the database. To do this, determine whether all or part of the needed data already exists in the form of a hierarchical database, so that you can use a logical database. You also examine the process design of the system to determine whether a secondary index is beneficial.

During the Physical Database Design phase, you again examine the intended method of processing the database to determine which physical database structure is best suited to the application. Generally, it's a good idea to minimize overhead by using the simplest structure that meets your needs.

SUMMARY

IMS is one of the most widely used hierarchical database managers. It consists of a DB component and a DC component. An IMS database can be diagrammed by using a hierarchy chart, which shows the parent-child relationships between segments. A segment can have a key, which allows you to use the GU function to directly access it.

Logical databases allow you to create a logical view that combines data from multiple physical databases. Secondary indexing allows you to logically treat a dependent segment in the databases as the root segment, allowing for more efficient access to the database for certain applications.

IMS does not require that a schema be completely defined. The schema and subschema are defined via the DBDGEN and the PSBGEN, which typically are created by the DBA. The DBDGEN defines the segments in the database and their hierarchical relationships, as well as fields that are key fields or that will be used in SSAs. The PSBGEN defines a program's view of the database, specifying the field-level sensitivity or the segment-level sensitivity of the program.

The two kinds of sequential access database structure are HSAM and HISAM. The two kinds of direct access database structure are HDAM and HIDAM. HSAM databases are sequential files. HISAM databases consist of primary databases, which are implemented via ISAM files or VSAM KSDSs, and overflow databases, which are implemented via OSAM files or VSAM ESDSs. HDAM databases consist of OSAM files or VSAM ESDSs. HIDAM databases use a structure similar to HDAM databases, except that an index is added; the index is implemented via either ISAM or VSAM.

DL/I is used by the application programmer to manipulate the database. You can use GN, GNP, or GU calls to read a database. To update a database, you must use either a GHN, GHNP, or GHU call, followed by a REPL call. If you want to delete a segment from a database, use a DLET call. When you need to add a segment to a database, use an ISRT call.

A DL/I call without an SSA is an unqualified call. On the other hand, a call with an SSA is a qualified call. An SSA that only specifies the segment name is an unqualified SSA. An SSA also can include a value and a relational operator to compare the value in the specified segment against. An SSA sometimes includes a command code. Some of the more useful command codes are "C" (concatenated key), "D" (pathcall), "L" (last), and "-" (null).

There are three different kinds of application programs: DL/I Batch Programs, MPPs, and BMPs. Each runs in a different environment. DL/I Batch Programs do not run under the control of IMS. They can access databases or other types of files, but a DBR command must be issued for any databases they are to access. MPPs run under the control of IMS. They can access databases and the message queue. The message queue can be used to store data for a BMP or to access a terminal. One way to access a terminal is through MFS. A BMP also runs under the control of IMS. It can access databases, the message queue, or other types of files.

To design a hierarchical database, you use much the same methodology as in designing a relational database. You replace the entity relation diagram with a hierarchy chart to show parent-child relationships. Instead of normalizing your design, you determine from your processing needs whether logical databases or secondary indexes are needed. During the Physical Database Design phase, you determine the database structure that best meets the needs of your application.

QUESTIONS

1. What are the major components of IMS? What is their function?
2. What is the function of a hierarchy chart?
3. What two DL/I calls must you use to update a segment?
4. Explain the macros in the AGENTDB DBDGEN in Figure 15.9.
5. Explain the fields in the physical structure of record 5 in Figure 15.18.
6. Who normally codes a DBDGEN?
7. What is the difference between field-level sensitivity and segment-level sensitivity?
8. Why do you use logical databases? Why do you use secondary indexes?
9. What are the three different kinds of IMS application programs? How do they differ?
10. What do you usually use the fields in the PCB mask for?
11. What DL/I calls do you use to update a segment?
12. What are some of the more useful command codes? What are they used for?
13. What is the purpose of the MID, the MOD, and the DIF/DOF?
14. How is security implemented in IMS?
15. A company with a large IMS database wants to investigate the possibilities of converting to DB2. Briefly discuss who should be on the task force responsible for this investigation.

CASE STUDY

Acme Grudznik Corporation is a large manufacturer of grudzniks, a space-saver kitchen appliance that has all of the features of a dishwasher, freezer, and microwave oven. Management has decided that an IMS database system is needed to manage parts inventory. Acme has several warehouses containing parts used in grudznik manufacture. Each part can be purchased from various suppliers. The data on warehouses, parts, and suppliers that Acme wants to keep is detailed below:

- Warehouse
  Warehouse number
  Location
- Part
  Part number
  Part description
  Quantity on hand
- Supplier
  Account number
  Name
  Location
  Quantity on order

The inputs and outputs of the Parts Inventory System are as follows:

1. Periodically, a batch report will be run showing quantity on order by supplier. These reports will be run at night, when the database is not needed for other purposes.
2. When parts ordered from a supplier arrive in a warehouse, Acme would like to be able to enter data on a terminal to immediately update the quantity on order and quantity on hand information in the database.
3. As parts are shipped from warehouses to manufacturing plants, Acme would like to be able to enter data on a terminal to update the quantity on hand information in the database. Because such transactions occur several times per day, however, Acme would like for the actual database update to be done in batch mode at night.

Questions

1. A hierarchy chart for the parts inventory database is included in the system documentation. Unfortunately, some modifications have been made to the database, and it is not known whether the documentation has been kept up to date. However, the source code for the DBDGEN for the current database is available:

```
DBD        NAME = PARTINDB
SEGM       NAME = WAREHOUS,PARENT = 0,BYTES = 85
FIELD      NAME = (WHOUSNO,SEQ),START = 1,BYTES = 5,
           TYPE = Z
SEGM       NAME = PART,PARENT = WAREHOUS,BYTES = 30
FIELD      NAME = (PARTNO,SEQ),START = 1,BYTES = 5,
           TYPE = Z
SEGM       NAME = SUPPLIER,PARENT = PART,BYTES = 110
FIELD      NAME = (ACCTNO,SEQ),START = 1,BYTES = 5,
           TYPE = Z
DBDGEN
```

Create a hierarchy chart of the database as defined by the DBDGEN.
2. Given the inputs and outputs for the system, would a secondary index be helpful?
3. Which type of IMS program would be most appropriate for each of the three inputs and outputs of the system?
4. Given the inputs and outputs of the system, which kind of database structure would be most appropriate?

16

Special Topics in Databases

Thus far in this text, we have examined both database technology currently in use (hierarchical databases implemented in COBOL) and state-of-the-art technology just beginning to see large-scale use (relational databases programmed via nonprocedural languages). In this chapter, we will examine some of the more esoteric aspects of databases. We will begin with concurrent database processing, which is the norm, at least in the mainframe world. Then we will examine distributed databases, which are beginning to see wide-scale implementation. We will conclude the chapter by examining several directions in database technology that show considerable promise and that are, to some extent, in their infancy: artificial-intelligence databases, object-oriented databases, and hypertext.

CONCURRENT DATABASE PROCESSING

Databases range from single-user systems, most frequently found on micro-computers, to large multiuser systems commonly found on mainframes. Note, however, that multiuser systems are becoming more and more common on microcomputer systems that employ LAN technology. We will examine this topic in more detail in the next section of this chapter. Multiuser systems require what is known as **concurrent database processing** because many users access the database concurrently.

The primary concern of concurrent processing is data integrity in a multiuser environment. Obviously, you do not want two users to be able to update the same database record simultaneously. In theory, your DBMS would have to decide which user should update the data first, and it would be very difficult to determine general criteria that could be designed into a system to make this decision. In practice, you probably would see partial updates, that is, the first user would update part of the record with part of his or her new data, while the second user would update the rest of the record with his or her new data. When this happens, data integrity is lost.

One solution for this problem is a strategy of **locking** the record when the first user begins to update the record. A locking strategy prevents partial updates by allowing only one user to access the record when the update operation begins. Other users are not allowed to access the record until the first user's update operation is complete. At this time, the lock is released.

An example of how a locking strategy can be implemented is found in IBM's DB2 database manager. This is a fairly complex locking strategy. Remember, a DB2 database is composed of pages within tablespaces. DB2 can lock at either the page or the tablespace level, so it can make either of these two groups of data, respectively, unavailable to users. Whether page locks or tablespace locks are used depend on several factors:

- Whether an index has been defined on the column or columns used to search the table
- Whether the internal search algorithms "decide" to use the index
- Whether the table was defined with page locks or tablespace locks
- Whether the user (or the user's software) issues a command to explicitly lock the tablespace

Even though DB2's locking strategy is complex, it allows considerable flexibility. The user or programmer has some control over how and when locks are established. Otherwise, locking is designed to achieve I/O efficiency.

DISTRIBUTED DATABASES

The basic concepts of distributed databases are:

- Data should exist close to the location that most often accesses it
- Data should be available to every location that needs it

Consider, for example, the case of a database with sales data for a company that does business nationwide. The business organizes its operations by geographical regions of the country,—the northern region, the southern region, the eastern region, and the western region. Each region has a sales manager who is responsible for that region. Each sales manager needs daily access to his or her region's sales data.

One way to meet the data processing needs in this example would be to implement a LAN with microcomputers. A LAN consists of at least one **file server** and several **workstations.** Figure 16.1 depicts a LAN for this example.

Each sales manager has a workstation, which is a microcomputer. The workstations are connected by communications links to the file server, which is also a microcomputer. The database with the sales data exists on the file server's storage media, usually a hard disk drive. Whenever one of the sales managers wishes to view data, the database software on the workstation must access the file server and request the data. The software on the file server will then download the data to the workstation, where the workstation software can display the data.

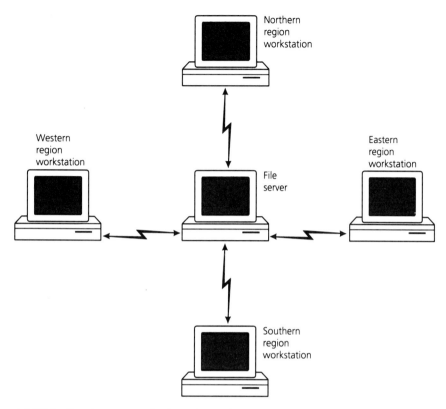

Northern
region
workstation

Western
region
workstation

File
server

Eastern
region
workstation

Southern
region
workstation

FIGURE 16.1   *A LAN for the sales managers for the various regions. The file server contains the actual data.*

Did you notice that the previous scenario does not use distributed data? Instead, the data is in a centralized location on the file server. This makes the data available to every location that accesses it, but the data does not exist at the immediate location, which can lead to undesirable results. If there is a large amount of activity to the database, I/O response might suffer because data cannot be accessed without the intervention of the file server. The file server then becomes a bottleneck to data access. Moreover, this scenario wastes the database-processing capability of the workstations. Remember, each workstation is a microcomputer which, with appropriate software, is capable of accessing a database on its own. In this scenario, we restrict the workstations to making requests to the file server. Both of these problems can be solved by using distributed data. To do this, subdivide the larger database into four smaller databases, each containing data for a specific region. You could allow the data for each region to reside on the workstation used by that region's sales manager. Now you have located data close to where it is used, and you have utilized some unused potential of your workstations. Because, in our example, each sales manager has a need only to look at his or her own region's data, the data is also available to all locations that need it.

SALES TABLE

SALE_NUMBER	SALE_AMOUNT	PRODUCT_KEY
101330	130.00	A06
239029	240.95	A07
123876	199.99	A03
198323	130.00	A06

PRODUCT TABLE

PRODUCT_KEY	PRODUCT_DESCRIPT
A03	DELUXE WIDGET
A06	STANDARD WIDGET
A07	TRACTOR GASKET

FIGURE 16.2   *Two tables used by the northern region sales manager. The PRODUCT table would be on the file server.*

If you are using relational database technology, you can easily refine the above scenario. Suppose that two of the tables used by the northern region's sales manager are as depicted in Figure 16.2.

Here are two tables in a relational database that are related via the foreign key PRODUCT_KEY. But note that although the data in the SALES table probably is specific to the northern region, and therefore will reside on that sales manager's workstation, the data in the PRODUCT table will be used in all four regions (i.e., widgets and tractor gaskets are sold in all four regions). In this case, the data cannot reside only on the northern region workstation. To do so would violate the concept that the data must be available to all locations that need it.

One alternative is to reproduce the PRODUCT table on all workstations. This produces data redundancy—which to some extent defeats the purpose of a relational database—but if the data in the table is relatively stable, this might be acceptable. A better solution, however, would be to keep the PRODUCT table on the file server while the SALES tables remain on the workstations

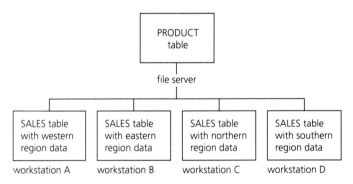

FIGURE 16.3   *Distributed data. Each region contains data unique to each site, while the file server contains general data for all regions.*

(see Figure 16.3). This means that the database software must be sophisticated enough to access tables in two different locations.

You can expand this example to involve a more sophisticated use of distributed databases. Suppose that each sales manager not only needs to access the data for his or her own region, but also needs to access the data from some other region. The best solution for this case, therefore, is for the network and database software to be sophisticated enough to access data not only on a workstation and on the file server, but also on other workstations. In this situation, software servicing a request for data will first search the workstation where the request was entered. If the data does not exist there, the software then searches for data on the file server. If the data does not exist on the file server, then the software searches other workstations for the data. And, although we have not considered this in our examples, if the data did not exist on the file server or on any workstation, the search might proceed through a communications link to a minicomputer or a mainframe (see Figure 16.4).

This last example, involving microcomputers, minicomputers, and mainframes, is an extremely sophisticated and flexible scenario for implementing distributed databases. It is noteworthy that this capability is part of the SAA commitment of IBM and will probably be implemented via DB2 on mainframes, SQL/400 on AS/400 minicomputers, and OS/2 Extended Edition Data Base Manager on microcomputer networks. All of these products provide relational database access via SQL.

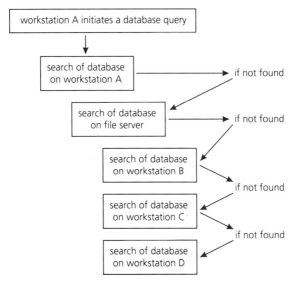

FIGURE 16.4   *A sophisticated search pattern for a distributed database. A query from one workstation initiates a search of the database on that workstation. If data satisfying the search criteria for the query is not found, the file server's database is accessed, followed by the databases on each of the workstations attached to the network.*

ARTIFICIAL INTELLIGENCE AND DATABASES

Artificial intelligence (AI) is a term that covers many concepts. Perhaps one of the simplest, but probably the best known, is an expert system. An **expert system** consists of three components: a knowledge engineer (an expert), a knowledge base (a database of rules), and an inference engine (a program that can apply the rules contained in the knowledge base). The basic premise of an expert system is that the knowledge engineer can use his or her expertise to devise a set of rules that are stored in the knowledge base. Nonexperts then can use the inference engine to apply the rules in the knowledge base to draw conclusions about matters outside their area of expertise.

There is an obvious connection between expert systems and databases, because the knowledge base is simply a type of database. It differs from most databases in that it contains rules about facts rather than just facts. For example, most databases contain data of a factual nature, such as "this driver's age is 24." A knowledge base contains both the data and a rule for that data, such as "if this driver's age is less than 25, increase his automobile insurance premium by ten percent." In either case, however, the same database structures and access methods could be used.

Most expert systems today have not emphasized the database portion of the system. Instead, the focus has been on the processing of the database via the inference engine. Most expert systems also involve considerable machine overhead. One direction toward a solution might be to optimize the system by using the latest in database technology.

Expert systems are a fairly simple application of AI technology. More complex applications can include heuristic algorithms, which attempt to emulate human reasoning processes and are capable of "learning," or neural networks, which use pattern-matching techniques to process "fuzzy," or imprecisely defined, input. Combining these techniques with modern database technology could lead to database systems that are capable of updating themselves.

OBJECT-ORIENTED PROGRAMMING AND DATABASES

An Object-oriented Programming System (OOPS) is a theoretical construct that has been implemented in many different programming languages (e.g., Smalltalk, Pascal, C++, and various extensions of LISP). At the core of OOPS is a concept that blurs the distinction between data and processing, the concept of objects.

An **object** is a self-contained entity that includes both data and operations performed on the data. This contrasts with traditional data processing techniques that perform various operations on a given piece of data. An object contains both the data and some relevant operation. Thus, in a traditional programming language, you might have various operations (such as addition, subtraction, multiplication, and division) that you can perform on any piece of data (such as a variable called "X"), whereas, in OOPS, you might have various objects (such as add_X, subtract_X, multiply_X, and divide_X) that contain both the data and the processing.

In OOPS, you do not perform operations on data, but instead you send a message to an object. This message causes the object to perform its defined processing on its defined data. You also can create new objects that can **inherit** the properties (the processing and data) of other objects allowing you to create more complex objects.

OOPS is still in its infancy—there is not yet a generally accepted method of implementing an OOPS application. There are several different programming languages that can be chosen for this task. In contrast, SQL has become an industry standard for implementing relational databases. Just as relational databases have merged the concepts of data entities and relationships between data entities, however, OOPS merges the concepts of data and processing. The result might be databases that are capable of causing processes to be executed when certain data entities are accessed.

HYPERTEXT

As the name implies, hypertext primarily is used for text displays; although in the future, it might be applied to other types of data displays. It can be viewed both as a data structure and an access method.

As an access method, it can present the user with a nonlinear method of accessing data. Consider the text display in Figure 16.5, which depicts a series of screens that present data in a linear fashion. The user must access each screen in sequence. When the user finishes viewing SCREEN 1, he or she displays the next screen by pressing a key (perhaps an "Enter" key). Figure 16.6 depicts the same series of screens viewed in a nonlinear fashion.

The user can view each screen sequentially in Figure 16.6 in the same manner as he or she can view the screens in Figure 16.5 (i.e., by pressing a key to proceed from one screen to the next).

Notice, however, the highlighted text in SCREEN 1. In a hypertext system, the user could move the cursor over one of the highlighted terms, for example, NUMERIC DATA, and press a key. In this case, the next screen presented would be SCREEN 3 rather than SCREEN 2. In other words, the user can "hop around" through the text to view the data that he or she wishes to view in any desired sequence.

As a data structure, hypertext is implemented via a file that contains the screens of text to be displayed and one or more linked lists. The structure of the text file generally employs some method of identifying the text that is to be highlighted, perhaps by enclosing it with special symbols. For example, the text in SCREEN 1 in Figure 16.5 might look like:

SCREEN 1

COBOL ALLOWS US TO DEFINE TWO BASIC TYPES OF DATA:
ALPHANUMERIC DATA AND NUMERIC DATA. ALPHANUMERIC DATA IS USED
FOR OUTPUTTING DATA ON TERMINALS OR PRINTOUTS, AS WELL AS FOR
INPUTTING DATA FROM TERMINALS OR CARD IMAGES. NUMERIC DATA IS
USED FOR MATHEMATIC CALCULATIONS.

SCREEN 2

ALPHANUMERIC DATA IS DEFINED BY USING THE PICTURE X CLAUSE.
FOR EXAMPLE, IF WE WISH TO DEFINE AN ALPHANUMERIC FIELD FOR A
PERSON'S NAME WITH A MAXIMUM LENGTH OF 40 BYTES, WE WOULD
CODE:

          77 NAME   PICTURE X(40).

SCREEN 3

NUMERIC DATA IS DEFINED BY USING THE PICTURE 9 CLAUSE. FOR
EXAMPLE, IF WE WISH TO DEFINE A NUMERIC FIELD FOR A PERSON'S
SALARY WHICH COULD CONTAIN A VALUE WITH A MAXIMUM OF FIVE
DIGITS, WE WOULD CODE:

          77 SALARY   PICTURE 9(5).

FIGURE 16.5   *Sample screens that present data in a linear fashion. The user must access each screen in sequence.*

SCREEN 1

Note the   -------------
highlighted
fields here! ──▶ COBOL ALLOWS US TO DEFINE TWO BASIC TYPES OF DATA:
                    ALPHANUMERIC DATA AND **NUMERIC DATA.** ALPHANUMERIC DATA IS
                    USED FOR OUTPUTTING DATA ON TERMINALS OR PRINTOUTS, AS WELL AS
                    FOR INPUTTING DATA FROM TERMINALS OR CARD IMAGES. NUMERIC
                    DATA IS USED FOR MATHEMATIC CALCULATIONS.

SCREEN 2

ALPHANUMERIC DATA IS DEFINED BY USING THE PICTURE X CLAUSE.
FOR EXAMPLE, IF WE WISH TO DEFINE AN ALPHANUMERIC FIELD FOR A
PERSON'S NAME WITH A MAXIMUM LENGTH OF 40 BYTES, WE WOULD
CODE:

          77 NAME   PICTURE X(40).

SCREEN 3

NUMERIC DATA IS DEFINED BY USING THE PICTURE 9 CLAUSE. FOR
EXAMPLE, IF WE WISH TO DEFINE A NUMERIC FIELD FOR A PERSON'S
SALARY WHICH COULD CONTAIN A VALUE WITH A MAXIMUM OF FIVE
DIGITS, WE WOULD CODE:

          77 SALARY   PICTURE 9(5).

FIGURE 16.6   *Sample screens from Figure 16.5 that present data in a nonlinear fashion. The user need not access*
screens in sequence. He or she moves the cursor to either of the highlighted fields and presses a key
to access another screen based on that field.

COBOL ALLOWS US TO DEFINE TWO BASIC TYPES OF DATA:
{ALPHANUMERIC DATA} AND {NUMERIC DATA}. ALPHANUMERIC DATA
IS USED FOR OUTPUTTING DATA ON TERMINALS OR PRINTOUTS,
AS WELL AS FOR INPUTTING DATA FROM TERMINALS OR CARD
IMAGES. NUMERIC DATA IS USED FOR MATHEMATIC
CALCULATIONS.

Notice braces ("{" and "}") are used to enclose the two highlighted phrases, ALPHANUMERIC DATA and NUMERIC DATA.

A linked list is used to store the screens the user accesses. In the last example, where the user "hopped" from SCREEN 1 to SCREEN 3, this list might contain the following data:

LIST ITEM	SCREEN CHOSEN	PREVIOUS SCREEN
1	SCREEN 1	NULL
2	SCREEN 3	SCREEN 1

Using backward pointers (PREVIOUS SCREEN) allows the user to return to a previous start point and continue accessing the data in a linear fashion.

SUMMARY

Although the future of databases is uncertain, there are several directions that may attain prominence in the field. These include concurrent database processing, distributed databases, artificial-intelligence databases, object-oriented databases, and hypertext.

Concurrent databases are the norm for mainframe databases. They also are found frequently on microcomputer LANs. They typically address the need for data integrity in a multiple-user environment through various locking strategies. Such strategies can give the user and programmer some flexibility while optimizing I/O efficiency.

Distributed databases are based on the concepts that data should exist close to the location where it is used most often, and data should be available to every location where it is used at all. Traditional database implementations keep all data in centralized locations, violating the first concept and wasting the capability of intelligent workstations. Data can, however, be distributed across a LAN with pieces of a database existing on workstations where it is used most often. This strategy works best with relational databases, because tables that are used in all locations can be kept on the file server. With more sophisticated software, databases on each workstation or even on a mainframe or minicomputer can be accessed from any workstation.

The best-known example of artificial intelligence is the expert system. An expert system consists of a knowledge engineer, a knowledge base, and an inference engine. A knowledge base is a type of database that might benefit in the future from utilizing state-of-the-art database technology. In addition, such techniques as heuristic algorithms for learning and neural networks for processing fuzzy input data might result in database systems that can update themselves.

Object-oriented Programming Systems consist of objects that contain both data and processing. You can create objects that inherit the properties of other objects. Although OOPS is still in its infancy, it can lead to databases that can invoke processes automatically.

Hypertext is used primarily for storing and displaying text. Its main feature is its ability to access data in a nonlinear fashion. It is implemented typically via a file that stores the text with markers to indicate what is to be highlighted on the screen and a linked list that keeps track of the screens that have been chosen by the user.

Questions

1. What are the basic concepts of distributed data?
2. What is a file server?
3. Why can centralized data be inefficient?
4. Which database technology best lends itself to distributed data?
5. What are the components of an expert system? Define each.
6. How does a knowledge base differ from a traditional database?
7. What is an object?
8. Give an example of accessing data in a linear fashion. Give an example of accessing data in a nonlinear fashion.
9. What kind of data structure does hypertext usually employ? Why do we use backward pointers?

A Short Discussion on Defining COBOL Variables

A COBOL program has two main areas: a Data Division and a Procedure Division. The data's description is defined in the Data Division and the logic for the manipulation of that data is placed in the Procedure Division.

THE DATA DIVISION

Data is organized into logical entities and placed into a series of 01 level groupings. In COBOL, group labels are 01, 02, 03, . . ., 49. "02" group labels are subdivisions of some 01 label, "03" group labels are subdivisions of some 02 group label, etc. For example, the record description in Figure A.1 can include any of the group labels of Figure A.2.

When labeling group levels, you are not required to follow a sequential numbering sequence. The only requirement is that higher-numbered group levels subdivide lower-numbered group levels. That is, the following two groupings are identical:

```
01 RECORD-A.                      01 RECORD-A.
   02 FULL-NAME.                      05 FULL-NAME
      03 LAST-NAME                        10 LAST-NAME
      03 FIRST-NAME                       10 FIRST-NAME
   02 FULL-ADDRESS                    05 STREET-ADDRESS
      03 STREET-ADDRESS               05 CITY
      03 CITY                         05 STATE
      03 STATE                        05 ZIP
      03 ZIP
```

The names you assign the variables can be from one to thirty-two characters in length. Be careful when naming the variables because the COBOL language has an extensive list of reserved names, including MOVE, PAGE, and ADD. The name cannot contain a blank. A common symbol that most COBOL programmers use to make the variable more readable is the dash ("-").

FIGURE A.1   *Record description for name and address.*

Use a PICTURE clause to describe the type of variable that will be stored in the variable name. The descriptor PIC X defines a one-byte alphanumeric field and the descriptor PIC 9 defines a one-byte numeric field.

Although a PIC A exists to identify an alphabetic field, it is not commonly used in actual COBOL programs. Fields longer than one byte are described by using repetitive Xs or 9s. That is, the descriptor PIC XXX defines a three-byte alphanumeric field and PIC 9999999 defines a seven-byte numeric field.

Obviously, for an alphanumeric field containing 20 bytes, the PIC clause can get cumbersome. Hence, we can abbreviate the clause using parentheses. The descriptor PIC X(15) defines a 15-byte alphanumeric field and the descriptor PIC 9(5) defines a 5-byte numeric field.

The letter V is used to indicate the logical placing of a decimal point within a number. The descriptor PIC 999V99 defines a five-byte field having three digits to the left of the decimal and two digits to the right of the decimal. The "V" is not counted in the length of the field. For example, the "01" description of the typical input record in Figure A.3 is:

```
01 RECORD-A.
      05 LAST-NAME        PIC X(25).
      05 FIRST-NAME       PIC X(25).
      05 ADDRESS          PIC X(25).
      05 HOURS-WORKED     PIC 999V9.
      05 FILLER           PIC X(5).
      05 RATE-OF-PAY      PIC 999V99.
```

In this example, the reserved word "FILLER" is used to represent a field that will not be used by the program. This description identifies an 89-byte long record in Figure A.3.

```
01 TOTAL-RECORD.              01 RECORD-A.
                                  02 FULL-NAME.
option A                              03 LASTNAME
                                      03 FIRSTNAME
01 RECORD-A.                      02 FULL-ADDRESS
   02 FULL-NAME.                      03 STREET-ADDRESS
   02 FULL-ADDRESS.                   03 CITY
                                      03 STATE
option B                              03 ZIP

                                  option C
```

FIGURE A.2   *Group labels.*

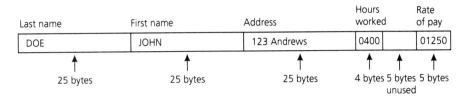

FIGURE A.3 *Record description for alphanumeric and numeric fields. Hours worked is 40.0 and the rate of pay is $12.50 per hour.*

You can assign a value to a variable by using the keyword "VALUE". For example, you can place the value "YES" in the variable ARE-THERE-MORE-RECORDS and the value "0.2345" in the variable PAY-MULTIPLIER using the following 01 level:

```
01 MISCELLANEOUS-VARIABLES.
    05 ARE-THERE-MORE-RECORDS    PIC XXX      VALUE 'YES'.
    05 PAY-MULTIPLIER            PIC V9999    VALUE 0.2345.
```

B

Using DL/I in an
Application Program

Remember that the format of the DL/I calls you used in Chapter 15 is not the same format that you must use in an application program. To begin with, DL/I functions ans SSAs are passed as parameters in subroutine calls. Therefore, you need to allocate storage for them that contains the proper values for segment names, relational operators, and so on. Also, there are some "housekeeping" functions that the application program must perform to be able to execute in an IMS environment. We will examine these differences by studying a COBOL application program.

Figure B.1 lists an application program that is designed to create a report listing the contents of the POLICY database (see Figure 15.3 in Chapter 15). The report will simply list the database segments in hierarchical sequence, beginning with one or more lines of policyholder data for each policyholder in the database. Each group of lines for a policyholder will be followed by one or more lines of policy data for each policy owned by that policyholder. Each group of lines for a policy will be followed by one or more lines for claims, bills, and payments for that policy. Figure B.1 does not list the entire program. Instead, the figure lists only the COBOL code that deals with processing the IMS database.

The logic of the program is simple. You read each PLCYHLDR segment with a GN call until you receive a status code that indicates you have reached the end of the database. For each policyholder, you read each PLCY segment with a GNP call until you receive a status code that tells you there are no more PLCY segments under this PLCYHLDR segment. Finally, for each policy, you use the same logic to read each CLAIM segment, each BILL segment, and each PAYMENT segment with GNP calls.

What is not so obvious is the way the program will execute in an IMS environment. An application program is called by IMS as a subroutine. Don't forget this when examining the program, beginning with the DATA DIVISION.

In an IMS COBOL program, you have to allocate storage for the parameters for each call and initialize it with certain values. At the beginning of the WORKING-STORAGE SECTION, you see this done for the DL/I functions you will

```
DATA DIVISION.

WORKING-STORAGE SECTION.

01  DLI-CALLS.
    03  GN-FUNCTION                          PIC X(4)
                                             VALUE 'GN '.
    03  GNP-FUNCTION                         PIC X(4)
                                             VALUE 'GNP '.
    03  GU-FUNCTION                          PIC X(4)
                                             VALUE 'GU '.

01  PLCYHLDR-SEGMENT
    03  PLCYHLDR-SOC-SEC-NO                  PIC 9(9).
    03  PLCYHLDR-NAME.
        05  PLCYHLDR-NAME-FIRST              PIC X(20).
        05  PLCYHLDR-NAME-MIDDLE             PIC X(20).
        05  PLCYHLDR-NAME-LAST               PIC X(20).
    03  PLCYHLDR-ADDR.
        05  PLCYHLDR-ADDR-STREET.
            07  PLCYHLDR-ADDR-STREET-1       PIC X(40).
            07  PLCYHLDR-ADDR-STREET-2       PIC X(40).
            07  PLCYHLDR-ADDR-STREET-3       PIC X(40).
        05  PLCYHLDR-CITY                    PIC X(20).
        05  PLCYHLDR-STATE                   PIC X(2).
        05  PLCYHLDR-ZIP                     PIC 9(5).
    03  PLCYHLDR-BIRTH-DATE.
        05  PLCYHLDR-BIRTH-DATE-YEAR         PIC 9(2).
        05  PLCYHLDR-BIRTH-DATE-MONTH        PIC 9(2).
        05  PLCYHLDR-BIRTH-DATE-DAY          PIC 9(2).

01  PLCY-SEGMENT.
    03  PLCY-NO                              PIC 9(10).
    03  PLCY-TERM                            PIC 99.
        88  PLCY-TERM-ANNUAL                 VALUE 1.
        88  PLCY-TERM-SEMIANNUAL             VALUE 2.
        88  PLCY-TERM-QUARTERLY              VALUE 4.
        88  PLCY-TERM-MONTHLY                VALUE 12.
    03  PLCY-PREMIUM                         PIC 9(4)V99.
    03  PLCY-DATE-SIGNED
        05  PLCY-DATE-SIGNED-YEAR            PIC 9(2).
        05  PLCY-DATE-SIGNED-MONTH           PIC 9(2).
        05  PLCY-DATE-SIGNED-DAY             PIC 9(2).
    03  PLCY-STATE-SIGNED                    PIC XX.
    03  PLCY-BENEFIT-LIMIT                   PIC 9(5)V99.

01  CLAIM-SEGMENT.
    03  CLAIM-NO                             PIC 9(10).
    03  CLAIM-AMOUNT                         PIC 9(5)V99.
    03  CLAIM-DISPOSITION                    PIC 9.
        88  CLAIM-ACCEPTED                   VALUE 0.
        88  CLAIM-CONTESTED                  VALUE 1.
```

FIGURE B.1   *A sample IMS application program. This program is designed to print a report on the contents of the POLICY database. The entire program is not shown.*

```
      03 CLAIM-PAID-DATE.
          05 CLAIM-PAID-DATE-YEAR              PIC 9(2).
          05 CLAIM-PAID-DATE-MONTH             PIC 9(2).
          05 CLAIM-PAID-DATE-DAY               PIC 9(2).
  01 BILL-SEGMENT.
      03 BILL-NO                               PIC 9(10).
      03 BILL-DATE.
          05 BILL-DATE-YEAR                    PIC 9(2).
          05 BILL-DATE-MONTH                   PIC 9(2).
          05 BILL-DATE-DAY                     PIC 9(2).
  01 PAYMENT-SEGMENT.
      03 PAYMENT-NO                            PIC 9(10).
      03 PAYMENT-DATE.
          05 PAYMENT-DATE-YEAR                 PIC 9(2).
          05 PAYMENT-DATE-MONTH                PIC 9(2).
          05 PAYMENT-DATE-DAY                  PIC 9(2).
  01 PLCYHLDR-SSA.
      03 FILLER                                PIC X(9)
                                               VALUE 'PLCYHLDR '.
  01 QUALIFIED-PLCYHLDR-SSA.
      03 FILLER                                PIC X(19)
                                               VALUE 'PLCYHLDR(PLCYHSSN ='.
      03 SSA-PLCYHSSN                          PIC 9(9).
      03    FILLER                             PIC X
                                               VALUE ')'.
  01 PLCY-SSA.
      03    FILLER                             PIC X(9)
                                               VALUE 'PLCY    '.
  01 QUALIFIED-PLCY-SSA.
      03    FILLER                             PIC X(17)
                                               VALUE 'PLCY   (PLCYNO ='.
      03 SSA-PLCYNO                            PIC 9(10).
      03    FILLER                             PIC X
                                               VALUE ')'.
  01 CLAIM-SSA.
      03    FILLER                             PIC X(9)
                                               VALUE 'CLAIM   '.
  01 BILL-SSA.
      03    FILLER                             PIC X(9)
                                               VALUE 'BILL    '.
  01 PAYMENT-SSA.
      03    FILLER                             PIC X(9)
                                               VALUE 'PAYMENT '.
  01 SWITCHES.
      03 END-OF-PLCYHLDR-SEGMENT-SWITCH        PIC X.
          88 END-OF-PLCYHLDR-SEGMENT           VALUE 'Y'.
      03 END-OF-PLCY-SEGMENT-SWITCH            PIC X.
          88 END-OF-PLCY-SEGMENT               VALUE 'Y'.
```

FIGURE B.1   *Continued.*

be using in this program, such as, GN, GNP, and GU. The 01-level data item
consists of a four-byte field for each function that is initialized to the proper
function code and padded with blanks as needed. You will see later how these
fields are used in conjunction with other fields as parameters to DL/I calls.

```
LINKAGE SECTION.

01  PCB-MASK.
        03  DBDNAME                          PIC X(8).
        03  SEGMENT-LEVEL                     PIC XX.
        03  STATUS-CODE                       PIC XX.
            88  END-OF-DATABASE               VALUE 'GB'.
            88  END-OF-SEGMENT                VALUE 'GE'.
        03  PROCOPT                           PIC X(4).
        03  RESERVED-DLI                      PIC S9(5).
        03  SEGMENT-NAME-FEEDBACK-AREA        PIC X(8).
        03  KEY-LENGTH-FEEDBACK-AREA          PIC S9(5).
        03  SENSEG-FEEDBACK-AREA              PIC S9(5).
        03  KEY-FEEDBACK-AREA                 PIC X(49).

PROCEDURE DIVISION.

    ENTRY 'DLITCBL' USING PCB-MASK.
    PERFORM GET-PLCYHLDR-DATA
        UNTIL END-OF-DATABASE.
    GOBACK.

GET-PLCYHLDR-DATA.
    CALL 'CBLTDLI' USING GN-FUNCTION
                PCB-MASK
                PLCYHLDR-SEGMENT
                PLCYHLDR-SSA.
    IF NOT END-OF-DATABASE
        PERFORM PRINT-PLCYHLDR-DATA
        MOVE 'N' TO END-OF-PLCY-SEGMENT-SWITCH
        PERFORM GET-PLCY-DATA
                UNTIL END-OF-PLCY-SEGMENT.

GET-PLCY-DATA.
    MOVE PLCYHLDR-SOC-SEC-NO TO SSA-PLCYHSSN.
    CALL 'CBLTDLI' USING GU-FUNCTION
                PCB-MASK
                PLCYHLDR-SEGMENT
                QUALIFIED-PLCYHLDR-SSA.
    CALL 'CBLTDLI' USING GNP-FUNCTION
                PCB-MASK
                PLCY-SEGMENT
                PLCY-SSA.
    IF NOT END-OF-SEGMENT
        PERFORM PRINT-PLCY-DATA
        MOVE 'N' TO END-OF-PLCY-SEGMENT-SWITCH
```

FIGURE B.1 *Continued.*

The next five 01-level data items are the segment data layouts from Figure 15.3. These will be used as I/O buffers in your DL/I calls. After a successful "get" call, DL/I will place the data from the segment you requested (via an SSA) in the buffer you specified.

The next seven 01-level data items allocate storage for the SSAs you will be using and initialize them to the proper values. The unqualified SSAs (e.g., PLCYHLDR-SSA) are relatively simple to code. Because an unqualified SSA simply consists of the segment name followed by a blank, you need only allocate

```
            MOVE PLCY-NO TO SSA-PLCYNO
            CALL 'CBLTDLI' USING GU-FUNCTION
                        PCB-MASK
                        PLCY-SEGMENT
                        QUALIFIED-PLCY-SSA
            PERFORM GET-CLAIM-DATA
                        UNTIL END-OF-PLCY-SEGMENT
            MOVE 'N' TO END-OF-PLCY-SEGMENT-SWITCH
            PERFORM GET-BILL-DATA
                        UNTIL END-OF-PLCY-SEGMENT
            MOVE 'N' TO END-OF-PLCY-SEGMENT-SWITCH
            PERFORM GET-PAYMENT-DATA
                        UNTIL END-OF-PLCY-SEGMENT
        ELSE
            MOVE 'Y' TO END-OF-PLCY-SEGMENT-SWITCH.

    GET-CLAIM-DATA.
        CALL 'CBLTDLI' USING GNP-FUNCTION
                    PCB-MASK
                    CLAIM-SEGMENT
                    CLAIM-SSA.
        IF NOT END-OF-SEGMENT
            PERFORM PRINT-CLAIM-DATA
        ELSE
            MOVE 'Y' TO END-OF-PLCY-SEGMENT-SWITCH.

    GET-BILL-DATA.
        CALL 'CBLTDLI' USING GNP-FUNCTION
                    PCB-MASK
                    BILL-SEGMENT
                    BILL-SSA.
        IF NOT END-OF-SEGMENT
            PERFORM PRINT-BILL-DATA
        ELSE
            MOVE 'Y' TO END-OF-PLCY-SEGMENT-SWITCH.

    GET-PAYMENT-DATA.
        CALL 'CBLTDLI' USING GNP-FUNCTION
                    PCB-MASK
                    PAYMENT-SEGMENT
                    PAYMENT-SSA.
        IF NOT END-OF-SEGMENT
            PERFORM PRINT-PAYMENT-DATA
        ELSE
            MOVE 'Y' TO END-OF-PLCY-SEGMENT-SWITCH.
```

FIGURE B.1   *Continued.*

nine bytes and initialize it with the segment name (padded with blanks on the right if needed to take up eight bytes) followed with a blank.

Qualified SSAs are somewhat more complicated, however. QUALIFIED-PLCYHLDR-SSA, for example, consists of three parts. The first part allocates and initializes storage for the segment name, the beginning parenthesis, and the relational operator, while the third part allocates and initializes storage for the closing parenthesis. In between is the second part, which is not initialized. Here, you will move the value of the key of the segment occurrence you want to access. Because you will want to access several different segment

occurrences, you will initialize the key field of the SSA in the PROCEDURE
DIVISION.

The WORKING-STORAGE SECTION ends with some switches that will be
used by the program.

The LINKAGE SECTION is required in an IMS program, as it is in most
subroutines, and contains what is known as the PCB Mask. The PCB Mask is
used to communica⁺ᵉ between IMS and the application program. One PCB
Mask is required f₋. each database specified in the PSBGEN for the program.

Most of the fields in the PCB Mask are used by the program only rarely,
if at all. Such fields are used primarily either internally by IMS or for debugging
purposes by the programmer. The STATUS-CODE field, however, is an exception. Its use by the program is critical. After a DL/I call, IMS updates this field
to indicate the effect of the call. Note that you have coded 88-level values to
indicate the status code returned when you have read to the end of the
database with GN calls ("GB") and to the end of a parent segment with GNP
calls ("GE").

Table B.1 lists the fields in the PCB Mask and their uses.

You begin the PROCEDURE DIVISION with an ENTRY statement which does
the following:

- Identifies the PCB Mask coded in the LINKAGE SECTION
- Establishes an entry point for DL/I to use to pass control to your
  program

The entry point name is always DLITCBL (DL/I to COBOL). This program
ends, as do all subroutines, with a GOBACK statement. In between is the code

TABLE B.1   *Fields in the PCB Mask and their uses. The STATUS-CODE field is the one used pri-*
marily by the application program

Field	Use
DBDNAME	Initialized by IMS at start of program to database name in PSBGEN
SEGMENT-LEVEL	Updated by IMS after DL/I call to hierarchical level of seg-ment accessed
STATUS-CODE	Updated by IMS after DL/I call to show effect of call
PROCOPT	Initialized by IMS at start of program to processing options in PSBGEN
RESERVED-DLI	Used internally by IMS
SEGMENT-NAME-FBA	Updated by IMS after DL/I call to name of segment accessed
KEY-LENGTH-FBA	Updated by IMS after DL/I call to length of concatenated key of segment accessed
SENSEG-FBA	Updated by IMS at start of program to number of sensitive segments in PSBGEN
KEY-FBA	Updated by IMS after DL/I call to concatenated key of seg-ment accessed

that causes paragraph GET-PLCYHLDR-DATA to execute until you receive the "GB" status code.

Paragraph GET-PLCYHLDR-DATA shows the format of a DL/I call. You call DL/I via the entry point CBLTDLI (COBOL to DL/I). The elements of the call (i.e., the DL/I function, the SSAs, etc.) are passed as parameters in the call. In COBOL, this means you should initialize data items with the values of the elements and pass these data items in the CALL statement. You pass, in order, the DL/I function, the PCB Mask, the I/O buffer, and any SSAs. In this case, you can use an unqualified SSA, because you don't care which particular PLCYHLDR segment you retrieve, as long as it is the next one. On the first time through this loop, the unqualified SSA will cause the program to access the first PLCYHLDR segment in the database.

Now you can execute code that will perform the paragraph that prints the PLCYHLDR segment data and will cause paragraph GET-PLCY-DATA to be performed until you receive the "GE" status code. None of the "print" paragraphs are shown in Figure B.1. The code in GET-PLCY-DATA begins by setting the value in the qualified SSA for the PLCYHLDR segment to the key of the PLCYHLDR segment in its I/O buffer (i.e., the segment that has most recently been retrieved). The program then issues a GU call for that PLCYHLDR segment. The reason for this has to do with a concept involving GNP calls that is known as "parentage." The logic of the program is essentially as follows:

```
Issue GN call for PLCYHLDR segment until end of database;
for each PLCYHLDR segment:
        Issue GNP call for PLCY segment until end of PLCYHLDR
        segment; for each PLCY segment:
                Issue GNP call for CLAIM segment until end of PLCY
                segment.
                Issue GNP call for BILL segment until end of PLCY
                segment.
                Issue GNP call for PAYMENT segment until end of
                PLCY segment.
```

Don't forget, however, that the GNP call reads all segments that are children of the parent accessed in the most recent GN or GU call. Thus, with this logic, the GNP calls for the CLAIM, BILL, and PAYMENT segments will read all segments that are dependents of a given PLCYHLDR segment, because you have not issued a GN or GU call for the PLCY segment. In other words, parentage has been set at the PLCYHLDR segment level. You only want to read the occurrences of those segments that are dependents of the PLCY segment, however. Thus, you need to issue a GU call for the PLCY segment before attempting to access its dependent segments with a GNP call—you need to set parentage at the PLCY segment level. Thus, the logic becomes:

```
Issue GN call for PLCYHLDR segment until end of database;
for each PLCYHLDR segment:
```

> Issue GNP call for PLCY segment until end of PLCYHLDR segment; for each PLCY segment:
>> Issue GU call for PLCY segment (to set parentage).
>> Issue GNP call for CLAIM segment until end of PLCY segment.
>> Issue GNP call for BILL segment until end of PLCY segment.
>> Issue GNP call for PAYMENT segment until end of PLCY segment.

There is still one problem with this logic, however—there are two loops at the beginning. The first loop consists of reading each PLCYHLDR segment and the second loop consists of reading each PLCY segment. The second loop is followed by three loops at the end of the logic that consist of reading the CLAIM, BILL, and PAYMENT segments. After reading all of these segments for a given PLCY segment, you will reexecute the second loop and read the next PLCY segment using a GNP call. But within the second loop, you have set parentage at the PLCY segment level. To properly use a GNP call for that segment, you have to reset parentage to the PLCYHLDR segment. This is the purpose of the GU call in the GET-PLCY-DATA paragraph. The logic is now as follows:

> Issue GN call for PLCYHLDR segment until end of database;
> for each PLCYHLDR segment:
>> Issue GU call for PLCYHLDR segment (to reset parentage).
>> Issue GNP call for PLCY segment until end of PLCYHLDR segment; for each PLCY segment:
>>> Issue GU call for PLCY segment (to set parentage).
>>> Issue GNP call for CLAIM segment until end of PLCY segment.
>>> Issue GNP call for BILL segment until end of PLCY segment.
>>> Issue GNP call for PAYMENT segment until end of PLCY segment.

This is not the only way—or even the best way—to address parentage concerns. It was chosen solely as a simple manner in which to illustrate one practical approach to the concept of parentage with GNP calls.

The remainder of the program consists of using GNP calls to access the data in the child segments of the PLCY segment. It operates in a straightforward manner and does not introduce any techniques we have not already examined.

C | *Introduction to SQL/DS*

Although SQL/DS is almost identical to DB2, there are some minor differences between the two products. DB2 runs under MVS while SQL/DS runs under VM. The two operating systems, therefore, require different procedures in linking the database entities to the system. Unlike DB2, SQL/DS does not have a SYSADM, DBADM, and so forth. In SQL/DS, the administrative authority is the **DBA**. Also, unlike DB2, SQL/DS does not have tablespaces and storage groups. In SQL/DS, a tablespace is called a **dbspace** and it resides on a **minidisk.** Tables are created in a dbspace. To obtain dbspace for storing tables, use the following statement:

ACQUIRE dbspace-type DBSPACE NAMED dbspace-name

where "dbspace-type" is PUBLIC or PRIVATE and "dpspace-name" is a name assigned to the dbspace. "Dbspace-name" can be from one to eight characters in length and cannot begin with the letters "SYS." For example, the statement:

ACQUIRE PRIVATE DBSPACE NAMED PAYROLDB

establishes a private dbspace called PAYROLDB. You must have RESOURCE authority to acquire a private dbspace and DBA authority to acquire a public dbspace. A DBA assigns RESOURCE authority to the account DB001 using the following command:

GRANT RESOURCE TO DB001

A PUBLIC dbspace lets multiple users access tables within the dbspace concurrently, while a PRIVATE dbspace lacks the ability to concurrently process data.

You use the following command to drop a dbspace:

DROP DBSPACE PAYROLDB

Before creating a table in a PUBLIC dbspace, you must have CONNECT authority. A DBA must issue the statement:

CONNECT DB001 TO PAYROLDB

to connect user DB001 to the database USERBASE. After you connect to a database, you can ACQUIRE a dbspace using the following statement:

ACQUIRE PUBLIC DBSPACE NAMED PAYROLDB

Here, DBA must issue the following statement:

GRANT CONNECT TO DB001

before DB001 can connect to a database.

RUNNING QUERIES IN BATCH MODE

You can execute SQL statements in batch mode by entering XEDIT and creating a standard Xedit file containing the SQL statements.

In VM/CMS you can enter the statement:

XEDIT LAB1 CTL A1

to activate Xedit and identify the file as LAB1 CTL. Then you can enter one or more SQL statements and exit Xedit by typing "FILE" on the editor's command line. Next, you can execute the SQL batch file using the VM/CMS statement:

SQLDBSU SYSIN (LAB1 CTL A1)

"SQLDBSU SYSIN" is an exec in VM/CMS that executes SQL statements in batch. The term "exec" in VM/CMS is the same as the term PROC in MVS.

RUNNING QUERIES ONLINE

You can execute SQL statements online by entering the statement:

ISQL

and typing the statement into the Interactive SQL facility. Because ISQL only provides a simple two line screen for the writing of queries, however, using the batch facility is more practical and efficient.

D Acronyms and Their Meanings

1NF First Normal Form—each row contains the same number of columns

2NF Second Normal Form—every column that is not part of the key is functionally dependent on the whole key

3NF Third Normal Form—every column that is not part of the key is functionally dependent only on the key

4GL Fourth-Generation Language—a language that generates code usually via a menuing process

4NF Fourth Normal Form—a record should not contain two or more independent multivalued facts about an entity

5GL Fifth-Generation Language—a declarative language where only a goal and rules exist

5NF Fifth Normal Form—when data in a table can no longer be decomposed into smaller tables without each row in the smaller tables having the same primary key

ABEND Abnormal End—an abnormal end to a program, task, or job

ADS/A Application Development System/Applications—an IDMS/R facility that links responses and functions together and provides the communications link between the screens

ADS/G Application Development System/Generation—an IDMS/R facility that links dialogs, screens, and other entities to database data and creates the application structure

ADS/O Application Development System/Online—an IDMS/R applications development tool that develops and executes online applications

ASCII American Standard Code for Information Interchange—a coding system that converts alphanumeric data into a bit configuration, usually found on PCs and non-IBM minis and mainframes

ASSIST an end-user interface in dBASE

BIND a DB2 facility that creates a PLAN using a DBRM

BMP Batch Message Processing—a batch job that runs under the control of IMS and is used to access IMS databases, the message queue, or other files

CALC   a location mode in IDMS/R that places a record on a random page within a predefined database space

CASE   Computer Assisted Software Engineering—represents a wide range of products that automate the various phases of system development

CGA   Color Graphic Adaptor—a type of PC video terminal

CHAR   Character—an option in the CREATE TABLE statement for defining the table's alphanumeric fields of fixed length

CICS   Customer Information Control System—an IBM product that manages programs that communicate with terminals in a multiprogramming environment

CL   Control Language—a component of SQL that handles security for DB2; it includes the GRANT and REVOKE commands

COBOL   Common Business Oriented Language—a business oriented computer language

CODASYL   Conference on Data Systems Languages—issues a proposal for three distinct database languages: schema, subschema, and DML

CUA   Common User Access—an IBM concept stating that all applications should look and feel the same to the user

DASD   Direct Access Storage Device—the disk packs and drives on a mainframe computer system

DB/DC   Database/Data Communication—two components in IMS that manage database I/O (DB) and terminal I/O (DC)

DB2   Database 2—a relational database management system from IBM that is available only on MVS systems

DB2I   Database 2 Interactive—a menu driven facility to access DB2 databases online

DBA   Database Administrator—the person or persons responsible for the database management system

DBADM   Database Administrator—a DB2 term identifying a specific authorization for someone who manages a database

dBASE   A database management system for PCs from Borland International (formerly Ashton-Tate, Inc.)

DBD   Database Definition—a series of statements that define an IMS database and its entities

DBDGEN   Database Definition Generation—uses a set of macros to define an IMS database

DBEDIT   Database Edit—an IBM software product that automatically creates screens for inserting, deleting, updating, and selecting data in DB2 tables

DBMS   Database Management System—a unified set of software and procedures for managing a database

DBRM Database Request Module—a sequential file containing all the embedded SQL statements of a program, created by the precompiler

DBSPACE Database Space—found in SQL/DS and is similar to a tablespace in DB2

DCLGEN Declare Generation—an option in DB2 for the translation of database table descriptions into a COBOL description

DDL Data Definition Language—a language in SQL for the defining of database entities using the CREATE, ALTER, and DROP statements

DFD Data Flow Diagram—a graphical representation of a subsystem, system, or project that is used in a systems analysis and design methodology

DL/I Data Language I—a language that accesses data in IMS databases

DMCL Device Media Control Language—a vendor facility that maps the file and record areas in the schema to physical DASD units

DOS Disk Operating System—an operating system for an IBM PC or IBM PC-compatible; it also refers to a 1960s IBM mainframe operating system

DXT Data Extractor—an IBM software product used to convert certain non-DB2 files to DB2 tables

EBCDIC Extended Binary Coded Decimal Interchange Code—an eight-bit coding system that translates alphanumeric characters into machine language and is used by IBM mainframes

EEPROM Electronically Erasable and Programmable Read Only Memory—similar to EPROM except it can be both programmed and erased electronically

EGA Enhanced Graphics Adoptor—a type of PC video terminal

EOF End-Of-File—a hexadecimal indicator to identify the end of a file, placed in the file by the system

EOR End-Of-Record—a hexadecimal indicator to identify the end of a record, placed in the file by the system

EPROM Erasable and Programmable Read Only Memory—a ROM chip that can be programmed and later erased using special equipment (usually electronically programmable and ultraviolet light erasable)

EUSC End User Support Center—usually a department or section of a company that trains end users on the use of computer hardware and software

EUSG End User Support Group—same as EUSC

EXEC see PROC

FAT File Allocation Table—a file containing the name and locations of all files on a PC's diskette, minidisk, or hard drive

FORTRAN Formula Translation—a computer language used by scientists, mathematicians, and engineers

HDAM Hierarchical Direct Access Method—a type of database structure where data is stored via a randomizing algorithm

HIDAM Hierarchical Indexed Direct Access Method—a type of database structure where data can be stored and retrieved either randomly or sequentially

HIPERSPACE High Performance Space—a data space in central storage that can be made to act like DASD, but at a higher rate of speed

HISAM Hierarchical Indexed Sequential Access Method—sequential files containing database segments in hierarchical sequence and containing an index; ISAM and OSAM are two types of HISAM methods

HSAM Hierarchical Sequential Access Method—sequential files containing database segments in hierarchical sequence

HYPERTEXT used for nonlinear accessing of text displays; also HIPERTEXT—High Performance Text—from IBM

I/O Input/Output—an abbreviation for input and/or output

IDD Integrated Data Dictionary—the main dictionary containing all the definitions and entities created by IDMS/R

IDMS/R Integrated Database Management System—a network database and application development product from Computer Associates (formerly Cullinet)

IMS Information Management System—a hierarchical database from IBM

IPL Initial Program Load—performed by the hardware when the system is first turned on to create the various sections of memory and load the supervisor into central storage

ISAM Indexed Sequential Access Method—an earlier IBM file accessing method that was capable of accessing records either sequentially or randomly; was replaced by VSAM

ISPF Interactive System Productivity Facility—a programmer's tool to edit, browse, create, copy, and compile data sets, with two components—ISPF/PDF and ISPF/DMS

ISPF/PDF see PDF

ISQL Interactive Structured Query Language—a facility used for the on-line execution of SQL statements

JCL Job Control Language—language used to control jobs on IBM mainframes and consisting of the JOB, EXEC, and DD statements

JES2 Job Entry System 2—a job scheduler in MVS

JES3 Job Entry System 3—a job scheduler in MVS

LAN Local Area Network—a group of PCs having a file server and several workstations both physically and logically linked

LRF Logical Record Facility—an IDMS/R facility that contains the accessing strategy for the extraction of records from an IDMS/R database

MFS Message Formatting Service—a facility to manage terminal access on IBM mainframes

MIP Millions of Instructions per Second—a measurement of the speed of a computer system

MPP Message Processing Programs (also known as DC programs)—an on-line program that runs under the control of IMS and is used to access the IMS database

MVS/ESA Multiple Virtual Storage/Enterprise Systems Architecture—an IBM mainframe operating system

MVS/XA Multiple Virtual Storage/Extended Architecture—an IBM mainframe operating system

OLM Online Mapping—an IDMS/R facility that is used by programmers to generate screens and application prototypes

OLQ Online Query—an IDMS/R language used to access database records

OS/2 Operating System 2—a sophisticated IBM PC-based operating system

PCB Program Communication Block—a macro in IMS that identifies the database that the program will access

PDF Program Development Facility—a menu-driven user interface in ISPF

PDS Partitioned Data Set—a grouping of data sets into a library containing one or more data sets and a directory of all the data sets within it

PLAN One of the results of a BIND in DB2 or SQL/DS. The plan contains the accessing strategy, security modules, and other procedures for accessing DB2 or SQL/DS databases

PROC Procedure—a set of routines, commands, or procedures that performs a task

PROM Programmable Read Only Memory—Read Only Memory that can be programmed

PSB Program Specification Block—defines a view of an IMS database

PSBGEN Program Specification Block Generation—used to create the PSB (the view) of an IMS database

QMF Query Management Facility—a user friendly menu-driven facility used for the accessing of DB2 or SQL/DS databases and the creating of reports

RAM Random Access Memory—Main memory that can be read and changed by the user

RDBMS Relational Database Management System—a database management system (DBMS) for relational databases

RID Record ID—refers to the relative pointers on pages of a DB2 database; these pointers contain the actual addresses of the rows on each page

ROM Read Only Memory—memory that is usable but not changeable and is generally installed by the hardware manufacturer

SAA Systems Application Architecture—an IBM set of guidelines for how end-user applications can be developed

SPUFI An option in DB2I for the interactive processing of SQL statements

SQL Structured Query Language—a language to access relational databases, consisting of DDL (CREATE, ALTER, DROP), DML (SELECT, UPDATE, DELETE, INSERT), and CL (GRANT, REVOKE) commands

SQL/DS SQL Data Systems—an IBM relational database management system similar to DB2 and available on VM systems

SQLCA SQL Communication Area—an area created by DB2 containing status codes for DB2 database calls

STOGROUP Storage Group—a group of one or more DASD volumes assigned to store a DB2 database

SYSADM Systems Administrator—a DB2 term identifying a specific authorization for someone who manages the DB2 software

TELON A 4GL product from Computer Associates' (formerly from Pansophic Corp.) that generates COBOL or PL/I code using menus

TSO Time Sharing Option—a time sharing facility that permits multiple users to access the computer system at the same time

VARCHAR Variable Character—an option in the CREATE TABLE statement for defining the table's alphanumeric fields of variable length

VGA Video Gate Array—a type of PC video terminal

VIA a location mode in IDMS/R that places a record on or near the page containing the record's owner

VSAM Virtual Storage Access Method—an IBM storage method that replaced ISAM

VTAM Virtual Telecommunication Access Method—a facility that interfaces the user's terminal to the system and handles all terminal I/O

VTOC Virtual Table of Contents—contains the names and locations of all data sets on a DASD volume

VM Virtual Machine—an IBM operating system for mainframes

Index